# PSYCHOLOGICAL TESTING AND ASSESSMENT

## Ninth Edition

**LEWIS R. AIKEN**

Pepperdine University

**ALLYN AND BACON**

**Boston London Toronto Sydney Tokyo Singapore**

Executive Editor: Mylan Jaixen
Editorial Assistant: Susan Hutchinson
Marketing Manager: Karon Bowers
Editorial Production Service: Raeia Maes, Maes Associates
Manufacturing Buyer: Megan Cochran
Cover Administrator: Linda Knowles

Copyright © 1997, 1994, 1991, 1988, 1985, 1982, 1979, 1976 by Allyn & Bacon
A Viacom Company
Needham Heights, MA 02194

The first edition was published under the title,
*Psychological and Educational Testing,* © 1971 by Allyn and Bacon, Inc.

**Library of Congress Cataloging-in-Publication Data**

Aiken, Lewis R.
    Psychological testing and assessment / by Lewis R. Aiken.—9th
ed.
        p.  cm.
    Includes bibliographical references and indexes.
    ISBN 0–205–18679–3
    1. Psychological tests.   I. Title.
BF176.A48   1997
150′.28′7—dc20                                                96–7850
                                                                 CIP

Printed in the United States of America

10  9  8  7  6  5  4  3  2        01  00  99  98  97

Whatever exists at all exists in some amount.     *Thorndike, 1918*

Anything that exists in amount can be measured.     *McCall, 1939*

# CONTENTS

# PREFACE

There has been much criticism of psychological testing and assessment during the past three decades. The use of standardized tests in educational and employment contexts, in particular, has been repeatedly attacked. Numerous legal suits and court cases concerned with testing have occurred, and in certain states legislation pertaining to test standards and usage has been passed. Most of these events, however, have had salutary effects, and psychological testing has continued to flourish. Increased public and professional attention to the usefulness and limitations of testing has stimulated a desire for greater care in designing and distributing psychological tests and other assessment materials. The need for better training of test users and greater public and professional awareness of the personal and social consequences of psychological and educational assessment has also become increasingly obvious. Psychometricians and other persons who are knowledgeable about tests and testing are concerned that these devices be constructed and used not only with attention to their technical features, but also with sensitivity to the needs and rights of examinees and society as a whole. This outlook is reflected in *The Standards for Educational and Psychological Testing* (American Educational Research Association et al., 1985), *Developing a Code of Fair Testing Practices in Education* (Fremer, Diamond, & Camara, 1989), and *Principles for the Validation and Use of Personnel Selection Procedures* (Society for Industrial & Organizational Psychology, 1987).

Consistent with these concerns and aspirations, the major objective of this textbook is to improve the knowledge, understanding, and practices of persons who construct tests, take tests, or merely ponder over the meaning and value of test scores. Like its predecessors, the current edition is designed primarily as a text for college students. However, it may also serve as a source of information and procedures for professional psychologists, educators, and other individuals who use tests and test results. The material in the book is appropriate for a one-semester course in testing and assessment at the undergraduate or beginning graduate level in psychology or education.

In writing this text I have tried to be comprehensive without being exhaustive, so instructors who adopt it will find that they have not been replaced by a book. Ample opportunity remains for the instructor to serve as a selector and interpreter, as well as an elaborator or expander on the text material. The *Questions and Activities* at the end of each chapter are also designed to extend and supplement the material discussed in the respective chapters.

The basic structure of the ninth edition of *Psychological Testing and Assessment* remains essentially the same as it was in previous editions. Consequently, instructors who used earlier editions of the book will find themselves in familiar territory that has changed here and there, but has not been radically altered. Since publication of the eighth edition, several notable, if not revolutionary, changes in psychological and educational testing have taken place. Among these are revisions in the content and format of college entrance examinations, new editions of various tests, and a renewed interest in the "politics of intelligence testing." Increasing attention is also being given to adaptive testing, item-response theory, the use of microcomputers in psychological testing, neuropsychological testing, and applications of testing in a variety of contexts. Users of previous editions will note that the methodology material in Part One has been expanded to five chapters and that Chapter 8, on research and theories concerning cognitive abilities, has been restored to its proper place. The high interest on the part of students and others in the results of research and theorizing on intelligence, as witnessed by the best-seller status of Herrnstein and Murray's book *The Bell Curve* (1994), prompted my decision to reinstate this material as a separate chapter.

As with previous editions of the text, my goal in preparing the ninth edition was to introduce psychological testing and assessment as an interesting, important field of study, not only to students who plan to become professional psychologists or educators, but also to those who will enter a wide range of educational, health-related, law-related, and other organizational areas in the world of work. To assist in attaining this goal, greater emphasis has been placed on applications of psychological testing in educational/school, clinical/ counseling, and industrial/organizational settings. Although the use of tests and other assessment instruments is discussed throughout the book, Chapter 13 is devoted exclusively to applications.

Many end-of-chapter exercises, some of which make use of computer programs written for this textbook, have been included. The package *Computer Programs for Psychological Assessment* includes programs for computing a variety of statistics and for the graphical display of results; programs for constructing, administering, and scoring tests, inventories, and other psychometric devices; and programs for assessing the user's own cognitive abilities and personality characteristics. A MS-DOS-based diskette containing the programs and directions for their use is available free of charge to instructors who adopt the text for their assessment courses. To obtain these materials, instructors may write directly to Lewis R. Aiken, 12449 Mountain Trail Court, Moorpark, CA 93021. An *Instructor's Manual to Accompany Psychological Testing and Assessment* (9th ed.) containing several hundred multiple-choice and true–false test items, as well as other course-related materials and instructional suggestions, is available from the publisher. The manual is also recorded on computer diskette as an ASCII file for instructors who wish to construct course tests on a word processor. Copies of this diskette will be sent on request to instructors who adopt the text.

Also accompanying the ninth edition of *Psychological Testing and Assessment* is a detailed *Study Guide* divided into 15 chapters and four appendixes. Each of the 15 chapters and Appendix A consists of six parts: Overview, Terms and Names, Completion Exercises, Practice Tests (true–false and multiple choice), Problems and Projects, and Suggested Readings.

I am grateful to the many students and colleagues who worked their way through the eight previous editions of the book and provided constructive criticisms and suggestions. I also wish to thank the reviewers of this edition, Richard Draper, Montclair State University, Linda S. Hynan, Baylor University, and R. Kevin Rowell, The University of Central Arkansas, the production editor, Raeia Maes; and the copy editor, William O. Thomas, for their untiring efforts and expertise. I sincerely hope that the results of their labors and mine are evident in the finished product.

# Part One

# Methodology of Assessment

# 1

# FOUNDATIONS OF PSYCHOLOGICAL MEASUREMENT

Anyone who has attended grade school or college, served in the armed forces, or applied for a job during the past 50 years or so has undoubtedly taken one or more tests. Testing has come to have an important influence on the lives and careers of people throughout the world. Whenever information is needed to help make decisions about people or to assist them in selecting courses of action pertaining to their future educational or occupational status, some form of test may be administered. Tests are used extensively in schools, psychological clinics, industry, and the civil and military services for diagnostic evaluation, selection, placement, and promotion purposes. In addition to their applications in practical decision making, tests are used extensively in research.

Considering its many functions, it is not surprising that testing itself has become a big business. According to the Association of American Publishers, the total sales figure for standardized tests administered in grades K–12 alone was an estimated $167.3 million in 1995. Commercial organizations such as those listed in Appendix C specialize in the publication and distribution of psychological tests and other instruments for assessing the abilities, personality, interests, and other characteristics of individuals of all ages and in various circumstances.

## HISTORICAL PERSPECTIVE

The fact that people differ in cognitive abilities, personality characteristics, and behavior and that these differences can be assessed in some way has been recognized since the dawn of human history. Plato and Aristotle wrote about individual differences nearly 2500 years ago, and even they were preceded by the ancient Chinese (Bowman, 1989; Doyle, 1974). As early as the 2200 B.C., a civil-service system was instituted by the Chinese emperor to determine if government officials were fit to perform their duties. This system, according to which officials were examined every three years for proficiency in music, archery, horsemanship, writing, arithmetic, and public and private rites and ceremonies, was continued by later Chinese rulers to include knowledge of civil law, military affairs, agriculture, revenue, geography, composition, and poetry (Green, 1991). During the nineteenth century, the British, French, and German governments patterned their civil service examinations after this system.

Interest in individual differences, at least from a scientific viewpoint, was almost nonexistent in Europe during the Middle Ages. In the social structure of medieval European society, a person's activities were dictated by the social class into which he or she was born. Little freedom was provided for personal expression or development. By the sixteenth century, however, European society had become more progressive and less doctrinaire; the idea that people are unique and entitled to assert their natural gifts and improve their position in life was growing. Thus, the Renaissance can be viewed not only as a period during which interest in scholarship and creativity was reawakened but also as a rebirth of individualism. The spirit of freedom and individual worth, which flourished with the political and economic stimulation provided by capitalism and democracy, found expression in art, science, and government. Not until the late nineteenth century, however, did the scientific study of individual differences in abilities and personality actually begin.

## Mental Measurement in the Nineteenth Century

Early in the nineteenth century, scientists generally viewed individual differences in sensorimotor and mental abilities as more of a nuisance than anything else. Before the invention of precise, automatic instruments for measuring and recording physical events, the accuracy of scientific measurements of time, distance, and other physical variables depended to a great extent on the perceptual-motor abilities of human observers. Most of these observers were highly trained and very careful in making such measurements, but measurements by different people and by the same person on different occasions still varied appreciably. Because the search for general laws of nature is difficult when measures of natural phenomena are unreliable, physical scientists directed their attention to the construction of instruments that would be more consistent and precise than unaided human observation.

Stimulated by the writings of Charles Darwin on the origin of species and by the emergence of scientific psychology, interest in the study of individual differences grew during the latter half of the nineteenth century. Darwin was an Englishman, but psychology was actually christened a science in Germany during the last quarter of the century. During that time, Gustav Fechner, Wilhelm Wundt, Hermann Ebbinghaus, and other experimental psychologists demonstrated that psychological phenomena could be expressed in quantitative, rational terms. Events occurring in France and the United States were also important to psychological testing. The research of French psychiatrists and psychologists on mental disorders influenced the development of clinical assessment techniques and tests, and the increased attention given to written examinations in American schools resulted in the development of standardized measures of scholastic achievement.

As is true of the history of any field, many people in a number of countries played significant roles in the pioneering phase of mental measurement. Especially important during the late 1800s were Francis Galton, J. McKeen Cattell, and Alfred Binet. Galton, a mentally gifted cousin of the naturalist Charles Darwin, was an English gentleman who became interested in the hereditary basis of intelligence and in techniques for measuring human abilities.

Galton was particularly concerned with the inheritance of genius, but he also constructed a number of sensorimotor tests and devised several methods for investigating individual differences in abilities and temperament. Using these simple tests, Galton made measurements on over 9000 people, ranging in age from 5 to 80 years. Among his many methodological contributions was the technique of "co-relations," which has continued to be a popular method for analyzing test scores.

J. McKeen Cattell was an American who, on returning from Germany after receiving the Ph.D. under Wilhelm Wundt, stopped over in England and became acquainted with Galton's methods and tests while serving as his assistant. Later, at Columbia University, Cattell tried relating scores on these *mental tests* of reaction time and sensory discrimination to school marks. The relationships, or correlations, between performance on the tests and scholastic achievement were, however, very low. It remained for a Frenchman, Alfred Binet, to construct the first mental test that was an effective predictor of scholastic achievement.

## Testing in the Early Twentieth Century

The French psychologist Alfred Binet (Figure 1–1) and his physician–associate Théodore Simon were commissioned in 1904 by the Parisian minister of public instruction to develop a procedure for identifying children who presumably could not benefit sufficiently from instruction in regular school classrooms. For this purpose, Binet and Simon

**FIGURE 1–1** Alfred Binet.
(Reprinted by permission of Culver Pictures, Inc.)

constructed an individually administered test consisting of 30 problems arranged in order of ascending difficulty. The problems on this first workable *intelligence test,* which was published in 1905, emphasized the ability to judge, understand, and reason. A revision of the test, containing a large number of subtests grouped by age levels from 3 to 13 years, was published in 1908. In scoring the 1908 revision of the Binet–Simon Intelligence Scale, the concept of *mental age* was introduced as a way of quantifying a person's overall performance on the test. A further revision of the Binet–Simon scale, published after Binet's untimely death in 1911, extended the test to the adult level.

Other pioneers in psychological testing and assessment included Charles Spearman in test theory, Edward Thorndike in achievement testing, Lewis Terman in intelligence testing, Robert Woodworth and Hermann Rorschach in personality testing, and E. K. Strong, Jr. in interest measurement. The work of Arthur Otis on group-administered tests of intelligence led directly to construction of the Army Examinations Alpha and Beta by a committee of psychologists during World War I. These two tests, the Army Alpha for literates and the Army Beta for illiterates, were administered on a group basis to measure the mental abilities of thousands of U.S. soldiers during and after the war.

Many individuals have contributed to the theory and practice of psychological and educational testing since World War I. The names of many of these pioneers, which are listed in Table 1–1, are still to be found in titles of tests and in references to techniques, procedures,

**TABLE 1–1   Selected Events in the History of Psychological and Educational Assessment**

| | |
|---|---|
| 1845 | Printed examinations first used by Boston School Committee under the guidance of the educator Horace Mann |
| 1864 | George Fisher, an English schoolmaster, constructs a series of scales consisting of sample questions and answers as guides for evaluating students' answers to essay test questions |
| 1869 | Scientific study of individual differences begins with publication of Francis Galton's *Classification of Men According to Their Natural Gifts* |
| 1884 | Francis Galton opens Anthropometric Laboratory for International Health Exhibition in London |
| 1888 | J. M. Cattell opens a testing laboratory at the University of Pennsylvania |
| 1893 | Joseph Jastrow displays sensorimotor tests at Columbian Exhibition in Chicago |
| 1897 | J. M. Rice publishes his research findings on spelling abilities of U.S. schoolchildren |
| 1904 | Charles Spearman describes his two-factor theory of mental abilities; first major textbook on educational measurement, E. L. Thorndike's *Introduction to the Theory of Mental and Social Measurement,* published |
| 1905 | First Binet–Simon Intelligence Scale published; Carl Jung uses word-association test for analysis of mental complexes |
| 1908 | Revision of Binet–Simon Intelligence Scale published |
| 1908–1909 | Objective arithmetic tests published by J. C. Stone and S. A. Courtis |
| 1908–1914 | E. L. Thorndike develops standardized tests of arithmetic, handwriting, language, and spelling, including *Scale for Handwriting of Children* (1910) |

**TABLE 1–1  Continued**

| | |
|---|---|
| 1916 | Arthur Otis develops the first group test of intelligence, based on Terman's Stanford Revision of the Binet–Simon scales |
| 1916 | Stanford–Binet Intelligence Scale published by Lewis Terman |
| 1917 | Army Alpha and Army Beta, the first group intelligence tests, constructed and administered to U.S. Army recruits |
| 1927 | First edition of Strong Vocational Interest Blank for Men published; Kuhlmann–Anderson Intelligence Tests first published |
| 1937 | Revision of Stanford–Binet Intelligence Scale published |
| 1938 | Henry Murray publishes *Explorations in Personality;* O. K. Buros publishes first *Mental Measurements Yearbook* |
| 1939 | Wechsler–Bellevue Intelligence Scale published |
| 1942 | Minnesota Multiphasic Personality Inventory published |
| 1949 | Wechsler Intelligence Scale for Children published |
| 1960 | Form L-M of Stanford–Binet Intelligence Scale published |
| 1970 | Increasing use of computers in designing, administering, scoring, analyzing, and interpreting tests |
| 1971 | Federal court decision requiring that tests used for personnel selection purposes must be job relevant *(Griggs et al. v. Duke Power)* |
| 1974 | Wechsler Intelligence Scale for Children–Revised published |
| 1980 | Development of item-response theory |
| 1981 | Wechsler Adult Intelligence Scale–Revised published |
| 1985 | *Standards for Educational and Psychological Testing* published |
| 1989 | MMPI–II published; Wechsler Preschool and Primary Scale of Intelligence–Revised published |
| 1990 | Wechsler Intelligence Scale for Children–III published |
| 1995 | Twelfth edition of *Mental Measurements Yearbook* published |

and other developments to which they contributed. Among these developments were improvements in statistical methodology and technological advances in the preparation and scoring of tests and the analysis of test results.

## TESTING AS A PROFESSION

The field of psychological testing has grown rapidly since the 1920s, and hundreds of tests are now produced and distributed commercially. After World War II, standardized testing, especially the testing of academic achievement or performance, spread throughout the world. Many American-made tests of ability and personality were translated from English into other languages. In addition to published standardized tests, hundreds of unpublished test materials are available. These tests, which are cited in professional journals and books, are in use in North America, Europe, and other countries throughout the world.

## Sources of Information

Information concerning psychological tests and other assessment instruments can be found in the catalogs of companies that distribute tests (see Appendix C) or, in more detail, in manuals accompanying the tests themselves. A number of reference books dealing with tests have also been published. *Tests in Print III* (Mitchell, 1983) and *Tests in Print IV* (Murphy, Conoley, & Impara, 1994), for example, contains descriptive information on thousands of commercially available tests. Another important source is *The Mental Measurements Yearbook* (Buros, 1978 and earlier; Mitchell, 1985; Conoley & Kramer, 1989; Kramer & Conoley, 1992; Conoley & Impara, 1995), the twelve editions of which contain descriptions and reviews of tests. Information on a wide variety of published tests may also be found in the volume *Tests* (Sweetland & Keyser, 1991), and reviews of tests are given in *Test Critiques* (Keyser & Sweetland, 1984–1994). Useful information on tests in specific areas (personality, reading, intelligence, English, foreign languages, mathematics, science, social studies, vocations) is provided in a series of monographs prepared by O. K. Buros (1970, 1975a, 1975b, and others) and in the *ETS Test Collection Catalog* (Educational Testing Service, Princeton, NJ). Also available in the ETS test collection are 200 annotated Test Collection Bibliographies and a quarterly newsletter, *News on Tests*.

Among the many other books of annotated lists and reviews of published tests are *Tests and Measurements in Child Development* (Johnson & Bommarito, 1971; Johnson, 1976), *Tests in Education: A Book of Critical Reviews* (Levy & Goldstein, 1984), *Testing Children* (Weaver, 1984), *Testing Adolescents* (Harrington, 1986), and *Testing Adults* (Swiercinsky, 1985). Information on available computer software and test-scoring services may be found in *Psychware Sourcebook* (Krug, 1993) and *Computer Use in Psychology: A Directory of Software* (Stoloff & Couch, 1992). Computer databases containing information on published tests include the *Mental Measurements Online Database* (Buros Institute of Mental Measurements, Lincoln, Nebraska) and the ETS Test Collection Database (The Test Collection, Educational Testing Service, Princeton, New Jersey).

Details on unpublished tests and scales may be found in sources such as the *Directory of Unpublished Experimental Mental Measures* (Goldman & Busch, 1978, 1982; Goldman & Mitchell, 1990; Goldman & Osborne, 1985; Goldman & Saunders, 1974), *Measures for Psychological Assessment* (Chun, Cobb, & French, 1976), *A Consumer's Guide to Tests in Print* (Hammill, Brown, & Bryant, 1992), and *Index to Tests Used in Educational Dissertations* (Fabiano, 1989).

Information on published and unpublished measures for clinical situations is given in *A Source Book for Mental Health Measures* (Comrey, Bacher, & Glaser, 1973) and the *Handbook of Psychiatric Rating Scales,* second edition (Lyerly, 1978). For information on unpublished measures of attitudes, the series of volumes produced at the University of Michigan's Institute for Social Research (Robinson, Athanasiou, & Head, 1974; Robinson, Rush, & Head, 1973; Robinson, Shaver, & Wrightsman, 1991), in addition to the volume by Shaw and Wright (1967), should be consulted. The HAPI (*Health and Psychosocial Instruments*) and PsychINFO databases are other useful sources of information on unpublished psychometric instruments.

Reviews of selected tests are published in a number of professional journals, for example, the *American Educational Research Journal,* the *Journal of Educational Mea-*

*surement, Measurement and Evaluation in Counseling and Development, Personnel Psychology,* and *Psychoeducational Assessment.* Articles on the development and evaluation of psychological tests and measures are included in such professional journals as *Applied Psychological Measurement, Educational and Psychological Measurement,* the *Journal of Clinical Psychology, Psychological Assessment: A Journal of Consulting and Clinical Psychology,* the *Journal of Counseling Psychology,* and the *Journal of Vocational Behavior.* Citations of sources of information on specific tests may also be found in *Psychological Abstracts, Education Index,* and *Current Index to Journals in Education.* In addition, entire books have been written on single tests, such as the Minnesota Multiphasic Personality Inventory (MMPI), the Rorschach Inkblot Test, and the Wechsler intelligence scales.

## Test Classification

As is true of any other profession, psychological testing has its own special vocabulary. The glossary at the back of the book provides definitions of the most frequently used terms, many of which refer to types of tests or methods of classifying tests. One such test classification is the dichotomy *standardized versus nonstandardized.* A *standardized test,* which was constructed by professional test makers and administered to a representative sample of people from the population for which the test is intended, has fixed directions for administration and scoring. Various types of converted scores, or *norms,* may be computed from the raw test scores of the *test standardization group;* these norms serve as a basis for interpreting the scores of people who take the test later. Even more common than published standardized tests are nonstandardized classroom tests, which are usually constructed in an informal manner by school teachers.

Tests are also classified as *individual* or *group.* An *individual test,* such as the Binet–Simon Intelligence Scale, is administered to one examinee at a time. A *group test,* such as the Army Examination Alpha, can be administered simultaneously to many examinees.

Whereas the dichotomy *individual versus group* is related to the efficiency of administration, the dichotomy *speed versus power* pertains to the time limits of a test. A pure *speed test* consists of many easy items, but the time limits are very strict and almost no one finishes in the allotted time. The time limits on a *power test* are ample for most examinees, but it contains more difficult items than those on a speed test.

A third classification dichotomy, *objective versus nonobjective,* is concerned with the method of scoring a test. An *objective test* has fixed, precise scoring standards and can be scored by a clerk. Scoring essay tests and certain types of personality tests is, on the other hand, quite subjective, and different scorers may obtain different results.

Tests may also be classified according to the content or task presented to examinees. Some tests contain only *verbal* materials (for example, diagrams and puzzles). A test may also require the examinees to manipulate objects, such as putting pegs into holes, in which case it is referred to as a *performance test.*

Another broad classification of tests according to content or process is *cognitive versus affective. Cognitive tests* attempt to quantify the processes and products of mental activity and may be classified as measures of achievement and aptitude. An *achievement test,* which assesses knowledge of some academic subject or occupation, focuses on the examinee's past behavior (what he or she has already learned or accomplished). An *aptitude test* focuses on future behavior, that is, what a person is capable of learning with appropriate training. Thus, tests of mechanical aptitude and clerical aptitude are designed to assess the ability to profit from further training in mechanical and clerical tasks, respectively. Achievement and aptitude, however, are not separate entities; what a person has accomplished in the past is usually a fairly good indicator of how he or she can be expected to perform in the future. In fact, some psychologists prefer not to use the terms *achievement* and *aptitude* at all as ways of classifying tests; they refer to both kinds of tests as measures of *ability.*

*Affective* tests are designed to assess interests, attitudes, values, motives, temperament traits, and other noncognitive characteristics of personality. Various techniques, such as behavioral observation, paper-and-pencil inventories, and projective pictures, have been designed for this purpose.

Certain institutions and organizations that maintain collections of psychological and educational tests have formal systems for classifying these instruments. One of the most comprehensive classification systems is that of *The Mental Measurements Yearbook.* In this system, the major headings of which are listed in Table 1–2, tests are classified into 18 broad content categories.

**TABLE 1–2  Major Categories of Tests Listed in the Twelfth Mental Measurements Yearbook**

Achievement
Behavior Assessment
Developmental
Education
English
Fine Arts
Foreign Languages
Intelligence and Scholastic Aptitude
Mathematics
Miscellaneous
Multi-Aptitude Batteries
Neuropsychological
Personality
Reading
Sensory-Motor
Social Studies
Speech and Hearing
Vocations

*Source:* Reproduced from *The Twelfth Mental Measurements Yearbook* by permission of The Buros Institute of Mental Measurements of the University of Nebraska–Lincoln. Copyright 1995.

## Purposes and Uses of Testing

Psychological tests and other assessment instruments are administered in a wide range of organizational contexts: schools and colleges, businesses and industries, psychological clinics and counseling centers, government and military organizations, and research situations. Personnel psychologists, clinical psychologists, counseling psychologists, school psychologists, guidance and marriage counselors, and many other applied and research-oriented specialists in human behavior spend a substantial portion of their professional time administering, scoring, and interpreting psychological tests.

The main purpose of psychological testing today is the same as it has been throughout this century: to evaluate behavior, mental abilities, and other personal characteristics in order to assist in making judgments, predictions, and decisions about people. More specifically, tests are used for the following purposes:

1. To screen applicants for jobs and educational and training programs
2. To classify and place people in educational and employment contexts
3. To counsel and guide individuals for educational, vocational, and personal counseling purposes
4. To retain or dismiss, promote, and rotate students or employees in educational and training programs and in on-the-job situations
5. To diagnose and prescribe psychological and physical treatments in clinics and hospitals
6. To evaluate cognitive, intrapersonal, and interpersonal changes due to educational, psychotherapeutic, and other behavior intervention programs
7. To conduct research on changes in behavior over time and evaluate the effectiveness of new programs or techniques.

In addition to describing and analyzing individual characteristics, tests may be used to assess psychological environments, social movements, and other psychosocial events.

No one knows precisely how many of each kind of commercially and noncommercially available tests are administered, and in what situations, for what purposes, and by whom they are administered during a given year. A rough indication of test usage can be found, however, in the results of various surveys (Brown & McGuire, 1976; Wade & Baker, 1977; Harrison et al., 1988; Piotrowski & Keller, 1989; Archer et al., 1991; Butler, Retzlaff, & Vanderploeg, 1991). Understandably, the findings of these surveys depend on the kinds of practitioners and/or researchers included in the survey sample. The results presented in Table 1–3 were obtained from a sample of 413 outpatient mental health facilities in the United States with at least one psychologist on staff. The 30 most frequently mentioned tests are listed in order in Table 1–3. These data, which were collected in 1988, are similar to those obtained a few years earlier by Lubin, Larsen, & Matarazzo, 1984.

The findings of a survey of randomly selected members of the Division of Counseling Psychology of the American Psychological Association (Watkins, Campbell, & McGregor, 1988) are summarized in Table 1–4. The 630 persons on whom these data were collected were employed in private practice, college and university counseling centers, hospital settings, and community mental health centers. The findings in Table 1–4 do not overlap completely with those in Table 1–3, but identical results should not be expected. This is true not

**TABLE 1–3   Psychological Tests Used Most Frequently in Outpatient Mental Health Centers, Clinics, and Services in the United States**

| Test | Usage rank |
| --- | --- |
| Minnesota Multiphasic Personality Inventory | 1 |
| Wechsler Adult Intelligence Scale–Revised | 2 |
| Bender Visual Motor Gestalt Test | 3 |
| Wechsler Intelligence Scale for Children/Wechsler Preschool and Primary Scale of Intelligence | 4 |
| Human Figure Drawings | 5 |
| Sentence Completion (all kinds) | 6 |
| House–Tree–Person | 7 |
| Rorschach Inkblot Test | 8 |
| Thematic Apperception Test | 9 |
| Wide Range Achievement Test | 10 |
| Peabody Picture Vocabulary Test | 11 |
| Beck Depression Inventory | 12 |
| Wechsler Memory Scale | 13 |
| Children's Apperception Test | 14 |
| Vineland Social Maturity Scale | 15 |
| Stanford–Binet Intelligence Scale | 16 |
| Strong Vocational Interest Blank | 17 |
| Sixteen Personality Factor Questionnaire | 18 |
| Millon Clinical Multiaxial Inventory (I & II) | 19 |
| Personality Inventory for Children | 20 |
| Benton Visual Retention Test | 21 |
| Halstead–Reitan Neuropsychological Battery | 22 |
| Graham–Kendall Memory-for-Designs Test | 23 |
| Luria–Nebraska Neuropsychological Battery | 24 |
| California Psychological Inventory | 25 |
| Interview for Recent Life Events | 26 |
| Millon Behavioral Health Inventory | 27 |
| Taylor Manifest Anxiety Scale | 28 |
| Symptom Checklist–90 & Revised | 29 |
| Children's Depression Inventory | 30 |

*Source:* From Piotrowski, C., & Keller, J. W. (1989). Psychological testing in outpatient mental health facilities: A national study. *Professional Psychology: Research and Practice, 20,* 423–425.

only because of differences in the times when the surveys were conducted, but also because different kinds of psychological practitioners were sampled in the two surveys. The results of another survey, this one of psychological tests administered to adolescents, are presented in Table 1–5.

**TABLE 1–4   Assessment Instruments Used Most Frequently by Counseling Psychologists**

| Test | Usage rank |
| --- | --- |
| Minnesota Multiphasic Personality Inventory | 1 |
| Wechsler Adult Intelligence Scale–Revised | 2 |
| Strong–Campbell Interest Inventory | 3 |
| Sentence Completion Blanks | 4 |
| Bender–Gestalt Test | 5 |
| Wechsler Intelligence Scale for Children–Revised | 6 |
| House–Tree–Person Test | 7 |
| Draw-a-Person Test | 8 |
| Thematic Apperception Test | 9 |
| Rorschach Inkblot Test | 10.5 |
| Sixteen Personality Factor Questionnaire | 10.5 |
| Wide Range Achievement Test | 12 |
| Edwards Personal Preference Schedule | 13.5 |
| Kuder Occupational Interest Survey | 13.5 |
| California Psychological Inventory | 15 |
| Wechsler Memory Scale | 16 |
| Wechsler Preschool and Primary Scale of Intelligence | 17 |
| Differential Aptitude Test | 18 |

*Source:* Adapted from Watkins, Campbell, and McGregor, 1988.

**TABLE 1–5   Psychological Assessment Instruments Used with Adolescents in Order of Usage Frequency**

Wechsler Intelligence Scales
Rorschach Inkblot Test
Bender–Gestalt Test
Thematic Apperception Test
Sentence Completion Tests
Minnesota Multiphasic Personality Inventory
Human Figure Drawings
House–Tree–Person Test
Wide Range Achievement Test
Kinetic Family Drawing
Beck Depression Inventory
Millon Adolescent Personality Inventory
MacAndrew Alcoholism Scale
Child Behavior Checklist
Woodcock Johnson Psychoeducational Battery

*Continues*

**TABLE 1–5    Continued**

---

Peabody Picture Vocabulary Test
Conners Behavior Rating Scale
Developmental Test of Visual-Motor Integration
Reynolds Adolescent Depression Scale
Children's Depression Inventory
Vineland Adaptive Behavior Scale
Vineland Social Maturity Scale
Roberts Apperception Test
Benton Visual Retention Test
Piers–Harris Children's Self-concept Scale
Stanford–Binet Intelligence Scale
Personality Inventory for Children
Peabody Individual Achievement Test
Halstead–Reitan Neuropsychological Battery
High School Personality Inventory

---

*Source:* Archer et al., 1991.

## TEST STANDARDS AND ETHICS

The increasing use of standardized tests of all kinds has brought with it a recognition of the need for greater public awareness of the advantages and limitations of tests and the motivations and practices of those who sell and use psychological and educational tests. A continuing concern of professional organizations of psychologists and educators is that commercially available tests should be useful and measure what the test authors, publishers, and distributors claim. Contributing to this goal is a booklet of technical standards, the *Standards for Educational and Psychological Testing,* which was prepared by representatives of the American Educational Research Association, the American Psychological Association, and the National Council on Measurement in Education (1985). Test authors, publishers, and consumers should be familiar with these *Standards,* which are referred to throughout this book. Also concerned with the matter of test standards are the *Guidelines for Computer-based Tests and Interpretations* (American Psychological Association, 1986) and the *Principles for the Validation and Use of Personnel Selection Procedures* (Society for Industrial & Organizational Psychology, Inc., 1987).

### Qualifications of Test Users

Qualifications for administering, scoring, and interpreting tests are not uniform; they vary with the particular types of test. Qualification standards are more stringent for users of individual tests than for group tests and for intelligence and personality tests than for tests of achievement and special abilities. Whoever the users are and whatever their qualifications may be, the ethical responsibility for ensuring that tests are sold only to qualified persons rests squarely on the shoulders of test publishers and distributors. The qualifications required to administer and interpret specific tests must be spelled out and enforced by these organizations.

Reputable commercial test publishers require that their customers satisfy certain requirements, depending on the nature of the test and/or the degree of training needed to administer it. An example is the three-level (A, B, and C) qualification system of The Psychological Corporation. Level A tests may be purchased by schools and other organizations by submitting the organization's or agency's official purchase number or by an official letterhead signed by the person authorized to purchase. Qualification at level B requires a master's degree in psychology or education, equivalent training relevant to assessment, or membership in a professional association that requires appropriate training in assessment of its members. Qualifications at level C, the highest level, requires a Ph.D. in psychology or education, the equivalent in training in assessment, or verification of licensure or certification requiring appropriate training and experience in psychological assessment.

## Ethical Codes

The ethical use of tests can be controlled to some extent by a code of ethics to which professional testers and publishers subscribe. Both the American Psychological Association (APA) and the American Personnel and Guidance Association (APGA) have ethical codes pertaining to test administration and other psychological services. The APA and APGA ethical codes cover many of the same matters of test administration, standardization, reliability, and validity as *Standards for Educational and Psychological Testing* (American Educational Research Association et al., 1985). Both codes stress the importance of considering the welfare of the examinee or client and guarding against the misuse of assessment instruments.

With respect to evaluation and diagnosis, "Ethical Principles of Psychologists and Code of Conduct" (American Psychological Association, 1992) emphasizes providing evaluation and diagnosis only in a professional context by trained, competent test users and the administration of appropriate tests. Emphasis is also placed on the applications of scientific procedures in designing and selecting tests and techniques that are appropriate for specified populations, the judicious interpretation of test results, the careful use of test scoring and interpretation services, the clear but careful explanation of assessment findings, and the need for maintaining test security.

The mere existence of high-quality tests and a set of standards or principles for test publishers, test distributors, and test consumers does not guarantee that tests will be administered and interpreted properly. Responsibility for using tests correctly rests with the test administrators and interpreters themselves, a responsibility that has been increasingly recognized by professional psychologists. Unfortunately, the skills and knowledge possessed by many counselors, clinicians, and other professionals are inadequate for administering certain tests. Therefore, mental testers must be made aware of the limitations of their professional qualifications, the need for further training, and the necessity of relying on other professionals and up-to-date sources of information for assistance. Furthermore, testers must be able to make sound ethical judgments by being sensitive to the needs of examinees as well as the institution and society as a whole.

In 1984, the three professional organizations (AERA, APA, and APGA) that were responsible for developing *Standards for Educational and Psychological Testing* formed a Joint Committee on Testing Practices (JCTP). The purpose of this committee was to work with test publishers in an attempt to improve the quality of testing practices in the public interest (Fremer, Diamond, & Camara, 1989). One result of the committee's efforts was a Code of Fair Testing Practices in Education. As shown in Figure 1–2, the 21 points of this code are grouped into four sections: A. Developing/Selecting Appropriate Tests, B. Interpreting Scores, C. Striving for Fairness, and D. Informing Test Takers. Each section contains a set of recommendations that test developers and users should follow in their respective activities. It was hoped that distribution of the code and adherence to its principles and procedures would improve the validity and fairness of tests and the manner in which they are administered, scored, and interpreted. Complementing the code is a booklet, *Responsible Test Use* (Eyde et al., 1993), an interdisciplinary casebook consisting of actual cases from various contexts in which specific tests were administered, scored, or interpreted improperly.

## A  Developing/Selecting Appropriate Tests*

Test developers should provide the information that test users need to select appropriate tests.

Test users should select tests that meet the purpose for which they are to be used and that are appropriate for the intended test-taking populations.

**Test Developers Should:**

1. Define what each test measures and what the test should be used for. Describe the population(s) for which the test is appropriate.

2. Accurately represent the characteristics, usefulness, and limitations of tests for their intended purposes.

3. Explain relevant measurement concepts as necessary for clarity at the level of detail that is appropriate for the intended audience(s).

4. Describe the process of test development. Explain how the content and skills to be tested were selected.

5. Provide evidence that the test meets its intended purpose(s).

6. Provide either representative samples or complete copies of test questions, directions, answer sheets, manuals, and score reports to qualified users.

7. Indicate the nature of the evidence obtained concerning the appropriateness of each test for groups of different racial, ethnic, or linguistic backgrounds who are likely to be tested.

8. Identify and publish any specialized skills needed to administer each test and to interpret scores correctly.

**Test Users Should:**

1. First define the purpose for testing and the population to be tested. Then, select a test for that purpose and that population based on a thorough review of the available information.

2. Investigate potentially useful sources of information, in addition to test scores, to corroborate the information provided by tests.

3. Read the materials provided by test developers and avoid using tests for which unclear or incomplete information is provided.

4. Become familiar with how and when the test was developed and tried out.

5. Read independent evaluations of a test and of possible alternative measures. Look for evidence required to support the claims of test developers.

6. Examine specimen sets, disclosed tests or samples of questions, directions, answer sheets, manuals, and score reports before selecting a test.

7. Ascertain whether the test content and norms group(s) or comparison group(s) are appropriate for the intended test takers.

8. Select and use only those tests for which the skills needed to administer the test and interpret scores correctly are available.

**FIGURE 1–2**  Code of Fair Testing Practices in Education.
(From Fremer, Diamond, & Camara, 1989.)

## B  Interpreting Scores

| Test developers should help users interpret scores correctly. | Test users should interpret scores correctly. |

**Test Developers Should:**

9. Provide timely and easily understood score reports that describe test performance clearly and accurately. Also explain the meaning and limitations of reported scores.

10. Describe the population(s) represented by any norms or comparison group(s), the dates the data were gathered, and the process used to select the samples of test takers.

11. Warn users to avoid specific, reasonably anticipated misuses of test scores.

12. Provide information that will help users follow reasonable procedures for setting passing scores when it is appropriate to use such scores with the test.

13. Provide information that will help users gather evidence to show that the test is meeting its intended purpose(s).

**Test Users Should:**

9. Obtain information about the scale used for reporting scores, the characteristics of any norms or comparison group(s), and the limitations of the scores.

10. Interpret scores taking into account any major differences between the norms or comparison groups and the actual test takers. Also take into account any differences in test administration practices or familiarity with the specific questions in the test.

11. Avoid using tests for purposes not specifically recommended by the test developer unless evidence is obtained to support the intended use.

12. Explain how any passing scores were set and gather evidence to support the appropriateness of the scores.

13. Obtain evidence to help show that the test is meeting its intended purpose(s).

## C  Striving for Fairness

| Test developers should strive to make tests that are as fair as possible for test takers of different races, gender, ethnic backgrounds, or handicapping conditions. | Test users should select tests that have been developed in ways that attempt to make them as fair as possible for test takers of different races, gender, ethnic backgrounds, or handicapping conditions. |

**Test Developers Should:**

14. Review and revise test questions and related materials to avoid potentially insensitive content or language.

15. Investigate the performance of test takers of different races, gender, and ethnic backgrounds when samples of sufficient size are available. Enact procedures that help to ensure that differences in performance are related primarily to the skills under assessment rather than to irrelevant factors.

16. When feasible, make appropriately modified forms of tests or administration procedures available for test takers with handicapping conditions. Warn test users of potential problems in using standard norms with modified tests or administration procedures that result in non-comparable scores.

**Test Users Should:**

14. Evaluate the procedures used by test developers to avoid potentially insensitive content or language.

15. Review the performance of test takers of different races, gender, and ethnic backgrounds when samples of sufficient size are available. Evaluate the extent to which performance differences may have been caused by inappropriate characteristics of the test.

16. When necessary and feasible, use appropriately modified forms of tests or administration procedures for test takers with handicapping conditions. Interpret standard norms with care in the light of the modifications that were made.

**FIGURE 1–2**  Continued

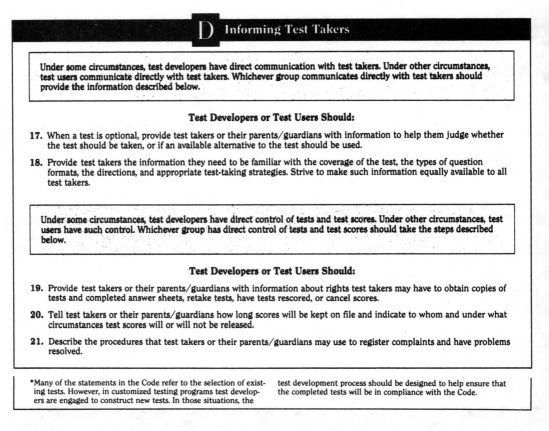

Under some circumstances, test developers have direct communication with test takers. Under other circumstances, test users communicate directly with test takers. Whichever group communicates directly with test takers should provide the information described below.

**Test Developers or Test Users Should:**

17. When a test is optional, provide test takers or their parents/guardians with information to help them judge whether the test should be taken, or if an available alternative to the test should be used.

18. Provide test takers the information they need to be familiar with the coverage of the test, the types of question formats, the directions, and appropriate test-taking strategies. Strive to make such information equally available to all test takers.

Under some circumstances, test developers have direct control of tests and test scores. Under other circumstances, test users have such control. Whichever group has direct control of tests and test scores should take the steps described below.

**Test Developers or Test Users Should:**

19. Provide test takers or their parents/guardians with information about rights test takers may have to obtain copies of tests and completed answer sheets, retake tests, have tests rescored, or cancel scores.

20. Tell test takers or their parents/guardians how long scores will be kept on file and indicate to whom and under what circumstances test scores will or will not be released.

21. Describe the procedures that test takers or their parents/guardians may use to register complaints and have problems resolved.

*Many of the statements in the Code refer to the selection of existing tests. However, in customized testing programs test developers are engaged to construct new tests. In those situations, the test development process should be designed to help ensure that the completed tests will be in compliance with the Code.

**FIGURE 1–2**  Continued

## Informed Consent and Confidentiality

Improper disclosure of test data, especially data identified by the examinee's name, is a continuing cause of concern to professionals in psychological assessment. The expanding use of computers and associated data banks has increased the need for vigilance in ensuring that test scores maintained in electronic files in particular are adequately protected against improper disclosure. Unless otherwise required by law, *informed consent* of test takers or their legal representatives is needed to release test results by name of examinee to any person or institution. Informed consent implies that an individual who has agreed to have personal information released knows what the information consists of and with whom it will be shared. Figure 1–3 is an informed consent form that should be read and signed by the examinee or another responsible party before a psychological examination is conducted. As stated on this form, before any tests or other psychometric procedures are administered, examinees must be told the nature and purposes of the examination, why they are being tested, who will have access to the information, and how it will be used. In addi-

---

INFORMED CONSENT FOR A PSYCHOLOGICAL EXAMINATION

I, _____ , voluntarily give my

consent to serve as a participant in a psychological examination conducted by _____ .
I have received a clear and complete explanation of the general nature and purpose(s) of the examination and the
specific reason(s) why I am being examined. I have also been informed of the kinds of tests and other procedures
to be administered and how the results will be used.

   I realize that it may not be possible for the examiner to explain all aspects of the examination to me until it has
been completed. It is also my understanding that I may terminate my participation in the examination at any time
without penalty. I further understand that I will be informed of the results and that the results will be reported to no
one else without my permission. At this time, I request that a copy of the results of this examination be sent to:

_____

_____

_____        _____
Signature of Examinee                 Examiner Prints Name Here

_____        _____
Date                                  Signature of Examiner

---

**FIGURE 1–3**   Form for Obtaining Informed Consent for Administering a
Psychological Examination.

tion to the rights of informed consent and confidentiality, the "least stigmatizing label"
should be applied in reporting the presence of certain psychological symptoms, disorders,
or other conditions. For example, "mentally impaired" is clearly less personally and socially
stigmatizing than "feeble-minded," "idiotic," or "moronic," and "adolescent adjustment
reaction" is less stigmatizing than "psychopathic personality."

   From a legal standpoint, psychological test data are considered a *privileged communication* to be shared with others only on a need-to-know basis. People should be told at testing
time why they are being tested, who will have access to the information, and how the information will be used. After being tested, they also have a right to know their scores and what
they mean. Except under unusual circumstances, as when the examinee is dangerous to
himself or other people, test information is confidential and should not be released without
the necessary informed consent. Even with informed consent, the information may be *privileged*. This means that, other than the examinee and, in the case of a minor or legally
incompetent person, the parent(s) or guardian, only the examinee's attorney, physician, or
psychologist may view the information.

   Not only do legally responsible examinees have the right of access to the findings in
their own test reports, but they can also arrange for transmittal of their test scores to educational, clinical, or counseling agencies for any appropriate use. At the same time, every
effort should be made to maintain confidentiality of test scores and other personal information. The Family Educational Rights and Privacy Act of 1974 specifies, for example, that test
results and other student records maintained by educational institutions receiving federal
funds can be made available in a personally identifiable way to other people only with the
written consent of the student or his or her parents. However, this act does permit parents

and school personnel with a "legitimate education interest" to review student records, as does Public Law 94-142 in the case of handicapped children.

## SUMMARY

The roots of psychological testing and assessment can be traced to ancient Greece and China, but a concerned, scientific approach to the measurement of individual differences in abilities and personality was not made until the late nineteenth century in Europe and the United States. The field of psychological and educational testing has grown rapidly during the twentieth century; tests of various kinds are used extensively in educational, clinical, business, government, and military situations.

Of the many sources of information about tests, *The Mental Measurements Yearbook* is the most comprehensive. Tests are classified in various ways: standardized or nonstandardized, individual or group, speed or power, objective or nonobjective, verbal or nonverbal, paper-and-pencil or performance, and cognitive, affective, or psychomotor.

During the past half-century, psychological and educational testing has come to be a big business, but the growth of the field has been accompanied by issues concerning the utility and ethics of educational and psychological testing and its practitioners. Information obtained by administering psychological tests should be kept confidential and, with some exceptions, shared with other people only after the written consent of the examinee or his or her legal guardian(s) or counsel has been obtained.

To counter the misuse of tests, the American Psychological Association, the American Educational Research Association, and the American Personnel and Guidance Association prepared codes of ethics, a list of standards, and a code of fair testing practices. Adherence to these codes and standards helps to ensure that psychological tests and other psychometric instruments and procedures are used by qualified persons in a sensible and sensitive manner.

## QUESTIONS AND ACTIVITIES

1. Identify the contributions made by each of the following men to psychological and educational assessment: Alfred Binet, J. McKeen Cattell, Francis Galton, Hermann Rorschach, Charles Spearman, Lewis Terman, Edward Thorndike, and Robert Woodworth. Consult articles or book chapters on the history of psychological and educational testing (for example, French & Hale, 1990; Goldstein & Hersen, 1990; McReynolds, 1986; Sokal, 1987) for more information.

2. Describe various ways of classifying psychological tests and other assessment instruments, and evaluate each of them.

3. Examine copies of *The Mental Measurements Yearbook* (Conoley & Impara, 1995, and previous editions), *Tests* (Sweetland & Keyser, 1991), and *Test Critiques* (Keyser & Sweetland, 1984–1994) in your library. Also obtain a copy of *Standards for Educational and Psychological Testing* (American Educational Research Association et al., 1985) from your instructor or library. Describe the various kinds of information contained in these reference sources.

4. Some writers, particularly in the physical sciences, have questioned whether test scores and other forms of psychological and educational measurement actually deserve to be called "measurement." Read a discussion of the logic of mental measurement in an appropriate source (for

example, Aiken, 1973, Section III), and defend the thesis that mental measurement is true measurement.

5. Assuming that psychologists are both professionals with the welfare of the public uppermost in mind and scientists whose search for truth does not entail the exploitation of other people, why is it necessary to have an explicit code of ethics governing the practice of psychology?

6. How do the concepts of *informed consent* and *confidentiality* in psychological testing differ from that of *privileged communication* as used in law and medicine?

7. What procedures or instruments were used to assess the abilities and personalities of people in ancient times, and how were the results of the assessments used?

# 2

# TEST DESIGN
# AND CONSTRUCTION

The amount of effort involved in constructing a psychological or educational test varies with the type of test and the purposes for which it is intended. Most classroom teachers probably spend relatively little time preparing essay or short-answer tests for evaluating pupil progress in a unit of instruction. On the other hand, the tests of ability and personality designed by specialists in psychological measurement usually require the efforts of many individuals working for extended periods of time.

The procedures employed in constructing a test also vary with the type of test and the aims of the users. Preparing a paper-and-pencil inventory of interests or personality entails different problems than constructing a test of achievement or aptitude. Similarly, the complex procedures followed by professional test designers are unfamiliar to the majority of teachers. Whatever the kind of test or the goals of the users may be, some content planning of content is necessary before the items comprising the test are written.

## PLANNING A TEST

Constructing a test demands careful consideration of its specific purposes. Tests serve many different functions, and the process of construction varies to some extent with their particular purposes. For example, different procedures are followed in constructing an achievement test, an intelligence test, a test of special aptitude, and a personality inventory. Ideally, however, the construction of any test or psychometric device begins by defining the variables or constructs to be measured and outlining the proposed content.

### Screening Tests

Constructing an aptitude test to screen applicants for a particular job starts with a detailed analysis of the activities comprising the job. A task analysis, or *job analysis,* consists of specifying the components of the job so that test situations or items can be devised to predict employee performance. These specifications may include *critical incidents*—behaviors that are critical to successful or unsuccessful performance—as well as other information describing job activities. Because the description of a particular job is usually long and involved, the finished test will not measure all aspects of employee performance. It will deal with only a sample of behaviors important to the job, a sample that should, at best, represent all tasks comprising the job.

## Intelligence Tests

Procedures for designing intelligence tests are described in detail in Chapter 7, so only a brief description will be given here. As in constructing any other test, a pool of items that presumably measures some aspect of the construct "intelligence" is assembled. These items may be constructed according to a specific theory of intelligent behavior or simply with reference to the kinds of tasks that highly intelligent people presumably perform more effectively than those of lower intelligence. The selection of items for the final test may be made on the basis of the relationships of item responses to criteria such as chronological age, as well as the relationships among the test items themselves.

## Personality Inventories and Scales

Various approaches, some based on common (or educated) sense, others on personality theories, and still others on statistical procedures, are employed in constructing personality inventories and rating scales. As described in Chapters 11 and 12, many recently published personality assessment instruments have been constructed by combining theoretical, rational, and empirical approaches. One or more of these approaches may be employed at different stages of instrument development.

## Achievement Tests

More attention has been devoted to procedures for constructing scholastic achievement tests than other kinds of tests. This is understandable when one realizes that more achievement tests are administered than all other types of tests combined. Despite the widespread use of achievement tests, most classroom teachers, who presumably are well acquainted with their subject matter, do not devote enough time to the evaluation of student progress. Too often teachers view testing as a somewhat disagreeable adjunct to teaching, rather than as an integral, formative part of the educational process. Used effectively, however, the results of testing are not limited to evaluating and motivating students. They also provide information to teachers, school administrators, and parents concerning the extent to which specific educational objectives have been attained. By providing data on the effectiveness of the school curriculum and teaching procedures, test scores can contribute to the planning of instruction for individual students or for entire classes and school districts.

### Questions for Test Planners

Planners of classroom achievement tests should begin by answering the following questions:

1. What are the topics and materials on which students are to be tested?
2. What kinds of questions should be constructed?
3. What item and test formats or layouts should be used?
4. When, where, and how should the test be given?
5. How should the completed test papers be scored and evaluated?

Questions 1, 2, and 3 are discussed in this chapter and questions 4 and 5 in Chapter 3.

### Taxonomies of Educational Objectives

Just as the construction of a screening test for use in personnel selection requires a prelim-inary job analysis, the preparation of a test to measure specific instructional objectives is most effective when the behaviors to be assessed are clearly defined at the outset. Since the mid-1950s, much attention has been given to formal, standard systems of classifying the cognitive, affective, and psychomotor objectives of instruction. The major categories of four such taxonomies of cognitive objectives are listed in Table 2–1. The six principal categories of the first taxonomy, the *Taxonomy of Educational Objectives: The Cognitive Domain* (Bloom & Krathwohl, 1956) are listed in order from simplest to most complex. These cate-gories are not exclusive, but rather progressively inclusive. For example, both "Knowledge" (category I) and "Comprehension" (category II) are basic to "Application" (category III) and are therefore included in the third category. Descriptions of the categories in this taxonomy are given in Table 2–2.

**TABLE 2–1   Illustrative Outlines of Cognitive Objectives**

| | |
|---|---|
| *Bloom and Krathwohl (1956)* | Ability to explain or illustrate |
|    Knowledge |    (understanding of relationships) |
|    Comprehension | Ability to calculate (numerical problems) |
|    Application | Ability to predict (what is likely to happen |
|    Analysis |    under specified conditions) |
|    Synthesis | Ability to recommend appropriate action |
|    Evaluation |    (or some specific practical problem |
| *Educational Testing Service (1965)* |    situations) |
|    Remembering | Ability to make an evaluative judgment |
|    Understanding | *Gerlach and Sullivan (1967)* |
|    Thinking |    Identifying |
| *Ebel (1979)* |    Naming |
|    Understanding of terminology |    Describing |
|       (or vocabulary) |    Constructing |
|    Understanding of fact and principle |    Ordering |
|       (or generalization) |    Demonstrating |

**TABLE 2–2    Categories of the *Taxonomy of Educational Objectives: The Cognitive Domain***

---

I. *Knowledge* involves the recall of specific facts. Sample verbs used in knowledge items are *define, identify, list,* and *name.* A knowledge item is "List the six major categories of *The Taxonomy of Educational Objectives: The Cognitive Domain.*"

II. *Comprehension* means understanding the meaning or purpose of something. Sample verbs in comprehension items are *convert, explain,* and *summarize.* A comprehension item is "Explain what the test reviewer means when he says that the test is unreliable."

III. *Application* involves the use of information and ideas in new situations. Sample verbs in application items are *compute, determine,* and *solve.* A sample application item is "Compute the mean and standard deviation of the following group of scores."

IV. *Analysis* is breaking down something to reveal its structure and the interrelationships among its parts. Sample verbs are *analyze, differentiate,* and *relate.* A sample analysis item is "Analyze this instructional unit into its several behavioral and content categories."

V. *Synthesis* is combining various elements or parts into a structural whole. Sample verbs are *design, devise, formulate,* and *plan.* A sample synthesis item is "Design a table of specifications for a test on elementary statistics."

VI. *Evaluation* is making a judgment based on reasoning. Sample verbs are *compare, critique, evaluate,* and *judge.* A sample evaluation item is "Evaluate the procedure used in standardizing this test."

---

*Source:* From *Taxonomy of Educational Objectives: The Classification of Educational Goals: Handbook I: The Cognitive Domain* by Benjamin S. Bloom et al. Copyright © 1956, renewed 1984 by Longman Publishing Group. Reprinted with permission.

Another taxonomy outlined in Table 2–1, one proposed by Gerlach and Sullivan (1967), emphasizes the examinee's behavior in identifying, naming, describing, constructing, ordering, or demonstrating something. In *identifying,* examinees must indicate which member of a set belongs in a particular category. In *naming,* the correct verbal label for a referent or set of referents must be supplied. In *describing,* relevant categories of objects, events, properties, or relationships are reported. In *constructing,* a product is created according to certain specifications. In *ordering,* two or more referents are arranged in a specific order, and in *demonstrating,* examinees perform certain actions to accomplish a specified task.

Following any of the taxonomies outlined in Table 2–1 should encourage the test designer to go beyond simple recognitive or rote memory items and devise items to measure higher-order educational objectives that require thinking. The following items, which may be presented in either essay or objective test format, are illustrative:

What is the formula for computing the standard error of measurement?    (*Knowledge*)

Examine the graph and determine how many items must be added to a 50-item test to increase its reliability from .60 to .80.    (*Comprehension*)

Compute the standard error of estimate for a test having a correlation of .70 with a criterion having a standard deviation of 10.   (*Application*)

Differentiate between a classroom achievement test and a standardized achievement test in terms of what each measures and how each is used.   (*Analysis*)

Formulate a theory relating interests to personality; cite appropriate supporting research evidence.   (*Synthesis*)

Evaluate the criticisms of Ralph Nader and Allen Nairn concerning the Scholastic Aptitude Test (SAT).   (*Evaluation*)

## Affective and Psychomotor Objectives

An important function of education is instilling certain attitudes, values, and other affective states in the learner. A completely satisfactory method of classifying the affective objectives of instruction does not exist, but a number of classification systems have been proposed. One such classification system is the *Taxonomy of Educational Objectives: Affective Domain* (Krathwohl, Bloom, & Masia, 1964). The major categories of this taxonomy are I. Receiving or Attending; II. Responding or Participating; III. Valuing or Believing in the Worth of Something; IV. Organizing Values into a System; and V. Characterization by a Value or Value Complex.

Taxonomies of educational objectives in the psychomotor domain have also been proposed (for example, Simpson, 1966; Harrow, 1972). The six categories in Harrow's Taxonomy of the Psychomotor Domain, for example, are Reflex Movements, Basic–Fundamental Movements, Perceptual Abilities, Physical Abilities, Skilled Movements, and Nondiscursive communication.

## Table of Specifications

Most test designers do not adhere rigidly to a formal taxonomy in specifying the objectives to be measured. Nevertheless, it is helpful in test planning to construct a two-way table of specifications. In preparing such a table, the behavioral objectives to be assessed are listed as row headings and the content (topical) objectives as column headings. Then the descriptions of specific items falling under the appropriate row and column headings are written in the body (cells) of the table.

A table of specifications should be fairly detailed in terms of the knowledge and skills examinees are expected to demonstrate, but it is important not to place undue emphasis on one particular objective. It may be easier to construct items that assess knowledge of terms and facts than items measuring the ability to analyze and evaluate, although items in the last two categories should also be included on the test.

Table 2–3 is a table of specifications for a unit on the preparation, administration, and item analysis of tests. Note that the percentage of the total number of items to be devoted to each topic is given in parentheses below the particular topic. Once a set of objectives for a course of study has been determined and a topical outline prepared, test items can be constructed to measure the extent to which students have attained the objectives listed for each topic.

**TABLE 2–3    Specifications for a Test on the Preparation and Administration of Tests**

| Behavioral objective | Content (topic) | | | | |
| | Preparation | Construction | Adminis-tration | Scoring | Item analysis |
| --- | --- | --- | --- | --- | --- |
| Knowledge of terminology | Job analysis critical inci-dents; repre-sentative sample (3 items) | Matching item; spiral omnibus; response set (5 items) | Rapport; halo effect (2 items) | Strip key; composite score; machine scor-ing (3 items) | Criterion; inter-nal consis-tency; test homogeneity (3 items) |
| Knowledge of specific facts | Categories in *Taxonomy of Educational Objectives* (2 items) | Advantages and disad-vantages of essay items and objective items (4 items) | Factors affecting testing perfor-mance (3 items) | Rules for scoring essay and objective tests (3 items) | Methods of determining item validity; purposes of item analysis (3 items) |
| Comprehension | Explanation of purposes of making a test plan (2 items) | (0 items) | (0 items) | Effects of item weight-ing on total score (1 item) | Explanation of relationship between *p* and *D* (1 item) |
| Application | Specifications for a unit on testing (1 item) | Examples of multiple-choice items to measure compre-hension, application, analysis, synthesis, and evalua-tion (4 items) | Directions for a test (2 items) | Correction for guessing; confidence weighting; use of nomo-graph for scoring rearrange-ment item (4 items) | Computation of difficulty and discrimi-nation indexes; distribution of responses to distracters (4 items) |
| Total | (8 items) | (13 items) | (7 items) | (11 items) | (11 items) |

Certain types of test items are more appropriate than others for measuring the attainment of specific objectives. Short-answer and completion items are suitable for assessing knowledge of terminology, but they are inadequate for assessing higher-order cognitive abilities. For this reason, the table of specifications for a test should be inspected closely before deciding what varieties of items and how many of each are appropriate for a particular test. Practical considerations such as cost, time available for administration, item arrangement, and testing conditions must also be considered in planning a test.

## PREPARING TEST ITEMS

The primary goal of test planning is preparation of a detailed outline, such as a table of specifications, to serve as a guide in constructing items to assess or predict certain objectives. Once a table of specifications or detailed content outline of the test has been prepared, the next step is to construct the actual items. It is generally recommended that, on objective tests, about 20 percent more items than are actually needed should be written initially so that an adequate number of good items will be available for the final version of the test. Commercial testing organizations such as Educational Testing Service employ as item writers persons who possess both a thorough knowledge of the subject matter of the test and skill in constructing test items. Anyone who wants to learn how to construct good test items can profit from inspecting a sample of items on published tests because they are among the best available.

All test items represent procedures for obtaining information about individuals, but the amount and kinds of information vary with the nature of the tasks posed by different types of items. Telling examinees to compare the Battle of the Bulge with the Battle of Hastings demands a different kind of response from that obtained when they are simply told to indicate which of a series of listed events occurred in each battle. Complex integrating and organizing abilities are required by the first item, whereas only recognitive memory is needed to answer the second.

Various methods of classifying items according to format, or the form of response required, have been suggested. *Supply* versus *selection, recall* versus *recognition,* and *constructed response* versus *identification* are ways of differentiating between items on which examinees are required to write or construct an answer and those on which they are asked to indicate which of several alternatives is correct. Another popular method of classifying items is *essay* versus *objective,* examples of which are given in Table 2–4. All essay items are of the supply type in that an examinee's answer is constructed, rather than simply being identified.

Objective items may be of either the supply or selection type, depending on whether examinees must construct a response or merely select the best answer from a list of alternatives. The crucial feature of objective items is not the form of the response, but rather how objectively the items can be scored. Two or more scorers of an essay item often disagree to some extent on the correctness of a given answer and how many points it should receive. Barring clerical errors, however, different scorers of an objective test will assign the same score to a given test paper.

### Essay Items

The most important advantage of essay items is that they can measure the ability to organize, relate, and communicate, behaviors that are not so easily assessed by objective items. An essay test also takes less time to prepare, and it is unlikely that examinees will get essay items right by guessing. However, the questions may be so general that they are interpreted differently by different examinees. Furthermore, the number of essay questions that can be answered in a typical class period—approximately six half-page answers in 50 minutes—may not adequately determine a person's knowledge of the subject matter of the test. One

**TABLE 2–4   Examples of Various Kinds of Test Items**

**I. Essay Items**
*Directions:* Write a half-page answer to each of the following items.
1. Contrast the advantages and disadvantages of essay and objective test items.
2. Explain the reasons for performing an item analysis of a classroom test.

**II. Objective Items**
A. Short answer
*Directions:* Write the appropriate word(s) in each blank.
1. The only thing that is objective about an objective test is

_____ .

2. What is the first formal step in constructing a test to predict the degree of success on a particular job?

_____ .

B. True–false
*Directions:* Circle T if the statement is true; circle F if it is false.
T  F  1. The most comprehensive test classification system is that of *The Mental Measurements Yearbooks.*
T  F  2. The social-desirability response set is the tendency to rate an examinee high on one trait simply because he or she is rated high on another trait.

C. Matching
*Directions:* Write the letter corresponding to the correct name in the appropriate marginal dash.
___ 1. group intelligence test            A. Binet
___ 2. individual intelligence test       B. Darwin
___ 3. interest inventory                 C. Galton
___ 4. personality inventory             D. Otis
___ 5. product–moment correlation         E. Pearson
___ 6. sensorimotor tests                 F. Rorschach
                                          G. Spearman
                                          H. Strong
                                          I. Woodworth

D. Multiple choice
*Directions:* Write the letter of the correct option in the marginal dash opposite the item.
___ 1. Qualifying words such as *never, sometimes,* and *always,* which reveal the answer to an examinee who has no information on the subject of the item, are called
A. glittering generalities
B. interlocking adverbs
C. response sets
D. specific determiners
___ 2. Jimmy, who is 8 years, 4 months old, obtains a mental age score of 9 years, 5 months. What is his ratio IQ on the test?
A. 88
B. 90
C. 113
D. 120

should not expect the answers to be as comprehensive or detailed as those demanded by the items in Box 2–1, but they should tap some in-depth understanding of the material. Other shortcomings of essay tests are that scoring them is subjective and time consuming, and they are susceptible to bluffing by verbally adept but uninformed examinees.

A history teacher whom I knew administered an essay test that included the question, "What were the causes and consequences of the Battle of Hastings?" One unmotivated student who had not taken time to go back farther than the fourteenth century in the study of English history began his answer to the question with the statement, "Far be it from me to comment on the Battle of Hastings, but let's turn our attention to the Hundred Years War." This is a fairly blatant example of the tendency of uninformed examinees to answer a slightly different question from the one being asked in order to emphasize what they do know, rather than what they don't. One way to cope with this problem, although laborious to both test takers and scorers, is the famous Chinese examination procedure of having students write down everything they know! However, it is possible that what would be measured by such a procedure is susceptibility to fatigue rather than general knowledge.

As a rule, essay items should not be used when it is possible to make the same evaluation with objective items. If essay questions are asked, the item writer should try to make the questions as objective as possible. This can be done by (1) defining the task and wording the items clearly, for example, asking examinees to "contrast" and "explain" rather than "discuss"; (2) using a small number of items, all of which should be attempted by all examinees; (3) structuring the items in such a way that subject-matter experts agree that one answer is demonstrably better than another; and (4) having examinees answer each item on a separate sheet of paper.

## Short-answer, True–False, and Matching Items

Objective items are not limited to the traditional four (short-answer or completion, true–false, matching, and multiple choice), but these are the most popular. Among the advantages claimed for objective tests are that they can be scored easily and objectively, and, because less time is needed to answer each item, a broader sampling of content is permitted than on essay tests. In preparing objective tests, care should be taken to make the items clear, precise, and grammatically correct. They should be written in language suitable to the reading level of the group for whom the test is intended. All information and qualifications needed to select a reasonable answer should be included in the item, omitting non-functional or stereotyped words and phrases.

It is tempting to construct objective items by lifting statements verbatim from textbooks or other sources, but this practice emphasizes rote memory. Item writers should also be careful not to include irrelevant clues to the correct answers and to avoid interrelated or interlocking items. Two items are *interrelated* when the wording of one item provides a clue to the answer to the other. Two items are *interlocked* when it is necessary to know the answer to one of them in order to get the other one right.

***Short-answer Items***    A short-answer item is a supply-type task on which examinees are required to complete or fill in one or more blanks of an incomplete statement with the

**Box 2–1**

**A Comprehension Senior Social Science Test**

1. Describe the history of the papacy from its origins to the present, concentrating especially but not exclusively on its social, political, economic, religious, and philosophical impact on Europe, Asia, Africa, and America.
2. Based on your knowledge of their works, evaluate the emotional stability, degree of adjustment, and repressed frustrations of Alexander of Aphrodisias, Ramses II, Gregory of Nicea, and Hammurabi. Support your answers with quotations from each man's work, citing appropriate references.
3. Develop a realistic plan for reducing the national debt. Trace the effects of your plan on cubism, the Donatist controversy, and the wave theory of light. Outline a method for preventing these effects. Criticize this method from all possible points of view. Point out the deficiencies in your point of view, as demonstrated by your answer to the preceding question.
4. Sketch the development of human thought. Estimate its significance, and compare it with the development of any other kind of thought—animal or alien.
5. Assume that 2500 riot-crazed aborigines are storming the classroom. How would you calm them? You may use any ancient language except Latin or Greek and any nonverbal technique other than violence.
6. Take a stand for or against logic and truth. How would you go about testing the validity of your position without involving anyone else or endangering your own sanity?

correct words or phrases or to give a brief answer to a question. In terms of the length of the constructed response, short-answer items fall somewhere between essay and recognition items. Short-answer items are among the easiest to construct, requiring examinees to supply the correct answer rather than simply recognize it. Although they are especially useful for assessing knowledge of terminology, short-answer items have serious limitations: They are not appropriate for measuring complex instructional objectives, and, because there may be more than one correct answer, scoring is not always entirely objective.

The following guidelines should be followed in constructing short-answer items:

1. Questions are preferable to incomplete statements.
2. If an incomplete statement is used, the blank should come at the end.
3. Avoid multiple blanks in the same item, especially if they make the meaning of the task unclear.

**True–False Items**   One of the simplest types of test items to construct, but probably the most criticized by professional testers, is the true–false item. True–false items can be written and read quickly, and so they permit a broad sampling of subject content. A notorious short-coming of these items is that they are often concerned with trivial information or are con-structed by lifting statements verbatim from textbooks. Consequently, they are said to encourage rote memorization and thereby misdirect efforts to learn. Other criticisms of true–false items are that they are often ambiguous and cannot be used to measure more complex instructional objectives. Furthermore, because the total score on a true–false test can be affected by the tendency of an examinee to guess when in doubt or to agree (or dis-agree), the accuracy of the score may be questionable.[1]

On the average, examinees will get 50 percent of the items on a true–false test right simply by guessing. Scores may be inflated even more when items contain *specific determiners*–words such as *all, always, never,* and *only,* which indicate that the state-ment is probably false, or *often, sometimes,* and *usually,* which suggest that the statement is true.

Despite these shortcomings, true–false items do not have to be trivial or ambiguous or misdirect learning. In defense of true–false items, Ebel (1979) maintained that "the extent of students' command of a particular area of knowledge is indicated by their suc-cess in judging the truth or falsity of propositions related to it" (page 112). He considers such propositions to be expressions of verbal knowledge—the essence of educational achievement.

Ebel's defense of true–false items can be questioned, but there is no questioning the fact that well-designed true–false items can measure more than rote memory. For example, by including two concepts, conditions, or events in a true–false item, the examiner can ask if it is true that they are moderately to strongly related (Diekhoff, 1984). Other possibilities are to ask if (1) one concept, condition, or event implies or is a consequence of another event; (2) one concept, condition, or event is a subset, example, or category of another event; or (3) both concepts, conditions, or events are true. Such items can measure understanding as well as significant knowledge of concepts and events.

Whatever the objectives of a true–false test may be, in constructing items of this type it is advisable to attend to the following suggestions:

1. Make certain that the statements deal with important (nontrivial) matters.
2. Make the statements relatively short and unqualifiedly true or false.
3. Avoid negatively stated items, especially those containing double negatives.
4. Avoid ambiguous and tricky items.
5. As a rule, avoid specific determiners. If specific determiners are used to trip up unknowledgeable but testwise examinees, they should be included in true items as often as in false ones.
6. On opinion statements, cite the source or authority.

---

[1]The tendency to agree when in doubt (*acquiescence*) is a response set. *Response sets* are tendencies on the part of examinees to answer test items on the basis of their form, that is, on the way items are worded, rather than on the basis of content.

7. Make true and false statements about the same length, and make the number of true statements approximately equal to the number of false statements. It can be argued that, because false items tend to be more discriminating than true items, the number of false statements should be greater than the number of true statements. However, if the teacher follows this practice on successive tests, students may become aware of it and begin to answer "false" when in doubt about the answer.

8. Make wrong answers more attractive by wording items in such a way that superficial logic, popular misconceptions, or specific determiners suggest that the wrong answers are correct. False statements having the ring of truth may also trip up unknowledgeable examinees.

**Matching Items**   Both true–false and multiple-choice items are, in a sense, varieties of matching items. On all three types of items, a set of response options is matched to a set of stimulus options (premises). The distinction is that true–false and multiple-choice items have only one stimulus option (the *stem* of the item) and two or more response options, whereas matching items have multiple stimulus options and multiple response options. The examinee's task on a matching item is to pair the response options with the correct stimulus options. Matching is usually one to one (one response per stimulus), but it may well be one to many, many to one, or many to many. Examinees should, of course, be told which of these procedures is applicable on a particular item.

Matching items are easier to construct and cover the material more efficiently than many other types of items, but they usually measure only rote memory of facts.[2] In addition, the necessity of making the options homogeneous (all options of the same kind, such as dates, places, or names) limits the type of material that can be fitted into a matching framework. Some guidelines for constructing matching items are:

1. Place the stimulus (premise) and response options in a clear, logical column format, with the stimulus options in the left column and the response options in the right column.

2. Number the stimulus options successively, and place letters (a, b, c, and so on) before the response options.

3. Use between six and fifteen stimulus options, with two to three more response options than stimulus options.

4. Clearly specify the basis for matching.

5. Place the entire item on a single page.

A special type of matching item is the *rearrangement item,* on which examinees are required to sort a group of options into a fixed number of predetermined categories. On a

---

[2]However, at least one study (Shaha, 1984) found that matching items can be designed to be equal or even superior to multiple-choice items as measures of the subject domain of interest and in the attitudes of test takers toward them.

THE CHRONICLE OF HIGHER EDUCATION

"Look, Harvey, the only reason you're depressed is that you're letting yourself be bound by conventional standards. I think that writing 5,383 multiple-choice questions is a contribution to literature."

**FIGURE 2–1**    Test Item Writing as a Passage to Fame.
(Courtesy of Vivian Scott Hixson.)

particular type of rearrangement known as a *ranking item,* a set of options is to be arranged in rank order from first to last.

## Multiple-choice Items

No one knows who constructed the first multiple-choice test item, but from the viewpoint of psychological assessment it was a momentous event.[3] Multiple-choice items are the most versatile of all objective test items in that they can be used to measure both simple and complex learning objectives at all grade levels and in all subject-matter areas. Although answering essay items demands greater organizational ability than selecting answers to multiple-choice items, responding correctly to a well-prepared multiple-choice item requires good discriminating ability and not merely skill in recognizing or recalling the correct answer. Scores on multiple-choice items are also less affected by guessing and other response sets than are scores on other objective items. Furthermore, useful diagnostic information can be obtained from an analysis of the incorrect options (*distracters*) selected by examinees.

[3]Arthur Otis should probably be credited with originating the multiple-choice item format, which appears to have been first used on his group intelligence test in 1916–1917.

Among the shortcomings of multiple-choice items are that (1) good ones are difficult to construct, especially items on which all options are equally attractive to examinees who do not know the correct answer; (2) they emphasize recognition rather than the recall and organization of information; and (3) they require more time to answer and may sample the subject-matter domain less adequately than true–false items. It has also been alleged, although not proved, that multiple-choice tests favor shrewd, nimblewitted, rapid readers and penalize more thoughtful, profound thinkers (Hoffman, 1962).

**_Guidelines for Writing Multiple-choice Items_**   The following guidelines should facilitate construction of high-quality multiple-choice items:

1.  Either a question or an incomplete statement may be used as the stem, but the question format is preferred. If the stem is an incomplete statement, place the blank at the end of the statement.
2.  State the specific problem of the question or incomplete statement clearly in the stem and at a reading level appropriate for the examinees, but avoid taking questions or statements verbatim from textbooks.
3.  Place as much of the item as possible in the stem. It is inefficient to repeat the same words in every option, and examinees have less difficulty scanning shorter options.
4.  Employ opinion questions sparingly; when they are used, cite the authority or source of the opinion.
5.  Four or five options are typical, but good items having only two or three options can also be written. With students in the lower grades, three options are preferable to four or five.
6.  If the options have a natural order, such as dates or ages, it is advisable to arrange them accordingly. Otherwise, arrange the options in random or alphabetical order (if alphabetizing does not provide clues to the correct answer).
7.  Make all options approximately equal in length, grammatically correct, and appropriate in relation to the stem. However, don't let the stem give away the correct option by verbal associations or other clues.
8.  Make all options plausible to examinees who don't know the right answer, but make only one option correct or "best." Popular misconceptions or statements that are only partially correct make good distracters.
9.  In constructing each distracter, formulate a reason why an examinee who doesn't know the correct answer might select that distracter.
10. Avoid, or at least minimize, the use of negative expressions such as "not" in either the stem or options.
11. Although a certain amount of novelty and even humor is appropriate and may serve to interest and motivate examinees, ambiguous or tricky items and options should not be used.
12. Use "none of the above," "all of the above," or "more than one of the above" sparingly. Also, avoid specific determiners such as "always" or "never."
13. Place the options in stacked (paragraph) format rather than in tandem (back to back); use numbers to designate items and letters for options.

14. Prepare the right number of items for the grade or age level to be tested, making each item independent of other items (not interlocking or interrelated).
15. Make the difficulty levels of items such that the percentage of examinees who answer correctly is approximately halfway between the chance (random guessing) percentage and 100 percent: % correct $= 50(k + 1)/k$, where $k$ is the number of distracters per item.

Simply following these guidelines, which are primarily the products of logic and experience rather than research, will not ensure the construction of a good multiple-choice test. Rather than blindly following a set of rules, constructing good items depends as much or more on knowledge of the subject matter of the test, understanding what students should know and are unlikely to know about the subject matter, and the art or skill of asking questions. Even when the guidelines are not followed precisely, multiple-choice items tend to be fairly robust in their ability to measure knowledge and understanding.

**Constructing Distracters**    A critical factor in determining the effectiveness of multiple-choice items is the selection or construction of distracters (incorrect options). Either a rational or an empirical approach to item selection may be employed. The *rational* approach requires the test constructor to make personal judgments as to which distracters are appropriate. In contrast, the *empirical* approach consists of selecting distracters according to the number of responses given to the stems of items administered as open-ended statements. There is no consensus as to which approach produces better distracters, but examiner judgment appears to be at least as effective as the empirical approach (Owens, Hanna, & Coppedge, 1970; Hanna & Johnson, 1978).

**Constructing Complex Items**    Test designers usually have more difficulty constructing items that measure understanding and thinking than those that measure straightforward knowledge of the subject matter. Various ways of composing objective items to assess more complex instructional objectives have been proposed. Options such as "all of the above," "none of the above," "two of the above," "all except one of the above," or "one of the following," can make an examinee's choice more difficult. In addition, making all options correct (or incorrect) and requiring examinees to select the best or most nearly correct option for each item complicate the task. Other ways of making an examinee's decision more demanding are to (1) include multiple-answer items in which a variable number of options is correct and the examinee must indicate which (if any) options are correct or incorrect; (2) have examinees select an answer and improve on it; and (3) ask examinees to identify the correct setup (such as an equation or method of solution) on problem-solving tasks. Additional procedures for increasing the complexity of multiple-choice items are illustrated in Figure 2–2. All of these techniques are designed to make the choice of the correct option a thoughtful, analytical process in which various mental abilities, rather than just recognitive memory, are brought into play.

1. **Classification.** *The examinee classifies a person, object, or condition into one of several categories designated in the stem:*
Jean Piaget is best characterized as a _____ psychologist.
   a. clinical
   c. psychometric
   b. developmental
   d. social

2. **If–Then Conditions.** *The examinee must determine the correct consequence of one or more conditions being present:*
If the true variance of a test increases but the error variance remains the same, which of the following will occur?
   a. reliability will increase
   c. observed variance will decrease
   b. reliability will decrease
   d. neither reliability nor observed variance will change

3. **Multiple Conditions.** *The examinee uses the two or more conditions or statements listed in the stem to draw a conclusion:*
Given that Mary's raw score on a test is 60, the test mean is 59, and the standard deviation 2, what is Mary's *z* score?
   a. −2.00
   c. .50
   b. −.50
   d. 2.00

4. **Multiple True–False.** *The examinee decides whether one, all, or none of the two or more conditions or statements listed in the stem is (are) correct:*
Is it true that (1) Alfred Binet was the father of intelligence testing, and (2) his first intelligence test was published in 1916?
   a. both 1 and 2
   c. not 1 but 2
   b. 1 but not 2
   d. neither 1 nor 2

5. **Oddity.** *The examinee indicates which option does not belong with the others:*
Which of the following names does not belong with the others?
   a. Alfred Adler
   c. Carl Jung
   b. Sigmund Freud
   d. Carl Rogers

6. **Relations and Correlates.** *The examinee determines the relationship between concepts 1 and 2 and indicates which of the concepts (a, b, c, d, etc.) listed in the options is related to concept 2 in the same way that concepts 1 and 2 are related:*
Mean is to standard deviation as median is to:
   a. average deviation
   c. semi-interquartile range
   b. inclusive range
   d. variance

**FIGURE 2–2** Some Complex Forms of Multiple-choice Items.

## ASSEMBLING AND REPRODUCING A TEST

After the items for a test have been prepared, it is always advisable to have them reviewed and edited by another knowledgeable person. Even the most painstaking efforts do not necessarily produce a good test, and a friend or associate can frequently spot errors and make valuable suggestions for improving items.

Assuming that the test designer has constructed a sufficient number of satisfactory items, final decisions concerning several matters must be made before assembling a test:

1. Is the length of the test appropriate for the time limits?
2. How should the items be grouped or arranged on the pages of the test booklet?
3. Are answers to be marked in the test booklet, or will a special answer sheet be used?
4. How will the test booklet and answer sheet be reproduced?
5. What information should be included in the test directions?

## Test Length

The decision on how many items to include on a test depends on the time limits, the grade and reading level of the examinees, and the length and difficulty of the items. Shorter items and/or those requiring only rote memory for facts can be answered in less time than longer items requiring laborious computations and/or abstract reasoning. On tests of moderate difficulty administered at the secondary school level and beyond, a good rule of thumb is to allow 1 minute for each multiple-choice or short-answer item and 1 minute for every two true–false items. Thus, a 50-item multiple-choice or short-answer test and a 100-item true–false test are usually appropriate for a typical 50-minute class period at the junior or senior high school level. Five or six half-page essay questions can be answered in this same period of time. Unless the items are very long or extremely difficult, at least 90 percent of the students in a typical secondary school class will be able to finish the test in the allotted time. The test length and time limits will need to be adjusted downward or upward when testing elementary school pupils and college students.

There are, of course, differences among students in the time it takes them to finish a test. It might be expected that students who are most knowledgeable or skilled in the subject matter of the test would finish first, but this is not always so. Less informed students may simply guess or "give up" and leave early if permitted to do so. Furthermore, the test-taking habits of high-scoring examinees may lead them to review the test items several times in order to make certain that they did not miss or misunderstand something. Certain students, both high and low scoring, will also have heard that their first answer is more likely to be correct, and therefore that it is not a good idea to reconsider their initial answers. All these factors make it difficult to predict how long a given student will take to complete a test. It depends on a complex interaction between the preparedness, personality, and temporary emotional and physical state of the student, the nature and difficulty of the test material, and the testing environment [noise and other distractions, behavior of the examiner or proctor(s), and so on]. It is likely that the examiner can make actual time-on-task more uniform across examinees by requiring them to remain in their seats after finishing the test, but even with this restriction there will be individual differences in the time needed to complete the test.

## Arrangement of Items

It has been alleged that examinees show position preferences in answering multiple-choice items, in that they are more likely to select certain options (say *b* and *c*) than other options (*a* and *d*) when they are not certain of the answer. Although research has failed to demonstrate that such position preferences have a significant effect on test scores (Wilbur, 1970; Jessell & Sullins, 1975), it is advisable to arrange multiple-choice and true–false items so that the answers follow no set pattern. Arranging the options for multiple-choice items in alphabetical order may be satisfactory, but a better strategy is to randomize the order of options within items. This will ensure that at least the test constructor was unbiased in positioning the correct options. Of course, when "all of the above" and/or "none of the above" are used as options, they should be placed in the last position.

Recommendations for arranging other types of items may also prove helpful. For example, placing short-answer items in groups of five or so reduces errors in taking and scoring a test. On matching or rearrangement items, it is more convenient for examinees and it facilitates scoring if all options appear on the same page. Finally, sufficient space should be provided for answering short-answer and essay items, whether the answers are written in the test booklet or on a separate answer sheet.

Concerning the layout of the test as a whole, it might be expected that the examinee's task would be easier if items of the same type (multiple choice, true–false, and so on) and items dealing with the same topic were grouped together. Although it is true that arranging items in groups according to type or topic may make test preparation, administration, and scoring simpler, there is no evidence that this practice improves test scores.

It is also reasonable to suppose that test scores will be higher if subsets of items are arranged in order from easiest to most difficult. Success in answering easier items would presumably create positive anticipations of further success and hence encourage examinees to exert more effort on more difficult items appearing later. Again, however, research findings have not always confirmed this supposition (Allison, 1984; Gerow, 1980; Klimko, 1984). An occasional easy item may improve performance on subsequent items, but, in general, arranging items in order of difficulty seems to have little or no effect on multiple-choice test scores. There are exceptions to this conclusion, for example, tests that are speeded (Plake et al., 1982) or very difficult (Green, 1984; Savitz, 1985). On either a speeded test or one that is very difficult, placing the hardest items at the end of the test seems to improve overall scores somewhat.

A logical conclusion from research findings on the effects of ordering items according to difficulty level is that, in constructing tests of easy to moderate difficulty, test designers would do well to be less concerned with item arrangement and more concerned with making certain that the items are well written and measure what they are supposed to measure. But when a test is very difficult or speeded, arranging the items in order from easiest to most difficult may ensure more efficient use of the examinee's time, as well as improve motivation and thereby result in higher test scores.

## Answer Sheets

For most classroom tests, especially in the lower grades, it is advisable to have students mark their answers in the test booklets. This results in fewer errors in indicating answers. On objective items, requiring examinees to write the appropriate letters or answers in marginal spaces on the left of the questions also facilitates scoring.

Separate answer sheets, which are easier to score, can be used at the upper elementary school level and beyond. Commercially distributed answer sheets will have to be used if the test is to be machine scored (Figure 2–3). On these answer sheets, examinees respond by

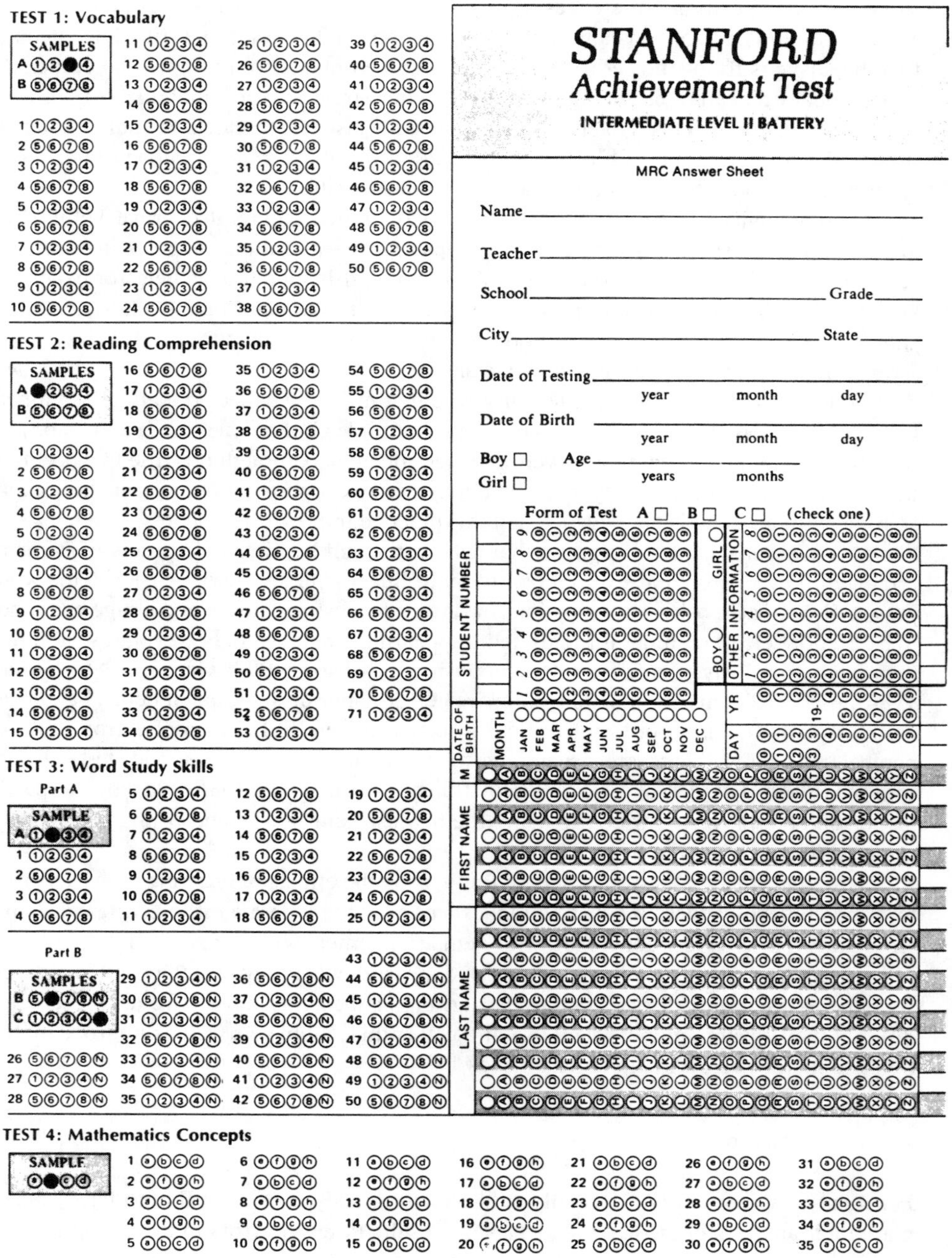
TEST 1: Vocabulary
SAMPLES
TEST 2: Reading Comprehension
SAMPLES
TEST 3: Word Study Skills
Part A
SAMPLE
Part B
SAMPLES
TEST 4: Mathematics Concepts
SAMPLE
STANFORD
Achievement Test
INTERMEDIATE LEVEL II BATTERY
MRC Answer Sheet
Name
Teacher
School
Grade
City
State
Date of Testing
year month day
Date of Birth
year month day
Boy
Girl
Age
years months
Form of Test A B C (check one)
STUDENT NUMBER
GIRL
BOY
OTHER INFORMATION
DATE OF BIRTH
MONTH
JAN FEB MAR APR MAY JUN JUL AUG SEP OCT NOV DEC
YR
DAY
M
FIRST NAME
LAST NAME

**FIGURE 2–3** Machine-scorable Answer Sheet.
(Reproduced from MRC Answer Sheet for Stanford Achievement Test: 8th Edition. Copyright © 1988 by The Psychological Corporation. Reproduced by permission. All rights reserved.)

filling in the corresponding numbered or lettered circle or space next to the item number. If the test is to be scored by hand, the classroom teacher can easily make up an answer sheet and have it reproduced in quantity. To illustrate, an answer sheet for a 75-item multiple-choice test might have the following format:

| | | | | | | | | | | | | | | | | |
|---|---|---|---|---|---|---|---|---|---|---|---|---|---|---|---|---|
| 1. | a | b | c | d | e | 26. | a | b | c | d | e | 51. | a | b | c | d | e |
| 2. | a | b | c | d | e | 27. | a | b | c | d | e | 52. | a | b | c | d | e |
| | . . . | | | | | | . . . | | | | | | . . . | | | |
| 25. | a | b | c | d | e | 50. | a | b | c | d | e | 75. | a | b | c | d | e |

Examinees are instructed to mark a slash ($/$) or a cross ($X$) through the letter corresponding to the correct answer to each item. SCANTRON answer sheets that can be scored either by machine or by hand are also widely available.

## Reproducing a Test

Every educational institution has facilities for reproducing written or printed materials for classroom use. Grade schools and colleges throughout the United States have replaced the mimeograph and ditto machines of yesteryear with photocopy machines. These machines can be used to duplicate test booklets in one- or two-sided printing format, sometimes in color. If the same type of answer sheet is to be used for different tests, a large quantity can be printed in a single run of the machine and stored for other test administrations.

## Test Directions

Upon receiving their test booklets and answer sheets, students often "plunge ahead" and begin marking their answers without first reading the directions. This is particularly true on classroom tests, since many students assume that they already know how to take tests and that reading the directions is a waste of time. Therefore, the examiner should read the general directions aloud to the class before distributing the test booklets and answer sheets. After the general directions have been read and any questions answered, the answer sheets can be distributed and the directions for marking answers on the answer sheet read aloud. Then the test booklets should be distributed face down and not turned over by the students until the signal to begin the test has been given. In this way, all examinees start the test at the same time, and no examinee can claim that he or she scored poorly because the examiner failed to explain how the answers should be marked, how much time was available, or other matters concerned with taking the test.

The test directions should tell the examinees what they are supposed to do and how long they have in which to do it. More specifically, the directions should indicate in relatively simple language the purpose of the test, the time limits, how answers are to be recorded, and how the test will be scored. The directions should also indicate whether it is advisable to guess when in doubt about an answer. A fairly detailed set of directions for a test on the preparation, administration, and scoring of classroom tests is as follows:

Write your name in the upper right-hand corner of the answer sheet; do not write anything on the test booklet. The purpose of this test is to determine your knowledge and understanding of test preparation, administration, and scoring. There are 50 items, and you will be given 50 minutes to finish the test. Answer every item by filling in the space on the answer sheet below the letter corresponding to the answer. Your score on the test will be the total number of items you answer correctly. Therefore, you should make an informed guess when in doubt about the answer. Do not omit any items. If you finish before time is up, please sit quietly until everyone has finished.

## ORAL TESTING

Oral testing is defined as an evaluation situation in which examinees respond to questions orally: The questions may be presented orally, in writing, or both. Oral achievement testing is more common in European educational institutions than in the United States, where oral testing has declined during this century and is less common in the higher than in the lower grades.

Many students do not like oral tests and feel that they are unfair measures of knowledge and understanding. However, teachers of speech, dramatics, English, and foreign languages often deplore the current inattention to the assessment of spoken language skills and feel that the consequence of such neglect is a citizenry that is unable to speak correctly, comprehensibly, or comfortably. While many teachers of languages and other subjects in which the development of speaking skills is important admit the desirability of oral exercises and evaluations, they also realize that oral tests are not only subjective but often inefficient (Platt, 1961; Crowl & McGinitie, 1974).

### Advantages of Oral Tests

Since the early part of this century, oral achievement tests have tended to be perceived as lacking in efficiency and psychometric rigor. They have also been criticized as being too time consuming, as providing a limited sample of responses, and as being poorly planned in most instances.

Despite the shortcomings of oral tests, even their critics admit that such tests possess some advantages over written tests. One advantage is the interactive social situation provided by oral examinations, permitting the evaluation of personal qualities such as appearance, style, and manner of speaking. The face-to-face situation also makes cheating and perhaps bluffing less likely. Other advantages of oral tests are that they frequently require responses at a higher intellectual level than written tests and provide practice in oral communication and social interaction. They also encourage more careful review of the test material and can be completed in less time than comparable written examinations. Oral examiners may be better able to follow the thought processes of examinees and locate the boundaries of their knowledge and understanding of the subject matter more readily. These boundaries can be determined by asking examinees to explain, defend, or elaborate on their answers. Finally, the time needed to prepare and evaluate oral answers may be less than that for written tests (Glovrozov, 1974; Platt, 1961).

Oral tests are especially appropriate for primary school children and others who experience difficulties in reading or writing. Even at higher grade levels, the administration of an occasional oral test is justified when time and/or facilities for duplicating test materials are in short supply (Green, 1975). And in subjects such as speech, foreign languages, and dramatics, oral examinations are crucial.

Oral examinations, which are actually structured interviews, are often administered to applicants for positions in governmental and industrial organizations, sometimes over the telephone for applicants who cannot travel to the examination site. Some standardization and control can be introduced into such tests by presenting the same questions to all examinees, limiting the time in which they have to answer them, and electronically recording their answers for later playback and evaluation.

## Oral versus Written Examinations

The fact that scores on oral achievement tests are only moderately correlated with scores on comparable written tests suggests that the two types of evaluation measure different aspects of achievement. In general, knowledge of specific facts can be determined more quickly with objective written tests, so oral examinations should not contain large numbers of these kinds of questions. On the other hand, as with essay tests, oral tests are more appropriate when the questions call for extended responses.

Because the achievements or behaviors assessed by oral tests are arguably just as important as those measured by written tests, more attention should be given to the major source of error in oral testing: the examiners or evaluators themselves. A thorough knowledge of the subject matter and a keen awareness of the appropriate responses are needed by oral examiners. Furthermore, the categories used by the examiners in describing or rating examinees' responses should cite specific, observable behaviors, rather than nebulous concepts such as *creative potential, character, general ability,* or *interpersonal effectiveness.* These undefined, and perhaps undefinable, concepts are no more easily measured by oral tests than by written ones.

# PERFORMANCE TESTING

Paper-and-pencil tests are the most efficient and objective of all types of testing, but they are vicarious rather than direct demonstrations of applicable knowledge and skills. Knowledge of the subject matter can be demonstrated fairly thoroughly in a short period of time by means of an essay, multiple-choice, or other written test. Unfortunately, possessing a body of information about a topic or being able to explain how to do something is not the same thing as using the information or skills in practical situations. I once conducted a human relationships workshop with a group of assembly-line supervisors. Although all the supervisors were able to do well on my written tests and they concurred that a democratic approach to employees was superior to an authoritarian approach, when these same supervisors returned to the assembly line, the majority resumed their "bull-of-the-woods," authoritarian approach to supervision. There are many other examples that are situation specific, in which students learn to give the correct answer in class or on a paper-and-pencil test, but abandon it when confronted with a real-life situation where it might apply.

Most of the learning that goes on in classrooms is, to some extent, related to behavior in nonacademic contexts, but the relationship is far from perfect. Generalization of knowledge and skills from the classroom to real-life situations is particularly tenuous in the case of verbal knowledge. Teachers realize that, if schooling is to prepare students for life, then skills as well as knowledge must be taught in a such a way that they will transfer to job situations and other nonschool contexts. Teachers of science, athletics, dramatics, music, industrial arts, speech, foreign languages, penmanship, agriculture, and numerous other subject-matter areas recognize the need for students to engage in repeated practice and to have practical experiences in the skills if they are to be well learned and transferrable. Science labs and projects, psychomotor skills learned in games and sports, playing musical instruments and singing, acting in plays, constructing or applying useful objects in shop, practicing public speaking and conversation in English and other languages—all provide opportunities to learn skills that are potentially useful outside class and will serve as a foundation for later practical experiential learning.

Although it may not be necessary to follow a taxonomy of psychomotor objectives like those proposed by Simpson (1966) and Harrow (1972) in planning a test to measure how well a person has learned a particular skill, it is useful to construct a detailed list of the behaviors that are indicative of a range of proficiency in that skill. Decisions should be made beforehand as to how much (numerical) weight will be assigned to each aspect of the performance and what deductions (if any) will be made for mistakes, slowness, and sloppiness.

A performance test should focus mainly on the product or end result of performing a skill, but the way in which it is performed (the process) is also important. For example, what counts most in playing golf is how many strokes the player takes to get the ball in the hole, but all golf instructors realize that form or style is also important. On performance tests involving a tangible finished product, not only the quantity and quality of that product but also how efficiently it was made should be noted.

Both the products and processes of performance are typically evaluated subjectively, primarily by observation, combined with a written or electronic record and a checklist or rating scale (see Figure 3–2). In particular, careful observation, as free as possible of bias, is critical to the accurate evaluation of performance. Structured performance tests, in which every examinee is tested under the same conditions, are usually more objective than unstructured ones, in which students are observed and evaluated surreptitiously during class, in the hall, or on the school grounds. But even when the utmost care is taken, by their very nature performance tests are less objective, and consequently less reliable, than written tests. In addition, performance tests take more time than written tests and often require expensive equipment and other time-consuming arrangements. For these reasons, whenever the cost and inefficiency of a performance test are not offset by its real-world character, a written test is preferred.

## SUMMARY

This chapter deals primarily with procedures for designing and constructing educational achievement tests, but the principles discussed can also be applied to other kinds of psychological and educational assessment instruments.

The first step in constructing an achievement test is to prepare a list of the behavioral objectives to be assessed. A table of specifications giving the number of items needed in each content (topical) category for each behavioral objective should then be constructed. Various taxonomies, or methods of classifying behavioral objectives in the cognitive, affective, and psychomotor domains, have been proposed. The most popular taxonomy of educational objectives is Bloom and Krathwohl's *Taxonomy of Educational Objectives: Cognitive Domain.*

Both essay and objective tests possess advantages and disadvantages. Essay items are easier to construct, but objective items can be scored more quickly and accurately. Objective tests also provide a more representative sample of subject content. Short-answer, true–false, multiple-choice, and matching questions are varieties of objective test items. Of these, multiple-choice items are the most versatile and popular.

In assembling a test, attention should be given to such factors as test length and format, the method of recording responses, facilities for reproducing the test, and directions for administration. Directions for administering a test include information on the purpose(s), time limits, scoring procedure, and advisability of guessing when in doubt.

Oral tests are not employed as much as written tests, but when carefully planned, administered, and evaluated, they can provide information that is not usually obtained by other assessment methods. In a sense, both written and oral tests are measures of performance, but the concept of *performance testing* has typically focused on nonverbal behavior. Performance tests are more realistic than verbal tests in that, rather than simply telling how to do something or what was done, the examinee demonstrates the process. Such tests are used extensively for evaluating learned abilities in both laboratory and field situations, ranging from the science laboratory to the sports arena and other applied contexts.

## QUESTIONS AND ACTIVITIES

1. Choose a topic for a test in an area of interest to you, state your behavioral and content objectives, construct a table of specifications, and design a 1-hour objective test on the topic using various types of items.

2. Design your own classroom system for educational objectives in the cognitive domain. How does your system differ from those described in the text? What particular advantages and disadvantages does it possess?

3. Describe the relative strengths and weaknesses of essay and objective tests. For what purposes and under what conditions is each type of test most appropriate?

4. Why are multiple-choice items generally considered superior to other types of objective test items? Can you think of any situation in which true–false, completion, or matching items would be preferable to multiple-choice items?

5. Write five short-answer (completion) items, five true–false items, and five multiple-choice items based on the following selection adapted from Aiken (1980):

> One reason for the shortage of psychometric data on older adults is that people in this age group, whose behavior is less susceptible to control by psychologists and educators, are frequently reluctant to be tested. There are many reasons for the uncooperativeness of older adult examinees, including lack of time, perception of the test tasks as trivial or meaningless, and the fear of doing badly and appearing foolish. Older adults, to an even greater extent than more test-conscious younger adults, do not relish performing tasks that make them look ridiculous or are perceived as having no significance in their lives.
>
> Because older adults have low motivation to be tested in the first place, sensitivity and tact on the part of psychological examiners are required to obtain valid responses in testing them. Unfortunately, it is often questionable whether technically proficient but young examiners can establish sufficient rapport with older examinees to communicate the test directions adequately and stimulate examinees to do their best. Relatively few psychometrists appear to have sufficient training and experience in the psychological examination of

older adults to do a credible job. Most examiners find, however, that once older persons agree to be tested, they are as highly motivated as younger examinees to do their best.

Even when older adults are cooperative and motivated to do well, the time limits on many tests, the presence of sensory defects, as well as distractibility and easy fatigability, make it difficult for them to perform satisfactorily. For example, one of the most characteristic things about being older is that reflexes and physical movements tend to be slower. For this reason, explanations of the age-related decline in test scores in such areas as learning and memory must take into account the fact that older adults typically do not react as quickly as their younger counterparts.

Although older people are usually at a disadvantage on timed tests, their performance improves significantly when they are given sufficient time to respond. Consequently, on untimed tests older adults show little or no inferiority in comparison with younger adults.

Sensory defects, especially in the visual and auditory modalities, can also interfere with performance in old age. Special test materials, such as large-face type and trained examiners who are alert to the presence of sensory defects, can help. Occasionally, however, an alleged sensory defect may actually be a mask for a problem in reading and auditory comprehension. For example, the writer had the experience of preparing to test an elderly man who, embarrassed by his poor reading ability, conveniently forgot his glasses and hence was unable to read the test materials.

6. What are the advantages and disadvantages of oral tests compared with written tests? Under what circumstances are oral tests appropriate? How should they be designed, administered, and scored?

7. What do performance tests measure that cannot be measured by means of paper-and-pencil (written) tests or oral tests? Describe two or three performance tests that you have taken.

8. Use program 1, "Constructing an Objective Test," in category B ("Programs on Test Construction, Administration, and Scoring") of *Computer Programs for Psychological Assessment* to prepare a short (10-item) multiple-choice test on a topic of interest to you. Then use program 2 in category B to administer your test to several classmates and score it. The passwords are "makit" for program B-1 and "takit" for program B-2.

# 3

# TEST ADMINISTRATION
# AND SCORING

No matter how carefully a test is constructed, the results are worthless unless it is administered and scored properly. The necessity of having established procedures or guidelines for administering and scoring psychological and educational tests is recognized by all professional organizations concerned with testing. *Standards for Educational and Psychological Testing* (American Educational Research Association et al., 1985) consists of a set of 180 standards for evaluating, administering, scoring, and interpreting tests and other psychometric instruments. Five of these standards pertaining specifically to test administration and scoring are listed in Table 3–1. These standards stress the importance of uniform test administration and

**TABLE 3–1 Standards for Test Administration and Scoring**

**Standard 15.1**   In typical applications, test administrators should follow carefully the standardized procedures for administration and scoring specified by the test publisher. Specifications regarding instructions to test takers, time limits, the form of item presentation or response, and test materials or equipment should be strictly observed. Exceptions should be made only on the basis of carefully considered professional judgment, primarily in clinical applications.

**Standard 15.2**   The testing environment should be one of reasonable comfort and with minimal distractions. Testing materials should be readable and understandable. In computerized testing, items displayed on a screen should be legible and free from glare, and the terminal should be properly positioned.

**Standard 15.3**   Reasonable efforts should be made to assure the validity of test scores by eliminating opportunities for test takers to attain scores by fraudulent means.

**Standard 15.7**   Test users should protect the security of test materials. *Comment:* Those who have test materials under their control should take all steps necessary to assure that only individuals with a legitimate need for access to test materials are able to obtain such access.

**Standard 15.10**   Those responsible for testing programs should provide appropriate interpretations when test score information is released to students, parents, legal representatives, teachers, or the media. The interpretations should describe in simple language what the test covers, what scores mean, common misinterpretations of test scores, and how scores will be used. *Comment:* Test users should consult the interpretive material prepared by the test developer or publisher and should revise or supplement the material as necessary to represent the local and individual results accurately and clearly.

scoring procedures and of making certain that the test directions are clear and that distractions are kept to a minimum. Furthermore, the security of test materials must be maintained, cheating should be controlled, and interpretations of scores should be understandable by persons who will read them.

## TEST ADMINISTRATION

The procedure to be followed in administering a test depends on the kind of test (individual or group, timed or nontimed, cognitive or affective), as well as the characteristics of the examinees (chronological age, education, cultural background, physical and mental status). Whatever the type of test and the kinds of people who take it, factors such as the extent to which the examinees are prepared and their level of motivation, anxiety, fatigue, and health can also affect performance.

Just as preparedness, test wiseness, and motivation of test takers can affect their scores, factors that vary with the examiner and the situation also have an influence. The skill, personality, and behavior of the examiner, particularly on individual tests, affect the performance of examinees. Administrators of most individual tests must be formally licensed or certified by an appropriate state agency or supervised by a licensed examiner. Such requirements help to ensure that examiners possess the requisite knowledge and skills to administer, score, and interpret psychometric instruments of various kinds.

Situational variables, including the time and place of testing and environmental conditions such as illumination, temperature, noise level, and ventilation, may also contribute to the motivation, concentration, and performance of examinees. For this reason, the examiner must make careful preparations before administering a test.

### Examiner's Duties before Test Administration

***Scheduling the Test***   In scheduling a test, the examiner should take into account activities that the examinees usually engage in at that time. Obviously, it is unwise to test schoolchildren during lunchtime, playtime, when other pleasurable activities typically occur or are being anticipated, or even when enjoyable or exciting events have just taken place (such as immediately after a holiday). The testing period should seldom be longer than 1 hour when testing elementary school children or $1\frac{1}{2}$ hours when testing secondary school students. Because 30 minutes is about as long as preschool and primary school children can remain attentive to test tasks, more than one session may be required for administering longer tests to young children.

With respect to classroom tests, students should be informed well in advance when and where the test will be given, what sort of material it will contain, and what kind of test (objective, essay, oral) it will be. Students deserve an opportunity to prepare intellectually, emotionally, and physically for a test. For this reason, "pop quizzes" and other unannounced tests are usually inadvisable. If the teacher feels that occasional pop quizzes help to ensure that students keep up with the course material, such quizzes should not carry the same weight as regular examinations.

***Informed Consent***    In many states, administration of an intelligence test or other psychodiagnostic instrument to a child requires the informed consent of a parent, a guardian, or someone else who is legally responsible for the child. *Informed consent* consists of an agreement between an agency or professional and a particular person or his or her legal representative. Under the terms of the agreement permission is given to administer psychological tests to the person and/or to obtain other information for evaluative or diagnostic purposes.

Informed consent should be obtained from test takers or their legal representatives before testing is done except (a) when testing without consent is mandated by law or governmental regulation (e.g., statewide testing programs); (b) when testing is conducted as a regular part of school activities (e.g., school-wide testing programs and participation by schools in norming and research studies; or (c) when consent is clearly implied (e.g., application for employment or educational admissions). When consent is not required, test takers should be informed concerning the testing process. (American Educational Research Association et al., 1985, page 85)

The requirement of informed consent is usually satisfied by obtaining the signature of the legally responsible person on a standard form supplied by the school district or other relevant agency. The form specifies the purpose(s) of the examination, the uses to be made of the results, the parent's or other guardian's rights, and the procedure for obtaining a copy of the final report or interpretation. An illustration of such a form is given in Figure 3–1 (see also Figure 1–3).

***Becoming Familiar with the Test***    When the examiner and the test author are one and the same, he or she is obviously familiar with the material and the administration procedure. But because the person administering a standardized test is seldom the one who constructed it, the manual accompanying the test should be studied carefully before attempting to administer it. It is particularly important to become familiar with the directions for administration and the content of the test. To acquire this familiarity, the examiner should take the test before administering it to anyone else. Finally, it is advisable to review the directions and other procedural matters just prior to administration. Test booklets, answer sheets, and other materials should also be checked and counted beforehand. *Secure tests* bearing serial numbers, such as the Scholastic Aptitude Test and the Graduate Record Examinations, must be inspected closely and arranged in numerical order.

If a child or an adult is referred by an outside agency or by a person such as a physician or court judge for an individual psychological examination, the tests and other diagnostic procedures that are administered will depend on the kinds of information requested by the referral source and the purposes for which the diagnostic information will be used. Consequently, it is important for the referring person to specify precisely what information is needed and what will be done with it. In any event, the examiner should be thoroughly familiar with the instruments administered and for what kinds of individuals and conditions they are appropriate.

***Ensuring Satisfactory Testing Conditions***    Examiners should make certain that seating, lighting, ventilation, temperature, noise level, and other physical conditions in the testing situation are appropriate. A room familiar to the examinees and relatively free from distractions is preferred. A "Testing—Do Not Disturb" sign on the closed door of the examination

Date Signed
Assessment
Plan is Received
Date IEP to be held

**LOS ANGELES UNIFIED SCHOOL DISTRICT**
Division of Special Education

**ASSESSMENT PLAN AND PARENTAL CONSENT FOR ASSESSMENT**

Procedural Safeguards
Due Process Procedures
( )Given ( )Mailed
To Parent on:

By: _____

TO THE PARENT/GUARDIAN OF: _____ Date: _____

Birthdate: _____   _____   Primary Language:_____
         Mo.   Day   Yr.              School

English Proficiency_____ Measured by Instrument (Specify)_____ Date:_____

WE REQUEST YOUR CONSENT FOR ASSESSMENT OF YOUR SON/DAUGHTER WHO ( ) MAY BENEFIT FROM SPECIAL EDUCATION OR ( ) IS ALREADY RECEIVING SPECIAL EDUCATION AND ADDITIONAL ASSESSMENT IS NEEDED.

QUALIFIED PROFESSIONALS WHO MAY CONTRIBUTE TO THE MULTIDISCIPLINARY ASSESSMENT ARE INDICATED BELOW BY THEIR INITIALS AND TITLES SUCH AS PSYCHOLOGIST, RESOURCE SPECIALIST, PHYSICIAN, SPEECH SPECIALIST, ADAPTIVE P.E. TEACHER, EDUCATIONAL AUDIOLOGIST, SCHOOL NURSE/PHYSICIAN, SPECIAL EDUCATION TEACHER AND OTHERS. REPRESENTATIVE TYPES OF TESTS ARE LISTED ON THE BACK OF THIS PLAN.

PLEASE REVIEW THE PLAN AND INDICATE IN THE PARENT CONSENT SECTION BELOW WHETHER OR NOT YOU CONSENT TO THIS ASSESSMENT. IF YOU HAVE ANY QUESTIONS ABOUT THE PLAN OR THE PROCEDURAL SAFEGUARDS/DUE PROCESS PROCEDURES YOU RECEIVED WITH THE PLAN, PLEASE CONTACT:

_____   _____   ( )_____
        NAME                      TITLE                    PHONE

**PROPOSED SPECIAL EDUCATION ASSESSMENT PLAN**

| TYPE AND PURPOSE OF ASSESSMENT | ASSESSMENT RESPONSIBILITIES (Indicate Initials and Title) |
|---|---|
| **ACADEMIC/PREACADEMIC ACHIEVEMENT** - To assess basic reading skills and reading comprehension; mathematics calculation and reasoning; spelling; written expression and, if appropriate, pre-reading skills | |
| **COGNITIVE LEVEL** - To assess specific skills, learning rate and problem solving ability. **NO STANDARDIZED INTELLIGENCE (I.Q.) TESTS WILL BE GIVEN.** | |
| **COMMUNICATION/LANGUAGE FUNCTIONING** - To measure the ability to understand, relate to and use language/speech clearly and appropriately. | |
| **SOCIAL/EMOTIONAL STATUS** - To assess level of social maturity, ability to function independently and inter-personal skills. | |
| **MOTOR ABILITIES** - To assess the coordination of body movements in large and small muscle activities. | |
| **MEDICAL** - To assess general physical condition by a history and physical examination. | |
| **AUDIOLOGICAL ASSESSMENT** - To measure the nature and degree of possible hearing loss. | |
| **OTHER** Purpose: | |

**PARENT CONSENT FOR ASSESSMENT**

**PLEASE INDICATE BY A CHECK MARK AND YOUR SIGNATURE**

1. ( ) I CONSENT TO THE ASSESSMENT PLAN

2. ( ) I DO NOT CONSENT TO THE ASSESSMENT PLAN

SIGNATURE _____   _____   ( )_____   ( )_____
              Parent/Guardian          Date         Home Phone        Work Phone

In addition, I wish to submit a written report(s) from the following person(s) who has evaluated my son/daughter:

_____              _____
        Name                                   Title

27.805B (Rev. 6/88)    RETURN THE WHITE COPY AS INDICATED IN THE COVER LETTER. KEEP THE YELLOW COPY FOR YOUR RECORDS

**STUDENT FILE COPY**

**FIGURE 3–1**   Los Angeles Unified School District: Assessment Plan and Parental Consent Form for Assessment.
(Reprinted by permission of the Los Angeles Unified School District.)

room may help to eliminate interruptions and other distractions. Adequate exits and restroom facilities should also be available.

It is best to administer an individual test in a private room, with only the examiner and the examinee (and, if necessary, the parent, guardian, or other responsible person) present. In administering either an individual or a group test, special provisions may also have to be made for physically handicapped or physically different (for example, left-handed) examinees.

**Minimizing Cheating**   Well-trained examiners are quite cognizant of the need for test security, both before and after a test is administered, and for accepting the responsibility for making certain that it is maintained. Before the test, comfortable seating that minimizes cheating should be arranged. Although preferable, it is not always possible for examinees to sit one seat apart or in such a way that cheating is difficult. Preparing multiple forms (different items or different item arrangements) of the test and distributing different forms to adjacent examinees can reduce cheating on group-administered tests. Another possibility is to use multiple answer sheets, that is, answer sheets having different layouts. None of these procedures eliminates the need for proctors, and several roving proctors should be employed whenever a large group of people is tested. Proctors may assist in distributing and collecting test materials, as well as answering procedural questions. The presence of proctors also discourages cheating and unruliness during a test.

Proctoring and other procedures designed to guard against cheating are taken quite seriously in the administration of secure standardized tests such as the Scholastic Assessment Test and the Graduate Record Examinations. These tests, which are carefully inventoried both before and after they are administered, are closely supervised; examinees are required to show proper identification before they can take the test.

### Examiner's Duties during the Test

**Following Test Directions**   Carefully prepared test directions, which are read slowly and clearly when presented orally, inform examinees of the purposes of the test and how to indicate their answers. Examiners of a standardized test are required to follow the directions for administration carefully even when further explanation might clarify the task. Departure from standard directions may result in a different task from the one the test designers had in mind. If the directions are not identical to those given to the sample of people on whom the test was standardized, the scores will not have the same meaning as those of the standardization group. The result will be the loss of a useful frame of reference for interpreting scores.

In typical applications, test administrators should follow carefully the standardized procedures for administration and scoring specified by the test publisher. Specifications regarding instructions to test takers, time limits, the form of item presentation or response, and test materials or equipment should be strictly observed. Exceptions should be made only on the basis of carefully considered professional judgment, primarily in clinical applications. (American Educational Research Association et al., 1985, page 83)

Testers in clinical and educational contexts sometimes go beyond the test directions. They attempt to "test the limits" of an examinee's abilities or personal characteristics by employing "dynamic testing" procedures to obtain additional cues for purposes of interpretation or diagnosis. Illustrative of such dynamic assessment are Feuerstein's *learning potential assessment* (Feuerstein et al., 1987) and Embretson's (1987) computer-based approach for finding an examinee's performance level. Both of these approaches involve a test–teach–test format in which the examinee is tested (pretested), then given practice on the test materials, and finally tested again (posttested). The change in performance level from pretest to posttest is calculated as a measure of the examinee's learning potential.

**Remaining Alert**   When administering a group test, whether standardized or nonstandardized, the examiner should be alert to cheating, as well as talking and other unnecessary noise. Making certain that a messenger is available in case of medical emergencies or other problems is also a wise precaution. On teacher-made tests or even on standardized tests if the directions permit, students may be informed periodically of how much time is remaining by writing the time on a chalkboard or other visible surface.

**Establishing Rapport**   On both individual and group tests, the behavior of the examiner can have a significant effect on the motivation and behavior of examinees. Sometimes even a smile provides enough encouragement to anxious or inadequately prepared examinees so that they will remain calm, try hard, and perform as well as they can. Because there is a better opportunity to observe examinees in individual than in group testing situations, low motivation, distractibility, and stress are more likely to be detected when administering an individual test. An attempt may then be made to cope with these problems or at least to take them into account in interpreting the scores. In a group testing situation, where personal interaction with every examinee is usually impossible, the examiner is more limited in sensing how well each person is feeling and doing. On both individual and group tests, a good rule to follow is to be friendly but objective, authoritative but not authoritarian, appropriate in manner and dress, and in charge of the testing situation. Such behavior on the part of the examiner tends to create a condition of *rapport*—a cordial, accepting relationship that encourages examinees to respond honestly and accurately.

**Preparing for Special Problems**   In some circumstances, examiners need to be especially active and encouraging. A testing situation creates a certain amount of tension in almost anyone, and sometimes an examinee becomes quite anxious. Testing the very young or very old, mentally disturbed or mentally retarded, and physically handicapped or culturally disadvantaged persons presents special problems. In certain situations, questions and answers may have to be given orally, rather than in print, or in a language other than English. Not only must the examiner be familiar with the test material, but also alert, flexible, warm, and objective. These qualities are not easily taught; experience in a variety of testing situations plays an important role in acquiring them.

**Flexibility**   Some flexibility is usually permitted in administering nonstandardized tests and even certain standardized instruments. In testing with these measures, sensitivity and patience on the part of the examiner can provide a better opportunity for handicapped individuals and those with other special problems to demonstrate their capabilities. Other recommended procedures, which have been adapted from well-known instructional techniques, are as follows:

1. Provide ample time for examinees to respond to the test material.
2. Allow sufficient practice on sample items.
3. Use relatively short testing periods.
4. Watch for fatigue and anxiety and take them into account.
5. Be aware of and make provisions for visual, auditory, and other sensory of perceptual-motor defects.
6. Employ a generous amount of encouragement and positive reinforcement.
7. Don't try to force examinees to respond when they repeatedly decline to do so.

***Oral Testing***   Students frequently regard oral examinations with mixed feelings and often considerable apprehension. Consequently, efforts to calm their fears and provide alternative testing methods for those who become emotionally distraught in oral testing situations can improve the effectiveness of these kinds of tests. Examiners who make special efforts to establish rapport with examinees discover that the latter may even come to enjoy oral tests.

## Taking a Test

In general, "pop quizzes" are not considered fair. Students deserve a chance to prepare for a test, so letting them know in advance not only when and where the test will be given, but also what it will cover and what kind of test it will be, is recommended procedure. With respect to the expected format of a test, both classroom and laboratory studies have found that people make higher scores on recall (essay, short-answer) tests when they are told in advance that this kind of test will be given (for example, May & Thompson, 1989). Expecting a recognition (multiple-choice, true–false) test encourages more concentrated study of details, whereas expecting a recall test results in greater efforts to remember higher-order units, trends, and themes in the material (Schmidt, 1983).

Classroom studies have found that announcing in advance that an objective will be given is associated with higher scores on multiple-choice, true–false, and other recognition tests. However, the results of laboratory studies are more complex (Lundeberg & Fox, 1991). Furthermore, other factors, such as mental ability, test wiseness, guessing, and careful reading and consideration of items, appear to have as much effect on test scores as knowing what type of test will be administered.

***Test Wiseness***   When responding to objective test items, examiners often employ quite different methods from those intended by the item writer. Not all examinees read the items carefully, and they often fail to use all the information given. This may not be essential in every case, because students often recognize the correct answers to multiple-choice items without having read the material on which the questions are based. Sometimes they are able to eliminate wrong options by noting that certain answers are worded incorrectly or are too broad or too narrow. Alliterative associations, grossly unrelated options, inclusionary language, correct options that are more precise than other options, grammatical cues, and giveaways that are answered in other items are additional cues that can reveal the correct answers to multiple-choice items.

Observations of students taking multiple-choice tests, combined with posttest interviews, indicate that, although they sometimes answer an item simply by eliminating obviously incorrect choices, a more common practice is to make comparative judgments among options. Knowledge of the teacher's idiosyncrasies is also an aspect of test wiseness. *Test wiseness* appears to be a nongeneral, cue-specific ability that develops as students mature and share information on test-taking skills (Evans, 1984). For example, the length, technicality, and exoticness of options act as cues to the correct answers (Strang, 1980; Tidwell, 1980). Boys appear to be more testwise than girls (Preston, 1964), and verbal items are more susceptible than numerical items to test wiseness (Rowley, 1974). Some aspects of test wiseness or test sophistication can also be taught (Millman & Pauk, 1969; American College, 1978). At the very least, students who wish to become more testwise should review the suggestions in Box 3–1.

***Changing Answers***    Often examinees must decide whether to change their first responses to test items. It is sometimes maintained that, because initial answers tend to be right, going over a test and changing answers that have already been thought through is a waste of time and counterproductive (Benjamin, Cavell, & Shallenberger, 1984). The results of a number of investigations indicate, however, that examinees tend to make higher scores when they reconsider their answers and change those about which they have second thoughts (for example, Geiger, 1990, 1991a, 1991b). Answers are more likely to be changed from wrong to right than vice versa, although the actual number of changed answers tends to be relatively small.

***Guessing***    Directions for objective tests often include advice concerning whether to omit an item or to guess when in doubt about the correct answer. Guessing, which is more likely to occur when items are difficult or wordy, results in greater score inflation on true–false than on multiple-choice tests. In general, it is advisable for test takers to guess only when they can eliminate one or more options or they have some idea about which option is correct. Because it is almost always possible to eliminate at least one option on an item, guessing rather than omitting items usually results in higher test scores. This is true whether or not scores are "corrected" for guessing.

Understandably, examinees guess less when they are informed that a penalty for guessing will be subtracted from their scores than when no directions concerning guessing are given or they are told to guess when in doubt. However, examinees do not always follow or even read the test directions carefully. Even those who read every word of the directions do not always interpret them in the same way. Regardless of what the test directions advise or do not advise, some examinees are reluctant to guess when they are uncertain of the correct answer. This characteristic has been referred to as "intolerance of ambiguity" or "low risk taking."

## Examiner's Duties after the Test

After administering an individual test, the examiner should collect and secure all test materials. The examinee should be reassured concerning his or her performance, perhaps given a small reward in the case of a child, and returned to an appropriate place. In clinical testing,

**Box 3–1**

**How to Improve Your Test Scores**

1.  Don't wait until the day before a test to begin studying when the test has been announced well in advance.
2.  Ask the instructor for old copies of tests that you can legitimately examine.
3.  Ask other students what kinds of tests the instructor usually gives.
4.  Don't make studying for the test a social occasion; it is usually better to isolate yourself when preparing for a test.
5.  Don't get too comfortable when studying. Your body assumes that you want to sleep when you lie down or get too comfortable.
6.  Study for the type of test (multiple choice, true–false, essay) that has been announced.
7.  If the type of test to be administered is not announced, it is probably best to study for a recall (essay) test.
8.  Apply the Survey Q3R (survey, questions, reading, recitation, review) when studying for a test. Survey the material, ask yourself questions about it, read it attentively with an intent to remember, recite the material to yourself after reading it, and review it just prior to the test.
9.  Try to form the material you are studying into test items, for example, into multiple-choice items if a multiple-choice test is to be given or into essay items if an essay test is announced.
10. Read the test directions carefully before beginning the test. If certain information, such as time limits, correction for guessing, item weighting, or the like, has been omitted, don't hesitate to ask the test administrator.
11. On essay tests, think about the questions and formulate answers in your mind and/or on scratch paper before you begin writing.
12. Pace yourself in taking a test. For example, on a multiple-choice test you should have answered $1/n$th of the items when $1/n$th of the time has elapsed.
13. Whether or not a correction for guessing is used in scoring a test, don't leave an item unanswered if you can eliminate even one option.
14. Skip more difficult items and return to them later. Don't panic if you can't answer an item; circle it and come back to it after you have answered other items. Then if you still aren't certain of the answer, make an educated guess.
15. When time permits, review your answers; don't be overly eager to hand in your test paper before time has expired.

it is usually important to interview a parent or other person who has accompanied the examinee, perhaps both before and after the test. Also after the test, some information on what will be done with the results can be given to the examinee and/or the accompanying party. The examiner reassures those concerned, promising to communicate the results and interpretations to the proper person(s) or agency and to recommend any further action.

Following administration of a group test, the examiner should collect the test materials (booklets, answer sheets, scratch paper, pencils, and so on). In the case of a standardized test, the test booklets and answer sheets must be counted and collated and all other collected materials checked to make certain that nothing is missing. Only then are the examinees dismissed or prepared for the next activity and the answer sheets arranged for scoring.

## TEST SCORING

Professional test designers do not wait until a test is constructed and administered before deciding what scoring procedure to use. Similarly, if a teacher-made test consists of a series of parts dealing with different content or different types of items, the teacher may wish to obtain separate scores on the various parts and a composite score on the test as a whole. Whether to subtract a correction for guessing, whether to assign different scoring weights to different items or sections, and whether to report the results in raw-score form or to convert them in some way must also be decided. For standardized tests, the classroom teacher does not have to make all these decisions; answer sheets can be scored by machine. And even when answer sheets must be scored by hand, scoring stencils provided by the test publisher can be used according to the directions given in the manual.

### Scoring Essay Tests

Essay questions can be made more effective by structuring the task clearly so that the interpretation of a question does not vary widely from person to person. Scoring can then be based on the quality of the answer. Similarly, the scoring procedure for essay items should be as structured and as objective as possible so that the scores will depend less on noncontent, impressionistic factors and more on the level of knowledge and understanding demonstrated. Scoring on the basis of penmanship rather than quality of the answers,[1] being overly general (*leniency error*), and giving a high score to an answer simply because an examinee scores high on other items (*halo effect*) are among the errors that can affect scores on essay items.

A number of things can be done to make the scores on essay tests more objective and reliable. To begin, the scorer must decide whether to score the question as a whole or to assign separate weights to different components. Whole (*global* or *holistic*) scoring is common, but it is perhaps more meaningful to use an analytic scoring procedure in which points are given for each item of information or skill included in the answer. On the first essay

---

[1]Interestingly enough, scores on essay tests are not always positively related to penmanship quality. In a study by Chase (1990–1991), for example, essays in poor handwriting were assigned higher marks than those in good handwriting.

item in Table 2–4, for example, one point might be awarded for each correct advantage or disadvantage listed and a maximum of five points for the manner in which the answer is organized. The maximum number of points allotted to an item is determined not only by the examiner's judgment of the importance of the item, but also by the assigned length of the answer. When the directions specify a half-page answer, the item should be weighted less than when a whole-page answer is required.

Whatever scoring weights are assigned to specific questions and answers, it is advisable for the test designer to prepare ideal answers to the questions. It is also recommended that the names of examinees be blocked out before inspecting the test papers so they can be scored anonymously. Other recommendations are as follows:

1. Score all answers to one question before going on to the next question.
2. Score all answers to an item during the same scoring period.
3. If both style (mechanics, quality of writing) and content are to be scored, evaluate each separately.
4. Have a second person rescore each paper, and make the final scores the average of the number of points assigned by the separate scorers.
5. Write comments next to the examinee's responses, and mark error corrections on the papers.

Corrections and comments written on classroom test papers are a valuable supplement to the number of points or the grade assigned. A student is more likely to learn something if the responses to a test are corrected and commented on, rather than merely being given a number or letter grade.

## Scoring Objective Tests

A unique advantage of objective tests is the efficiency and accuracy with which they can be scored. Whereas scorers of essay tests spend hours reading answers and evaluating their correctness, a clerk can score an objective test quickly and accurately with a scoring stencil or machine. Therefore, the test papers can be returned to the examinees while the material remains fresh in their minds.

A strip key or stencil for handscoring test booklets or answer sheets can be easily prepared. A strip of cardboard containing the correct answers at positions corresponding to the spaces in the test booklet where answers are to be written makes a satisfactory strip key. A scoring stencil for use with a special answer sheet can be prepared from a blank sheet of paper or cardboard by punching out the spaces where the correct answers should be.

*Machine Scoring*    Although the majority of answer sheets for commercially distributed tests can be scored by hand or machine, tests distributed by National Computer Systems and certain other organizations are scored only by machine. After a test is administered, the answer sheets may be mailed to a special scoring service or returned to the distributor for machine scoring.

Machine scoring of objective tests has been possible for over a half-century, and the widespread availability of computers has made test scoring much more rapid, flexible, and economical. Optical scanners connected to computers are used by numerous scoring services and can score hundreds of answer sheets in an hour.

**Human Scoring Errors**   Computer scoring of tests is not completely error free, and it is recommended that test-scoring services monitor their error frequencies and issue corrected score reports when errors are found in test scores (American Educational Research Association et al., 1985). Compared with hand scoring, however, the error rates in computer scoring are small indeed.

   Considering the fact that in some cases the directions for scoring many individual tests of intelligence and personality are not entirely clear, it is not surprising that different scores may be assigned to the same response. Although the variability of scores is probably greater with less experienced scorers (Slate & Jones, 1990), even highly experienced scorers make mistakes. It has been found, for example, that errors in both administration and scoring occur when graduate students in psychology and even professional psychologists administer individual intelligence tests (Franklin & Stillman, 1982; Ryan, Prefitera, & Powers, 1983). In a number of cases, the errors are of sufficient magnitude to result in assigning individuals to the wrong intelligence level. Trained clinical personnel also make mistakes in hand scoring personality inventories, some being serious enough to alter clinical diagnoses (Allard et al., 1995). Other studies have found that scoring is affected by the examiner's or scorer's liking for the examinee. Perception of the examinee as a warm person (Donahue & Sattler, 1971) or as bright or dull (Sattler, Hillix, & Neher, 1970; Sattler & Winget, 1970) can also affect scoring. Errors in converting raw scores to standard or scaled scores may occur when the examinee's exact chronological age is unknown or computed incorrectly.

**Scoring Weights for Multiple-choice and True–False Items**   It might seem that on objective tests, as on essay items, the number of points assigned to an answer should vary with the kind of item and the quality of the response. Many studies of the effects of a priori weighting of responses to conventional objective test items, that is, allocating different numbers of points to different item types and different responses, have been conducted. Some research has found weighting to be more discriminating and reliable than conventional scoring (Serlin & Kaiser, 1978; Willson, 1982; Hsu, Moss, & Khampalikit, 1984). The advantages of a priori weighting, however, do not seem to be justified by the increased scoring time and cost (Kansup & Hakstian, 1975). On tests of 20 or more items, simply assigning a score of 1 to each correct response and 0 to each incorrect response is as satisfactory as using different weights. Thus, possible scores on a conventionally scored 50-item multiple-choice or true–false test scored by this procedure range from 0 to 50.

   Assigning different weights to different responses might be more effective if the type of required response were changed. One interesting variation on the true–false format is to have examinees indicate how confident they are in their answers. Table 3–2 illustrates one such confidence-weighting procedure for true–false items. Although this procedure may represent an improvement over conventional 0–1 scoring of true–false items, the latter is probably satisfactory for most classroom tests consisting of 30 or more objective test items.

**Scoring Ranking Items**   As with true–false and multiple-choice items, short-answer and matching items may be scored by assigning 1 point to correct responses and 0 points to incorrect responses or omissions. Because of the large number of different orders in which

**TABLE 3–2 Confidence-weighting Procedure for True–False Items**

| | The statement is actually: | |
| --- | --- | --- |
| Examinee says that: | True | False |
| The statement is probably true | 2 | −2 |
| The statement is possibly true | 1 | 0 |
| I have no idea | .5 | .5 |
| The statement is possibly false | 0 | 1 |
| The statement is probably false | −2 | 2 |

*Source:* Robert L. Ebel, *Measuring Educational Achievement,* © 1965, p. 131. Adapted by permission of Prentice Hall, Upper Saddle River, NJ.

a group of items can be arranged, scoring ranking items presents a special problem. For example, the error of assigning to second place an item that actually belongs in first place is not as serious as placing the same item in fourth place.

Two formulas that can be used for scoring ranking items are

$$S_1 = c\left[1 - \frac{2\sum |d|}{c^2 - j}\right] \tag{3.1a}$$

$$S_2 = c\left[1 - \frac{3\sum d^2}{c(c^2 - 1)}\right] \tag{3.1b}$$

In these formulas, $c$ = the number of things ranked, the $d$'s are the differences between the ranks assigned by the examinee and the keyed ranks, and $k = 0$ if $c$ is even and 1 if $c$ is odd. To illustrate the use of these formulas, assume that five cities are to be arranged in rank order according to population by assigning a rank of 1 to the city with the largest population, 2 to the next largest city, and so on. The names of the five cities are given in the first column of Table 3–3, the keyed ranks in the second column, and the ranks assigned by a hypothetical examinee in the third column. The fourth column contains the absolute values of the differences between the correct rank for each city and the keyed rank, and the fifth column contains the squares of those differences. The sum of the absolute values of the differences between the examinee's ranks and the keyed ranks is 10, and the sum of the

**TABLE 3–3 Scoring an Illustrative Rearrangement Item**

| City | Correct rank | Ranking by examinee | Absolute value of difference | Square of difference |
| --- | --- | --- | --- | --- |
| Philadelphia | 4 | 1 | 3 | 9 |
| Chicago | 3 | 2 | 1 | 1 |
| Los Angeles | 2 | 3 | 1 | 1 |
| San Francisco | 5 | 4 | 1 | 1 |
| New York | 1 | 5 | 4 | 16 |
| | | Sums | 10 | 28 |

squared differences is 28. Substituting $c = 5$, $\sum |d| = 10$, and $j = 1$ in formula 3.1a yields $5[1 - 2(10)/(5^2 - 1)] = .83 \approx 1$. Substituting $c = 5$ and $\sum d^2 = 28$ in formula 3.1b yields $5\{1 - 3(28)/[5(5^2 - 1)]\} = 1.5 \approx 2$. The results of applying these two formulas do not agree because, compared with formula 3.1a, formula 3.1b gives more weight to larger differences in ranks and less weight to smaller differences in ranks. Either formula is satisfactory, depending on whether the scorer chooses to penalize responses that are quite different from the keyed ones more than those that are less different. In any event, no way of scoring test items is best in all respects: it depends on one's philosophy and goals.

**Correction for Guessing**    After the total raw score on an objective test has been determined, the question arises as to whether the score is an accurate indicator of the examinee's true standing on the test or whether it has been inflated by successful guessing. People do guess on objective tests, and the chances of improving their scores in this way, especially on items having few options, can be quite high. If a person does not know the correct answer and all options are equally attractive, the chances of selecting the correct option by guessing are $100/k$ out of 100, where $k$ is the number of options per item. Thus, the chances of guessing the correct answer are 50 out of 100 on a true–false item, but only 25 out of 100 on a four-option multiple-choice item. Obviously, guessing the answer to a large number of items will have a more serious effect on the scores on true–false than on multiple-choice tests.

To correct for the effects of guessing on certain standardized tests (for example, the SAT and GRE), a portion of the number of wrong answers is subtracted from the number of right answers. The reasoning behind correction-for-guessing formulas need not concern us here, except for the questionable assumption that examinees guess blindly when in doubt. The most popular correction-for-guessing formula is

$$S = R - \frac{W}{k - 1} \tag{3.2}$$

where $S$ is the corrected score, $R$ is the number of items the examinee gets right, $W$ is the number of items the examinee gets wrong, and $k$ is the number of options per item. This formula has been criticized for yielding scores that are too low when examinees are less familiar with the test material and too high when they are more familiar with the material (Little, 1962, 1966). An alternative formula proposed by Little (1962) is

$$S = R - \frac{W}{2(k - 1)} \tag{3.3}$$

Professional testers generally agree that correction-for-guessing formulas do not really correct for guessing and typically have little effect on the rank order of scores. Exceptions occur when the number of unanswered items varies greatly from person to person and when certain items are more likely to be guessed at than others. These formulas, which involve procedures similar to that of assigning differential weights to different items, is not generally recommended in scoring classroom tests. The formulas are probably most helpful in scoring true–false and speeded tests, where guessing is more of a factor, than on other types of tests. Negative scores, which occasionally occur when formula 3.2 is applied to true–false tests ($S = R - W$), are usually changed to zeros. In any event, examinees have a right to know if their scores will be corrected for guessing. Information on how a test is scored, including whether a correction for guessing is employed, should be included in the test directions.

**Converted Scores**    It is usually not worthwhile to alter raw scores on objective tests by differential item weighting or correction-for-guessing formulas, but the scores are often changed in other ways to make them more meaningful. As described in the section on norms in Chapter 4, the process of interpreting test scores is facilitated by transforming them to percentile ranks, standard scores, or converted scores.

***Scoring Oral Tests***    Although errors are more likely to occur in scoring responses to oral questions than to written ones, special forms for rating performance can improve the objectivity of scoring oral tests (see Figure 3–2). Careful attention to the design of questions, construction of model answers to questions before administering the test, use of multiple raters or scorers, and training examiners to avoid favoritism and other rater biases can also decrease errors in scoring oral tests. If the time allotted to scoring is not critical, the accuracy with which oral tests are scored can be improved by electronically recording examinees' responses for later playback and (re)evaluation (see Aiken, 1983a).

## Score Evaluation and Grading

After a test has been administered and scored, the scores then need to be evaluated. In the case of teacher-made tests, score evaluation usually implies the assignment of letter grades or marks. Grade assignment is a fairly subjective process, depending not only on the test

---

*Directions:* For each of the questions listed below, rate the oral report on a scale of 1 to 10, 1 being very low and 10 being very high. Write the appropriate number (1 to 10) in the marginal dash.

_____  1. What is the level of the student's knowledge of the subject matter in the report?

_____  2. How well organized was the report?

_____  3. How effective was the introduction to the report in capturing your attention?

_____  4. How clearly and distinctly did the student speak?

_____  5. How interesting was the topic?

_____  6. How effectively used were audiovisual materials (films, posters, chalkboard, and the like)?

_____  7. To what extent did the student look at the class during the report rather than looking at his or her notes?

_____  8. How effectively did the student use gestures, body postures, and other nonverbal messages to communicate?

_____  9. To what extent did the student refer to research or other primary sources in presenting the report?

_____  10. How would you rate the closing (summary of major points, presentation of thought questions, and the like) of the report?

*Comments:*

---

**FIGURE 3–2**   Form for Evaluating Oral Reports.

itself, but also on the expectations of the evaluator and the scores obtained by other students. Some teachers grade strictly on the curve, whereas others grade in terms of a fixed performance standard or criterion. The majority, however, probably employ a combination of curve and fixed-standard grading. In one curve-grading procedure, the *Cajori method,* A's are assigned to the top 7 percent of test papers, B's to the next 24 percent, C's to the next 38 percent, D's to the next 24 percent, and F's to the lowest 7 percent. A disadvantage of this method is its failure to consider that tests vary in difficulty and that the overall ability level of students in different classes is not the same. An alternative curve-grading procedure establishes letter-grade boundaries on classroom tests when the ability level of the class, the class's test performance relative to that of other classes, and the test scores themselves are all taken into account (Aiken, 1983b).

The traditional grading system, in which A is considered excellent or superior, B is above average or good, C is average, D is below average or poor, and F is failing, is a form of score interpretation or performance evaluation. Every public or private organization has standards that its students, employees, or members are expected to meet. The standards may be flexible, but at some time individuals who belong to the organization are usually evaluated on their level of proficiency or participation. The penalty for receiving a negative evaluation may consist of remedial work, demotion, suspension, or even expulsion. The rewards for a good evaluation include prizes, privileges, and promotions.

Letter grading implies evaluation of scholastic performance by administering various kinds of achievement tests to students. Scores on other tests of ability and personality also require interpretation if they are to be used for certain purposes: for placement in special classes or jobs, for psychodiagnosis, or for psychological treatment or other interventions. Procedures for interpreting scores on such tests can be very complex, depending on the type of test and the purposes(s) for which it is administered. These procedures are described throughout this book, beginning with the discussion of norms in Chapter 4.

## SUMMARY

Procedures for administering and scoring tests vary to some extent with the type of test and the people for whom it is intended. It is particularly important for test takers to be prepared, motivated to do well, and relatively free from stress and other disruptive conditions. Test administrators should be trained, familiar with the particular test, and confident that everything is in order before giving a test. In general, the testing situation should be physically and psychologically comfortable so that examinees will be inclined to do as well as they can.

As a rule, examinees should be informed of the purpose(s) of a test, where and when it will be administered, the format of the test, and the material with which it deals. Examiners should follow the test directions carefully, taking precautions to minimize cheating, and being prepared to handle emergencies and other special problems. Some flexibility is usually permitted in administering both teacher-made and standardized tests, but sharp deviations from the directions for administration will invalidate the use of norms on the latter type of test. Examiners should also attempt to establish rapport with examinees, especially on individually administered tests.

Test wiseness, successful guessing, changing answers, and cheating are some of the factors that can inflate scores on objective tests; bluffing, a sophisticated writing style, and good penmanship can do the same on essay tests. The effects of test wiseness are minimized by constructing items carefully, thus avoiding cues such as item length, specific determiners, grammatical errors, stylistic giveaways, and heterogeneous (nonparallel) options. Correction-for-guessing formulas are sometimes applied to reduce the effects of guessing. With the possible exception of true–false items, however, conventional correction-for-guessing formulas are usually not worth the time or effort in scoring classroom tests.

Essay tests may be scored holistically or analytically, but in either case examinees should be informed as to how the test will be scored. Scoring the responses of all examinees to a specific essay question before going on to the next one is recommended, as is scoring responses separately for content and style. In addition to a numerical score, written comments, corrections, and explanations are often helpful in providing feedback on essay test performance.

Many objective tests are scored by computers or other special machines. Machine scoring is generally superior in terms of speed and accuracy, but less flexible than hand scoring. The scoring of many individual tests of intelligence and personality is not completely objective and may result in serious errors on the part of professionals and trainees alike.

The effects of assigning different scoring weights to different kinds of objective items or to different responses to an item have been investigated extensively. In general, a priori scoring weights are not recommended on tests consisting of 20 items or more.

Raw test scores are often converted to percentile ranks or standard scores for purposes of computing averages, making comparisons, and interpreting scores. Scores on classroom tests are also converted to grades, either by using a fixed set of percentages such as those specified by the Cajori method or in a more subjective manner.

## QUESTIONS AND ACTIVITIES

1. Define *test wiseness,* and describe test-taking behaviors that are indicative of test wiseness. What can a test designer do to minimize the effects of test wiseness on scores?

2. Question a group of your fellow students about the techniques they use in selecting answers to items on a multiple-choice test when they have not studied the material thoroughly. What techniques are most popular, and how effective are they?

3. You have undoubtedly observed that the speed of completing a classroom test can vary markedly from student to student. Some students finish a 2-hour examination in less than an hour, while others continue working even after time has expired. From your observations and conversations, what do you believe are the major factors that determine how quickly students finish a test?

4. John takes a 50-item, four-option, multiple-choice test. He gets 30 items right, 16 items wrong, and leaves 4 items blank. What is his total score on the test, both corrected and uncorrected for guessing? If all items were of the true–false variety and he gave the same number of correct and incorrect answers as listed above, what would his total score be, both corrected and uncorrected for guessing?

5. A test on British history contains a rearrangement item consisting of a list of seven battles. Students are asked to arrange the seven battles, from first to last, according to their dates of occurrence. The

correct order is Battle of Hastings, Battle of Bunker Hill, Battle of Yorktown, Battle of Trafalgar, Battle of Waterloo, Battle of the Marne, Battle of Britain. John listed these battles in the following order: Waterloo, Hastings, Yorktown, Trafalgar, Marne, Britain, Bunker Hill. What was his score on the item? Jenny listed the seven battles in the order: Hastings, Waterloo, Yorktown, Bunker Hill, Trafalgar, Marne, Britain. What was her score?

6. Applying the percentages designed by the Cajori method, assign letter grades to the scores on the $X$ distribution in Exercise 3 of Appendix A. Then assign grades to the $Y$ distribution in the same exercise. You can use program 7 ("Grade Assignment by the Modified Cajori Method") in category B of the set of *Computer Programs for Psychological Assessment* to solve this problem. Let the maximum score equal 50, the minimum score equal 0, and the median ability of the class equal 50.

# 4

# ITEM ANALYSIS
# AND NORMS

This chapter deals with two somewhat technical but important topics: item analysis and test standardization. Both topics involve the computation of certain statistics that must be examined closely to determine if all items on a test are working as they should and how the test scores may be interpreted. Item analysis focuses on the functioning of the individual items, whereas standardization is concerned with the normative interpretation of scores on the test as a whole or on the several parts or subtests comprising the test.

## ITEM ANALYSIS

Even after a test has been administered and scored, it is not always certain that it has done its job well. When a test is tried out initially, it is likely that a number of problems will be encountered. This is one reason why commercially distributed tests are administered first to a sample of people who are representative of the group for whom the test is ultimately intended. The responses of this pilot sample can then be analyzed to determine if the items are functioning properly.

Whatever the type of test—standardized or teacher made, ability or personality—a postmortem or post hoc analysis of results is just as necessary as it is in medicine or in any other human enterprise. Among the questions that need to be answered are the following: Were the time limits adequate? Did the examinees understand the directions? Were the testing conditions appropriate? Were emergencies handled properly? Rarely is every problem or contingency that arises during a test anticipated, but a post hoc analysis can provide information and motivation for anticipating and coping with similar situations in future administrations. The questionnaire in Figure 4–1, administered immediately after the test has been taken, can provide qualitative information on student perceptions of the fairness of the test, whether they felt prepared for it, whether it met their expectations, and how they responded to the test items.

An analysis of responses given by a group of people to the individual items on a test serves several functions. The major aim of such an *item analysis* is to help to improve the test by revising or discarding ineffective items. Another important function of an item analysis, especially of a classroom achievement test, is to provide diagnostic information on what examinees know and do not know.

*Directions:* Complete this form after you finish the test. Circle your response to each item, and fill in the blanks if appropriate.

Yes  No  1. Was the testing environment (seating, temperature, ventilation, and the like) satisfactory? If not, explain. _____

_____

Yes  No  2. Did you read the directions carefully before beginning the test?

Yes  No  3. Were the directions for the test clear?

Yes  No  4. Was the layout of the test (kinds of items, arrangement, answer sheet, and the like) satisfactory? If not, explain. _____

_____

Yes  No  5. Did the test cover the assigned material adequately? If not, explain. _____

_____

Yes  No  6. Were the test questions of appropriate difficulty? If not, explain.

_____

Yes  No  7. Did you study enough for the test? Why not? _____

_____

Yes  No  8. Did you study the right material? Why not? _____

_____

Yes  No  9. Do you think you answered any questions wrong? Which ones?

_____

Yes  No  10. Did you guess at any answers? How many? _____ Which ones? _____

Yes  No  11. Did you omit any items? How many? _____

Yes  No  12. Did you have enough time to finish the test? Why not? _____

_____

Yes  No  13. After you finished the test, did you go back and check your answers?

Yes  No  14. Were you very anxious (emotionally upset) during the test?

Yes  No  15. Was the test fair? Why not? _____

16. In general, was this a good test? Why not? _____

_____

17. What grade do you expect to get on the test? _____

**FIGURE 4–1** Test Evaluation Form.

## Criterion-Referenced Tests and Mastery

The procedure employed in evaluating the effectiveness of test items depends to some extent on the purposes of the test. For example, the examiner may merely be interested in determining how much an examinee knows of the test material, not in comparing the latter's performance with that of other people. In this case the performance is compared with a criterion or standard established by the classroom teacher or by institutional policy. The purpose of such *criterion-referenced testing* is not to determine how people score in relation to other people, but rather to determine where each person stands with respect to certain educational objectives. A particular type of criterion-referenced test designed to measure the attainment of a limited range of cognitive skills is known as a *mastery test.* A person's score on a mastery test, or on any other criterion-referenced test, is expressed as a percentage of the total number of items answered correctly; a perfect score indicates 100 percent mastery of the test material.

## Individual Differences and Item Validity

Because it is often difficult to obtain agreement on how much someone should know about a particular subject or what constitutes mastery of the material, a score on a psychological or educational test is more often interpreted by comparing it with the scores of other people. Psychological tests have been devised primarily to assess the differences among individuals in cognitive and affective characteristics, so the history of testing is interwoven with the study of individual differences. People differ in their abilities and personalities, and psychologists attempt to evaluate these differences with various kinds of tests. The more carefully this is accomplished, the more precisely behavior can be predicted from test scores. Consequently, professional test constructors try to devise items that differentiate among people in terms of whatever is to be measured. By so doing, the variability of total test scores is increased, and a given score becomes a more accurate index of a person's standing in relation to that of other people.

To assess the usefulness of an item as a measure of individual differences in ability or personality characteristics, testers need some external criterion measure of the characteristic. If the test is being constructed to predict performance on a job or in school, then an appropriate criterion is a measure of job performance, such as supervisors' ratings, or of school achievement, such as teacher-assigned marks. The *validity* of an item for predicting the particular external criterion measure may be determined by correlating scores on the item (0's for wrongs and 1's for rights) with scores on the criterion measure. Different types of correlation coefficients have been used for this purpose, the most common being the *point-biserial coefficient.* A formula for computing the point-biserial coefficient is

$$r_{pb} = \frac{(\overline{Y}_p - \overline{Y})\sqrt{n_t n_p / [(n_t - n_p)(n_t - 1)]}}{s} \qquad (4.1)$$

where $n_t$ = the total number of examinees, $n_p$ = the number of examinees who get the item right, $\overline{Y}_p$ = the mean criterion scores of examinees who get the item right, $\overline{Y}$ = the mean of all criterion scores, and $s$ = the standard deviation of all criterion scores. The criterion may be an external one or even total scores on the test itself.

To illustrate the computation of the point-biserial coefficient, assume that the mean and standard deviation of the total test scores of a group of 30 people are 75 and 10, respectively. Also assume that the mean score of the 17 examinees who get a certain item right is 80. Substituting these numbers in formula 4.1 yields

$$r_{pb} = \frac{(80 - 75)\sqrt{30(17) / [13(29)]}}{10} = .58$$

The higher the item–criterion correlation, the more useful the item is for predicting the criterion. Whether an item is retained or discarded depends on the size of this coefficient. Although items having correlations as low as .20 with the criterion may contribute to predicting it, higher coefficients are preferred. Certainly, an item having a correlation close to or less than .00 with the criterion should be revised or discarded. The usefulness of an item for predicting a specified criterion, however, depends not only on the item–criterion correlation, but also on the correlation of the item with other items on the test. Items having high correlations with the criterion but low correlations with other items are best because they make a more independent contribution to the prediction of criterion scores.

## Item Difficulty and Discrimination Indexes

On classroom achievement tests, there is usually no external criterion against which to validate items, so a different, *internal consistency* procedure is used. As with any other test, an item analysis of a classroom test entails determining the percentage of examinees who pass the item and the correlation of the item with a criterion measure. But in this case the criterion consists of total scores on the test itself. Use total scores as the criterion in determining the internal consistency because it is assumed that the set of items as a whole is an adequate measure of achievement in the subject, even though a few items are not.

A shortcut procedure is to sort the examinees into three groups according to their scores on the test as a whole: an upper group consisting of the 27 percent making the highest scores, a lower group composed of the 27 percent making the lowest scores, with the remaining 46 percent in a middle group. When the number of examinees is small, upper and lower 50 percent groups on total test scores are sometimes used. In any event, the following statistical indexes are computed from scores on the upper and lower groups:

$$p = \frac{U_p + L_p}{U + L} \tag{4.2}$$

and

$$D = \frac{U_p - L_p}{U} \tag{4.3}$$

$U_p$ and $L_p$ are the numbers of examinees in the upper and lower groups, respectively, who get the item right; $U$ and $L$ are the total number of examinees in the upper and lower groups (note that $U = L$). The value of $p$ is referred to as an *item difficulty index* and $D$ as an *item discrimination index*. To illustrate the computation of these indexes, assume that 50 people take a test. Then the upper and lower groups can be formed from the top 14 and the bottom 14 examinees on total test scores. If 12 of the examinees in the upper group and 7 of those in the lower group pass item A, then $p = (12 + 7)/28 = .68$ and $D = (12 - 7)/14 = .36$.

The item difficulty index has a range of .00 to 1.00. An item with $p = .00$ is one that no examinee answered correctly, and an item with $p = 1.00$ is one that all examinees answered correctly. The optimum $p$ value for an item depends on a number of factors, including the purposes of the test and the number of response options. If the purpose of a test is to identify or select only a small percentage of the best applicants, then the test should be fairly difficult, as reflected in a lower mean value of $p$. If the test is designed to screen out only a few very poor applicants, then a high mean value of $p$ is best.

The optimum value of $p$ depends on the purposes of the test. For example, the optimum $p$ is fairly low for items on a test designed to assign scholarships or for advanced placement, but fairly high on a test designed to select students for remedial programs. On a test designed to measure a broad range of ability, the optimum $p$ value is closer to .50. As shown in Table 4–1, the optimum mean value of $p$ for such a test also varies with the number of response options ($k$). The $p$'s for acceptable items fall within a fairly narrow range, approximately .20, around these tabled values.[1] Although several very easy and several very difficult items are often included on a broad-range test, they actually add very little to the overall effectiveness of the test in distinguishing among examinees who possess different amounts of knowledge, skill, or understanding of the test material.

The item discrimination index ($D$) is a measure of the effectiveness of an item in discriminating between high and low scorers on a test. The higher the value of $D$, the more effective the item is in discriminating between high and low scorers on the test as a whole. When $D$ is 1.00, all examinees in the upper group on total test scores and none of those in the lower group answered the item right. Rarely, however, is $D$ equal to 1.00, and an item is usually considered acceptable if its $D$ index is .30 or higher. But $D$ and $p$ are not independent indexes, and the minimum acceptable value of $D$ varies with the value of $p$. A $D$ value somewhat less than .30 is acceptable as $p$ becomes increasingly higher or lower than the optimum value, particularly when the sizes of the upper and lower comparison groups are large (Aiken, 1979b). Furthermore, an item having a low $D$ index is not automatically discarded: it may be possible to save the item by modifying it. Constructing good test items is a time-consuming process, so defective items should be revised if possible.

## Group Differences on Speeded Tests

The results of an item analysis often vary substantially with the specific group tested, especially when the number of examinees is small. Certain items may be answered differently by males than by females or by one ethnic or socioeconomic group or another. In constructing a standardized test, it has become common practice to examine each item and its associated statistics for indications of group discrimination or bias. Simply because the way

**TABLE 4–1  Optimum Mean Item Difficulty Indexes for Test Items Having Various Numbers of Options**

| Number of options (k) | Optimum mean difficulty index (p) |
|---|---|
| 2 | .85 |
| 3 | .77 |
| 4 | .74 |
| 5 | .69 |
| Open-ended (essay, short answer) | .50 |

*Source:* Constructed from data provided by F. M. Lord, *Psychometrika, 17* (1952), 181–194.

[1]The range of $p$ should be less than this in a *peaked test* designed to measure well within a fairly narrow range of ability.

in which an item is answered varies from group to group, it does not necessarily mean that the item is biased against one of the groups. Technically, an item is biased only when it measures something different—a different characteristic or trait—in one group than another. If item scores reflect true differences in ability or whatever characteristic the item was designed to measure, the item is technically unbiased. Conducting a separate item analysis for each group should reveal the presence of item bias, that is, whether the item discriminates effectively between high and low scorers in both groups.

Problems also occur in the item analysis of speeded tests, on which the time limits are short and not all examinees have time to finish. On a speeded test, items near the end of the test are attempted by relatively few people. If those who reach and therefore attempt an item are the most able examinees, the discrimination index ($D$) will probably be greater than it would be if the time limits were ample. On the other hand, if the most careless responders are more likely to reach and attempt items toward the end of the test, the $D$ values of those items will tend to be smaller than the $D$ values of items near the beginning of the test. Various procedures have been proposed for coping with problems encountered in analyzing items toward the end of speeded tests, but none of them is completely satisfactory.

The time allotted for taking a test is not the only factor that can affect the item difficulty and discrimination indexes. Nevertheless, these two indexes provide useful information on the functioning of individual items. In general, it has been found that item analyses can result in significant improvements in test effectiveness. The item discrimination index in particular is a fairly good measure of item quality. Along with the difficulty index ($p$), $D$ can serve as a warning that something is wrong with an item. Consequently, these two indexes, together with the nature and size of the group tested, should be recorded on the back of an index card containing the item. When this process is repeated for all items, the result is a library of items from which future tests can be constructed.

## Internal Consistency versus Validity

The concept of item validity usually refers to the relationship of an item to an external criterion. But $D$ is a measure of the relationship of an item to total test score, rather than to an external criterion. Selecting items having high $D$ values will result in an internally consistent test on which the correlations among items are highly positive. Scores on an internally consistent test, however, are not necessarily highly correlated with an external criterion. To construct a test having a high correlation with an external criterion, items having low correlations with each other, but high correlations with the criterion, should be selected. Thus, selecting items on the basis of the $D$ statistic yields a different kind of test than one composed of items selected for their high correlations with an external criterion. Which of these procedures is superior depends on the purposes of the test. If an internally consistent measure of a characteristic is desired, the discrimination index ($D$) should be used in selecting items. If the most valid predictor of a particular external criterion is needed, the item–criterion correlations should be used. Sometimes a combination of the two approaches is appropriate: a composite test is constructed from subtests having low correlations with each other and substantial correlations with an external criterion, but the items within each subtest are highly intercorrelated.

## Criterion-referenced Test Items

Difficulty and discrimination indexes may also be computed on criterion-referenced test items. In this case, the examinees are divided into two groups: an upper group consisting of the $U$ examinees whose total test scores meet the criterion of mastery, and a lower group consisting of the $L$ examinees whose total scores fail to meet the criterion. For a particular item, $U_p$ is the number in the upper group (above criterion level) who get the item right, and $L_p$ is the number in the lower group (below criterion level) who get the item right. Then the item difficulty index is defined by formula 4.2. Because $U$ and $L$ are not necessarily equal, the item discrimination index is defined as

$$D = \frac{U_p}{U} - \frac{L_p}{L} \qquad (4.4)$$

An external criterion may also be used in forming the upper and lower groups. In the case of a criterion-referenced achievement test, for example, examinees may be sorted into two groups: those who received instruction in the subject matter associated with the test ($U$) and those who did not receive such instruction ($L$). The $U$ and $L$ groups may also consist of the same individuals, both before ($L$) and after ($U$) instruction. In either case, formula 4.4 can be used to determine an item discrimination index (Popham, 1981, pages 300–303).

## Analysis of Distracters

The analysis of multiple-choice items typically begins with the computation of difficulty and discrimination indexes for each item. A second analysis is concerned with the functioning of the $k - 1$ distracters for each item. The algebraic sign and magnitude of the item discrimination index ($D$) provide some information on the functioning of the distracters as a whole. A positive $D$ means that examinees in the upper group (on total test score) tended to select the correct answer, while those in the lower group tended to select the distracters; the magnitude of $D$ indicates the extent of this tendency. On the other hand, a negative $D$ indicates that the distracters on the whole were chosen more frequently by the upper group than the lower group and that the item needs revising. However, the sign and magnitude of $D$ do not reveal whether all distracters functioned properly.

The simplest method of determining whether all distracters are working as they should is to count the number of times each distracter is selected as the right answer by examinees in the upper group and by those in the lower group. If, on an otherwise satisfactory item, too many examinees in the upper group or too few of those in the lower group selected a given distracter, that distracter should be edited or replaced. Ideally, all $k - 1$ distracters should be equally plausible to examinees who do not know the correct answer to an item; consequently, every distracter should be selected by approximately the same number of people.

## Item Characteristic Curves

Even acceptable values of $p$ and $D$ do not guarantee that an item is functioning effectively across all levels of overall test performance. To be most effective, the proportion of people who answer a test item correctly should increase steadily with increases in total scores on the test or subtest. Whether a test item functions in this manner is determined from the *item characteristic curve*. In constructing an item characteristic curve, the proportion of examinees who gave the keyed answer is plotted against their scores on an internal criterion (for example, total test scores) or an external criterion such as academic or occupational performance. Once the characteristic curve for a particular item has been constructed, the difficulty level and discrimination index for the item can be determined. The *difficulty level (b)* is the criterion score at which 50 percent of the examinees gave the correct (keyed) answer; the *discrimination index (a)* is the slope of the item-response curve at the 50 percent point. In the two item characteristic curves shown in Figure 4–2, item 1 has a lower difficulty level but a steeper slope, and hence a greater discrimination index, than item 2. These two indexes are similar to the $p$ and $D$ indexes of traditional item analysis, but an item characteristic

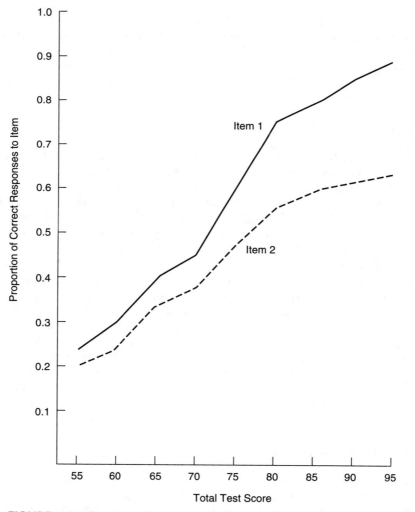

**FIGURE 4–2**   Two Item Characteristic Curves. See text for explanation.

curve goes further in providing a detailed picture of how the item is functioning across the entire range of criterion scores.

## Item-Response Theory

An extension of the item characteristic curve approach is *item-response theory (IRT)*. An item-response curve is constructed by plotting the proportion of people who answer an item according to the keyed response against estimates of the true standing of these people on a unidimensional latent trait or characteristic (see Figure 4–3). These estimates are derived by a mathematical function known as a logistic equation. The precise mathematical equations

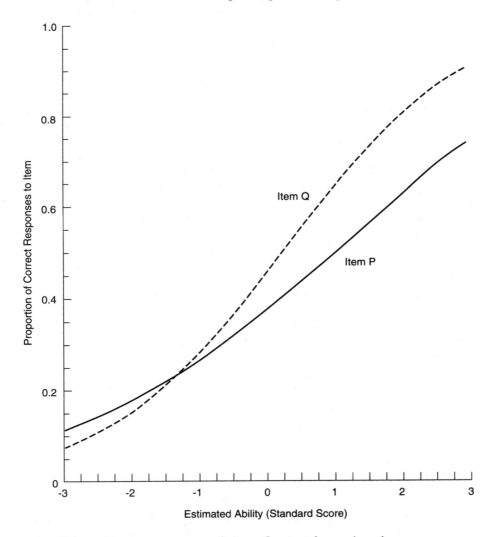

**FIGURE 4–3** Two Item–response Curves. See text for explanation.

involved in IRT vary with the assumptions and estimation procedures prescribed by the approach.

An item-response curve can be constructed either from the responses of a large group of examinees to an item or, if certain parameters are estimated, from a theoretical model. In the one-parameter IRT model, known as the *Rasch model,* an item-response curve is drawn by estimating only the item difficulty parameter ($b$). In the two-parameter model, which is probably the most popular IRT model, construction of an item-response curve involves both difficulty ($b$) and discrimination ($a$) parameters. Finally, in the three-parameter model, difficulty ($b$), discrimination ($a$), and guessing ($c$) parameters are estimated. Figure 4–3 illustrates item-response curves constructed according to a two-parameter model. For item $P$, the difficulty parameter ($b$) is 1.00 and the discrimination parameter is .5; for item $Q$, $b = .25$ and $a = .75$. Therefore, item $Q$ is easier but more discriminating than item $P$.

## TEST STANDARDIZATION AND NORMS

Data on the performance of a large group of individuals like those on whom the instrument was designed are useful for purposes of score interpretation. To accomplish this task, the test, inventory, rating scale, or other psychometric device must be standardized.

Any standardized test has standard directions for administration and scoring that should be followed closely, leaving little room for personal interpretation or bias. Standardization also involves administering the test to a large sample of people (the *standardization sample*) selected as representative of the *target population* of persons for whom the test is intended.

The major purpose of the standardization procedure is to determine the distribution of raw scores in the standardization group (*norm group*). The obtained raw scores are then converted to some form of derived scores, or *norms*. These norms include age equivalents, grade equivalents, percentile ranks, and standard scores. Most test manuals contain tables of norms listing raw scores and some type of converted scores corresponding to them. Then a person's standing on a test can be evaluated by referring to the appropriate norms table and finding the converted score equivalents of his or her raw scores(s). In this way, norms serve not as standards of desirable performance, but simply as a frame of reference for interpreting scores. Norms indicate a person's standing on the test relative to the distribution of scores obtained by people of the same chronological age, grade, sex, or other demographic characteristics.

In terms of sample size and representativeness, group tests, and achievement tests in particular, are often standardized more adequately than individual tests. Norms for group tests may be based on as many as 100,000 people, whereas the size of the norm group for a carefully standardized individual test is more likely to be 2000 to 4000. A large standardization sample, however, does not guarantee that the sample is representative of the population of interest. The sample must be carefully selected in order to be representative of this *target population.*

### Selecting a Standardization Sample

To serve effectively in the interpretation of test scores, norms must be appropriate for the group or individual being evaluated. For example, a particular fourth-grader's score may surpass that of 80 percent of fourth-grade children and 60 percent of sixth-graders. Although it may be of some interest to compare a fourth-grader's score with scores of third- and sixth-graders, a student's standing in his or her own (fourth grade) group is of primary concern. Whenever a test score is converted by referring to a table of norms, it is important to note the nature (age, sex, ethnicity, educational and socioeconomic status, geographical region) of the particular norm group and to include this information in all communications regarding the person's test performance. Another important consideration is when (on what date) the norms were obtained. Norms on certain tests can become outdated during times of rapid social and educational change. For example, changes in school curricula may necessitate restandardizing and perhaps modifying or reconstructing an achievement test every five years or so.

The manner in which a standardization sample is selected from a population varies from simple random sampling to more complex sampling strategies, such as stratified random sampling and cluster sample. In *simple random sampling,* every person in the target population has an equal chance of being selected. However, randomness does not ensure representativeness. Consequently, a more appropriate way to standardize a test is to begin by categorizing, or *stratifying,* the population on a series of demographic variables (sex, age, socioeconomic status, geographical region, and the like) that are presumably related to scores on the test. Then the number of individuals selected at random from each category or stratum is made proportional to the total number of people in the population who fall in that stratum. When this *stratified random sampling* procedure is employed, the likelihood of selecting an atypical, or biased, sample is minimized. Then the obtained norms will provide a better basis for interpreting scores on the test than will norms obtained on a simple random sample.

Cluster sampling is more economical than stratified random sampling and more likely than simple random sampling to produce a representative sample of the target population. *Cluster sampling* consists of dividing a designated population of geographical areas or other relevant units into blocks or clusters. Then a specified percentage of the clusters is chosen at random, and within each cluster a certain number of subunits (schools, residences, and so on) are randomly selected. The final step is to administer the test to everyone in each subunit, or at least a random sample of people having certain designated characteristics.[2]

Administering all items on a test to a stratified random sample or a cluster sample of individuals is tedious and time consuming, so less costly strategies for obtaining norms have been proposed. One such strategy is to sample items as well as individuals. In *item sampling,* different samples of items are administered to different, randomly selected samples of people. One group answers one set of items, and other groups answer other sets. The process is efficient in that more items can be administered to a large number of persons in a fairly short period of time. Item analyses can then be conducted, and norms based on the scores of representative samples can be determined for a wide range of test content. Norms obtained by item sampling are very similar to those obtained by the traditional but more laborious procedure of administering the entire test to a large representative sample.

## Types of Norms

Figure 4–4, a report of the scores of a student who took the Gates–MacGinitie Reading Tests, illustrates several types of norms: national and local percentile ranks, national and local stanines, grade equivalents (grade norms), and standard scores. Among the norms not shown in this report are age equivalents (age norms) and certain types of standard score norms.

---

[2]Programs C-5, C-6, and C-7 of *Computer Programs for Psychological Assessment* can be used to select random, stratified random, and multistage cluster samples from a designated population.

**FIGURE 4–4** Individual Student Score Report, Gates–MacGinitie Reading Tests, Third Edition.
(Reproduced from Gates–MacGinitie Reading Tests, Third Edition, Copyright © 1989. Reproduced by permission of The Riverside Publishing Company.)

***National, Regional, and Local Norms*** The norms published in test manuals are useful for comparing an examinee's score with the scores of a sample of people from various localities, sometimes a cross section of the entire nation. But teachers are typically more interested in knowing how well students performed in comparison with other students in the school, school system, state, or region, rather than with a national sample. When interest is restricted to the test scores of a particular school, the test administrator will want to convert raw test scores to *local norms* by the procedures discussed in the following sections. Local norms are often used for selection and placement purposes in schools and colleges.

***Age and Grade Norms*** Among the most popular types of norms, primarily because they are easily understood by test users, are age norms and grade norms. An *age norm* (age equivalent, educational age) is the median score on a test obtained by persons of a given chronological age; a *grade norm* (age equivalent) is the median score obtained by students at a given grade level. Age norms are expressed in 12 one-month intervals. To illustrate, age norms for the tenth year range from 10 years, 0 months to 10 years, 11 months. Grade norms, on the other hand, are expressed in 10 one-month intervals: it is assumed that growth in the characteristic of interest is inconsequential during the summer months. For example, the range of grade norms for the fifth grade is 5-0 to 5-9, in one-month intervals from the first to the last month of the school year.

Despite their popularity, age and grade norms have serious shortcomings. The main problem is that growth in cognitive, psychomotor, or affective characteristics is not uniform over the entire range of ages or grades. Thus, a difference of two months growth in achievement at grade 4 (say, from 4-2 to 4-4) is not educationally equivalent to two months' growth in achievement at a later grade level (say, from 8-2 to 8-4). Actually, age and grade units become progressively smaller with increasing age or grade level. Since age and grade norms incorrectly imply that the rate of increase in tested abilities is constant from year to year, their use is frequently discouraged by educational measurement specialists. Norms in which the unit of measurement is less variable are preferred.

Because of their convenience, age and grade norms continue to be used at the elementary school level, where the growth units are more nearly constant across time. Even at this level, however, age and grade norms should be supplemented with the percentile norms or standard score norms for a particular age or grade.

***Modal Age Norms*** Typically, students in a given grade on whom grade norms are determined have a rather wide range of ages; the scores of certain students who are actually much older (or younger) than the average student in that grade are included in the norms. To provide a more accurate index of the average score of students at a given grade level, the scores of students who are much older or much younger than the modal age are sometimes omitted, and the median score is computed only on those who are of the appropriate age for that grade. These restricted norms are referred to as *modal age norms*. Modal age norms, which are rarely found in contemporary achievement test manuals, are mentioned here primarily for their historical interest.

***Mental Age Norms*** The term *mental age* will be recalled from the brief discussion in Chapter 1 of the history of mental measurement. This concept, which was introduced by Alfred Binet, is a type of age norm employed on various intelligence tests. The mental age score of a particular examinee corresponds to the chronological age of the subgroup of children (all of the same chronological age) in the standardization group whose median score is the same as that of the examinee. The practice in many schools for the mentally retarded has been to group such children according to mental age, rather than chronological age, for instructional purposes.

***Quotients*** An older practice in testing, which has virtually disappeared, is to convert age norms to quotients by dividing the age scores of examinees by their chronological ages and multiplying the resulting quotients by 100. The *intelligence quotient (ratio IQ)* on the older Stanford–Binet Intelligence Scale, for example, was defined as

$$IQ = 100\left(\frac{MA}{CA}\right) \tag{4.5}$$

where MA and CA are the examinee's mental and chronological ages in months. Similarly, an *educational quotient* on certain achievement tests was computed as the ratio of educational age (age norm on an educational achievement test) to chronological age in months. By comparing the results of an intelligence test with those of an educational achievement test, an *accomplishment quotient* could be computed as the ratio of educational age to mental age. Some of these quotients are still calculated in evaluating test scores, but the practice is discouraged by psychological measurement specialists.

**Percentile Norms**    Percentile norms consist of a table of percentages corresponding to particular raw scores. The raw scores are referred to as *percentiles,* and the percentage of the norm group falling below a particular score is the *percentile rank* of that score. Columns 2 and 5 of the distribution in Table 4–2 show that, for this group of scores, the percentile rank of a score of 775 is approximately 99 and the percentile rank of a score of 475 is approximately 23. Alternatively, the 99th percentile is 775 and the 23rd percentile is 475.

Because percentile norms are often needed for selection and placement purposes in a given school or grade group, the procedure for computing them will be described in some detail. Columns 1 and 3 of Table 4–2 are a frequency distribution of 250 scores obtained on a scholastic aptitude test, and column 2 gives the midpoints of the score intervals. To compute the entry in column 4 (cumulative frequency below midpoint) for a particular interval, the frequencies on all intervals up to that interval are summed. To this sum is added one-half of the frequency on that interval. For example, the entry 227.0 for the interval 650–699 is computed as $1 + 13 + 25 + 38 + 65 + 49 + 27 + \frac{1}{2}(18) = 227.0$. Since the entry for a particular interval in column 4 is the cumulative frequency below the midpoint of that interval, the percentile rank of a given interval midpoint may be computed by dividing the cumulative frequency in column 4 by the total number of scores ($n$) and multiplying the resulting quotient by 100. For the data in Table 4–2, $n = 250$, so each of the percentile ranks in column 5 is equal to 100 times the corresponding cumulative frequency in column 4 divided by 250. Therefore, the percentile rank of the midpoint 674.5 is $100(227/250) = 90.8 \approx 91$.

**TABLE 4–2    Percentile Ranks and Standard Scores Corresponding to Midpoints of a Frequency Distribution of Test Scores**

| (1) Score interval | (2) Midpoint | (3) Frequency | (4) Cumulative frequency below midpoint | (5) Percentile rank | (6) z | (7) Z | (8) $z_n$ | (9) T | (10) NCE |
|---|---|---|---|---|---|---|---|---|---|
| 750–799 | 774.5 | 3 | 248.5 | 99.4 (99) | 2.59 | 76 | 2.51 | 75 | 103 |
| 700–749 | 724.5 | 11 | 241.5 | 96.6 (97) | 2.03 | 70 | 1.82 | 68 | 88 |
| 650–699 | 674.5 | 18 | 227.0 | 90.8 (91) | 1.48 | 65 | 1.33 | 63 | 78 |
| 600–649 | 624.5 | 27 | 204.5 | 81.8 (82) | .92 | 59 | .91 | 59 | 69 |
| 550–599 | 574.5 | 49 | 166.5 | 66.6 (67) | .37 | 54 | .43 | 54 | 59 |
| 500–549 | 524.5 | 65 | 109.5 | 43.8 (44) | −.19 | 48 | −.16 | 48 | 47 |
| 450–499 | 474.5 | 38 | 58.0 | 23.2 (23) | −.74 | 43 | −.73 | 43 | 35 |
| 400–449 | 424.5 | 25 | 26.5 | 10.6 (11) | −1.30 | 37 | −1.25 | 38 | 24 |
| 350–399 | 374.5 | 13 | 7.5 | 3.0 (3) | −1.85 | 31 | −1.88 | 31 | 11 |
| 300–349 | 324.5 | 1 | .5 | .2 (0) | −2.41 | 26 | −2.88 | 21 | −10 |

Percentile ranks are easy to compute and understand and, consequently, more popular than other types of norms. Tables of percentile norms within grades, chronological ages, gender, occupations, and other demographic groups are listed in the manuals accompanying many psychometric instruments. Unfortunately, the problem of unequal score units, which was referred to earlier in the discussion of age and grade norms, is not solved by percentile norms. Percentile ranks are ordinal-level rather than interval-level measures, and hence the units are not equal on all parts of the scale. The distance between two percentile ranks on either the high or low end of the *percentile equivalents* scale (see Figure 4–5) is greater than the distance between two percentile ranks closer to the center of the scale. Although the numerical differences between the ranks are the same, the size of the percentile-rank unit becomes progressively larger as one goes from the center to the extremes of the scale.

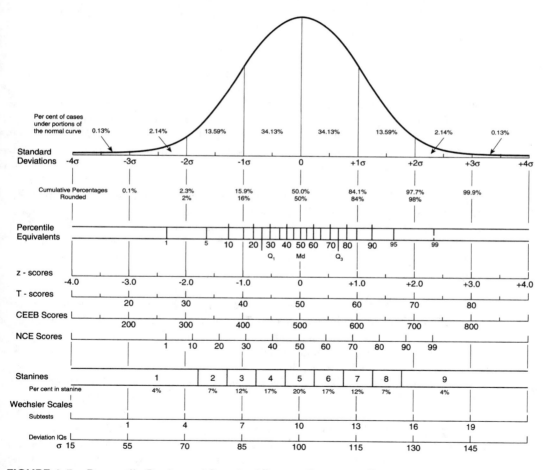

**FIGURE 4–5** Percentile Ranks and Standard Scores Corresponding to Various Points on the Baseline of a Normal Distribution of Scores.
(H. G. Seashore, *Methods of expressing test scores*, The Psychological Corporation Test Service Bulletin, No. 48, 1955.)

The tendency of the units to bunch up in the middle and spread out at the extremes of the percentile-rank scale causes difficulty in the interpretation of changes and differences in these transformed scores. Thus, the difference in ability between a person with a percentile rank of 5 and one with a rank of 10 on an achievement test is not equal to the difference in ability between a person with a percentile rank of 40 and one with a percentile rank of 45. On the percentile-rank scale, 10 minus 5 is greater than 45 minus 40, because the unit of measurement for the first difference is larger. To interpret percentile norms accurately, one must simply remember to give greater weight to percentile-rank differences at the extremes than to the same differences nearer to the middle of the scale.

**Standard-score Norms**   Unlike percentile ranks, standard scores represent measurement on an interval scale. *Standard-score norms* are converted scores having any desired mean and standard deviation. There are many different types of standard scores: z scores, Z scores, CEEB scores, deviation IQ scores, stanine scores, T scores, and NCE scores.

   *z Scores*   The z score equivalents of a particular distribution of raw scores may be determined as

$$z = \frac{X - \overline{X}}{s} \tag{4.6}$$

where $X$ is a given raw score, $\overline{X}$ is the arithmetic mean, and $s$ is the standard deviation of the scores. Transforming raw scores to z scores results in a score distribution having the same shape as, but a different mean and standard deviation from, the raw score $(X)$ distribution. The mean of z scores is 0, and the standard deviation is 1. In fact, the term *z score* is an abbreviation for "zero mean plus or minus 1."

   The z scores corresponding to the interval midpoints listed in column 2 of Table 4–2 are given in column 6. It may be determined by procedures described in Appendix A that the mean and standard deviation of the distribution of scores in Table 4–2 are 541.5 and 90.3, respectively. Therefore, the z score corresponding to the midpoint 774.5 is $(774.5 - 541.5)/90.3$ = 2.58. The z scores of the midpoints of other intervals may be found in the same way. The z scores corresponding to various points along the base line of the normal curve are given in Figure 4–5.

   *Z Scores*   The fact that z scores can be negative or positive decimal numbers creates some difficulty in manipulating these scores. This problem can be solved by multiplying the z scores by a constant and adding another constant to the products. Multiplying z by 10, adding 50 to the product, and rounding the result to the nearest whole number produces a Z score. The mean of these Z scores is 50, and their standard deviation is 10, but the frequency distribution of the Z scores has the same shape as the original raw-score distribution (see column 7 of Table 4–2).

   *CEEB Scores*   Instead of having a mean of 50 and a standard deviation of 10, the scores on the two sections (Verbal and Mathematical) of the Scholastic Aptitude Test (SAT) were originally transformed by multiplying the corresponding z scores by 100 and adding 500 to the products. This was done to the results of the tests administered in 1941, yielding a new score distribution having a mean of 500 and a standard deviation of 100. Subsequently, however, the scores obtained by students taking the SAT were not transformed in this manner. Rather, to ensure a constant score unit for comparing test results from year to year, beginning in 1941 the SAT scales were based on the results of the test administered in that year.[3]

**AGCT and Wechsler Scores**    The score scale on the Army General Classification Test (AGCT), which was formerly employed in selecting and placing U.S. soldiers, had a mean of 100 and a standard deviation of 20. Raw scores on the subtests of the Wechsler intelligence scales were transformed to have a mean of 10 and a standard deviation of 3, whereas the Verbal, Performance, and Full Scale scores for the standardization samples on the Wechsler tests were converted to have means of 100 and standard deviations of 15 (see the last two lines of Figure 4–5).

**Normalized Standard Scores**    The standard-score norms described above are simple linear transformations of raw scores. The mean and standard deviation of the transformed scores are different from those of the raw-score distribution, but the shapes of the two distributions are identical. If the raw-score distribution is symmetrical, the distribution of transformed scores will also be symmetrical.

To make the scores from different tests more directly comparable, a transformation procedure is used that not only affects the mean and standard deviation, but also changes the shape of the distribution of raw scores to that of a normal distribution. Transformation of a group of raw scores to *normalized standard scores* begins with the computation of the percentile ranks of the raw scores. Then, from a table of areas under the normal curve (Appendix B), the $z$ score corresponding to each percentile rank is found. For example, assume that the midpoints (column 2) of the distribution in Table 4–2 are to be converted to normalized standard scores. Since the percentile ranks of these midpoints have already been found (column 5), we begin by converting the percentile ranks to proportions (for example, 99.4 becomes .994). Then, from the table in Appendix B, the $z$ scores below which the given proportions of the area lie may be determined. Thus, the $z$ score $(z_n)$ below which .994 of the area under the curve lies is 2.51. The other normalized $z$ scores in column 8 of Table 4–2 were obtained similarly. To eliminate decimal points and negative numbers, these $z_n$ scores were transformed to $T$ scores by the formula $T = 10z_n + 50$ (column 9) and to NCE (normal curve equivalent) scores by the formula $NCE = 21z_n + 50$. $T$ scores range from approximately 20 to 80 and NCE scores from approximately 0 to 100.

The $z_n$ scores may be transformed to normalized scores having any desired mean and standard deviation. Another popular scale, which has been used by the U.S. Air Force and for grading purposes in certain academic institutions, is the *stanine* (standard nine) scale. The stanine scale, illustrated by the third scale from the bottom in Figure 4–5, is a normalized standard scale having a mean of 5 and a standard deviation of approximately 2. There are nine different ranges, or stanines, on the scale.[4] These ranges are designated by the numbers 1 through 9, and, as shown in the figure, a certain percentage of a normal distribution

---

[3]Scoring the latest version of the SAT, renamed the Scholastic Assessment Test, is based on the performance of 1 million students who took the test in 1994. Based on the performance of that group, SAT scores were *recentered* to have a mean of 500 and a standard deviation of 100.

[4]A *sten scale* consisting of 10 units (Canfield, 1951) and a *C scale* consisting of 11 unit (Guilford & Fruchter, 1973) have also been proposed, but only the former scale has been used to any extent.

of scores falls within the interval represented by a given stanine. The stanine scale, however, is not a true standard score scale because the first and ninth stanines are open ended. Notice in Figure 4–5 that the widths of stanines 2 through 8 are equal, indicating equal standard score units, but that stanines 1 and 9 are much wider.

One advantage of stanine scores is that they represent ranges rather than specific points. This helps to combat the tendency to view test scores as precise, unvarying measures of individual differences. Another procedure having the same effect is to report not only the percentile rank or standard score corresponding to a given raw score, but also a percentile-rank or standard-score interval within which the examinee's true standing on the test might reasonably be expected to fall. This practice is a recognition of the fact that scores on psychological and educational tests are not exact measurements, but are subject to errors of measurement.

## Parallel and Equated Tests

In many situations involving applications and research with psychological tests, more than one form of a test is needed. *Parallel forms* of a test are equivalent in the sense that they contain the same kinds of items of equal difficulty and are highly correlated. Therefore, the scores made on one form of a test are very similar to the scores of the same examinees on a second form at the same age or grade levels as the first form. The construction of two parallel tests is, unfortunately, a rather expensive and time-consuming process. It begins with the preparation of two tests having the same number and kinds of items and yielding the same means and standard deviations when standardized on the same group of people. The resulting parallel forms are then "equated" by converting scores on one form to the same units as those on the other form. This may be done, for example, by the *equipercentile method* of changing the scores on each form to percentile ranks. Then a table of equivalent scores on the two forms is prepared by equating the *p*th percentile on the first form to the score at the *p*th percentile on the second form.

The process of equating, or rather making comparable, two tests of the same difficulty level (for example, the same grade), is referred to as *horizontal equating*. Equating may also be done *vertically,* as when scores on two tests at different difficulty levels (for instance, different grades) are equated. In general, the process of equating involves anchoring the tests to a common test or pool of items, as has been done every year with the Scholastic Aptitude Test (SAT). By using a set of common anchor items that were the same as a subset of items on at least one earlier form of the test, scores on each new form of the SAT administered each year were statistically equated to previous forms on the test.

*Item-response theory (IRT)* was discussed previously in connection with item analysis. The IRT approach, which prescribes methods of calibrating a set of test items on an operationally defined latent trait continuum (usually represented by standard scores on the horizontal axis of an item-response curve), has also been applied to the task of equating tests. The IRT approach to equating involves finding a linear equation that transforms the item parameters (difficulty and discrimination indexes) of one form of a test to those of a second form. The methodology by which the appropriate constants for the linear transformation equations are determined so that the corresponding parameters on the two tests will be on the same scale is referred to as *linking*. Linking procedures require that the two tests share some common (anchor) items or that a subset of examinees take both tests or a third test measuring the same trait. The equating procedures of item-response theory are economical in that item sampling, in which randomly selected subsets of items are administered to different randomly selected groups of people, is also involved.

Whatever the method of attempting to equate two tests may be (equipercentile, item response, linear or nonlinear score transformations), tests that either measure different psychological characteristics or have different reliabilities cannot, strictly speaking, be equated. In almost every case, about the best that can be done is to make the two tests or other psychometric instruments "comparable."

## SUMMARY

The major purpose of an item analysis is to improve a test by revising or discarding ineffective items. Item analysis also provides specific information on what examinees know and do not know.

Test items may be analyzed by comparing item responses with scores on an external criterion, such as teacher-assigned marks or ratings by supervisors, or with an internal criterion such as total test scores. If the goal of the test constructor is to produce a test that is most predictive of scores on an external criterion, then the items should be validated against that criterion.

Various statistics are computed to validate test items against external or internal criteria. These statistics, which are indexes of the relationship between dichotomously scored (right–wrong) items and scores on the criterion measure, provide a basis for accepting or rejecting specific items.

Two simple coefficients that may be computed in an item analysis of a teacher-made test are the item difficulty index ($p$) and the item discrimination index ($D$). These indexes are applicable to both norm-referenced and criterion-referenced items. The optimum value of $p$ depends on the purposes of the test and the number of options per item. In most situations, a $D$ value of .30 or higher is required for an item to be acceptable.

In addition to computing the difficulty and discrimination indexes, test items should be examined for bias, ambiguity, and the effects of speededness. Marked variations from a uniform frequency distribution of responses to the distracters is a sign of a poorly functioning item.

In constructing an item characteristic curve, the proportion of examinees who give the keyed response to an item is plotted against scores on an internal (total test scores) or external criterion. An extension of the item characteristic curve approach known as item-response theory involves inserting difficulty, discrimination, and guessing parameters into a logistic equation or deriving values of these parameters from such an equation. The logistic equation relates the proportion of examinees who answered the item correctly to estimates of their scores on a specified continuum of ability or another unidimensional characteristic.

Standardization consists of administering a test to a representative sample of people under standard (uniform) conditions and scoring it by a standard procedure. Norms computed from the obtained test scores provide a frame of reference for interpreting scores made by people who subsequently take the test. Test norms have traditionally been determined by testing a sample (random, stratified random, cluster) of the population of people for whom the test is intended. Less expensive and more efficient than traditional test-standardization procedures are item-sampling techniques in which not only people but also test items are sampled, with different groups of examinees answering different sets of items.

Depending on the needs and resources of test users, norms may be computed on local, regional, or national samples. Age and grade norms, which are determined most often for tests of achievement, permit comparisons of individual test scores with the average scores of children of a certain age or grade. The main shortcoming of age and grade norms is that growth in achievement or ability is not uniform over age or grade levels. Percentile norms, in which raw test scores are converted to the percentages of people in the standardization group who made those scores or lower, also suffer from the problem of unequal score units. Age, grade, and percentile norms are fairly easy to understand and convenient to use, so they will undoubtedly continue to be popular.

Standard score norms are converted scores having a designated mean and standard deviation. Unlike the ordinal measures represented by age, grade, and percentile norms, standard scores ($z$, $T$, CEEB, and others) are interval-level measures. Not all standard scores are normally distributed, but they can be converted to normalized scores.

Scores on parallel tests may be scaled to achieve comparability, if not strictly equated, in various ways. Tests have traditionally been equated by the equipercentile method, but recent approaches entail more technically sophisticated item-response models.

## QUESTIONS AND ACTIVITIES

1. What are the difficulty ($p$) and discrimination ($D$) indexes of a test item administered to 75 people if 18 of those in the upper group (upper 27 percent on total test score) and 12 of those in the lower group (lower 27 percent on total test score) get the item right? Note that rounding yields 20 people in the upper group and 20 people in the lower group. Use formulas 4.2 and 4.3 to solve this problem.

2. Compute the difficulty ($p$) and discrimination ($D$) indexes of an item on a criterion-referenced test taken by 50 people, 30 of whom scored at or above the criterion level and 20 of whom scored below the criterion level. Of those who scored at or above the criterion level, 20 percent got the item right; of those who scored below the criterion level, 10 got the item right.

3. The following two-way table indicates whether each of 20 people got each of the 10 items on a four-option multiple-choice test right (r) or wrong (w). Classifying examinees A through J in the upper group and examinees K through T in the lower group on total test score (see the last line of the table), compute the difficulty and discrimination indexes for each item. Write these values in the last two columns of the table. By inspecting the $p$ and $D$ indexes, decide which items are acceptable and which need revising or discarding.

*Examinee*

| Item | A | B | C | D | E | F | G | H | I | J | K | L | M | N | O | P | Q | R | S | T | p | D |
|------|---|---|---|---|---|---|---|---|---|---|---|---|---|---|---|---|---|---|---|---|---|---|
| 1 | r | r | r | w | w | w | r | r | r | r | w | r | r | w | w | w | r | w | w | w | | |
| 2 | r | r | w | r | w | r | w | r | w | r | r | w | w | r | w | w | w | w | r | w | | |
| 3 | r | w | r | r | r | w | r | w | r | w | w | r | r | w | w | r | w | w | w | w | | |
| 4 | r | r | r | r | r | w | r | w | r | r | w | w | r | r | w | w | w | w | w | w | | |
| 5 | r | r | w | r | r | r | r | r | w | w | w | r | w | w | w | w | w | w | w | w | | |
| 6 | r | r | r | r | r | r | w | r | r | r | r | w | r | r | w | r | w | r | w | r | | |
| 7 | r | w | w | w | r | r | r | r | w | r | w | w | r | w | r | w | w | r | r | w | | |
| 8 | r | r | r | r | r | w | w | w | r | w | r | r | w | w | w | r | r | w | w | w | | |
| 9 | r | r | r | r | w | r | r | w | r | r | r | r | w | r | r | w | w | w | w | w | | |
| 10 | r | r | r | w | r | r | r | w | r | w | w | w | w | w | w | w | r | w | w | w | | |

Score  10  8  7  7  7  7  6  6  6  6  5  5  4  4  3  3  3  2  2  1

4. Using the diskette of *Computer Programs for Psychological Assessment,* run program 3 ("Item Characteristic Curves and Item Response Curves") in category C to plot item characteristic curves (ICCs) for the 10 items in exercise 3. What conclusions concerning the functioning of these items can you draw from inspecting the ICC curves?

5. Suppose that George makes a raw score of 65 on an arithmetic test having a mean of 50 and a standard deviation of 10, but makes a raw score of 80 on a reading test having a mean of 75 and a standard deviation of 15. What are George's $z$ scores and $Z$ scores on the tests? Is he better in arithmetic or reading?

6. By referring to a table of areas under the normal curve (Appendix B), find the $z$ scores corresponding to the 10th, 20th, 30th, 40th, 50th, 60th, 70th, 80th, and 90th percentile ranks. Then convert the $z$ scores to $T$ scores, CEEB scores, NCE scores, and stanines.

7. Using Table 4–2 as a model, construct a frequency distribution of the following 30 scores (let $i = 3$). Then compute the percentile rank, $z$, $Z$, $z_n$, and $T$ scores corresponding to the interval midpoints.

| | | | | | | | | | |
|---|---|---|---|---|---|---|---|---|---|
| 82 | 85 | 70 | 91 | 75 | 88 | 78 | 82 | 95 | 79 |
| 86 | 90 | 87 | 77 | 87 | 73 | 80 | 96 | 86 | 81 |
| 85 | 93 | 83 | 89 | 92 | 89 | 84 | 83 | 79 | 74 |

8. Why are standard score norms considered superior to age norms, grade norms, and percentile norms?

# 5

# RELIABILITY
# AND VALIDITY

Standardization is an important step in designing and evaluating psychological tests and other assessment instruments, but it is not the last step. Before a test can be used with some assurance that it is an accurate measure of the psychological construct it is supposed to measure, information concerning the reliability and validity of the test must be obtained.

## RELIABILITY

No assessment device can be of value unless it is a consistent, or *reliable*, measure of something. Consequently, one of the first things that should be determined about a newly constructed assessment instrument is whether it is sufficiently reliable to measure what it was designed to measure. If, in the absence of any permanent change in a person due to growth, learning, disease, or injury, scores on the instrument vary appreciably from time to time or situation to situation, the test is probably too unreliable to be used in explaining or making predictions about a person's behavior. Note that *reliability* is not the same thing as *stability*: in determining the reliability of a measuring instrument, it is assumed that the instrument is measuring a relatively stable characteristic. Unlike instability, unreliability is the result of measurement errors produced by temporary internal states, such as low motivation or indisposition, or external conditions, such as a distracting or an uncomfortable testing environment.

### Classical Reliability Theory

In classical test theory, it is assumed that a person's observed score on a test is composed of a "true" score plus some unsystematic error of measurement. A *true score* is defined as the average of the scores a person would obtain if he or she took the test an infinite number of times. It should be emphasized that a person's true score can never be measured exactly; it must be estimated from the person's observed score on the test. It is also assumed in classical test theory that the variance of the observed scores $(s_{obs}^2)$ of a group of people is equal to the variance of their true scores $(s_{tru}^2)$ plus the variance due to unsystematic errors of measurement $(s_{err}^2)$:

$$s_{obs}^2 = s_{tru}^2 + s_{err}^2 \qquad (5.1)$$

Then the reliability $(r_{11})$ of the scores is defined as the ratio of true score variance to observed score variance, or the proportion of observed variance that is accounted for by true variance:

$$r_{11} = \frac{s_{tru}^2}{s_{obs}^2} \qquad (5.2)$$

The proportion of observed variance accounted for by error variance, or unaccounted for by true variance, can be determined from formulas 5.1 and 5.2 to be

$$\frac{s_{err}^2}{s_{obs}^2} = 1 - r_{11} \qquad (5.3)$$

The reliability of a set of test scores is expressed as a positive decimal number ranging from .00 to 1.00; $r_{11} = 1.00$ indicates perfect reliability, and $r_{11} = .00$ indicates total unreliability of measurement. Because the variance of true scores cannot be computed directly, reliability is usually estimated by analyzing the effects of variations in conditions of administration and test content on test scores. As noted previously, reliability is not influenced by systematic changes in scores that have a similar effect on all examinees, but only by unsystematic changes that have different effects on different examinees. Such unsystematic factors influence the error variance and hence the reliability of scores obtained on a test. Each of the several methods of estimating reliability (test–retest, parallel forms, internal consistency) takes into account somewhat different conditions that may produce these unsystematic changes in test scores and consequently affect the magnitude of the error variance and the index of reliability obtained when the test is administered under certain conditions to a specific group of people.[1]

## Test–Retest Coefficient

To determine whether an instrument measures consistently from one time to another, a *test–retest* coefficient is determined. This coefficient, also known as a *coefficient of stability*, is found by correlating the scores obtained by a group of people on one administration of a test with their scores on a second administration. The test–retest procedure takes into account errors of measurement resulting from differences in conditions associated with the two occasions on which the test is administered. Because the same test is administered on both occasions, errors due to different samples of test items are not reflected in a test–retest coefficient. Furthermore, differences between conditions of administration are likely to be greater after a long time interval than a short one. As a result, the magnitude of a test–retest

---

[1] Strictly speaking, a test itself is neither reliable nor unreliable. Rather than being a characteristic of a test, reliability is a property of the *scores* obtained when the test is administered to a *particular* group of people on a specific occasion and under certain conditions (Thompson, 1994).

reliability coefficient tends to be larger when the interval between initial test and retest is short (a few days or weeks), rather than long (months or years).

## Parallel-forms Coefficient

When the time interval between initial test and retest is short, examinees usually remember many of the responses they made on the initial test. This obviously affects their responses on the second administration, a fact which by itself would not change the reliability coefficient if everyone remembered equal numbers of responses. However, some people usually recall more answers than others, reducing the correlation between test and retest. What seems to be needed to overcome this source of error is a parallel form of the test, one consisting of similar items, but not the same items. Then a *parallel-forms coefficient,* also known as a *coefficient of equivalence,* can be computed as an index of reliability.

The parallel-forms idea is reasonable in principle: by administering a parallel form after a suitable interval following administration of the first form, a reliability coefficient reflecting errors of measurement due to different items and different times of administration can be computed. To control for the confounding effect of test form with administration time, one form should be administered first to half the group and a second form to the other half; then, on the second administration, the first group takes the second form and the second group takes the first form. The resulting correlation between scores on the two forms, known as a *coefficient of stability and equivalence,* takes into account errors due to different times of administration and different test items.

## Internal Consistency Coefficients

Parallel forms are available for a number of tests, particularly tests of ability (achievement, intelligence, special aptitudes). But because a parallel form of a test is expensive and often very difficult to construct, a less direct method of taking into account the effects on reliability of different samples of test items was devised. This is the *method of internal consistency,* including Spearman's split-half method, the Kuder–Richardson formulas, and Cronbach's alpha. Errors of measurement, caused by different conditions or times of administration, are, however, not reflected in an internal consistency coefficient. Consequently, internal consistency coefficients cannot be viewed as truly equivalent to either test–retest or parallel-forms coefficients.

*Split-half Method*    It is often convenient to conceptualize a single test as composed of two parts (parallel forms), each of which measures the same thing. Thus, a test can be administered and separate scores assigned to every examinee on two arbitrarily selected halves of the test. For example, the odd-numbered items may be scored separately from the even-numbered items. Then the correlation ($r_{oe}$) between the two sets of scores is a parallel-forms reliability coefficient for a test half as long as the original test. Assuming that the two halves are equivalent, having equal means and variances, the reliability of the test as a whole can be estimated by the *Spearman–Brown prophecy formula:*

$$r_{11} = \frac{2r_{oe}}{1 + r_{oe}} \tag{5.4}$$

To demonstrate the use of formula 5.4, assume that the correlation between total scores on the odd-numbered items and total scores on the even-numbered items of a test is .80. Then the estimated reliability of the entire test is $r_{11} = 2(.80)/(1 + .80) = .89$.

*Kuder–Richardson Method*   A test can be divided into two halves containing equal numbers of items in many different ways. Because each way may yield a somewhat different value of $r_{11}$, it is not clear which halving strategy will result in the best estimate of reliability. One solution to the problem is to take the average of the reliability coefficients obtained from all half-splits as the overall reliability estimate. But even with a test of, say, 20 items, a computer is needed to determine and average the resulting 92,378 split-half coefficients!

Under certain conditions, the mean of all split-half coefficients can be estimated by one of the following formulas:

$$r_{11} = \frac{k\left[1 - \sum p_i(1 - p_i)/s^2\right]}{k - 1} \tag{5.5}$$

$$r_{11} = \frac{k - \overline{X}(k - \overline{X})/s^2}{k - 1} \tag{5.6}$$

In these formulas, $k$ is the number of items on the test, $\overline{X}$ is the mean of total test scores, $s^2$ is the variance of total test scores (computed with $n$ instead of $n - 1$ in the denominator), and $p_i$ is the proportion of examinees giving the keyed response to item $i$. The sum of the $p_i$'s is taken over all $k$ items. Formulas 5.5 and 5.6 are known as Kuder–Richardson (K–R) formulas 20 and 21, respectively. Unlike formula 5.5, formula 5.6 is based on the assumption that all items are of equal difficulty; it also yields a more conservative estimate of reliability and is easier to compute than formula 5.5.

To demonstrate the application of formula 5.6, assume that a test containing 75 items has a mean of 50 and a variance of 100. Then, by formula 5.6, $r_{11} = [75 - 50(75 - 50)]/100]/74 = .84$.

*Coefficient Alpha*   Formulas 5.5 and 5.6 are special cases of the more general coefficient alpha (Cronbach, 1951). *Coefficient alpha* is defined as

$$\alpha = \frac{k\left(1 - \sum s_i^2/s_t^2\right)}{k - 1} \tag{5.7}$$

where $k$ is the number of items, $s_i^2$ is the variance of scores on item $i$, and $s_t^2$ is the variance of total test scores. Although the Kuder–Richardson formulas are applicable only when test items are scored 0 or 1, coefficient alpha is a general formula for estimating the reliability of a test consisting of items on which two or more scoring weights are assigned to answers.

All internal consistency procedures (split-half, Kuder–Richardson, coefficient alpha) overestimate the reliability of speeded tests, which most examinees do not finish in time. Consequently, internal consistency procedures must be modified to provide reasonable estimates of reliability when a test is speeded. One recommendation is to administer two split halves of the test at different times, but with equal time limits. The correlation between scores on the two separately timed halves is computed, and the resulting coefficient is corrected by formula 5.4. Test–retest and parallel-forms procedures may also be used to estimate the reliabilities of speeded tests.

The reliability coefficients of affective instruments such as personality and interest inventories are typically lower than those of cognitive tests. Sometimes, however, the reliability coefficients obtained on affective measures are fairly high and the reliabilities obtained from administering cognitive instruments very modest. How high must the reliability coefficient be for a test to be useful? The answer depends on what one plans to do with the test scores. If a test is used to determine whether the mean scores of two groups of people are significantly different, a fairly modest reliability coefficient (.60 to .70) may be satisfactory. But if the test is used to compare one person's score with that of another person, a reliability coefficient of at least .85 should be obtained.

## Interscorer Reliability

Barring clerical errors, the scores computed by two different scorers of an objective test will be identical. Scoring essay and oral tests, in addition to certain other evaluative judgments (personality ratings, projective test scoring) is, however, a fairly subjective process. In evaluating scores involving subjective scorer judgment, it is important to know the extent to which different scorers agree on the numerical values assigned to the responses of different examinees and items. The most common approach to determining this *interscorer* or *interrater reliability* is to have two persons score the responses of a sizable number of examinees and then compute the correlation between the two sets of scores. Another approach is to have many persons score the test responses of one examinee or, better still, have many persons score the responses of a number of examinees. The last approach yields an *intraclass coefficient* or *coefficient of concordance,* which is a generalized interscorer or interrater reliability coefficient. Programs for computing these and other reliability coefficients are included in the set of computer programs accompanying this text (category D). Special procedures for computing test–retest and internal consistency reliability indexes from rating-scale data and for conducting statistical tests of significance of the indexes have also been devised by the author (Aiken, 1985).

## Reliability of Oral Tests

Oral tests are not known for their high reliabilities, but special forms for rating oral performances can improve the objectivity, and hence the reliability, with which they are judged (see Figure 3–2). Although oral examinations typically have lower reliabilities than comparable written tests, careful attention to the design of oral questions, the construction of model answers to questions before the test is administered, and the use of multiple raters or scorers can enhance the reliability of scores on these tests. Such procedures have resulted in interscorer reliability coefficients in the .60s and .70s for oral tests administered in certain undergraduate, graduate, and professional school courses. Other suggestions for improving the reliability of oral performance evaluations include requiring examinees to delay answering until they have thought about the question for a while and electronically recording responses for later playback and reevaluation by scorers.

## Variability and Reliability

As with other measures of relationship, reliability coefficients tend to be higher when the variance of the variables of interest (test scores, item scores, ratings) is large than when it is small. Because test score variance is related to test length, one method of increasing reliability is to make the test longer.[2] The general Spearman–Brown formula is an expression of the effect on reliability of lengthening a test by including more items of the same general type. This formula, a generalization of formula 5.4, is

$$r_{mm} = \frac{mr_{11}}{1 + r_{11}(m - 1)} \tag{5.8}$$

where $m$ is the factor by which the test is lengthened, $r_{11}$ is the reliability of the original, unlengthened test, and $r_{mm}$ is the estimated reliability of the lengthened test. For example, if a 20-item test having a reliability coefficient of .70 is made three times as long by adding 40 more items, the estimated reliability of the lengthened test will be $3(.70)/[1 + 2(.70)] = .875$. To determine how many times longer a test of reliability $r_{11}$ must be to obtain a desired reliability ($r_{11}$), solving formula 5.8 for $m$ yields

$$m = \frac{r_{mm}(1 - r_{11})}{r_{11}(1 - r_{mm})} \tag{5.9}$$

In addition to being dependent on the number of items, the variance and reliability of a test are affected by the heterogeneity of the sample of people who take the test. The greater the range of individual differences on a certain characteristic, the larger will be the variance of the scores on a measure of that characteristic. Consequently, the reliability coefficient of a test or other assessment instrument will be higher in a more heterogeneous group, which has a larger test score variance. The fact that the reliability of a test varies with the nature of the group tested is reflected in the practice of reporting separate reliability coefficients for different age, grade, gender, and socioeconomic groups.

The association between the variance and reliability of a test is also reflected in the fact that tests comprised mostly of items of intermediate difficulty ($p$ values of around .50) tend to be more reliable than tests on which most of the items have high or low difficulty indexes.

## Standard Error of Measurement

The reliability of a test cannot be computed directly from formula 5.2 because the variance of true scores is unknown. Given an estimate of reliability, however, true score variance can be computed from formula 5.2, or, of greater interest, error variance can be computed from formula 5.3. Solving formula 5.3 for $s_{err}$ yields

$$s_{err} = s\sqrt{1 - r_{11}} \tag{5.10}$$

where $s$ is the standard deviation of the observed test scores and $r_{11}$ is the test–retest reliability coefficient. This statistic, known as the *standard error of measurement* ($s_{err}$), is an

---

[2]Simply including more items on a test does not necessarily increase reliability. The new items must be of the same general type and measure the same variable as the items already on the test. In fact, adding items that measure something different from whatever the original items measure can lead to a reduction in reliability.

estimate of the standard deviation of a normal distribution of test scores that would presumably be obtained if a person took the test an infinite number of times. The mean of this hypothetical score distribution is the person's true score on the test.

To illustrate the computation and meaning of the standard error of measurement, assume that the standard deviation of a test is 6.63 and the test–retest reliability coefficient is .85; then $s_{err} = 6.63\sqrt{1 - .85} = 2.57$. If a certain person's raw test score is 40, it can be concluded with 68 percent confidence that the person is one of a group of people having observed scores of 40 whose true scores on the test fall between $40 - 2.57 = 37.43$ and $40 + 2.57 = 42.57$. To obtain the 95% confidence interval for a person's true score, we compute the following: observed score $\pm 1.96 s_{err}$.

As can be seen from formula 5.10, the standard error of measurement increases as the reliability coefficient decreases. When $r_{11} = 1.00$, there is no error at all in estimating a person's true score from his or her observed score; when $r_{11} = .00$, the error of measurement is a maximum and equal to the standard deviation of observed scores. Of course, a test having a reliability coefficient close to .00 is useless because the correctness of any decisions made on the basis of the scores will be no better than chance.

## Percentile Bands

An examinee's score on certain tests is expressed not as a single number, but rather as a score band, or *percentile band,* having a width of one standard error of measurement (or the percentile rank equivalents of $s_{err}$) on both sides of a person's observed test score. This practice is an acknowledgment of the fact that a test score is not a fixed, unvarying measure of a characteristic, but only an approximation. The standard error of measurement is an estimate of the average error in that approximation.

When a person's scores on several tests are plotted in the form of a profile, it is useful to draw a band having a width of one or two standard errors of measurement around the score points. Then small differences between the scores of the same person on two different tests or the scores of two persons on the same test are less likely to be viewed as significant. As a rule of thumb, the difference between the scores of two persons on the same test should not be viewed as significant unless it is at least twice the standard error of measurement of the test. On the other hand, the difference between the scores of the same person on two tests should be greater than twice the larger standard error of measurement in order for the difference to be interpreted as significant. This is so because the standard error of the difference between scores on two tests is larger than the standard error of measurement of either test by itself.

## Reliability of Criterion-referenced Tests

The traditional concept of reliability pertains to norm-referenced tests, which are designed primarily to differentiate among individuals who possess various amounts of a specific characteristic. The greater the range of individual differences in test scores is, the higher the reliability of the test. On the other hand, the goal in constructing most criterion-referenced tests is to assign people to one of two groups. One group consists of those whose scores equal or exceed the criterion (mastery) level on the ability being assessed, and the other group consists of those whose scores do not reach the criterion level. In this situation, traditional correlational procedures for determining test–retest, parallel-forms, and internal consistency coefficients are inappropriate.

The *coefficient of agreement* ($p_0$), which is the proportion of scores falling above or below the criterion level on both administrations or both forms, is one measure of the reliability of a criterion-referenced test. A second measure is the *kappa coefficient* ($K$), which is somewhat more difficult to compute, but a statistically sounder index than the coefficient of agreement. Both coefficients, their confidence limits, and the right-tail probabilities associated with them can be computed by program D-4 of the computer program package accompanying the text.

## Generalizability Theory

Since the 1950s, there has been increasing dissatisfaction with the classical test theory that was developed during the first half of this century, and a number of alternative approaches have been proposed. These approaches are based on modern statistical theory and have also been influenced by advances in high-speed computing. An example is *generalizability theory,* which considers a test score as a single sample from a universe of possible scores. The reliability of that score is the precision with which it estimates a more generalized universe value of the score (the "true score"). The computations of generalizability theory involve the application of analysis of variance statistical techniques to determine the generalizability, or *dependability,* of test scores as a function of changes in the person(s) taking the test, different samples of items comprising the test, the situations or conditions under which the test is taken, and the methods or people involved in scoring it. A *generalizability coefficient,* which is similar to a traditional reliability coefficient, may then be computed as the ratio of the expected variance of scores in the universe to the variance of scores in the sample. Finally, a *universe value* of the score, similar to the true score of classical reliability theory, can be estimated (Cronbach et al., 1972). The effects of various samples of items, conditions of administration, or other *facets* on the accuracy with which the universe values of scores are determined are of particular interest.

Generalizability theory, item-response theory, covariance structures analysis, and other modern statistical methods are certainly more technically sophisticated than classical test theory. Be that as it may, test development and applications still rely greatly on the traditional concepts of reliability and validity and the procedures derived from these concepts.

# VALIDITY

Traditionally, the *validity* of a test has been defined as the extent to which the test measures what it was designed to measure. A shortcoming of this definition is the implication that a test has only one validity, which is presumably established by a single study to determine whether the test measures what it is supposed to measure. Actually, a test may have many different validities, depending on the specific purposes for which it was designed, the target population, and the method of determining validity.

The methods by which validity may be determined include (1) an analysis of the content of the test, (2) computing the correlation between scores on the test and those on the criterion measure of interest, and (3) investigating the particular psychological characteristics or constructs measured by the test. All these procedures are useful to the extent that they increase our understanding of what a test measures, which is important if the scores are to provide information for making decisions about people. Furthermore, we need to ask how much the particular test adds to the prediction and understanding of criteria that are already being predicted. This is the notion of incremental validity, to which we shall return later.

Unlike reliability, which is influenced only by unsystematic errors of measurement, the validity of a test is affected by both unsystematic and systematic (constant) errors. For this reason, a test may be reliable without being valid, but it cannot be valid without being reliable. Reliability is a necessary but not a sufficient condition for validity. Technically, the criterion-related validity of a test, as indicated by the correlation between the test and an external criterion measure, can never be greater than the square root of the parallel-forms reliability coefficient of either the test or the criterion.

## Content Validity

The physical appearance of a test with regard to its particular purposes (*face validity*) is certainly an important consideration in marketing. The concept of *content validity,* however, refers to more than just face validity. Content validity is concerned with whether the content of a test elicits a range of responses representing the entire domain or universe of skills, understandings, and other behaviors that the test is supposed to measure. Examinees' responses to the sample of items on a well-designed test are representative of what their responses would be to the entire universe of behaviors being measured.

An analysis of content validity occurs most often in connection with achievement tests, for which there is usually no external criterion. Content validity is also of concern on measures of aptitude, interest, and personality, although perhaps less so than criterion-related or construct validity. The content validity of an achievement test is determined by evaluating the extent to which the composition of the test represents the objectives of instruction. One way of doing this is to compare the content of the test with an outline or table of specifications concerning the subject matter presumably covered by the test (see Chapter 2). If subject-matter experts agree that the test looks and acts like an instrument that was designed to measure whatever it is supposed to, then the test is said to possess content validity. Such judgments involve not only the appearance of the test items, but also an analysis of the cognitive processes involved in arriving at answers to the items. Obviously, the process of evaluating content validity should not wait until the test has been constructed. Expert judgments concerning what items to include are necessary from the very beginning of the test-construction process. By defining the universe of content of the test and the sample of that universe to be included, test constructors are engaging in content validation.

## Criterion-related Validity

The validation of all tests consists of relating test scores to performance on criterion measures—standards or variables with which test performance can be compared. Traditionally, however, the term *criterion-related validity* has referred to validation procedures in which the test scores of a group of people are compared with ratings, classifications, or other behavioral or mental measurements. Examples of criteria against which tests are validated are school marks, supervisors' ratings, and number or dollar amount of sales. Whenever a criterion measure is available at the time of testing, the *concurrent validity* of the test can be determined. When scores on the criterion do not become available ("mature") until sometime after the test has been administered, it is the *predictive validity* of the test that is of interest.

**Concurrent Validity**   Concurrent validation procedures are employed whenever a test is administered to people in various categories, such as clinical diagnostic groups or socio-economic levels, for the purpose of determining whether the average scores of people in the various categories are significantly different. If the average score varies substantially from category to category, then the test might be used as another, perhaps more efficient, way of assigning people to those categories. For example, scores on the Minnesota Multiphasic Personality Inventory (MMPI) are useful in identifying specific mental disorders, because it was found that people diagnosed as having a particular disorder tend to score differently on certain groups of items (*scales*) than people in general.

**Predictive Validity**   Predictive validity is concerned with how accurately test scores predict criterion scores, as indicated by the correlation between the test (predictor) and a criterion of future performance. Predictive validity is of concern primarily with respect to aptitude or intelligence tests, since scores on these kinds of instruments are often correlated with ratings, marks, achievement test scores, and other criteria of success.

The magnitude of a predictive validity coefficient is limited by the reliabilities of both the predictor and criterion variables, being no greater than the square root of the products of those two reliabilities. For this and other reasons, the correlation between a predictor and a criterion variable, computed by procedures described in Appendix A, varies with the specific criterion, but is seldom greater than .60. Because the proportion of variance in the criterion that can be accounted for by the predictor is equal to the square of the correlation between predictor and criterion, typically not more than 36 percent of the variation in criterion scores can be predicted from scores on a test or other prediction instrument. This leaves 64 percent of the criterion variance unaccounted for or unpredicted. Considering that the predictive validity of most tests is less than .60, it is understandable why claims concerning the ability of psychological tests to predict behavior must be made cautiously.

**Standard Error of Estimate**   The section on regression and prediction in Appendix A describes the procedure for finding a regression equation (prediction equation) for forecasting the criterion scores of a group of people from their scores on tests or other variables. However, entering a person's test score into a regression equation yields only an estimate of what score the person will actually obtain on the criterion variable. If the predicted criterion score of a certain person is viewed as the mean of a normal distribution of the criterion scores of a group of people who make the same score on the predictor test as that person, then the standard deviation of this distribution is an index of the average error in such predictions. This statistic, known as the *standard error of estimate* ($s_{est}$), is approximately equal to

$$s_{est} = s\sqrt{1 - r^2} \tag{5.11}$$

where $s$ is the standard deviation of the criterion scores and $r$ is the product–moment correlation between the predictor (test) and the criterion.

Assume, for example, that the standard deviation of a criterion measure is 15 and the correlation between test and criterion is .50; then $s_{est} = 15\sqrt{1 - .50^2} = 13$. If the predicted criterion score is 50, the chances are 68 out of 100 that the person will obtain a criterion score between 37 and 63 ($Y_{pred} \pm s_{est}$) and approximately 95 out of 100 that he or she will obtain a criterion score between 25 and 75 ($Y_{pred} \pm 1.96s_{est}$). More precisely, the chances are 68 out of 100 that the person is one of a group of people having a test score of 50 whose criterion scores fall between 37 and 63. Similarly, the chances are approximately 95 out of 100 that the individual is one of a group of people with a test score of 50 whose obtained criterion scores fall between 25 and 75. As illustrated by this example, when the correlation between test and criterion scores is low, a person's obtained criterion score may be very different from his or her predicted score. For this reason, caution must be exercised in interpreting predicted scores when the correlation between test and criterion is modest. The smaller the correlation coefficient is, the larger the standard error of estimate and the less accurate the prediction from test to criterion.

***Factors Affecting Criterion-related Validity***   The criterion-related validity of a test can be affected by a number of factors, including group differences, test length, criterion contamination, and base rate. The incremental validity of a test should also be considered in deciding whether to use the test for purposes of selection and placement.

*Group Differences*   The characteristics of a group of people on whom a test is validated include such variables as sex, age, and personality traits. Referred to in this context as *moderator variables,* these factors can affect the correlation between a test and a criterion measure. The magnitude of a validity coefficient, like that of a reliability coefficient, is also influenced by the degree of heterogeneity of the validation group on whatever the test measures. Validity coefficients tend to be smaller in more homogeneous groups, that is, groups having a narrower range of test scores. The size of a correlation coefficient is a function of both the predictor and criterion variables, so narrowing the range of scores on either variable will tend to lower the predictive validity coefficient.

Because the magnitude of a validity coefficient varies with the nature of the group tested, a newly constructed test that is found to be a valid predictor of a particular criterion variable in one group of people should be cross-validated on a second group. In *cross-validation,* a test is administered to a second sample of people to determine whether the test retains its validity across different samples. Due to the operation of chance factors, the magnitude of a validity coefficient usually shrinks somewhat on cross-validation. Consequently, the correlation between predictor and criterion obtained on cross-validation is considered in most instances to be a better index of predictive validity than the original test–criterion correlation. Cross-validation, which is one way of determining the validity generalization of a test, may also involve a different (parallel) sample of test items. In any case—different samples of examinees, different samples of test items, or both—there is typically some shrinkage of the validity coefficient on cross-validation. Formulas for correcting for such shrinkage have been proposed, but they entail certain assumptions that are not always met.

*Test Length*   Like reliability, validity varies directly with the length of the test and the heterogeneity of the group of people who are tested. Up to a point, scores on a longer test and scores on a test administered to a group of individuals who vary greatly in the characteristics being measured have larger variances. On the other hand, scores obtained on shorter tests or tests administered to more homogeneous groups of people have smaller variances. Formulas that correct for the effects of range restriction and curtailed test length on validity have been proposed, but they are appropriate only under certain special circumstances.

*Criterion Contamination*   The validity of a test is limited not only by the reliabilities of the test and criterion, but also by the validity of the criterion itself as a measure of the variable of interest. Sometimes the criterion is made less valid, or becomes *contaminated,* by the particular method of determining the criterion scores. For example, a clinical psychologist who knows that a group of patients has already been diagnosed as psychotic may misperceive psychotic signs in the personality test responses of those patients. Then the method of contrasting groups, in which the test scores of the psychotics are compared with those of normals, will yield false evidence for the validity of the test. Such contamination of the criterion (psychotic versus normal) can be controlled by *blind analysis,* that is, by making available to the diagnostician no information about the examinees other than their test scores. Many clinical psychologists maintain, however, that blind analysis is unnatural in that it is not the way in which tests are used in practice to identify consistencies or congruences among the various kinds of data when making a diagnosis or treatment recommendation.

*Incremental Validity*   When trying to decide whether administering a particular assessment instrument for predictive or diagnostic purposes is justified by the cost, *incremental validity* should also be considered. Incremental validity is concerned with the question of how much more accurate predictions and diagnoses are when a particular instrument is included in a battery of assessment procedures. It is possible that other, less expensive methods of assessment (observation, interview, biographical inventory) can adequately fulfill the purposes of assessment.

## Construct Validity

Predictive validity is of greatest concern in occupational or educational selection and placement. Ability tests of various kinds, and sometimes personality and interest tests, are used for selection and placement purposes. Of even greater concern with respect to personality tests is construct validity. The *construct validity* of a psychological assessment instrument refers to the extent to which the instrument measures a particular *construct,* or psychological concept such as anxiety, achievement motivation, extroversion–introversion, or neuroticism. Construct validity, which is the most general type of validity, is not determined in a single way or by one investigation. Rather, it involves a network of investigations and other procedures designed to determine whether an assessment instrument that purportedly measures a certain psychological construct is actually doing its job.

*Evidence for Construct Validity*   The following are sources of evidence for the construct validity of a test:

1. Experts' judgments that the content of the test pertains to the construct of interest
2. An analysis of the internal consistency of the test
3. Studies of the relationships, in both experimentally contrived and naturally occurring groups, of test scores to other variables on which the groups differ
4. Correlations of the test with other tests or measures with which it is expected to have a certain relationship and factor analyses of these correlations
5. Questioning examinees or raters in detail about their responses to a test or rating scale in order to reveal the specific mental processes involved in responding to the items

As seen in this list, various kinds of information may contribute to establishing the construct validity of a psychometric instrument. The information may be obtained from rational or statistical analyses of the variables assessed by the instrument and studies of its ability to predict behavior in situations where the construct is known to be operating. Experimental demonstrations such as those used in the construct validation of the Taylor Manifest Anxiety Scale (TMAS) (Taylor, 1953) are particularly important in establishing construct validity. According to Hullian learning theory, anxiety is a drive, and hence more anxious people should be easier to condition than less anxious ones. Assuming that this theory is correct, people with a high anxiety level should acquire a conditioned eyeblink in a light–airpuff–eyeblink classical conditioning situation more quickly than people having a low anxiety level. So if the TMAS is a valid measure of the construct *anxiety,* high scorers on the instrument should condition more readily in this situation than low scorers. Verification of this prediction contributed significantly to acceptance of the construct validity of the TMAS.

**Convergent and Discriminant Validation**   A construct-validated instrument should have high correlations with other measures of or methods of measuring the same construct (*convergent validity*) and low correlations with measures of different constructs (*discriminant validity*). Evidence for the convergent and discriminant validity of a psychometric instrument can be obtained by comparing correlations between measures of the following:

1. The same construct using the same method
2. Different constructs using the same method
3. The same construct using different methods
4. Different constructs using different methods

The construct validity of a psychometric instrument is demonstrated by this *multitrait–multimethod approach* (Campbell & Fiske, 1959) when correlations between the same construct measured by the same and different methods are significantly higher than correlations between different constructs measured by the same or different methods. Unfortunately, the results of such comparisons are not always as desired; sometimes correlations between different constructs measured by the same method are higher than correlations between the same construct measured by different methods. This means that the method (paper-and-pencil inventory, projective technique, rating scale, interview, and so on) is more important in determining whatever is measured than the construct or trait that is presumably being assessed.

## USING TESTS IN PERSONNEL DECISION MAKING

The topic of predictive validity was introduced earlier in the chapter. In this section, we shall describe how predictive validity information on tests is applied to the very practical tasks of selecting, classifying, and placing people in organizations.

Since antiquity people have been selected, classified, and placed in positions to perform various duties. Often, however, the procedures followed in personnel selection, classification, and placement have been haphazard and unsystematic. A variety of procedures for personnel selection and appraisal, many of which were based on casual observation and intuition, have been employed. For example, at one time great importance was attached to physical features, such as head shape, eye movements, and overall body appearance. Cultural and familial origins were also significant in determining who was appointed to a position, hired for a specific job, or accepted for a certain educational program.

### Screening

Traditionally, personnel selection has been concerned with identifying, from a pool of applicants, those who are most able to perform designated tasks. In this approach, psychological tests are used, together with nontest information (personal history, physical characteristics, recommendations, and so on), to assist in selecting applicants who can perform particular jobs immediately or following appropriate training.

A personnel selection procedure may be fairly simple or very complex, depending on the nature of the organization and the task for which applicants are being selected. The most straightforward approach is the sink-or-swim strategy in which all who apply are selected or admitted, but only those who perform effectively are retained. In some ways this is an ideal selection strategy, but it is also expensive to both the organization and the applicants. Consequently, almost all organizations use some kind of *screening* procedure by which applicants who are clearly unsuitable for the task (job, program, and so on) are rejected immediately. If the screening instrument is a psychological test of some kind, applicants who make a specified minimum score (*cutoff score*) or higher on the test are accepted, whereas those who make below the cutoff score are rejected. This procedure is fairly impersonal, and it may occasionally seem unkind from the applicant's perspective. However, both product-making and service-providing organizations must run efficiently in order to reach their goals. Obviously, they will run most efficiently when the members of the organization perform their assigned tasks effectively and efficiently.

### Classification and Placement

Initial screening is usually followed by *classification* and the assignment of those who have been selected to one of several occupational categories. Classification decisions may involve grouping people on the basis of their scores on more than one psychological test, such as classifying military inductees into occupational specialties on the basis of their scores on the Armed Services Vocational Aptitude Battery. Screening and classification are frequently followed by *placement* of those who have been selected to a particular level of a certain job or program.

The process of personnel selection usually consists of a sequence of stages entailing a series of yes–no decisions based on information obtained from application blanks, letters of reference, telephone calls, personal interviews, observations, and psychological tests. The purpose of collecting such information is identical to that of any other application of psychology: to make better predictions of future behavior on the basis of past and present behavior. The more reliable and valid the information is, the greater the likelihood of making accurate predictions of on-the-job or in-the-program behavior and hence the sounder the selection decisions. The reliability and validity of psychological assessment instruments and procedures for making selection decisions cannot, of course, be determined merely by inspecting the assessment materials. Reliability and validity must be evaluated empirically, which is one of the primary tasks of the personnel psychologist.

## An Expectancy Table

When tests are used for selection purposes, it is not essential to determine the test–criterion correlation and the regression equation linking performance on the criterion variable to scores on the test. Correlational methods are applicable to the construction of theoretical expectancy tables, but an empirical expectancy table can be constructed without computing a correlation coefficient or any other statistic except frequencies and percentages. Assume, for example, that Table 5–1 was constructed from a joint frequency distribution of the scores of 250 job applicants on an Occupational Selection Test (OST) and the ratings given to the applicants by their work supervisors six months after being hired. The OST score intervals are listed on the left side of the table, and the performance ratings (on a scale of 1 to 8) across the top. The non-parenthesized entries in the cells of the table are the numbers of employees who obtained OST scores within a specified 5-point range and the performance rating indicated at the top of a given column. For example, 10 employees whose OST scores were between 81 and 85 were given a performance rating of 5 by their supervisors, and 14 employees whose OST scores fell between 66 and 70 were given a performance rating of 4.

The numbers in parentheses in Table 5–1 are the percentages of people having OST scores in a given interval whose performance ratings were equal to the value in the given cells or higher. Thus, 85 percent of employees whose OST scores fell in the interval 81 to 85 received performance ratings of 5 or higher, and 61 percent of those having OST scores between 66 and 70 had performance ratings of 4 or higher.

To illustrate how this kind of information is applied to the process of occupational selection, assume that John, a potential employee from a group similar to that on which Table 5–1 was constructed, makes a score of 68 on the Occupational Selection Test. Then it can be estimated that John's chances of receiving a rating of 4 or higher on job performance by his supervisor six months after beginning the job are 61 out of 100, but his chances of obtaining a performance rating of 6 or higher are only 5 out of 100. If a rating of 4 or higher is acceptable, then John will be hired.

**TABLE 5–1  Empirical Expectancy Table**

| Occupational selection test score | Performance rating | | | | | | | |
|---|---|---|---|---|---|---|---|---|
| | 1 | 2 | 3 | 4 | 5 | 6 | 7 | 8 |
| 96–100 | | | | | | (100) 1 | | (67) 2 |
| 91–95 | | | | | (100) 2 | | (82) 5 | (36) 4 |
| 86–90 | | | | (100) 1 | (94) 8 | (50) 3 | (33) 4 | (11) 2 |
| 81–85 | | | | (100) 4 | (85) 10 | (48) 7 | (22) 5 | (4) 1 |
| 76–80 | | | (100) 6 | (88) 12 | (63) 16 | (31) 13 | (4) 2 | |
| 71–75 | | (100) 4 | (94) 7 | (83) 25 | (45) 21 | (12) 5 | (5) 3 | |
| 66–70 | | (100) 5 | (87) 10 | (61) 14 | (24) 7 | (5) 2 | | |
| 61–65 | (100) 1 | (96) 6 | (72) 8 | (40) 5 | (20) 4 | (4) 1 | | |
| 56–60 | (100) 2 | (85) 5 | (46) 4 | (15) 2 | | | | |
| 51–55 | (100) 1 | | | | | | | |

## Factors Affecting Predictive Accuracy

The accuracy with which an applicant's criterion score can be predicted depends not only on the size of the correlation between the predictor and criterion variables. It is also affected by several other factors, including false positive and false negative errors, the selection ratio, and the base rate.

If the cutoff score on a test is set very low, there will be many incorrect acceptances, or *false positives*. These are applicants who were selected but do not succeed on the job or in the program. On the other hand, if the cutoff score is set very high, there will be many incorrect rejections or *false negatives*. These are applicants who were not selected but would have succeeded if they had been. Since the purpose of personnel selection is to obtain as many "hits" as possible—to reject potential failures and select potential successes—a cutoff score must be set carefully.

To illustrate these concepts, refer again to Table 5–1. Suppose that the cutoff score on the OST is set at 66 and that a 4 is considered a minimum acceptable job performance rating. Then $4 + 5 + 6 + 7 + 10 = 32$ of the employees represented in Table 5–1 will be classified as false positives: they scored at least 66 on the OST but had performance ratings of less than 4. On the other hand, $5 + 2 + 4 + 1 = 12$ employees will be false negatives: they scored below 66 on the OST but received performance ratings of 4 or higher. Observe that raising the cutoff score on the OST results in the number of false positives being decreased, but the number of false negatives being increased. The opposite effect—an increase in false positives and a decrease in false negatives—will occur if the cutoff score on the OST is lowered.

Another important factor to consider when setting a cutoff score on a test or test composite is the *selection ratio*: the proportion of applicants to be selected. The lower the selection ratio is, the higher the cutoff score, and vice versa. Because the number of false positive and false negative errors is affected by where the cutoff score is set, one might argue that the selection ratio should be determined by the relative seriousness with which these two types of errors are viewed. Is the error made in accepting an applicant who fails to perform the task satisfactorily (false positive) more or less serious than rejecting an applicant who could have performed the task successfully if he or she had been selected (false negative)? Such errors should be taken into account, but at least as important in determining the selection ratio is the total number of applicants. For example, when the labor market is tight, the number of applicants will be small. Then the selection ratio will need to be high and, consequently, the cutoff score on the test must be lowered in order to select the desired number of people. On the other hand, in a free, or open, labor market, the number of applicants is large, so the selection ratio will be low. A low selection ratio means that the cutoff score on the test will need to be set fairly high, leading to a smaller number of accepted applicants and false positives but a larger number of rejected applicants and false negatives. Not only does the percentage of successful applicants vary inversely with the selection ratio; it varies directly with the validity of the test or other selection device. In general, a more valid test leads to a greater percentage of "hits" and a smaller percentage of false positives and false negatives.

Another factor that affects the accuracy with which a test can identify people who will behave in a certain way is the *base rate,* the proportion of people in the population of interest who would be expected to perform satisfactorily on a job if provided with an opportunity to do so. As with the selection ratio, a test designed to predict a particular type of behavior is most effective when the base rate is 50 percent and least effective when it is either very high or very low. For this reason, a test designed to select people for a highly complex job on which relatively few people can do well would not be as effective as a test designed to select people for a job that half the applicant population can perform satisfactorily. The concept of base rate is not limited to personnel selection; it is also important in clinical diagnosis. For example, because the incidence of suicide in the general population is very low, a test designed to identify potential suicides would not be very effective. But a test designed to identify neurotics would do better because the percentage of neurotics is much higher than that of potential suicides.

The amount of information contributed by a test beyond the base rate can be determined by consulting the *Taylor–Russell table* for the specified base rate (Taylor & Russell, 1939). The numbers in one such table, that for a base rate of .60, have been graphed in Figure 5–1. This table depicts the percentage of selected applicants who would be expected to succeed on a job or in another selection situation as a function of the validity coefficient of the test and the selection ratio. Note that the percentage who are expected to succeed varies directly with the validity coefficient, but inversely with the selection ratio. Thus, the percentage of successful applicants is higher when the selection ratio is low. For example, with a base rate of .60, a validity coefficient of .50, and a selection ratio of .90, only 64% of the applicants would be

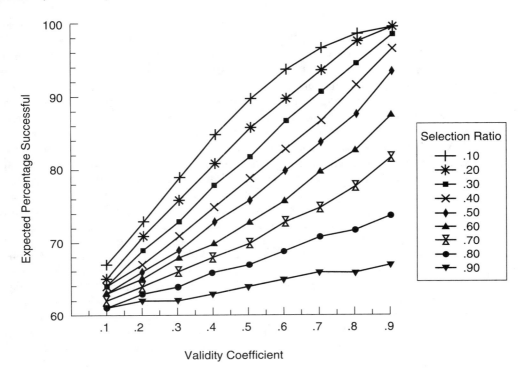

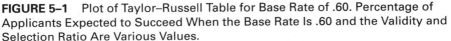

**FIGURE 5–1** Plot of Taylor–Russell Table for Base Rate of .60. Percentage of Applicants Expected to Succeed When the Base Rate Is .60 and the Validity and Selection Ratio Are Various Values.
(Based on data from Taylor, H. C., & Russell, J. T. (1939). The relationship of validity coefficients to the practical effectiveness of tests in selection: Discussion and tables. *Journal of Applied Psychology, 23,* 565–578.)

expected to succeed—an increase of a mere 4% over the base rate. But for the same base rate and validity coefficient, 90% of the applicants would be expected to succeed when the selection ratio is .10, an increase of 30% over the base rate. In general, at an intermediate base rate and with a low selection ratio, even scores on a test having a quite modest validity coefficient can produce a substantial increase in the number of "hits" in a selection situation.[3]

## Multiple Cutoff and Multiple Regression

Setting the cutoff score on a selection or placement test is a complex judgmental process. In addition to the factors just discussed, the cutoff score and the usefulness of a test in general are affected by other information available on an applicant.

[3]Use of the Taylor–Russell tables assumes a clear, discrete, dichotomous definition of success (versus failure) in the selection situation. Similar approaches involving continuous criteria of success based on decision and utility theory have been devised, but they are complex and beyond the scope of this text (see Cronbach & Gleser, 1965; Cascio & Ramos, 1986; Schmitt & Robertson, 1990; Raju, Normand, & Burke, 1990).

Frequently, a set of test scores and other measures are combined in making selection and classification decisions. One procedure for combining scores, referred to as *successive hurdles* or *multiple cutoff,* is to set separate cutoff scores on each of several measures. Then an applicant must score at the cutoff point or higher on each separate measure in situations where a high score on one measure does not compensate for a low score on another measure. For example, the ability to differentiate between tones of different pitches is essential to effective performance as an orchestra conductor. Regardless of how high their scores tests of cognitive abilities may be, people who are tone deaf will not do well in this profession.

A more mathematical approach to combining the scores of a large sample of people on several measures is to determine a *multiple-regression equation* in which different statistically assigned weights are applied to scores on different tests. A procedure for computing these regression weights is described in Appendix A. Once the regression weights have been determined, a single predicted criterion score for each applicant can be computed by multiplying the applicant's score on each variable by the appropriate weight, adding the products, and subtracting a constant. For example, a multiple-regression equation employed for admission purposes at one college was $GPA_{pred} = .002 (SAT-V) + .001 (SAT-M) + .030 (HSR) - 2.00$, where SAT–V and SAT–M are the applicant's scores on the Verbal and Mathematical sections of the Scholastic Assessment Test, HSR is a $T$ score measure of the applicant's rank in his or her high school graduating class, and $GPA_{pred}$ is the predicted freshman year grade-point average of the applicant. If a particular applicant's scores on the two sections of the SAT are 600 and 500 and his or her high school rank is 70, then the applicant's predicted grade-point average is $GPA_{pred} = .002(600) + .001(500) + .030(70) - 2.00 = 1.8$, which is equivalent to a low C.

In the multiple-regression approach, a high score on one predictor variable can compensate for a low score on another predictor variable. Consequently, this approach should not be used when a minimum score on any of the predictors is essential for effective performance on the criterion. When the multiple-regression approach is used, a *multiple correlation coefficient* ($R$), which is an index of the relationship of a weighted combination of the predictor variables to the criterion variable, should be computed. The procedure for computing $R$, which ranges from .00 to 1.00 and is interpreted in a manner similar to that for the product–moment coefficient, is described in Appendix A.

## SUMMARY

Reliability refers to the relative freedom of test scores from errors of measurement. In classical test score theory, reliability is defined as the ratio of a test's true score variance to its observed score variance. Because true score variance cannot be computed directly, reliability must be estimated by one of several procedures that take into account various sources of measurement error. Three traditional methods for estimating the reliability of a test or other assessment instrument are test–retest, parallel forms, and internal consistency. The method of parallel forms, which considers errors due to different administration times as well as errors due to different samples of test items, is the most satisfactory. Because parallel forms are expensive and time consuming to construct, test–retest and internal consistency procedures are more popular sources of evidence for reliability. Internal consistency approaches, which are less appropriate for speeded tests, include split half, Kuder–Richardson, and coefficient alpha.

The standard error of measurement, which varies inversely with the magnitude of the reliability coefficient, is used to compute confidence intervals for true scores on a test. The larger the standard error of measurement is, the wider the range of scores that can be said, within a specified degree of confidence, to contain a person's true score on the test.

The reliability of a test varies directly with the number of items and the heterogeneity of the group taking the test. Reliability also varies with the difficulty level of the items comprising the test, being highest with items of intermediate difficulty.

Procedures for determining the consistency among different scorers or raters (interscorer or interrater reliability) and the reliability of criterion-referenced tests were discussed briefly in this chapter. Some attention was also given to generalizability theory, which conceptualizes a test score as a sample from a population and therefore an estimate of a true score or universe value.

Reliability is a necessary but not a sufficient condition for *validity*—the extent to which a test measures what it was designed to measure. Information on the validity of a test may be obtained in various ways: by analyzing the test's content (*content validity*), by correlating test scores with scores on a criterion measure obtained at the same time (*concurrent validity*), by correlating test scores with scores on a criterion measured at a later time (*predictive validity*), and by a systematic study of the adequacy of the test in appraising a specified psychological construct (*construct validity*). Achievement tests are usually content validated, whereas predictive validity is of greater interest with respect to aptitude tests. Concurrent and construct validity are more important on personality tests.

The amount of error made in predicting a person's criterion score from his or her score on a test is estimated by the standard error of estimate, which varies inversely with the size of the criterion-related validity coefficient. Both the criterion-related validity coefficient and the standard error of estimate are affected by a number of factors, including group differences, test length, and criterion contamination. The magnitudes of validity coefficients can also be affected by chance factors, and therefore tests used for predictive purposes should be cross-validated. It is also important to consider how much test scores contribute to the process of making good decisions about people (incremental validity).

Information on the construct validity of a test as a measure of a particular psychological construct (characteristic or trait) can be obtained in a variety of ways. Especially helpful is an analysis of correlations between the test and other measures of the same construct obtained by the same or different methods, as well as measures of different constructs obtained by the same or different methods (multitrait–multimethod matrix).

Psychological tests are administered in occupational settings for purposes of employment selection, classification, promotion, and periodic appraisal of employees. Some of the statistical procedures that are used for these purposes are expectancy tables, selection ratios, and multiple-cutoff and multiple-regression methods.

## QUESTIONS AND ACTIVITIES

1. Calculate both split-half (odd–even) and Kuder–Richardson reliability (formulas 5.5 and 5.6) coefficients on the following scores of 10 examinees for the 10 items on an achievement test, where 1 indicates a right answer and 0 a wrong answer.

|      | *Examinee* |   |   |   |   |   |   |   |   |   |
|------|---|---|---|---|---|---|---|---|---|---|
| *Item* | *A* | *B* | *C* | *D* | *E* | *F* | *G* | *H* | *I* | *J* |
| 1    | 1 | 1 | 0 | 1 | 1 | 0 | 1 | 0 | 1 | 0 |
| 2    | 1 | 0 | 0 | 0 | 0 | 1 | 0 | 0 | 0 | 1 |
| 3    | 1 | 1 | 1 | 1 | 1 | 0 | 1 | 0 | 0 | 0 |
| 4    | 1 | 1 | 1 | 0 | 0 | 1 | 0 | 1 | 0 | 0 |
| 5    | 1 | 0 | 1 | 1 | 0 | 0 | 0 | 0 | 0 | 0 |
| 6    | 1 | 1 | 1 | 0 | 1 | 1 | 1 | 0 | 0 | 0 |
| 7    | 1 | 0 | 1 | 1 | 0 | 0 | 1 | 1 | 0 | 1 |
| 8    | 1 | 1 | 1 | 0 | 1 | 1 | 0 | 0 | 1 | 0 |
| 9    | 1 | 1 | 0 | 1 | 1 | 1 | 0 | 1 | 0 | 0 |
| 10   | 1 | 1 | 1 | 1 | 1 | 0 | 0 | 0 | 1 | 0 |
| Totals | 10 | 7 | 7 | 6 | 6 | 5 | 4 | 3 | 3 | 2 |

The mean $(\overline{X})$ of the total scores is 5.30, and the variance $(s^2)$ is 5.21.

2. Compute the standard error of measurement $(s_{err})$ of a test having a standard deviation of 10 and a parallel-forms reliability coefficient of .84. Then use the obtained value of $s_{err}$ to find the 95 percent confidence interval for the true scores corresponding to obtained scores of 40, 50, and 60.

3. A test consisting of 40 items has a reliability coefficient of .80. Approximately how many more items of the same general type must be added to the test to increase its reliability to .90?

4. Plot a set of curves on a single graph illustrating how test reliability $(r_{mm})$ varies as a function of test length $(m)$ and initial reliability $(r_{11})$. Let $m$ equal 2, 3, 4, 5, and 6 and $r_{11}$ equal .50, .60, .70, .80, and .90. The horizontal axis of your graph should be $r_{11}$ and the vertical axis $r_{mm}$. Plot one curve for each value of $m$ and state appropriate conclusions concerning the effects of lengthening a test on its reliability.

5. A criterion-referenced test is administered twice to the same group of 100 examinees. The criterion level is reached by 70 examinees on both administrations, 10 examinees on the first administration only, 15 examinees on the second administration only, and 5 examinees on neither administration. Using program D-4 in the package of computer programs accompanying the text, compute and evaluate the agreement index $(p_0)$ and the kappa coefficient for these data.

6. What is the standard error made in estimating grade-point averages from scores on an aptitude test if the standard deviation of the criterion is .50 and the correlation between test and criterion is .60? Interpret the results.

7. Construct an empirical expectancy table for the paired $X, Y$ scores in Table A–2 in Appendix A. Let $X$ be the predictor (row) variable and $Y$ the criterion (column) variable. Use an interval width of 7 for both variables in setting up the score intervals for $X$ and $Y$.

# Part Two

# Assessment of Abilities

# 6

# STANDARDIZED ACHIEVEMENT TESTS

Chapters 1 through 5 are concerned with the background, methodology, and professional status of psychological and educational testing. In the next two parts of this textbook, specific kinds of cognitive and affective instruments and what they measure are surveyed. Achievement testing, known in the United Kingdom as *attainment testing,* is discussed in this chapter. Other cognitive instruments, tests of general intelligence, and special abilities are dealt with in Chapters 7 through 9. Affective assessment, including measures of interests, attitudes, values, and personality, is considered in Chapters 10 through 12.

## ACHIEVEMENT TESTING IN PERSPECTIVE

Tests of *achievement,* defined as the level of knowledge, skill, or accomplishment in an area of endeavor, are the most popular of all kinds of tests. Counting all classroom tests constructed by teachers and the standardized tests sold to schools and other organizations, the number of achievement tests administered easily exceeds all other types of psychological and educational measures. The majority of standardized achievement tests are in the areas of reading and language arts, although millions of dollars are also spent each year on tests in mathematics, science, social studies, and other subject-matter areas.

Any test of ability—general intelligence, special abilities, or achievement—actually measures what individuals have achieved. The items on tests of intelligence and special abilities, like those on achievement tests, require examinees to demonstrate some accomplishment. Scores on achievement tests may also be used for many of the same purposes as scores on other tests of general or specific abilities. These purposes include not only global and diagnostic assessment of individual abilities, but also evaluation of the effectiveness of instruction or a specific educational program.

Achievement tests are often better predictors of school marks than tests of intelligence or special abilities, but this does not mean that tests of achievement in a specific subject can entirely replace tests of intelligence and special abilities. The accomplishments or achievements measured by general intelligence tests are usually broader and produced by less formal and presumably less recent learning experiences than those measured by standardized tests of achievement. Achievement tests usually assess knowledge of something that has been explicitly taught, so scores on these tests tend to be influenced more by coaching than are scores on intelligence tests.

A distinction between achievement tests and tests of intelligence and special abilities can also be made in terms of their emphases. Achievement tests focus more on the present, that is, what a person knows or can do right now. Tests of intelligence and special abilities focus on the future: they measure *aptitude* for learning—what a person should be able to achieve with further education and training.

## Historical Overview

Written examinations in composition and poetry, recopied and judged by two graders, were first used in China around A.D. 1370. Following the introduction of paper making into Europe, a skill that had been learned from the Arabs in the twelfth century and in turn by them from the Chinese in the eighth century, written examinations began to replace oral examinations in some European universities. The first educational use of written tests in a European university was reportedly made at Cambridge, England, in 1702, and the University of London was chartered as an examining center in 1836 (Green, 1991). Not until 1845, however, were written examinations administered on a large scale in the United States (Greene, Jorgensen, & Gerberich, 1954). Despite the fact that the number of students had grown too large for the periodic administration of oral examinations in U.S. cities, until the latter half of the nineteenth century oral testing was the principal method employed in evaluating pupil achievement in the United States. In the middle of the nineteenth century, the Boston educator Horace Mann argued persuasively that written examinations, administered and scored under uniform conditions, were better measures of achievement than oral examinations. Mann's influence led the Boston schools to begin giving written examinations to pupils every year. It was hoped that this practice would help to determine "the condition, improvement or deterioration of our schools" (Fish, 1941, page 23). Despite the efforts of Horace Mann and other educators, oral examinations continued for many years to be the principal method of assessing school achievement and were only gradually replaced by written tests.

The first objective test of achievement, one that could be reliably scored, was a handwriting scale constructed by the Englishman George Fisher in 1864. One year later, New York State initiated the Regents Examinations in an effort to raise educational standards. Another important step was taken some years later in 1897 by J. M. Rice, who is credited with inventing the comparative test and being the father of educational research in America (Ross & Stanley, 1954). Rice first designed objective spelling tests for his classic survey of the spelling abilities of schoolchildren. With these tests he found little relationship between the length of time spent daily in spelling drill and proficiency in that subject. The results of administering a 50-word spelling test to 33,000 children led Rice to conclude that as much was learned in 15 as in 40 minutes of daily instruction in spelling. In later studies, he assessed the language skills of 8000 children and the arithmetic achievement of 6000 children. The beginnings made by Rice, whose work is generally viewed as the forerunner of standardized achievement testing and the beginning of educational research, were subsequently built on by Thorndike and other educational psychologists.

A number of standardized achievement tests were published during the early years of the twentieth century under the direction of E. L. Thorndike, who is considered the father of the educational testing movement (Ross & Stanley, 1954). These included C. L. Stone's Arithmetic Test for the Fundamental Operations and the Arithmetic Reasoning Test in 1908, S. A. Courtis's Arithmetic Tests Series in 1909, and E. L. Thorndike's Scale of Handwriting for Children in that same year. Demonstrations of the unreliability of grades assigned by teachers, even in more exact subjects such as mathematics (Starch & Elliott, 1913), led to an increased interest in objective, standardized testing. By the end of the 1920s, numerous standardized achievement tests were available, including batteries of measures such as the Stanford Achievement Test (1923) for elementary school pupils and the Iowa High School Content Examination (1924). Shortly thereafter, in 1926, the multiple-choice Scholastic Aptitude Test replaced the essay tests that had been previously administered by the College Entrance Examination Board (Donlon, 1984). The new multiple-choice format, together with the invention of automated scoring machines, led to a rapid increase in the use of standardized tests for evaluating pupil achievement.

Rather than being motivated solely by educational and scientific concerns, the growth of achievement testing in the United States is attributable in part to the fact that both sides in a political debate over public schools found the advocacy and results of testing useful in their arguments (Levine, 1976). As seen in debates over nationwide standardized achievement examinations and alternative approaches to such assessment, even today standardized testing in the schools continues to have significant political ramifications.

Despite the passage of time and hundreds of research studies, the question of the relative merits of essay and objective tests has never been completely settled. In fact, it has often been alleged that teachers have gone overboard in their use of objective tests to the detriment of students' composition skills. Nevertheless, it is clear that carefully designed objective tests can measure not only memory for facts, but also many of the more complex objectives of instruction that were formerly presumed to be assessed only by essay examinations. A noteworthy trend in the past three decades has been toward tests that measure higher-order instructional objectives, such as application, analysis, and evaluation. Another trend has been away from standardized achievement tests that attempt to assess broad educational objectives and toward tests designed specifically for particular textbooks and teaching programs. Finally, in response to the criticism that objective tests foster poor writing and self-expression techniques, greater emphasis is now being placed on standardized essay tests of written expression. Constructed response tests in mathematics and science, protocols from laboratory experiments, and portfolios of work are also being studied and encouraged in an attempt to expand the assessment of student achievement (Linn, 1992).

## Uses of Achievement Tests

The basic function of achievement tests is to determine how much people know about certain topics or how well they can perform certain skills. This function—the assessment of achieved competence—is the first purpose listed in Table 6–1. The results of achievement testing inform students, as well as teachers and parents, about students' scholastic accomplishments and deficiencies. Other functions of achievement testing include advanced placement, course credit, and certification. Such tests can also act as a stimulus for student learning, provide teachers and school administrators with information for planning or modifying the curriculum for a student or group of students, and serve as a means of evaluating

**TABLE 6–1   The Many Purposes of Achievement Testing**

1. Assessment of achieved competence
2. Diagnosis of strengths and weaknesses
3. Assignment of grades
4. Certification and promotion
5. Advanced placement and credit by examination
6. Curriculum and program evaluation
7. Accountability
8. Information for educational policy

*Source:* Linn, R. L. (1992). Achievement testing. In M. C. Alkin
   (Ed.), *Encyclopedia of educational research* (6th ed., pp. 1–12).
   New York: Macmillan.

the instructional program and staff. Scores on achievement tests are obviously not the only means of evaluating the effectiveness of instruction, but they provide a measure of the quality of education and can thereby contribute to its improvement.

Admittedly, achievement tests cannot assess all objectives or goals proposed by educational philosophers. For example, they do not directly measure such affective variables as delight and confidence in thinking, interest in educational subject matter, pleasure in using skills, enjoyment of reading, learning to learn and to cope with change, or the development of interpersonal and social skills. What these tests can measure, however, and more accurately than teachers' ratings or other subjective judgments, is the extent to which students have attained certain cognitive objectives of instruction (Levine, 1976).

***Teacher-made versus Standardized Tests***   Standardized achievement tests represent only a fraction of the number of tests administered in the schools; students spend much more time taking teacher-made tests (Dorr-Bremme & Herman, 1986). Be that as it may, the functions of achievement testing described in the preceding paragraphs apply to both classroom tests prepared by teachers and to standardized tests constructed by professionals in educational measurement. But teacher-made tests differ from standardized tests in certain important respects. A teacher-made test is more specific to a particular teacher, classroom, and unit of study and is easier to keep up to date than a standardized test. Consequently, a teacher-made test is more likely to reflect the current educational objectives of a given school or teacher. Standardized tests, on the other hand, are built around a core of educational objectives common to many different schools. These objectives represent the combined judgments of subject-matter experts, who cooperate with test-construction specialists in developing tests. Standardized achievement tests also focus more on understanding and thinking processes than on knowledge of specifics. Clearly, teacher-made tests and standardized tests are complementary rather than opposing methods of evaluating achievement. They measure somewhat different but equally important things, and, depending on the objectives of the particular classroom or school, both kinds of tests should be employed. When a given standardized test does not assess the educational goals of a particular school system, other standardized tests or even a teacher-made test should be considered.

In addition to being more carefully constructed and having broader content coverage than teacher-made tests, standardized achievement tests have norms and are usually more reliable. For these reasons, standardized achievement tests are particularly helpful in comparing individual pupils for the purpose of class placement and in evaluating different curricula by assessing the relative achievements of different groups of schools. The diagnostic function of a test, whereby a person's abilities and disabilities in a certain subject or area are determined, may be served by both teacher-made and standardized tests, although standardized tests are somewhat more effective for this purpose. Decisions pertaining to the individualization of instruction, the placement of students at particular levels of instruction, and remedial education are also usually made on the basis of scores on standardized rather than teacher-made tests.

***Accountability and Performance Contracting***   Test scores have been used not only to assess student performance, but also to evaluate teachers and schools. *Accountability*—holding teachers accountable for their degree of success in teaching students—has been a controversial topic in education for many years. Should teachers, who typically are not permitted to select their students, but must attempt to educate every student who is assigned to them, be rewarded only when these students attain the objectives of instructions and not rewarded or even penalized when they do not? As a result of increasing public concern over the failure of schools to do an adequate job of educating students, particular attention has been given to accountability or responsibility for teaching effectiveness. During the 1970s and 1980s, efforts were made in both the public and private sectors to make teachers accountable for student learning. In keeping with these efforts, the competencies that must be attained by students to complete a given grade or course of study or to graduate from high school were specified. Evaluation of instructional effectiveness was then based on the achievement of these competencies, as indicated largely by scores on achievement tests.[1]

Accountability and competency-based instruction are associated with *performance contracting,* that is, making the pay checks of teachers commensurate with their degree of success in educating students. If tests are to be employed as a means of determining the extent to which teachers have fulfilled contracts to teach the educational material to students, the same tests may be administered at both the beginning and the end of instructional units. Consequently, the greater the gains in student achievement from pretest to posttest, the higher the teacher's pay. A frequent result of such "high stakes" testing is, unfortunately, overattentiveness to the content of the tests at the expense of other important instructional objectives.

When combined with other measures of performance, achievement test scores can and should contribute to decisions concerning accountability, but they have definite limitations when used for this purpose. One problem is that the reliability of the differences between pretest and posttest scores is lower than the reliability of either the pretest or the posttest. In addition, tests do not measure everything of value that students gain from schools: attainment

---

[1]Unfortunately, some students and parents view formal education from a rather narrow vendor–consumer perspective, in which schools are seen as markets that "sell" educational products to student customers. Such a perspective places the responsibility for student learning almost completely on the teachers, the educational materials, and the structure and dynamics of organizations in which learning takes place. Teachers realize, however, that it is difficult if not impossible to teach students who are not interested in learning the subject material and/or who fail to accept some of the responsibility for their own education. Thus, in addition to "teacher accountability," the importance of "student responsibility" and "parent responsibility" for the learning process needs to be emphasized.

of living skills or competencies and life satisfaction depend on social interactions and other nontested behaviors that are also crucial aspects of human development.

**Summative and Formative Evaluation**   Traditional practice calls for administering an achievement test at the end of a unit or course of study to determine whether students have attained the objectives of instruction. Technically, this procedure is known as *summative evaluation;* a test score is viewed as an end product, or summing up, of large units of educational experience. In contrast to summative evaluation, the need for *formative evaluation* is a consequence of the belief that the processes of instruction and evaluation should be integrated. The purpose of formative evaluation is "to help both the learner and the teacher focus upon the particular learning necessary for movement toward mastery" (Bloom, Hastings, & Madaus, 1971, page 61). When evaluation is formative, testing and other methods of assessing educational progress take place continuously during the process of instruction. A direct result of the concept of formative evaluation is the development of instructional units that include testing as an ongoing, integral part of instruction, rather than a termination of the process. In this way, the learner's performance is monitored throughout the learning process and can serve to direct review and further learning.

**Norm-referenced and Criterion-referenced Measurement**   Not only has educational measurement traditionally been summative; it has also been norm referenced rather than criterion referenced. A person's score on a norm-referenced test is interpreted by comparing it with the distribution of scores obtained from some norm (standardization) group, but a person's score on a criterion-referenced test is interpreted by comparing it with an established standard or criterion of effective performance. This standard may be formulated from a consensus of a group of people from all walks of life who are concerned with education—school teachers and administrators, parents, measurement experts, and politicians. In terms of their content, norm-referenced tests are typically broader and contain more complex tasks than criterion-referenced tests. Consequently, the range of individual differences in scores on a norm-referenced test tends to be greater than on a criterion-referenced test.

   Despite differences in the purpose and design of norm- and criterion-referenced tests, a particular achievement test can function in both ways. How much material a student has learned (criterion-referenced function) and how his or her performance compares with that of other students (norm-referenced function) can frequently be determined from the same test (Carver, 1974).

   Among the many single-subject criterion-referenced tests that are commercially available are the California Diagnostic Reading Test and the California Diagnostic Mathematics Test (both from CTB/McGraw-Hill). Batteries of criterion-referenced tests, such as the National Proficiency Survey Series and the Cultural Literacy Test, can also be purchased. Another product offered by certain testing companies are single-subject tests combined with matching instructional strategies in those subjects. Several testing companies also prepare customized criterion-referenced tests or make available banks of criterion-referenced items in a number of subjects. These custom-built tests possess the advantage of being tailored to the objectives of a particular school system, but they also have a number of shortcomings. In addition to the problem of deciding on an acceptable passing score or mastery level on each test, the need for a large number of subtests to measure many different educational objectives necessitates making each subtest relatively short, and hence its reliability is fairly low. Furthermore, the problem of how the reliabilities and validities of the various subtests and the test as a whole should be determined has not been completely resolved.

**The National Assessment of Educational Progress**    A criterion-referenced approach has guided the National Assessment of Educational Progress (NAEP), a continuing nationwide survey of the knowledge, skills, understandings, and attitudes of young Americans. The purpose of NAEP "is to improve the effectiveness of our Nation's schools by making objective information about student performance in selected learning areas available to policy makers at the national, state, and local levels" (Public Law 100-297, sec. 3401). NAEP assesses the abilities of large samples of four age groups (9, 13, 17, and 25 to 35 years) in 10 subject areas: art, career and occupational development, citizenship, literature, mathematics, music, reading, science, social studies, and writing. Two or three subjects are assessed in a given year and reassessed on a 3- to 6-year cycle (see Table 6–2).

A stratified random sampling procedure is used by NAEP to select a certain number of persons of each gender, socioeducational status, and race from four geographical regions and four types of communities. Although many questions are asked concerning each topic, the fact that both examinees and items are sampled necessitates only one relatively short testing period (50 minutes) for each person. Adults are assessed individually, and younger persons are assessed on both an individual and a group basis. Because the results are expressed in terms of the percentages of people in each age group who possess certain skills and knowledge, the names of those persons do not appear on the test papers.

**TABLE 6–2    Subject Areas Assessed by NAEP**

| Assessment period | Subject area |
| --- | --- |
| 1969–79 | Science |
| 1970–71 | Reading, Literature |
| 1971–72 | Music, Social Studies |
| 1972–73 | Science, Mathematics |
| 1973–74 | Career and Occupational Development, Writing |
| 1974–75 | Reading, Art, Index of Basic Skills |
| 1975–76 | Citizenship/Social Studies, Mathematics |
| 1976–77 | Science, Basic Life Skills, Reading, Health |
| 1977–78 | Mathematics, Consumer Skills |
| 1978–79 | Writing, Art, Music |
| 1979–80 | Reading/Literature, Art |
| 1981–82 | Science, Mathematics, Citizenship/Social Studies |
| 1984 | Reading, Writing |
| 1986 | Competence, Literature, U.S. History |
| 1988 | Reading, Writing, Civics, U.S. History, Geography |
| 1990 | Reading, Mathematics, Science, Writing |
| 1992 | Reading, Mathematics, Writing |

*Source:* The National Assessment of Educational Progress.

NAEP was planned as a continuing program to provide the U.S. public, and especially legislators and educators, with information on the status and growth of educational accomplishments in the United States and the extent to which the nation's educational goals are being met. It was not designed, as some have feared, to evaluate the achievements of specific schools or school districts or as a means of federal control over public school curricula. However, the findings have been analyzed by geographical area (state-by-state comparisons were begun in 1990), size and type of community, gender, parental education, and ethnic group. Of particular interest are analyses of the effects of federal support and specific types of programs on educational attainment.

## Types of Standardized Achievement Tests

There are four general types of standardized achievement tests: survey test batteries, survey tests in special subjects, diagnostic tests, and prognostic tests. Some of these tests are designed to be administered individually to one person at a time, but the great majority are group tests. The market for highly specialized tests in a particular subject area is rather limited, so standardized achievement tests typically cover broad content areas and deal with matters of general knowledge. Because the curriculum becomes more specialized in the upper grade levels, administration of standardized achievement tests is less common after junior high school.

***Survey Test Batteries***    The most comprehensive way of assessing achievement is to administer a *survey test battery,* a group of subject-matter tests designed for particular grade levels. The major purpose of administering a battery of tests is to determine an individual's general standing in a group, rather than his or her specific strengths and weaknesses. Consequently, each test in a survey battery contains a fairly limited sample of the content and skills in a given subject. Because all tests in a battery are standardized on the same group of people and the scores are expressed on the same numerical scale, a person's performance in different subjects can be compared directly.

Although they provide a more comprehensive assessment of pupil achievement than single tests, test batteries have a number of drawbacks. Despite the longer total administration time for a battery, the tests are shorter than single-survey tests and consequently tend to have lower reliabilities. Of course, not all the tests in a battery need to be administered to a given group of students; the examiner may administer just those tests that yield relevant information pertaining to the particular goals of assessment.

***Single-subject Survey Tests***    In addition to the individual subject tests in a survey battery, a number of single-subject tests are available. These survey tests are usually longer and more detailed than comparable tests in a battery and thereby permit a more thorough evaluation of achievement in a specific area. Single-subject tests, however, typically yield only an overall score and perhaps a couple of subscores and make no real attempt to determine the specific causes of high or low performance in the subject. Because of greater uniformity among different schools in reading and mathematics instruction than in other subjects, standardized tests in these two areas tend to be more valid than, for example, science and social studies tests.

***Diagnostic Tests***   Certain tests have the diagnostic function of identifying specific difficulties in learning a subject. To construct a *diagnostic test* in a basic skill such as reading, arithmetic, or spelling, performance in the subject as a whole must be analyzed into subskills and then groups of items devised to measure performance in these subskills. Unlike survey tests, which focus on total scores, diagnostic tests yield scores on each of several subskills. Because differences among scores on the various parts of the tests are interpreted in making diagnoses, the number of items for measuring a particular subskill must be sufficient (10 or more) to ensure that the differences between part scores are reliable. Unfortunately, the number of items comprising part scores are often small, and scores on the parts are correlated, resulting in difference scores having low reliability.

Most diagnostic tests are in the area of reading, but diagnostic tests in mathematics and spelling have been constructed. A diagnostic test contains a greater variety of items and usually takes longer to administer than a survey test in the same subject. It may also involve special apparatus, such as a tachistoscope to present reading material for only a brief period of time and an eye-movement camera to track the direction in which the eyes move in reading.

In addition to diagnostic tests in specific subjects such as reading and mathematics, certain individually administered survey or *global* tests are used for educational diagnosis in reading, mathematics, and spelling. Examples are the Kaufman Test of Educational Achievement and the Peabody Individual Achievement Test–Revised (from American Guidance Service). Even more global in its diagnostic aims is the Woodcock–Johnson Psychoeducational Battery (from Teaching Resources Corporation), an individually administered multiple-skills test battery designed to assess cognitive abilities, scholastic aptitude, academic achievement and interests of people aged 3 to 80 years.

Administration of a survey test battery is a reasonable first step in a testing program, because it provides an overall picture of a person's standing in various subjects. If a second assessment of a person's achievement in a particular area is needed, a single test in the specific subject can be given. Finally, if it is desirable to make a detailed analysis of an individual's disability in reading or mathematics and to determine the causes of the disability, a diagnostic test should be administered.

***Prognostic Tests***   Prognostic tests, which are designed to predict achievement in specific school subjects, contain a wider variety of items than survey achievement tests in the same subject. They are similar to aptitude tests in their function as predictors of later achievement. For example, the purpose of a *reading readiness test* administered to a kindergartner or first grader is to predict whether the child is prepared to benefit from instruction in reading. At a higher grade level, prognostic tests in mathematics (algebra, geometry) and foreign languages are available for predicting ease of learning those subjects.

## Selecting a Standardized Test

Selecting a standardized achievement test is basically a matter of finding an instrument with a content that matches the instructional objectives of the particular organization, class, school, or school system. This means that the level of knowledge or ability of the examinees and the content and objectives of the curriculum must be determined before deciding what test(s) to administer. Furthermore, the reasons for testing and the way in which the scores are to be used should be considered; there is little purpose in administering a test merely because it "looks good" and then letting the unused results gather dust in a file drawer.

***Purposes and Practical Considerations***    The manual accompanying a test frequently details its possible uses (evaluation, placement, diagnosis of learning disabilities, readiness to learn, curriculum evaluation) and refers to supporting evidence. Consequently, before a test is selected, the specific ways in which the scores are to be used should be clarified and test manuals consulted to determine what tests are appropriate for these purposes. In addition to reading the manual, prospective purchasers should examine a copy of the test and even take it themselves to determine whether it is suitable for its intended use. Many testing companies publish specimen sets of tests, consisting of a test booklet, an answer sheet, a manual, a scoring key, and other associated materials; test catalogs are also available on request. These materials are helpful in deciding which tests to administer.

Another consideration in selecting a test is the degree of cooperation that can be expected from the school staff in administering the test and interpreting the findings. Also of importance are practical matters such as cost and time for administration, scoring, and analyzing the results. The machine-scoring services provided by commercial testing firms greatly facilitate the scoring and analysis processes and are usually fairly reasonable in cost.

***Reliability, Validity, and Norms***    Frequently overlooked in selecting an achievement test, but often crucial, are its statistical characteristics. The reliabilities of most achievement tests are in the .80's and .90's, but the meaning of these high coefficients depends on the procedures by which they were obtained. A parallel-forms coefficient is preferable to a test–retest coefficient or an internal-consistency coefficient because the last two are more likely to be spuriously high. When an achievement test is administered for the purpose of predicting later achievement, as in the case of a readiness or prognostic test, evidence of its predictive validity is important. In deciding whether an achievement test is valid, it is essential to obtain evidence of content validity by comparing the content of the test with the objectives of the instructional program of interest. An adequately prepared test manual describes the system for classifying content and behavioral objectives used in constructing the test, and prospective purchasers must decide whether these objectives correspond to their own.

Another statistical characteristic to be examined in selecting any test is the adequacy and appropriateness of the norms. Most well-constructed achievement tests are standardized on representative, national samples, sometimes stratified according to age, sex, geographical region, socioeconomic status, and other relevant variables. Test purchasers who plan to report scores in terms of such norms should make certain that the characteristics of the norm group are similar to those of the students to be examined. For purposes of placement and other comparisons within a given school or school system, local norms may be even more meaningful than national norms.

Users of standardized achievement tests also need to be aware of the fact that, in plotting a student's academic growth by means of normed scores on a standardized achievement test administered at successive grade levels, the assumption is being made that the different grade-level groups on which the test was standardized are equivalent. If there is any reason to believe that differences among the norm groups on variables other than those that are growth related are significant, then a student's grade-norm scores, percentile-rank scores, or standard scores on a test cannot be compared accurately across grade levels.

Another caveat on purchasing a test is to be careful not to be misled by a name. Experienced test users are well aware of the "jingle fallacy" of assuming that instruments having the same name measure the same thing and the "jangle fallacy" of assuming that instruments having different names measure different things. Before deciding what achievement tests to purchase, novices and experienced testers alike can profit from consulting volumes of *The Mental Measurements Yearbook* and test reviews in professional journals.

## ACHIEVEMENT TEST BATTERIES

Achievement test batteries represent efforts to measure broad cognitive abilities and skills produced by basic educational experiences in core areas. These multilevel batteries of tests assess basic skills in reading, mathematics, language arts, and, at the appropriate grade levels, study skills, social studies, and science.

A representative list of the most popular achievement test batteries is given in Table 6–3. Descriptions of these and other commercially available achievement test batteries can be found in the various editions of *The Mental Measurements Yearbook, Tests in Print, Tests,* and *Test Critiques,* and in the catalogs available from test publishers (see Appendix C). These batteries were designed to assess the formal educational achievements of students in kindergarten through senior high school, with an emphasis on the elementary and junior high years.

The testing programs of many schools are based on achievement test batteries administered during the fall and spring to grade-school pupils for the purpose of measuring general educational attainment and growth. Such tests have many different uses: grouping

**TABLE 6–3    Representative Achievement Test Batteries**

---

*California Achievement Test* (CAT) (CTB/Macmillan/McGraw-Hill)

*Comprehensive Test of Basic Skills* (CTBS) (CTB/McGraw-Hill)

*Iowa Tests of Basic Skills* (ITBS) (Riverside Publishing Company; grades K–8)

*Iowa Tests of Educational Development* (ITED) (Riverside Publishing Company; grades 9–12)

*Metropolitan Achievement Tests* (MAT) (The Psychological Corporation; grades K–12)

*Sequential Tests of Educational Progress* (STEP-III) (CTB/McGraw-Hill; grades K–12)

*SRA Achievement Series* (Science Research Associates, Inc.; grades K–12)

*Stanford Achievement Test Series* (The Psychological Corporation; grades K–12)

*Tests of Achievement and Proficiency* (TAP) (Riverside Publishing Company; grades 9–12)

---

(placement), identification of individuals for more detailed study, curriculum evaluation, and curriculum planning. The test results are of interest to teachers, parents, and curriculum advisers and, of course, to the students themselves. A limitation of the battery approach is that some of the tests may not correspond to the particular objectives of a school or school system. Furthermore, not all tests in a given battery have equal reliabilities or equal content validities.

## Battery Norms

The various subtests at a particular grade level of an achievement test battery were standardized on the same group of people. Consequently, the resulting unified set of norms permits direct evaluation of a person's relative achievement in several subject areas. Because different grade levels of a test battery are standardized on comparable groups of students, the scholastic growth of students may be charted by comparing their scores on the tests comprising the battery over a period of several years. However, this should not be done if there is any doubt about the equivalence or comparability of the different grade-level samples of students on whom the battery was standardized. Furthermore, the norms against which students' scores are compared should have been obtained from administering the test(s) to the standardization group during the same time of year (fall or spring) as the students whose scores are being evaluated.

## Content of Achievement Test Batteries

***Elementary School Level***   Because of the greater uniformity of instructional content in elementary school, achievement test batteries are administered more frequently at this level. A typical elementary school battery consists of subtests for measuring reading vocabulary, reading comprehension, language usage, spelling, arithmetic fundamentals, and arithmetic comprehension. Subtests to measure study skills, social studies, and science may also be included, but the emphasis at the elementary level is on the measurement of achievement in basic verbal and quantitative skills. Figure 6–1, a report of the scores obtained by one fourth-grader on the Stanford Achievement Test, illustrates the variety of linguistic and quantitative skills measured by an achievement test battery at the elementary school level. Other popular achievement test batteries at this level are the California Achievement Tests, the Comprehensive Tests of Basic Skills, the Iowa Tests of Basic Skills, and the Metropolitan Achievement Tests. These batteries also contain kindergarten and secondary school levels of tests.

***Secondary School Level***   Because of greater variability in the academic programs of different high school students, achievement test batteries are less useful at this level. Secondary school test batteries continue to emphasize basic skills in reading, language, and arithmetic, but tests in social studies, science, and study skills are also common. At both the elementary and secondary levels, achievement tests emphasize general educational development and are not tied to specific courses in particular schools. Illustrative items appearing at successive levels in five of the tests on one achievement battery—the Comprehensive Tests of Basic Skills—are shown in Figure 6–2. Also of interest at the high school level are

## STANFORD

ACHIEVEMENT TEST SERIES, EIGHTH EDITION

| | | |
|---|---|---|
| TEACHER: | JOHN WILLIAMS | |
| SCHOOL: | LAKESIDE ELEMENTARY | GRADE: 4 |
| DISTRICT: | NEWTOWN | TEST DATE: 4/89 |

NORMS: SPRING
LEVEL: INTER 1
FORM: J

STANFORD GRADE 4 NATIONAL
OLSAT GRADE 4 NATIONAL E 1

STUDENT SKILLS ANALYSIS
FOR
BRIAN ELLIOTT

| TESTS | NO. OF ITEMS | RAW SCORE | SCALED SCORE | NATL PR-S | LOCAL PR-S | GRADE EQUIV | AAC RANGE | NATIONAL GRADE PERCENTILE BANDS |
|---|---|---|---|---|---|---|---|---|
| Total Reading | 94 | 70 | 143 | 50-5 | 45-5 | 4.8 | LOW | |
| Vocabulary | 40 | 27 | 148 | 52-5 | 46-5 | 5.1 | LOW | |
| Reading Comp. | 54 | 43 | 143 | 5 | 44-5 | 4.8 | LOW | |
| Total Math | 118 | 58 | 143 | 5 | 45-5 | 4.6 | LOW | |
| Concepts of No. | 34 | 14 | 137 | 32-4 | 26-4 | 3.8 | LOW | |
| Computation | 44 | 22 | 145 | 50-5 | 56-5 | 4.8 | MIDDLE | |
| Applications | 40 | 22 | 145 | 50-5 | 53-5 | 4.8 | LOW | |
| Total Language | 60 | 47 | 149 | 61-6 | 56-5 | 5.4 | MIDDLE | |
| Lang Mechanics | 30 | 21 | 148 | 60-6 | 54-5 | 5.4 | MIDDLE | |
| Lang Expression | 30 | 26 | 150 | 62-6 | 58-5 | 5.4 | MIDDLE | |
| Spelling | 40 | 22 | 143 | 40-5 | 34-4 | 4.0 | LOW | |
| Study Skills | 30 | 21 | 142 | 50-5 | 44-5 | 4.8 | LOW | |
| Science | 50 | 31 | 139 | 44-5 | 38-4 | 4.6 | LOW | |
| Social Science | 50 | 42 | 161 | 82-7 | 76-6 | 6.2 | MIDDLE | |
| Listening | 45 | 25 | 130 | 49-5 | 45-5 | 4.7 | LOW | |
| Using Information | 70 | 35 | 152 | 59-5 | 55-5 | 5.2 | MIDDLE | |
| Thinking Skills | 101 | 45 | 146 | 52-5 | 53-5 | 4.9 | LOW | |
| Basic Battery | 387 | 243 | 143 | 50-5 | 45-5 | 4.8 | LOW | |
| Complete Battery | 487 | 316 | 145 | 52-5 | 47-5 | 4.9 | LOW | |

1  10  30  50  70  90  99

| OTIS-LENNON SCHOOL ABILITY TEST | RAW SCORE | SAI | AGE PR-S | AGE NCE | SCALED SCORE | GRADE PR-S | GRADE NCE |
|---|---|---|---|---|---|---|---|
| Total | 72 | 53 | 116 | 84-7 | 70.9 | 290 | 82-7 | 69.3 |
| Verbal | 36 | 27 | 117 | 85-7 | 71.8 | 295 | 83-7 | 70.1 |
| Nonverbal | 36 | 26 | 115 | 82-7 | 69.3 | 285 | 80-7 | 67.7 |

AGE 10 YRS 2 MOS

| READING GROUP | MATHEMATICS GROUP | COMMUNICATIONS GROUP | LANGUAGE GROUP |
|---|---|---|---|
| GROUP 3 | GROUP 2 | GROUP 1 | GROUP 2 |

| CONTENT CLUSTERS | RAW SCORE/ NUMBER OF ITEMS | BELOW AVERAGE | AVERAGE | ABOVE AVERAGE |
|---|---|---|---|---|
| Reading Vocabulary | 27/ 40 | | ✓ | |
| Synonyms | 17/ 24 | | ✓ | |
| Context | 5/ 8 | | ✓ | |
| Multiple Meanings | 5/ 8 | | ✓ | |
| Reading Comprehension | 43/ 54 | | ✓ | |
| Recreational | 12/ 18 | | ✓ | |
| Textual | 15/ 18 | | ✓ | |
| Functional | 16/ 18 | | | ✓ |
| Literal | 18/ 21 | | ✓ | |
| Inferential | 22/ 26 | | ✓ | |
| Critical | 3/ 7 | | ✓ | |
| Concepts of Number | 14/ 34 | | ✓ | |
| Whole Numbers | 6/ 16 | ✓ | | |
| Fractions | 3/ 4 | | | ✓ |
| Decimals | 2/ 3 | | ✓ | |
| Operations and Properties | 3/ 11 | ✓ | | |
| Mathematics Computation | 22/ 44 | | ✓ | |
| Add and Subtract/Whole Nos | 7/ 12 | | ✓ | |
| Multiplication/Whole Numbers | 6/ 12 | | ✓ | |
| Division/Whole Numbers | 5/ 10 | | ✓ | |
| Add and Subtract/Decimals | 2/ 6 | ✓ | | |
| Add and Subtract/Fractions | 2/ 4 | | ✓ | |
| Mathematics Applications | 22/ 40 | | ✓ | |
| Problem Solving | 12/ 22 | ✓ | | |
| Graphs and Charts | 4/ 6 | | | ✓ |
| Geometry/Measurement | 6/ 12 | | ✓ | |

| CONTENT CLUSTERS | RAW SCORE/ NUMBER OF ITEMS | BELOW AVERAGE | AVERAGE | ABOVE AVERAGE |
|---|---|---|---|---|
| Language Mechanics | 21/ 30 | | ✓ | |
| Capitalization | 5/ 7 | | ✓ | ✓ |
| Punctuation | 8/ 11 | | ✓ | |
| Applied Grammar | 8/ 12 | | ✓ | |
| Language Expression | 26/ 30 | | | ✓ |
| Sentence Correctness | 16/ 20 | | ✓ | |
| Sentence Effectiveness | 10/ 10 | | | ✓ |
| Spelling | 22/ 40 | | ✓ | |
| Study Skills | 21/ 30 | | ✓ | |
| Library/Reference Skills | 10/ 17 | | ✓ | |
| Information Skills | 11/ 13 | | ✓ | ✓ |
| Science | 31/ 50 | | ✓ | |
| Physical Science | 9/ 16 | | ✓ | |
| Biological Science | 15/ 20 | | ✓ | |
| Earth/Space Science | 7/ 14 | ✓ | | |
| Social Science | 42/ 50 | | ✓ | |
| Geography | 12/ 13 | | ✓ | |
| History | 8/ 8 | | ✓ | |
| Political Science | 6/ 10 | | | ✓ |
| Economics | 9/ 10 | | ✓ | |
| Psych/Sociol/Anthro | 7/ 9 | | ✓ | |
| Listening | 25/ 45 | | ✓ | |
| Vocabulary | 9/ 15 | ✓ | | ✓ |
| Listening Comprehension | 16/ 30 | | ✓ | |
| Using Information | 35/ 70 | | ✓ | |
| Thinking Skills | 45/101 | | ✓ | |

**FIGURE 6–1** Sample Skills Analysis Report for Stanford Achievement Test Series.

batteries of tests such as the American College Tests (ACT), which are administered annually for college admissions purposes. The ACT is actually an achievement test battery, but it is somewhat like an aptitude test in that its broad range of content is less related to specific school experiences than that of most achievement tests.

Test 1.   READING Vocabulary (Selecting the word that means the same or about the same as the underlined word)

| Level 1 (Grades 2.5–4) | Level 2 (Grades 4–6) |
|---|---|
| mend the tire | approved his behavior |
| ○ patch | F conscience |
| ○ clean | G rights |
| ○ change | H decision |
| ○ fill | J actions |

| Level 3 (Grades 6–8) | Level 4 (Grades 8–12) |
|---|---|
| adequate supplies | complete solitude |
| F adjusted | F pacification |
| G actual | G seclusion |
| H sufficient | H confusion |
| J extra | J classification |

Test 3.   LANGUAGE Mechanics (Identifying mistakes in capitalization)

Level 1 (Grades 2.5–4)

| In America we | celebrate a holiday | on July 4. | None |
|---|---|---|---|
| ○ | ○ | ○ | ○ |

Level 2 (Grades 4–6)

F   This selection comes        G   from "the silent world,"
H   a book about exciting       J   deep-sea diving adventures.    K   None

Level 3 (Grades 6–8)

A   The villain was        B   finally apprehended at        C   Dulles international airport
D   near Washington.       E   None

Level 4 (Grades 8–12)

F   When football magazine        G   featured him on its cover,        H   his fame became
J   truly nationwide.             K   None

Test 5.   LANGUAGE Spelling (Identifying misspelled words)

| Level 1 (Grades 2.5–4) | Level 2 (Grades 4–6) |
|---|---|
| ○ full | A jerney |
| ○ cake | B event |
| ○ football | C contain |
| ○ rabit | D spoon |
| ○ None | E none |

| Level 3 (Grades 6–8) | Level 4 (Grades 8–12) |
|---|---|
| F recommend | F constantly |
| G allowance | G interpret |

**FIGURE 6–2**   Sample Items from Comprehensive Tests of Basic Skills.
Copyright © 1968, 1981, 1989 by McGraw-Hill. Reprinted by permission
of CTB/McGraw-Hill.

| H | literature | H | benefit |
| J | profit | J | explenation |
| K | None | K | None |

## Test 7.    ARITHMETIC Concepts

*Level 1 (Grades 2.5–4)*

What goes in the box?

$5 + 4 = 10 - \square$

   0     1     9    10

  ○    ○    ○    ○

*Level 2 (Grades 4–6)*

What should be next in this series:

57, 64, 71, 78, _____?

   F  79

   G 81

   H 85

   J  88

*Level 3 (Grades 6–8)*

In 5963.427 the digit in the hundredths place is

   A    2

   B    5

   C    6

   D    7

*Level 4 (Grades 8–12)*

If $R < S$ and $S < T$, then

   F    $R = T$

   G    $R > T$

   H    $R < T$

   J    $R + S = T$

## Test 9.    STUDY SKILLS (Using reference materials)

*Level 1 (Grades 2.5–4)*

Which one of these words would be *first* in abc order?

  pair      paint      polish      point

  ○         ○         ○         ○

*Level 2 (Grades 4–6)*

Which reference book would you use to find information on: A history of shipbuilding?

   A    almanac

   B    dictionary

   C    encyclopedia

   D    atlas

*Level 3 (Grades 6–8)*

The library catalog subject card for Amusements would be found in the tray labeled

   F    A—ALK

   G    ALL—ANH

   H    ANI—ANS

   J    ARO—BAH

*Level 4 (Grades 8–12)*

In preparing a report about Carl Sandburg, which would be a primary source of information?

   F    a collection of his writings

   G    a review of a collection of his poems

   H    a talk with an old friend of his

   J    a biography by a well-known writer

**FIGURE 6–2**    Continued

## Basic Education and GED Tests

Several achievement test batteries have been designed specifically to measure proficiency in the basic skills of adults having less than a high school education. Examples are the Tests of Adult Basic Education (TABE) (from CTB/McGraw-Hill) and the Adult Basic Learning Examination (ABLE) (from The Psychological Corporation). Both of these multilevel tests, which were standardized on adults, emphasize skills in reading, mathematics, and language.

Despite the availability of adult basic skills tests such as TABE and ABLE, a survey of 595 U.S. and Canadian companies found that only about one-third of these organizations actually tested their employees for literacy. As a consequence, at least one out of every four employees is functionally illiterate and must "bluff it out" in performing a job requiring reading skills. Another survey of 1728 employers found that 63 percent knew that they had workers who could not read, write, perform computations, or comprehend English. Not only are illiterate employees more likely to have accidents, but they are also handicapped in their ability to advance in an organization ("Fewer Firms Testing Employee Literacy," 1992).

The Tests of General Educational Development (GED) were designed to measure the educational achievements of people with a high school education or equivalent. The full battery of GED tests, which takes about 7 hours, consists primarily of multiple-choice items in five areas: writing skills, social studies, science, reading skills, and mathematics. The writing skills test also includes an essay. Rather than stressing specific facts and details, items on the GEDs deal with broad concepts and generalizations based on competencies and knowledge dealt with in secondary school curricula. Many colleges and business organizations, as well as the U.S. armed forces, accept scores on these *general equivalency diploma* tests on the same basis as a high school diploma.

## ACHIEVEMENT TESTS IN SPECIFIC AREAS

Administration of an achievement test battery has priority in a typical school testing program. When more information on pupil achievement in a particular subject is needed, the usual procedure is to follow the battery with the administration of a specific test on that subject. These specific achievement tests have certain advantages over comparable tests in a battery. For example, the fact that a specific subject-matter test contains more items and has a broader subject content than a single test on an achievement battery makes it likely that the former will represent the instructional objectives of a wide range of classrooms and schools more adequately.

A line from an old song, "Reading and writing and 'rithmetic, taught to the tune of a hickory stick," is a testimonial to the time-honored prominence of these subjects in the elementary school curriculum—but with less stress on corporal punishment nowadays. Hundreds of specific subject-matter tests in reading, mathematics, language, science, social studies, the professions, business, and the skilled trades are available. Other areas in which standardized achievement tests are available are health, home economics, industrial arts, library usage, literature, the Bible, music, speech, spelling, and driver education. In addition to traditional norm-referenced survey, diagnostic, and prognostic instruments, there are many criterion-referenced tests in specific subjects. Furthermore, during the past two decades the emphasis on basic skills competency testing for high school graduation has led to publication of a number of proficiency tests for assessing the knowledge and skills of junior and senior high students in reading, writing, and mathematics. These "survival skills" are considered essential for coping with the demands of everyday living.

## Reading Tests

Many of the difficulties experienced by children in learning school subjects are related to problems in reading, a frequent reason for referring a child for psychoeducational evaluation. Because problems with reading are cumulative and affect performance in almost all schoolwork, it is important to assess reading level and diagnose deficiencies in this subject early and regularly. Because of their many uses, more reading tests are administered than any other kind of achievement test. In fact, there are so many different reading tests that a separate volume of the Buros series, *Reading Tests and Reviews II* (Buros, 1975a), has been devoted to them. Various types of reading tests are available; three major categories are survey tests, diagnostic tests, and reading readiness tests. Other ways of classifying reading tests are norm-referenced versus criterion-referenced (or both) and silent versus oral reading.

***Survey Reading Tests***    The main purpose of administering a survey reading test is to determine a person's overall reading ability. Tests of this type contain sections of vocabulary items and sections of paragraphs or passages about which questions are asked. A measure of word knowledge is obtained from the vocabulary items, whereas speed and level of reading comprehension are measured from the paragraphs. Noteworthy examples of survey reading tests are the Gates–MacGinitie Reading Tests, the Nelson–Denny Reading Test, the Gray Oral Reading Tests–Revised, and the MAT6–Reading Survey Test. The first three of these tests are available from Riverside Publishing Company and the last two from The Psychological Corporation.

***Diagnostic Reading Tests***    Diagnostic reading tests, which are by far the most common type of diagnostic test, attempt to assess many different factors that affect reading: eye–hand coordination, visual and auditory perception, understanding of concepts, and even motivation. They contain subtests on visual and auditory discrimination, sight vocabulary and vocabulary in context, phoneme/grapheme: vowels and consonants, silent and oral reading, and spelling, reading comprehension, and rate of comprehension—all for the purpose of discovering the causes of a student's disability in reading. Because correlations among these subtests are often substantial, the various skills measured by diagnostic reading tests are not necessarily independent. In addition, the reliabilities of the subtests and the test as a whole are frequently not as high as might be desired. Representative of tests in this category are the California Diagnostic Reading Tests (from CTB/McGraw-Hill), the MAT Reading Diagnostic Tests and Stanford Diagnostic Reading Tests (from The Psychological Corporation), and the Woodcock Reading Mastery Tests (from American Guidance Service).

***Reading Readiness Tests***    As a measure of the extent to which a child possesses the skills and knowledge necessary for learning to read, a reading readiness test often predicts achievement in first grade better than a general intelligence test. For this reason, reading readiness tests, which usually take less time to administer than intelligence tests, may be given to kindergartners and first-graders when intelligence test scores are not available. Certain reading tests contain both diagnostic and prognostic components. For example, the Woodcock Reading Mastery Tests is not only a diagnostic reading test, but also contains a reading readiness test. Furthermore, reading readiness tests contain many of the same types of items as diagnostic reading tests—measures of visual discrimination, auditory blending and discrimination, vocabulary, letter recognition, and visual–motor coordination. Illustrative of tests of this type are the CTBS Readiness Test (from CTB/McGraw-Hill), the Linguistic Awareness in Reading Readiness (from American Guidance Service), and the Metropolitan Readiness Tests (from The Psychological Corporation). The latter is unique in that it combines a reading readiness test with a mathematics readiness test.

## Mathematics Tests

In a manner similar to achievement tests in reading, mathematics achievement tests may be classified as survey, diagnostic, and prognostic.

*Survey Mathematics Tests*    The field of mathematics education has changed appreciably during the past 30 years, most recently in the reform movement of the late 1980s. A variety of approaches to instruction are represented by current mathematics tests, including more traditional emphases in mathematics curricula as well as more modern emphasis on problem solving, concept development, and reasoning. Certain tests are designed to encompass both modern and traditional emphases in the mathematics curriculum, and instruments reflecting more specialized instructional approaches from primary school through college are available. In general, norm-referenced mathematics tests of the survey type, such as the MAT6 Mathematics Survey Tests and the Stanford Mathematics Tests (from The Psychological Corporation), require students to demonstrate an understanding of quantitative concepts and operations and the ability to apply this understanding in solving problems. Tests of proficiency in high school mathematics are also available through the College-Level Examination Program (CLEP) of the College Entrance Examination Board.

*Diagnostic Tests in Mathematics*    Although less widely administered than diagnostic reading tests, diagnostic tests in mathematics also represent attempts to break down a complex subject involving a variety of skills into its constituent elements. The items on diagnostic tests of arithmetic and mathematics are based on an analysis of skills and errors in the subject. Skills and the knowledge required for applications involving numeration, fractions, algebra, and geometry are tapped by these tests. Three examples of diagnostic mathematics tests are the Stanford Diagnostic Mathematics Test and the MAT6 Mathematics Diagnostic Tests (from The Psychological Corporation) and KeyMath (from American Guidance Service). The first two instruments are group tests designed to diagnose the specific strengths and weaknesses in basic mathematical concepts and operations of children in grades 1–12 and in grades 1–9, respectively. KeyMath Revised: A Diagnostic Inventory of Essential Mathematics is an individually administered test designed to measure the understanding and application of basic mathematics concepts and skills in grades K–9.

***Prognostic Tests in Mathematics***   A number of tests have been designed to forecast performance in specific mathematics courses, but, compared with prognostic tests in reading (reading readiness tests), they are not widely used. Examples are the Orleans–Hanna Algebra Prognosis Test–Revised (from The Psychological Corporation) and the Iowa Algebra Aptitude Test (from Riverside Publishing Company). Designed to identify, prior to instruction, which students will be successful and which will encounter difficulties in learning algebra, the Orleans–Hanna test assesses aptitude and achievement, as well as interest and motivation, in algebra of junior and senior high school students. The questionnaire and work sample items on the test take 40 minutes to complete. The percentile rank and stanine score norms are based on three groups of students: those completing seventh grade mathematics, those completing eighth grade mathematics, and those from the first two groups who completed a 1-year course in algebra during the following year. Somewhat newer than the Orleans–Hanna is the Iowa Algebra Aptitude Test, also designed to assess readiness for Algebra I. Requiring a total of 50 minutes administration time, the four subtests measure pre-algebra skills in interpreting graphs and written mathematical information, translating word problems into algebraic or equation format, identifying functions, and using symbols. The norms on the two forms of this test are based on a large national standardization in 1991.

## Language Tests

Language, as the term is generally construed, refers to any means of communication. Although language tests are primarily of the verbal type, measures of nonverbal communication for use with hearing-impaired and, more recently, normal-hearing people have been developed.

Both oral and written language is taught at all levels, and tests appropriate for the entire range of grades are available. Failure to understand certain concepts can act as a communication barrier between pre- and primary-school pupils and teachers and consequently have serious effects on children's learning. In recognition of this fact, the Boehm Test of Basic Concepts–Revised (for grades K–2) and the Boehm Test of Basic Concepts: Preschool Version (for ages 3–5 years) were designed to measure a young child's mastery of basic concepts of space, quantity, and time (see Figure 6–3). Kits of materials to help young children master basic concepts, the *Boehm Resource Guide for Basic Concept Teaching* and the *Bracken Concept Development Program,* are also available from The Psychological Corporation.

Despite the existence of tests such as the Boehm, most achievement tests in the language category were designed for secondary school and college students. These instruments, which include both English and foreign language tests, are frequently administered in high schools and colleges for the purpose of placing students in English or foreign language courses appropriate to their level of competence.

***English Language Tests***   Some of the most severe criticisms of objective tests have come from teachers of English, but it is generally recognized that such tests do a fairly respectable job of measuring knowledge of grammar and vocabulary and, to some extent, skill in oral and written expression. English language skills are assessed as a part of achievement test batteries, but there are also many separate tests of proficiency in English. Examples are

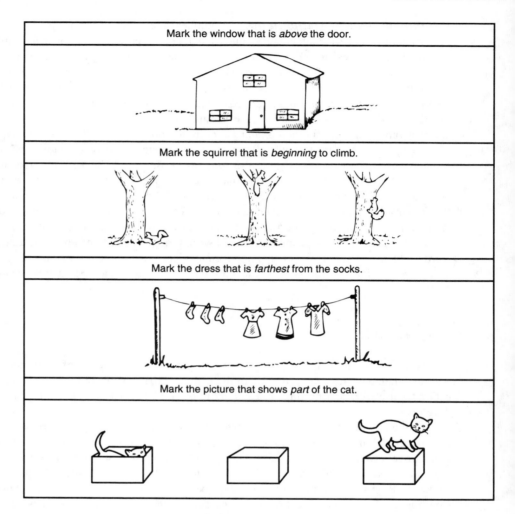

Mark the window that is *above* the door.

Mark the squirrel that is *beginning* to climb.

Mark the dress that is *farthest* from the socks.

Mark the picture that shows *part* of the cat.

**FIGURE 6–3**  Sample Items from the Boehm Test of Basic Concepts–Revised.
The Examinee Marks an X on the Selected Option.

the Purdue High School English Test, the Business English Test, and the College English
Placement Test (all from Riverside Publishing Company). These tests assess knowledge of
vocabulary, grammar, syntax, and spelling. Separate tests of spelling, such as the Test of
Written Spelling–3 (pro.ed), are also available.

Listening, speaking, and writing are obviously part of English usage, and a number of
tests have been designed to measure these skills. A good example of a listening test is the
Goldman–Friscoe–Woodcock Auditory Skills Test Battery (from American Guidance Service). Among measures of children's abilities to articulate speech sounds are the Test of
Articulation Performance (from pro.ed) and the Goldman–Friscoe Test of Articulation

(from American Guidance Service). Understanding and meaningful use of spoken words, different aspects of grammar, and the ability to speak words correctly and to distinguish between similar-sounding words can be assessed by the Test of Language Development (from pro.ed). Examples of writing tests are the Test of Written Language–3 (from pro.ed) and the MAT6 Writing Test (from The Psychological Corporation). These two writing tests, for students in grades 2–12, are free-response, work-sample measures on which examinees write stories about a set of pictures shown to them (see Figure 6–4). The stories may be scored on several variables, including theme, vocabulary, syntax, spelling, and style. Many other achievement tests, such as the CEEB Advanced Placement Tests, also contain a writing (essay) component.

Non-native English speakers from foreign countries who apply for admission to U.S. colleges and universities typically take the Test of English as a Foreign Language (TOEFL). TOEFL, a 3-hour, multiple-choice examination administered by Educational Testing Service, consists of three parts: Listening Comprehension, which measures the ability to understand spoken English; Structure and Written Expression, which measures the ability to recognize language inappropriate for standard written English; and Vocabulary and Reading Comprehension, which measures the ability to understand technical reading material. A number of tests, such as The Psychological Corporation's Language Assessment

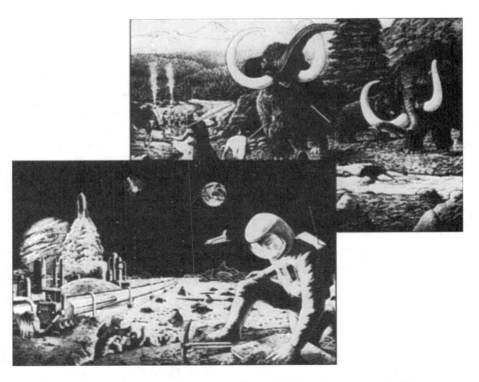

**FIGURE 6–4**  Sample Pictures from the Test of Written Language–3. The Examinee Makes up a Story about Each of a Series of Pictures Like These Two. (Reprinted by permission of pro.ed, Inc., Austin, TX.)

Scales, have also been developed to assess the English reading, writing, and speaking skills of minority students.

***Foreign Language Tests***   Survey tests of proficiency in a foreign language typically consist of different forms for students who have completed different amounts of training in the language. Certain tests reflect the more traditional grammatical approach to language instruction, whereas others emphasize comprehension of spoken and written language. In addition to survey (placement) tests in foreign languages, there are several prognostic tests. The content of these tests, which are designed to predict success in learning specific foreign languages, varies with the particular instrument. A typical test includes measures of rote memory, interest in studying a foreign language, sensitivity to grammatical structure, and the ability to associate sounds and symbols. An example of foreign language tests of the survey type is the MLA–Cooperative Foreign Language Tests. These tests, published by the Modern Language Association of America and Educational Testing Service, are available in French, German, Spanish, Russian, and Italian. Also available in the foreign language category are several prognostic tests, such as the Modern Language Aptitude Test (from The Psychological Corporation). This instrument, which was designed to predict how easily and rapidly English-speaking students can progress in a typical foreign language program, consists of a series of exercises in learning the vocabulary and grammar of an artificial language.

## Social Studies Tests

Topics in social studies, history, economics, and political science are generally thought of in connection with secondary school and college curricula. But social studies, perhaps in a less formal sense, is also taught in the elementary grades. Representative of tests of achievement in social studies at the secondary school level are the CAT End-of-Course Tests in World History, American History, and Consumer Economics (from CTB/McGraw-Hill) and the Emporia American Government Test (from Bureau of Educational Measurements). General examinations in the social sciences and history are also available through the College-Level Examination Program (CLEP) of the College Entrance Examination Board.

## Science Tests

Instruction in science, like instruction in mathematics, has changed markedly during the past three decades, making many older tests inappropriate for today's science curricula. The Biological Sciences Curriculum Study (BSCS) and the Physical Sciences Study Committee (PSSC) led to the design of specific tests in biology and physics. Comprehensive testing programs in other sciences, such as the American Chemical Society's Cooperative Chemistry Tests, also reflect contemporary approaches to science education. These approaches emphasize the teaching of science content so it will be usable and important for decision making in everyday life. With this goal in mind, more recently developed science tests require students to discover patterns in sets of data and interpret the meanings of those patterns, rather than merely recalling them. Many older tests have also been revised in an attempt to assess performance in either a modern or traditional science program. Examples of tests of instructional effectiveness in specific sciences are the End-of-Course Tests in Biology, Chemistry, and Physics (from CTB/McGraw-Hill) for senior high students and the natural sciences tests of the College-Level Examination Program (CLEP).

## Tests in Higher Education and the Professions

Many institutions of higher learning permit students to earn credit for college courses by making acceptable scores on standardized achievement tests, such as those administered by the College Board's Advanced Placement Program (APP), the College-level Examination Program (CLEP), and the ACT Proficiency Examination Program. In addition, colleges, universities, and professional schools use scores on standardized achievement tests as criteria for selecting students. These tests are usually restricted or secure in the sense that they are sold or rented only to certain organizations for administration in connection with specific educational programs.

A set of standardized achievement tests used in selecting students for graduate programs are the Subject Tests of the Graduate Record Examinations (GRE). The GRE Subject Tests, which consist of tests in major fields of college work, may be taken, along with the GRE General Test, by college students in their senior year who intend to apply for admission to graduate school. Other examples of standardized tests used for purposes of admission to graduate or professional schools are the National Teacher Examination (NTE) Programs, the Medical College Admission Test (MCAT), the Law School Admission Test (LSAT), the NLN Achievement Tests in Nursing, and the Graduate Management Aptitude Test (GMAT). Certification or licensing as a certified public accountant, physician, lawyer, registered nurse, or professional in certain other fields is also contingent on passing a series of achievement tests (board examinations, bar examinations) in the particular field.

## Tests for Business and the Skilled Trades

Business is a school subject in itself, and business education tests are designed to assess a person's knowledge of the subject. In addition to evaluating the degree of accomplishment in a school subject, achievement tests are used in business and industry for purposes of selection, placement, and promotion. Tests of proficiency in typing, filing, word processing, computing, and other office skills are perhaps the most popular of these measures. Examples of tests in this category are the Office Skills Tests (see Figure 6–5) and the Word Processor Assessment Battery distributed by London House.

Tests of knowledge and skill in a particular trade (*trade tests*) are widely used for purposes of employee selection, placement, and licensing. A trade test may consist of a series of questions to be answered orally or in writing, or it may be a work-sample task requiring demonstration of a particular skill. Examples of trade, or occupational competency, tests are those devised under Educational Testing Service's National Occupational Competency Program. This program has been responsible for the development of dozens of occupational tests, including proficiency examinations for auto mechanics, bartenders, beauticians, contact lens dispensers, fire fighters, foreign service officials, police officers, professional golfers, and many other specialties. These tests often involve quite different performances from those

**Sample Item   Typing**

*missing person, Ramona Woodstock,
526 Vine, had been told to be home
from visiting Mary Tyne no later
than 2390 hours. Contact of family
was made at 0200 hours and
missing person had not yet returned home.*

**Sample Item   Forms Completion**

At 8:30 a.m. on Oct. 15, 1977, Today's Sound Center reported a burglary at their location at 3907 Palm Ave., Wista, California. Tel: 689-7734. Four tape decks, two amplifiers, and two cases of blank tape cassettes were reported missing. Rear door was damaged to obtain entry. It is possible arson in adjoining store was intended to divert suspicion of burglary. Offense 789A3 reported.

```
                    CITY OF WISTA
                 POLICE DEPARTMENT

   OFFENSE REPORTED  789A3            CR# _____

   DATE REPORTED  OCT. 15, 1977  TIME REPORTED  8:30 A.M.

   NAME OF VICTIM (FIRM IF BUSINESS)  TODAY'S SOUND CENTER

   ADDRESS OF INCIDENT  3907 PALM AVE., WISTA  PHONE 689-7734

   EXTENT OF LOSS  4 TAPE DECKS    2 AMPLIFIERS
        2 CASES  BLANK  TAPE CASSETTES
```

**Sample Item   Filing**

You are to look at the item in the "To Be Filed" column and find the number of the item in the "Existing File" that this new item should *follow*. Mark an "X" on *that* number in the row of circled numbers on the right. If there is no number given for your choice, put an "X" in the *blank* circle.

|              | Existing File          | To Be Filed   |                                  |
|--------------|------------------------|---------------|----------------------------------|
| **1.**       | Philip Jenkins         |               |                                  |
| **2.**       | J. C. Kile             | A. B. Reynolds | ① ② ③ ⊗ ○                       |
| **3.**       | Thomas Morris Company  |               |                                  |
| **4.**       | Paulson Company, Inc.  | John Jones    | ② ③ ④ ⑤ ⊗                       |
| **5.**       | Sally White            |               |                                  |

**Sample Item   Coding**

In this test you will be given code lists similar to these.

**34** male
**21** female
**M** adult
**U** teenager
**Z** child

Below the code lists you will find a list of items. Each item is followed by circles containing five possible codes. Your task is to find the correct code combination for the item and mark an "X" in the appropriate circle. Look at the following examples. An "X" has been placed on the answer for example 1. What would you mark for example 2?

Examples:

1. female adult    (34U) (34M) (86Z) (⊗) (21U)
2. male child       (21Z) (34Z) (34U) (21U) (34M)

**FIGURE 6–5**   Sample Items from the Office Skills Test.
(Reprinted by permission of London House.)

required by traditional paper-and-pencil examinations. In the test for foreign service officials, for example, there is an "assessment day" on which the candidate's ability to take appropriate action on each of a set of memoirs and other communications of the sort usually found in an executive's in-basket, as well as the ability to handle a leaderless group negotiation interview, is evaluated. These kinds of tasks obviously go beyond the domain of ability testing and into the realm of attitude and personality assessment.

## SUMMARY

More tests of achievement—the level of knowledge, skill, or accomplishment in an area of endeavor—are administered than all other types of tests combined. During the twentieth century, written examinations, especially those of the objective variety, have become increasingly popular. Objective tests can measure not only knowledge of facts, but comprehension and higher-order thinking as well. They have been criticized, however, for fostering poor skills in written composition.

Standardized achievement tests reflect general educational objectives, whereas teacher-made tests are more likely to reflect the goals of a particular teacher or school system. The results of standardized achievement testing are used to evaluate students for purposes of grade assignment, promotion, placement, diagnosis of learning difficulties, determination of readiness to learn, and evaluation of curricula and teaching effectiveness (accountability).

The emphasis on formative evaluation, in which testing is an integral part of the instructional process, and criterion-referenced testing is indicative of the changing roles of educational achievement testing. Also of significance is the use of tests in large-scale educational assessment and planning, as in the National Assessment of Educational Progress.

Four types of achievement tests are single-subject survey tests, survey test batteries, diagnostic tests, and prognostic tests. Survey tests provide an overall appraisal of achievement in a subject, whereas diagnostic tests analyze the specific strengths and weaknesses in a person's knowledge of a particular subject. Readiness, aptitude, and other prognostic tests attempt to forecast achievement by determining a person's ability to learn certain material.

Sources of information concerning achievement tests include publishers' catalogs, test reviews in professional journals, *The Mental Measurements Yearbooks, Tests,* and *Test Critiques,* and specimen sets of tests. The reliabilities of most achievement tests are in the .80's or .90's. In evaluating achievement tests, content validity is of greater concern than other types of validity.

Various multilevel achievement test batteries are commercially available. Examples are the Stanford Achievement Tests, the Comprehensive Tests of Basic Skills, and the Iowa Tests of Basic Skills. These batteries are commonly administered in elementary and junior high school. Single-subject tests in reading, mathematics, science, social studies, English foreign languages, and other areas are also widely administered. Survey reading tests typically measure knowledge of vocabulary as well as speed and level of comprehension. The Gates–MacGinitie Reading Tests are a good example of survey reading tests.

Diagnostic tests, which are designed to assess specific strengths and weaknesses in a particular subject, are found in reading, arithmetic, and spelling. Examples are the Woodcock Reading Mastery Test–Revised and the Stanford Diagnostic Mathematics Test. Various prognostic tests in reading (reading readiness tests), mathematics, and languages (language aptitude tests) are available. Examples of prognostic tests are the Metropolitan Readiness Tests (reading), the Orleans–Hanna Algebra Prognosis Test (mathematics), and the Modern Language Aptitude Test.

Achievement tests in social studies (history, economics, political science) and in the natural sciences (general science, biology, chemistry, physics) are available for a wide range of grades and different types of curricula. Tests for admission to schools of nursing (NTE), medicine (MCAT), law (LSAT), management (GMAT), and other professional programs and for determining proficiency in various business occupations and the skilled trades are also used extensively.

## QUESTIONS AND ACTIVITIES

1.  Compare standardized achievement tests with teacher-made tests, listing the merits and shortcomings of each.
2.  What is accountability in education? How is accountability related to performance contracting? List arguments supporting and opposing performance contracting in the schools.
3.  Distinguish between norm-referenced and criterion-referenced measurement. What are the advantages and disadvantages of each?
4.  How does formative evaluation differ from summative evaluation? How do the two approaches to evaluation complement each other? In what way is formative evaluation related to criterion-referenced measurement?
5.  Compare the purposes and design of survey tests, diagnostic tests, and prognostic tests.
6.  Why is it better to administer an achievement test battery rather than a series of single subject-matter tests? Why not?
7.  Name at least one standardized achievement test in each of the following school subjects: English, science, reading, mathematics, foreign languages.
8.  Most departments of psychology and education keep on file specimen sets of standardized achievement tests, including test booklets, answer sheets, scoring keys, manuals, and perhaps other interpretive materials. Select one of these tests for review, using an outline such as the following. Whenever possible, you should fill in this outline from information obtained by reading the test manual and examining the test itself. You should wait until you have completed your own reviews before consulting published reviews of the test in *The Mental Measurements Yearbooks, Test Critiques,* or other sources.

### *Outline of a Test Review*

*Content.*   List the title, author(s), publisher, date and place of publication, forms available, type of test, and cost. Give a brief description of the sections of the test, the kinds of items of which the test is composed, and the mental operations or characteristics the test is supposed to measure. Indicate how the test items were selected and whether the construction procedure and/or theory on which the test is based are clearly described in the manual.

*Administration and Scoring.*   Describe any special instructions, whether the test is timed, and, if so, the time limits. Give details concerning scoring: as a whole, by sections or parts, and so on. Indicate whether the directions for administration and scoring are clear.

*Norms.*   Describe the group(s) (demographic characteristics, size, and so on) on which the test was standardized and how the samples were selected (systematic, stratified random, cluster, or other). What kinds of norms are reported in the test manual or technical supplements? Does the standardization appear to be adequate for the recommended uses of the test?

*Reliability.*   Describe the kinds of reliability information reported in the manual (internal consistency, parallel forms, test–retest, and so on). Are the nature and sizes of the samples on which reliability information is reported adequate with respect to the stated uses of the test?

*Validity.* Summarize available information on the validity (content, predictive, concurrent, construct) of the test included in the manual. Is the validity information satisfactory in terms of the stated purposes of the test?

*Summary Comments.* Prepare a summary statement of the design and content of the test, and comment briefly on the adequacy of the test as a measure of what it was designed to measure. Does the manual provide satisfactory descriptions of the design, content, norms, reliability, and validity of the test? What further information and/or data are needed to improve the test and its uses?

9. Run programs B-8 ("Randomly Generated Arithmetic Tests") and B-9 ("A Spelling and Word Usage Test") in the computer program package accompanying the text. What do you see as the advantages and disadvantages of this method of taking an achievement test compared with a paper-and-pencil version of the same test?

# 7

# INTELLIGENCE: TESTS AND DISTRIBUTION

Although more standardized achievement tests are sold than all other types of tests combined, it was by administering intelligence tests that large numbers of aspiring psychologists discovered that they could make a living in their profession by doing something other than teaching and research. For this reason, intelligence testing has sometimes been called "the bread and butter of psychology." Today, "Binet testing" is no longer the exclusive occupation of applied psychologists, but the assessment of cognitive abilities still forms a part of the activities of psychologists in a variety of clinical, educational, and other organizational settings.

## HISTORY AND TERMINOLOGY

*Intelligence,* a common term in the vocabulary of most people today, was almost unknown in everyday speech a century ago. During the latter part of the nineteenth century, many scholars and scientists became proponents of Charles Darwin's theory that differences among species evolved by natural selection. Two of these individuals, the philosopher Herbert Spencer and Darwin's cousin Francis Galton, became interested in intraspecies differences in mental characteristics and behavior. These men and their followers maintained that there exists in human beings an inborn degree of general mental ability, which they referred to as *intelligence.*

Unlike Spencer, Galton was not content merely to speculate and argue about the nature of intelligence. He attempted to demonstrate a hereditary basis for intelligence by studies of family trees and devised a number of tests of sensory discrimination and reaction time to measure its components. These and other sensorimotor tests (measures of movement speed, muscular strength, pain sensitivity, weight discrimination, and the like) were studied extensively by the American psychologist J. McKeen Cattell. Unfortunately, these tests proved to be relatively useless as predictors of accomplishment in schoolwork and other tasks that presumably require intelligence.

The approach taken by the French psychologist Alfred Binet was radically different from the analytic procedure of trying to measure the components of intelligence. Binet maintained that intelligence is manifested by performance on a variety of tasks and can be measured by responses to a sample of those tasks. Because his work in designing the first successful intelligence tests was motivated by the problem of identifying mentally retarded children in the Paris school system, it is natural that the sample of tests selected by Binet was heavily loaded with school-type tasks.

Binet and his physician associate, Théodore Simon, published their first set of intelligence tests—30 short tests arranged in order from easiest to most difficult—in 1905. Further work led to the publication in 1908 of a revised Binet–Simon scale consisting of 58 tasks arranged at age levels from 3 to 13 years. The tasks were grouped by chronological age according to what Binet's research had indicated normal children of a given age could do. A child's mental age (MA) was determined by the number of subtests he or she passed at each level; a mental age strikingly lower than the child's chronological age was considered indicative of mental retardation. A final revision of the scale was published in 1911 (Table 7–1), but after Binet's untimely death during that same year, the scene of later developments in intelligence testing shifted to the United States and Great Britain.

**Definitions of Intelligence**    Ever since Binet and Simon produced the first practical intelligence tests, psychologists have tried to come to grips with a workable definition of the concept. Binet's definition emphasized judgment, understanding, and reasoning. Other definitions have described intelligence as the ability to think abstractly, the ability to learn, or the ability to adapt to the environment. Each of these definitions has been criticized for one reason or another. Adaptability is obviously necessary for survival, but it is perhaps too broad a definition of intelligence. On the other hand, Lewis Terman's definition of intelligence as the ability to do abstract thinking appears to be too narrow: abstract thinking ability is an important aspect of intelligence, but certainly not the only one. Finally, the popular conception of intelligence as the ability to learn is inadequate if intelligence tests are accepted as measures of intelligence. Scores on these tests are not highly correlated with rate or speed of learning new things, although they are more closely related to the level or amount of learning of which a person is capable.

To traditional definitions of intelligence such as "the ability to learn and profit from experience" and "the ability to think or reason abstractly," Sternberg (1981, 1982) added two other components: "the ability to adapt to the vagaries of a changing and uncertain world" and "the ability to motivate oneself to accomplish expeditiously the tasks that need to be accomplished." Sternberg maintained that traditional intelligence tests do a fairly good job of assessing the first two components, but that there is a need for better measures of practical problem solving and motivation. Stimulated to a great extent by advances in computer technology and research on artificial intelligence, other psychologists have conceptualized intelligence in terms of attentiveness, information processing, and planning (Naglieri, 1989; Naglieri, Das, & Jarman, 1990) (see Chapter 8).

Rather than attempting to formulate a universally acceptable definition of intelligence, certain psychologists have suggested that it may be better to abandon the term altogether. If an alternative term is needed, one might use *general mental ability, scholastic aptitude,* or *academic ability.* The last two terms are a recognition of the fact that traditional intelligence tests are primarily predictors of success in schoolwork. But however strong opposition to the term *intelligence* may be, it is certainly less intense than opposition to *IQ.* Because of the controversy surrounding IQ and its implications of being a

**TABLE 7–1    The Fifty-four Subtests on the 1911 Binet–Simon Scale**

*Age 3*

Points to nose, eyes, and mouth.
Repeats two digits.
Enumerates objects in a picture.
Gives family name.
Repeats a sentence of six syllables.

*Age 4*

Gives own sex.
Names key, knife, and penny.
Repeats three digits.
Compares two lines.

*Age 5*

Compares two weights.
Copies a square.
Repeats a sentence of 10 syllables.
Counts four pennies.
Unites the halves of a divided rectangle.

*Age 6*

Distinguishes between morning and
    afternoon.
Defines familiar words in terms of use.
Copies a diamond.
Counts 13 pennies.
Distinguishes pictures of ugly and pretty
    faces.

*Age 7*

Shows right hand and left ear.
Describes a picture.
Executes three commands given
    simultaneously.
Counts the value of six sous, three of which
    are double.
Names four cardinal colors.

*Age 8*

Compares two objects from memory.
Counts from 20 to zero.
Notes omissions from pictures.
Gives day and date.
Repeats five digits.

*Age 9*

Gives change from 20 sous.
Defines familiar words in terms superior to
    use.
Recognizes all the (nine) pieces of money.
Names the months of the year in order.
Answers or comprehends "easy
    questions."

*Age 10*

Arranges five blocks in order of weight.
Copies two drawings from memory.
Criticizes absurd statements.
Answers or comprehends "difficult
    questions."
Uses three given words in not more than
    two sentences.

*Age 12*

Resists suggestion as to length of lines.
Composes one sentence containing three
    given words.
Names 60 words in 3 minutes.
Defines three abstract words.
Discovers the sense of a disarranged
    sentence.

*Age 15*

Repeats seven digits.
Finds three rhymes for a given word in 1
    minute.
Repeats a sentence of 26 syllables.
Interprets pictures.
Interprets given facts.

*Adult*

Solves the paper-cutting test.
Rearranges a triangle in imagination.
Gives differences between pairs of abstract
    terms.
Gives three differences between a president
    and a king.
Gives the main thought of a selection that
    he has read.

fixed measure of cognitive ability, many psychologists who have devoted their lives to the study of intelligence have expressed a willingness to abandon the term altogether (Vernon, 1979).

Not all instruments discussed in this chapter are specifically labeled *intelligence tests;* rather, they have been proposed as measures of *general* mental ability. In this sense, they are to be distinguished from the measures of *special abilities* considered in Chapter 9. The distinction between tests of general mental ability (intelligence) and tests of special abilities is, however, not sharp, and certain scholastic ability tests described in the present chapter might fit equally well in Chapter 9.

The items on intelligence tests represent attempts to assess individual differences in the effects of experiences common to nearly everyone, particularly in Western culture. It is assumed that, when exposed to the same experiences, persons of higher intelligence will benefit more from those experiences than persons of lower intelligence. Consequently, to the extent that test makers are successful, differences among individuals' scores on intelligence tests should be more a matter of variations in basic mental ability that variations in experience.

**Individual versus Group Tests**   Despite the common aim of measuring a unitary capacity, not all tests of general intelligence are alike. On some tests, the order of the items is mixed or alternated and there is a single time limit; on other tests, the items are grouped as sets of separately timed subtests.

The most common way of classifying intelligence tests is by the dichotomy *individual* versus *group*. Individual intelligence tests, which are administered to one person at a time, have a somewhat different focus than group intelligence tests, which can be administered to many people at the same time. The focus of individual tests is more global or holistic: their major purpose is to assess a general trait (Tyler & Walsh, 1979). The focus of group tests, on the other hand, tends to be narrower: to predict academic or occupational performance. Furthermore, administering an individual intelligence test is usually more time consuming than administering a group test. However, in administering individual tests examiners can pay more attention to the examinees and thereby encourage and observe them more closely. An examinee's approach to the test, that is, anxiety, confidence, problem-solving strategies, frustrations, distractibility, and the like, can be observed when administering individual tests, but not as easily on group tests. Scores on individual tests are also not as dependent on reading ability as are scores on group tests.

The greater economy of administering a group test in certain situations is seen by the fact that many more group than individual tests are given. Also, in spite of what advocates of individual tests have sometimes declared, some group tests of intelligence have even higher validity coefficients than individual intelligence tests.

Group intelligence tests are more often used for initial screening in educational and employment situations, to be followed by individual testing in cases where the examinee scores lower and/or more information on strengths and weaknesses is needed. Individual intelligence tests are preferred by psychologists in clinics, hospitals, and other settings in which clinical diagnoses are made. In these settings such tests may serve not only as measures of general mental ability, but also as a means of obtaining insight into personality functioning and specific disabilities.

## INDIVIDUALLY ADMINISTERED INTELLIGENCE TESTS

The instruments stemming from the work of Lewis Terman and David Wechsler have been the most popular individually administered tests of intelligence. Over the years, these tests have been used to evaluate the intellectual abilities of children and adults in many different settings. Other individual tests, some representing variations or extensions of Terman's and Wechsler's tests, have been designed specifically to assess the mental abilities of young children and persons with linguistic and/or physical handicaps.

### Older Editions of the Stanford–Binet Intelligence Scale

There were three English translations and adaptations of the Binet–Simon scale in the United States. One was prepared by H. H. Goddard of the Vineland Training School, one by Frederic Kuhlmann of the University of Minnesota, and a third by Lewis Terman of Stanford University. The most popular of these revisions, the Stanford–Binet Intelligence Scale, was published by Terman in 1916.

***The 1916 Scale*** Like the earlier Binet–Simon scales, the 1916 Stanford–Binet was an age scale on which the subtests were grouped into chronological age levels. Terman selected items from the Binet–Simon scales, as well as completely new items representing a broad sample of tasks that presumably require intelligence. Efforts were also made to include tasks that were not so dependent on specific school learning experiences.

One criterion for including an item on the Stanford–Binet was that an increasing percentage of children at successive age levels should be able to answer the item correctly. For certain statistical reasons having to do with maintaining a fairly constant intelligence quotient (IQ) scale across age levels, the percentage-passing requirement was set lower for items included in subtests at higher-year levels than for items at lower-year levels. In any event, the percentage-passing criterion served as an objective means of making certain that every item on the test was placed at an appropriate age level.

An examinee's mental age (MA) and intelligence quotient on the Stanford–Binet depended on the number of subtests passed at successive age levels. An IQ was determined by dividing the examinee's mental age (MA)—the total number of months credit earned on the test—by his or her chronological age (CA) in months and then multiplying the resulting quotient by 100. In symbols, this *ratio IQ* was computed as

$$IQ = \frac{MA}{CA} \times 100 \qquad (7.1)$$

For many years, the Stanford–Binet Intelligence Scale served as a standard for evaluating other intelligence tests. Nevertheless, it had a number of shortcomings. For example, the 1916 version was standardized on only 1000 children and 400 adults. The sample was, by present-day standards, not selected carefully and was certainly not representative of the U.S. population at the time. Two other shortcomings were inadequacies in testing adults and very young children and the lack of a second form to permit immediate retesting. Therefore, in 1937, Terman and his associate, Maud Merrill, published a revised, updated version of the scale.

**The 1937 Scale**    The 1937 version of the Stanford–Binet Intelligence Scale had a lower *floor* and a higher *ceiling* than the 1916 scale, two parallel forms (L and M), and better standardization. The 1937 scale was standardized in stratified fashion on 100 children at each half-year age interval from ages $1\frac{1}{2}$ through $5\frac{1}{2}$ years, 200 children at each year age interval from 6 through 14 years, and 100 children at each year age interval from ages 15 through 18. Equal numbers of boys and girls were tested in 17 communities of 11 states, but the sampling was limited to native-born whites who, as a group, were somewhat above average in socioeconomic status. Consequently, the sample was not truly representative of the entire U.S. population.

Three criteria were used for including an item on the scale. These were (1) the item was judged to be a measure of intelligent behavior, (2) the percentage of children passing the item accelerated with chronological age, and (3) children who passed the item had a significantly higher mean mental age than those who failed the item. Items were grouped at half-year intervals (levels) from Year II through Year V and at yearly intervals from Year VI through Year XIV; there was also an Average Adult level and three Superior Adult levels (Superior Adult I, II, and III). The six subtests at each level from Year II through Year V were given 1-month credit each; from Year VI through Year XIV, the subtests were given 2 months' credit each; and the six subtests at Superior Adult levels I, II, and III were given 4, 5, and 6 months' credit each, respectively.

In testing a child with the Stanford–Binet, the examiner first established the child's basal age. The *basal age* was the highest year level at which the child passed all subtests. Testing then continued until the *ceiling age,* the lowest year level at which the child failed all subtests, was reached. Mental age was computed by adding to basal age the number of months' credit received for passing each subtest up to the ceiling age. Then the IQ was computed by formula 7.1.

**The 1960 Scale**    The third edition of the Stanford–Binet Intelligence Scale, published in 1960, consisted of an updating of the best items from the 1937 L and M forms. Like its predecessors, the third edition was used to measure the intelligence of individuals from age 2 to adulthood. The procedure for administering the test was similar to that for the 1937 scale, although certain changes were introduced. One of these consisted of the addition of an alternative subtest at each age level for use when a particular subtest was not administered or was administered incorrectly. Testing time could also be shortened in certain instances by administering only four selected subtests instead of six at each year level. Another change was the provision for deviation IQs. The ratio IQ, like any other age norm, did not satisfy the requirement of equality of age units. Furthermore, it was meaningless when applied to adults, because there was no satisfactory answer to the question of what chronological age should be used as the denominator of the MA/CA ratio when examining adults. Fourteen years, 16 years, and 18 years had all been claimed as the age at which mental growth stops, and hence any one of those ages might be a suitable denominator in computing the IQ. Because of such problems in determining the ratio IQ, it was decided to change from a ratio IQ to a deviation IQ scale having a mean of 100 and a standard deviation of 16. The older ratio IQ was still reported on occasion, and tables for computing it were supplied in the 1960 Stanford–Binet manual.

The standardization group for the 1960 Form L–M of the Stanford–Binet consisted of 4500 children aged $2\frac{1}{2}$ through 18 years who had taken either Form L or M of the 1937 scale between 1950 and 1954. Realizing the need for updated norms, the publisher arranged for the test to be administered in 1972 to a stratified national sample of 2100 children (100 children at each half-year interval from 2 through $5\frac{1}{2}$ years and at each year interval from 6 through 18 years). The sample was more representative than earlier normative samples of the general U.S. population. Based on the 1972 standardization, a revised manual for the third edition was published (Terman & Merrill, 1973). The manual listed test–retest reliability coefficients of over .90 and, as with the first two editions, moderate correlations with school grades and achievement test scores (.40 to .75).

### Fourth Edition of the Stanford–Binet

The fourth edition of the Stanford–Binet Intelligence Scale (SB–IV) (Thorndike, Hagen, & Sattler, 1986) was constructed with the needs of clinical, school, and other psychologists who use intelligence test information in mind. SB–IV maintains historical continuity with the older versions of the Stanford–Binet, but in terms of its theoretical and psychometric bases, its content, and administration procedure, it represents a distinct departure from its predecessors. Like many modern tests, it was constructed by using sophisticated psychometric procedures, such as item-response theory (Rasch scaling) and ethnic-bias analysis. In addition, it was designed not only to assist in identifying mentally retarded and mentally gifted individuals, but also to provide diagnostic information concerning specific learning disabilities. With respect to sex and ethnic bias, items judged to be unfair or that showed atypical statistical differences between the sexes or ethnic groups were omitted.

***Theoretical Model and Tests***  As diagrammed in Figure 7–1, the model on which SB–IV is based consists of a three-level hierarchy with a general intelligence factor ($g$) at the first level, three broad factors (crystallized abilities, fluid-analytic abilities, and short-term memory) at the second level, and three factors (verbal reasoning, quantitative reasoning, and abstract-visual reasoning) at the third level. The verbal and quantitative reasoning factors at the third level comprise the crystallized abilities factor at the second level, and the abstract-visual factor at the third level comprises the fluid-analytic abilities factor at the second level.

Like its predecessors, the fourth edition of the Stanford–Binet was designed to measure intelligence from age 2 years to adulthood. It consists of fifteen tests: three to four tests in each of the three broader categories of Level 3 (Verbal Reasoning, Quantitative Reasoning, Abstract-visual Reasoning), plus four Short-term Memory tests. Each test is arranged in a series of levels consisting of two items each; almost all tests include sample items for familiarizing examinees with the nature of the specific task.

***Administration***  Total testing time for the entire SB–IV scale is approximately 75 minutes, varying with the age of the examinee and the number of tests taken. The adaptive or multistage nature of the scale calls for giving the Routing (Vocabulary) Test first to determine the entry level on the other tests. The entry level on the Routing Test is determined by the examinee's chronological age (CA). Administration of the Routing Test continues until the examinee fails three or four items at two consecutive levels, the higher of which is the *critical level*. The entry level for the remaining 14 tests is determined from a table by a combination of the critical level on the Routing Test and the examinee's CA. Administration of each test begins

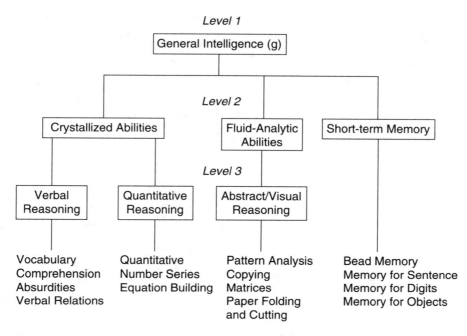

**FIGURE 7–1**    Theoretical Model and Tests for Stanford–Binet IV.
(Reproduced by permission of Riverside Publishing Company.)

at the entry level and continues downward until the examinee passes both items at two consecutive levels (*basal level*) and upward until he or she fails three or four items at two consecutive levels. The higher of these levels is the examinee's *ceiling age* for that test.

***Scoring***    The raw scores on each of the 15 tests are equal to the number of items passed. These scores are converted, within each age group, to standard age scale (SAS scores) having a mean of 50 and a standard deviation of 8. Raw scores on the four areas (Verbal Reasoning, Abstract-visual Reasoning, Quantitative Reasoning, Short-term Memory), each of which is equal to the sum of the raw scores on the three or four tests comprising that area, are converted to standard scale scores (area SAS scores) having a mean of 100 and a standard deviation of 16. Finally, an overall composite score consisting of the sum of the four area scores is converted to a standard age score scale having a mean of 100 and a standard deviation of 16. The range of the overall composite scores is 36 to 164, which is equivalent to a *z*-score range of –4 to +4 (see Figure 7–2).

***Standardization***    The fourth edition of the Stanford–Binet was standardized on 5013 individuals between the ages of 2 years and 23 years, 11 months in 47 states and the District of Columbia. The standardization sample was 48 percent male and 52 percent female, 75 percent white, 14 percent black, 6 percent Hispanic, 3 percent Asian/Pacific Islander, and 2 percent other ethnic groups. Student examinees were also stratified according to relative standing in their school class. Despite efforts to select a standardization sample that was truly representative of the U.S. population, the sample contained disproportionate numbers of

9-74539

**STANFORD-BINET INTELLIGENCE SCALE**

**RECORD BOOKLET**

# Stanford-Binet Intelligence Scale: Fourth Edition

Name **John C.**

Sex **M**

Ethnicity  NA  H  B  (W/NH)  O/AA  PI  Other _____

|  | YEAR | MONTH | DAY |
|---|---|---|---|
| Date of Testing | 86 | 6 | 29 |
| Birth Date  **B** | 72 | 1 | 18 |
| Age | 14 | 5 | 11 |

School **Hillview High School**

Grade **9th**  **A**

Examiner **Robinson**

Father's Occupation: **Civil engineer**

Mother's Occupation: **Social worker**

FACTORS AFFECTING TEST PERFORMANCE
Overall Rating of Conditions  **C**

Optimal   Good   (Average)   Detrimental   Seriously detrimental

|  | 1 | 2 | 3 | 4 | 5 |  |
|---|---|---|---|---|---|---|
| **Attention** | | | | | | |
| a) Absorbed by task | | | | ✓ | | Easily distracted |
| **Reactions During Test Performance** | | | | | | |
| a) Normal activity level | | | | ✓ | | Abnormal activity level |
| b) Initiates activity | | | ✓ | | | Waits to be told |
| c) Quick to respond | | ✓ | | | | Urging needed |
| **Emotional Independence** | | | | | | |
| a) Socially confident | | | | ✓ | | Insecure |
| b) Realistically self-confident | | | | ✓ | | Distrusts own ability |
| c) Comfortable in adult company | | | ✓ | | | Ill-at-ease |
| d) Assured | | | | ✓ | | Anxious |
| **Problem-Solving Behavior** | | | | | | |
| a) Persistent | | | | ✓ | | Gives up easily |
| b) Reacts to failure realistically | | | ✓ | | | Reacts to failure unrealistically |
| c) Eager to continue | | | ✓ | | | Seeks to terminate |
| d) Challenged by hard tasks | | | ✓ | | | Prefers only easy tasks |
| **Independence of Examiner Support** | | | | | | |
| a) Needs minimum of commendation | | | | ✓ | | Needs constant praise and encouragement |
| **Expressive Language** | | | | | | |
| a) Excellent articulation | | | | ✓ | | Very poor articulation |
| **Receptive Language** | | | | | | |
| a) Excellent sound discrimination | | | ✓ | | | Very poor sound discrimination |

Was it difficult to establish rapport with this person?
Easy  ✓  Difficult

**D**

| | RAW SCORE | STANDARD AGE SCORE ✱ |
|---|---|---|
| **Verbal Reasoning** | | |
| 1  Vocabulary | 27 | 47 |
| 6  Comprehension | 39 | 61 |
| 7  Absurdities *(Est. ceiling)* | 31 | 57 (Est.) |
| 14  Verbal Relations | | |
| Sum of Subtest SAS's ③ | | 165 |
| Verbal Reasoning SAS | | (171) |
| **Abstract/Visual Reasoning** | | |
| 5  Pattern Analysis | 40 | 56 |
| 9  Copying | | |
| 11  Matrices | 14 | 48 |
| 13  Paper Folding & Cutting | | |
| Sum of Subtest SAS's ② | | 104 |
| Abstract/Visual Reasoning SAS | | (105) |
| **Quantitative Reasoning** | | |
| 3  Quantitative | 19 | 39 |
| 12  Number Series | 6 | 37 |
| 15  Equation Building | | |
| Sum of Subtest SAS's ② | | 76 |
| Quantitative Reasoning SAS | | (73) |
| **Short-Term Memory** | | |
| 2  Bead Memory | 28 | 51 |
| 4  Memory For Sentences | 32 | 60 |
| 8  Memory For Digits *(Est. basal)* | 12 | 47 (Est.) |
| 10  Memory For Objects | 9 | 55 |
| Sum of Subtest SAS's ④ | | 213 |
| Short-Term Memory SAS | | (108) |
| Sum of Area SAS's | | 397 |

| | COMPOSITE SCORE ✱ |
|---|---|
| **Test Composite** ........................... | (99) |
| Partial Composite ........................... | 109 |
| Partial Composite based on **VR, A/VR, STM** | |

✱ Be sure that all Standard Age Scores (SAS's) are based on the tables in the *Guide* with the number 9-74502 on the cover.

**The Riverside Publishing Company**

Robert L. Thorndike
Elizabeth P. Hagen
Jerome M. Sattler

1986 The Riverside Publishing Company All rights reserved

**FIGURE 7–2**  Front Cover of Record Booklet of the Stanford–Binet Intelligence Scale: Fourth Edition.
(Reproduced with permission of the Riverside Publishing Company from page 7 of *Stanford–Binet Intelligence Scale Examiner's Handbook: An Expanded Guide for Fourth Edition Users* by E. A. Delaney and T. F. Hopkins. Copyright 1987, © The Riverside Publishing Company.)

individuals in the upper socioeconomic and higher educational levels. An attempt was made to correct for this problem in scoring the test, but it was not completely successful. Other problems are that the factors measured by the scale are not uniform across age levels and the reliability information in the manual is inadequate. However, split-half and test–retest coefficients, computed on measures obtained over a time interval of 2 to 8 months, indicate that the reliabilities of the 15 tests, the four areas, and the composite are satisfactory.

## Wechsler's Tests

Although subtests at the adult level have been included on the Stanford–Binet since the 1937 revision, the test was not a very satisfactory measure of adult intelligence. Consequently, in 1939 David Wechsler, a psychologist at Bellevue Hospital in New York, published an individual intelligence test designed specifically for adults. To this test, the Wechsler–Bellevue Scale Form I, Wechsler added a second form in 1947, the Wechsler–Bellevue Scale Form II. A complete revision and restandardization of Form I was published in 1955 by The Psychological Corporation as the Wechsler Adult Intelligence Scale (WAIS). The WAIS itself was revised, restandardized, and republished in 1981 as the Wechsler Adult Intelligence Scale–Revised for assessing the intelligence of adults between 16 and 74 years of age.

***Wechsler Adult Intelligence Scale–Revised (WAIS–R)***   As described in Table 7–2, the six verbal subtests on the WAIS–R are Information, Digit Span, Vocabulary, Arithmetic, Comprehension, and Similarities; the five performance subtests are Picture Completion, Picture Arrangement, Block Design, Object Assembly, and Digit Symbol. Verbal and performance subtests are administered alternately in the order listed in Table 7–2 in approximately 75 minutes total time for all eleven subtests. Within each subtest, the items are arranged in order of increasing difficulty. Testing on a particular subtest is discontinued when the examinee fails a specified number of items in succession.

Raw scores on the 11 WAIS–R subtests are converted to a standard score scale having a mean of 10 and a standard deviation of 3. Then, by referring to a special table in the manual, the sum of the scaled scores on the verbal subtests can be converted to a Verbal IQ, the sum of the scaled scores on the performance subtests to a Performance IQ, and the sum of the scaled scores on all 11 subtests to a Full Scale IQ. These are deviation IQs, expressed as numbers on a standard score scale having a mean of 100 and a standard deviation of 15 (see Figure 7–3).

*Standardization*   The WAIS–R was standardized on a carefully selected national sample of 1880 "normal" adults in nine age groups (16–17, 18–19, 20–24, 25–34, 35–44, 45–54, 55–64, 65–69, 70–74) within the range of 16 through 74 years. The sample in each age category was stratified by sex, geographical region, white versus nonwhite, education, and occupation. Other characteristics, such as urban versus rural residence, were controlled but did not serve as stratification variables. Standardization of the WAIS–R differed from that of the WAIS primarily in stratification of the sample by ethnic group and provision for more representative sampling of older adults.

*Diagnostic Significance of WAIS and WAIS–R Scores*   In designing the WAIS, Wechsler planned to obtain more than just an estimate of a person's overall mental

**TABLE 7–2    Descriptions of Verbal (V) and Performance (P) Subtests on the Wechsler Adult Intelligence Scale–Revised (WAIS–R)**

**Information** (V).    The material on this subtest consists of 33 general information questions to be answered in a few words or numbers. The questions are arranged in easy-to-difficult order. Testing begins with item 5; items 1 to 4 are administered if the examinee fails either item 5 or 6. Testing is discontinued when the examinee fails seven items in a row. Responses are scored 0 or 1 and are affected by familial and cultural background.

**Picture Completion** (P).    The material on this subtest consists of 27 pictures on cards, each having a part missing. The examinee is allowed 20 seconds to indicate what is missing in a picture. Testing begins with item 1 and is discontinued when the examinee fails seven consecutive items. Responses are scored 0 or 1. The subtest was designed to measure visual alertness, memory, and attention to details.

**Digit Span** (V).    On this subtest, seven series of digits are to be recited forward and seven series are to be recited backward. Testing on "Digits Forward" begins with three digits read aloud (one digit per second) by the examiner. The examinee is directed to repeat each series as soon as the examiner has finished. Two trials are given on each series length (two different sets of digits). Testing on "Digits Forward" continues until the examinee fails both trials of a series or succeeds on nine digits forward. On "Digits Backward," the examinee is directed to say the digits backward after the examiner has finished saying them forward. Testing begins at two digits backward and continues until the examinee has failed both trials of a series or succeeded on eight digits backward. The score on each set of "Digits Forward" or "Digits Backward" is 0, 1, or 2; total score is the sum of part scores on "Digits Forward" and "Digits Backward." This subtest was designed to measure immediate rote memory, but scores are affected by attention span and comprehension.

**Picture Arrangement** (P).    The material on this subtest consists of 10 sets of cards, with each card in a set containing a small picture. The examinee is directed to arrange the pictures in each set of cards into a sensible story. The time limits are 60 seconds on sets 1 to 4, 90 seconds on sets 5 to 8, and 120 seconds on sets 9 and 10. Testing is discontinued when the examinee fails five consecutive sets. Responses are scored 0, 1, or 2, depending on their accuracy. This subtest measures ordering or sequencing ability, as well as social planning, humor, and the ability to anticipate.

**Vocabulary** (V).    On this subtest, 37 words to be defined are presented in order of ascending difficulty. Testing starts with item 1 for examinees having poor verbal ability, otherwise with item 4. Testing is discontinued when the examinee fails six words in a row. Responses to each word are scored 0, 1, or 2, depending on the degree of understanding of the word that is expressed. The subtext was designed to measure knowledge or words, a skill that is highly related to general mental ability.

**Block Design** (P).    The materials on this subtest consist of 10 red and white geometric designs on cards and nine red-and-white blocks. The examinee is instructed to duplicate each design with four or nine blocks. Two attempts are permitted on the first two designs and one attempt on each succeeding design. Testing is discontinued when four designs in a row are failed. Base scoring is 0, 1,

**TABLE 7–2  Continued**

or 2 points on designs 1 and 2 and 0 or 2 points on designs 3 to 10; bonus points are given for rapid, perfect performance. The subtest was designed to measure the ability to perceive and analyze a visual pattern into its component parts. In terms of its correlations with total scores on the Performance Scale and scores on the test as a whole, "Block Design" is considered to be one of the best performance tests of intelligence.

**Arithmetic** (V).   On this subtest, 15 arithmetic problems are presented in order of increasing difficulty. Testing begins with item 3 and is discontinued after five consecutive failures; items 1 and 2 are given if items 3 and 4 are failed. Fifteen seconds is allowed on problems 1 to 4, 30 seconds on problems 5 to 10, 60 seconds on problems 11 to 14, and 120 seconds on problem 15. Responses are scored 0 or 1; bonus points are given for rapid, perfect performance on certain problems. This subtest measures elementary knowledge of arithmetic, together with the ability to concentrate and reason quantitatively.

**Object Assembly** (P).   The materials on this subtest consist of four cardboard picture puzzles presented to the examinee in a prearranged format, with directions to put the pieces together to make something. All four puzzles are presented; the time limits are 120 seconds on puzzles 1 and 2 and 180 seconds on puzzles 3 and 4. The score for each puzzle is determined by the number of "cuts" that are correctly joined; bonus points are given for rapid, perfect performance. The subtest was designed to measure thinking, work habits, attention, persistence, and the ability to visualize a final form from its parts.

**Comprehension** (V).   On this subtest, 18 questions requiring detailed answers are presented in order of ascending difficulty. The questions are asked until the examinee fails six consecutive items. The responses are scored 0, 1, or 2, depending on the quality and degree of understanding expressed. The subtest measures practical knowledge, social judgment, and the ability to organize information.

**Digit Symbol** (P).   On this subtest, the examinee is directed to fill in each of 93 boxes with the appropriate coded symbol for the number appearing above the box. Testing begins with a practice series, after which the examinee is given 90 seconds to copy the correct symbols from a key into the boxes. The score range is 0 to 93 points. This subtest was designed to measure attentiveness and persistence in a simple perceptual-motor task.

**Similarities** (V).   The materials on this subtest are 14 items of the type "In what way are A and B alike?" The items are presented in order of ascending difficulty until the examinee fails five in a row. The responses are scored 0, 1, or 2, depending on the quality and degree of understanding expressed. The subtest is designed to measure logical or abstract thinking—the ability to categorize and generalize.

ability. A significant difference between a person's Verbal and Performance IQs and the pattern of scores (scatter) on the 11 subtests was thought to be characteristic of certain types of mental disorders and therefore potentially useful in clinical diagnosis. Unfortunately, the results of research failed to confirm Wechsler's hypotheses concerning the diagnostic significance of subtest scatter.

NAME _James L. Clarke_ AGE _24_ SEX _M_
MARITAL STATUS _Single_ HANDEDNESS _Right_
OCCUPATION _Store Clerk_ EDUCATION _H.S. Grad_
PLACE OF TESTING _Midwestern College_
TESTED BY _Lewis R. Aiken_
REFERRED BY _Self_
REASON FOR REFERRAL _Vocational and Educational Testing_

## WAIS-R® EXPANDED RECORD FORM

|  | Year | Month | Day |
|---|---|---|---|
| Date Tested | 1995 | 12 | 10 |
| Date of Birth | 1971 | 9 | 15 |
| Age | 24 | 2 | 25 |

### TABLE OF SCALED SCORE EQUIVALENTS*

| Scaled Score | Information | Digit Span | Vocabulary | Arithmetic | Comprehension | Similarities | Picture Completion | Picture Arrangement | Block Design | Object Assembly | Digit Symbol | Scaled Score |
|---|---|---|---|---|---|---|---|---|---|---|---|---|
| 19 | — | 28 | 70 | — | 32 | — | — | — | 51 | — | 93 | 19 |
| 18 | 29 | 27 | 69 | — | 31 | 28 | — | — | — | 41 | 91-92 | 18 |
| 17 | — | 26 | 68 | 19 | — | — | 20 | 20 | 50 | — | 89-90 | 17 |
| 16 | 28 | 25 | 66-67 | — | 30 | 27 | — | — | 49 | 40 | 84-88 | 16 |
| 15 | 27 | 24 | 65 | 18 | 29 | 26 | — | 19 | 47-48 | 39 | 79-83 | 15 |
| 14 | 26 | 22-23 | 63-64 | 17 | 27-28 | 25 | 19 | — | 44-46 | 38 | 75-78 | 14 |
| 13 | 25 | 20-21 | 60-62 | 16 | 26 | 24 | — | 18 | 42-43 | 37 | 70-74 | 13 |
| 12 | 23-24 | 18-19 | 55-59 | 15 | 25 | 23 | 18 | 17 | 38-41 | 35-36 | 66-69 | 12 |
| 11 | 22 | 17 | 52-54 | 13-14 | 23-24 | 22 | 17 | 15-16 | 35-37 | 34 | 62-65 | 11 |
| 10 | 19-21 | 15-16 | 47-51 | 12 | 21-22 | 20-21 | 16 | 14 | 31-34 | 32-33 | 57-61 | 10 |
| 9 | 17-18 | 14 | 43-46 | 11 | 19-20 | 18-19 | 15 | 13 | 27-30 | 30-31 | 53-56 | 9 |
| 8 | 15-16 | 12-13 | 37-42 | 10 | 17-18 | 16-17 | 14 | 11-12 | 23-26 | 28-29 | 48-52 | 8 |
| 7 | 13-14 | 11 | 29-36 | 8-9 | 14-16 | 14-15 | 13 | 8-10 | 20-22 | 24-27 | 44-47 | 7 |
| 6 | 9-12 | 9-10 | 20-28 | 6-7 | 11-13 | 11-13 | 11-12 | 5-7 | 14-19 | 21-23 | 37-43 | 6 |
| 5 | 6-8 | 8 | 14-19 | 5 | 8-10 | 7-10 | 8-10 | 3-4 | 8-13 | 16-20 | 30-36 | 5 |
| 4 | 5 | 7 | 11-13 | 4 | 6-7 | 5-6 | 5-7 | 2 | 3-7 | 13-15 | 23-29 | 4 |
| 3 | 4 | 6 | 9-10 | 3 | 4-5 | 2-4 | 3-4 | — | 2 | 9-12 | 16-22 | 3 |
| 2 | 3 | 3-5 | 6-8 | 1-2 | 2-3 | 1 | 2 | 1 | 1 | 6-8 | 8-15 | 2 |
| 1 | 0-2 | 0-2 | 0-5 | 0 | 0-1 | 0 | 0-1 | 0 | 0 | 0-5 | 0-7 | 1 |

### SUMMARY

|  | Raw Score | Scaled Score | Age-Scaled Score¹ |
|---|---|---|---|
| **VERBAL SUBTESTS** | | | |
| Information | 20 | 10 | 11 |
| Digit Span | 12 | 8 | 8 |
| Vocabulary | 44 | 9 | 10 |
| Arithmetic | 13 | 11 | 11 |
| Comprehension | 15 | 7 | 7 |
| Similarities | 18 | 9 | 9 |
| Verbal Score | | 54 | |
| **PERFORMANCE SUBTESTS** | | | |
| Picture Completion | 13 | 7 | 7 |
| Picture Arrangement | 6 | 6 | 6 |
| Block Design | 27 | 9 | 9 |
| Object Assembly | 28 | 8 | 8 |
| Digit Symbol | 45 | 7 | 7 |
| Performance Score | | 37 | |

¹Scaled score equivalents of raw scores for a specific age range( see Manual, Table 21). Not to be used for determination of IQ.

*Clinicians who wish to draw a profile may do so by locating the examinee's raw scores on the table above and drawing a line to connect them. See Chapter 4 in the Manual for a discussion of the significance of differences between scores on the subtests.

|  | Scaled Score | IQ | Percentile Rank | Classification |
|---|---|---|---|---|
| Verbal Score | 54 † | 94 | 34 | Average |
| Performance Score | 37 ‡ | 80 | 9 | Low Average |
| Full Scale Score | 91 | 86 | 18 | Low Average |

†Prorated from 5 subtests, if necessary.
‡Prorated from 4 subtests, if necessary.

**FIGURE 7–3** WAIS-R Record Form.
(Reproduced by permission from the Wechsler Adult Intelligence Scale–Revised. Copyright © 1981, 1951 by The Psychological Corporation. All rights reserved.)

Two problems in attempting to analyze subtest score scatter on the WAIS–R are that scores on the subtests are not highly reliable and some subtests have substantial correlations with each other. Consequently, the difference between a person's scores on two given subtests must be quite large before it can be viewed as significant or meaningful. Large differences between subtest scaled scores and between Verbal and Performance IQs are, however, of some use in the diagnosis of organic brain damage and psychopathology and in differentiating between intelligence and opportunity. A significantly lower Verbal than Performance IQ, for example, may be the result of limited linguistic experience or "cultural deprivation."

**Wechsler Intelligence Scale for Children–Third Edition (WISC–III)**   The Wechsler Intelligence Scale for Children (WISC), a downward extension of the Wechsler–Bellevue Scale Form I, was published in 1949. A revision of the WISC, the WISC–R, was published by The Psychological Corporation in 1974, and a second revision, the Wechsler Intelligence Scale for Children–Third Edition (WISC–III), was published in 1991. The WISC–III, designed for children from 6 through 16 years 11 months, consists of the following six Verbal subtests and seven Performance subtests:

| *Verbal Subtests* | *Performance Subtests* |
|---|---|
| Information | Picture Completion |
| Similarities | Coding |
| Arithmetic | Picture Arrangement |
| Vocabulary | Block Design |
| Comprehension | Object Assembly |
| Digit Span (supplementary) | Symbol Search (supplementary) |
|  | Mazes (supplementary) |

The 10 core subtests can be administered in 50 to 70 minutes, and the supplementary subtests in 10 to 15 minutes. As with the WAIS–R, the Verbal and Performance subtests on the WISC–III are administered alternately. Verbal, Performance, and Full Scale IQs, based on the same standard score scale as that of the WAIS–R, are determined by adding the scaled score equivalents of raw scores on the five Verbal and the five Performance subtests that are administered. Additionally, WISC–III may be scored for four factors: Verbal Comprehension, Perceptual Organization, Freedom from Distractibility, and Processing Speed.

The WISC–III was standardized on representative U.S. samples of 100 boys and 100 girls in each of 11 age groups from 6 to 16 years. The samples were also stratified by geographical region, parental educational level, and race. Other samples of children were tested with both the WISC–III and either the WAIS–R or the WPPSI–R, depending on their ages. The test–retest reliabilities of the WISC–III, obtained by readministering the scale after 4 to 8 weeks, are satisfactory. In addition, a number of validation studies have been conducted with various clinical groups of children.

**Wechsler Preschool and Primary Scale of Intelligence–Revised**   The third member of the Wechsler family of tests, the Wechsler Preschool and Primary Scale of Intelligence (WPPSI), was first published in 1967 and a revision, the WPPSI–R, in 1989. The six verbal (V) and six performance (P) subtests on the WPPSI–R, in order of administration, are Object Assembly (P), Information (V), Geometric Design (P), Comprehension (V), Block Design (P), Arithmetic (V), Mazes (P), Vocabulary (V), Picture Completion (P), Similarities (V), Animal Pegs (P), and Sentences (V). The last two are supplementary subtests. Designed for children aged 3 to 7 years, the WPPSI–R was standardized during 1987–1989 on a national sample of U.S. children aged 3 to 7 years. Stratifying the sample by gender, ethnicity, and parents' educational and occupational level made it more representative of the U.S. population in this age range. Like the WAIS–R and the WISC–III, the WPPSI–R yields separate Verbal, Performance, and Full-scale IQs based on a standard score scale having a mean of 100 and a standard deviation of 15.

## Other Wide-Range Individual Intelligence Tests

Although they are the most popular individual tests of intelligence in the United States, the Stanford–Binet and Wechsler series of tests are by no means the only wide-range batteries for assessing general mental ability. Nor are they the most popular tests of mental ability in other countries. Especially noteworthy in the United Kingdom are the British Ability Scales (BAS), which The Psychological Corporation revised and restandardized in the United States as the Differential Ability Scales (DAS).

***Differential Ability Scales (DAS)***    The basic purpose of the DAS, like that of the BAS, is to provide ability profiles for analyzing and diagnosing children's learning difficulties, to assess changes in abilities over time, and to identify, select, and classify children (ages $2\frac{1}{2}$ to 17 years) with learning disabilities. The DAS consists of 19 subtests: Similarities, Matrices, Sequential and Quantitative Reasoning, Picture Similarities, Pattern Construction, Block Building, Copying, Matching Letterlike Forms, Recall of Digits, Recall of Designs, Recognition of Pictures, Recall of Objects, Naming Vocabulary, Word Definitions, Verbal Comprehension, Word Reading, Spelling, Basic Number Skills, and Speed of Information Processing. The subtests are grouped into four ability areas: verbal, nonverbal, spatial, and diagnostic. Eight to twelve subtests, requiring a total time of 45 to 65 minutes, are administered at a particular age level. In addition, three achievement subtests (Word Reading, Spelling, and Basic Number Skills), requiring a total of 15 to 20 minutes testing time, are included in the battery. Raw scores on each subtest are converted to ability scores independent of the examinee's age. The ability scores can then be converted to $T$ scores and percentile ranks based on the scores obtained by a sample of 3475 U.S. children matched against 1988 census data. Scores on the various subtests are also used to compute Verbal Ability, Nonverbal Reasoning Ability, and General Conceptual Ability scores based on a mean of 100 and a standard deviation of 15.

***Detroit Test of Learning Aptitude***    Another noteworthy intelligence test battery is the Detroit Test of Learning Aptitude (available from pro.ed). Administration of the primary edition of this battery (DTLA–P:2), which was designed for children aged 3 to 9 years, takes 15 to 20 minutes. The subtests include Articulation, Conceptual Matching, Design Reproduction, Digit Sequences, Draw-a-Person, Letter Sequences, Motor Directions, Object Sequences, Oral Directions, Picture Fragments, Picture Identification, Sentence Imitation, Symbolic Relations, Visual Discrimination, Word Opposites, and Word Sequences.

The third edition of the Detroit Test of Learning Aptitude (DTLA–3) was designed for children aged 6 to 17 and takes 50 to 90 minutes to administer. The DTLA–3 subtests include Word Opposites, Design Sequences, Sentence Imitation, Reversed Letters, Story Construction, Design Reproduction, Basic Information, Symbolic Relations, Word Sequences, Story Sequences, and Picture Fragments. Standard scores, percentile ranks, age equivalents, and various composite scores can be computed on both the DTLA–P:2 and the DTLA–3. Although these two test batteries represent improvements over earlier editions of the DTLA, problems concerning the reliabilities of some of the subtests and the representativeness of the standardization sample remain.

## Individual Pictorial Tests

Less ambitious in concept that the Stanford–Binet and Wechsler tests, but useful when testing time is limited and/or the examinee's reading skills are poor, are intelligence tests that employ only pictures as test materials. Examples are the Peabody Picture Vocabulary Test and the Columbia Mental Maturity Scale.

***Peabody Picture Vocabulary Test–Revised (PPVT–R)***   The materials on the PPVT–R are 175 pictorial plates, arranged in ascending order of difficulty by age level and containing four pictures each. The examiner presents a plate, says a word, and instructs the examinee to point to the one picture out of four on the plate that best illustrates the meaning of the word. The PPVT–R takes 10 to 20 minutes to administer and score and can be used with a wide age range of examinees ($2\frac{1}{2}$ years to adulthood). Because no verbal response is required, the test can be given to persons with speech impairments, cerebral palsy, or reading problems and to mentally retarded, withdrawn, or distractible children. Standardization of the first edition (the PPVT) was quite limited, but Forms L and M of the revised edition were standardized in 1979 on a national sample of 4200 people from $2\frac{1}{2}$ to 18 years of age and 800 adults ranging in age from 19 to 40. A study designed to equate PPVT–R scores with those on the PPVT was conducted on 1849 children aged 3 to 18 years. The test norms are expressed as standard scores, percentile ranks, stanines, and age equivalents.

***Columbia Mental Maturity Scale, 3rd Edition (CMMS)***   On this test (available from The Psychological Corporation), the child selects the drawing that does not belong in each series of pictorial and figure drawings. The 92 items on the CMMS are arranged in eight overlapping levels, but only 51 to 65 items are administered to a given person. The test takes 10 to 20 minutes to administer and is appropriate for children $3\frac{1}{2}$ to 10 years of age. It is particularly suitable for nursery school or kindergarten children and/or those with impaired physical or mental functioning. The CMMS was standardized in the early 1970s on 2600 children, comprising a national quota sample stratified by sex, race, parents' occupation, and geographical residence. Scores are expressed as age deviations, corresponding percentile ranks and stanines, and maturity indexes.

## Nonverbal Tests for the Handicapped

Psychometric instruments such as the PPVT–R and the CMMS, which require pointing, manipulating objects, or some other nonverbal response, rather than speaking or writing, are referred to as *nonverbal tests*. Performance on certain tasks on these tests may be facilitated by verbal language, but its use is minimized.

The fact that the Wechsler scales contain separate verbal and performance measures makes them more suitable than older versions of the Stanford–Binet for examining persons with physical, linguistic, or cultural differences. The Wechsler performance subtests tend to be more accurate measures of mental ability in hearing-handicapped and culturally different children, whereas the verbal subtests are more valid measures for the blind and partially sighted. A special version of the WISC–R, The Adaptation of WISC–R Performance Scale for Deaf Children,[1] has been designed for deaf children. In testing blind persons, a series of specially designed performance tests known as the Haptic Intelligence Scale for Adult Blind,[2] is sometimes used in conjunction with the WAIS–Verbal Scale. An instrument designed specifically to assess the cognitive abilities of hearing-impaired children is the Hiskey–Nebraska Test of Learning Aptitude (Hiskey, 1966).[3] It consists of 12 nonverbal subtests administered with pantomimic directions to deaf children or verbal directions to normal children, administered in unspeeded fashion and yielding a mental age and an intelligence quotient.

Adaptations of the Stanford–Binet and other intelligence tests have been used to assess the intelligence of blind and partially sighted persons. Examples are the Perkins–Binet Tests of Intelligence, the Haptic Intelligence Scale, and the Blind Learning Aptitude Test (BLAT) (Newland, 1969). The last of these is an untimed test consisting of tactile items in an embossed (bas-relief) format with dots and lines similar to those used in Braille. The six different kinds of behavioral tasks are adaptations of items on the Culture Fair Intelligence Test and the Raven Progressive Matrices. The BLAT, which covers the range of school grades from kindergarten through twelfth grade, was standardized on a stratified (by geographical region, age, sex, race, and socioeconomic status) sample of 961 blind students in residential schools in 12 states and 55 day schools throughout the United States.

**Single-task Tests**    One of the oldest nonverbal tests, the Seguin Form Board, was introduced in 1866. It was not until the early part of the twentieth century, however, that Knox, Porteus, and other psychologists made serious efforts to standardize such tests. In addition to many types of form boards, other nonverbal tasks were investigated and standardized. These included puzzles of various kinds, sequential tapping of cubes, matching problems, block designs, and mazes.

Mazes have been used extensively in psychological laboratories and clinics and have been included on a number of standardized tests. The Porteus Mazes, viewed by its designer as a measure of foresight and planning ability, was introduced in 1914. It consists of a series of mazes arranged in order of increasing difficulty. On each maze the examinee is directed to draw the shortest path between the start and finish points without lifting the pencil or entering a blind alley. The Porteus is particularly suitable as a brief test (25 minutes) for the verbally handicapped and has been employed in a number of anthropological studies. It is also reported to be sensitive to brain damage, but, as is true

[1] Available from the Office of Demographic Studies, Gallaudet College, Washington, DC 20002.
[2] Available from Psychological Research, Box 14, Technology Center, Chicago, IL 60616.
[3] Available from Marshall S. Hiskey, 5640 Baldwin, Lincoln, NE 68507.

of scores on intelligence tests in general, Porteus scores are affected by education and experience.

Another nonverbal performance test for the handicapped consists of block designs such as those on the Wechsler scales and the Differential Ability Scales. One of the earliest of these tests was the Kohs Block Design. The materials on the Kohs are 16 colored cubes and 17 cards with colored designs to be duplicated by the examinee. The Kohs Block Design was considered especially appropriate for language- and hearing-handicapped children, but it is seldom administered anymore.

***Performance Test Batteries***    The first battery of standardized performance tests to be distributed commercially was the Pintner–Paterson Scale of Performance Tests (1917). Equally well known is the Arthur Point Scale of Performance Tests, published initially by Grace Arthur in 1925. Two performance test batteries used rather extensively with speech- and hearing-handicapped children are the Leiter International Performance Scale and the Hiskey–Nebraska Tests of Learning Aptitude.

The Leiter International Performance Scale, which can be administered entirely without verbal language, consists of 54 blocks arranged in an age scale-format. The examinee, aged 2 to adulthood, must select the blocks bearing the proper symbols or pictures and insert them into the appropriate recesses of a frame. The Leiter was developed on various ethnic Hawaiian groups and also employed in studies of native Africans. It is viewed as a measure of intelligence in people of foreign or non-Western cultural background, as well as in illiterates and persons with physically based language handicaps. An abbreviated version of the test, the Arthur Adaptation of the Leiter, was designed for children from 2 to 12 years of age.

## Developmental Scales for Infants and Young Children

Testing infants (0 to $1\frac{1}{2}$ years) and preschoolers ($1\frac{1}{2}$ to 5 years) can be difficult because of their short attention span and greater susceptibility to fatigue. Young children may also lack the motivation to pursue the test tasks, which frequently assess characteristics that are particularly unstable in early childhood. For these reasons, the reliabilities and validities of tests administered to preschoolers tend to be lower than those designed for school-age children. Infant tests have very low correlations with scores on intelligence tests administered to the same children in later years and are not very accurate predictors of later intellectual development (Lewis & McGurk, 1972).

One reason why correlations between scores on infant intelligence tests and scores on tests such as the Stanford–Binet administered at a later age are low is because the types of tasks on the two kinds of tests are different. Infant tests are primarily measures of sensorimotor development, whereas Binet-type tests are heavily loaded with verbal material. Nevertheless, infant tests are frequently useful in identifying mental retardation and organic brain damage.

Stimulated to some extent by research on child development and training, in the past few decades efforts to construct measures of the cognitive abilities of preschoolers have increased. Furthermore, educational television programs for young children have tried to familiarize them with tests and develop their test-taking skills. The success of these programs is revealed by the finding that time spent viewing them is directly related to improvements in test-taking skills.

**Older Developmental Scales**   Research begun by Arnold Gesell at the Yale Clinic of Child Development in the 1920s led to an extensive series of investigations of infancy and early childhood that continued for 40 years. A guiding assumption of these studies was that human development follows an orderly, sequential maturational pattern. Normative data on the development of motor, linguistic, and personal–social skills, as well as adaptive behavior, from birth to age 6 were collected. Detailed information on each child was obtained by various methods: home record, medical history, daily record, anthropometric measurements, material observations, reports of the child's behavior at the clinic, normative examination, and developmental ratings. The following excerpt is characteristic of the normative behavioral descriptions provided by Gesell and his co-workers (Gesell & Amatruda, 1941, page 41):

The baby can reach with his eyes before he can reach with his hand; at 28 weeks a baby sees a cube; he grasps it, senses surface and edge as he clutches it, brings it to his mouth, where he feels its qualities anew, withdraws it, looks at it on withdrawal, rotates it while he looks, looks while he rotates it, restores it to his mouth, withdraws it again for inspection, restores it again for mouthing, transfers it to the other hand, bangs it, contacts it with the free hand, transfers, mouths it again, drops it, resecures it, mouths it yet again, repeating the cycle with variations—all in the time it takes to read this sentence.

Scores on the Gesell Developmental Schedules, determined from the presence or absence of specific behaviors characteristic of children at certain ages, were summarized in terms of a *developmental age* (DA). As with the ratio IQ, a child's DA could be converted to a *developmental quotient* (DQ) by the formula DQ = 100 (DA/CA). However, Gesell did not consider the DQ as equivalent to an IQ.

The Gesell Developmental Schedules were probably used more by pediatricians than by psychologists from the 1920s through the 1940s. Psychologists, particularly those with a strong psychometric or statistical orientation, criticized the Gesell Schedules as being too subjective and as poorly standardized. However, a later version of the scales provided more objective observational procedures. The age range on the revised scales is 4 weeks to 5 years, and five behavioral categories are covered: adaptive (alertness, intelligence, constructive exploration), gross motor (balance, sitting, locomotion, postural reactions), fine motor (manual dexterity), language (facial expression, gestures, vocalizations), and personal–social (feeding, playing, toilet training). Knobloch and Pasamanick (1974) provided detailed instructions for making observations on the revised Gesell Developmental Schedules and interpreting them. Norms for preschoolers ($2\frac{1}{2}$ to 6 years) by half-year intervals, but not for infants, have also been published (Ames et al., 1979).

Other noteworthy older tests of infant and preschool development are the Merrill–Palmer Scale and the Cattell Infant Intelligence Scale. The Merrill–Palmer Scale was designed for children from $1\frac{1}{2}$ to 6 years of age, whereas the Cattell, which is a downward extension of the Stanford–Binet, has an age range of 3 months to $2\frac{1}{2}$ years.

**Brazelton Neonatal Behavioral Assessment Scale**   Reaching lower in age than either the Merrill–Palmer or the Cattell Scale is the Neonatal Behavioral Assessment Scale (NBAS) (Brazelton, 1973, 1984), with an age range of 3 days to 4 weeks. The NBAS is scored on 26 behavioral items and 20 elicited responses, including measures of neurological, behavioral, and social functioning. The items involve hand–mouth coordination, habituation to sensory stimuli, startle responses, reflexes, stress responses, motor maturity, and cuddliness. Few normative or validity data are provided, and the published reliability coefficients are fairly low (Sameroff, 1978). Despite its shortcomings, the NBAS is a popular research instrument. This scale, which emphasizes the individuality of the infant in its interactions with the mother and other features of the environment from the moment of birth, will probably continue to be used by pediatricians and child psychologists.

***Bayley Scales of Infant Development***   These scales are based on the results of an extensive research program (the Berkeley Growth Study) directed by Nancy Bayley. The second edition of the scales (Bayley–II), designed for children between 1 and 30 months who are suspected of being "at risk," was published by The Psychological Corporation in 1993. The three parts of Bayley–II, a Mental Scale yielding a Mental Development Index, a Motor Scale yielding a Psychomotor Development Index, and a Behavior Rating Scale to supplement information from the Mental and Motor Scales, can be administered in 25 to 35 minutes to children under 15 months and in a maximum of 60 minutes to children over 15 months old. Bayley–II was standardized on 850 boys and 850 girls selected in stratified random fashion from four geographical regions according to the demographic breakdown of the 1988 U.S. Census. Data on a number of clinical samples are also included in the manual. An accompanying instrument, the Bayley Infant Neurodevelopmental Screen (BINS), was designed to assess basic neurological functions, auditory and visual receptive functions, and social and cognitive processes in children aged 3 to 24 months.

***McCarthy Scales of Children's Abilities***   Taking up where the Bayley scales leave off, the McCarthy Scales of Children's Abilities (MSCA) were designed for children aged $2\frac{1}{2}$ to $8\frac{1}{2}$ years of age. These scales yield six measures of intellectual and motor development: verbal, perceptual performance, quantitative, general cognitive, memory, and motor. The MSCA was standardized on samples of approximately 100 children in each of 10 age groups within the designated age range, stratified by race, region, socioeconomic status, and urban–rural residence. Data on the validity of the MSCA, published only after the author's death, remain rather meager.

***Kaufman Assessment Battery for Children (K–ABC)***   This test battery (from American Guidance Service) was designed by A. S. and N. L. Kaufman to assess the abilities of $2\frac{1}{2}$- to $12\frac{1}{2}$-year-old children to solve problems requiring simultaneous and sequential mental processing. The K–ABC also includes an Achievement Scale to measure acquired skills in reading and arithmetic. Based on extensive research in neuropsychology and cognitive psychology, the K–ABC was designed especially for preschool, minority, and exceptional children. As shown in the Individual Test Record in Figure 7–4, scores are obtained in four global areas: Sequential Processing, Simultaneous Processing, Mental Processing Composite (sequential plus simultaneous), and Achievement. Thirteen of the 16 gamelike subtests comprising the K–ABC can be administered in 30 to 50 minutes to a preschooler and in 50 to 80 minutes to an older child.

The standardization sample for the K–ABC, stratified for race (white, black, Hispanic, Asian, Native American) and including a representative group of exceptional children, was

## K·ABC  Kaufman Assessment Battery for Children
by Alan S. Kaufman and Nadeen L. Kaufman

**INDIVIDUAL TEST RECORD**

Name _Mary B._  Sex _F_

Parents' names _Rita and James_

Home address _807 S. Lincoln_

Home phone _782-4602_

Grade _4_  School _Central Elementary_

Examiner _Norma Ehrhardt_

SOCIOCULTURAL INFORMATION (if pertinent)

Race _black_

Socioeconomic background _Mother finished 3rd grade, housewife; father finished 6th grade, construction worker_

| | YEAR | MONTH | DAY |
|---|---|---|---|
| Test date | 83 82 | 8 17 | 15 |
| Birth date | 72 | 8 | 11 |
| Chronological age | 10 | 9 | 4 |

| Achievement Subtests X = 100; SD = 15 | Standard score – band of error 90 % confidence | Nat'l %ile rank Table 4 | Socio-cultural %ile rank Table 5 | S or W Table 11 | age eq. Other data | grade eq. |
|---|---|---|---|---|---|---|
| 11. Expressive Vocabulary | ± | | | | | |
| 12. Faces & Places | 87 ± 8 | 19 | 35 | | 8-9 | |
| 13. Arithmetic | 92 ± 8 | 30 | 70 | | 9-6 | |
| 14. Riddles | 99 ± 9 | 47 | 90 | S | 10-6 | |
| 15. Reading/ Decoding | 73 ± 8 | 4 | 10 | W | 7-6 | 2.4 |
| 16. Reading/ Understanding | 67 ± 8 | 1 | 5 | W | 7-3 | 1.9 |

Sum of subtest scores **418**

Transfer sum to Global Scales. *Sum of subtest scores column*

| Mental Processing Subtests X = 10; SD = 3 | Scaled Score | | | Nat'l %ile rank Table 4 | S or W Table 11 | age eq. Other data |
|---|---|---|---|---|---|---|
| | Sequential | Simultaneous | Non-verbal | | | |
| 1. Magic Window | | | | | | |
| 2. Face Recognition | | | | | | |
| 3. Hand Movements | 10 | | | 50 | | 11-9 |
| 4. Gestalt Closure | | 14 | | 91 | S | above 12-6 |
| 5. Number Recall | 11 | | | 63 | | above 12-6 |
| 6. Triangles | | 8 | | 25 | | 8-0 |
| 7. Word Order | 6 | | | 9 | W | 6-6 |
| 8. Matrix Analogies | | 9 | | 37 | | 9-9 |
| 9. Spatial Memory | | 7 | | 16 | | 8-3 |
| 10. Photo Series | | 9 | | 37 | | 9-9 |

Sum of subtest scores **27  47**

Transfer sums to Global Scales. *Sum of subtest scores column*

| Global Scales X = 100; SD = 15 | Sum of subtest scores | Standard score ± band of error 90 % confidence Table 2 | Nat'l %ile rank Table 4 | Socio-cultural %ile rank Table 5 | age eq. Other data |
|---|---|---|---|---|---|
| Sequential Processing | 27 | 93 ± 8 | 32 | 50 | 11-9 |
| Simultaneous Processing | 47 | 95 ± 6 | 37 | 80 | 9-9 |
| Mental Processing Composite | 74 | 93 ± 6 | 32 | 70 | 9-9 |
| Achievement | 418 | 81 ± 4 | 10 | 30 | 8-9 |
| Nonverbal | | | | | |

### Global Scale Comparisons

| | Indicate < or ≈ | | Circle the significance level |
|---|---|---|---|
| Sequential | ≈ | Simultaneous (Table 10) | (NS) 05 01 |
| Sequential | ≈ | Achievement (Table 10) | (NS) 05 01 |
| Simultaneous | > | Achievement (Table 10) | NS 05 (01) |
| M P C | > | Achievement (Table 10) | NS 05 (01) |

**AGS** *
© 1983, American Guidance Service, Inc.
Circle Pines, Minnesota 55014
No part of this test record may be photocopied or otherwise reproduced.

**FIGURE 7–4**  Individual Test Record of Kaufman Assessment Battery for Children.
(Kaufman Assessment Battery for Children, by Alan S. Kaufman and Nadeen L. Kaufman.
© 1983 American Guidance Service, Inc., 4201 Woodland Road, Circle Pines, Minnesota
55014-1796. Reproduced with permission of the publisher. All rights reserved.)

based on statistics reported in the 1980 U.S. census. Separate percentile norms were determined by race and socioeconomic level for white and black children. Split-half reliability coefficients for the four global scales are in the high .80s and .90s. Information on the construct, concurrent, and predictive validities of the test is also given in the manual.

# GROUP-ADMINISTERED INTELLIGENCE TESTS

During the early part of this century, Lewis Terman regularly taught a course at Stanford University on the Stanford–Binet Intelligence Scale. It was reportedly in a section of the course that a student, Arthur Otis, conceived the idea of adapting selected Stanford–Binet tasks to paper-and-pencil format. Shortly thereafter, many of Otis's adapted tasks and others were combined as the first group intelligence test, the Army Examination Alpha.

The Army Alpha and the Army Beta, a nonlanguage test for non-English speakers and illiterates, were administered to nearly 2 million U.S. Army recruits during and after World War I for purposes of military selection and job classification. The Army Alpha, which consisted of items involving analogies, arithmetic problems, number series completions, synonyms and antonyms, cube analysis, digit symbols, information, and practical judgment, laid the groundwork for later group tests of intelligence and academic aptitude. After World War I, Otis and other psychologists published their own group tests of intelligence, and by the 1930s many such instruments were commercially available.

A typical group intelligence test consists of a series of multiple-choice questions arranged in a spiral-omnibus format, or as a series of separately timed subtests. In the *spiral-omnibus format,* several types of items comprising the test are mixed together and arranged in order of increasing difficulty; items with the same degree of difficulty are grouped together. Examples of spiral-omnibus tests are the Otis–Lennon Mental Ability Tests and the Henmon–Nelson Tests of Mental Ability. In contrast to the spiral-omnibus format are tests consisting of a series of separately timed subtests, such as the Test of Cognitive Skills and the Cognitive Abilities Test.

## Multilevel Group Intelligence Tests

The rationale underlying the construction of a multilevel intelligence test is to provide a series of tasks for comparing the intellectual growth of children over several years. The Stanford–Binet and Wechsler instruments are individually administered, multilevel intelligence tests. More extensively used than these are group tests such as the Otis–Lennon Mental Ability Tests, the Cognitive Abilities Test, and the Wonderlic Personnel Test.

***Otis Tests*** The Otis–Lennon School Ability Test (OLSAT) is a revision of earlier tests in the Otis series: the Otis Self-administering Tests of Mental Ability, the Otis–Lennon Mental Ability Test, and the Otis Quick-Scoring Mental Ability Tests. Like its predecessors, the sixth edition of the OLSAT consists of a variety of pictorial, verbal, figural, and quantitative items to measure Verbal Comprehension, Verbal Reasoning, Pictorial Reasoning, Figural Reasoning, and Quantitative Reasoning from kindergarten through grade 12. There are two forms and seven levels of the OLSAT. A maximum of 75 minutes, depending on which level is administered, is required to complete the test. The norms, based on a large national sample, are expressed as percentile ranks, stanines, and NCEs by grade. Comparisons between ability and achievement can also be made when the OLSAT is administered with the Stanford Achievement Test 8 or the Metropolitan Achievement Test 7.

***Cognitive Abilities Test (CogAT)*** The fifth edition of CogAT is designed to assess the abilities of schoolchildren to reason and solve problems by using verbal, quantitative, and spatial (nonverbal) symbols. CogAT is a multilevel test, with Levels 1 and 2 for grades

K–3 and Levels A–H for grades 3–12, and takes approximately 90 minutes to complete. Each level contains a Verbal Battery, a Quantitative Battery, and a Nonverbal Battery consisting of two to three subtests. Separate scores obtained on the three batteries and an overall composite score may be converted to various types of norms (standard age scores, national grade and age percentile ranks, grade and age stanines, and normal curve equivalents) based on a national standardization in 1992.

**Wonderlic Personnel Test**    The Wonderlic Personnel Test is a brief (2 to 3 minutes for reading directions, 12 minutes for taking the test), 50-item instrument based originally on the Otis Self-Administering Test of Mental Ability. Questions on the Wonderlic, which are illustrated in Figure 7–5, consist of analogies, definitions, logical, arithmetic problems,

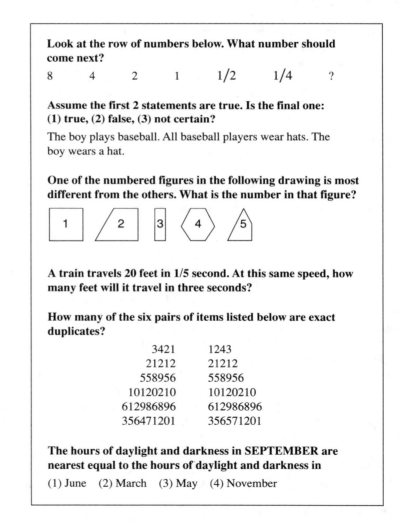

**FIGURE 7–5**    Sample Items from the Wonderlic Personnel Test.
(Reprinted by permission of Wonderlic Personnel Test, Inc., Libertyville, IL.)

spatial relations, word comparisons, and direction finding. This test has been used extensively as a screening device in employment situations for many years, and research indicates that it is a fair and valid selection device for a wide range of jobs. Despite the brevity of the Wonderlic, its reliability coefficients and correlations with scores on other measures of intelligence reportedly reach into the .90s.

## Administration, Scoring, and Reporting of Group Intelligence Tests

Group intelligence tests can be administered to small groups of children as young as 5 or 6 years or to adults of any age. When testing young children, examiners must be particularly careful to ensure that the examinees understand the directions, turn to the right page, start and stop on time, and so forth. In scoring group intelligence tests, raw scores, whether part or global, can be converted to percentile ranks, standard scores, or other numerical units. Because they are fairly short, tests such as the OLSAT are reliable enough to yield only one score; longer tests are needed to provide reliable scores on several parts.

Scores on group tests, even more than on individual tests, should be interpreted cautiously and against a background of other information (school grades and interview–observational data) about the examinee. Report 7–1 illustrates how the findings from a group intelligence test may be reported and interpreted, along with other relevant information about the examinee. Interpretative profiles of scores can also be prepared by a test-scoring service. Examinees with very low scores should be followed up with additional testing, preferably individual, before diagnostic or placement decisions are made.

### REPORT 7–1    Report of Group Intelligence Test Results

| | |
|---|---|
| Name of Examinee: Jane N. Brown | Sex: Female |
| Birth Date: March 11, 1973 | Age: 21 years, 11 months |
| Address: 12449 Mount Olive Street | Education: College senior |
| Thousand Oaks, CA | Date of Testing: 2/15/95 |

Tests Administered: Otis–Lennon School Ability Test, Advanced Form R

Jane Brown, a young woman of approximately average height and weight (5'5", 120 pounds), volunteered to take the intelligence test because of a personal interest in her mental abilities and as a favor to the examiner. The test was administered as an assignment in Psychology 405 (Psychological Assessment) at Western College during the spring semester of 1994.

At the time of the examination, Jane was in her final semester as an accounting major at Western College. She reported her overall grade-point average as 3.2. Jane indicated that she would like to attend graduate school in business eventually to work toward an MBA degree, but that immediately after graduation she planned to work full time at an accounting firm in the Los Angeles area.

Jane's father is a college graduate, and her mother completed two years of college. Both the father and mother work in the family business, a tax-assistance firm. Jane has reportedly made good grades (B's and A's) throughout her school career, but she confessed that "I'm no scholar!" She seems to be very practical minded in her interests, as indicated not only by her chosen major but also by her plans and other statements made to the examiner.

Jane showed moderate interest in the test questions and appeared relaxed but involved during the testing process. She worked attentively and uninterruptedly during the entire 40 minutes. Testing conditions were good; no disruptions or other distractions occurred.

### *Test Results and Interpretations*

Jane completed all the test questions during the allotted time (40 minutes). She obtained the following scores on the Otis–Lennon:

Raw score = 65
School Ability Index = 116
Percentile Rank (18+ years group) = 84
Stanine (18+ years group) = 7

These scores are approximately average for college seniors, indicating an overall intellectual ability in the "High Average" range for the general population. A brief analysis of the 16 items that Jane answered incorrectly indicated that she has somewhat greater difficulty with nonverbal reasoning than with verbal reasoning. However, there is no significant pattern in the errors that she made; they are fairly random.

### Conclusions and Recommendations

In a posttest interview, Jane indicated that she had done her best on the test and did not have to hurry to finish on time. She completed the test in 35 minutes and spent the last 5 minutes checking her answers. She indicated that the School Ability Index, which the examiner reported to her, was within five points of an IQ score that she made on an intelligence test she took in high school. She could not remember the name of the test.

Taking into account the conditions of testing, the examinee's observed behavior, and her statements after the test, the results are considered valid at this time. Jane's career plans and aspirations appear suitable for her intellectual ability, although she will probably have to work very hard to obtain an MBA from an accredited institution.

*Laura F. Green*
Laura F. Green
Senior Psychology Major
Western College

---

## Academic Ability and Admissions Tests

Many group intelligence tests have been designed specifically to measure aptitude for scholastic work and are referred to as *academic ability tests*. Some group intelligence tests have a broader focus than this, but they are still similar in content to academic ability measures: they are often heavily loaded with verbal, numerical, and other school-type items.

A number of different tests have been used over the years for college admissions purposes, including the American Council on Education Psychological Examination (ACE), the School and College Ability Tests (SCAT), the College Entrance Examination Board's Scholastic Aptitude Test (now called the Scholastic Assessment Test) (SAT), and the American College Testing Program Assessment (ACT). Because of their widespread use, the last two of these test batteries will be described in some detail.

***Scholastic Assessment Test (SAT)***    Prior to 1994, the SAT consisted of two sections yielding two scores: Verbal (SAT–V) and Mathematical (SAT–M). Verbal analogies, antonyms, information, reading, comprehension, and sentence-completion items made up the Verbal section; arithmetic, algebra, geometry, charts and graphs, and logical reasoning items made up the Mathematical section. Both sections were scored on a standard score scale having a mean of 500 and a standard deviation of 100; the scores ranged from 200 to 800. Although new forms of the SAT were developed every year, scores on each new form were previously scaled back to the 1941 standardization group. This group consisted of 10,000 mostly white male students from upper-income groups in the northeastern United States who were applying for admission to Ivy League schools. Understandably, high school students in the early 1990s scored somewhat lower than the mean of 500 achieved by that group.

The current version of the SAT, which was first administered on a nationwide basis in March 1994, consists of two sections—SAT I: Reasoning and SAT II: Subject Tests. SAT I consists of Verbal Reasoning and Mathematical Reasoning sections lasting 75 minutes each. The Verbal Reasoning section consists of 78 multiple-choice items on Analogies, Sentence Completions, and Critical Reading. The Mathematical Reasoning section consists of 60 items on Regular Mathematics, Quantitative Comparisons, and Student-produced Responses. Students are urged to bring their own hand calculators to the test so that they can compute the answers to the questions on the mathematical subtests.

As on earlier versions of the SAT, raw scores on the Reasoning Tests are converted to a standard score scale having a mean of 500 and a standard deviation of 100. Scoring of the revised version of the SAT (the Scholastic Assessment Test) is based on the performance of more than 1 million students who took the test in 1994. The scores were "recentered" to reflect the larger and more diverse student population of today, resulting in an increase in the average Verbal Reasoning score of approximately 80 points and the average Mathematical Reasoning score of around 20 points. Understandably, this caused some confusion among students (and their parents) who took the new test in 1995 and attained higher scores than they expected. In addition to standard scores on the Reasoning Tests, raw scores and percentile ranks for each subtest, score ranges based on the standard error of measurement of the tests, and national and state percentile equivalents for college-bound seniors are given in the score report.

The SAT Subject Tests consist of 18 tests in foreign languages, history, mathematics, the sciences, and other subject-matter areas. A direct sample of the examinee's writing skills is obtained, and multiple-choice questions concerning written English, diction, and logical expression are also administered. Like the SAT–I, SAT–II scores are reported on a standard score scale having a mean of 500 and a standard deviation of 100.

***American College Tests (ACT)***    The second most widely administered college admissions test is the ACT, which is given five times each year at 4000 centers in the United States and four times a year at 200 centers in foreign countries. A revision of the ACT, the Enhanced ACT Assessment Program, was first administered on a nationwide basis in October 1969. Like its predecessors, the new version consists of four subtests: English Test, Mathematics Test, Reading Test, and Science Reasoning Test. Changes in these tests include a better measure of "pure" reading ability and comprehension, more difficult mathematics items, and a science reasoning measure.

In addition to scores on the four subtests, a composite score and seven subscores are reported to takers of the ACT. Scores on the four subtests and the composite (the average of four subtest scores rounded to the nearest integer) range from 1 to 36, with a mean of 18; the seven subscores range from 1 to 18, with a mean of 9. The reliabilities of the four subtest scores range from .78 for Science Reasoning to .91 for English, with internal consistency coefficients being somewhat higher than parallel-forms coefficients. As might be expected because of their shorter length, the reliabilities of the subscores are lower, ranging from .67 for Plane Geometry/Trigonometry to .85 for English Usage/Mechanics.

The ACT Vocational Interest Inventory, which yields scores on the examinee's interests in science, the creative arts, social service, business contact, business detail, and technical areas, is administered along with the ability tests. Scores on the interest inventory and ability tests may be used, in combination, for purposes of vocational and academic counseling.

***Graduate Record Examinations***   The most popular test for admission to graduate school is the Graduate Record Examinations, consisting of a General Test to measure aptitude for graduate work and a Subject Test to measure achievement in a particular subject-matter area. The General Test consists of seven tests of 30 minutes each. Two of the seven tests are verbal, two are quantitative, two are analytical, and one is reserved for research purposes. The verbal tests consist of analogies, antonyms, sentence completions, and reading comprehension. The quantitative tests consist of quantitative comparisons, discrete quantitative, and data interpretation problems. The analytical tests consist of analytical reasoning and logical reasoning exercises. The General Test yields separate Verbal (GRE–V), Quantitative (GRE–Q), and Analysis (GRE–A) scores having the same standard score scale as the SAT. The GRE Subject Tests are 3-hour examinations in any one of 15 or so different subject-matter fields.

Several other standardized tests are used in the selection of students for professional schools, the most widely administered being the Graduate Management Aptitude Test (GMAT), the Law School Admissions Test (LSAT), and the Medical College Admissions Test (MCAT). Although these examinations are primarily achievement oriented, certain sections are similar to those found on tests of academic aptitude.

## Nonverbal and Culture-fair Group Intelligence Tests

Performance tests designed as individually administered measures of the intellectual abilities of persons with language or cultural handicaps were discussed earlier in the chapter. Complementary instruments that can be administered on a group basis have been constructed for the physically and culturally disadvantaged. The grandfather of these nonverbal tests was the Army Beta of World War I, which included tasks such as cube analysis, digit symbols, geometrical constructions, mazes, and picture completions. The Army Beta, which also proved useful in testing unskilled civilian workers, was updated, restandardized, and republished by The Psychological Corporation in 1978 as the Revised Beta Examination, Second Edition. Another example of a nonverbal test suitable for group (or individual) administration is the Goodenough–Harris Drawing Test. Unlike the Revised Beta Examination, which is a multiple-task test, the Goodenough–Harris requires only that the examinee accomplish the task of drawing a human figure.

***Goodenough–Harris Drawing Test*** This test is a revision of the Goodenough Draw-a-Man Test, together with the similar Draw-a-Woman Test and an experimental Self-Drawing scale. The man and woman figures drawn by the examinee are scored for body and clothing details, proportionality among the various body parts (for example, head to trunk), and other characteristics, rather than according to artistic merit. The test is untimed, but it usually takes from 10 to 15 minutes to complete. Norms for children from age 3 to 15 years are reported as standard scores and percentile ranks, separately by sex.

For many years, designers of intelligence tests have been besieged by the criticism that these instruments are loaded with the cultural biases of middle-class Western society. It was the hope of Goodenough and Harris that their test would measure basic intelligence relatively free of cultural influences, but it has become clear that the task of drawing a human figure is significantly affected by specific sociocultural experiences. There have been several other noteworthy, but largely unsuccessful, attempts to develop a culture-free intelligence test, and subsequently the aim was modified to that of constructing a culture-fair test. On a *culture-fair test* of intelligence, efforts are made to include only items related to experiences common to a wide range of cultures. Consequently, items involving specific linguistic constructions and other culture-loaded tasks, such as speed of responding, are not included. In this sense, the Goodenough–Harris test is culturally fair. Two other widely used tests that probably come as close as any others to being culturally fair are Raven's Progressive Matrices and the Culture Fair Intelligence Test.

***Raven's Progressive Matrices*** This test, which may be administered on either an individual or a group basis, requires examinees to indicate which of several figures or designs belongs in a given matrix. Developed in Great Britain as a measure of Spearman's general intelligence factor, the Raven's is available in three forms: Standard, Coloured, and Advanced Progressive Matrices. The Standard Form, suitable for ages 6 to 80, can be obtained in five black-and-white sets of 12 problems each and completed in 20 to 45 minutes. The Coloured Form, designed for children aged 5 to 11 years, elderly persons, and mentally and physically impaired persons, takes 15 to 30 minutes. The Advanced Form has a range of age 11 through adulthood and takes 40 to 60 minutes to complete. The most recent norms, based on British and American samples, are available on the Advanced Form, but all three forms need restandardizing.

Similar to but more recently developed than Raven's Progressive Matrices is the Matrix Analogies Test. It consists of nonverbal reasoning items organized in four groups: Pattern Completion, Reasoning by Analogy, Serial Reasoning, and Spatial Visualization. Examinees (aged 5 to 17 years) are tested in 20 to 25 minutes on 64 abstract designs of the standard progressive matrix type, one design per page. The norms are based on a large, representative sample of individuals aged 5 to 17 years living in the United States. Raw scores are converted to standard scores, percentile ranks, and stanines by half-year intervals and to age equivalents ranging from 5 to 17 years 11 months. A Matrix Analogies Test–Short Form, consisting of 34 items, is also available.

***Culture Fair Intelligence Test*** This series of tests is composed of three scales: Scale 1 for children aged 4 to 8 years and adult retardates; Scale 2 for children 8 to 14 years and adults of average intelligence; and Scale 3 for college students, executives, and others of above-average intelligence. As illustrated by the sample problems in Figure 7–6, each scale is composed of four subtests (Series, Classifications, Matrices, and Conditions) for measuring the ability to

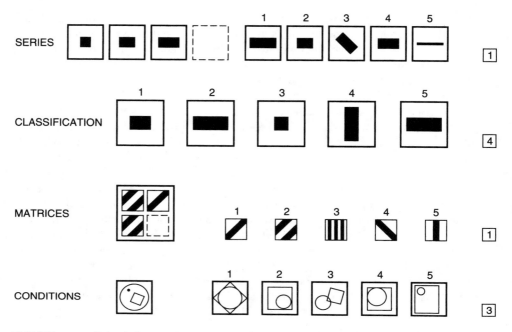

**FIGURE 7–6**   Sample Items from the Culture Fair Intelligence Test.

perceive relationships. In addition to these four culture-fair subtests, Scale 1 contains four subtests for assessing cultural information and verbal comprehension. Testing time is 40 to 60 minutes for Scale 1 and 25 to 30 minutes for each of the two forms of Scales 2 and 3.

Raven's Progressive Matrices and the Culture Fair Intelligence Test represent commendable efforts to develop tests on which different cultural groups score equally well. It is now recognized, however, that constructing test items that measure abilities independent of experience is probably impossible. Middle-class Caucasian groups typically score higher on both verbal, "culturally loaded" intelligence tests and culture-fair tests. Furthermore, culture-fair tests are poorer predictors of academic achievement, job performance, and other indicators of success in Western culture.

## DISTRIBUTION AND CLASSIFICATION OF INTELLIGENCE TEST SCORES

Scores on intelligence tests, and IQ scores in particular, depend on what test is administered. A Wechsler (WISC–III or WAIS–R) IQ of 130, for example, is not precisely equivalent to a Stanford–Binet or Otis–Lennon IQ of 130. A person's score on an IQ test varies somewhat from test to test. Consequently, whenever the IQ is reported, it is important to include the name and form of the test on which it was obtained.

Despite variations from test to test in the meaning of an intelligence quotient, the shape of the IQ distribution for well-standardized individual intelligence tests is approximately normal (bell shaped). One reason why the distribution is not precisely normal is the hump at the extreme lower end of the curve produced by low scores obtained by many children who have suffered accidents or diseases resulting in brain damage. In addition, because of assortative mating (mating among persons with similar characteristics), the distribution of intelligence test scores is often flatter than the normal curve. It has been argued that the flatness of the IQ distribution, which results from a larger number of very low and very high scores than in a normal distribution, is just what one would expect if intelligence is substantially influenced by heredity.

## Mental Retardation

Alfred Binet's principal reason for constructing the first practical test of intelligence was to identify children who had little chance of making reasonable progress in regular school classrooms. Therefore, it is not surprising that one of the most popular uses of general intelligence tests has been in diagnosing mental retardation.

According to the American Association on Mental Deficiency (AAMD),

Mental retardation refers to significantly subaverage general intelligence functioning resulting in or associated with concurrent impairments in adaptive behavior and manifested during the developmental period. (Kidd, 1983, pages 243–244)

Although this definition does not mandate the use of IQ tests in diagnosing mental retardation, intelligence test scores, along with measures of academic and vocational achievement, psychomotor skills, socio-emotional maturity, and other *adaptive behaviors,* are taken into account in making the diagnosis. Adaptive behaviors may be assessed by an informal analysis of the person's history and present behavior or by administering a standardized instrument such as the Vineland Adaptive Behavior Scale or the AAMD Adaptive Behavior Scale. The psychological examiner fills out a Vineland or AAMD Adaptive Behavior Scale from information supplied by a parent, teacher, or other person who is well acquainted with the child's behavior.

Socially derogatory labels such as *moron, imbecile,* and *idiot,* which were once used to categorize different degrees of mental retardation, are no longer applied by professional psychologists and educators in the United States. In fact, there have been efforts to replace the term mental retardation with a perhaps less stigmatizing term, such as *mental impairment* or *developmental disability.* In any event, various systems for classifying mental retardation have been proposed. One of the most widespread classification systems is recommended by the American Association of Mental Deficiency (Kidd, 1983):

Mild mental retardation:   IQ = 50–55 to approximately 70

Moderate mental retardation:   IQ = 35–40 to 50–55

Severe mental retardation:   IQ = 20–25 to 35–40

Profound mental retardation:   IQ = below 20 or 25

When a child's behavior is sufficiently impaired and judged to be due to deficits in reasoning and judgment, the limit of 70 on the mild mental retardation category may be extended upward to 75 or more if the test is sufficiently reliable. However, the term *marginal intelligence* is sometimes applied to IQs in the 70 to 85 range (Maloney & Ward, 1976).

The AAMD classification system, which is approved by some psychologists but considered confusing by others, is not uniformly adhered to by all 50 states. Although an IQ of 75 is generally accepted as the cutoff score, the definition and procedures for identifying mental retardation vary from state to state (Frankenberger, 1984). As advocated by Public Law 94-142 and by the AAMD, both adaptive behavior and IQ are usually considered in making the diagnosis.

Other systems of classifying the degree of mental retardation have been proposed by the National Association for Retarded Children (NARC) and the American Psychiatric Association (APA). The more functional NARC system consists of the following categories: marginally independent (IQ = 50 to 75); semidependent (IQ = 25 to 50); dependent (IQ = 0 to 25). The American Psychiatric Association (1994, page 50) lists three requirements for a diagnosis of mental retardation:

Significantly subaverage intellectual functioning: an IQ of approximately 70 or below on an individually administered IQ test (for infants, a clinical judgment of significantly subaverage intellectual functioning).

Concurrent deficits or impairments in present adaptive functioning (i.e., the person's effectiveness in meeting the standards expected for his or her age by his or her cultural group) in at least two of the following areas: communication, self-care, home living, social/interpersonal skills, use of community resources, self-direction, functional academic skills, work, leisure, health, and safety.

The onset is before age 18.

The four levels of severity in the APA system of classifying mental retardation are mild mental retardation (IQ level 50–55 to approximately 70); moderate mental retardation (IQ level 35–40 to 50–55); severe mental retardation (IQ level 20–25 to 35–40); profound mental retardation (IQ level below 20 or 25).

Another classification system sometimes used in schools to emphasize adaptive behavior rather than mental deficiency is *educable mentally impaired* for children who are mildly retarded, *trainable mentally impaired* for those who are moderately retarded, and *severely mentally impaired* for children who are severely mentally retarded.

In the United States, mild mental retardation is associated with a number of demographic variables related to low socioeconomic status: low educational level, minority group membership, unemployment or low employment levels, poor nutrition, poor health, and generally substandard living conditions. Heredity is undoubtedly a significant factor in mild retardation, but the inadequate language models, insufficient intellectual stimulation, and unstructured and unpredictable environments in which a large percentage of these children live contribute substantially to the degree of retardation.

Descriptions of the characteristic behaviors of children in the four categories designated by the American Psychiatric Association at three periods of development are given in Table 7–3. As shown in the table, expected behaviors vary with both the degree of retardation and the chronological age of the person. These behaviors are, of course, norms or averages, and the extent to which a particular person's behavior corresponds to the norms varies

## TABLE 7–3 Age-related Behavioral Changes in the Mentally Retarded

### Profound Mental Retardation (IQ below 20)

*Preschool age (0–5)*
Extreme retardation in all areas; minimal sensorimotor abilities; requires nursing
  care.

*School age (6–21)*
Obviously delayed in all areas of development; responds with basic emotions and
  may benefit from training in use of limbs and mouth; must be closely supervised.

*Adult (21 and over)*
May be able to walk and talk in a primitive way; benefits from regular physical
  activity; cannot take care of self, but requires nursing care.

### Severe Mental Retardation (IQ = 20–34)

*Preschool age (0–5)*
Pronounced delay in motor development; little or no speech; benefits from self-help
  (e.g., self-feeding) training.

*School age (6–21)*
Usually walks unless locomotor disability present; can understand and respond to
  speech; can profit from training in health and other acceptable habits.

*Adult (21 and over)*
Follows daily routines and contributes to self-maintenance; needs direction and
  close supervision in controlled environment.

### Moderate Mental Retardation (IQ = 35–49)

*Preschool age (0–5)*
Most development noticeably delayed, particularly in speech; can be trained in
  variety of self-help activities.

*School age (6–21)*
Learns to communicate and take care of elementary health and safety needs; learns
  simple manual skills but makes little or no progress in reading and arithmetic.

*Adult (21 and over)*
Performs simple unskilled or semiskilled tasks under supervised conditions;
  participates in simple games and travels alone in familiar places; incapable of self-
  maintenance.

### Mild Mental Retardation (IQ = 50–70)

*Preschool age (0–5)*
Slower than average to walk, feed self, and talk, but casual observer may not notice
  retardation.

*School age (6–21)*
Learns perceptual-motor and cognitive skills (reading and arithmetic) on third- to
  sixth-grade level by late teens; can learn to conform socially.

*Adult (21 and over)*
Usually achieves social and vocational skills needed for maintaining self; requires
  guidance and help when under unusual economic or social stress.

with sociocultural background, other skills or characteristics possessed by the individual, and additional circumstances.

The extreme retardation of persons falling in the severe and profound categories, and in some cases in the moderate category, may be caused by a variety of disorders leading to central nervous system damage: major gene problems such as galactosemia, gargoylism, phenylketonuria, and Tay–Sachs disease; genetic-dependent conditions such as cretinism, hydrocephaly, and microcephaly; chromosomal abnormalities such as Down's syndrome and Klinefelter's syndrome; and intrauterine infections, birth trauma (head injury, oxygen deprivation or oversupply), and diseases contracted during infancy (meningitis, encephalitis, lead poisoning, and others). These conditions account for a relatively small percentage of the total number of retarded children in more developed countries, where good maternal and infant health care are the rule. In less-developed countries, where malnutrition is more common and health care is less adequate, disorders of malnutrition account for a higher proportion of retarded individuals.

## Mental Giftedness

At the other end of the intelligence continuum from mental retardation is mental giftedness. The most comprehensive longitudinal study of persons with high IQs was conducted by Lewis Terman and his associates (Terman & Oden, 1959). Several hundred children who had scored in the top 1 percent of the distribution of IQs on the Stanford–Binet Intelligence Scale were followed throughout their lives at 5-year intervals from 1921 onward. After Terman's death in 1956, the study was continued by Oden (1968) and Sears (1977). The purpose of the study was to obtain information on the occupational success, physical and mental health, social adjustment, and other variables associated with high intelligence. Details on the childhood, education, personality, career(s), family, physical and mental health, and life stresses of the participants, as well as their adjustment to old age, were obtained from questionnaires.

### *Characteristics of Terman's Kids*   The results of the Terman study seemed to contradict a number of popular myths concerned the gifted: that bright children are sickly, that they burn out early ("early ripe, early rot"), and that genius is akin to insanity. The mentally gifted were physically superior to other children: they were heavier at birth and remained heavier than the average child; they walked and talked earlier and matured at an earlier age than average; and their general health was better. Furthermore, they maintained their mental and physical qualities as adults. Follow-up data revealed that, compared with average adults, they earned more degrees, attained higher occupational success and salaries, had equivalent or better personal and social adjustment, achieved greater marital success, and were physically healthier. The greater occupational success of the gifted appears, however, to have been due to their higher educational attainments, rather than their higher IQs per se. When educational level was controlled for, IQ scores obtained in childhood had no relationship to occupational achievement.

Terman's findings of better adjustment and a lower rate of mental disorders among the mentally gifted did not go unchallenged. Hughes and Converse (1962) suggested that the fact that the children were selected initially on the basis of teachers' ratings as well as IQ may have biased the sample in favor of better-adjusted persons. Terman's gifted children also tended to be of higher socioeconomic status, which is associated with better adjustment.

**Personalities of the Gifted**   Subsequent research also posed questions concerning personality adjustment in the gifted. Webb and Meckstroth (1982) characterized gifted children as more inquisitive, active, and energetic, but also as being perceived as obnoxious, unruly, strong willed, mischievous, unmanageable, and rebellious. These researchers noted that intellectually gifted children who are also highly creative are often troublesome to their parents and feel troubled themselves. Realizing that they are different from other children, they are presumably aware of the envy of their playmates and burdened by high expectations. Those who are particularly sensitive and under great stress to perform publicly may become depressed, use drugs, fail to perform up to their capacity, and occasionally drop out of society altogether.

**Mathematically Gifted Children**   Many other investigations of mentally gifted children have been conducted. Particularly noteworthy are the studies of mathematically precocious youth conducted by Julian Stanley and his colleagues (Stanley, Keating, & Fox, 1974; Keating, 1976). A special search was made for youngsters who by age 13 scored 700 or above on the Scholastic Aptitude Test–Mathematical (SAT–M). The children were then given various psychological tests and monitored while they took part in college mathematics courses.

As is true of other gifted children, those who are mathematically talented frequently learn complex material without being explicitly taught. Stanley and his co-workers also found that not only did such children benefit from college-level instruction in mathematics, but, despite initial fears that they would be unable to adjust to a college environment, they actually adapted quite well. Unlike some other findings concerning the mentally gifted and creative persons, the mathematically talented adolescents in Stanley's study tended to be personally well adjusted and highly motivated (especially in mathematics!).

# SUMMARY

*Intelligence,* an ancient Latin term reintroduced during the last century, refers to general mental ability. Various sensorimotor tests were used in early attempts to assess this ability, but the first practical measure of intelligence was devised by Alfred Binet and Théodore Simon during the first decade of the twentieth century. The Binet–Simon scale, a series of school-related tasks arranged in order of ascending difficulty, yields a mental age score for each examinee. Of the many translations and revisions of the Binet–Simon scale, the Stanford–Binet Intelligence Scale was the most popular. The Stanford–Binet, authored by Lewis Terman, was first published in 1916 and revised in 1937 and 1960. The test yielded a ratio IQ, defined as IQ = 100(MA/CA), although a deviation IQ could also be computed on the 1960 revision.

The fourth edition of the Stanford–Binet Intelligence Scale was a major departure from previous editions of the scale. Construction of the fourth edition, which involved more sophisticated theory and psychometric methodology, provided for separate scores on 15 tests and four areas, as well as a composite score. The emphasis in designing the fourth edition was not only on the identification of mental retardation, but also on providing information for diagnosing specific causes of learning disabilities.

For many years earlier editions of the Stanford–Binet were a standard against which other intelligence tests could be compared. During the past four decades, however, the Wechsler intelligence scales have become increasingly popular. Unlike subtests on the Stanford–Binet, which are grouped according to age levels, subtests on the Wechsler scales are grouped into 10 or so categories according to content. Also, scores on the Wechsler scales yield three kinds of deviation IQs: Verbal, Performance, and Full Scale. In addition to three IQs, the pattern of subtest scaled scores on the WAIS–R may provide clinical information useful in the diagnosis of certain personality characteristics and disorders.

Among the many special-purpose, individually administered intelligence tests are pictorial tests, such as the Peabody Picture Vocabulary Test and the Columbia Test of Mental Maturity, as well as other single-task tests, such as the Porteus Mazes and the Kohs Block Designs. Other nonverbal tests for individuals with language or physical handicaps include performance test batteries, such as the Blind Learning Aptitude Test, the Hiskey–Nebraska Test of Learning Aptitude, and the Leiter International Performance Scale.

An extensive amount of research has contributed to the construction of various developmental scales for infants and young children. The Brazelton Neonatal Behavioral Assessment Scale, the Bayley Scales of Infant Development, and the McCarthy Scales of Children's Abilities are illustrative of tests in this category. Having a wider age range than either the Bayley or the McCarthy is the Kaufman Assessment Battery for Children (K–ABC). The K–ABC represents a different approach to the assessment of children's cognitive abilities, an approach based on the notion of simultaneous and sequential mental processing.

Used more extensively than individual tests of intelligence are group-administered tests of intelligence. These tests stem from the Army Examinations Alpha and Beta, based on the pioneering work of Arthur Otis and other psychologists during World War I. Examples of current group intelligence tests are the Otis–Lennon School Ability Test, the Test of Cognitive Skills, the Cognitive Abilities Test, and the Wonderlic Personnel Test. Certain group tests of academic ability, the Scholastic Assessment Test (SAT), the American College Tests (ACT), and the Graduate Record Examinations, in particular, are used extensively for college, university, and professional school admissions. Nonverbal group intelligence tests for people with language handicaps are also available, an example being the Goodenough–Harris Drawing Test.

Traditionally, it has been assumed that the items on intelligence tests deal with common experiences, at least for people in a given culture. It was maintained that people with higher innate ability benefit more from these common experiences than people of lesser ability. Not only is this assumption questionable, but it has also been recognized that Binet-type tests, which are heavily loaded with verbal materials, are not always fair to examinees whose life experiences have been different from those of people in the Western middle class. Unfortunately, attempts to develop culture-free or even culture-fair intelligence tests have not proved very successful. Illustrative of such efforts are Raven's Progressive Matrices and the Culture Fair Intelligence Test.

The frequency distribution of intelligence test scores in the general population is roughly normal in shape. Individuals falling at the extreme low and high ends of this score distribution are referred to, respectively, as mentally retarded or mentally gifted, and much research has focused on both groups. Not only IQ but adaptive behavior and other characteristics play a role in the diagnosis of mental retardation. With respect to giftedness, creative performance is known to be not only a function of intelligence but also of motivation, special training, and perhaps other psychological abilities. Neither the mentally retarded nor the mentally gifted are free from problems of adjustment, but the former group has greater difficulties in this regard. For various reasons, research and special programs have concentrated more on the retarded than the gifted.

## QUESTIONS AND ACTIVITIES

1. What is the ratio IQ of a child who is 8 years, 9 months old if his or her score on the Stanford–Binet Intelligence Scale is equal to a mental age of 6 years, 5 months?

2. Why are deviation IQ scores considered psychometrically superior to ratio IQ scores?

3. Trace the development of the Stanford–Binet Intelligence Scale from Binet's early tests through the fourth edition of the scale.

4. List and describe current editions of the Wechsler series of intelligence tests, including the age range for which each is appropriate and the subtests on each test.

5. Compare the Wechsler tests with the older and newer editions of the Stanford–Binet in terms of age range, types of abilities measured, fairness of the tests to physically or culturally disadvantaged people, and other relevant features.

6. What intelligence test(s) would you recommend for administration to each of the following individuals? (a) a 5-year-old child suspected of being mentally retarded; (b) a group of South Sea island aborigines; (c) a 10-year-old child with cerebral palsy; (d) a normal, English-speaking adult; (e) a 7-year-old totally blind child; (f) an adult schizophrenic; (g) a group of culturally disadvantaged elementary school children.

7. Select one of the following categories of intelligence tests discussed in this chapter and two representative published instruments in the category: individual pictorial tests; developmental scales for infants and young children; multilevel group intelligence tests; nonverbal group intelligence tests. Obtain as much information on the two tests as you can from textbooks on testing, *The Mental Measurements Yearbooks, Tests, Test Critiques,* and other sources (consult the *Psychological Abstracts* and *Education Index* in particular). Write a comparative review of the tests, focusing on design and format, procedures for administering and scoring, norms, reliability, validity, and research concerned with the tests (see question 8 in Chapter 6). Draw appropriate conclusions regarding the relative merits of the two tests.

8. Describe the classification systems for mental retardation advocated by the American Association on Mental Deficiency, the National Association for Retarded Children, and the American Psychiatric Association.

9. Because the method of diagnosing mental retardation, including the cutoff IQ, varies from state to state, it is possible for a child to be mentally retarded in one state and "borderline" or "low average" in another state. What consequences might this have?

10. More government funds are spent on education of the mentally retarded than the gifted. Is this justified? Why or why not?

11. Run all the programs in category E ("Problem Solving and Thinking") of the *Computer Programs for Psychological Assessment.* Compare your results with those of your classmates or friends.

# 8

# INTELLIGENCE: RESEARCH AND THEORIES

Ever since their introduction during the first decade of this century, intelligence tests have been a part of numerous investigations concerned with the characteristics, causes, and effects of mental abilities. The findings of these investigations have stimulated much theorizing and controversy concerning the nature and the development of learning, thinking, and problem-solving skills. Because of the central importance of the concept of intelligence in psychological measurement, a brief review of research findings and theories should be helpful in understanding not only the concept of general intelligence, but also its relationship to other variables.

The research literature on individual and group differences in mental abilities is voluminous, and no attempt will be made here to provide a comprehensive review. These investigations, which were initiated by Francis Galton during the latter part of the nineteenth century, have too often been unsystematic and a reflection of convenient correlational methods rather than sound research design. Still, even when the results are difficult to interpret meaningfully, they are provocative and must be taken into account by anyone who decides to theorize about the nature and development of human cognition.

## AGE CHANGES IN INTELLIGENCE

Because of the popular misconception that a person's IQ is absolutely constant from year to year and from test to test, it is important to emphasize that IQs are not fixed or unvarying numbers. All intelligence tests are less than perfectly reliable; consequently, a person's score on one of these tests will change somewhat with time and testing conditions. It is true, however, that, given a relatively stable life situation and optimal testing conditions, scores on intelligence tests are fairly stable during the school years. The scores tend to be less stable during early and middle childhood, but they are more consistent during adolescence. A child's IQ score on an individual intelligence test varies about 5 points on the average, although changes of 20 points or more can occur. However, large fluctuations in IQ are usually traceable to rather dramatic variations in health or living conditions. Psychological factors, such as a traumatic emotional experience or the removal of an emotional problem, may also produce unusual changes in IQ.

The older definition of the intelligence quotient as 100 times the ratio of mental age to chronological age implies that mental age must increase as chronological age increases if a child's IQ is to remain stable from year to year. The same assumption applies to tests that do not yield ratio IQs: raw scores and mental ages on intelligence tests should increase with age during childhood. The exact form of the function relating raw test scores or mental ages to chronological age depends, of course, on the specific test and the intellectual components it measures.

## Cross-sectional and Longitudinal Studies

Conclusions from earlier studies of changes in general intelligence with age were almost always based on cross-sectional data (Yerkes, 1921; Jones & Conrad, 1933; Doppelt & Wallace, 1955). In an analysis of scores on the Army Examination Alpha administered to U.S. soldiers during World War I, Yerkes (1921) found that average scores on this group-administered test of intelligence declined steadily from the late teens through the sixth decade of life. In another early study, Jones and Conrad (1933) administered the Army Alpha to 1200 New Englanders between the ages of 10 and 60 years. The general form of the curve relating intelligence to age in this investigation was a linear increase in scores from age 10 to 16, followed by a gradual decline to the 14-year level by age 55. Scores on the Wechsler Adult Intelligence Scale–Revised also indicate that intelligence peaks in youth, although at a somewhat older age than found in earlier studies. As shown in Figure 8–1, the mean of Full Scale scaled scores on the WAIS–R reaches a peak in the early 20s, remains fairly constant from that point until the late 20s or early 30s, and then declines steadily throughout later life.

There are, of course, problems in attempting to interpret the results of cross-sectional studies. In contrast to *longitudinal studies,* which compare the same group of people at different ages, *cross-sectional studies* compare people of different cohorts, that is, groups of people brought up in different environmental circumstances. Differences among cohorts in factors such as educational opportunity, which is closely related to intelligence test scores, make it difficult to match people of different ages. Consequently, it is impossible to compare different age groups on intelligence without confounding the effects of education with other test-related experiences.

The steady rise in average educational and socioeconomic levels of Americans during the twentieth century must be taken into account when interpreting the apparent age decline in cognitive abilities. Because intelligence test scores are positively related to both educational level and socioeconomic status, it is understandable how older adults, who had less formal education and fewer test-related experiences, might make significantly lower test scores than younger adults.

It can be argued that, because longitudinal studies of intelligence have most often been conducted on college graduates or other intellectually favored groups, the findings do not necessarily apply to the general population (Bayley & Oden, 1955; Nisbet, 1957; Campbell, 1965; Owens, 1953, 1966). However, longitudinal investigations conducted on people of average intelligence (Charles & James, 1964; Eisdorfer, 1963; Tuddenham, Blumenkrantz, & Wilkin, 1968) and noninstitutionalized mentally retarded adults (Baller, Charles, & Miller, 1967; Bell & Zubek, 1960) have yielded similar findings. Mean intelligence test

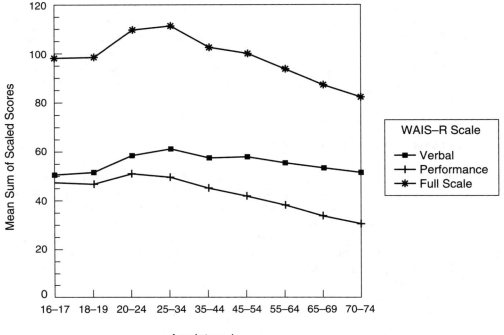

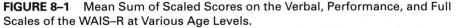

**FIGURE 8–1**   Mean Sum of Scaled Scores on the Verbal, Performance, and Full Scales of the WAIS–R at Various Age Levels.
(The data from which this figure was constructed are from the Wechsler Adult Intelligence Scale–Revised. Copyright © 1981, 1955 by The Psychological Corporation. Reproduced by permission. All rights reserved.)

scores increase by small amounts during early adulthood and reach a plateau between the ages of 25 and 30. People who are below average or fail to make adequate use of their abilities decline somewhat in intelligence after then. On the other hand, individuals of above-average intelligence may show no decline at all or even continue to improve until age 50. Although the results of both cross-sectional and longitudinal studies reveal substantial declines in cognitive abilities during the 70s and 80s, it has been found that such abilities can increase even after age 70 (Baltes & Schaie, 1974; Schaie & Hertzog, 1983; Busse & Maddox, 1985). These studies have been interpreted as indicating that the magnitude of intellectual decline with aging varies with the task and the individual.

### Specific Abilities

General intelligence tests measure a combination of several cognitive abilities, and the pattern of change in performance with age depends on the specific ability that is measured. As seen in the age-related pattern of subtest scaled scores on the WAIS–R (Wechsler, 1981), scores on vocabulary and information tests typically show no appreciable changes with aging, but perceptual–integrative abilities and comprehension of numerical symbols decline more rapidly.

Both cross-sectional and longitudinal methods have shortcomings, and investigations combining the two approaches are required to reach valid conclusions regarding intellectual growth with age. One such study concerning the differential effects of aging on cognitive abilities was conducted by Schaie and Strother (1968). Fifty people in each 5-year age range from 20 to 70 were tested with the Primary Mental Abilities Test, and as many as could be located were retested 7 years later. The greatest age-related decline in abilities was found with the cross-sectional method, a decline that also began earlier than with the longitudinal method and varied with the specific ability. In a later longitudinal study, Baltes and Schaie (1974) found an age decline on the factor of "visuomotor flexibility" but no significant change in "cognitive flexibility." Increases during the later years occurred in "crystallized intelligence" and "visualization," two other cognitive factors that were tested. It has also been noted that age-related declines are less likely to be found in vocabulary knowledge and similar skills that are highly dependent on lifelong learning than in performance on unfamiliar problems of logic and other skills requiring new learning. Similarly, Horn and Cattell (1966) found a greater age-related decline in the ability to reason and solve problems involving visual and geometric stimuli ("fluid intelligence") than in verbal skills ("crystallized intelligence").

As the preceding results make clear, whether a decrease, no change, or even an increase in cognitive abilities is observed with age depends not only on the research methodology (longitudinal, cross sectional, or variations on these methods), but also on the specific ability and the person tested. Variations in cognitive abilities during adulthood depend to some extent on the kinds of experiences relevant to test performance a person has during these years. People who remain intellectually active typically show less decline in intelligence test scores than those who fail to continue in academic-type pursuits (Botwinick, 1977). Furthermore, even when older people do poorly on intelligence tests, they may possess highly specialized knowledge and skills in areas not covered by the tests. Such abilities enable them to be even more competent than younger adults in dealing with the problems of daily living. There has been some disagreement among psychologists such as John Horn and Warner Schaie regarding the magnitude, quality, and generality of age changes in cognitive abilities. For example, Horn and Donaldson (1976) concluded that decrements in a number of the important abilities comprising intelligence are likely to occur if one lives long enough. In fact, Horn maintained that intelligence may begin to decline as early as the 20s and 30s. The decline becomes particularly noticeable during middle age and is more apparent in fluid intelligence than in crystallized intelligence.

Schaie (1983) recognized that there are differences between the cognitive abilities of older and younger adults, but he felt that such differences are related more to variations in the experiences of young and old cohorts than to age or time of measurement. Agreeing that some age-related decline occurs, Schaie maintained that it is much less than Horn and his colleagues asserted. To Schaie, the existence of interindividual variations in intelligence and its growth and decline, together with its multidimensionality, modifiability, and the interaction between age and cohort, leads to the conclusion that intelligence is a very plastic variable. Schaie (Schaie, 1983; Schaie & Hertzog, 1986) maintained that a favorable environment, one with varied opportunities for intellectual stimulation and the maintenance of a flexible life-style, can help to sustain a high level of functioning intelligence in later life.

### Terminal Drop

An apparent exception to the conclusion that no abrupt decline in cognitive abilities occurs in old age is a phenomenon referred to as the *terminal drop*. This is a deterioration in cognitive functioning (IQ, memory, cognitive organization), sensorimotor abilities such as reaction time, and personality characteristics such as assertiveness during the last few months or years of life. Prompting research on the terminal drop was the claim made by a nurse in a home for the aged that she could predict which patients were going to die soon merely by observing that they "seem to act differently" (Lieberman, 1965, page 181). Subsequent research findings revealed declines in various areas of cognitive and sensorimotor functioning and in the ability to cope with environmental demands in patients who died within a year after being tested (Granick & Patterson, 1972; Lieberman & Coplan, 1969; Reimanis & Green, 1971; Riegel & Riegel, 1972). Riegel and Riegel (1972) noted that the drop becomes evident as long as 5 years before death, but subsequent research results indicate that it may not begin until about 2 years before death and occurs only in certain skills (White & Cunningham, 1988).

Studies of deceased men who had participated in a longitudinal study of aging conducted by Duke University researchers found no terminal drop on tests of physical functioning, but scores on intelligence tests tended to fall sharply a few months or years before death (Palmore, 1982; Palmore & Cleveland, 1976; Siegler, McCarty, & Logue, 1982). A decline was more likely to occur on nonspeeded tests such as vocabulary, which is apparently little affected by age until late in life, than on speeded tests of a perceptual or problem-solving nature. On the other hand, patients who did not show such declines in cognitive functioning and behavior did not die until a significantly longer period after being tested.

## OTHER DEMOGRAPHIC VARIABLES

The relationships of intelligence test scores to a multitude of demographic variables, including family size, birth order, occupation, socioeconomic status, education, nationality, and culture, have been examined in hundreds of studies. The methodology and findings of these investigations constitute a substantial portion of the subject matter of courses on differential psychology.

### Family Size and Birth Order

For over a century, psychological researchers have noted the tendency for mentally duller persons to have larger families. It has been found that, on the average, intellectual ability declines as family size increases (Belmont & Marolla, 1973; Kellaghan & MacNamara, 1972; Zajonc, 1976). The negative correlation between family size and intelligence is not due entirely to socioeconomic differences between large and small families, because it remains significant even when those differences are taken into account. Such a finding might be cause for alarm except for the fact that the death rate is also higher among people of lower intelligence.

Also commonly observed is that high achievement is more often associated with first-born than later-born children. Summarizing the results of studies up through the mid-1960s,

Altus (1966) concluded that first-borns constitute a greater percentage of the intellectually superior portion of the population than they do of the population as a whole. First-borns also talk earlier and more clearly, learn to read earlier, and are better at problem-solving and perceptual tasks than later-borns. One possible explanation for these differences is that parents usually treat first-borns (particularly boys) differently from later-borns. Both parents tend to be more attentive and stimulating to first-born babies, spend more time with them, and provide greater encouragement and assistance in walking, talking, reading at the appropriate age, and other developmental tasks (Kilbride, Johnson, & Streissguth, 1977; Mac-Phee, Ramey, & Yeates, 1984). These differences in parental treatment are thought to be responsible for first-borns being more serious, responsible, studious, and competitive, while later-borns are more outgoing, relaxed, imaginative, and athletic.

## Occupational Status

In an open, competitive society such as ours, it is reasonable to expect more highly intelligent people to enter occupations demanding higher ability. Likewise, persons of lower intelligence tend to enter occupations requiring less ability. Related to this point is one of the most widely cited findings in mental testing—differences in the mean scores on the Army General Classification Test (AGCT) scores of World War II military inductees who had been employed in various civilian occupations (Harrell & Harrell, 1945). The mean AGCT scores computed on over 70 occupational groups showed accountants, lawyers, and engineers to be at the top. Teamsters, miners, and farmers were at the bottom, and other occupational groups were arranged in between in a hierarchy according to their mean scores on the AGCT. As might be expected, there was a wide range of scores within each occupation. For example, some truck drivers scored higher than some teachers, proving that the former are not necessarily the opposite of "wise guys." Nevertheless, the data clearly demonstrate the importance of the intelligence variable in the prediction of occupational membership. In general, intelligence test scores are reasonably good predictors of performance in a variety of occupations (Brody, 1992).

The role of education, which is significantly related to both intelligence and occupational status, in the positive link between the last two variables is not entirely clear. Cronin et al. (1975) maintained that the relationship between intelligence and occupational status is due to the fact that both variables are correlated with social-class background. They concluded that middle- or upper-class backgrounds are more likely than lower-class backgrounds to prepare children to do well on intelligence tests and in schoolwork, thus paving the way for them to enter higher-status occupations. The effect sequence may also be something like this: scoring high on a test of intelligence or scholastic aptitude is usually a requirement for admission to a good college, and graduation from a good college or university (and/or a professional school in some cases) is a requirement for entering a more prestigious occupation.

## Socioeconomic Status

One of the most consistent findings of research on individual and group differences in psychological characteristics is the positive correlation between IQ and socioeconomic status

(SES), where SES is defined in terms of parental income, education, and occupation. Higher average IQs among children in higher social classes have generally been found in these studies, a distinction that holds on both conventional and culture-fair tests of intelligence (Speath, 1976). Whether social-class differences in ability are primarily the results of heredity or environment is debatable, but it is generally agreed that a supportive home environment can exert a significant effect on cognitive abilities (Skodak & Skeels, 1949; Hunt, 1961).

Because socioeconomic status and educational level are closely related, it is difficult to conclude whether observed differences in IQs are due to differences in education or to some other variable associated with socioeconomic status. Children who score low on intelligence tests tend not only to have less formal education, but also to come from homes that are alienated from the dominant culture and are under greater than average economic stress. A language other than standard English is typically the primary means of communication in these homes, and the parents do not emphasize the importance of academic skills or know how to help their children acquire them.

Despite the significant positive correlation between intelligence test scores and socioeconomic status, the two variables are far from interchangeable. Consider, for example, the results of a study conducted by Thomas, Alexander, and Eckland (1979) of the relationships of these variables to school marks: it was found that the positive correlation between IQ and educational attainment remained significant even when socioeconomic status was statistically controlled. On the other hand, when IQ was statistically controlled, the correlation between socioeconomic status and educational attainment was slightly negative. These findings suggest that the correlation between IQ and school marks is not, as some psychologists believe, due primarily to differences in social-class background. Rather, it seems that intellectual ability affects both socioeconomic status and educational level. For this reason, it can be argued that a major reason why students from middle-class backgrounds are more likely than others to end up in the top half of their school classes is because they possess greater intellectual ability (Thomas, Alexander, & Eckland, 1979).

## Urban versus Rural Residence

Place of residence (urban versus rural) is related to both occupational membership and socioeconomic status, as well as intelligence. Studies conducted in the United States during the first half of this century (see McNemar, 1942) found that children living in rural areas had significantly lower mean IQs than those living in urban areas. Although this urban–rural difference in intelligence test scores has persisted, it is not as pronounced as it was a generation or two ago. Because of television, better access to schools, and other sources of information and intellectual stimulation, rural children of today are exposed to a wider range of environmental stimuli than their parents and grandparents were. Increased exposure to the wider culture has improved the vocabularies, level of knowledge, and general intellectual awareness of rural children. Furthermore, studies conducted among the Venda of South Africa, the Malays and Chinese of Malaysia, and Nigerians support the conclusion that group differences in performance on intelligence tests reflect differences in social class and education, rather than urban versus rural environment per se (Cronbach & Drenth, 1972; Scribner & Cole, 1973). The same could presumably be said for differences in the test scores of children living in different sections of metropolitan areas.

## Teacher Expectations

Cognitive abilities certainly have an effect on educational achievement, but education also influences abilities. The effects of education on cognitive abilities are sometimes indirect, as revealed by studies of teacher expectations. The *looking-glass theory*—that people tend to adapt their behavior and self-perceptions to how they believe they are perceived by other people—was first proposed by the sociologist C. H. Cooley (1922). More recently, investigations stemming from the observation that the expectations of researchers can affect their research findings was extended to the classroom situation. These investigations, which frequently involved socially disadvantaged children, have been concerned with the influence of teachers' expectations and attitudes on observed changes in the test scores and behaviors of students. The most famous, albeit somewhat controversial, experiment of this kind was conducted by Rosenthal and Jacobson (1968) in the elementary schools of a south San Francisco school district.

The purpose of the Rosenthal and Jacobson experiment was to determine the effects of telling teachers that certain pupils would show a "potential spurt" in intellectual growth during the ensuing school year. In September, verbal, reasoning, and total IQ scores for all children in the school were obtained by having them take nonverbal intelligence tests, the Tests of General Ability (TOGA). Then 20 percent of the children were labeled "potential spurters," ostensibly on the basis of their TOGA scores but actually at random, in a report to their teachers. TOGA was readministered to all the children one semester, 1 year, and 2 years later. Comparisons were then made between the IQ gains of the experimental groups ("potential spurters") and those of control groups of children who had not been labeled potential spurters. The experimental groups in grades 1 through 3 made greater average gains than the controls, but there were no differences between the experimentals and controls in grades 4 through 6. Mexican-American children and those in the medium-ability track showed the greatest initial gains in total IQ. Boys showed greater average gains in verbal IQ and girls in reasoning IQ. The experimentals also showed greater gains in reading marks and were rated by their teachers as happier, more intellectually curious, and less in need of social approval than the controls.

Rosenthal and Jacobson could not identify the specific teacher behaviors that produced the changes in IQs for the experimental groups, but they speculated that teachers' higher expectations for these children were communicated by means of facial expressions, postures, touch, and other nonverbal cues. The findings of this experiment were not completely replicated by other investigators, and the experiment was criticized for a number of methodological flaws. A subsequent meta-analysis of studies of the expectancy effect strongly supported the hypothesis that the more closely acquainted teachers are with their pupils, the smaller is the expectancy effect (Raudenbush, 1984).

## Nationality

According to popular dogma, certain nationalities and ethnic groups possess specific personality and behavioral characteristics that distinguish them from other groups of people. Although these stereotypes contain an element of truth, they are usually overgeneralizations that may serve as justifications for differential treatment or even mistreatment of particular national and ethnic groups. Nevertheless, social scientists have shown considerable interest in the relationships of cognitive variables to nationality, ethnicity, and culture.

A number of early investigations concerned with group differences in intelligence focused on nationality. An influential study conducted in the 1920s concluded that Jewish, Scandinavian, and German immigrants (along with native-born Americans) had higher average intelligence test scores than other immigrant groups in the United States (Hirsch, 1926). These results, which suggested that immigrants from countries in Northern and Western Europe were more intelligent than those from other countries, so impressed the psychologist H. H. Goddard that he lobbied for immigration laws that would restrict admission of all immigrants to the United States except those from Northern and Western Europe (Gould, 1981). Hirsch's (1926) findings, combined with those of Yerkes (1921), Brigham (1923), and others, were subsequently interpreted as being due to selective migration; significant nationality differences were not found when people were tested in their native countries and in their native language. Brigham (1930), in particular, repudiated his statements concerning nationality differences on the Army Alpha and concluded that the methods used were wrong and that the tests measured familiarity with American language and culture rather than innate intelligence. Other studies of immigrants found that scores on American intelligence tests vary with the similarity between the examinees' native culture and that of the dominant American culture.

## Ethnicity

One of the most controversial issues in the measurement of cognitive abilities has concerned racial differences in IQ. A general finding of research on this topic is that although the mean IQ scores of Asian-Americans are usually equal to or greater than the mean IQ of Caucasian-Americans, the mean IQs of Native Americans, Hispanic-Americans, and black Americans are significantly lower. Among the various group comparisons, attention has focused on black–white differences, a matter that is related to the heredity–environment controversy.

***Black–White Differences*** In a summary of the pre-1960 literature on black–white differences in abilities, Dreger and Miller (1960) concluded that, as a group, whites are superior to blacks in psychophysical, psychomotor, and intellectual functions, but the differences are not as large in young children as in older children and adults. Many social scientists (Lee, 1951; Klineberg, 1963) have attributed the results of research on racial differences in cognitive abilities to differences in the cultural environments to which black and white children are subjected; others believe that the differences have a genetic basis (Jensen, 1969; Eysenck, 1971). After analyzing the results of research on black–white differences in intelligence, Jensen (1969) concluded that the frequency of genes carrying higher intelligence is lower in the black population as a whole than in the white. The consequence, he maintained, is that blacks, although equal to whites in rote learning ability, are poorer in abstract reasoning and problem solving.

One set of research findings cited by Jensen (1981) to counter a strictly environmentalist explanation of racial differences in intelligence is that Hispanic-American and Native American children who were living under even worse environmental conditions than blacks made higher mean scores on nonverbal intelligence tests than the last group. Furthermore, despite the fact that their parents and grandparents were subjected to severe discrimination during the nineteenth and twentieth centuries, persons of Chinese and Japanese ancestry in the United States now excel Caucasians in mean nonverbal intelligence test scores, as well as in educational and occupational achievement, and are equal to Caucasians in verbal intelligence test scores. Finally, Jews, who themselves are no strangers to social discrimination, have consistently scored higher than other groups on measures of verbal intelligence (Vernon, 1985). In many of these groups, however, there are cultural traditions and family characteristics that encourage high achievement even when native endowment is not necessarily superior.

Despite the arguments of Jensen (1980, 1981), Herrnstein and Murray (1994), and others, the question of racial differences in intelligence is far from settled. Research findings indicate that whites outscore blacks by approximately one standard deviation on both the WAIS–R (Reynolds et al., 1987) and the Stanford–Binet: Fourth Edition (Thorndike et al., 1986). There is, however, a great deal of overlap between the IQ distributions of the two ethnic groups: an estimated 15 percent of blacks obtain higher IQs than the average white, and 15 percent of whites score lower than the average black person (Vernon, 1985). These racial differences in intelligence test scores can be attributed to an interactive combination of factors, including the inadequacies of the tests, differences in environments, and genetic differences, but the relative importance of these three sources of variability has not been determined.

***Japanese–American Differences***   Interest in the question of nationality and ethnic-group differences in intelligence was stimulated anew some years ago with the finding of significantly higher mean IQs in Japanese than in American children (Lynn, 1982). It has been known for many years that children of Asian immigrants to the United States tend to score at least as high as Caucasian children in this country. Lynn (1982) reported that the difference in mean IQ between Americans and Japanese reared in their own countries is approximately 11 points in favor of the latter group. In fact, it has been estimated that at least 10 percent of the Japanese population, compared with only 2 percent of Americans and Europeans, have IQs of 130 or greater.

Several possible explanations have been offered for the difference in mean IQs of Japanese and American children, a difference that has reportedly increased gradually since World War II. Assuming that the samples of Japanese and American children who were tested were equally representative of the specific populations and that the tests were equally appropriate, the most obvious explanation points to differences in child rearing and formal education practices in the two cultures. One biological explanation for the rise in IQ is that, due to improvements in health and nutrition, Japanese children today are better off physically and mentally than their counterparts in the pre-World War II days. Another suggestion is that the IQ increase has been caused by heterosis (hybrid vigor) resulting from a decline in consanguineous (kinship) marriages as large numbers of Japanese moved from small villages to large cities after World War II. Finally, Lynn (1987) proposed that differences in intelligence between Caucasians and people with Asian backgrounds are due to genetic differences in brain functioning. He maintained that in people of Asian backgrounds the left cerebral hemisphere evolved structures capable of processing visuo-spatial information. The result, according to Lynn, is that in Asians a higher proportion of cortical tissue is devoted to the processing of spatial information, but a smaller proportion of cortical tissue is available for processing verbal information. Consequently, linguistic communication, as in reading and writing Kanji, in Japanese involves spatial skills that normally depend on the right cerebral hemisphere. As reasonable as this explanation of the superior test scores of

Japanese children may sound, however, Brody (1992) concluded that the evidence for Lynn's theory is not persuasive.

## BIOLOGICAL FACTORS AND COGNITIVE ABILITIES

Modern scientists recognize that the brain is the organ of mental activity, but efforts to relate specific brain structures to mental abilities have not been very successful. Some of the smallest brains on record have been those of recognized geniuses (for example, Walt Whitman and Anatole France), and some of the largest brains were those of severely retarded individuals. Still, research reviews have concluded that the overall size of the brain has a small positive correlation with intellectual ability (Broman et al., 1987; Jensen & Sinha, 1991; Stott, 1983; Willerman et al., 1989). In a study of 139 infants who had low birth weights (less than 1.5 kilograms), it was found that head circumference at 8 months after birth was a significant predictor of Stanford–Binet IQs at 3 years of age (Hack & Breslau, 1985). This remained true even when medical and sociodemographic variables, which were significant but poorer predictors than head circumference of later IQs, were statistically controlled. Although compensatory growth of the brain during the first 8 months after birth offset the lowering of later IQs in some infants, little catch-up brain growth was observed after 8 months. Thus, it would appear that, at least in infants, head size may forecast later intellectual status (see Wilson, 1985).

### Cerebral Localization of Cognitive Functions

One might wish that it were possible to increase intelligence dramatically by surgical or chemical techniques, but at present this is only science fiction. A popular hypothesis—that higher-order mental processes take place in the frontal lobes of the brain—has received some support from PET (positron emission tomography) scan data (Haier, 1991). Furthermore, patients who had prefrontal lobotomies, a brain operation widely used at one time in the treatment of chronic schizophrenia, showed no consistent changes in scores on intelligence tests. However, some postoperative deterioration in specific intellectual abilities was noted in lobotomized patients (DeMille, 1962).

Changes in specific cognitive abilities are also associated with injury to other areas of the brain. For example, damage to the left temporal lobe, the dominant hemisphere for most people, disrupts verbal–symbolic performance more than perceptual–spatial performance. Damage to the right temporal lobe, however, affects perceptual–spatial performance more than verbal–symbolic performance. Also to be considered in assessing the effects of brain injury is the age of the patient. The intellectual development of a young child may be greatly affected by the same kind of brain injury that has no measurable effect on the intellectual abilities of an older person.

### Sex Differences

Occasionally, a difference between males and females in general intelligence is found, but it is usually insignificant. The results of research indicate, however, that there are sex differences in specific cognitive and perceptual-motor abilities. Females tend to be superior to males in verbal fluency, reading comprehension, finger dexterity, and clerical skills; males tend to surpass females in mathematical reasoning, visuo-spatial ability, and speed and coordination of large bodily movements (Minton & Schneider, 1980). It is recognized that these findings are, at least in part, a function of differences in the ways in which boys and girls are treated in our society. For example, girls are usually expected to be more accomplished in linguistic and social skills, whereas boys are supposed to do better in mathematical, mechanical, and related problem tasks. In any event, differences between males and females in mathematical and spatial reasoning abilities have reportedly declined in recent years (Linn & Hyde, 1989).

Not only sex (gender) but also sex hormones have been found to be related to cognitive abilities. For example, Hier and Crowley (1982) found a positive correlation between spatial ability and secretions of male sex hormones during puberty. The results of several investigations also suggest that testosterone slows development of the left hemisphere and enhances development of the right hemisphere of the brain, which is associated with the kinds of reasoning skills need to solve mathematical problems (Christiansen & Knussman, 1987). Finally, Hampson reported that women perform better on tests of motor coordination and verbal facility but poorer on tests of spatial reasoning during times of the month when estrogen levels in their blood are highest (Hampson, 1990; Kimura & Hampson, 1993).

## Diet and Chemicals

***Malnutrition***    It is reasonable to suppose that prenatal and postnatal nutrition affect intelligence, and research findings tend to support this hypothesis (for example, Lucas et al., 1992). The results of numerous studies document the effects of fetal and infant malnourishment on low intelligence (for example, Stoch & Smythe, 1963) and the persistence of such effects (Zeskind & Ramey, 1981). Attempts to reverse the malnutrition-related deficit in intelligence by supplementing the diets of malnourished young children and exposing them to a care-giving environment have not been entirely successful in erasing the intellectual deficit, although such intervention can help to arrest the decline (Barba, 1981; Zeskind & Ramey, 1981).

***Genetic Disorders and Diet***    Very low intelligence is found in individuals having certain rare genetic disorders that are affected by diet. An example is phenylketonuria (PKU), a genetic disorder caused by failure to inherit a gene that directs production of an enzyme responsible for oxydizing phenylalanine. The result is an accumulation of phenylalanine in the blood and a drastic depression of intellectual abilities. PKU can be detected by a simple medical test at the time of birth and alleviated and, consequently, the intelligence decline averted when the child is placed on a phenylalanine-free diet.

PKU and certain other genetic disorders characterized by low intelligence, for example, Tay–Sachs disease and galactosemia, are transmitted by recessive genes. Tay–Sachs is associated with an accumulation of a fatty substance in the central nervous system, while galactosemia is associated with an accumulation of galactose in the blood. Like PKU, galactosemia is treatable by placing the patient on a special diet, one free of galactose in this case.

***Drugs***   The list of drugs or substances that have at one time or another been thought to be associated with improvements in learning and retention is legion: gerovital, Dexedrine, glutamic acid, ascorbic acid, magnesium pemoline, vinpocetine, sex hormones, and various dietary and vitamin supplements. Although many drugs have seemed initially to enhance memory, the improvement is usually temporary or attributable to improvements in motivation and general health or to a placebo effect. Recently, a drug known as deprenyl has received a great deal of media attention for its apparent ability to improve learning ability in rats. If deprenyl, which is believed to be a "nerve growth hormone," works in humans, it could be particularly useful in the treatment of Alzheimer's patients and other individuals with memory problems.

***Exposure to Lead***   Intelligence may be affected by either too little or too much of a substance. Certain drugs, when taken by pregnant women to control for symptoms such as morning sickness, anxiety, insomnia, leg cramps, and seizures or to prevent premature delivery can pass through the placental membrane and affect the physical and mental development of the fetus. Evidence also indicates that postnatal exposure to a high concentration of substances like lead, which exists in housing, food, soil, and air, has a debilitating effect on intelligence (Needleman et al., 1978, 1990; Thatcher et al., 1983). In one of these investigations, the persistence of lead-related mental defects into adulthood was demonstrated in a reexamination of 132 of the 270 young adults who had been examined initially when they were in primary school. It was found that those with higher lead levels more often failed to graduate from high school and had increased absenteeism, reading disabilities, and lower scores on tests measuring vocabulary, grammatical reasoning, fine motor skills, and eye–hand coordination (Needleman et al., 1990). These findings, combined with those of other investigators (for example, Fulton et al., 1987; McMichael et al., 1988), provide support for the hypothesis that exposure to high levels of lead during early childhood has an adverse effect on intellectual development.

## Heredity and Intelligence

Belief in the genetic determination of intelligence goes back at least as far as the time of Francis Galton in the late nineteenth century. Alfred Binet did not reject the idea that intelligence is genetically determined, but he was more interested in the possibility of modifying intellectual abilities by education, training, and environmental intervention (Eysenck, 1984). One of the staunchest early believers in the notion that intelligence is fixed by heredity was the psychologist H. H. Goddard, who advocated the reconstruction of society along IQ lines (Goddard, 1920).

Most psychologists, child development specialists, and educational researchers would probably agree that general intelligence, or at least a predisposition to develop intellectually, is to some extent inherited (Snyderman & Rothman, 1987). Although many geneticists consider the matter of genetic differences in intelligence to be an open question, certain genetics researchers view intelligence as a *polygenic* characteristic, that is, one that is determined by the interaction of many minor genes rather than a single major gene.

***Genetic Research Methods***   The least ambiguous method of obtaining information concerning the effects of environment on cognitive abilities is to conduct an experiment with pairs of identical twins, who have identical heredities. Some twin pairs would be separated at birth by assigning them to different experimentally contrived environments, while other twin pairs would be kept together in the same environment. If greater differences in abilities were found between twin pairs reared in different environments than between those reared in the same environment, the results would support the hypothesis that environment influences cognitive abilities.

Because society will not permit even well-intentioned scientists to move children around like chess pieces, nonexperimental methods for determining the relative effects of heredity and environment have been employed. One approach is to compare, at various chronological ages, the IQs of identical twins who have been reared apart. In this way, heredity is effectively held constant while environment is varied, albeit in an unsystematic, uncontrolled manner. Furthermore, the IQs of individuals who have different heredities but live in similar environments, such as nonidentical siblings or unrelated children reared together, can be compared. Finally, comparisons can be made between the IQs of persons having different heredities and different environments, such as nonidentical siblings and unrelated individuals reared apart.

Despite the difficulty of locating pairs of identical twins who have been reared apart, several noteworthy investigations of this kind have been conducted (see Bouchard & McGue, 1981; Bouchard et al., 1990; Plomin, 1988, 1989). The results of these studies reveal that the correlation between the IQs of identical twins reared together is greater than that of identical twins reared apart, although both correlations are highly positive. The correlations listed in Table 8–1, which are the averages of results obtained from numerous studies, demonstrate that the more similar the heredities of pairs of individuals, the more closely related are their intelligence test scores. These statistics also suggest that the effects of environment on the IQs of persons having different degrees of genetic similarity are not nearly as great as those of heredity. Findings such as these have been

**TABLE 8–1   Average Correlations between IQs of Persons with Different Degrees of Kinship**

| Comparison | Average correlation |
| --- | --- |
| Monozygotic twins reared together | .86 |
| Monozygotic twins reared apart | .72 |
| Dizygotic twins reared together | .60 |
| Siblings reared together | .47 |
| Siblings reared apart | .24 |
| Half-siblings | .35 |
| Parent and offspring (together) | .42 |
| Parent and offspring (apart) | .24 |
| Cousins | .15 |
| Nonbiological siblings reared together | .29 |
| Nonbiological siblings reared apart | .34 |
| Adoptive parent and offspring | .19 |

*Source:* Bouchard, T. J., & McGue, M. (1981). Adapted from Loehlin (1989). Copyright 1989 by the American Psychological Association and adapted by permission.

offered as evidence for the relatively greater importance of heredity than environment in determining intelligence.

**Heritability Index**   Population geneticists often express the results of studies of hereditary differences in terms of a *heritability index* ($h^2$), defined as the ratio of the test score variance due to heredity to the test score variance due to both heredity and environment. Although heritability estimates as high as .72 (Plomin, 1990) have been reported, average estimates of $h^2$ for intelligence in the general population are around .50. This means that an estimated 50 percent of the variance in IQ scores is attributable to genetic factors. It should be cautioned that these numbers reveal nothing about the relative importance of heredity and environment in determining the intelligence of a specific individual; they apply only to populations.

**Heredity–Environment Interaction**   Even the strongest supporter of the genetic bias of intelligence on the one hand or an extreme environmentalist on the other recognizes that *both* heredity and environment are important in the formation of cognitive abilities. *Environment* in this context refers not only to the psychosocial, or experiential, environment of the person, but also to the prenatal and postnatal biological environment (nutrition, accidents, and so forth). One interpretation of the research data bearing on this matter is that heredity establishes a kind of upper limit to intelligence, a limit that is attainable only under optimal environmental conditions (Weinberg, 1989). A corollary to this proposition is that the higher the hereditarily determined upper limit on a person's intelligence, the greater are the potential effects of environment.

One can discuss heredity and environment as if they were independent influences, but the difficulty of separating their effects has been demonstrated in research by Sandra Scarr and her associates. The sample of individuals in a study by Scarr and Weinberg (1976) consisted of 130 black and racially mixed children who had been adopted into "advantaged" white families but whose biological parents had only average educations. The influence of an advantaged environment was seen in the fact that the adopted children scored above the overall averages for white children on tests of intelligence and achievement. But the influence of heredity was demonstrated by the finding that the biological children of the adoptive parents scored even higher on the tests than the adopted children.

The results of this study indicated that heredity and environment interact in shaping intelligence, but in discussing the findings of a later investigation, Scarr emphasized the importance of the former variable. Summarizing the results obtained in comparing children adopted during the first few months of life with children reared by their natural parents, Scarr drew two conclusions: "(a) individuals differ genetically in ways that affect how much they learn from similar exposures to material, and (b) among whites in this culture there seem to be average genetic differences in IQ and test scores by social class" (Scarr & Yee, 1980, page 20).

## THEORIES OF INTELLIGENCE

Theories of intelligence, or rather theories of intelligent behavior, are based on psychometric, developmental, or information-processing models (Pellegrino & Varnhagen, 1985). The first two of these are traditional approaches, and the last is of more recent origin. The psychometric approach, which has resulted in many tests of intelligence and a variety of statistical methods for analyzing scores on those tests, has stressed individual differences in cognitive abilities and a search for the causes of those differences. The developmental tradition, which stems from research on human developmental psychology, has emphasized uniformities or interindividual similarities in cognitive growth rather than individual differences. The information-processing approach, which stems primarily from research and theory in the physical sciences and their applications to human psychology, emphasizes understanding the brain as an information-processing system or machine that works more efficiently in some people than others. No approach, however, has succeeded in providing a completely satisfactory explanation of how intelligence develops and changes, the causes of individual differences in intelligence, and the specific cognitive and physiological processes that are responsible for intellectual activity.

## Theories Based on Factor Analysis

The statistical technique of factor analysis, which is discussed briefly in Appendix A, was introduced early in this century by the British psychologist–statistician Charles Spearman. Spearman (1927) proposed a two-factor theory of intelligence, which he felt could explain the pattern of correlations among the group of cognitive tests he was analyzing. In its simplest form, the theory stated that performance on any cognitive task depends on a general factor ($g$) plus one or more specific factors ($s_1, s_2, s_3, \ldots, s_n$) unique to the particular task. Two tests that have been viewed as relatively pure measures of Spearman's $g$ factor are the Raven Progressive Matrices and the Culture Fair Intelligence Test (see Chapter 7).

Criticisms of Spearman's two-factor theory have not been lacking, and many alternative factor theories have been proposed. The pioneer American psychologist E. L. Thorndike, for example, formulated a theory and devised a test—the CAVD (the letters stand for completions, arithmetic, vocabulary, and understanding of directions and discourse)—as an expression of his view that intelligence is a composite of many different abilities interconnecting in the brain. One proposal made by Thorndike for three kinds of intelligence (social, concrete, and abstract) was probably the first multifactor theory of cognitive abilities. This theory, however, was not based on the results of factor analyses of ability tests. It remained for L. L. Thurstone and his coworkers to make the first serious assault on Spearman's two-factor theory.

***Thurstone's Primary Mental Abilities***    As a result of applying his *centroid method* of factoring and oblique rotation to the correlations among many different cognitive measures, Thurstone extracted seven important group factors. These *primary mental abilities,* as he labeled them, are as follows:

> *Verbal meaning (V)*: Understanding ideas and word meanings, as measured by vocabulary tests.
>
> *Number (N)*: Speed and accuracy of performing arithmetical computations.
>
> *Space (S)*: The ability to visualize form relationships in three dimensions, as in recognizing figures in different orientations.

*Perceptual speed (P)*: The ability to distinguish visual details and the similarities and differences between pictured objects quickly.

*Word fluency (W)*: Speed in thinking of words, as in making rhymes or in solving anagrams.

*Memory (M)*: The ability to memorize words, numbers, letters, and the like, by rote.

*Inductive reasoning (I)*: The ability to derive a rule from given information, as in determining the rule for a number series from only a part of the series.

Thurstone's multidimensional conception of cognitive abilities established a frame of reference for future factor-analytic research on intelligence in the United States, and his list of seven primary mental abilities was subsequently expanded to approximately 25 (Ekstrom, French, & Harman, 1979). Prominent among these multifactor theorists were J. P. Guilford in the United States and Godfrey Thomson in the United Kingdom. British factor analysts continued to follow Spearman's lead in emphasizing a general intelligence factor (*g*). It is noteworthy that in a further factor analysis of the seven primary mental ability factors Thurstone found evidence of a second-order factor that could be interpreted as *g*. The results of many factor analyses of ability tests in both countries led British psychologists to represent intelligence as a general factor that could be broken down into more specific factors, whereas U.S. psychologists emphasized specific (primary) abilities that could be combined to form more general abilities. This difference became associated with a greater emphasis on general aptitude testing in the United Kingdom as contrasted with differential aptitude testing in the United States.

### Guilford's Structure-of-Intellect Model

Holding the record for the largest number of cognitive factors is J. P. Guilford's model of the structure of intellect (Guilford, 1967; Guilford & Hoepfner, 1971). In what was basically an extension of Thurstone's primary mental abilities theory, Guilford proposed that performance on any cognitive task could best be understood by analyzing it into the kind of mental *operation* or process performed, the type of *content* or test material on which the mental operation is performed, and the resulting *product* of performing a particular operation on a certain type of test content. The original structure-of-intellect model contained 120 different factors, which were assumed to be independent and for which Guilford and his associates attempted to design separate tests. A modification of the original model conceptualized intelligence as consisting of five possible kinds of *operation* (cognition, memory, divergent thinking, convergent thinking, and evaluation), five types of *content* (figural—auditory and visual, symbolic, semantic, and behavioral), and six *products* (units, classes, relations, systems, transformations, and implications). This implied the existence of $5 \times 5 \times 6 = 150$ possible intellectual tasks comprising the structure of intellect. Although he initially assumed that these 150 factors were independent of each other, research failed to support this assumption (Kelderman, Mellenberg, & Elshout, 1981). Guilford subsequently replaced the modified structure-of-intellect model of intelligence with a hierarchical ability model consisting of 150 first-order factors, 85 second-order factors, and 16 third-order factors (Guilford, 1981, 1985). This last model has not been thoroughly evaluated by research, but Brody (1992) concluded that it is not an acceptable alternative to a hierarchical model that includes a general (*g*) factor at the apex.

Other factor-analytic models of intelligence have been proposed, but none of them is considered totally satisfactory. An effort to combine the results of the various factorial conceptions of cognitive abilities into a logical whole is represented by Philip Vernon's hierarchical model, which has been more popular than the complex multifactor approach of Guilford.

***Vernon's Hierarchical Model***    Figure 8–2 is a diagram of the hierarchical, tree-shaped model of mental abilities proposed by Vernon (1960). A general cognitive factor (*g*) is at the top of the hierarchy, with two major group factors, verbal–educational (*v:ed*) and practical–mechanical–spatial (*k:m*), at the next level. The *v:ed* and *k:m* factors are broken down further into a number of minor group factors. For example, *v:ed* comprises abilities such as verbal fluency, numerical ability, and perhaps creativity. Some of the minor group factors under *k:m* are mechanical comprehension, psychomotor ability, and spatial relations. And at the bottom of the hierarchy are factors that are specific to particular tests.

In this hierarchical model of intelligence, the higher a factor is on the tree, the broader it is or the wider the range of behaviors it encompasses. Consequently, Vernon's model retains Spearman's general intelligence factor while relegating Thurstone's primary mental abilities and Guilford's structure-of-intellect factors to a subordinate status under *g*. Vernon's hierarchy is a plausible way of combining the findings and interpretations of various factor-analytic studies into a single theory.

***Cattell's Fluid and Crystallized Intelligences***    Donald Hebb (1949) distinguished between *intelligence A,* the portion of overall intelligence due to heredity, and *intelligence B,* the portion due to environment. Related to Hebb's distinction is R. B. Cattell's (1963) theory that general intelligence is composed of two "major general" factors: *fluid intelligence* (*g_f*) and *crystallized intelligence* (*g_c*). Cattell viewed these two types of intelligence as distinct but correlated. Both entail the ability to perceive relationships, but fluid intelligence is more biologically or genetically determined and consequently more nonverbal or culture free. Compared with crystallized intelligence, fluid intelligence changes less over

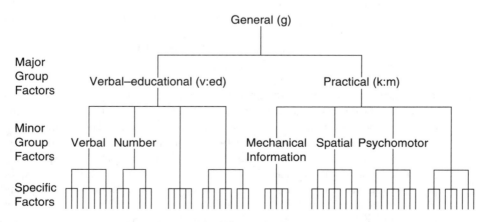

**FIGURE 8–2**    Vernon's Hierarchical Model of Intellectual Abilities.
(After Vernon, 1960, page 22. Reprinted with permission of Routledge.)

short time periods and is more adversely affected by brain injury. It is involved in many different areas of endeavor, being applied more extensively on tasks requiring adaptation to new situations. On the other hand, crystallized intelligence, which develops from the application of fluid intelligence to a specific environmental or cultural context, is used more on tasks where habits have become fixed.

As measured by culture-fair tests such as the Raven Progressive Matrices and the Culture Fair Intelligence Test, fluid intelligence appears to peak at around age 14 or 15. Crystallized intelligence, however, continues developing until age 25 or 30. The Stanford–Binet Intelligence Scale and similar scholastic-type intelligence tests are considered better measures of crystallized than fluid intelligence.

Like Vernon's hierarchical model, Cattell's theory of fluid and crystallized abilities is a compromise between the theories of Spearman and Thurstone. From his extensive factor analyses of cognitive abilities tests, Cattell also found three less general factors: visual abilities $(g_v)$, memory retrieval $(g_r)$, and performance speed $(g_s)$. Cattell's theory, as extended by Horn (1979), depicts numerous oblique factors comprising fluid and crystallized intelligence. A person's standing on 20 of these factors is assessed by the Comprehensive Ability Battery.

## Piaget's Theory of Cognitive Development

Research and theorizing on the nature and origins of intellectual abilities have not been limited to factor analysts and other psychometric psychologists. Experimental and developmental psychologists, as well as professionals in other disciplines, have formulated ideas concerning the development of learning, thinking, problem solving, and other cognitive processes. Illustrative of these efforts is Jean Piaget's theory of cognitive development.

Jean Piaget's writings, which are a source of many observations and speculations pertaining to child development, represent more than a theory of intellectual growth. Piaget was both an epistemologist and a psychologist: his writings are concerned not only with intelligence, but also with the question of how human beings acquire knowledge and understanding about the world in which they live. In Piaget's epistemology, children are depicted as active, interacting scientists who are constantly striving to make sense out of their experiences by organizing them, constructing hypotheses, and testing these hypotheses against their experiences. As a result, they generate practical knowledge that can be applied to future interactions with the environment.

***Assimilation and Accommodation***    According to Piaget, a child comes to know and understand the environment by interacting with it and adapting to it, a process referred to as *adaptation* or *equilibration*. Equilibration involves both assimilation and accommodation. *Assimilation* consists of fitting new experiences into preexisting mental structures (*schemata*), and *accommodation* is the modification of these schemata as a result of experience.

Young children assimilate whenever they take in or use (grasp, suck, explore, shake, probe, and so on) the environment. For example, when an infant tries to use one hand to grasp a glass container after having just grasped a rattle with that hand, he or she is attempting to assimilate the glass into a preexisting schema for grasping. If the infant is unsuccessful in grasping the glass with one hand, that behavior will have to be modified by using both hands.

The process of accommodation occurs whenever the environment resists, moves, hurts, rewards, punishes, or, in other words, *reacts*. As the child matures, the grasping schema and other mental structures and the associated patterns of behavior are elaborated and refined in response to experience. Thus, an intelligent adult might be forced to modify his schema of pacifism when physically attacked. Finally, the tendency to combine elementary schemata into higher-order, integrated schemata is referred to as *organization*.

***Periods of Intellectual Development***    Piaget maintained that cognitive growth, which takes place by the actions of assimilation and accommodation in the external world, occurs in a sequence of four stages or periods. These stages constitute a hierarchy of development in that successful equilibrations in preceding stages are necessary for an individual to progress to succeeding ones. During the first stage (*sensorimotor period*), which occurs between birth and 2 years of age, the child learns to exercise simple reflexes and coordinate various perceptions. In the second stage (*preoperational period*), between ages 2 and 7, the child acquires language and other symbolic representations of reality; this is a concrete, egocentric period of development. During the stage of *concrete operations,* between 7 and 11 years, the child develops organized systems of operations by the process of social interaction, with a corresponding reduction in self-centeredness. A child has reached the final stage of cognitive development, that of *formal operations* (ages 11 to 15 years), when he or she can use logic and verbal reasoning and perform higher-level, more abstract operations.

The sequence of four periods is normally completed by age 15, and what increases thereafter is not intelligence but achievement. In Piaget's system, intelligence, which he defined as the ability to solve new problems, supposedly declines slowly after age 15. For Piaget, the terminal age of intellectual growth is the same age as that at which Cattell maintains that fluid intelligence is normally fully developed.

Although Piaget's theorizing has been more influential in educational planning and remediation than in the design of tests to predict academic performance or to assess cognitive disorders, a number of tests have been devised within the Piagetian framework. The major purpose of these instruments has been to determine a child's stage of cognitive development or the extent to which the child possesses one of the several mental processes described by Piaget: object permanence, operational causality, object relations in space, schemata development, means-end relations, and imitation. Among the more general-purpose instruments designed for these purposes are the Ordinal Scales of Psychological Development (Uzgiris & Hunt, 1975) and the Piaget Task Kit. A test designed with the more limited aim of determining the degree to which young children understand the physical principle of conservation is the Concept Assessment Kit–Conservation. Another test within a Piagetian framework, the Cognitive Diagnostic Battery, was designed for a specific population—psychiatric patients. These and other Piagetian assessment devices are discussed in some detail by Clarizio (1982).

## Information-processing Models and Theories

The rapid development of computer technology and communication systems during the past few years has led to a reevaluation and reconceptualization of the human brain as a kind of computing machine that operates similarly to a computer. Research in neurophysiology and cognitive psychology has also contributed to these *information-processing models* of human problem solving and thinking. The models are concerned with identifying the processes or operations by which information is encoded, stored, retrieved, and utilized by the brain in performing cognitive tasks like those on intelligence tests.

Rather than conceptualizing intelligence as a complex of mental structures or factors or as developing through a series of stages at which different cognitive strategies are preferred, information-processing theorists attempt to provide a detailed, exhaustive description of the steps involved in solving a problem. In addition to using data obtained from traditional correlational studies of individual differences, these theorists apply the findings of laboratory investigations of learning, thinking, and problem solving to develop and confirm theoretical propositions. Applying the functionally oriented language of representations, strategies (planning, monitoring, shifting, and the like), and processes, the goal of many information-processing theories is to simulate human cognitive performance on a computer and describe the cognitive processes in computer-oriented language.

Computer models of thinking and problem solving view the human brain as an information-processing system having a large storage capacity. The storage contains, among other things, complex programs or strategies that can be evoked by particular stimulus inputs. In these models, intelligence is analyzed in terms of variables such as storage capacity, speed of performing basic operations, and speed of access to storage, in addition to the number, variety, and complexity of programs on file in storage. An example of this kind of theorizing is the general information-processing model, or communication system for problem solving (SIPS), based on concepts provided by information theory and Guilford's structure-of-intellect model (Guilford & Tenopyr, 1968). Unfortunately, efforts to develop a realistic, workable computer model of human intellectual functioning have not been very successful. As Vernon (1979) pointed out, it is extremely difficult to observe and measure the various stages or processes between the input and output of an information-processing system (initial filtering, short-term rehearsal, chunking, coding, and long-term storage, retrieval, and decoding). Intelligence is involved in all of these stages, as well as in controlling strategies derived from past experience.

Two mental processes that have been the subjects of theory and research on human information processing are attention and processing speed. Research on attention has been concerned with such questions as whether more intelligent people are able to mobilize and distribute their attention better than less intelligent people. For example, can more intelligent individuals shift their attention better than the less intelligent when presented with two tasks at the same time? Although there is still some controversy over whether attention is a motivational rather than a cognitive variable, the results of a number of studies indicate that individuals with higher intelligence are more flexible in their attentiveness and can mobilize a greater amount of attention in performing a task (Eysenck, 1987; Hunt, 1980; Hunt & Lansman, 1983; Larson and Saccuzzo, 1989).

Another variable that has been studied from an information-processing perspective is processing speed. A fundamental question here is whether the brains of people of high intelligence process information faster than those of low intelligence. Research has found small positive correlations between response time in performing mental tasks and measures of nonverbal intelligence (Carlson, Jensen, & Widaman, 1983; Vernon, 1987). Hunt (1983, 1987) also determined that speed of performing tasks requiring rapid access to memory is only modestly related to scores on reasoning and general comprehension tests. From these results it would appear that processing speed plays a relatively minor role in intelligent behavior.

**The PASS Model**   Attentional processes have been incorporated in the PASS (planning–attention–simultaneous processing–successive processing) model for intelligence (Das, Naglieri, & Kirby, 1994). PASS is based on Aleksandr Luria's theory that the cognitive activity of the human brain is divided into three functional units. The *first functional unit,* which is considered to be associated with the upper brain stem and the limbic system, is concerned with arousal or attention and discrimination among stimuli. Although not responsible for receiving and analyzing information, this unit is crucial to cognitive processing because it provides a general state of readiness and a focus of attention. The *second functional unit,* thought to be associated with the posterior regions of the cerebral hemispheres, including the visual (occipital), auditory (temporal), and general sensory (parietal) areas, is concerned with the reception, elaboration, and storage of information by means of simultaneous and successive processing. The *third functional unit,* associated with anterior parts of the cerebral hemispheres, particularly the prefrontal region, is responsible for the programming, regulation, and verification of cognitive activity. This unit regulates the activities of the first functional unit so that behavior will be consistent with the individual's conscious goals and motives. In summary, the first functional unit is said to be responsible for arousal and attention; the second for reception, analysis, and storage using simultaneous and successive reasoning processes, and the third for planning, regulating, and verifying mental activity. Both input and output may be serial or concurrent.

A diagram of the PASS cognitive processing model is given in Figure 8–3. As shown in the diagram, the model conceptualizes the three functional units of Luria's theory as operating on the individual's knowledge base. The knowledge base consists of all the information, in both long- and short-term memory, that is available to the individual at processing time. For processing to be effective, this knowledge base must be integrated with the *planning* (third functional unit), arousal/attention (first functional unit), and *simultaneous and successive* processes (second functional unit) as they are demanded by the particular task. The result of processing, or *output,* involves speaking, writing, or other motoric activities.

**Sternberg's Theories**   Another illustration of a theory of intelligence within the information-processing camp is Sternberg's triarchic theory. According to Sternberg (1982), mental components, or cognitive processes for operating on information and solving problems, fall into five classes: metacomponents, performance components, acquisition components, retention components, and transfer components. The metacomponent processes involved in problem solving are used for executive planning and decision making. The decisions and plans made through the operation of these metacomponent processes are implemented by performance component processes, and learning of new information occurs through acquisition component processes. The retrieval of information that is stored in memory is carried out by retention components, and the carrying over of retained information from one situation to another is effected by transfer components.

Among the many components constituting intelligence in Sternberg's framework, two of the performance component processes, encoding and comparing, are critical to effective problem solving. In *encoding,* the examinee forms a mental representation of the essential elements of a problem. The encoded representations are then *compared* to find an answer.

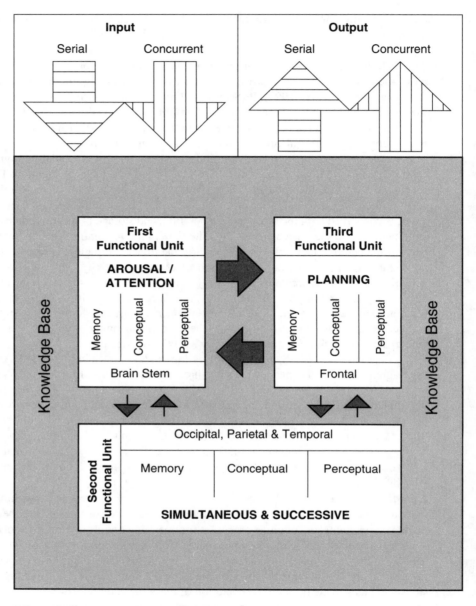

**FIGURE 8–3**  The PASS Model of Ability.
(From Das, Naglieri, & Kirby, 1994, page 21. Reprinted with permission.)

People who are able to encode and compare rapidly are more intelligent than those who require more time to carry out these processes.

Unlike the structural approach of factor-analytic models of intelligence, the component process approach provides a more functional analysis of the processes involved in problem solving. However, like traditional psychometric procedures, the emphasis is on diagnosis and remediation. Thus, an analysis of the component processes involved in a person's attack on specific problems results in a diagnostic profile of his or her strengths and weaknesses in the various components. Poor strategy selection points to a metacomponent deficiency, inaccurate recall of relevant information reveals a retention component deficiency, and poor ability to generalize learned approaches to problem solving indicates a transfer component deficiency.

Sternberg revised and expanded his component process theory to include two subtheories in addition to the componential subtheory: an experiential subtheory and a contextual subtheory. In this *triarchic theory,* the componential subtheory was somewhat condensed to include metacomponents, performance components, and knowledge-acquisition components. The second part of the triarchic theory, the experiential subtheory, is concerned with the ability to formulate new ideas by combining seemingly unrelated facts or information. A high standing on this dimension indicates good ability at identifying critical information and combining seemingly unrelated facts. The third part of the theory, the contextual subtheory, is concerned with the ability to adapt to changing environmental conditions and to shape the environment in such a way that one's strengths are maximized and one's weaknesses are compensated for. A high standing on the contextual dimension indicates high practical intelligence.

In an even later modification of his theory, Sternberg proposed the concept of *mental self-government,* which represents an attempt to combine the concept of intelligence with that of personality (Sternberg, 1988, 1989). The ways in which the three types of intelligence delineated by the triarchic theory—componential, experiential, and contextual—are brought to bear in solving everyday problems are characterized in this theory as *intellectual styles.* Whether a particular intellectual style works is said to depend on the extent to which it matches the person's intellectual ability, his or her preferred style, and the nature of the immediate problem to be solved. Like most theories of intelligence, Sternberg's triarchic theory is supported to some extent by the data (Sternberg, 1985, 1986), but it is by no means the final theory of intelligence or cognition.

## Gardner's Theory of Multiple Intelligences

Other theoretical approaches to intelligence have attempted to combine the results of research on individual differences with both factor-analytic and information-processing models. For example, Gardner (1983) takes a *symbol systems* approach. He maintains that the distinctiveness of human cognition and information processing involves the deployment of various symbol systems, which are characteristic forms of perception, memory, and learning. Thus, a person may be good in language, but not at music, manipulation of the spatial environment, or interpersonal interactions.

Elaborating on the symbol systems that humans employ, Gardner makes a case for seven forms of intelligence: linguistic, logical–mathematical, spatial, musical, bodily kinesthetic, and two forms of personal intelligence (intrapersonal and interpersonal). The first three forms on this list are measured by conventional intelligence tests, but the last four seem more like special aptitudes than intelligences. Bodily kinesthetic intelligence is seen more in athletes, craftspeople, dancers, and surgeons. Spatial intelligence is needed by sculptors and surveys, and musical intelligence by composers, musicians, and singers. The two personal intelligences are interpersonal intelligence—being able to detect the moods of other people and to lead them—and intrapersonal intelligence—knowledge of one's own feelings and understanding how to use that self-knowledge productively.

Defining intelligence as the "ability to solve problems or to create products which are valued in one or more cultural settings," Gardner emphasizes the findings of cross-cultural research to document the role of cultural values in determining the intellectual competencies developed by humans. Linguistic and logical–mathematical intelligences are most highly valued in Western culture, bodily kinesthetic intelligence is more important in hunting cultures, and interpersonal intelligence is very important in highly ordered societies such as the Japanese. Spatial, bodily kinesthetic, and interpersonal intelligences have been more valued in apprenticeship systems, and linguistic and intrapersonal intelligences were most esteemed in old-fashioned religious schools.

Gardner finds support for his theory of multiple intelligences in a variety of sources, including research in biology. He points out that injury to a particular area of the brain does not affect all mental abilities equally. Damage to the left cerebral hemisphere has a pronounced effect on linguistic intelligence, but little if any effect on musical, spatial, or interpersonal intelligence. Damage to the right cerebral hemisphere affects musical, spatial, and interpersonal intelligences, but leaves linguistic intelligence intact. A patient who has become totally aphasic as a result of left hemisphere damage, and hence can hardly speak or understand, may still be able to draw, sing, or even compose music well. It appears that the brain is wired differently for musical sounds and therefore analyzes them in a different way from linguistic sounds.

Gardner also draws on research with children to demonstrate the independence of the seven intelligences. For example, a child's artistic ability is not related to his or her ability with language, logic, or dealing with people. The developmental basis of the theory is seen in the hypothesis that the forms of the seven intelligences change from infancy to old age. Logical–mathematical intelligence, for example, is said to decline fairly rapidly with age, whereas interpersonal intelligence shows a smaller age-related decrement.

Gardner's theory of multiple intelligences, although not based as completely on the results of factor analysis, is a structure-of-intellect model rather than a process theory, such as Sternberg's triarchic conceptualization. The theory has enjoyed wide popularity, especially among educators, but Gardner's ideas are based more on reasoning and intuition than on the results of empirical research studies. With respect to criticisms of the theory, Brody (1992) argues that the list of seven intelligences is arbitrary and that the omission of a general intelligence factor is simply wrong.

So which theory is correct? Probably all of them are right to some extent, but certainly none of them is completely correct. For the present, it seems that information-processing theories offer the best chance for a logical and empirically based conception of cognitive abilities, but the situation could change. In any event, one thing is certain: other theories of intelligence will be forthcoming, and their value will be determined by their effectiveness in predicting and explaining human learning and thinking.

## SUMMARY

Given a relatively stable home environment, adequate nutrition, and appropriate educational experiences, the IQ score of an individual remains fairly stable after early childhood. The results of cross-sectional studies depict intelligence as rising into young adulthood and then declining gradually into old age; longitudinal studies find less decline with age. The rate of decline, or even rise in some cases, is a function of the kinds of activities engaged in by individuals throughout their lifetime; people who continue to pursue intellectual activities show less intellectual decline. The question of whether intelligence declines abruptly in the last weeks or months before death in old age, the *terminal drop,* has not been answered satisfactorily.

Larger family size is associated with lower average IQs, and first-born children tend to be intellectually superior to later-borns. Occupational status and socioeconomic status are positively correlated with each other and with intelligence, but it is not clear whether the advantages of higher social-class membership result in children with higher IQs or whether both higher IQs and higher social position are consequences of genetic factors. Other demographic variables associated with IQ scores are urban versus rural residence, educational level, nationality, and ethnicity. With respect to education, teachers' attitudes concerning what children are capable of achieving (teacher expectations) may also play a role in whether a child fulfills his or her potential.

No specific area in the brain has been found that can be considered the seat of intelligence. However, research on cerebral localization of cognitive functions has found that certain structures play important roles in higher-order mental processes.

Studies have revealed no consistent gender differences in general mental ability, but each sex tends to be superior to the other in certain specific abilities. Girls are better at rote memory, language-type tasks, perceptual speed and accuracy, and numerical computations. Boys are better in mathematical reasoning, visuo-spatial ability, mechanical ability, and speed and coordination of large bodily movements. The physiological bases of these differences are not well understood; they appear to be related to differences in the development and functioning of the left and right hemispheres of the brain.

Various hormones and drugs have been found to be related to mental abilities, but a pill guaranteed to improve memory or learning ability has not been discovered. When chemical substances have an effect on mental abilities, in many instances they do so by improving motivation or general health rather than abilities. Malnutrition, especially during the late prenatal or early postnatal period, can result in lower IQs. In addition, certain genetically based disorders (PKU, Tay–Sachs disease, and galactosemia, for example) associated with low IQs can be treated with special diets if detected soon enough.

Of the various issues and controversies surrounding intelligence testing for a good part of this century, the most debated has concerned the relative contributions of heredity and environment in shaping cognitive abilities. Evidence from dozens of investigations underscores the relationship of heredity to general mental ability, while not denying that both heredity and environment are important and interactive in their effects on intelligent behavior. This issue has been particularly controversial because of its association with the question of racial differences in intelligence.

Although the findings of numerous investigations have led to the conclusion that in an assortatively mating population the heritability coefficient (proportion of variance in the intelligence test scores of the general population accounted for by heredity) is as high as .70, it is also clear that the biological and psychosocial environments have important influences on intelligence.

Among the theories or models of cognitive abilities stemming from the results of factor analyses are Spearman's two-factor theory (consisting of a general factor plus several specific factors for each test), Thurstone's multifactor theory of seven primary mental abilities, Guilford's structure-of-intellect model, and Vernon's hierarchical model. Vernon's model consists of a general factor at the first level, verbal–educational and practical–

mechanical–spatial factors at a second level, and a number of minor group factors at a third level.

Cattell's theory of two kinds of intelligence, fluid and crystallized, is also based on the results of factor analysis and is related to Hebb's intelligence A and intelligence B. The relative roles of heredity and environment in differentiating factors of intellect are not clear, although Cattell's fluid intelligence is considered to be more genetically determined, and his crystallized ability is the result of fluid ability acting on the environment.

Another influential theory of the development and functioning of intellectual abilities is Piaget's conception that cognition develops from the actions of assimilation and accommodation on the external world. By interacting with the environment, the growing child creates schemata, or mental structures, to serve as explanatory maps and guides to behavior. In the development of cognition, children normally mature intellectually through a series of progressive stages: sensorimotor, preoperational, concrete operational, and formal operational. Piaget believed that the growth of intelligence ceases at around age 15, but a number of researchers have taken issue with this assertion.

Information-processing models of problem solving and thinking are concerned with identifying the mental processes or operations by which the brain deals with stimulus input in learning and thinking. Research on attention and processing speed has received particular emphasis from an information-processing perspective.

The PASS (planning, attention, simultaneous processing, successive processing) model of intelligence is based on Luria's theory that cognitive activity in the brain is describable in terms of three functional units. The validity of PASS and a test battery developed from the theory are still under scrutiny.

In his component process approach to intelligence, Sternberg conceptualizes the brain as an information-processing (and problem-solving) organ. He initially hypothesized five classes of component processes by which the brain operates on information and solves problems. Among the various components in these five classes, encoding and comparing are especially critical for effective problem solving. In an extension of his component process theory, Sternberg proposed a triarchic theory that includes three subtheories: a componential subtheory, an experiential subtheory, and a contextual subtheory. In the notion of mental self-government, Sternberg has tried to combine the concepts of intelligence and personality; he describes how different intellectual styles lead to different methods of solving everyday problems.

Gardner's proposal that there are many different kinds of intelligence is reminiscent of factor theories, but it actually owes more of a debt to Piaget and information-processing models of intellect. Gardner makes a case for seven forms of intelligence: linguistic, logical–mathematical, spatial, musical, bodily kinesthetic, interpersonal, and intrapersonal. He argues that Western culture has overemphasized the first two forms, but in many societies and circumstances the other five forms of intelligence are more important and highly valued.

## QUESTIONS AND ACTIVITIES

1. What demographic variables are related to scores on intelligence tests? Which of these variables appear to be the most important? Which have a causal relationship to intelligence?

2. What biological factors have been shown to affect intelligence? Which of these are the most important?

3. Design a study to test the hypothesis that there is no significant difference between the mean IQs of blacks and whites. Don't be concerned so much with the feasibility of the study, but make certain that as many extraneous (confounded) variables as possible are controlled.

4. The data in Table 8–1 indicate that the median correlation between the IQs of same-sex dizygotic twins reared together is .60, and the median correlation between the IQs of monozygotic twins reared together is .85. A suggested formula for computing the heritability coefficient is

$$h^2 = 2\,(r_m - r_d)$$

where $r_m$ is the correlation between the IQs of monozygotic twins and $r_d$ is the correlation between the IQs of same-sex dizygotic twins reared together. Use this formula to compute $h^2$ and interpret the result.

5. Is there a difference between "practical" and "academic" intelligence? How would you go about designing a test of "practical intelligence"?

6. What implications do Piaget's theory of cognitive development and Gardner's theory of multiple intelligence have for teaching and other educational practices?

7. Compare the theories of Robert Sternberg and Howard Gardner in terms of their (a) reasonableness, (b) consistency with research findings, (c) practical utility, and (d) social responsibility. Defend your choice.

8. What implications does the conceptualization of the human brain as an information-processing system have for theories of intelligence and the design of intelligence tests?

# 9

# TESTING SPECIAL
# ABILITIES

The term *aptitude* has traditionally been defined as the ability to profit from education or training in a designated field, whereas *achievement* refers to the degree of ability already attained. The measurement of aptitude focuses on the future, the measurement of achievement on the past. Thus, aptitude tests have been devised primarily to assess potential achievement or to predict future performance in some field of endeavor.

A person's aptitudes are assessed for purposes of academic and occupational counseling and placement. With aptitude test information in hand, a counselor or placement director should be able to do a better job of advising people or placing them in the appropriate programs of education and training or in suitable occupations.

## CONCEPTS AND CHARACTERISTICS

When they first appeared during the 1920s, tests of special aptitudes were viewed as measures of specific innate or hereditary talents not based on experience. In a sense, the term *aptitude* is a misnomer if it is meant to imply that what is being measured is an inborn, unchangeable characteristic. Early mental testers did aspire to measure hereditary characteristics, for they assumed that all people whom they examined had equal opportunities to learn the material on which the tests were based. This assumption, however, was incorrect: learning opportunities are never exactly the same for different people, particularly people of different social classes or cultures.

Today it is recognized that aptitude tests are actually measures of achievement, a complex product of the interaction between hereditary and environmental influences. Conversely, if *aptitude test* designates a psychometric instrument that can predict future accomplishment, then achievement tests that predict school marks and other performance criteria also qualify as measures of aptitude.

Because of confusion over the difference between aptitude and achievement, it has been recommended that the terms be replaced with the single term *ability*. Then, depending on the purpose for which it is used—to assess current knowledge and understanding or to predict future performance—a test of ability could be either a measure of achievement or aptitude.

It would be a mistake, however, to assume that the distinction between aptitude and achievement is inconsequential. As an illustration of the functional difference between measures of these two variables, consider the results of a study by Carroll (1973). It was found that performance in a foreign language course by students whose precourse scores on a foreign language achievement test were zero could be predicted from their scores on a test of aptitude for learning foreign languages. At the end of the course, the two tests were read-ministered. As would be expected if the training had improved achievement but had not affected aptitude, scores on the achievement test increased significantly but aptitude test scores remained essentially unchanged.

## General and Specific Abilities

The intelligence tests discussed in Chapters 7 and 8 are measures of *general* aptitude, in that scores on these tests represent a composite of cognitive abilities and can be used to forecast achievement and other behaviors in a wide range of situations. In fact, scores on general intelligence tests are often better predictors of success in educational and employment situations than are combined scores on measures of special abilities. But the fact that general intelligence tests measure a hodgepodge of specific aptitudes or abilities is a two-edged sword. In this fact lie both the strength and weakness of these kinds of tests.

Intelligence tests measure an assortment of abilities and hence they have what Cronbach (1970) referred to as broad *bandwidth*. Because of their broadness, these tests have proved moderately effective in predicting various criteria. A longer test of one of the special abilities measured by an intelligence test, that is, an instrument with a narrower bandwidth, would have greater *fidelity*. In other words, it would measure whatever it measures more precisely and do a better job of predicting a narrower range of criteria.

Having noted the significant positive correlations among measures of special abilities, Vernon (1960) concluded that general intelligence is more important than special abilities in determining occupational success. Correlations among tests of special abilities are, however, not particularly high, since people often perform much better on some kinds of tasks than others. Whether performance varies because of differences in work motivation or differences in the special abilities required by certain occupations, or both, is arguable.

## Origins of Vocational Testing

One of the events that stimulated the development of tests of special abilities during the first half of this century was the growth of *scientific management*. Proponents of scientific management in business and industry felt that both employees and employers would benefit if psychological tests could be devised to help match people to jobs. Employees would be selected for and placed on jobs they could perform more effectively, and hence they would be more productive and thereby earn higher wages. Similarly, the selection of more competent employees and placement of them on jobs for which they were best suited would benefit employers by improving production efficiency.

During the Great Depression years of the 1930s, when matters related to employment (or, rather, unemployment!) became of great concern to government, research and development programs at the University of Minnesota and elsewhere resulted in the construction of a series of special abilities tests for use in vocational counseling and in employee selection and placement. From these programs and subsequent efforts came not only numerous single-ability measures, but also several batteries of tests.

## Validity of Special Abilities Tests

Because aptitude tests are designed with differential prediction in mind, it is reasonable to ask how successful they are in predicting who will succeed and who will fail in particular occupations or job training programs. That is, just how valid are vocational aptitude tests? The answer is that, in general, the validities of these tests are not very high. Ghiselli's (1973) summary of the average validity coefficients of different kinds of aptitude tests used to predict performance in various job categories revealed that the coefficients are typically in the .20s and almost never above the .30s. These very modest coefficients underscore the limitations of tests of special abilities for predicting performance on the job. Despite their limitations, such tests can still assist in determining what occupation or training program is most suitable for a given person. The tests are certainly limited when used alone, but their value increases when the scores are combined with other kinds of information about the person.

Even the relatively modest validity coefficients of most special abilities tests are not fixed: they vary with the nature of the criterion, the situation, and the people being examined. For example, a validity coefficient is likely to be higher when a test is validated against grades in a training program than when validated against ratings of actual on-the-job performance. A validity coefficient also tends to be higher when the test is administered and the criterion data collected fairly close together in time than when there is a long delay between administration of the test administration and collection of the criterion data.

Situational variability in the validity coefficient is seen when the correlation between scores on an ability test and ratings of job performance are lower in one manufacturing or service organization than another. Validity also varies with the characteristics of the people who are tested. It may depend on the sex, ethnicity, and socioeconomic status of the examinees, as well as their vocational interests, motivation, and personality characteristics. Such individual and group differences influence, or moderate, the correlation between a test and a criterion measure and are therefore referred to as *moderator variables*.

The fact that the magnitude of a validity coefficient depends on the criterion, the situation, and the group tested underscores the wisdom of validating a test against the specific criterion, in the specific situation in which it is to be used, and with a representative sample of the population to which it is intended to be administered. Although many vocational aptitude tests have significant validity coefficients in a variety of situations or contexts (Schmidt & Hunter, 1977, 1981), it is frequently wise, from both an economic and a legal standpoint, to collect additional validity evidence when a test is used in a new situation.

Organizations are like people in that they desire not only to survive but to grow; in fact, in our dynamic society organizations must grow or, in the long run, they will die. Consequently, from the perspective of the organization an important factor in deciding whether to use a specific test in selecting, placing, or promoting personnel is whether the test contributes to the economic well-being of the organization. The cost of administering the test must be weighed against the benefits to the organization from using it, and studies of the validity of the test can contribute to measuring those benefits. Not only should a test be a valid predictor of job performance, it should be an independently valid predictor. Why use the test if other, cheaper methods of identifying good workers and predicting how they will perform are available? Still, economic benefit to the organization is not the only reason for determining how valid a test is for a specific purpose in a specific situation. An important legal reason for conducting validity studies in business and industry centers on the question of bias or fairness. For example, it may be that the test-criterion correlation is significantly higher with one ethnic group than another. If so, it is unfair to use the same prediction equation with both groups. The *fairness,* or relative freedom from bias, of the test must be demonstrated if it is to be used for selection or classification purposes.

## Performance versus Paper-and-Pencil Tests

The first measures of special abilities to be devised were performance tests that required examinees to construct something or manipulate physical objects in certain ways. These "apparatus" tests are frequently more interesting than paper-and-pencil tests, especially to examinees who have reading problems. But the reliabilities of speeded performance tests are typically lower than those of comparable paper-and-pencil tests, and the tests are time consuming and expensive to administer. Furthermore, correlations between scores on performance tests and paper-and-pencil measures of the same ability are far from perfect. Despite the shortcomings of performance tests, *work-sample tests* (or *job-replica tests*), which require examinees to complete a sample of tasks similar to those comprising a certain job, are among the most useful measures of ability in specific occupational contexts.

## In-basket Technique and the Assessment Center

An interesting example of a work-sample test is the *in-basket technique.* This procedure was originally devised as a job-replica test for school administrators, but it was used subsequently in evaluating other kinds of administrators and executives as well. Candidates for an administrative position are presented with samples of items of the sort typically found in an administrator's in-basket (letters, memos, notes, directives, reports, telephone messages, FAXs) requiring some kind of action. They are asked to indicate what action should be taken on each item, and their responses are evaluated according to experts' judgments of the type of administrative response deemed most appropriate.

The assessment center approach, which was introduced by the American Telephone and Telegraph Company in the 1950s, combines the in-basket technique with other simulation tasks, such as management games and group problem-solving exercises (as in the Leaderless Group Discussion Test). Interviews, psychological tests, and other methods of appraisal are also used in this approach. The assessment center has been employed less as a selection technique than as a means of evaluating managerial-level personnel for promotion and classification. Six to twelve candidates are brought to a specific location, where they are observed and assessed by other executives and by each other for several days. The principal criteria on which the candidates are evaluated are degree of active participation, organizational skills, and decision-making ability.

Because the in-basket technique and other simulation tasks are realistic, it might seem that they would be highly valid. The candidates, however, are aware of being "on stage," as it were, and may role play or in other ways act differently from how they would in an actual administrative situation. Expense and time constraints also prohibit using such simulation techniques for anything other than the assessment of fairly high level managerial personnel.

## SENSORY-PERCEPTUAL AND PSYCHOMOTOR SKILLS TESTS

Although strictly speaking they are not mental tests, tests of sensory-perceptual and psychomotor skills are important sources of information on the ability of a person to perform certain work-related tasks. There is little relationship between mental and physical abilities, but task performance may depend as much on the latter as the former. Test of sensory-perceptual and psychomotor abilities are useful as screening devices in the selection, placement, and classification of employees and military personnel for jobs or training programs, as well as in vocational and educational diagnosis and counseling.

### Sensory-Perceptual Tests

Performance in school or on the job is obviously affected by vision and hearing, so most educational and work organizations make arrangements for determining the presence of visual and auditory defects. Sensory screening tests are typically administered once a year in the elementary school grades, followed by a more thorough examination of children with sensory deficits. In addition, for reasons of safety and proficiency, tests of vision and hearing are administered periodically on many business, industrial, and government jobs. Complementing the simple screening instruments that measure a single visual or auditory function are more complex instruments for assessing several different sensory and perceptual functions.

***Illustrative Single-purpose Instruments***   A single-purpose instrument measures only one function. There are separate single-purpose screening instruments for determining visual acuity, auditory acuity, color vision, and certain other sensory-perceptual functions.

*Visual Acuity*   One of the oldest instruments for measuring visual acuity at a distance is the *Snellen wall chart*. This chart is illustrated in Figure 9–1, but the illustration is actually much smaller than a standard Snellen chart. The standard testing situation requires the examinee to stand 20 feet in front of the chart and read the smallest row of letters that he or she can see clearly, first with one eye and then the other. If the row of letters is one that a person with normal eyes can read at 20 feet (row 7 in Figure 9–1), then visual acuity in that eye is expressed as 20/20. If the smallest line the examinee can read at 20 feet is one that people with normal vision can read at 40 feet (row 5), then the former's visual acuity is 20/40. If the smallest line the examinee can read at 20 feet is one that people with normal vision can read only by moving up to 15 feet (row 8), then visual acuity in that eye is 20/15. Thus, a ratio under 1.00 indicates poorer-than-normal visual acuity, while a ratio over 1.00 indicates better-than-normal visual acuity.

*Auditory Acuity*   A crude assessment of auditory acuity can be made with a "dollar watch"; depending on how quiet the room is, a person with normal hearing should be

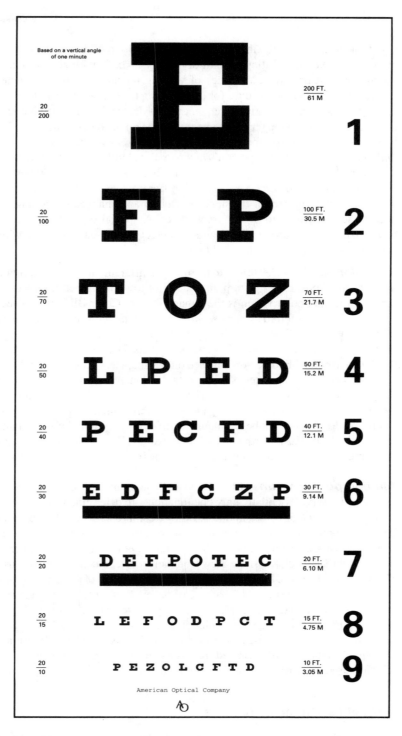

**FIGURE 9–1** Snellen Chart.
(Reproduced by permission of American Optical Corporation.)

able to hear the watch ticking from a distance of 30 to 40 inches from the ear. However, a more accurate determination of auditory acuity is made with an *audiometer*, an electronic instrument that presents pure tones of varying intensities and frequencies in the normal range of hearing. The procedure for determining the hearing threshold in each ear is to present a series of tones of a given frequency, first decreasing and then increasing in intensity, until the person is no longer able to hear the tone on the decreasing intensity series or is just barely able to hear it on the increasing intensity series. The results may be plotted as an *audiogram*, a graph of the person's auditory threshold at each frequency and for each ear. The normal human ear can hear frequencies between 20 and 20,000 hertz and is most sensitive at around 2000 hertz. Persons with different degrees of deafness typically show relative insensitivity to certain frequencies. Due to age changes in the inner ear, older adults become less sensitive to higher frequencies. A special type of audiometric test know as *acoustic impedance audiometry* is used to detect middle-ear disorders, which are the major cause of hearing loss in young children.

*Color Vision*    The ability to distinguish different hues is an important requirement in many occupations, ranging from airplane pilot to yarn inspector. One of the oldest instruments for testing color vision is the Isihara Test for Color Blindness, a set of 14, 24, or 38 cards. Each card, referred to as a *pseudo-isochromatic plate*, consists of an aggregate of dots of different colors. A person with normal color vision perceives the aggregate as a numeral or other form on a background of contrasting dots. Depending on the nature and severity of the defect, a color-blind person may see only a shapeless collection of dots on the card.

Another color vision test similar to the Ishihara is the Dvorine Color Vision Test. The materials on this test, which takes about 2 minutes to administer, consist of 15 pseudo-isochromatic plates and 8 auxiliary plates for verification purposes. Numbers or geometric figures made of dots must be distinguished from a background of dots of another color. Also noteworthy is the Farnsworth Dichotomous Test for Color Blindness, on which the examinee is required to arrange, according to color, a series of 15 movable color caps attached to a rack.

**Multipurpose Instruments**    The visual and auditory acuity and color vision tests discussed so far serve essentially only one function—to determine visual acuity, auditory acuity, or degree and type of color blindness. If more comprehensive testing of sensory capacities is desirable, a multipurpose instrument must be employed. Illustrative of multipurpose instruments for visual screening are Bausch & Lomb's B & L Vision Tester, American Optical Company's Sight Screener, Keystone View Company's Telebinocular, and Titmus Optical's Titmus Vision Tester. The B & L Vision Tester consists of a series of 12 tests in four categories: vertical and lateral phoria (muscular balance of the eyes) at far (20 feet) and near (14 inches) distances; acuity (including six tests) in the right eye, the left eye, and both eyes together; stereopsis (depth perception); and color discrimination. The B & L Vision Tester has been used primarily as a screening instrument in industrial contexts, and profiles for a number of *visual job families* have been determined. A less expensive instrument is the Titmus Vision Tester, which is used primarily for visual screening (acuity and phoria) in school settings.

## Tests of Psychomotor Abilities

Tests of psychomotor skills were among the first measures of special abilities to be constructed. Many of the available tests in this category were introduced during the 1920s and

1930s to predict performance in certain skilled jobs or trades. Subsequently, the Air Force Personnel and Training Research Center made a comprehensive analysis of psychomotor abilities, in particular those skills involved in performance as a pilot. Particularly important in these analyses were performance on flight simulators such as the Link Trainer and the Complex Coordination Test. On the latter, the examinee uses three controls similar to a stick and rudder to match a pattern of stimulus lights on a vertical panel simulating the movements of an airplane in flight.

An extensive research program conducted by Fleishman (1954, 1972) and his associates found a high degree of specificity in measures of psychomotor skills. The correlations between performance tests and paper-and-pencil tests of psychomotor abilities, as well as correlations between measures of speed and quality of movement, were generally low. From the pattern of correlations among various tests, Fleishman identified 11 psychomotor factors: aim, arm–hand steadiness, control precision, finger dexterity, manual dexterity, multilimb coordination, rate control, reaction time, response orientation, speed of arm movement, and wrist–finger speed. It was also found that the reliabilities of psychomotor tests were lower on the average (.70s and .80s) than those of other tests of special abilities. One reason for the lower reliability coefficients is the fact that performance on psychomotor tests is highly susceptible to practice. Furthermore, the relationships of scores on specific tests to the psychomotor factors changed dramatically from the first trials to the point at which examinees reached proficiency (Fleishman, 1972). Thus, both the scores on psychomotor tests and what the tests measure are affected by practice.

Generally, tests of psychomotor abilities have not proved very useful in vocational counseling. Due in part to the effects of practice on scores on these tests, the validities tend to be lower than those for tests of mechanical or clerical ability. Psychomotor tests have been more helpful in predicting performance in training programs than in forecasting job proficiency. They also have higher validities for predicting success in repetitive jobs, such as routine assembly and machine operation, than in complex jobs involving higher-order cognitive and perceptual abilities.

To illustrate the available psychomotor skills tests, selected measures of gross movements, fine movements, or a combination of gross and fine movements are described next. The majority of these instruments are appropriate for both adolescents and adults and are scored in terms of the number of task units completed in a specified time or the time required to complete the entire task.

***Gross Manual Movements***    Two older tests that were designed to measure speed and accuracy of gross finger, hand, and arm movements are the Stromberg Dexterity Test and the Minnesota Rate of Manipulation Test. On the Stromberg Dexterity Test the examinee is required to place 54 biscuit-sized, colored discs (red, yellow, blue) in a prescribed sequence as rapidly as possible (Figure 9–2). The Minnesota Rate of Manipulation Test consists of a 60-hole board with blocks that are red on one side and yellow on the other. The test is divided into five subtests, on which the blocks are turned, moved, and placed in certain ways. On the Placing Test portion, for example, the blocks are placed into the holes on the board; on the Turning Test portion the blocks are turned over and replaced in the board.

***Fine Manual Movements***    Representative of tests requiring manipulation of small parts are the O'Connor Finger Dexterity Test, the O'Connor Tweezer Dexterity Test, and Purdue Pegboard, and the Crawford Small Parts Dexterity Test. On the O'Connor tests the

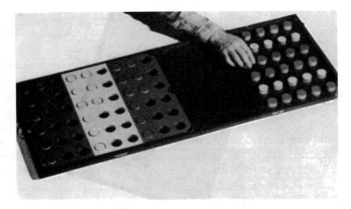

**FIGURE 9–2**   The Stromberg Dexterity Test.
(Copyright © 1945, 1951, 1981 by The Psychological
Corporation. Reproduced by permission. All rights reserved.)

examinee places small brass pins in the holes of a fiber plate by using the fingers or a pair of tweezers. The Purdue Pegboard, which is similar to the O'Connor tests, consists of five tasks for measuring manual dexterity and fine finger dexterity. On the first part of this test, the examinee puts pins into holes, first with the right hand, then with the left, and finally with both hands. On the second part of the test, the examinee puts a pin into a hole, places a washer and collar over the pin, puts another pin into a hole, and so on (Figure 9–3).

The Crawford Small Parts Dexterity Test consists of two parts. On the first part, examinees use tweezers to insert pins into holes and place collars over them. On the second part, the examinee places screws into threaded holes and screws them down with a screwdriver (Figure 9–4).

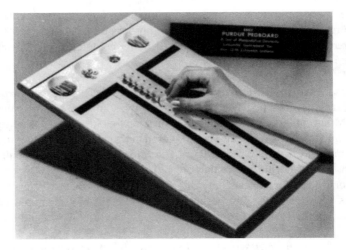

**FIGURE 9–3**   Purdue Pegboard.
(Courtesy of Lafayette Instrument Company.)

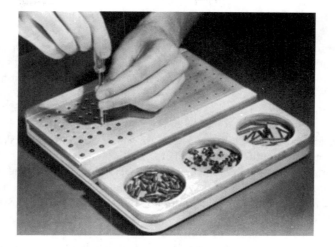

**FIGURE 9–4** The Crawford Small Parts Dexterity Test, Part II.
(Copyright © 1946, 1956, 1981 by The Psychological Corporation. Reproduced by permission. All rights reserved.)

***Gross and Fine Manual Movements*** Two psychomotor skills tests involving a combination of finger dexterity and gross movements of the arms and hands are the Pennsylvania Bi-manual Worksample and the Hand-Tool Dexterity Test. Both tests use nuts and bolts. On the Pennsylvania test, the examinee screws 100 nuts onto 100 bolts and places them into the holes of an 8- by 24-inch board. On the Hand-Tool Dexterity Test (Figure 9–5), the examinee is required first to unfasten 12 nuts from 12 bolts of three different sizes mounted on the left side of a frame and then to reassemble the nuts and bolts on the right side of the frame. Scores consist of the time it takes to complete the task. Norms are given in the manual for various groups of industrial applicants.

**FIGURE 9–5** The Hand-Tool Dexterity Test.
(Copyright © 1946, 1965, 1981 by The Psychological Corporation. Reproduced by permission. All rights reserved.)

## MECHANICAL ABILITY

A certain minimum level of psychomotor ability seems to be necessary for almost any occupation involving the operation of machinery, but above that level spatial perception, mechanical knowledge, and other cognitive abilities are more important determiners of performance. One of the first and most frequent kinds of special ability to be measured is mechanical ability. There is some evidence for a weak general factor of mechanical ability, but the tests that have been devised to measure it involve a variety of perceptual-motor and cognitive abilities. These are tests of psychomotor skills such as speed and muscular coordination, perception of spatial relations, and comprehension of mechanical relations. The psychomotor components of various mechanical ability tests, like psychomotor tests in general, have low correlations with each other. Nevertheless, total scores on different mechanical ability tests frequently have substantial positive correlations with each other.

One interesting, if not surprising, finding is the presence of gender differences in scores on tests of mechanical ability. Males typically score higher on spatial and mechanical comprehension items, whereas females score higher on items requiring fine manual dexterity and certain aspects of perceptual discrimination. These differences become more pronounced in junior and senior high school, and cultural factors undoubtedly play a role in producing them.

### Spatial Relations Tests

An intensive analysis of mechanical ability conducted by D. G. Paterson and his coworkers at the University of Minnesota during the late 1920s resulted in the construction of three tests: the Minnesota Mechanical Assembly Test, the Minnesota Spatial Relations Test, and the Minnesota Paper Formboard (Paterson et al., 1930). On the first of these, a work-sample test, the examinee reassembled a set of disassembled mechanical objects. The task required manual dexterity and space perception, in addition to mechanical comprehension. The second and third instruments in the series were tests of space perception, which had been shown to be an important factor in occupations involving mechanical tasks. As the name implies, tests of space perception measure the ability to visualize objects in three dimensions and manipulate them to produce a particular configuration.

One descendant of the preceding tests was the Minnesota Spatial Relations Test, Revised Edition. This instrument consists of four formboards (A, B, C, D) and two sets of geometrically shaped blocks. One set of blocks fits into the recesses of boards A and B; the second set fits into the recesses of boards C and D. The test begins with the blocks scattered outside the recesses, and the examinee must pick up the blocks and place them in their proper recesses on the board as quickly as possible.

Another descendant of the Minnesota Mechanical Ability Test is the Revised Minnesota Paper Formboard Test, a paper-and-pencil adaptation of the Minnesota Spatial Relations Test. This test consists of 64 multiple-choice items, each containing a frame showing a geometric figure divided into several parts and five answer frames containing an assembled form (Figure 9–6). The examinee's task is to select the one answer frame out of five showing how the disassembled geometric figure would look if the parts were fitted together.

There are two or more parts in the upper left-hand corner for each of the problems shown below. Choose from among the five figures labeled A, B, C, D, E, the one that shows how the parts in the upper left-hand corner would look if fitted together. The correct answer is shown for Problem 1.

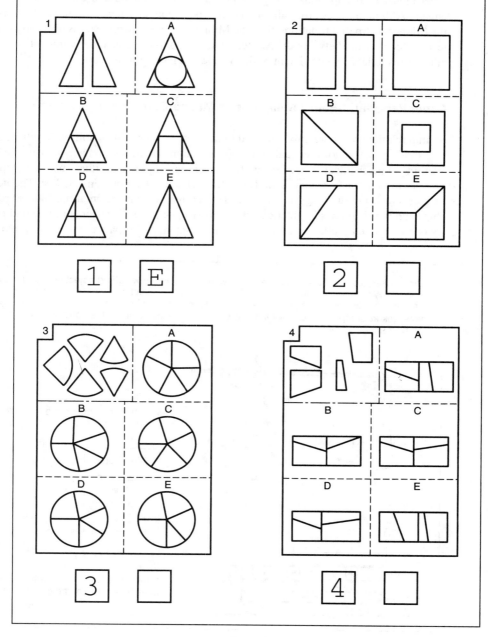

**FIGURE 9–6** Sample Items from the Revised Minnesota Paper Formboard Test. (Copyright © 1948, 1970 by The Psychological Corporation, Reproduced by permission. All rights reserved.)

The test has proved useful in predicting grades in shop and engineering courses, as well as supervisors' ratings and production records in inspection, packing, machine operation, and other industrial occupations. Scores on the test are also related to achievement in dentistry and art. Although it was originally intended to be a more efficiently administered version of the Minnesota Spatial Relations Test, the Minnesota Paper Formboard is not really the same test: the correlation between the two tests was found to be substantially lower than the parallel-forms reliability coefficient of the Minnesota Paper Formboard.

## Other Paper-and-Pencil Measures of Mechanical Ability

Spatial relations tests are only one kind of measure of mechanical ability. Another measure is provided by tests of mechanical comprehension, which are concerned with the understanding of mechanical principles involved in a range of practical situations. One of the most popular tests in this category is the Bennett Mechanical Comprehension Test. The items on this test consist of drawings and questions concerning the operation of mechanical relationships and physical laws in practical situations (Figure 9–7). The average score and reliability of the Bennett are lower for women than for men, and separate norms are provided by

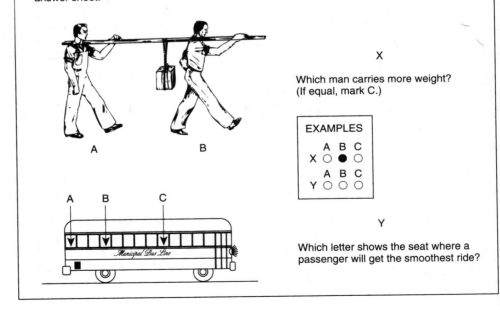

**FIGURE 9–7** Sample Items from the Bennett Mechanical Comprehension Test. (Copyright © 1942, 1967–1970, 1980 by The Psychological Corporation. Reproduced by permission. All rights reserved.)

sex. Evidence for the validity of the test is found in its modest correlations with performance in a variety of occupations requiring mechanical ability.

# CLERICAL AND COMPUTER-RELATED ABILITIES

Like many other categories of ability, clerical ability is not a unitary factor distinct from general intelligence. Although manual dexterity and speed of perceiving similarities and differences are necessary in clerical work, also important are verbal and quantitative abilities, which are aspects of general intelligence. Consequently, many tests of clerical ability contain items similar to those found on general intelligence tests, as well as items to measure perceptual speed and accuracy.

In addition to the more general tests of clerical ability, several tests have been designed to measure stenographic aptitude. Also available are tests of the ability to learn the complex clerical and problem-solving tasks of computer programming and computer operation.

## Representative Tests of General Clerical Ability

Commercially distributed tests of clerical ability vary in content from the simple number-and-name checking tasks of the Minnesota Clerical Test to the combined general intelligence and perceptual-motor tasks of the newer Clerical Abilities Measures. The Minnesota Clerical Test was designed for use in selecting clerks, inspectors, and other specialists in occupations involving speed of perceiving and manipulating symbols. It consists of two parts, Number Comparison and Name Comparison, on which the examinee inspects 200 pairs of numbers and 200 pairs of names for errors and checks identical pairs (Figure 9–8). Both parts are scored by the formula "rights minus wrongs," and the test–retest reliabilities of the scores are in the .70s and .80s. Percentile norms for students, by sex and grade (7 to 12), and for groups of clerical workers and applicants are given in the manual. The scores are moderately correlated with teachers' and supervisors' ratings on clerical work.

In contrast to the Minnesota Clerical Test, which measures only perceptual speed and accuracy, the Clerical Abilities Battery is composed of seven tests designed to measure a variety of clerical skills: Filing, Copying Information, Comparing Information, Using Tables, Proofreading, Addition and Subtraction, and Reasoning and Numbers. Testing time is 5 to 20 minutes for each subtest or 60 minutes for all seven subtests. Percentile norms based on several well-defined clerical populations are available on both forms A and B of the test.

## Computer-related Abilities

Rapid growth in the computer industry during the past three decades has led to a change in the nature of most clerical jobs and a demand for computer software—the programs of logical statements that tell computers what to do to achieve specific objectives. Learning how to program computers and to use the complex software that has already been designed requires a combination of the clerical and problem-solving abilities possessed by people in varying degrees. Therefore, it has become important to identify individuals who possess the aptitudes and skills for learning how to program and operate computers. Responding to this

If the two names or the two numbers of a pair are exactly the same make a check mark (✔) on the line between them; if they are different, make no mark on that line.

*Samples* done correctly
of pairs of *Numbers*

79542 _____ 79524

5794367 __✔__ 5794367

Samples done correctly
of pairs of Names

John C. Linder _____ John C. Lender

Investors Syndicate __✔__ Investors Syndicate

---

*Now try the samples below.*

(1) New York World _____ New York World

(2) Cargill Grain Co. _____ Cargil Grain Co.

(3) 66273894 _____ 66273984

(4) 527384578 _____ 527384578

**FIGURE 9–8**   Sample Items from the Minnesota Clerical Test.

need, measurement specialists have constructed tests of computer-programming aptitude, an example of which is the Computer Programmer Aptitude Battery (CPAB). This 75-minute battery, designed to evaluate and select applicants for computer-programming courses, consists of Verbal Meaning, Reasoning, Letter Series, Number Ability, and Diagramming subtests. Beginners and experienced programmers and systems analysts were used in developing the items, and percentile norms on total and subtest scores are reported in the manual. Validation studies have shown that the CPAB predicts relevant job success in a variety of production and service organizations.

Also available are tests that assess aptitude for operating computers; an example is the Computer Operator Aptitude Battery (COAB). The three subtests on this 45-minute battery are Sequence Recognition ("ability to recognize sequences quickly"), Format Checking ("ability to perceive conformity of numbers and letters to a specified format"), and Logical Thinking ("ability to analyze problems and visualize solutions logically"). The manual lists percentile norms, obtained on relatively small samples of experienced computer operators and inexperienced applicants or trainees, by subtest and total score.

# ARTISTIC, MUSICAL, AND OTHER CREATIVE ABILITIES

As the phrase "beauty is in the eye of the beholder" implies, the ultimate judge of artistic merit is the observer. Because taste in art varies greatly from person to person, from culture to culture, and from generation to generation, it is not surprising that criteria of artistic ability are difficult to specify. Notwithstanding the many problems of defining reliable criteria and constructing tests to predict those criteria, a number of tests of visual art ability and musical ability have been published. However, many of these tests are old and are no longer commercially available.

## Art Ability Tests

Many years ago researchers at the University of Minnesota found a positive correlation between scores on spatial perception tests, such as the Minnesota Paper Formboard, and artistic ability (Paterson et al., 1930). Spatial ability, of course, is not the only factor in artistic ability; judgment, manual dexterity, creative imagination, and other factors also play a role. Furthermore, a person who can recognize good art is not necessarily able to produce it. For this reason, it is important to distinguish between measures of aesthetic appreciation (judgment and perception) and work-sample measures of productive skill in art. Illustrative of tests of art judgment and perception are the Meier Art Tests (Art Judgment and Aesthetic Perception) and the Graves Design Judgment Test. Unlike the Meier, which uses famous works of art as test materials, the Graves employs two- and three-dimensional abstract designs to elicit artistic judgments. An example of a performance test in art is the Horn Art Aptitude Inventory, which requires the examinee to sketch common objects and geometric figures and to make sketches from sets of basic lines in rectangular frames.

## Musical Ability Tests

As with artistic ability, the correlations between scores on tests of musical ability and criteria of musical accomplishment are not high. There does appear, however, to be a weak general factor of musical ability, and a number of tests have been designed to measure it. Although scores on these tests are positively correlated with intelligence test scores, a high intellectual level is certainly not essential to musical ability. Both young children and the mentally retarded may be quite accomplished musically.

The oldest musical ability test, the Seashore Measures of Musical Talents, was a product of the pioneering research of Carl Seashore and his colleagues at the University of Iowa during the 1920s and 1930s (Seashore, 1939). In contrast to the musical ability tests that were developed later, the stimulus materials on the Seashore tests consisted of a series of musical tones or notes, rather than meaningful musical selections. This analytic, atomistic approach to measuring musical ability was severely criticized, and, as a result, several tests having more complex musical content were developed. Among these are omnibus measures such as the Wing Standardized Tests of Musical Intelligence, the Drake Musical Aptitude Test, and the Musical Aptitude Profile.

The Musical Aptitude Profile (MAP) is a tape-recorded test consisting of 250 original short selections for violin and cello played by professional musicians. No previous knowledge of musical or historical facts is required. Three basic musical factors (musical expression, aural perception, and kinesthetic musical feeling) are purportedly measured by the three tests (T, R, and S) on the MAP. There are two subtests (Melody and Harmony) on Test T (Tonal Imagery), two subtests (Tempo and Meter) on Test R (Rhythm Imagery), and three subtests (Phrasing, Balance, and Style) on Test S (Musical Sensitivity). Tests T and R, which have correct answers, require the examinee to indicate whether two stimuli are alike or different. Test S, which has multiple scoring, requires the examinee to indicate which of two tape-recorded renditions of a piece of music is more tasteful. The total battery takes 110 minutes to administer and is appropriate for grades 4–12.

A 3-year longitudinal predictive study of the Musical Aptitude Profile was perhaps the most carefully conducted of all investigations of musical ability (Gordon, 1967). Fourth- and fifth-grade children in eight classrooms in five cities were tested individually with the test and then given weekly instruction in playing musical instruments. The correlation between initial scores on the Musical Aptitude Profile and ratings of musical performance was .59 after 1 year of instruction and .74 after 3 years of instruction.

## Creativity

Tests of intelligence or scholastic aptitude administered to school-age children usually do a fair job of predicting short-term school achievement and related criteria. These tests, however, were not designed to measure situational variables, lifelong determination, motivation, or nonscholastic talent of the sort that may influence creative performance. It is noteworthy that few, if any, of the intellectually gifted individuals studied by Terman (Terman & Oden, 1959) attained the eminence of a Winston Churchill, an Albert Einstein, or an Ernest Hemingway. Nor did any of them become a famous composer, artist, or poet.

***Characteristics of Creative People***    Thomas Alva Edison held 1093 patents, Albert Einstein published 248 papers, Pablo Picasso averaged over 200 works of art a year, and Wolfgang Amadeus Mozart had composed more than 609 pieces of music by the time of his death at age 35. These cases illustrate the high inner drive that creative people reportedly possess (Haney, 1985). Other affective and cognitive traits said to be characteristic of creative people are ideational fluency, flexibility, unconventionalism, social sensitivity, nondefensiveness, a greater willingness to concede faults, and close ties with parents (MacKinnon, 1962).

Based on the results of investigations by MacKinnon (1962) and Wallach and Kogan (1965), it would seem that creativity, especially when accompanied by high intelligence, is not a bad characteristic to possess from a mental health standpoint. However, in a study of prominent British artists (novelists, painters, playwrights, poets, and sculptors), Jamison (1984) found that these individuals were much more likely than less creative people to have been treated for mood disorders (mania and depression). Similar results were found by Andreasen (1987) in a study of 30 faculty members in a writers' workshop: 80 percent exhibited depression or some other form of mood disorder, and 43 percent were diagnosed as manic-depressive. The meaning of these findings is not entirely clear, but at least they suggest that creative adults, like gifted children, are no strangers to unhappiness and poor adjustment.

***Tests of Creativity***    It is generally recognized that above-average intelligence is necessary but not sufficient for creative productivity. Beyond a minimum IQ of around 120, creative performance appears to depend more on motivation and special abilities than on general mental ability (MacKinnon, 1962). Therefore, investigations of creativity conducted during the past 30 years have focused on the identification of other cognitive and affective characteristics that distinguish creative from noncreative people. For example, efforts have been made to develop measures of divergent, as opposed to convergent, thinking ability (Guilford, 1967). On measures of *convergent thinking,* such as problems of the sort found on intelligence tests, there is only one correct answer. In contrast, on tests of *divergent thinking,* examinees are presented with a problem having a number of possible solutions and are scored on the originality of their responses. Rather than having a fixed number of possible answers, items on tests of divergent thinking are open ended. Unfortunately, this open-endedness leads to difficulties in scoring and determining the reliability and validity of these tests. Among the scoring procedures that have been advocated is evaluating answers for both the number of responses given by the examinee (fluency) and their originality or uncommonness (novelty).

**Examples of Creativity Tests**    The following are illustrative of items on tests of creativity:

> *Consequences Test.* Imagine all the things that might possibly happen if all national and local laws were suddenly abolished. (Guilford, 1954)

> *Remote Associates Test.* Find a fourth word that is associated with each of these three words: (a) rat–blue–cottage; (b) out–dog–cat; (c) wheel–electric–high; (d) surprise–line–birthday. (Mednick, 1962)

> *Unusual Uses Test.* Name as many uses as you can think of for: (a) a toothpick (b) a brick (c) a paper clip. (Guilford, 1954)

> *Word Association Test.* Write as many meanings as you can for each of the following words: (a) duck (b) sack (c) pitch (d) fair. (Getzels & Jackson, 1962; copyright © 1962. John Wiley & Sons, Inc. Reprinted by permission of John Wiley & Sons, Inc.)

**Creativity Test Batteries**    Two examples of creativity test batteries are the Structure-of-Intellect Abilities and the Torrance Tests of Creative Thinking. The tests on the Structure-of-Intellect Abilities (SOI), several of which are distributed by Consulting Psychologists Press as Guilford's Measures of Creativity, are by-products of the factor-analytic research of J. P. Guilford and his co-workers on the nature of human intelligence (Guilford, 1967, 1974). Included in this battery are Consequences and Unusual Uses subtests, four Christensen–Guilford fluency tests, other verbal subtests, such as Simile Interpretation, and nonverbal subtests, such as Sketches, Making Objects, and Decorations. The majority of these tests can be administered at the junior high level and beyond, but the scoring is complex. The split-half reliabilities of the tests range from .60 to .90.

The Torrance Tests of Creative Thinking (TTCT) consist of three picture-based exercises (Figural TTCT) and six word-based exercises (Verbal TTCT). An example of the kinds of items on the Verbal TTCT is to "Write out all the questions you can think of" about a given picture. On one part of the Figural TTCT, the examinee is asked to make a sketch from a basic line (Figure 9–9). The Verbal TTCT, which takes 45 minutes to complete, is scored on three variables: fluency, flexibility, and originality. The Figural TTCT, which

**FIGURE 9–9**  Sample Items from the Torrance Tests of Creative Thinking.
These Drawings from the Figural TTCT Illustrate the Humor That Is Presumably
More Characteristic of Creative Persons.
(Copyright © 1984 by Scholastic Testing Service, Inc. Reprinted by permission of
Scholastic Testing Service, Inc., from Torrance Tests of Creative Thinking, Streamlined,
Revised Manual, Figures A and B, by E. Paul Torrance and Orlow E. Ball.)

takes 30 minutes to complete, is scored on five variables: fluency, originality, elaboration, titles, and closure. The TTCT was restandardized in 1980, and national percentile ranks and standard scores from grade 1 through college and adult level are given in the manual. Although a number of researchers have concluded that the TTCT is an unbiased indicator of giftedness (for example, Esquivel & Lopez, 1988; Torrance, 1988), the reliabilities of the tests are quite variable and the results of validity studies are inconclusive (Hattie, 1980). Clearly, more work needs to be done with the TTCT before it can be used comfortably in applied settings as a measure of creativity.

***Evaluation of Creativity Tests*** The instruments that have been designed to assess creativity are intriguing, but it is important to heed the criticisms made by McNemar (1964) and other psychologists. Tests of creativity frequently have significant correlations with IQ tests, and the former are apparently no more effective than the latter in predicting "creative performance." All things considered, a reasonable conclusion is that it remains to be demonstrated whether effective measures of creativity can be constructed. Until a test can be designed to predict performance on a generally accepted criterion of creativity, it would be well to follow McNemar's (1964) advice not to dispose of our general intelligence tests.

## MULTIPLE-APTITUDE BATTERIES

The assessment of skills and knowledge in several different areas is often useful in vocational counseling, as well as in job classification and placement. The counselor may, of course, decide to administer a set of separate, single tests of abilities, but this can be very time consuming. More important, in all likelihood such a collection of single tests will have been standardized on as many different groups of people as there are tests. Because the norm groups for different tests may vary in significant ways, it may be difficult to compare a person's score on one test with his or her scores on other tests in any meaningful way.

Separate tests of special abilities certainly have a place, especially in personnel selection and screening. Such tests are, however, less useful in vocational counseling and classification. In an economic system such as ours, in which the emphasis has shifted somewhat from selecting only the "cream of the crop" to classifying and placing workers on jobs most suited to their abilities and needs, classification rather than selection has been increasingly emphasized. Consequently, multiple-aptitude tests, which are designed to match people having particular ability patterns to specific jobs, are seen as potentially more valuable than single tests designed to select only the best and screen out all others. Unlike single tests of special abilities, which may be of either the paper-and-pencil or performance type, a typical multiple-aptitude battery involves no apparatus other than paper and pencil. Therefore, it can be administered simultaneously to a large group of students, job applicants, military inductees, or other people.

Many school systems administer a multiple-aptitude test battery in the eighth or ninth grade. During the junior high years, students are beginning to make career plans and decisions on what courses to take. The information provided by an aptitude test battery can sharpen students' awareness of their strengths and weaknesses and thereby provide guidance in making occupational and educational decisions. Cognitive abilities are less specific during the elementary school years, becoming more differentiated with maturity and experience. This is one reason why administration of an expensive, time-consuming multiple-aptitude battery is usually not recommended prior to the junior high years.

Rather than administering a long series of special abilities tests or a multiple-aptitude battery, a vocational counselor may decide to use a general intelligence test plus one or more tests of special abilities. There is certainly nothing wrong with this strategy. The verbal and quantitative abilities measured by intelligence tests are important in a wide range of activities in Western culture. Consequently, scores on these instruments are among the best overall predictors of academic and occupational success in our society. In addition to evaluating several special abilities, many aptitude batteries contain a general intelligence test. This provides the combined advantages of more efficient administration and comparable norms on all tests.

## Score Differences and Profile Interpretation

The statistical procedures of factor analysis (see Appendix A) were used in the construction of a number of aptitude test batteries. Examples are the Primary Mental Abilities Test and the Guilford–Zimmerman Aptitude Survey. Even on batteries not constructed by factor-analytic methods, the results of studies employing these methods have usually been considered in preparing items and defining test variables.

Items on the Differential Aptitude Tests, a nonfactored battery, were selected to have high correlations with other items on the same subtest, but low correlations with items on other subtests. The final result was a set of internally consistent subtests having low correlations with each other. It was important for the correlations among subtests to be low; otherwise, the overlap among the abilities measured by different subtests would be too great for differential interpretation of subtest scores.

***Reliability and Standard Error of Score Differences***   Correlations among different subtests in the same battery are often sizable, and the fact that the subtests are fairly short results in relatively low subtest reliabilities. Not only does the reliability of the differences between scores on two tests vary directly with the reliabilities of the tests, it also varies inversely with the correlation between the tests. The combined effect of a sizable correlation between two given subtests and low reliabilities of those subtests is low reliability of the differences between scores on the subtests.

A formula for the reliability of the differences ($r_{dd}$) between the scores of the same people on two tests or subtests having equal variances is

$$r_{dd} = \frac{r_{11} + r_{22} - 2r_{12}}{2(1 - r_{12})} \tag{9.1}$$

where $r_{11}$ is the reliability of the first set of scores, $r_{22}$ is the reliability of the second set of scores, and $r_{12}$ is the correlation between the two sets of scores. For example, assume that the reliability of pretest scores is $r_{11} = .90$, the reliability of posttest scores is $r_{22} = .80$, and the correlation between pretest and posttest scores is $r_{12} = .70$. Then the reliability of the difference between pretest and posttest scores is $[.90 + .80 - 2(.70)]/[2(1 - .70)] = .50$.

When the reliability of the differences between scores on two subtests is low, the difference between a person's scores on the subtests must be fairly large to be viewed as significant. To illustrate this principle, suppose that the reliability of $T$ scores on the spatial relations test of an aptitude battery is .85 and the reliability of $T$ scores on the mechanical ability test of the same battery is .90. An approximate value of the standard error of the differences ($s_{est}$) between scores on two tests having equal standard deviations may be computed from

$$s_{est} = s\sqrt{2 - r_{11} - r_{22}} \qquad (9.2)$$

where $r_{11}$ and $r_{22}$ are the test–retest reliabilities of the two tests, and $s$ is the standard deviation of the scores on each test. Recalling that the standard deviation of $T$ scores equals 10, when scores on both tests are expressed as $T$ scores, formula 9.2 becomes

$$s_{est} = 10\sqrt{2 - .85 - .90} = 5$$

Consequently, to be fairly certain (say, with a probability of .95) that the difference between a person's scores on these two tests is not due to chance, the difference should be at least $1.96 \times 5 = 9.8$ $T$-score units.

***Score Profile***    The process of interpreting a person's score on a multiple-aptitude battery consisting of several tests standardized on the same or equivalent norm groups begins with the construction of a score profile. A *score profile,* which is a line graph or bar graph of scores on different tests, provides a picture of the person's strengths and weaknesses in various aptitude areas. From the norms, it is possible to construct a profile of a person's scores on the various tests for use in academic or vocational counseling. Rather than plotting test scores as points, they may be drawn as vertical bars spanning one standard error of measurement for the test on either side of the score. Then, if the vertical bars for two tests do not overlap, the difference between the examinee's scores on those two tests may be considered significant.

Comparing an individual's profile of scores on a multiple-aptitude battery with the average score profile of people in selected occupations can be of help in vocational counseling and occupational selection and placement. Although workers within the same occupation differ to some degree in their pattern of abilities, certain job families seem to require a particular set of abilities. Similar profiles on a multiple-aptitude battery indicate similar patterns of abilities.

## Differential Aptitude Tests

A number of aptitude test batteries have been designed for and standardized primarily in school situations and used as predictors of scholastic achievement. Most prominent of all batteries of this type are the Differential Aptitude Tests (DAT). The DAT was designed primarily for educational and vocational counseling of junior and senior high students, but it has also found uses in basic adult education, community college, vocational/technical, and correctional programs. There are two levels, Level 1 for grades 7–9 and Level 2 for grades 9–12, of the latest (fifth) edition of the DAT.

As illustrated by the sample items in Figure 9–10, eight tests comprise the DAT: Verbal Reasoning, Numerical Reasoning, Abstract Reasoning, Perceptual Speed and Accuracy, Mechanical Reasoning, Space Relations, Spelling, and Language Usage. Working time for the entire battery is 156 minutes, but a DAT Partial Battery consisting of the Verbal Reasoning and

### Verbal Reasoning* (25 min.)

Measures the ability to see relationships among words; may be useful in predicting success in business, law, education, journalism, and the sciences.

> **SAMPLE ITEM**
>
> Which answer contains the missing words to complete this sentence?
>
> . . . . is to fin as bird is to . . . .
>
>    **A** water – – feather
>    **B** shark – – nest
> ★ **C** fish – – wing
>    **D** flipper – – fly
>    **E** fish – – sky

### Numerical Reasoning* (30 min.)

Measures the ability to perform mathematical reasoning tasks; important in jobs such as bookkeeping, lab work, carpentry, and toolmaking.

> **SAMPLE ITEM**
>
> Which number should replace R in this correct addition example?
>
>     7R        ★ **A** 9
>    + R           **B** 6
>    ―――       **C** 4
>     88            **D** 3
>                   **E** None of these

### Abstract Reasoning (20 min.)

A nonverbal measure of the ability to reason using geometric shapes or designs; important in fields such as computer programming, drafting, and vehicle repair.

> **SAMPLE ITEM**
>
> Choose the Answer Figure that should be the next figure (or fifth one) in the series.
>
>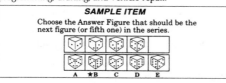
>
>   **A**  ★**B**   **C**   **D**   **E**

### Perceptual Speed and Accuracy (6 min.)

Measures the ability to compare and mark written lists quickly and accurately; helps predict success in performing routine clerical tasks.

> **SAMPLE ITEM**
>
> Look at the underlined combination of letters or numbers and find the same one on the answer sheet. Then fill in the circle under it.
>
> 1 XY Xy XX <u>YX</u> Yy     XY Yy YX XX Xy    nn mn nv ńm mm
> 2 6g <u>6G</u> G6 Gg g6     ○○ ● ○ ○     ○ ○ ○ ● ○
> 3 <u>nm</u> mn mm nn nv    g6 Gg 6g G6 6G    BD BB Bd Db Bb
> 4 Db <u>BD</u> Bd Bb BB    ○ ○ ○ ●     ● ○ ○ ○ ○

### Mechanical Reasoning (25 min.)

Understanding basic mechanical principles of machinery, tools, and motion is important for occupations such as carpentry, mechanics, engineering, and machine operation.

> **SAMPLE ITEM**
>
> Which load will be easier to pull through soft sand?
>
>   **A**        **B**        **C**
>
>

### Space Relations (25 min.)

Measures the ability to visualize a three-dimensional object from a two-dimensional pattern, and to visualize how this object would look if rotated in space; important in drafting, architecture, design, carpentry, and dentistry.

> **SAMPLE ITEM**
>
> Choose the one figure that can be made from the pattern.
>
>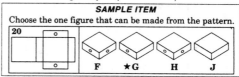
>
>   **F**  ★**G**   **H**   **J**

### Spelling (10 min.)

Measures one's ability to spell common English words; a useful skill in many academic and vocational pursuits.

> **SAMPLE ITEM**
>
> Decide which word is not spelled correctly in the group below.
>
> ★ **A** paragraf
>    **B** dramatic
>    **C** circular
>    **D** audience

### Language Usage (15 min.)

Measures the ability to detect errors in grammar, punctuation, and capitalization; needed in most jobs requiring a college degree.

> **SAMPLE ITEM**
>
> Decide which of the four parts of the sentence below contains an error. If there is no error, mark the space on your answer sheet for the letter next to No Error.
>
> Jane and Tom / is going / to the office / this morning.
>    **A** .   ★**B**       **C**        **D**
> **E** No Error

**FIGURE 9–10**   DAT Sample Items.

Numerical Reasoning tests requires only 90 minutes working time. In addition, there is a Computerized Adaptive version of the entire battery requiring only 90 minutes working time on the average. Using item-response theory, the adaptive version presents a subset of test items that are most appropriate for the person being tested.

    The fifth edition of the DAT was standardized on a representative national sample of junior and senior high students, stratified according to size of school district, geographical region, socioeconomic status of community, and type of school (public versus nonpublic). There are significant gender differences in DAT scores: females score higher than males on Perceptual Speed and Accuracy and Language Usage, whereas males score higher than females on Mechanical Reasoning and Space Relations. Because of these differences, the percentile rank, stanine, and scaled score norms are presented separately for males and females, as well as combined.

The internal consistency reliability coefficients of the eight tests on the DAT range from .82 to .95 and the parallel-forms coefficients from .73 to .90. The correlations among the tests range from nearly zero for Perceptual Speed and Accuracy to as high as .70 for the Reasoning and Language Usage tests. The manual presents extensive data that the tests on the DAT, and especially the Verbal Reasoning plus Numerical Reasoning composite, are valid predictors of high school and college grades. The tests are also useful in predicting job level within occupations, but the norms for various occupations are limited. Consequently, the DAT should be used cautiously as a differential predictor of vocational success.

## Multidimensional Aptitude Battery

The Multidimensional Aptitude Battery (MAB) is a group-administered adaptation of the Wechsler Adult Intelligence Scale–Revised. Like the WAIS–R, the MAB consists of two scales (Verbal and Performance) containing five subtests each. The five Verbal subtests are Information, Comprehension, Arithmetic, Similarities, and Vocabulary. The five Performance subtests are Digit Symbol, Picture Completion, Spatial, Picture Arrangement, and Object Assembly. The time limit for each subtest is 7 minutes, so the entire battery can be completed in less than $1\frac{1}{2}$ hours. IQs and standard scores on the Verbal, Performance, and Full Scale Batteries, as well as subtest scale scores, age-corrected scale scores, and a narrative report of the scores and their interpretation, may be obtained from the computer-scoring service of Sigma Assessment Systems.

The MAB manual (Jackson, 1984) reports test–retest reliabilities over a period of 45 days as .95 for Verbal, .96 for Performance, and .97 for Full Scale scores. In a study of 500 individuals aged 16 to 20, internal consistency coefficients for Verbal, Performance, and Full Scale IQs were found to be in the high .90s. Correlations between MAB scores and WAIS–R IQs in a sample of 145 adults were .94 for Verbal, .79 for Performance, and .91 for Full Scale WAIS–R scores. The results of factor analyses of scores on the MAB subtests indicate that, like the WAIS–R, the test measures a general intelligence factor as well as separate verbal and performance factors.

## General Aptitude Test Battery

Several multiple-aptitude batteries have been designed specifically for personnel selection and placement in business and industry. Among these are the General Aptitude Test Battery, the Flanagan Aptitude Classification Tests, the Flanagan Industrial Tests, and the Employee Aptitude Survey. One of the oldest of the industrially oriented test batteries was constructed in the 1930s by the staff of the Minnesota Employment Stabilization Research Institute (MESRI). The MESRI battery contained tests of general intelligence, as well as numerical ability, perceptual ability, mechanical ability, and psychomotor ability. Profiles of the average scores on the tests obtained by clerks, mechanical workers, salespersons, and many other occupational groups were established as a set of *occupational ability patterns* (OAPs) with which individual performance could be compared.

The OAP approach of the MESRI battery was retained in the development of the General Aptitude Test Battery (GATB) of the U.S. Employment Service. The GATB, designed on the basis of job analyses and a factor analysis of 59 tests, is composed of 8 paper-and-pencil and 4 apparatus tests. These 12 tests in combination yield scores on nine major aptitudes and skills required for occupational success: Intelligence (G), Verbal Aptitude (V), Numerical Aptitude (N), Spatial Aptitude (S), Form Perception (P), Clerical Perception (Q), Motor Coordination (K), Finger Dexterity (F), and Manual Dexterity (M). Raw scores on these nine variables are converted to percentile ranks or standard scores having a mean of 100 and a standard deviation of 20. Any person's standard scores on the GATB variables can then be compared with those of the 36 or so occupational ability patterns (OAPs) determined from an analysis of the GATB scores of people in over 800 jobs. An OAP consists of a set of minimum GATB scores considered essential for effective performance in that occupation.

The entire GATB takes $2\frac{1}{2}$ hours to administer and is appropriate for senior high students (usually twelfth graders) and adults. Test–retest and parallel-forms reliability coefficients of the separate tests range from .80 to .90, with a standard error of measurement of approximately 7 points for the standard scores. The validities of the nine aptitude scores and the 36 OAPs for predicting occupational and academic criteria of success range from .00 to the .90s. The GATB has been one of the most widely used vocational counseling and job placement tools for students in grades 9–12 and adults and is probably the most appropriate test battery for that purpose. However, the DAT is considered better for educational counseling purposes.

Because of the alleged unfairness of the GATB to minority groups, in 1981 a system of "race norming" of the scores was put in place as part of the affirmative action program of the U.S. Department of Labor. This policy consisted of using separate percentile norms for whites, blacks, and Hispanics and reporting only the in-group percentile ranks of applicants. Critics viewed this practice, however, as reverse discrimination, and in 1990 use of the GATB was suspended by the Department of Justice until such time as issues regarding fairness and reverse discrimination could be settled.

## Armed Services Vocational Aptitude Battery

Beginning with the Army Examinations Alpha and Beta in World War I, over the years various tests have been used to select and classify personnel in the U.S. Armed Services. The Army General Classification Test (AGCT) was administered to millions of military recruits during and after World War II to classify them for skilled and unskilled jobs, to select those who could profit from further training, and to reject those who, because of low mental ability, were considered unfit for military service. Some years after World War II, the Armed Forces Qualification Test (AFQT) replaced the AGCT for screening U.S. military applicants.

During the 1970s, the Armed Services Vocational Aptitude Battery (ASVAB) became the uniform selection and classification test for the joint armed services. The current form of this battery (ASVAB, 18/19), which is the most widely administered multiple-aptitude test in the United States, consists of 10 tests: General Science (GS), Arithmetic Reasoning (AR), Word Knowledge (WK), Paragraph Comprehension (PC), Numerical Operations (NO), Coding Speed (CS), Auto & Shop Information (AS), Mathematics Knowledge (MK), Mechanical Comprehension (MC), and Electronics Information (EI). Working time per test ranges from 3 minutes for Numerical Operations to 36 minutes for Arithmetic Reasoning, for a total of 144 minutes. Standard $T$ scores and percentile score bands are reported for each of the tests and three composites: Verbal Ability (VA = WK + PC), Math Ability (MA = AR + MK), Academic Ability (AA = 2VA + MA).

Internal consistency reliability coefficients ranging from .92 to .96 are given in the *Counselor's Manual* (U.S. Department of Defense, 1992) and the *ASVAB 18/19 Technical Manual* (U.S. Department of Defense, 1993). Alternative forms reliability coefficients range from .77 to .85 for the speeded tests (Numerical Operations and Coding Speed) and from .71 to .91 for the remaining (power) tests. The *Counselor's Manual,* the *Technical Manual,* and a review by Welsh, Kucinkas, and Curran (1990) contain extensive data on the validity of the ASVAB with military personnel. These sources also provide information on the validity of the ASVAB extrapolated to high school and college students, to whom the test battery was administered for career counseling purposes (also see U.S. Department of Defense, 1994).

## Longitudinal Studies of Aptitude Tests and Careers

One of the great success stories of applied psychology involved construction of the Aviation Cadet Classification Battery for the Army Air Corps during World War II. The problem facing the Air Corps psychologists was to predict success in learning to fly an airplane. Their solution was to construct a battery of instruments, including tests of general information, verbal and mathematical abilities, perceptual-motor skills, mechanical abilities, and an inventory of biographical data. Initially, all candidates took the battery of tests (the Aviation Cadet Classification Battery) and were accepted for the training program regardless of their scores. Subsequently, scores on the tests were correlated with success in completing flying training. Many different tests contributed something to the prediction of success in learning to fly, and, when used in combination as a selection battery, they saved the U.S. government a great deal of money on its pilot-training program. Use of the tests spared not only airplanes, but many student pilots and flight instructors as well!

Twelve years later, Thorndike and Hagen (1959) located 10,000 men who had taken the Air Corps test battery in 1943. By 1955, this group of men had entered over 100 occupations. The investigators correlated scores on the Air Corps tests taken a dozen years earlier with occupational membership and seven criteria of success in these occupations. Although near-zero correlations were found between scores on the tests and criteria of success within occupations, the average scores obtained by various occupational groups differed significantly. For example, airmen who later became scientists or college professors had scored above average on the tests of general intelligence, numerical ability, and perceptual–spatial ability in 1943. On the other hand, those who later became machinists or mechanics had scored higher than average on tests of mechanical and psychomotor abilities on the 1943 battery. Be that as it may, the average variability of scores within the same occupation was almost as great as the variability of scores across occupational groups.

A number of explanations were offered for the failure of the Aviation Cadet Classification Battery to forecast occupational membership and success more accurately. Among the explanations proposed by Thorndike (1963) are (1) the wide range of occupations within each occupational group, (2) differences among variables that were important in the training program and variables important on the job, (3) imprecise definitions of occupational success in occupations where pay and promotions had become institutionalized, and (4) contingency or "incidental" factors.

The fact that aptitude test scores alone are not very accurate predictors of academic and vocational performance was confirmed some years later by the results of Project TALENT, a nationwide sampling and longitudinal follow-up investigation of the abilities and interests of U.S. high school students. During the spring of 1962, a cross-sectional sample consisting of 440,000 students in high schools throughout the United States took a battery of 22 aptitude and achievement tests and filled out a student activities inventory, an interest inventory, and a personal information blank. The students were followed up in 1961, 1965, 1970, and 1980 to determine the relationships of their scores on the tests and inventories to their later educational attainments, vocational careers, and social contributions. An analysis of the 13 ability factors and 13 motivational factors indicated that the latter were some of the best predictors of college major and vocational placement (Cooley & Lohnes, 1968). Even when both ability and motivational factors were taken into account, however, prediction of career choice and other criteria was still a matter of probability rather than certainty.

Thus, it seems that although the pattern of scores on a multiple-aptitude test battery can serve as a rough indicator of a person's suitability for a particular job, occupational success cannot be predicted with accuracy from test scores alone. The range of tasks comprising most jobs is great enough so that people within a fairly wide span of abilities can adapt. Whether a person manages to adapt and succeed or becomes maladjusted and fails on the job or in other areas of life depends not only on that person's abilities, but also on his or her motivation, interest, temperament, situational variables, and, of course, the ever-elusive factor of chance.

## SUMMARY

Tests of aptitudes or special abilities focus on the future, that is, on measuring a person's ability to profit from further training or experience in a certain area. Tests of special abilities also have narrower bandwidths than conventional intelligence tests, in that they predict more specific accomplishments. Although certain tests of special abilities are of the work-sample or performance type, paper-and-pencil tests are more widely administered.

A variety of tests exist for measuring visual acuity, auditory acuity, color vision, and other aspects of sensation and perception. In addition, multipurpose instruments for visual screening and for measuring perceptual-motor skills are available.

Psychomotor abilities appear to be highly specific variables, and scores on tests of these abilities frequently have lower reliabilities than other ability tests; the scores are also very susceptible to practice effects. Illustrative of psychomotor tests are the Minnesota Rate of Manipulation Test for measuring gross manual movements, the Crawford Small Parts Dexterity Test for measuring fine manual movements, and the Hand-Tool Dexterity Test for measuring both gross and fine manual movements.

Tests of mechanical ability and clerical ability were among the first standardized measures of special abilities to be devised. However, neither mechanical ability nor clerical ability is a unitary psychological dimension. Tests of mechanical ability may involve psychomotor skills in addition to perception and mechanical comprehension. Tests of clerical ability may measure perceptual speed and accuracy, as well as verbal and numerical ability. Examples of tests of mechanical ability are the Bennett Mechanical Comprehension Test and the Test of Mechanical Concepts. Representative tests of clerical ability include the Minnesota Clerical Test and the Clerical Abilities Battery. A number of tests designed to measure aptitudes for computer programming and computer operation have also been constructed, including the Computer Programmer Aptitude Battery and the Computer Operator Aptitude Battery.

A number of tests of artistic and musical ability have been designed since the 1920s. Some of these tests measure art appreciation (judgment and perception), while others assess artistic performance or knowledge of art. The Meier Art Tests and the Graves Design Judgment Test have been two of the most popular tests of art appreciation.

The Seashore Measures of Musical Talents, the oldest published test of musical ability, emphasizes discrimination, judgment, and memory for tones or tonal combinations. Several other musical ability tests (for example, the Wing Standardized Tests of Musical Intelligence and the Musical Aptitude Profile) involve judgment and discrimination of meaningful music. Success in either music or art depends, however, on many factors other than talent. In any case, most of these tests of artistic and musical ability are no longer commercially available.

Creative performance is not only a function of relatively high intelligence, but also of high motivation, special training, and perhaps other psychological abilities. A major problem in developing useful measures of creativity is defining the criteria of creative performance. Tests such as Guilford's Structure-of-Intellect Abilities and the Torrance Tests of Creative Thinking are noteworthy examples of instruments designed to assess creativity. The results of recent research suggest that certain kinds of creative performance are related to mental illness, in particular mood disorders such as manic-depressive psychosis.

Multiple-aptitude batteries are designed to measure individual strengths and weaknesses in a variety of ability areas. Aptitude test batteries, which are typically not administered before the junior high years, are useful tools in academic and vocational counseling, selection, and placement. Certain multiple-aptitude batteries (for example, the Guilford–Zimmerman Aptitude Survey and the General Aptitude Test Battery) are based on the results of factor analysis, whereas other aptitude batteries (for example, the Differential Aptitude Tests) are not. Aptitude test batteries, which are usually not administered prior to the junior high years, are useful tools in academic and vocational counseling, selection, and placement. The Differential Aptitude Tests are generally considered the most useful battery for academic counseling, whereas the best battery for vocational counseling is the General Aptitude Test Battery. The Armed Services Vocational Aptitude Battery is used for selection and occupational placement purposes in the U.S. military.

Scores on an aptitude battery alone are inadequate for effective academic or vocational counseling. Past performance, interests and motivation, personality characteristics, and situational factors must also be taken into account.

## QUESTIONS AND ACTIVITIES

1.  Empirical support for a distinction between aptitude and achievement was obtained in a cross-sectional investigation by Burket (1973). It was found that achievement scores *increased* with increasing grade level when aptitude scores were held constant, but aptitude scores *decreased* with increasing grade level when achievement scores were held constant. These findings, combined with those of other investigators (for example, Carroll, 1973), may be interpreted in terms of the following equation: achievement = aptitude × experience. Explain.

2.  Identify at least two tests in each of the following categories: psychomotor abilities, mechanical ability, clerical ability, and creativity.

3.  Compare the work of test developers at the Minnesota Employment Stabilization Research Institute during the late 1920s with that of the designers of the Aviation Cadet Classification Battery during World War II.

4.  What are the advantages and disadvantages of administering an aptitude test battery rather than several single tests of special abilities?

5.  How do the purposes of personnel selection and screening differ from those of classification and placement? What kinds of tests are most appropriate for assisting the decision-making process in selection and/or screening? In classification and placement?

6.  Write a critical review of any of the separate tests of special abilities described in this chapter, following the outline given in question 8 of Chapter 6.

7.  Arrange to visit a local optometrist or ophthalmologist and ask him or her to describe the procedures and instruments used in testing a person's vision. What aspects of vision are measured routinely, and which ones are measured only under special circumstances? Prepare a report of your findings.

8.  Arrange to visit the administrative offices of your local school district and interview the school psychologist or director of special education about the psychological tests administered by these professionals. For example, what tests are used in assessing the special abilities or disabilities of students? How often are students tested or screened for visual problems? Prepare a report of your findings.

9.  John makes a *T* score of 65 on the verbal comprehension test and a *T* score of 75 on the numerical reasoning test of a multiple-aptitude test battery. If the reliabilities of the two tests are .90 and .85, respectively, can the examiner be 95 percent sure that John is poorer in verbal comprehension than in numerical ability? Support your answer with appropriate computations.

10. Run all seven programs in Category F ("Tests of Special Abilities") of *Computer Programs for Psychological Assessment.* Compare your results with those of your classmates.

# Part Three

# Assessment of Personality and Preferences

# 10

# INTERESTS, ATTITUDES, AND VALUES

Scores on tests of intelligence and special abilities are among the best predictors of educational and occupational success. Such tests are measures of *maximum performance,* in that they indicate what a person is capable of achieving under optimal conditions. Questionnaires and inventories of preferences and other affective variables do not typically contribute as much as cognitive measures to the prediction of success in school and on the job, but they are very useful in educational and vocational counseling. These measures of *typical performance* often add significantly to information obtained from measures of ability and past performance.

One shortcoming of affective assessment instruments is that most are not as objective and therefore not as reliable as cognitive tests. It is even debatable whether questionnaires, self-report inventories, and other affective measuring instruments deserve the title of *tests.* Nevertheless, many affective instruments have very respectable reliabilities, appreciable validities for certain purposes, and other characteristics of good tests.

Three affective variables that have received a great deal of research attention are *interests, attitudes,* and *values.* Measures of these variables, which serve both as predictors of outcomes and outcome criteria in their own right, are the topics of the present chapter. In Chapters 11 and 12, our survey of affective measures will be completed with an examination of various types of personality assessment procedures and instruments.

## INTERESTS AND INTEREST MEASUREMENT

Information on a person's *interests,* or preferences for certain kinds of activities and objects, can be obtained in various ways. The most direct method, simply asking a person what he or she is interested in, has its pitfalls. For example, people often have little insight into what their vocational interests are or what particular occupations entail. Nevertheless, these *expressed interests* are sometimes better predictors than less direct information and should not be overlooked in counseling situations. The results of one extensive investigation showed, for example, that the really large differences between occupational groups were in expressed interests rather than cognitive abilities (Flanagan, Tiedeman, & Willis, 1973). Engineering students scored much higher than average on mechanical–technical and physical science interests, whereas law students scored higher on public service (politics), literary–linguistic activity, business, and sales interests.

Other methods of determining interests include observations of behavior, such as participation in various activities, inferring interests from knowledge of special terminology or other information about specific occupations, and administering one of the more than 200 available interest inventories. These four approaches to interest measurement—asking for expressions of interests, deducing interests from observed behavior, inferring interests from performance on tests of abilities, and determining interests from paper-and-pencil inventories—are applicable to the assessment of the basic interest groups described by Super and Crites (1962). These eight interest groups are scientific, social welfare, literary, material, systematic, contact, esthetic expression, and esthetic interpretation.

## Historical Background and Uses

Beginning with the work of Thorndike (1912) and others, research on interests has not been limited to applied contexts; many research studies on the origins and dynamics of interests have been conducted. However, standardized methods of measuring interests were developed initially for purposes of vocational counseling and selection. James Miner is credited with the first systematic efforts to design criterion-related and content-validated measures of vocational interests. An interest questionnaire constructed by Miner in 1915 led to a historic seminar on interest measurement at the Carnegie Institute of Technology in 1919 and subsequently to the construction of standardized vocational interest inventories. A prominent figure in those developments was E. K. Strong, Jr., who, encouraged by the success of one of his doctoral students (K. Cowdery) in differentiating between engineers, lawyers, and physicians on the basis of their interests, expanded these efforts by launching a research program to differentiate among many different vocations in terms of interests. The research of Strong and his students led to the development of the Strong Vocational Interest Blank for Men and a companion instrument for women in the late 1920s and 1930s. Other noteworthy events in the history of interest measurement were the publication in 1939 of the Kuder Preference Record and the research on objective interest measures conducted by U.S. Army Air Corps psychologists during World War II. Many interest inventories were published after the war, but modifications of Strong's and Kuder's original instruments continued to be the most popular.

Today, interest inventories are administered for a number of reasons in a variety of settings. Traditionally, these instruments have been used principally in occupational and educational counseling in high schools, colleges, and vocational rehabilitation contexts. They have also been used extensively in research on individual and group differences, both in basic research to determine the nature, origins, and effects of interests and in applied research for vocational counseling, selection, and placement. Other applications of interest inventories include assistance in making avocational choices, mid-career decisions, and preretirement and retirement decisions (Hansen & Campbell, 1985). Although school counselors and psychological researchers are undoubtedly the largest groups of users of vocational interest inventories, industrial consultants, career development managers, and human resources practitioners also find them useful.

## Origins and Stability of Interests

The vocational interests of young children typically have an element of fantasy. Children fantasize about being glamorous, talented, heroic, or adventurous, but such fantasies may have little to do with their abilities or knowledge of what particular occupations entail. Children normally progress from a fantasy stage to a transition stage in late childhood and early adolescence and, finally, to a more realistic stage in the development of vocational interests during late adolescence and early adulthood.

Although vocational interests do not become very specific, realistic, or stable until high school or beyond, the general direction of a person's interests may be apparent fairly early in life. Young children tend to engage in activities that they view as appropriate and to avoid activities that they consider inappropriate for themselves (Tyler, 1964). They also make distinctions between people roles and life roles. According to Anne Roe and her coauthors (Roe & Siegelman, 1964; Roe & Klos, 1969), vocational interests, and hence career choices, result from the kinds of relationships children have with their families. A warm, accepting family atmosphere tends to create a "people" orientation, whereas a cold, aloof family atmosphere is more likely to result in an "object" or "thing" orientation. From a social learning perspective, interests are viewed as the results of differential reinforcement for engaging in certain activities, coupled with imitation and modeling of people who are important to the individual.

**The Role of Heredity**   Environment certainly affects interests to a substantial degree, but the findings of one study (Grotevant, Scarr, & Weinberg, 1977) suggest that a child is born with a hereditary predisposition to be interested in certain things. In this study of 114 biologically related families, many significant correlations between children's and parents' scores on an interest inventory were found. In contrast, few significant correlations were found between the interests of parents and children in 109 adoptive families. Biologically related children were more similar in their interest patterns than nonbiologically related children, and the interests of same-sex pairs of children were more similar than those of opposite-sex pairs. The results of a widely cited Minnesota study of identical twins reared apart also indicated that the correlations between the interests of identical twins are greater than those between the interests of other family pairs (Bouchard et al., 1983). Because identical twins have identical heredities, these findings have been interpreted as demonstrating the influence of heredity on interests.

A common belief is that parental behavior is more influential than heredity in shaping children's interests, but Scarr and her colleagues concluded that what parents do apparently has little effect on the children's interests (Grotevant, Scarr, & Weinberg, 1977). Rather than trying to force or lead them into certain interest areas, these researchers recommended that children be provided with a variety of experiences and models. They will then have a better opportunity to develop whatever interest predispositions or inclinations toward specific activities they naturally possess.

Granting that people tend to be interested in the things that they do well and that heredity plays a significant role in determining both abilities and temperament, it can be argued that heredity affects interests indirectly by way of abilities, temperament, and physical structure. For example, a person with a genetically based high level of activity but a modest level of intelligence will probably have little interest in becoming a theoretical physicist who spends most of the time thinking about scientific problems. On the other hand, a temperamentally energetic and physically able person may show a greater interest in becoming a professional athlete.

***Stability of Interests***   Individual patterns of likes and dislikes begin developing long before one has had experiences with specific occupations. These early interests are relatively unstable, but by the time a child has reached the ninth grade, and almost certainly by the eleventh grade, his or her preferences for specific types of activities are fairly well established. Longitudinal studies spanning two decades and more have demonstrated that interests are fairly stable after the late teens (Strong, 1955). On the other hand, a person's interests can change even in adulthood, and particular caution should be exercised in interpreting the results of interest inventories administered before the ninth grade (Crites, 1969).

## Validity of Interest Inventories

Because of the importance of academic and vocational guidance, commercially available interest inventories have been almost as popular as tests of general intelligence and special abilities. Compared with cognitive measures, however, interest inventories are not very accurate predictors of school grades or occupational performance. On the average, scores on interest inventories correlate around .20 to .30 with school marks, whereas scores on general intelligence tests correlate around .50 with the same criterion. Scores on interest inventories contribute to the prediction of occupational selection, persistence, and satisfaction, but job success is usually more closely related to ability than to interests (Kuder, 1963; Campbell & Hansen, 1981). Because people are more likely to avoid occupations that they dislike than they are to enter occupations that they like, low scores on interest inventories tend to be more predictive of what a person will not do than high scores are of what he or she will do (Dolliver, Irvin, & Bigley, 1972; Zytowski, 1976).

***Faking***   As is also true of ability tests, the validity of interest inventories in predicting occupational choice is affected by test-taking factors and personal characteristics. Whether or not they are intentionally faked, responses to interest inventories may not indicate the true interests of people. Certainly, they can fake them if they wish to. Bridgman and Hollenbeck (1961) found, for example, that, when directed to do so, college students filled out an interest inventory (Kuder Form D) in such a way that their responses were very similar to those of people who were employed in the specified occupations. Interest inventories are less useful when it is advantageous to give false reports, which is more likely when the scores are used for educational or employment selection purposes. Responding falsely to an interest inventory is, however, much less likely when the inventory is administered for purposes of academic and vocational counseling. Even when people might seem to benefit from giving untruthful answers to an interest inventory, they do not necessarily do so. For example, the Strong Vocational Interest Inventory was used for many years to select individuals for advanced training in the U.S. Navy. Under such circumstances, it might be supposed that faking would be a problem. However, this was not found to be the case (Abrahams, Neumann, and Gilthens, 1971). The mean scores of a group of young men who took the Strong as part of a Navy scholarship application were quite similar to the scores that they obtained in high school a year before or in college a year after applying for the scholarship. In addition, correlations between the interest score profiles obtained under the scholarship application condition and those obtained under routine testing conditions were in the .90s. It might have been advantageous for the applicants to produce a more favorable outcome by faking, but they did not do so to any appreciable degree.

***Response Sets***   Although not the same as intentional faking, the tendency to respond to the structure rather than the content of test items (*response sets*) can also result in inaccurate scores on interest inventories. Of particular concern are the response sets of *acquiescence* (agreeing rather than disagreeing when uncertain) and *social desirability* (giving a more socially desirable response). One technique designed to minimize these response sets is the *forced-choice* format. Items having this format consist of two or more descriptive statements that are equal in social desirability but different in content and validity. On a forced-choice interest item, examinees are instructed to indicate which of the activities described in the three or four choices they would like to do and which they would least like to do (see Figure 10–2 later). Unfortunately, people sometimes find the forced-choice format awkward and frustrating.

***Socioeconomic Status***   One demographic factor that is significantly related to responses, and consequently to the validity of interest inventories, is the socioeconomic status of the respondent. Working-class people do not always have an opportunity to cultivate their interests or to train for and enter occupations that are appealing to them. To these individuals, monetary security is a more important factor in employment decisions than satisfying one's interests. This is one reason why, for many years, psychologists showed little inclination to construct inventories to measure the vocational interests of people who were planning to enter unskilled, semiskilled, or even skilled occupations. Because money seemed to be a more important occupational determinant than satisfying one's vocational interests, the development of interest inventories for nonprofessional occupations was viewed as unproductive. Early interest inventories were designed almost entirely for use in counseling young people who planned to enter the professions. The situation changed somewhat after World War II, but the principal focus of interest inventories remains on the professions.

At the high end of the socioeconomic scale are children of the wealthy, who may have strong vocational interests, but for whom familial and societal expectations and traditions are often more influential than individual interests in determining career choices. Children in affluent families may not be permitted to do what they like, either because the status or monetary rewards of occupations consistent with their interests are not high enough or because parents expect their offspring to follow in their footsteps or even surpass the parents' own accomplishments. On the other hand, young people in the upwardly mobile middle class are more likely to try to improve their chances of success by entering occupations in which they have strong interests, perhaps even if they do not possess the requisite abilities. For this reason, vocational interests have traditionally been more important in determining occupational selection, and scores on interest inventories have been more predictive of occupational choice for middle-class than for upper-class and working-class people (McArthur & Stevens, 1955). In any event, it would seem that most occupations in the modern workplace do not provide for satisfaction of the interests of most workers (Warnath, 1975). So what do workers do when they find that there are large discrepancies between what they would like to do and what they have to do in order to survive? In most cases, rather than jeopardizing their security in a relentless pursuit of their vocational interests and ambitions, they are much more likely to adjust their aspirations to be closer to what they can actually attain (Gottfredson & Becker, 1981).

## STRONG AND KUDER INVENTORIES

### Strong Inventories

As a result of research conducted during the 1920s, E. K. Strong, Jr. discovered consistent, significant differences in reports by people of what they liked and disliked. Strong decided to construct an inventory to assess these individual differences in interests, and began by constructing a variety of items concerning preferences for specific occupations, school subjects, amusements, activities, and types of people. He then administered these items, in addition to a scale for rating one's abilities and characteristics, to groups of men employed in specific occupations. By comparing the responses of these occupational groups to those of men in general, Strong was able to develop several dozen occupational scales consisting of items that significant numbers of men in specific occupations answered differently from men in general. This Strong Vocational Interest Blank for Men was the first standardized and commercially produced measure of interests. Several years later, when it became clear that the interests of women were not limited to clerical work, school teaching, nursing and housewifery, a companion instrument, the Strong Vocational Interest Blank for Women, was devised.

For various reasons, including the desire to comply with Title IX of the Civil Rights Act of 1964 and to counter allegations of sexism, in 1974 the men's and women's forms of the Strong Vocational Interest Blank were combined into a single instrument, the Strong–Campbell Interest Inventory (SCII). An effort was made to remove sex bias in the content of the items and the occupational labels and to create a more gender-free inventory. It was recognized, however, that gender bias had been reduced but not entirely eliminated on the SCII.

***Format of the Strong Interest Inventory***   The latest (1994) edition of the instrument originated by Strong is the Strong Interest Inventory (SII). This inventory consists of 317 items grouped into the following eight parts:

*I. Occupations*   Each of 135 occupational titles is responded to with like (L), indifferent (I), or dislike (D).

*II. School Subjects*   Each of 39 school subjects is responded to with like (L), indifferent (I), or dislike (D).

*III. Activities*   Each of 46 general occupational activities is responded to with like (L), indifferent (I), or dislike (D).

*IV. Leisure Activities*   Each of 29 amusements or hobbies is responded to with like (L), indifferent (I), or dislike (D).

*V. Types of People*   Each of 20 types of people is responded to with like (L), indifferent (I), or dislike (D).

*VI. Preference between Two Activities*   For each of 30 pairs of activities, preference between the activity on the left (L) and the activity on the right (R) or no preference (=) is indicated.

*VII. Your Characteristics*   Each of 12 characteristics is responded to with Yes, ?, or No, depending on whether or not they are self-descriptive.

*VIII. Preference in the World of Work*   For each of six pairs of ideas, data, and things, preference between the item on the left (L) and the item on the right (R) or no preference (=) is indicated.

Although the items, format, and administration procedure of the Strong Interest Inventory were essentially unchanged from the preceding edition, the profile was expanded to include 211 occupational scales (102 pairs with separate scales for men and women and 7 scales for occupations represented by a single gender).

**Scoring**   The SII can be scored only by computer, the item weights and scoring procedures being a trade secret. Completed inventories are sent to the publisher (Consulting Psychologists Press) for scoring, profiling, and interpretation, or they can be scored and interpreted by software sold to users. The Strong Profile report presents and profiles the examinee's scores on hundreds of scales; other types of reports, such as the Strong Interpretive Report, which provides detailed graphic information on the examinee's occupational interests and tailored descriptions of the best occupations for him or her, are also available.

The SII is scored on five groups of measures: Administrative Indexes, General Occupational Themes, Basic Interest Scales, Occupational Scales, and Personal Style Scales. Before attempting to interpret a person's scores on the last four categories, scores on three Administrative Indexes should be checked: the Total Responses Index; the Like, Indifferent, and Dislike Percent Indexes; and the Infrequent Responses Index. The Total Responses Index should not fall below 300 (out of 317); the Like, Indifferent, and Dislike Percent Indexes should not fall outside the range of 14 to 60; and the Infrequent Responses Index should not be less than zero (Harmon et al., 1994). The Administrative Indexes are listed at the bottom of page 6 of the six-page "Snapshot: A Summary of Results."

As shown in Figure 10–1, the SII is scored on six General Occupational Themes. These themes are based on the six categories of Holland's (1985) "vocational personalities": Realistic (R), Investigative (I), Artistic (A), Social (S), Enterprising (E), and Conventional (C). The examinee's standard *T* score and his or her score position in the range of the middle 50 percent of the norm groups of men and women, on each RIASEC theme and the three to five Basic Interest Scales falling under it, are listed in the far right column of the appropriate box on page 2 of the summary. The 25 Basic Interest Scales were constructed by grouping items

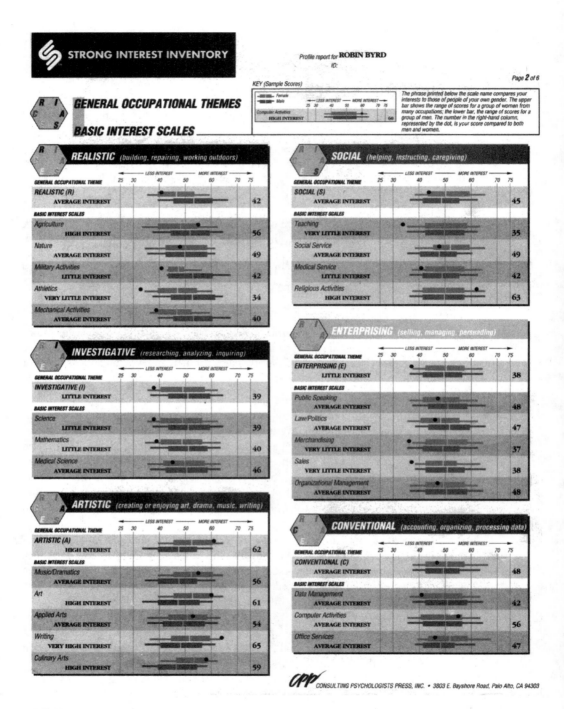

**FIGURE 10–1** Page 2 of Sample Snapshot Profile of Scores on the Strong Interest Inventory.

(Reprinted by special permission of the distributor, Consulting Psychologists Press, from the Strong Interest Inventory, by Lenore W. Harmon, Jo-Ida C. Hanson, Fred H. Borgen, and Allen C. Hammer. © Copyright 1994 by the Board of Trustees of Leland Stanford Junior University.)

with high intercorrelations. Scores on these scales represent the strength and consistency of special areas of interest (Agriculture, Science, Music/Dramatics, Teaching, Public Speaking, Data Management, and so on). $T$ scores on the scales are designated as Very Little Interest, Little Interest, Average Interest, High Interest, or Very High Interest.

$T$ scores on the 109 Occupational Scales, consisting of separate scores for men and women on 102 scales and combined gender scores on 7 scales, are listed under the appropriate RIASEC theme on pages 3 to 5 of the "Snapshot." Each of the Occupational Scales was constructed by comparing the responses of men or women employed in a particular occupation with the responses of a reference group of men or women in general. All but seven of the Occupational Scales were matched with opposite-gender scales and standardized separately by gender. A person's raw score on a given occupational scale is determined by adding the numerical weights assigned to his or her responses on the scale. The assigned weight depends on the direction in which the item discriminates between men or women employed in that occupation and men or women in general. After all weights corresponding to a person's responses to the items on a particular scale have been added, the obtained raw score is converted to a standard $T$ score that varies directly with the degree of similarity between the examinee's responses and those of the specific occupational group. $T$ scores are grouped into three categories: Dissimilar Interests, Mid-range, and Similar Interests.

Profiles of $T$ scores and ranges of the middle 50 percent of scores in the norm groups of men and women on the four Personal Style Scales are given on page 6 of the "Snapshot." These are bipolar scales with the following definitions:

Work style: "Works with ideas/data/things" versus "Works with people"

Learning environment: "Practical" versus "Academic"

Leadership style: "Leads by example" versus "Directs others"

Risk taking/adventure: "Plays it safe" versus "Takes chances"

Scores on the Personal Style Scales are also helpful in vocational counseling and career exploration.

**Psychometric Characteristics**   The developmental sample for the Strong Interest Inventory was a group of over 55,000 people in 50 occupations who took the inventory in 1992–1993. However, only 9467 women and 9484 men from this group were used as general reference samples. This was sufficient to permit accurate validation of old occupational scales and the development of new ones. With respect to the reliability of the SII, high internal consistency and test–retest coefficients on scores on the General Occupational Themes, the Basic Interest Scales, the Occupational Scales, and the Personal Style Scales have been obtained in groups of college students and employed adults. Cronbach alpha coefficients for the General Occupational Themes range from .90 to .94 in the reference sample of men and women, and test–retest coefficients over a 3 to 6 month interval in a sample of 65 employed women and 75 employed men range from .84 to .92. Alpha coefficients for the Basic Interest Scales range from .74 to .94 in the reference sample, and test–retest coefficients in a sample of approximately 200 men and women range from .82 to .94. For the Personal Style Scales, alphas range from 178 to 91 in the reference sample; test–retest coefficients (1 to 4 month interval) in a sample of 128 women and 103 men range from .81 to .92. The great majority of the test–retest coefficients in samples of college students and employed adults for the Occupational Scales were also in the .80s and .90s.

Various kinds of evidence concerning the validity—content, concurrent, predictive, construct—of the SII are reported in the manual (Harmon et al., 1994). Content validity is perhaps the easiest to establish: an analysis of the composition of the 1994 SII supports the claim of content validity for this instrument. Ranking mean scores on the General Occupational Themes, Basic Interest Scales, Personal Style Scales, and Occupational Scales on the 109 occupational groups provides evidence for concurrent and construct validity, as do correlations between similar measures on other interest inventories (for example, Holland's Vocational Interest Inventory). Similarly, differences in mean scores on the Personal Style Scales by educational level, educational major, and occupation reinforce the validity claim for these scales. The 1994 edition of the SII is still too new for extensive data on the long-term validity of this inventory to have been collected. However, the results of predictive validity studies conducted with previous editions of the Strong (Campbell, 1971; Hansen & Campbell, 1985) have been extrapolated to the 1994 edition.

### Kuder Interest Inventories

In contrast to the varied item format of the Strong Interest Inventory, G. F. Kuder employed a forced-choice item format in designing his interest inventories. To construct his first inventory, the Kuder Vocational Preference Record, Kuder administered a list of statements concerning activities to college students and determined from their responses which items clustered together. The results led him to construct 10 groups of items having low correlations across item groups but high correlations within groups. Then triads of items, each member of a triad belonging to a different interest group or area, were formed and administered in forced-choice format. In this way, interests in different areas were pitted against one another.

Items on the Kuder inventories consist of three statements of activities, and examinees are directed to indicate which of the three activities they *most* prefer and which they *least* prefer. Responses to the first item triad in Figure 10–2 indicate that this person would most like to visit a museum and least like to visit an art gallery. Of the activities listed in the second item triad, the person would most like to collect coins and least like to collect stones.

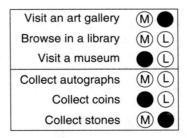

**FIGURE 10–2** Examples of Items on the Kuder General Interest Survey. (From the Kuder General Interest Survey, Form E, Answer Sheet, by G. Frederic Kuder. Copyright © 1985, 1976, 1963 by G. Frederic Kuder. Used by permission of the publisher, CTB/McGraw-Hill.)

There are both advantages and disadvantages to the forced-choice item format. Although it tends to minimize certain response sets (acquiescence, social desirability, and so forth), people sometimes find the forced-choice response format awkward. Another problem is the ipsative nature of responses to forced-choice items: by accepting or rejecting an activity in one area, the respondent does not select or reject an activity falling on another area. For this reason it is impossible to obtain uniformly high or uniformly low scores across all interest areas. A typical score pattern consists of high scores on one or more areas, low scores on one or more areas, and average scores on the remaining areas.

***Kuder General Interest Survey***   Form C of the Kuder Vocational Preference Record is still commercially available, but more popular are the Kuder General Interest Survey, Form E (KGIS), and the Kuder Occupational Interest Survey, Form DD (KOIS). The KGIS, which was designed for grades 6–12 and takes 45 to 60 minutes to complete, consists of 168 triads of statements describing various activities; one activity in each triad is to be marked Most Preferred and one Least Preferred. The KGIS is scored on 10 general interest areas: Outdoor, Mechanical, Computational, Scientific, Persuasive, Artistic, Literary, Musical, Social Service, and Clerical, plus a Verification (V) scale that indicates whether the responses were marked carefully and sincerely. Separate percentile norms for four groups (males and females in grades 6–8 and males and females in grades 9–12) were obtained in 1987. The availability of separate gender norms permits examinees to compare their KGIS scores with those of both boys and girls. The narrative report format provides a rank-order listing of percentiles in the 10 interest areas, as well as the three themes in Holland's RIASEC system on which the examinee ranks highest with respect to other males and with respect to other females. Although the provision of separate gender norms helps to control for gender bias resulting from combined norms, differences in the interests of males and females can be seen in the fact that, on the average, boys score higher on the Mechanical, Computational, Scientific, and Persuasive scales, while girls score higher on the Artistic, Literary, Musical, Social Service, and Clerical scales.

***Kuder Occupational Interest Survey***   The KOIS, which was designed for grade 11 through adulthood and takes 30 to 40 minutes to complete, consists of 100 triads of statements describing various activities: one activity in each triad is to be marked Most Preferred and one Least Preferred. In addition to the traditional paper-and-pencil form, a personal computer version of the KOIS (Kuder DD/PC) is available.

In scoring the KOIS, the responses of the examinee are compared with those of people who were reportedly satisfied with their occupational choices; responses are also compared with those of college students majoring in particular fields of study. A person's score on any of the KOIS occupational or college-major scales is a modified biserial correlation coefficient (*lambda coefficient*) between his or her responses to the items and the proportion of individuals in the specified occupational or college major group who endorsed each item. The higher the lambda coefficient is, the more closely the person's score resembles the interest pattern of the corresponding occupational group or major. The narrative report of scores on the KOIS lists the lambda coefficients for occupational and college-major scales by gender of the norm group. In interpreting a person's lambda coefficients, the highest coefficients are emphasized; the associated occupations or majors are those in which the examinee's interests are greatest. However, it is recommended that occupations or majors having lambda coefficients within .06 units of the highest coefficients also be considered.

***Reliability and Validity of the KGIS and KOIS***   The short-term test–retest reliability coefficients of the KGIS and KOIS scales are in the .80s and .90s, and the scores have been found to be fairly stable over a decade or more (Zytowski, 1976). In general, the evidence indicates that the content validities of both the KGIS and the KOIS are satisfactory. With respect to the predictive validity of the KOIS, Zytowski (1976) found that over half the individuals who had taken it 12 to 19 years earlier had entered occupations on which they had scored within .07 to .12 points of their highest lambda coefficients.

## OTHER GENERAL- AND SPECIAL-PURPOSE INTEREST INVENTORIES

Although the Strong and Kuder inventories have been the most popular of all standardized psychometric instruments for assessing interests, many other general- and special-purpose interest measures have been constructed. A representative sample of these instruments is listed in Table 10–1. The majority of these instruments focus on vocational interests, but several have also been designed primarily to measure school-related interests and interests in various kinds of leisure activities. In addition to surveying interests, one of them, the Campbell Interest and Skill Survey (CISS), provides for self-reports of the respondent's confidence in his or her ability to perform various skills. Many special-purpose inventories for assessing the interests of children, the disadvantaged, and people who plan to enter non-professional occupations have also been published.

### Jackson Vocational Interest Survey

One of the most carefully designed and validated of all general-interest inventories is the Jackson Vocational Interest Survey (JVIS). Based on the results of an extensive research program directed by D. N. Jackson, the JVIS consists of 289 forced-choice pairs of statements describing job-related activities. The statements comprising an item pair refer to two equally popular interests, and examinees are told to indicate a preference between them. Designed for high school age and beyond, the JVIS takes 45 to 60 minutes to complete. Initial scoring is on 34 basic interest scales representing 26 work-role and eight work-style dimensions. Definitions of these dimensions were refined by referring to job descriptions in the *Dictionary of Occupational Titles*. Another approach to scoring the JVIS is in terms of 10 occupational themes (Expressive, Logical, Inquiring, Practical, Assertive, Socialized, Helping, Conventional, Enterprising, Communication). These themes are based on Holland's six "vocational personalities" themes and a factor analysis of responses to the JVIS. Scores on the 10 themes are highly reliable (test–retest coefficients between .82 and .92), as are scores on the 34 basic interest scales (median $r = .84$). With respect to the validity of the JVIS, a large study conducted at Pennsylvania State University found that JVIS profiles did a better job of predicting choice of academic major than any previously reported combination of interest and aptitude measures.

**TABLE 10–1    Representative Vocational Interest Inventories[a]**

Adult Career Concerns Inventory (CPP)
Campbell Interest and Skill Survey (NCS)
Career Assessment Inventory–Enhanced Version (NCS)
Career Assessment Inventory–Vocational Version (NCS)
Career Attitudes and Strategies Inventory (PAR, Psychological Corporation)
The Career Beliefs Inventory (CPP)
Career Decision Scale (PAR)
Career Development Inventory (CPP)
Career Directions Inventory (Sigma)
Career Interest Inventory (Psychological Corporation)
Career Maturity Inventory (CTB/McGraw-Hill)
COPS Interest Inventory (EdITS)
COPS Intermediate Inventory (EdITS)
COPS Picture Inventory of Careers (EdITS)
Forer Vocational Survey: Men–Women (WPS)
Geist Picture Interest Inventory (WPS)
Gordon Occupational Check List II (Psychological Corporation)
Guilford–Zimmerman Interest Inventory (CPP)
Hall Occupational Orientation Inventory (STS)
The Harrington–O'Shea Career Decision-Making System (AGS)
IDEAS (NCS Assessments)
Jackson Vocational Interest Survey (Sigma, Psychological Publications)
Kuder General Interest Survey, Form E (CTB)
Kuder Occupational Interest Survey, Form DD (CTB)
Kuder Vocational Preference Record, Form C (CTB)
Occupational Aptitude Survey and Interest Schedule (pro.ed)
Ohio Vocational Interest Survey, Second Edition (Psychological Corporation)
Reading-Free Vocational Interest Inventory (Psychological Corporation)
School Interest Inventory (Riverside)
Self-Directed Search (Psychological Corporation, Psychological Publications)
16 PF Personal Career Development Profile (IPAT)
Strong Interest Inventory (CPP)
The Vocational Interest Inventory–Revised (WPS)
Vocational Preference Inventory (PAR)
Wide Range Interest–Opinion Test (Jastak, Psychological Corporation, CTB)

[a]Publishers and/or distributors are given in parentheses. See Appendix C for addresses.

Reviewers of the JVIS have praised its careful construction and factorially pure scales, but more evidence for its validity is needed (Davidshofer, 1985; Thomas, 1985). The JVIS is also a rather long inventory, taking more time to complete than an inventory with a similar format, the Kuder Occupational Interest Survey.

## Inventories for Children and the Disadvantaged

Because the vocational interests of children are often neither highly developed nor realistic, interest inventories have focused on students in junior high school and beyond. However, several interests inventories—the Hall Occupational Orientation Inventory–Intermediate and the Wide Range Interest–Opinion Test (WRIOT), for example—can be administered to elementary school children (grades 3–7). These inventories serve to introduce and familiarize children with a wide range of activities and occupations in relation to their current interests, experiences, abilities, and ambitions. The Intermediate Hall contains 110 school-related items designed to complement awareness/development programs and focuses on 22 work and personality characteristics.

The WRIOT and various other instruments (for example, the Geist Picture Interest Inventory and the Reading-Free Vocational Interest Inventory) were developed primarily for culturally and educationally disadvantaged young people. Rather than words, phrases, or statements, for test materials these instruments employ pictures of people engaged in certain activities. The WRIOT consists of 150 sets of three drawings, presented in booklet or filmstrip form, of people engaged in various activities with which physically and mentally handicapped individuals can identify. The WRIOT can be completed in 40 to 60 minutes by individuals ranging in age from 5 years to adulthood. Likes and dislikes are selected in a forced-choice format, and responses are scored on 18 interest clusters (such as art, sales, management, office work, mechanisms, machine operation, and athletics) and eight attitude clusters (sedentariness, risk, ambition, sex stereotype, and so on). Job title lists are available for each of the 18 interest clusters.

On each item of the Geist Picture Inventory, respondents circle the one of three pictures that they prefer. The inventory takes about 25 minutes to complete and is scored on 12 areas. On the Reading-Free Vocational Interest Inventory, the examinee marks his or her preference on each of 55 sets of three drawings depicting job tasks. The drawings represent the kinds of tasks or occupations in which mentally retarded individuals can be productive and proficient (automotive, building trades, clerical, animal care, food service, patient care, horticulture, housekeeping, personal service, laundry, or materials handling).

## Interests in Nonprofessional Occupations

Certain scales on the Strong Interest Inventory, the Kuder Occupational Interest Survey, and other general-interest inventories pertain to interests in nonprofessional occupations, but none of these inventories was designed specifically for this purpose. Since the 1950s, a number of inventories focusing on the skilled trades and somewhat simpler in content and vocabulary than the Strong and Kuder instruments have been constructed. One such instrument is the Career Assessment Inventory.

***Career Assessment Inventory***    The Vocational Version of the Career Assessment Inventory (CAI) was modeled after the Strong inventories and has sometimes been referred to as "the working man's Strong Interest Inventory." Responses to the 305 items on the CAI are on a 5-point scale (L = like very much, l = like somewhat, I = indifferent, d = dislike somewhat, and D = dislike very much). The items, written at a sixth-grade level and covering activities, school subjects, and occupational titles, can be answered in 30 to 45 minutes. The computer-based report of $T$ scores on the CAI consists of four sections: I. Administrative Indices (Total Responses, Response Consistency, Response Percentages on Activities, School Subjects, Occupations); II. General Themes (Realistic, Investigative, Artistic, Social, Enterprising, Conventional); III. Basic Interest Area Scales; and IV. Occupational Scales. The 25 Basic Interest Area Scales and the 111 Occupational Scales are grouped under Holland's six themes. Scores on four special Scales (Fine Arts–Mechanical, Occupational Extroversion–Introversion, Educational Orientation, and Variability of Interests), a computer-generated narrative report, and a counselor's summary are provided. From a psychometric viewpoint, the CAI is well designed and has good reliability. On the negative side, McCabe (1985) noted that no predictive validity information is reported in the manual and that the CAI is relatively expensive to score. Overall, however, he rates the CAI as a very important test that fills a significant need and is well developed and engineered to be easily and appropriately used. A 370-item Enhanced Version of the CAI, which can be scored on more professional occupations than the Vocational Version, was published in 1986. Both the Vocational and Enhanced Versions can also be scored on General Occupational Themes based on Holland's RIASEC model.

## Interests and Personality

According to a holistic conception of personality, interests and abilities are characteristics of personality. Unlike abilities or talents, which are more likely to be perceived as to some extent innate, interests have traditionally been viewed as acquired characteristics produced by fortuitous experiences. A more contemporary conception of interests is that, rather than developing by chance, they are reflections or expressions of deep-seated individual needs and personality traits (Darley & Hagenah, 1955). It follows from this viewpoint that, as psychoanalysts have maintained since Freud's time, vocational selection is influenced by personality traits. It might be surmised, for example, that becoming either a butcher or a surgeon is an expression of strong aggressive or sadistic impulses and that becoming an actor or other performer is a reflection of exhibitionistic needs.

With respect to the research evidence linking interests to personality, it has been found that the incidence of psychoneurosis is higher among people who have strong literary and esthetic interests, that introversion is more common among people with scientific interests, and that aggressiveness is related to an interest in selling (Darley & Hagenah, 1955; Osipow, 1983; Super & Bohn, 1970). Two psychologists whose research and theorizing on the relationships of interests to personality have been particularly influential are Anne Roe and J. L. Holland.

***Roe's Theory***   On the basis of observations and research on careers, Roe (1956) concluded that the primary factor in career choice is whether one is person oriented or nonperson oriented. Roe's revised theory contains two independent dimensions or continua. On the first dimension, occupational roles are classified as ranging from orientation to purposeful communication at one end through orientation to resource utilization at the other end. On the second dimension, occupational roles range from interpersonal relations at one extreme to orientation to natural phenomena at the other end. Although these two basic dimensions are a central feature of Roe's theory, it is actually much more elaborate and has influenced the development of several interest inventories. Three of these instruments are the COPS Interest Inventory, the Hall Occupational Orientation Inventory, and the Vocational Interest Inventory. The Hall Occupational Orientation Inventory, which focuses on 22 job and personality characteristics, is appropriate for individuals from grade 3 through adulthood. The Vocational Interest Inventory, designed for grade 3 through adulthood, consists of 112 forced-choice items focusing on eight occupational areas: Service, Business Contact, Organization, Technical, Outdoor, Science, General Culture, Arts and Entertainment.

***Holland's Instruments and Theory***    The notion that interest inventories are actually measures of personality is made explicit in J. L. Holland's Self-directed Search and Vocational Preference Inventory. One of the most widely used career interest inventories, the Self-Directed Search (SDS)–Form R 1994 Revision consists of an assessment booklet designed to help the user to make a thoughtful evaluation of his or her own interests and abilities and an Occupations Finder (Occu-Find) for actively exploring the entire range of possible occupations. As noted in the discussion of the SII, the six RIASEC scores yielded by the SDS are Realistic, Investigative, Artistic, Social, Enterprising, and Conventional (see Figure 10–3). The norms are incorporated in a three-letter occupational code, and the Occu-Find contains over 1100 occupational titles keyed to the code. The SDS and the Occu-Find have been used extensively in many contexts, not the least of which is the ASVAB Career Exploration Program of the U.S. Department of Defense (1994).

The Vocational Preference Inventory (VPI) is a supplement to the Self-directed Search and other interest inventories. It is based on Holland's theory that occupations can be described in terms of personality characteristics. Respondents indicate whether they like or dislike each of more than 160 different occupations, and their responses are scored on 11

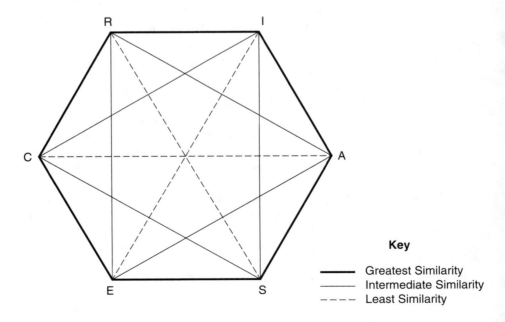

**Key**

—— Greatest Similarity
—— Intermediate Similarity
- - - Least Similarity

**FIGURE 10–3**   Holland's Hexagonal Model of Interests.

scales: Realistic, Investigative, Artistic, Scientific, Enterprising, Conventional, Self-Control, Status, Masculinity–Femininity, Infrequency, and Acquiescence. The first six (RIASEC) scores can be used with the SDS Occu-Find for purposes of career exploration and vocational guidance. Different patterns of high scores on these six types result in assignment of the examinee to different vocational categories. For example, a person who scores high on the Conventional, Enterprising, and Social scales falls in the same category as advertising agents and sales representatives.

**Gender Differences**    Also reflective of personality differences are the sex-stereotyped patterns of scores obtained on the Strong Interest Inventory, the Vocational Preference Inventory, the Vocational Interest Inventory (VPI), and other measures of interests. For example, women tend to score higher than men on the Social, Artistic, and Conventional themes, whereas men score higher on the Realistic, Investigative, and Enterprising themes of the VPI (Gottfredson, Holland, & Gottfredson, 1975; Prediger & Hanson, 1976). Similar gender differences have been found in scores on the Vocational Interest Inventory and the Strong Interest Inventory. It has been argued that such differences are due to items that focus on specific activities or materials with which one sex has more experience than the other. Examples are carpentry and automobile-repairing items on Holland's Realistic scale, which are more familiar to males; redesigning the items to include a sewing machine or a blender might make them more familiar to females.

It has been alleged, with some justification, that the Strong and other early interest inventories contributed to gender discrimination by directing young women into traditional women's occupations such as teaching, nursing, and clerical work (Diamond, 1979). Responding to the allegation of gender bias, developers of the Strong Interest Inventory and certain other psychometric instruments constructed unisex forms of the instruments. Furthermore, combined gender norms, as well as the traditional separate-sex norms, are provided. To eliminate gender differences in responses, certain instruments, such as the revised version of the Vocational Interest Inventory and the Unisex Edition of the ACT Interest Inventory, utilize sex-balanced items. Such items were endorsed by approximately equal percentages of men and women. Perhaps an even more effective way of reducing or eliminating gender differences in scores on interest inventories is to provide equal opportunities, encouragement, and experiences for both sexes in a variety of activities—both traditionally male and traditionally female.[1]

**Personality Inventories and Interests**    Personality inventories like those described in Chapter 12 usually contain a number of items concerning interests, attitudes, and values. For this reason, scores on many of these inventories provide information that is useful in academic and vocational counseling. One such inventory is the 16 Personality Factor Questionnaire (16 PF). As illustrated in Report 10–1, the 16 PF can be scored and interpreted by computer on occupational variables corresponding to Holland's RIASEC themes. The resulting profile of scores on these variables can be compared with the profiles of dozens of occupations to determine the similarity between the respondent's interests and those of each occupational group.

---

[1]Concern over sex discrimination, as well as the nature and origin of sex differences in psychological characteristics, also stimulated the development of a number of measures of gender role, prominent among which are the Bem Sex-Role Inventory and the Personal Attributes Questionnaire.

## REPORT 10–1    Vocational Interests Interpreted with Report 12–1.
(Copyright © 1994 by the Institute for Personality and Ability Testing, Inc. Reproduced by permission. "16 PF" is a registered trade mark of IPAT, Inc.)

```
Basic Interpretive Report                         NAME: Jody A. Good
Vocational Activities                             DATE: January 22, 1996
```

### Vocational Activities

Different occupational interests have been found to be associated with personality qualities.  The following section compares Mr. Good's personality to these known associations.  The information below indicates the degree of similarity between Mr. Good's personality characteristics and each of the six Holland Occupational Types (Self Directed Search; Holland, 1985).  Those occupational areas for which Mr. Good's personality profile shows the highest degree of similarity are described in greater detail.  Descriptions are based on item content of the Self Directed Search as well as the personality predictions of the Holland types as measured by the 16PF.

Remember that this information is intended to expand Mr. Good's range of career options rather than to narrow them.  All comparisons should be considered with respect to other relevant information about Mr. Good, particularly his interests, abilities, and other personal resources.

### Holland Themes

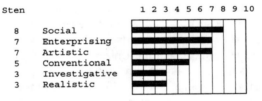

```
Sten                    1 2 3 4 5 6 7 8 9 10

   8    Social
   7    Enterprising
   7    Artistic
   5    Conventional
   3    Investigative
   3    Realistic
```

**Social = 8**
Mr. Good shows personality characteristics similar to Social persons, who indicate a preference for associating with other people.  Such interactions are distinguished by a nurturing, sympathetic quality.  Mr. Good may find it very easy to relate to all kinds of people.  In addition to being warm and friendly, Social persons are typically receptive to different views and opinions.  They feel most comfortable in positions that allow for regular social interaction.  It might be worthwhile to explore whether Mr. Good enjoys working with others and having them seek him out for advice or comfort.

```
        Occupational Fields: Teaching
                             Counseling
                             Psychology
                             Social Work
                             Health Services
```

---

**REPORT 10–1   Continued**

---

**Enterprising = 7**
Mr. Good shows personality characteristics similar to Enterprising persons, who
enjoy interacting with others in an assertive role.  Social interactions are warm
and animated; Enterprising persons may enjoy being the focus of attention.  Such
persons are socially bold and may try to persuade others or assume a position of
leadership.  It might be worthwhile to explore whether Mr. Good's interests and
experiences are very business-oriented, and whether he possesses good sales and/or
managerial skills.

    Occupational Fields: Business
                         Sales
                         Political Activity
                         Management
                         Law

**Artistic = 7**
Mr. Good shows personality characteristics similar to Artistic persons, who are
self-expressive, typically through a particular mode such as art, music, design,
writing, acting, composing, etc.  Like Artistic persons, Mr. Good may be venturesome
and open to different views and experiences.  Sometimes he may be preoccupied with
thoughts and ideas, which may relate to the overall creative process.  He may do his
best work in an unstructured, flexible environment.  It may be worthwhile to explore
whether Mr. Good appreciates aesthetics and possesses artistic, design, or musical
talents.

    Occupational Fields: Art
                         Music
                         Design
                         Theater
                         Writing

---

## Using Interest Inventories in Counseling

Young men and women are often unrealistic in making academic and vocational plans.
Many more high school students expect to graduate from college than actually do, and the
career aspirations of college graduates are often incompatible with their career possibilities.
Career aims and decisions are affected not only by environmental factors such as the economic situation and the kinds of jobs available, but also by gender, socioeconomic status,
physical and mental abilities, interests, and knowledge of particular occupations. Consequently, high school and college counselors should be informed about the world of work—
what particular jobs entail—and whether the abilities, interests, and resources possessed by
students are appropriate for entering or preparing for certain jobs. Properly trained counselors are prepared to obtain personal data from students and other counselees and to supply them with information on training programs and occupations.

Vocational counseling must be conducted with caution. Both jobs and students are mul-
tifaceted and dynamic: they possess many different features, and those features change with
time. The job of psychologist, for example, may involve different activities in different situations, and the nature of the job has changed over the years. Even in the same situational

context and time period, there is usually enough diversity in most jobs for people with different abilities and interests to adapt and perform satisfactorily.

**Interests Are Not Abilities**   Despite the need for a flexible, probabilistic approach to vocational counseling, counselors must make some interpretation of scores on psychological tests and inventories. One obvious distinction that counselors should make is between aspirations on the one hand and interests and abilities on the other. Aspirations are often colored by false perceptions of what a particular activity or occupation entails. For example, a child who aspires to become a nurse may picture herself (himself) as a Florence Nightingale, helping suffering humanity and reaping the praises and love of others. But the child may be unaware of the fact that nursing involves a great deal of standing and walking, emptying bed pans, and listening to endless complaints. Consequently, effectiveness in nursing may depend as much on possessing a strong pair of ankles and a high olfactory tolerance as on love for humanity.

In interpreting the results of an interest inventory, counselors should be aware of and attempt to clarify the difference between interests and abilities. It is not uncommon for a student to conclude from the results of an interest inventory that he or she has the requisite abilities to succeed in a certain occupation, when actually all that has been shown is that the student's interests are similar to those of employees in that occupation. Because students sometimes fail to distinguish between interests and abilities, it is unwise to leave the task of interpreting a self-administered inventory to the student alone. This is especially true of younger students.

The fact that correlations between measures of interests and abilities tend to be rather low indicates that many people do not have the abilities required for success on jobs in which they are interested and that others are not interested in jobs for which they have the necessary abilities. For this reason, scores on interest inventories should be employed in vocational counseling in the light of other information about the counselee. Other information that may facilitate vocational decision making can be obtained from accomplishments (grades, awards, extracurricular activities, community service, and the like), experiences, and level of motivation.

Realizing the difficulties of explaining to students, parents, and others the concepts of interests and abilities and how psychological differences among people relate to their academic and vocational goals, experienced vocational counselors should have available many sources of information and explanation pertaining to the world of work. In addition to books such as the *Dictionary of Occupational Titles,* the *Occupational Outlook Handbook,* the *Occupational Outlook for College Students,* and *The Guide for Occupational Exploration,* vocational counselors should have available the various career exploration and development materials published by commercial testing companies.

**Computer-based Career Counseling**   Over 24 computer-assisted guidance systems designed to help students to explore their interests, values, attitudes, and abilities and to make realistic career decisions are available. Prominent among career guidance programs are ETS's SIGI and SIGI PLUS, ACT's DISCOVER, the University of Oregon's Career Information System, and STM Systems Corporation's CHOICES (see Sampson & Reardon, 1990, for reviews). The System of Interactive Guidance and Information (SIGI PLUS), a program developed by Educational Testing Service to assist students and adults in making educational and career plans, presents a series of questions and problems to users and helps them to appraise their values, interests, skills, and resources (educational, financial, and other) and to relate these characteristics to the rewards, satisfactions, activities, and require- ments of career choices.[2]

Similar to SIGI PLUS are DISCOVER and DISCOVER for Adult Learners, which has versions for junior high and middle school students, high school students, college students and adults, human resource counseling in organizational settings, and retirement planning. Users reportedly find these programs enjoyable and profitable, and several sessions with them can be followed by discussions with an experienced career counselor. College students and counselors in training have given high ratings to SIGI, SIGI PLUS, and DISCOVER (Kapes, Borman, and Frazier, 1989; Sampson & Reardon, 1990).

## MEASUREMENT OF ATTITUDES

An *attitude* is a learned predisposition to respond positively or negatively to a specific object, situation, institution, or person. As such, it consists of cognitive (knowledge or intel- lective), affective (emotional and motivational), and performance (behavioral or action) components. Although the concept of attitude is not entirely distinct from that of interest, opinion, belief, or value, there are differences in the manner in which these terms are used. An *interest* is a feeling or preference concerning one's own activities. Unlike *attitude,* which implies approval or disapproval (a moral judgment), being interested in something simply means that a person spends time thinking about it or reacting to it, regardless of whether those thoughts and behaviors are positive or negative. An *opinion* is a specific reaction to certain occurrences or situations, whereas an *attitude* is more general in its effects on responses to a broad range of people or events. Furthermore, people are aware of their opin- ions, but they may not be fully conscious of their attitudes. Opinions are similar to beliefs, in that both are judgments or acceptances of certain propositions as facts, but the factual supports for opinions are usually weaker than those for beliefs. Finally, the term *value* refers to the importance, utility, or worth attached to particular activities and objects, usu- ally as ends but potentially as means as well.

### Methods of Measuring Attitudes

Different methods can be used to obtain information on a person's attitude toward some- thing, including direct observations of how the person behaves in relation to certain things. That is, what does the person actually do or say in situations in which the attitude object or event is present? Willingness to do a favor, sign a petition, and make a donation to some cause are examples of behavioral measures of attitudes.

Direct observation of behavior is informative, particularly with young children or when other methods are considered obtrusive. However, obtaining a representative sample of behavior, across time and situations, is time consuming and expensive. In addition,

[2]Because ETS felt that expressed interests are at least as accurate as inventoried interests, SIGI PLUS does not include an interest inventory.

behavioral measures of attitudes often yield different results from projective techniques and attitude questionnaires or scales.

Attitudes may be assessed projectively by showing a set of ambiguous pictures to people and instructing them to make up a story about each picture. Because the pictures can be interpreted in various ways, stories told by respondents should reveal something about their attitudes toward the characters, scenes, or situations in the pictures.

The most popular method of measuring attitudes is to administer an *attitude scale* consisting of a set of positive and negative statements concerning a topic of interest (a group of people, an institution, a concept). One of the first attitude scales was the Bogardus Social Distance Scale (Bogardus, 1925), on which respondents ranked various racial and religious groups in order of their acceptance to them. The Bogardus scale proved useful in research on regional differences and other variables associated with racial prejudice, but it permitted attitude measurement on only an ordinal scale and was somewhat crude by present-day standards. Better measures of attitudes resulted from the research of Louis Thurstone, Rensis Likert, Louis Guttman, and other psychometricians.

**Thurstone Scales**    During the late 1920s, Louis Thurstone and his co-workers attempted to measure attitudes on an interval level (see Appendix A) by using the methods of *pair comparisons* and *equal-appearing intervals.* Construction of an attitude scale by either of these methods begins by collecting a large number of statements expressing a wide range of positive and negative feelings toward a given topic. The next step in the method of pair comparisons is for a large number of experts to compare the statements with each other and indicate which statement in each pair expresses a more positive attitude toward the topic. Because making the numerous comparisons required by this procedure is rather cumbersome and time consuming, the method of equal-appearing intervals proved more popular.

In the method of equal-appearing intervals, the 200 or so statements expressing attitudes toward something (person, object, event, situation, or abstraction) are sorted into 11 categories by a large sample of judges. These categories range from least favorable (category 1) to most favorable (category 11) toward the thing in question. The judges are instructed to think of the 11 categories as lying at equal intervals along a continuum. After all judges have completed the sorting process for all statements, a frequency distribution is constructed for each statement by counting the number of judges who placed the statement in each category. Next, the median (*scale value*) and semi-interquartile range (*ambiguity index*) for each statement are computed from the corresponding frequency distribution. Then the statements are rank ordered according to their scale values, and 20 or so statements are selected for the finished scale. In a true interval scale, the difference between the scale values of any two adjacent statements will be equal to the difference between the scale values of any other pair of adjacent statements. Furthermore, the ambiguity indexes of all statements should be low.

A portion of one of the many attitude scales constructed by this method is shown in Figure 10–4. Note that the scale values of the statements, which are concerned with attitudes toward capital punishment, range from .1 (highly negative toward) to 11.0 (highly positive toward). A person's score on such a scale is the median of the scale values of the statements that she or he checks.

Despite the fairly high reliabilities of instruments constructed by the method of equal-appearing intervals, the procedure has been criticized for the great amount of work involved

This is a study of attitude toward capital punishment. Below you will find a number of statements expressing different attitudes toward capital punishment.

✔  Put a checkmark if you agree with the statement.
X  Put a cross if you disagree with the statement.

Try to indicate either agreement or disagreement for each statement. If you simply cannot decide about a statement, you may mark it with a question mark. This is not an examination. There are no right or wrong answers to these statements. This is simply a study of people's attitudes toward capital punishment. Please indicate your own convictions by a checkmark when you agree and by a cross when you disagree.

| Scale value | Item number | |
|---|---|---|
| (0.1) | 12 | I do not believe in capital punishment under any circumstances. |
| (0.9) | 16 | Execution of criminals is a disgrace to civilized society. |
| (2.0) | 21 | The state cannot teach the sacredness of human life by destroying it. |
| (2.7) | 8 | Capital punishment has never been effective in preventing crime. |
| (3.4) | 9 | I don't believe in capital punishment but I'm not sure it isn't necessary. |
| (3.9) | 11 | I think the return of the whipping post would be more effective than capital punishment. |
| (5.8) | 18 | I do not believe in capital punishment, but it is not practically advisable to abolish it. |
| (6.2) | 6 | Capital punishment is wrong but is necessary in our imperfect civilization. |
| (7.9) | 23 | Capital punishment is justified only for premeditated murder. |
| (9.4) | 20 | Capital punishment gives the criminal what he or she deserves. |
| (9.6) | 17 | Capital punishment is just and necessary. |
| (11.0) | 7 | Every criminal should be executed. |

**FIGURE 10–4.**  Twelve of the Twenty-four Items on a Scale of Attitudes Toward Capital Punishment.

in scale construction, the lack of uniqueness in a respondent's score, and the effects of the judges' own attitudes on the scale values of statements (Selltiz, Wrightsman, & Cook, 1976). Considering the availability of time-saving devices, the first criticism is not so serious. The second criticism refers to the fact that the same score, which is simply the median scale value of the statements checked, may be obtained by checking different statements. The third criticism refers to the fact that not everyone is capable of playing the role of neutral judge. Bruvold (1975) concluded, however, that careful instruction of the judges reduces the judgmental bias to a level that does not seriously distort the equal-interval properties of these scales. A final criticism, which is not limited to Thurstone-type attitude scales, is that these scales represent measurement at only an ordinal rather than an interval level. Actually, the level of measurement of equal-appearing interval scales probably lies somewhere between the ordinal and interval levels.

**Likert Scales**   As with Thurstone's method of equal-appearing intervals, Rensis Likert's *method of summated ratings* begins with the collection of a large number of item statements expressing a variety of positive and negative attitudes toward a specific object or event. Next, a group of 100 to 200 people, not necessarily expert judges, indicate on a 4- to 7-point scale the extent to which they agree or disagree with each item. In the typical case of a 5-point scale, positively worded items are scored 0 for strongly disagree, 1 for disagree, 2 for undecided, 3 for agree, and 4 for strongly agree; negatively worded items are scored 4 for strongly disagree, 3 for disagree, 2 for undecided, 1 for agree, and 0 for strongly agree. The respondent's total score on the initial set of attitude items is computed as the sum of scores on the individual items. After obtaining the total scores for all respondents on the initial item set, a statistical procedure (*t* test or item discrimination index) is applied to each item. Then equal numbers of positively and negatively worded items (typically 10 of each) that significantly discriminate between respondents whose total scores fall in the upper 27 percent from those whose total scores fall in the lower 27 percent are selected. An attitude scale constructed by this method is shown in Figure 10–5. A person's score on the scale is the sum of the numerical weights (0, 1, 2, 3, or 4) of the responses he or she checks.

Not all published attitude scales that are referred to as Likert scales were actually constructed by item-analysis procedures. In many cases, a set of declarative statements, each with five agree–disagree response categories, is simply put together as an instrument without any specific theoretical construct in mind or without following Likert's procedure. Consequently, one cannot be certain that a questionnaire that looks like a Likert scale was actually constructed by the Likert scaling procedure.

Despite misuses of the method of summated ratings, it has several advantages over the method of equal-appearing intervals (Selltiz, Wrightsman, & Cook, 1976). Because it does not require expert, unbiased judges, constructing a Likert scale is easier than constructing a Thurstone scale. Also, unlike Thurstone scales, Likert scales permit the use of items that are clearly related to the attitude being assessed as long as they are significantly correlated with total scores. Finally, a Likert scale is likely to have a higher reliability coefficient than a Thurstone scale consisting of the same number of items. Like Thurstone scales, however, Likert scales have been criticized for the fact that different patterns of responses can yield the same score and that, at best, the scores represent ordinal measurement.

**Guttman Scales**   The Thurstone and Likert attitude-scaling procedures have been widely used, but a third procedure, Louis Guttman's *scalogram analysis,* has been employed less often. The purpose of scalogram analysis (Guttman, 1944) is to determine whether responses to items selected to measure a given attitude fall on a single dimension. When the items constitute a true, unidimensional Guttman scale, the respondent who endorses a particular item also endorses every item having a lower scale value. The condition is more likely to be met with cognitive test items than with attitude statements or other affective items.

*Directions:* Write your name in the upper right corner. Each of the statements in this opinionnaire expresses a feeling or attitude toward mathematics (science). You are to indicate, on a five-point scale, the extent of agreement between the attitude expressed in each statement and your own personal feeling. The five points are: Strongly Disagree (SD), Disagree (D), Undecided (U), Agree (A), Strongly Agree (SA). Draw a circle around the letter(s) that best indicate(s) how closely you agree or disagree with the attitude expressed in each statement as it concerns you.

1. Mathematics (Science) is not a very interesting subject.   SD  D  U  A  SA

2. I want to develop my mathematical (science) skills and study this subject more.   SD  D  U  A  SA

3. Mathematics (Science) is a very worthwhile and necessary subject.   SD  D  U  A  SA

4. Mathematics (Science) makes me feel nervous and uncomfortable.   SD  D  U  A  SA

5. I have usually enjoyed studying mathematics (science) in school.   SD  D  U  A  SA

6. I don't want to take any more mathematics (science) than I absolutely have to.   SD  D  U  A  SA

7. Other subjects are more important to people than mathematics (science).   SD  D  U  A  SA

8. I am very calm and unafraid when studying mathematics (science).   SD  D  U  A  SA

9. I have seldom liked studying mathematics (science).   SD  D  U  A  SA

10. I am interested in acquiring further knowledge of mathematics (science).   SD  D  U  A  SA

11. Mathematics (Science) helps to develop the mind and teaches a person to think.   SD  D  U  A  SA

12. Mathematics (Science) makes me feel uneasy and confused.   SD  D  U  A  SA

13. Mathematics (Science) is enjoyable and stimulating to me.   SD  D  U  A  SA

14. I am not willing to take more than the required amount of mathematics (science).   SD  D  U  A  SA

15. Mathematics (Science) is not especially important in everyday life.   SD  D  U  A  SA

16. Trying to understand mathematics (science) doesn't make me anxious.   SD  D  U  A  SA

*(Continued)*

**FIGURE 10–5**   Scale for Measuring Attitudes Toward Mathematics or Science.
(Reprinted by permission of School Science and Mathematics Association.)

| | |
|---|---|
| 17. Mathematics (Science) is dull and boring. | SD  D  U  A  SA |
| 18. I plan to take as much mathematics (science) as I possibly can during my education. | SD  D  U  A  SA |
| 19. Mathematics (Science) has contributed greatly to the progress of civilization. | SD  D  U  A  SA |
| 20. Mathematics (Science) is one of my most dreaded subjects. | SD  D  U  A  SA |
| 21. I like trying to solve new problems in mathematics (science). | SD  D  U  A  SA |
| 22. I am not motivated to work very hard on mathematical (scientific) problems. | SD  D  U  A  SA |
| 23. Mathematics (Science) is not one of the most important subjects for people to study. | SD  D  U  A  SA |
| 24. I don't get upset when working on mathematical (scientific) problems. | SD  D  U  A  SA |

**FIGURE 10–5**  Continued

As with Bogardus's (1925) approach to attitude-scale construction, the goal of scalogram analysis is to produce a cumulative, ordinal scale. Guttman realized the difficulty of constructing a true interval scale with attitude items, but he felt that it could be approximated. The extent to which a true scale is obtained is indicated by the *reproducibility coefficient,* computed as the proportion of actual responses that fall into the perfect pattern of a true Guttman scale. That is, what proportion of the respondents who endorse a particular item endorse all items below it on the scale? An acceptable value of the reproducibility coefficient is .90 (Edwards, 1957).

***Other Attitude Measurement Procedures***   A number of other procedures have been applied to the process of attitude-scale construction, including the semantic differential technique, Q-technique, and facet analysis. The first two of these are discussed in Chapter 11. The last procedure, *facet analysis,* is a complex, multidimensional approach to item construction and analysis that can be applied to any attitude object or situation (Castro & Jordan, 1977). It has been used to construct attitude–behavior scales pertaining to a number of psychosocial conditions and situations, including mental retardation and racial–ethnic interaction (Jordan, 1971; Hamersma, Paige, & Jordan, 1973).

During the past three decades or so it has become increasingly clear that attitudes are multidimensional rather than unidimensional variables and that measuring them requires more complex assessment procedures than those of Thurstone and Likert. For example, factor analysis (see Appendix A) is now routinely used in constructing attitude instruments. The trend away from unidimensional scales is also seen in the increasing use of complex statistical procedures, such as multidimensional scaling, latent structure analysis, latent partition analysis, and the repertory grid technique (Duckworth & Entwhistle, 1974).

## Sources of Information and Psychometric Characteristics of Attitude Scales

Many different inventories and scales for assessing social attitudes (Robinson, Shaver, & Wrightsman, 1991), political attitudes (Robinson, Rush, & Head, 1973), and occupational attitudes (Robinson, Athanasiou, & Head, 1974) are described in a series of books published by the Institute for Social Research at the University of Michigan. Other sources include the *American Social Attitudes Data Sourcebook, 1947–1978* (Converse et al., 1980) and *A Sourcebook of Harris National Surveys: Repeated Questions, 1963–1976* (Martin & McDuffee, 1981). Dozens of attitude measures in a wide range of areas are also listed in *Tests in Microfiche* (Educational Testing Service) and in Volume 5 of the *ETS Test Collection Catalog* (1991). Among the attitudes which have been assessed and studied extensively are, in alphabetical order, attitudes toward aged (old) people, AIDS, computers, Congress, day care, drinking, the environment, gender role, gifted children, handicapped people, gays and Lesbians, mainstreaming, mathematics, politicians, premarital sex, the president, race (ethnic group), school, science, sex, smoking, teachers, testing, women, and work. Several publishers and distributors of psychological assessment instruments market attitude questionnaires and scales, a representative list of which is given in Table 10–2.

**TABLE 10–2   Representative Commercially Available Measures of Attitudes and Values**

**Alienation Index Survey** (from Psychological Surveys Corporation; assesses work-related attitudes of adult job applicants)

**Arlin–Hills Attitude Surveys** (by M. Arlin & D. Hills; from Psychologists and Educators, Inc.; measures attitudes of students in grades K–12)

**Attitude Survey Program for Business and Industry: Managerial Survey** (from London House, Inc.; measures attitudes of managers above first-line supervisors toward the company and provides an overview of company conditions)

**Attitude Survey Program for Business and Industry: Organization Survey** (from London House, Inc.; measures the attitudes of hourly employees and first-line supervisors toward the company and provides an overview of company conditions)

**Attitude Survey Program for Business and Industry: Professional Survey** [from London House, Inc.; measures attitudes of professions in staff positions (attorneys, editors, accountants, engineers, etc.) toward the company]

**Attitude Survey Program for Business and Industry: Sales Survey** (from London House, Inc.; measures attitudes of outside field sales representatives toward the company)

**Attitude Toward School Questionnaire** (by G. P. Strickland, R. Hoepfner, & S. P. Klein; from Monitor; measures attitudes toward school of students in grades K–3)

**Attitude Towards Disabled Persons Scale** (by H. E. Yuker & J. R. Block; from Center for the Study of Attitudes Toward Persons with Disabilities, Hofstra University; measures attitudes of students and adults toward disabled persons)

**Bloom Sentence Completion Attitude Survey** (by W. Bloom; from Stoelting; assesses attitudes relating to eight important factors in everyday living)

*(Continued)*

**TABLE 10–2    Continued**

**Canadian Comprehensive Assessment Program: School Attitude Measure** (from Guidance Center; evaluates affective responses of students in grades 4–9 to their school experiences)

**Career Attitudes and Strategies Inventory** (by J. L. Holland & G. D. Gottfredson; from Psychological Assessment Resources; assesses career attitudes and obstacles in employed and unemployed adults)

**Career Orientation Placement and Evaluation** (by L. F. Knapp & R. R. Knapp; from EdITS; designed to measure those personal values that have been observed to be related to the type of work one chooses and the satisfactions derived from the work one does)

**Employee Attitude Inventory** (from London House, Inc.; measures six variables designed to help to identify an organization's potential exposure to employee theft and counterproductive behavior)

**Marriage and Family Attitude Survey** [by D. V. Martin & M. Martin; from Psychologists and Educators, Inc.; assesses attitudes of adolescents and adults toward various aspects of marriage and family life (parenting, communication expectations and privacy rights, social needs, sexuality, sex roles, marriage and divorce, etc.)]

**Opinions Toward Adolescents** (by W. T. Martin; from Psychologists and Educators, Inc.; examines opinions and attitudes of adults toward adolescents on eight bipolar scales)

**Rokeach Value Survey** (by M. Rokeach; from Consulting Psychologists Press; assesses the relative importance of 18 instrumental values and 18 terminal values to the respondent)

**The Sales Attitude Checklist** (by E. K. Taylor; from SRA/London House; measures the attitudes and behaviors toward selling of sales applicants)

**Sex-Role Egalitarianism Scale (SRES)** (by L. A. King & D. W. King; from Sigma Assessment Systems; measures attitudes toward the equality of men and women and judgments about both men and women assuming nontraditional roles)

**Study Attitudes and Methods Survey** (by W. B. Michael, J. J. Michael, & W. S. Zimmerman; from EdITS; developed to assess dimensions of a motivational, noncognitive nature that are related to school achievement and that contribute to student performance beyond what is measured by traditional ability tests)

**Survey of Study Habits and Attitudes** (by W. F. Brown & W. H. Holtzman; from The Psychological Corporation; measures study methods, motivation for studying, and certain attitudes toward scholastic activities that are important in the classroom)

**Study of Values** [by G. W. Allport; from Riverside Publishing Company; measures six values (theoretical, economic, esthetic, social, political, religious), useful in vocational guidance, personnel work, personality research, and classroom demonstrations in psychology courses]

**Survey of Interpersonal Values** [by L. V. Gordon; from Science Research Associates; measures six values (support, conformity, recognition, independence, benevolence, leadership) involving relationships with others that are important in many work situations]

**Survey of Personal Values** [by L. V. Gordon; from Science Research Associates; measures six values (practical mindedness, achievement, variety, decisiveness,

**TABLE 10–2    Continued**

orderliness, goal orientation) that influence the manner in which people cope with
problems and choices of everyday living; provides information about how people
are likely to approach jobs or training programs]

**Temperament and Values Inventory** (by C. B. Johannson & P. L. Webber; from NCS
Assessments; measures personality factors that may affect contentment in work
situations)

**The Values Scale (2nd ed.)** (by D. E. Super & D. D. Nevill; from Consulting
Psychologists Press; measures extrinsic and intrinsic values related to career
development and most personally satisfying career)

**Work Values Inventory** (by D. E. Super; from Riverside Publishing Company;
measures the relative importance of work values in grades 7–12; provides
guidance counselors, teachers, and administrators with profiles of student values
for counseling them in occupational choices and course selections)

Because of their homogeneity of content, the internal consistency reliability coefficients of scores on attitude scales are usually in the .80s or even .90s. Test–retest reliabilities tend to run a bit lower, but are still fairly high for Thurstone and Likert-type scales. With
respect to their validity, scores on attitude scales tend to make a small but significant contribution to the prediction of performance in school subjects and to performance in organizational settings. Attitude measures have not generally correlated very highly with actual
behavior, and research reviews have concluded that they are not very accurate predictors of
specific behaviors. Ajzen and Fishbein (1977) maintained, however, that specific behavior
can be predicted from measures of attitude toward the specific behavior, especially when
attitude statements are expressed in behavioral terms.

## MEASUREMENT OF VALUES

The *values* held by a person—the usefulness, importance, or worth attached to particular
activities or objects—are related to but not identical to his or her interests and attitudes.
Milton Rokeach (1973), who conducted extensive international and cross-cultural research
on the topic, defined a value as "an enduring belief that a specific mode of conduct or end-
state of existence is personally or socially preferable to an opposite or converse mode of
conduct or end-state of existence" (page 5). To Rokeach there are two kinds of values: those
concerned with modes of conduct (*instrumental values*) and those concerned with end
states (*terminal values*). Although vocational psychologists have in large measure limited
their attention to terminal values, Rokeach defined several subcategories of both instrumental and terminal values and designed an instrument to measure them.

*Rokeach Value Survey*    Rokeach classified instrumental values as being of two kinds—
*moral values* and *competence values*. The former category is concerned with interpersonal
modes of conduct, which produce guilt feelings when violated. The latter category—competence values—has to do with intrapersonal, self-actualizing modes of conduct, violations

of which lead to feelings of inadequacy. Terminal values are also subdivided into *personal values* and *social values*. Personal values, which include such end states as peace of mind and salvation, are self-centered. Social values, which include end states such as equality and world peace, are societally centered.

The Rokeach Value Survey consists of a series of 18 instrumental and 18 terminal value terms or phrases for assessing the relative importance of these values to people. The respondent is directed to place the 18 items in each list in rank order according to their importance to him or her. No other instrument attempts to measure as many values, a fact that, coupled with speed of administration and scoring and inexpensiveness, may account for its popularity. The Rokeach has adequate reliability for differentiating between groups, a purpose for which it has been employed in hundreds of investigations for more than two decades. People of different nationalities and in different walks of life rank the items on the Rokeach Value Survey differently. For example, Israeli students assigned highest rankings to "a world at peace" and "national security," whereas U.S. students placed higher value on "a comfortable life" and "ambitious" (Rokeach, 1973).

**Study of Values**    Over the past several decades, many different instruments have been constructed by social and vocational psychologists to measure values. Undoubtedly the most popular of these instruments has been the Study of Values, a popularity attested to by its administration in numerous research investigations concerned with personality, perception, learning, social psychology, and vocational guidance. Based on Eduard Spranger's classification of people into six value types—theoretical, economic, esthetic, social, political, and religious—the Study of Values assesses the relative strength of a person's values in these six areas. Appropriate for high school and college students as well as adults, the Study of Values is untimed but takes approximately 20 minutes to complete. On the 30 items of Part I, respondents indicate a relative preference for two activities by dividing 3 points among them or by dividing the 3 points between affirmative and negative responses. On the 15 items of Part II, respondents rank four choices in order of preference. Scores on the six areas, which are ipsative in nature, are plotted as a profile showing the relative strength of the respondent's values. The manual lists mean scores on each of the six value areas for a sample of over 8000 college students of both sexes and various occupational groups. The most recent norms, based on a nationwide sample of 6000 high school students, were obtained in 1968. Test–retest reliabilities of the six value scales over a 2-month interval are in the .80s.

The theoretical foundation, the ipsative nature of the scoring system, and the fair amount of education required to understand the wording of items on the Study of Values have all been criticized (Rabinowitz, 1984). In addition, some of the content seems too old-fashioned for the 1990s, and the norms are obviously dated. Despite these shortcomings, the Study of Values continues to be used for instructional and research purposes.

**Vocational Values**    Although there is no reason why Rokeach's Value Survey and the Study of Values cannot be used for vocational counseling purposes, these instruments were not designed specifically for this purpose. More closely tied to work choices and satisfactions are instruments such as the Work Values Inventory, the Values Scale, and the Temperament and Values Inventory. The vocational values measured by these instruments vary from person and to person, within the same person from time to time, and with the nature of the job. Super (1973) found, for example, that people in upper-level occupations are more motivated by the need for self-actualization, which is an intrinsic goal, whereas extrinsic values are more likely to be subscribed to by people in lower-level occupations.

***Work Values Inventory*** This inventory, designed by Donald Super to assess 15 values deemed significant in vocational success and satisfaction, consists of 45 Likert-type items. Each of the values (for example, achievement, supervisory relations, independence, esthetics, and creativity) is measured by three items. Each item consists of a statement, and the respondent indicates, on a 5-point scale, the degree of importance that he or she attaches to the value represented by the statement. Percentile norms by grade (7–12) for each of the 15 values are based on data collected in the spring of 1968 on a representative national sample of approximately 9000 high school boys and girls. Test–retest reliability coefficients, obtained from retesting 999 tenth graders after 2 weeks, range from .74 to .88 for the 15 scales. Evidence for the content, concurrent, and construct validity of the Work Values Inventory is described in the manual.

The Work Values Inventory has been praised for its excellent psychometric foundations and its continuing research uses (Bolton, 1985), but it has not gone uncriticized. The manual needs to be brought up to date by including the results of research studies conducted since 1970. In addition, reliability data based on college students and adults, not just tenth graders, and new normative data are needed.

*The Values Scale* Developed by the Work Importance Study, an international consortium of vocational psychologists from North America, Asia, and Europe, this instrument possesses characteristics of both the Work Values Inventory and Rokeach's Value Survey. The purpose of the consortium and the Values Scale was to understand values that individuals seek or hope to find in various life roles and to assess the relative importance of the work role as a means of value realization in the context of other life roles. The Values Scale consists of 106 items and takes 30 to 45 minutes to complete. It is scored for 21 values (five items per value):

| | | |
|---|---|---|
| Ability utilization | Creativity | Social interaction |
| Achievement | Economic rewards | Social relations |
| Advancement | Life style | Variety |
| Esthetics | Personal development | Working conditions |
| Altruism | Physical activity | Cultural identity |
| Authority | Prestige | Physical prowess |
| Autonomy | Risk | Economic security |

The reliabilities of all scales are adequate for individual assessment at the adult level; the reliabilities of ten scales are high enough for individual assessment at the college level, and the reliabilities of eight scales are adequate at the high school level. The means and standard deviations for three samples (high school, college, adult), as well as data on the construct validity of the instrument, are given in the manual. The Values Scale appears to have good potential for research on vocational counseling and selection and particularly for cross-cultural or cross-national comparative studies.

## SUMMARY

Inventories are the most popular of all methods of assessing interests. The serious use of interest inventories in vocational and academic counseling and placement began with the construction of the Strong Vocational Interest Blanks in the 1920s and 1930s. Subsequent publication of the Kuder Vocational Preference Record and other interest inventories resulted in increased understanding of interests and improved the accuracy with which they could be measured.

Scores on interest inventories are not very good predictors of vocational success, but they do a better job of forecasting occupational choice and satisfaction. The results of longitudinal studies have shown inventoried interests to be fairly stable, although responses to such inventories can be faked and may be susceptible to response sets. Interests are generally considered to be learned, but there is some evidence of a hereditary basis for preferences for different types of people, activities, and things.

The most recent version of the Strong Interest Inventory consists of 317 items grouped into eight categories. It is scored on 6 general occupational themes, 25 basic interest scales, 211 occupational scales, 4 Personal Style Scales, and 3 Administrative Indexes. Scoring keys for the occupational scales were developed empirically by comparing the responses of people in general with those of people employed in particular occupations. Scores on the Strong Interest Inventory are fairly reliable and valid predictors of occupational persistence and satisfaction, but not necessarily occupational success.

G. F. Kuder constructed several interest inventories consisting of a series of forced-choice item triads. The Kuder Vocational Preference Record, the Kuder General Interest Survey, and the Kuder Occupational Interest Survey are three instruments of this sort. The last of these instruments, like the Strong Interest Inventory, can be scored on a number of empirically derived occupational sales, but the first two are scored only on general-interest scales. All these inventories, also like the Strong Interest Inventory, are appropriate for high school students and adults.

In addition to inventories scored according to broad interest areas and adult occupations, a number of instruments are available for assessing the interests of children, the disadvantaged, and those planning to enter nonprofessional occupations.

The relationships of interests to personality are emphasized in the research of Anne Roe and John Holland and instruments based on that research.

Vocational counseling requires a broad knowledge of the world of work and skilled integration of ability test scores, measures of interest, biographical data, and behavioral observations.

Attitudes are learned predispositions to respond positively or negatively to some object, person, or situation. As such, attitudes are characteristics of personality, although at a more superficial level than temperaments, values, and other affective characteristics. Attitudes can be assessed in a number of ways, the most popular being attitude inventories or scales. Procedures for constructing attitude scales were devised by Thurstone (method of equal-appearing intervals), Likert (method of summated ratings), and Guttman (scalogram analysis). Other attitude-scaling techniques include the semantic differential, Q-sorts, and a variety of multivariate statistical procedures.

Judging from the variety of instruments, one can have an attitude toward almost anything—any school subject, any vocation, any defined group, any institution, any proposed social action, any practice. The great majority of the hundreds of attitude scales and questionnaires listed in various reference sources have not been standardized; they were designed for a particular research investigation or application. However, a number of standardized instruments for assessing attitudes toward school and school subjects, work and work supervisors, and other kinds of human activities are available from commercial test distributors.

Values, or beliefs concerning the utility or worth of something, can be assessed by many different inventories, including the Rokeach Value Survey and the Study of Values. The Rokeach Value Survey and the associated theory have stimulated research on political–ideological values and conceptions of the good life. The Study of Values has been used extensively in research on perception, learning, and motivation. Research on work-related values has resulted in a number of psychometric instruments, such as the Work Values Inventory and the Values Scale.

## QUESTIONS AND ACTIVITIES

1. What are response sets? Why are they of particular concern in designing inventories to measure interests and personality characteristics? What can be done to counter the effects of response sets on scores on these inventories?

2. Arrange with your instructor to take the Strong Interest Inventory and have it scored by Consulting Psychologists Press. When a report of your scores is returned, get help from your instructor or counselor in interpreting the results.

3. Compare the Strong Interest Inventory with the Kuder Occupational Interest Survey (Form DD) in terms of design, scoring, and interpretation. Why are the correlations between occupational scales on the SII and the KOIS that have the same or very similar names often not very high? What theoretical and practical significance might this have?

4. Run all the programs in Category G ("Inventories of Interests, Attitudes, and Values") in the set of *Computer Programs for Psychological Assessment.* Compare your results with those of your classmates.

5. Consider the following four interest inventories:
   a. Career Assessment Inventory
   b. Kuder Occupational Interest Survey
   c. Self-directed Search
   d. Strong Interest Inventory
   e. Wide Range Interest–Opinion Test

   Which of these inventories would you recommend for the following situations?
   (1) Counseling a college freshman or sophomore on choice of major and vocation.
   (2) Setting up a counseling program for students admitted to a vocational high school with a variety of different trade programs.
   (3) Helping tenth graders to explore careers and consider various occupational choices.
   (4) Helping a group of physically and mentally handicapped individuals to consider a variety of activities with which they can identify.
   (5) Helping a counseling service work with college graduates who are uncertain about their future careers.
   (6) Introducing to and familiarizing a group of elementary school children with a wide range of career activities and occupations.

6. Defend the thesis that interests are personality characteristics and therefore that interest inventories are measures of personality. Cite specific theories, research findings, and instruments to support your position.

7. To construct an attitude scale by Thurstone's method of equal-appearing intervals, suppose that each of 50 judges sorts 200 attitude statements into 11 piles. The numbers of judges who place statements X, Y, and Z into each of the 11 categories are given in the three frequency distributions listed next. Compute the scale value (median) and ambiguity index (semi-interquartile range) of each statement by methods described in Appendix A. Use the pile number (1, 2, . . . , 11) plus .5 as the upper exact limit of the interval.

| Pile Number | Statement X | Statement Y | Statement Z |
|---|---|---|---|
| 1 | | | 8 |
| 2 | | | 17 |
| 3 | | 6 | 10 |
| 4 | | 10 | 9 |
| 5 | | 13 | 6 |
| 6 | 3 | 8 | |
| 7 | 7 | 6 | |
| 8 | 9 | 4 | |
| 9 | 13 | 3 | |
| 10 | 10 | | |
| 11 | 8 | | |

8. Make multiple copies of the attitude scale in Figure 10–4 (concerning attitudes toward capital punishment). Before administering the scale to several people, the statements in Figure 10–4 should be retyped in order of their item numbers with the scale values omitted. The respondent's total score on the scale of attitudes toward capital punishment is determined by adding the scale values of the statements that are checked and dividing the sum by the total number of statements (12). Ask the respondents to explain the reasons for their attitudes toward capital punishment and summarize the results. What personality variables do you believe are related to attitudes toward capital punishment?

9. Make multiple copies of the Mathematics or Science Attitude Scale in Figure 10–5 and administer the scale to several people. (*Note:* A computer-based version of the scale is available as program 4 in category G of *Computer Programs for Psychological Assessment.*) Compute their scores on the four parts of the scale: E (enjoyment of mathematics or science), M (motivation in mathematics or science), I (importance of mathematics or science), and F (fear of mathematics or science). Also determine a total score by adding the E, M, I, and F scores. The E score consists of the sum of responses to items 1, 5, 9, 13, 17, and 21; the M score is the sum of responses to items 2, 6, 10, 14, 18, and 22; the I score is the sum of responses to items 3, 7, 11, 15, 19, and 23; and the F score is the sum of responses to items 4, 8, 12, 16, 20, and 24. Responses to items 1, 4, 6, 7, 9, 12, 14, 15, 17, 20, 22, and 23 are scored as SD = 4, D = 3, U = 2, A = 1, SA = 0; responses to items 2, 3, 5, 8, 10, 11, 13, 16, 18, 19, 21, and 24 are scored as SD = 0, D = 1, U = 2, A = 3, SA = 4. The T (total) score is the sum of the four part scores (T = E + M + I + F). A high score on the four parts or total score of the Mathematics (or Science) Attitude Scale indicates a favorable attitude toward mathematics (or science); a low score indicates an unfavorable attitude toward mathematics (or science). Question your examinees on the causes of their attitudes toward mathematics and science, and summarize your findings.

10. Administer the following Educational Values Inventory (EVI) to several students of various backgrounds and compute their scores. (*Note:* A computer-based version of the EVI is available as program 6 in category G of *Computer Programs for Psychological Assessment.*) Construct and compare the profiles of scores of the students on the six value scales. Responses to each item on the EVI are scored on a scale of 1 to 5 from left (U or N) to right (E), respectively. The

sum of the scores on items 2, 7, 18, and 21 is the Aesthetic Value score. The sum of the scores on items 1, 8, 13, and 24 is the Leadership Value score. The sum of the scores on items 4, 9, 15, and 23 is the Philosophical Value score. The sum of the scores on items 5, 12, 16, and 19 is the Social Value score. The sum of the scores on items 6, 11, 17, and 22 is the Scientific Value score. The sum of scores on items 3, 10, 14, and 20 is the Vocational Value score.

## Educational Values Inventory

**Part I**   Each of the items in this section refers to a possible goal or emphasis of higher education. Check the appropriate letter after each of the following statements to indicate how important you believe the corresponding goal should be. Use this key: U =unimportant, S = somewhat important, I = important, V = very important, E =extremely important.

| | | |
|---|---|---|
| 1. | Ability to lead or direct other people. | U  S  I  V  E |
| 2. | Appreciation of the beautiful and harmonious things in life. | U  S  I  V  E |
| 3. | Preparation for a vocation or profession of one's choice. | U  S  I  V  E |
| 4. | Gaining insight into the meaning and purpose of life. | U  S  I  V  E |
| 5. | Understanding social problems and their possible solutions. | U  S  I  V  E |
| 6. | Understanding scientific theories and the laws of nature. | U  S  I  V  E |
| 7. | Acquiring the ability to express oneself artistically. | U  S  I  V  E |
| 8. | Understanding how to direct others in the accomplishment of some goal. | U  S  I  V  E |
| 9. | Development of a personal philosophy of life. | U  S  I  V  E |
| 10. | Learning how to succeed in a chosen occupation or field. | U  S  I  V  E |
| 11. | Learning about scientific problems and their solutions. | U  S  I  V  E |
| 12. | Understanding people of different social classes and cultures. | U  S  I  V  E |

**Part II**   Check the appropriate letter after each of the following items to indicate your estimate of how valuable the particular kinds of college courses are to students in general. Use this key: N = not at all valuable, S = somewhat valuable, V = valuable, Q = quite valuable, E = extremely valuable.

| | | |
|---|---|---|
| 13. | Courses concerned with how to direct and organize people. | N  S  V  Q  E |
| 14. | Courses in one's chosen vocation or professional field. | N  S  V  Q  E |
| 15. | Courses dealing with philosophical and/or religious ideas. | N  S  V  Q  E |
| 16. | Courses concerned with understanding and helping people. | N  S  V  Q  E |
| 17. | Courses in science and mathematics. | N  S  V  Q  E |
| 18. | Courses in music, art, and literature. | N  S  V  Q  E |

**Part III**   Check the appropriate letter after each of the following items to indicate how much attention you feel should be given to each kind of college course in the education of most college students. Use this key: N = no attention at all, L = little attention, M = a moderate degree of attention, A = above average attention, E = an extensive amount of attention.

| | | |
|---|---|---|
| 19. | Courses concerned with how to understand and be of help to other people. | N  L  M  A  E |
| 20. | Courses in the vocational or professional field of your choice. | N  L  M  A  E |
| 21. | Courses in art, literature, and music. | N  L  M  A  E |
| 22. | Courses in scientific and mathematical fields. | N  L  M  A  E |
| 23. | Courses concerned with philosophy and religion. | N  L  M  A  E |
| 24. | Courses concerned with organizing and directing people. | N  L  M  A  E |

# 11

# PERSONALITY ASSESSMENT: OBSERVATIONS, INTERVIEWS, AND RATINGS

The term *personality* has many different meanings. To some, it refers to a mysterious charisma possessed by Hollywood stars and other popular, influential people, but not by everyone. To others, personality is the same as temperament—a natural, genetically based predisposition to think, feel, and act in a particular way. To still others, personality consists of a person's unique mixture of emotional, intellectual, and character traits (honesty, courage, and so forth). To more behaviorally oriented psychologists, personality is not something internal, but rather an externally observable pattern of organized behavior typical of a person.

Perhaps an acceptable compromise is to define human *personality* as a composite of cognitive abilities, interests, attitudes, temperament, and other individual differences in thoughts, feelings, and behavior. This definition emphasizes the fact that personality is a unique combination of cognitive and affective characteristics describable in terms of a typical, fairly consistent pattern of individual behavior.

From the last definition, it follows that methods of assessing personality should include a broad range of cognitive and affective variables. Among these variables are the measures of achievement, intelligence, special abilities, interests, attitudes, and values discussed in Chapters 6 through 10. Other emotional, temperamental, and stylistic characteristics, which have traditionally been labeled *personality variables,* are also important in understanding and predicting human behavior. The observations, interviews, ratings, personality inventories, and projective techniques for assessing this second group of variables are described in this chapter and the next.

## FOUNDATIONS OF PERSONALITY ASSESSMENT

As was the case with intelligence testing, personality assessment developed partly from research on individual and group differences. Many antecedents of contemporary personality assessment can be found in the history of abnormal psychology and psychiatry.

## Pseudosciences and Other Historical Antecedents

The history of science is replete with examples of beliefs or doctrines that had many adherents at one time, but subsequently were proved to be partially or totally incorrect. Among these pseudoscientific doctrines are phrenology, physiognomy, and graphology.

*Phrenology,* which almost no one seriously believes in today, was taken quite seriously by many famous men and scholars during the late eighteenth and early nineteenth centuries. According to proponents of phrenology, the development of specific brain areas is associated with certain personality characteristics and mental disorders. Among the personality traits supposedly traced to particular protuberances of the skull are agreeableness, combativeness, and acquisitiveness (Figure 11–1). A natural consequence of this belief is that personality can be analyzed by fingering a person's head for "bumps" over brain areas presumably associated with certain characteristics. Phrenology had a great deal of influence on nineteenth-century psychiatry and on *faculty psychology,* a basically incorrect notion that affected the school curriculum of the time. According to faculty psychology, the mind

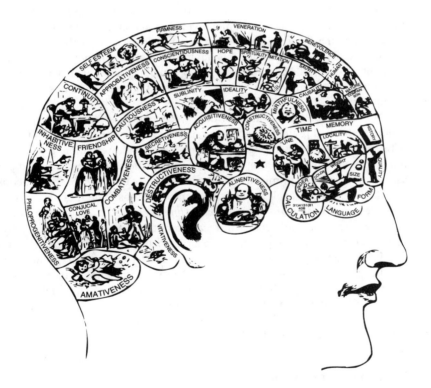

**FIGURE 11–1**   Localization of Various Affective and Cognitive Faculties as Depicted by a Nineteenth-century Phrenologist. Phrenology Was a Pseudoscience, and No One Places Much Credence in It Today.
(The Bettmann Archive.)

consists of a number of faculties that can be developed by mental exercise (for example, by studying Latin, Greek, geometry, and other difficult subjects), just as the body can be developed by physical exercise.

*Physiognomy,* another pseudoscience, is concerned with determining temperament and character from external features of the body and especially the face. Remnants of physiognomy can be seen in contemporary personnel evaluation and assessment procedures, for example, in the requirement that a photograph be submitted with an employment application and in the Szondi Test. This test consists of six sets of photographs, eight pictures per set, of mental patients having different diagnoses (for example, hysteria, catatonia, paranoia, depression, or mania). Examinees select the two pictures they like most and the two they dislike most in each set. The basic assumption underlying the Szondi Test is that the facial features of the mental patients depicted in the 12 selected and 12 rejected photographs have a personal meaning for the respondent. The respondent's needs and personality are presumably similar to those of the patients depicted in the photographs. Because no consistent evidence for the validity of the Szondi Test in personality analysis or psychiatric diagnosis has been found, it has been generally discredited.

Belief in *graphology,* which is concerned with analyzing personality by studying handwriting samples, is perhaps even more widespread than belief in physiognomy. Although it makes sense that handwriting, which is a type of stylistic behavior, reflects personality characteristics, even experienced handwriting analysts are not known for the accuracy of their interpretations. Physiognomy and graphology are somewhat more reputable than phrenology, but many of the claims of their proponents are just as wrong as those of the phrenologists.

Not all nineteenth-century efforts to develop a science of personality assessment should be labeled pseudosciences. For example, the efforts of Francis Galton, Emil Kraepelin, and Alfred Binet, though not always successful, were more reputable. In 1884, Galton proposed to measure emotions by recording changes in heartbeat and pulse rate and to assess good temper, optimism, and other personality traits by observing people in contrived social situations. Kraepelin, who is best known for his system of classifying mental disorders, developed the *word-association technique* in 1892. Also during the 1890s, Alfred Binet, whose name the reader will recall from the chapter on intelligence testing, devised methods for studying the personality characteristics of eminent persons.

Despite a few promising beginnings in the nineteenth century, genuine progress in personality assessment was not made until the twentieth century. Particularly noteworthy in this regard are Carl Jung's use of word-association tests to detect and analyze mental complexes (1905), the use of Robert Woodworth's Personal Data Sheet, the first standardized personality inventory, in military selection (1919), and the publication of Hermann Rorschach's Inkblot Test (1920).

## Theories of Personality

Almost everyone has some theory as to why people behave as they do. These theories of human nature and behavior typically consist of overgeneralizations or stereotypes, but they serve as rough guides to expectations and action. Sometimes our very survival depends on the ability to understand and predict the behavior of other people, and we engage in all kinds of verbal and nonverbal behaviors based on the assumptions that we make about others.

Realizing that everyone is different from everyone else and that human behavior can be very complex, personality theorists have learned to be suspicious of commonsense explanations. Certain psychologists, impressed by the individuality and intricacy of human actions, have despaired of finding general principles or laws to explain personality. They reject the *nomothetic approach*—the search for general laws of behavior and personality—as unrealistic and inadequate to the task of understanding the individual. Instead, they advocate an *idiographic approach* of viewing every personality as a lawful, integrated system to be studied in its own right (Allport, 1937).

There are many other differences among personality theories, one being the relative emphasis placed on heredity and environment as molders of behavior. Theorists also differ in the extent to which they emphasize internal, personal characteristics of the individual, rather than situational variables, as determinants of behavior. As these and other points of debate among psychologists suggest, there is no generally accepted theory of personality. On the contrary, theories and research findings pertaining to the origins, structure, and dynamics of personality are continually developing and changing. Still, it is important for anyone who is interested in psychological assessment to be aware of the various theories of personality and to be skeptical of untested theories. Despite their shortcomings, theories can serve as guides to the measurement and understanding of personality. They provide frames of reference—some ideas about the dynamics and development of personality and behavior—for interpreting assessment findings. In this respect, the theories proposed and tested by professional psychologists are presumably more useful than commonsense theories.

**Type Theories**   One of the oldest approaches to understanding personality is the notion of fixed categories or types of people. Galen, a physician in ancient Rome who subscribed to Hippocrates's doctrine of four body humors—blood, yellow bile, black bile, phlegm—maintained that there are four corresponding temperament types. The *sanguine type,* with an excess of blood, was said to be vigorous and athletic; the *choleric type,* with an excess of yellow bile, was easily angered. The *melancholic type,* with an excess of black bile, was generally depressed or sad, and the *phlegmatic type,* with an excess of phlegm, was chronically tired or lazy. Like phrenology and other pseudoscientific notions, the humoral theory is now only of historical interest (but see Figure 11–3). Based somewhat more securely on observational data, but still highly tentative and overgeneralized, are the body-type theories of Ernest Kretschmer, Cesare Lombroso, and William Sheldon.

The idea that personality is associated with physique has intrigued many philosophers and poets. Shakespeare declared as much in several of his plays. For example, in Act I, Scene II of *Julius Caesar,* Caesar says:

> Let me have men about me that are fat.
> Sleek-headed men, and such as sleep a-nights.
> Yond Cassius has a lean and hungry look;
> He thinks too much; such men are dangerous.

Less poetic but perhaps more systematic than the writings of famous authors were the descriptions of the scientist Ernst Kretschmer (1925). Kretschmer concluded that both a tall, thin body build (*asthenic*) and a muscular body build (*athletic*) are associated with withdrawing tendencies (schizoid personality). A short, stout body build (*pyknic*), on the other hand, is associated with emotional instability (cycloid personality). A related typology—a three-component somatotype system of classifying human physiques according to the degree of fatness (*endomorphy*), muscularity (*mesomorphy*), and thinness (*ectomorphy*)—was proposed by Sheldon, Stevens, and Tucker (1940) (Figure 11–2). These body builds are presumably related to the following respective temperament types: viscerotonia (sociable, jolly, loves food), somatotonia (athletic, aggressive), and cerebrotonia (introversive, studious).

Body-type theories are intriguing, but their scientific status is questionable. There are many exceptions to the hypothesized relationships between physique and temperament, and different interpretations have been given to those relationships. Furthermore, contemporary psychologists object to typologies because they place people in categories and assign labels to them. Not only does labeling overemphasize the internal causation of behavior, but it may also act as a self-fulfilling prophecy through which people become what they are labeled as being. Thus, a person who is labeled an *introvert* may be left alone by would-be friends, causing him or her to become even more socially isolated. Similarly, an *extrovert* may become more outgoing or sociable because other people expect him or her to behave in that way.

***Trait Theories***   Less general than personality types are personality traits. Gordon Allport, an early personality theorist, began his research on traits by listing 17,953 words in the

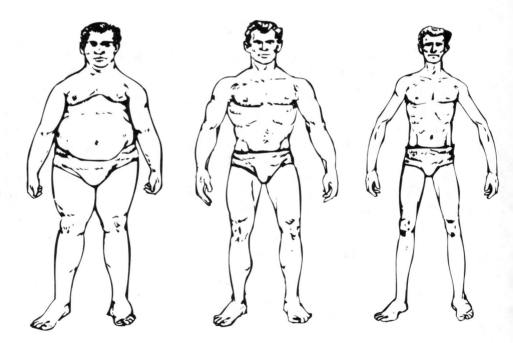

**FIGURE 11–2**   Sheldon's Somatotypes.
(From *Elements of Psychology* by David Krech and Richard S. Crutchfield. Copyright © 1958 by David Krech and Richard S. Crutchfield. Reprinted by permission of Alfred A. Knopf, Inc.)

English language that refer to characteristics of personality and then reducing them to a smaller list of trait names (Allport & Odbert, 1936). He defined a *trait* as a "neuropsychic structure having the capacity to render many stimuli functionally equivalent, and to initiate and guide equivalent (meaningfully consistent) forms of adaptive and expressive behavior" (Allport, 1961, page 347). To Allport, *personality* consisted of the dynamic organization of those traits that determine a person's unique adjustment to the environment.

Another trait theorist, R. B. Cattell, classified traits in four ways: common versus unique, surface versus source, constitutional versus environmental mold, and dynamic versus ability versus temperament. Common traits are characteristics of all people, whereas unique traits are peculiar to the individual. A person's surface traits are easily observed in behavior, but source traits can be discovered only by the statistical procedures of factor analysis (see Appendix A). Constitutional traits depend on heredity, and environmental-mold traits depend on environment. Finally, dynamic traits motivate the person toward a goal, ability traits determine the ability to achieve the goal, and temperament traits pertain to the emotional aspects of goal-directed activity. Cattell's trait theory, which is much more elaborate than this brief description suggests, has served as a framework for several personality inventories, including the 16 Personality Factor Questionnaire.

Many other psychologists, including Henry Murray, J. P. Guilford, and Hans Eysenck, constructed theories and conducted research on personality traits. The methods of factor analysis have been applied to much of this research, yielding a variety of personality dimensions. The two basic dimensions in Eysenck's system, introversion–extroversion and stability–instability, are depicted in Figure 11–3. The positions of the 32 traits on the axes of this figure indicate the direction and amounts of each of the two basic dimensions comprising each trait.

**Psychoanalytic Theory**    Sigmund Freud and other psychoanalysts viewed human personality as a kind of battleground where three combatants—the id, ego, and superego—vie for supremacy. The *id,* a reservoir of instinctive drives of sex and aggression housed in the unconscious part of the mind, acts according to the pleasure principle. It runs into conflict with the *superego* (the conscience), which acts according to the moral principle. Although the id is innate, the superego develops from internalization of the prohibitions and sanctions placed by parents on the child's behavior. Meanwhile, the *ego,* which functions according to the reality principle, attempts to serve as a mediator between the relentless pressures of the id and superego for control. The id says "Now!," the superego says "Never!," and the ego says "Later" to the individual's basic desires. Id impulses and the conflict of id with superego and ego are usually in the unconscious mind, but they are expressed in thoughts and behavior in various disguised forms.

Freud also believed that human personality develops through a series of *psychosexual stages.* During each stage, a different region of the body (*erogenous zone*) is the center of sexual stimulation and gratification, and at that stage conflicts pertaining to the particular body region predominate. The *oral stage* occurs from birth to $1\frac{1}{2}$ years, during which time pleasure is derived primarily from stimulation of the mouth and lips, as in sucking, biting, and swallowing. During the *anal stage,* from about age $1\frac{1}{2}$ to 3 years, interest and conflict center on the retention and expulsion of feces. Negativism, manifested by defiance of parental orders and frequently associated with toilet training, is most pronounced during the anal stage. Next in order is the *phallic stage,* from ages 3 to 6, when the body region of

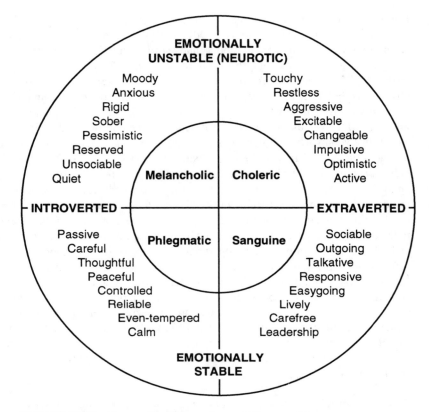

**FIGURE 11–3** Eysenck's Dimensions of Personality.
(From *Personality and Individual Differences* by H. J. Eysenck and M. W.
Eysenck, Plenum Publishing, New York, 1958. Reprinted by permission.)

greatest interest is the genital area. It is during this stage, when rubbing, touching, exhibit-
ing oneself, and looking are emphasized, that the Oedipus complex develops. The *Oedipus
complex,* viewed by Freud as a universal phenomenon, consists of a composite of sexual
feelings toward the mother and dislike of the father in 3- to 6-year-old boys. The comparable situation in girls—dislike of the mother and love of the father—is known as the *Electra
complex.*

Freud maintained that if a boy is to develop psychosexually beyond the phallic stage to
the *latency period* of relative sexual inactivity during middle childhood, the Oedipus complex must either be resolved or repressed. In most instances, it is resolved by the boy's
learning to identify with, that is, trying to act like, his father. At the onset of puberty the
child who has successfully passed through the previous psychosexual stages enters the *genital stage.* Interest in the opposite sex then becomes dominant, usually culminating in het-
erosexual mating.

Freud was one of the first personality theorists to recognize that "the child is father
to the man," that deprivation and conflict in childhood frequently have permanent effects

on personality. His theory of psychosexual stages maintains that frustration and conflict at a particular stage affect adult character structure by causing *fixation* (failure to progress psychosexually beyond a particular stage) or *regression* (partial or complete return to a pattern of behavior typical of an earlier stage of development). A person who is fixated at the oral stage, for example, is said to be characterized by overdependency, greed, and passivity; a person who is fixated at the anal stage is excessively orderly, obstinate, and stingy.

Freud's theory of personality was based almost entirely on uncontrolled clinical observations of approximately 100 patients, and many features of the theory have not been confirmed by research. Certain assumptions, for example that the Oedipus complex is universal and that there is a latency period in sexual development, are considered incorrect. Be that as it may, Freud and his followers were undoubtedly correct in pointing out the existence of childhood sexuality and its importance for personality development, the significant role played by unconscious motivation in shaping personality and behavior, and the functions of defense mechanisms in helping the individual cope with anxiety produced by intrapsychic conflict. The notion that children invariably pass through the sequence of psychosexual stages outlined above and that adult personality is shaped by childhood sexual conflicts is debatable and was modified by later psychoanalysts. Compared with Freud, modern psychoanalytic theory places more emphasis on social learning and culture than on biological instincts as determinants of personality.

***Phenomenological Theories***    Stemming from a philosophical tradition that emphasized the analysis of immediate, personal, subjective experience, phenomenological (humanistic or "self") theorists maintain that trait theorists and others who attempt to divide personality into a set of components do an injustice to its integrated, dynamic organization. Consequently, phenomenological theorists have been critical of psychoanalytic, trait-factor, and behavioral approaches to understanding personality. In contrast to traditional psychoanalysis, which emphasizes the fundamental importance of sexual and aggressive impulses, the unconscious, and psychosexual stages of development, phenomenologists stress perceptions, meanings, feelings, and the self. Phenomenologists see a person as responding to the world in terms of his or her unique, private perceptions of it. These perceptions are determined by experiences and the meanings attached to those experiences in an effort to fully realize one's potentialities. The part of the environment that is perceived and has meaning for the individual is known as the *phenomenal field,* a portion of which, the *self,* is related to the individual in a personal way. Finally, the totality of the good and bad evaluations given by a person to the self are referred to as the *self-concept.*

According to Abraham Maslow, Carl Rogers, and other phenomenological theorists, everyone strives to attain a state of *self-actualization,* a congruence or harmony between the real and ideal selves. The basic direction of existence is toward self-actualization and pleasant relations with others, but that effort can be inhibited in various ways. Carl Rogers pointed out that most people are not open to accepting or willing to accept the full range of their experiences. In the process of growing up, they learn that they are objects of *conditional positive regard,* in which their behavior is deemed acceptable by parents and other significant persons only if it conforms to expected standards (*conditions of worth*). Consequently, the child, who eventually becomes an adult, learns to recognize and accept only a part of his or her experiences. The result is an incompletely functioning individual who cannot become fully functioning until other people treat him or her with *unconditional positive regard*. This is a condition in which the individual is accepted regardless of what he or she is or does.

Clinical practitioners who espouse phenomenological theory tend to prefer case studies and open or unstructured interviews, rather than objective psychological tests and procedures. Carl Rogers was not a great believer in personality assessment instruments, and phenomenology or self theory has not been as influential as trait-factor and psychoanalytic theories in the development of such devices. Still, many instruments and procedures for assessing feelings and attitudes toward the self have followed a phenomenological theory of personality. Examples are Q-sorts (Stephenson, 1953) and inventories such as the Tennessee Self-Concept Scale, the Piers–Harris Children's Self-Concept Scale, and the Coopersmith Self-Esteem Inventories.

**Social Learning Theory**    Many other theoretical conceptualizations have influenced the development of personality assessment instruments. Among these are George Kelly's (1955) theory of personal constructs and the cognitive-behavioral approach of social learning theorists such as Julian Rotter, Albert Bandura, and Walter Mischel.

*Rotter's Theory*    The first *social learning theory* as such was that of Julian Rotter (1954), who attempted to integrate the traditional behavioristic position on the role of reinforcement in learning with the cognitive conceptualizations of Kurt Lewin and other field theorists. Rotter was not the first to note that most human behavior is learned in a social context, but he made a more conscious effort than his predecessors to develop a systematic theory of how this takes place. Rotter distinguished between reinforcements and cognitions: reinforcements result in movement toward or away from a goal, whereas cognitions are internal states such as expectancy and reinforcement value. The term *expectancy* refers to a person's estimate of the subjective probability that a specific behavior performed in a certain situation will lead to reinforcement. Two *generalized expectancies* measured and investigated by Rotter and others are internal–external locus of control and interpersonal trust. *Locus of control* refers to the typical direction from which people perceive themselves as being controlled (internal, or from within oneself, versus external, or by other people). *Interpersonal trust* is concerned with the extent to which a person believes that other people tell the truth.

According to Rotter, reinforcement is important for performance, but not all reinforcements are equally valued by the individual: even when the probabilities of occurrence of different reinforcements are equal, certain objects or actions will have greater *reinforcement value* than others. Both reinforcement value and expectancies are affected by the psychological relevance or meaning of the situation to the individual; this meaning must be understood in order to predict how the person will behave in that situation.

*Bandura's Observational Learning Theory*    More important for the development of techniques for modifying maladaptive behavior than for influencing the design of personality assessment instruments is Albert Bandura's social learning theory. Conceptualizing psychological functioning as the reciprocal interactions of behavioral variables, person variables (cognitions and other internal states), and environmental variables, Bandura emphasizes the fact that the individual is not a passive "push button" automaton that acts only when acted upon. People both influence and are influenced by the social environment, in which learning takes place by observation, imitation, and modeling. Unlike more traditional behaviorists, such as Clark Hull and B. F. Skinner, Bandura maintains that much learning takes place without reinforcement—in the absence of rewards and punishments—but that reinforcement is important in determining when learned behavior occurs. Particularly significant in the learning process is modeling the behavior of others. The effectiveness of modeling depends on the personal characteristics of the model and the learner's motivational level. Aggression, fears, sex-typed behaviors, and many other emotional and stylistic reactions are, according to Bandura, learned by observation and modeling.

Bandura also emphasizes the fact that learning and behavior are mediated by perceptions and cognitions: people use internal, symbolic representations of their environments, and it is these representations that mediate changes in behavior. By visualizing the consequences of certain actions, the individual learns to regulate his or her behavior.

## Empirical Approaches to Personality Assessment

Rather than being designed according to a specific theory of personality, many personality assessment instruments have been constructed on a purely empirical basis. For example, items on the various scales of the Minnesota Multiphasic Personality Inventory (MMPI) were selected on the basis of their ability to distinguish between two contrasting groups of people (normals and selected psychiatric patient groups). No specific theory of personality was implied or involved in this empirical procedure; the MMPI items were simply validated against the specific criterion of psychiatric diagnoses in various samples of mental patients.

A number of assessment instruments have been developed in the context of investigations of personality and behavior disorders. These efforts, although not completely devoid of theoretical foundations, have not been restricted to one particular theoretical position. Illustrative of such approaches are the research programs of the Harvard personologists and the psychologists at the Institute for Personality Assessment and Research at the University of California at Berkeley.

## Ethical and Measurement Problems

Personality assessment procedures and instruments are used in schools, clinics, hospitals, prisons, and other settings where the results contribute to the process of making decisions about people. Ideally, the results are treated conscientiously and with an awareness of the limitations of the assessments and the needs and rights of examinees. Unfortunately, the ethics of personality assessors are not always as they should be.

Among the methods used in personality assessment are observations, interviews, rating scales, checklists, self-report inventories, and projective techniques. Sometimes these methods have been misapplied by untrained or unethical persons, resulting in a black mark for psychological testing as a whole. It is not difficult for a person who has read a bit of psychology to obtain a few paper-and-pencil instruments and pretend to be a personality analyst.

Like fortune tellers and other charlatans, these would-be psychodiagnosticians deal in generalities, truisms, and other statements that seem specific to a given individual but actually apply to most people. To demonstrate this "Barnum effect," consider the following "personality profile":

You have a strong need for other people to like you and for them to admire you. You have a tendency to be critical of yourself. You have a great deal of unused capacity which you have not turned to your advantage. While you have some personality weaknesses, you are generally able to compensate for them. Your sexual adjustment has presented some problems for you. Disciplined and controlled on the outside, you tend to be worrisome and insecure inside. At times you have serious doubts as to whether you have made the right decision or done the right thing. You prefer a certain amount of change and variety and become dissatisfied when hemmed in by restrictions and limitations. You pride yourself as being an independent thinker and do not accept others' opinions without satisfactory proof. You have found it unwise to be too frank in revealing yourself to others. At times you are extroverted, affable, social, while at other times you are introverted, wary, reserved. Some of your aspirations tend to be pretty unrealistic (Forer, 1949).

Is this a fairly good description of your own personality? Thirty-seven in a group of 50 students to whom I showed this paragraph rated it a good or excellent description of their personalities.

A great deal of training and experience are needed to become a skilled observer and interpreter of human personality. Teachers, personnel managers, and other nonpsychologists can often apply rating scales and checklists in a sensitive, sensible manner, but the administration and interpretation of personality inventories and projective techniques are restricted to psychologists and other professionals with comparable training. Even then, it is questionnable whether many personality inventories and projectives should be used for anything other than research purposes. Very often personality tests focus more on symptoms of maladjustment and mental illness than on adjustment and mental health. Because these topics are very personal and should be handled with care, one needs to be cautious in administering and interpreting the results of any personality assessment device. Both the examinee's right to privacy and natural concern over his or her own emotional stability and mental health should be respected.

In addition to the question of privacy and other moral issues, the reliability and validity of personality assessment devices pose problems. Responding to test materials in terms of the most socially desirable answers or letting one's answers be determined by whatever role it is felt necessary to assume in the specific testing situation are types of response sets that can invalidate the results. More unobtrusive measures, which are less susceptible to faking or on which the procedure does not unduly interfere with obtaining valid results, may take care of response sets, but at the same time introduce problems of quantification and interpretation of the findings.

## Interpreting and Reporting Assessment Data

Even when the most carefully constructed and validated measures of personality are used, it is a cardinal rule that the resulting interpretations should be viewed as hypotheses to be confirmed or disconfirmed by behavioral observations and personal interviews. Certainly, the results of personality assessment are neither exact nor final, and they can be viewed in different ways by different examiners. This becomes embarrassingly obvious when different psychologists or psychiatrists, acting as expert witnesses in a court case, differ radically in their interpretations of the same assessment findings. Given the subjective nature of most psychological assessments, such embarrassment may be unavoidable when the two parties in a legal dispute have different objectives.

Several additional recommendations concerning the collection and interpretation of personality assessment data adapted from Sundberg (1977) can be made:

1. Survey the examinee's overall life situation and problems and then obtain more details in areas of particular relevance to the assessment.
2. Be sensitive to the sociocultural and ethnic background of the examinee, as well as his or her age and sex, if relevant.
3. Use more objective, as opposed to subjective, techniques and data whenever possible.
4. Obtain the *right kind* of information, not just *more* information, about the specific situation and purposes of the assessment.
5. Avoid too much speculation in interpreting results and predicting behavior; be especially careful in making predictions concerning behavior having a low probability of occurrence.
6. If possible, check your findings and interpretations with those of other psychological assessment specialists, and keep a record of your agreements and disagreements, successes and failures.
7. Communicate your findings in writing in a style that can be understood by the people for whom the report is intended.

Whatever the reasons for a psychological examination may be—to determine vocational competency, cognitive abilities, or emotional stability—some kind of written report of the results is usually required. The outline and length of the written report of a clinical case study vary with its purposes and the readers for whom it is intended, but the format in Figure 11–4 is representative.

When preparing a formal report of a psychological examination, the writer should keep clearly in mind the referral questions or principal complaint(s) (why the person was referred for psychological assessment or sought it) and how the assessment findings bear on answers to these questions or solutions to these problems. Information on the current mental status and emotional stability, as well as the probable outcomes (prognosis) of the patient's condition, should also be considered. The examinee's characteristics and their interrelationships should be described as fully and specifically as possible, avoiding vague generalizations, stereotypes, and banalities. It is also helpful for the writer to have a theory of personality, or at least some psychological framework, to serve as a basis for interpreting the findings. The report should be written in a succinct, clear style that is comprehensible to the reader. A psychological report is of little value if it is not understood or not read by those who are in a position to use the information that it contains to help to make decisions bearing on the life and well-being of the examinee.

**Format of a Psychological Assessment Report**

Name of Examinee _____

Age _____ Birth Date _____ Education _____

Examiner _____

Place of Examination _____ Date _____

**Tests Administered.**  List the names, including forms and levels, of all tests and inventories that were administered.

**Referral and Background Information.**  Why was the examinee referred for psychological testing? What was the purpose of the referral, and what person or facility made it? What background information relevant to the case was obtained from other sources (school records, interviews, etc.)? Give the examinee's own story, as well as that of other observers if available. Describe the examinee's physical and psychological history and characteristics, educational and employment situation. In the case of children in particular, information on the home and family (social status, characteristics of parents, siblings, etc.) is important. Serious sensory of psychomotor handicaps, as well as the presence of emotional disorder, should also be noted.

**Appearance and Behavioral Characteristics.**  Describe the appearance and behavior of the examinee during the examination. Describe the examinee's characteristics, his or her approach to the tasks, level of motivation and emotionality, and any other factors that might have influenced the results. What behaviors on the part of the examinee were symptomatic of particular physical, cognitive, or affective conditions or characteristics?

**Test Results and Interpretations.**  Give a detailed description of the results of the tests or other instruments administered and how they may be interpreted. If the examiner is interpreting the results according to a particular theory of personality or behavior, make certain that the reader understands the language and assumptions of that theory. Be as specific and individualized as possible in interpreting the results.

**Conclusions and Recommendations.**  Describe the conclusions (descriptive, dynamic, diagnostic) stemming from the observational, interview, and standardized or unstandardized test data. What recommendations are warranted by the results? Include appropriate interpretative cautions, but don't "hedge" or deal in generalities. Additional psychological assessment (be specific), neurological or other medical examinations, counseling or psychotherapy, special class placement and training, vocational rehabilitation, and institutionalization are among the recommendations that might be made. If a handicap or disability exists, is it remediable?

_____

Signature and Printed Name of Examiner

**FIGURE 11–4**  Format for a Psychological Assessment Report.

## OBSERVATIONS

The most widely employed and probably the most generally understood and acceptable method of personality assessment is some form of observation. When using the method of observation, which is basic to all science, the observer simply takes note of events, such as human behavior, and perhaps makes a record of what is observed. The most common procedure is the *uncontrolled observation* of behavior "on the wing" with no attempt to restrict it to a particular situation or set of conditions. Observing the activities of children on a playground and the behavior of people in a waiting line are examples of such uncontrolled, or *naturalistic,* observation. An illustration of uncontrolled observation in the world of work is the *critical incidents technique* (Flanagan, 1954). Supervisors and others who are familiar with a particular job are asked to identify specific behaviors that are critical to job performance or that distinguish between good and poor workers. These behaviors, or *incidents,* are critical because they have either highly positive or highly negative consequences. Examples are "secures machinery and tidies up place of work when finished" and "follows up customers' requests promptly." Identification of a large number of such incidents provides valuable information on the nature of the job and the requirements for effective performance.

### Observation as a Research Method

Observations may be uncontrolled and yet systematic and objective. For example, teachers can be trained to make objective observations of the behavior of schoolchildren and accurate *anecdotal records* of whatever behavior seems significant. A well-trained teacher–observer indicates in the anecdotal record precisely what was observed and distinguishes it from how it was interpreted. The observer realizes that when Johnny pinches Mary it is not always an act of aggression.

***Improving the Accuracy of Observations***　　Training observers to be as objective as possible, by not letting their own personal biases and needs affect what they observe and separating observation from interpretation, is one of several recommended guidelines for improving the validity of observational data. Another recommendation is to observe a limited number of specific behaviors, which are defined beforehand. Employing several observers and collecting a large, representative sample of observations can also improve the accuracy of observations. Obtaining a representative sample of behavior is, however, time consuming and expensive. To reduce the volume of data collected in continuous observation, the *incident sampling* technique of noting and recording only specific events or incidents, say of aggressive behavior, is appropriate. Further improvements in the efficiency of observation may be obtained by *time sampling*—making a series of observations lasting only a few minutes each over a period of a day or so (Wright, 1960).

***Participant Observation***　　Also relatively uncontrolled is *participant observation,* in which the observer is a part of the observational situation. Participant observation has been used extensively by cultural anthropologists, so much so that at one time it was remarked that a typical aborigine family consisted of a mother, a father, two children, and a cultural anthropologist! Realizing that they must take into account the likelihood that the observer's own behavior will affect the reactions of other people in the situation, proponents of this research method argue that active involvement in a situation can provide insights that are unobtainable by other means.

## Controlled Observations and Situational Testing

In addition to relatively uncontrolled observations, prearranged, contrived, or controlled observations are made with the purpose of determining how people (and animals) behave in various situations. For example, a developmental psychologist may set up an observational situation beforehand to determine if a child will cheat or behave honestly under a pre-arranged set of conditions.

A classic series of studies that used a controlled observational procedure known as *situational testing* was the Character Education Inquiry (Hartshorne & May, 1928). In these investigations, children were surreptitiously given an opportunity to demonstrate their honesty, altruism, and other character traits. For example, to test for honesty, the investigators placed a child in a situation where some coins could be stolen and in another situation where test answers could be copied, presumably without being detected. Among the findings of the studies were that older children, less intelligent children, children of lower socioeconomic status, and more emotionally unstable children tended to be less honest in all the situations. Perhaps the most important outcome of the Hartshorne and May studies was that honesty and other character traits varied as much with the specific situation as with the individual. In other words, the degree of honesty, altruism, or other ethical behavior manifested by children depended greatly on the situations in which they were observed.

Situational testing of military personnel was introduced by the Germans and subsequently adapted by the British and U.S. Armed Forces during World War II. A series of simulated situational tests for selecting espionage agents was designed by the U.S. Office of Strategic Services (OSS), the forerunner of the CIA. As in the Hartshorne and May (1928) studies, deception of the candidates was involved. For example, in the "wall problem" a group of men was assigned the task of crossing a canyon. Unknown to the real candidate, the men designated to assist him were "plants," rather than actual candidates. One of these plants acted as an obstructor by making unrealistic suggestions and insulting or worrisome remarks; another plant pretended not to understand the task and passively resisted directions from the candidate. Not realizing that the others were in league with the examiners, the real candidate was observed during his efforts to complete the task in the face of these frustrating circumstances. It was difficult to determine the effectiveness of these procedures as selection methods, however, and they were never adequately validated.

Situational testing has been used in other assessment programs, for example, in the selection of clinical psychologists (Kelly & Fiske, 1951). One interesting variation is the Leaderless Group Discussion (LGD) test, in which a group of executive candidates discusses an assigned topic for 30 to 50 minutes while their individual performances are rated by observers. The ratings of these observers, as well as ratings made by the other candidates, may be in terms of the degree of ascendance, task facilitation, and sociability shown by the candidate. In spite of the real-life quality of situational testing, it is never possible to duplicate real situations in detail. Even in the OSS assessment program, some candidates realized that the tests were rigged. For these and other reasons, the reliabilities and predictive validities of situational tests are frequently too low to justify the cost.

In situational testing, the behavior of the examinee may be observed through a television monitor. By remaining unseen, the observer does not intrude on or affect the behavior of the people who are being observed. Whenever people realize that they are being observed, they may behave unnaturally or act as if they were on stage (role playing). For this reason, observations for the purposes of personality assessment are usually made as unobtrusively as possible. In unobtrusive observation, the performer is unaware of the observer's presence, and therefore the behavior of the former is not influenced by the knowledge of being watched. Either controlled or uncontrolled observation may be unobtrusive, and even participant observation can be relatively unobtrusive when the observer takes steps to be accepted by the people who are being observed.

## Clinical Observations

A clinical or school psychologist who is examining a child interacts with the child as a special kind of participant observer. Consequently, a psychological examiner must be careful not to let his or her own presence and actions provoke atypical responses in the child. As implied in the report format in Figure 11–4, the examiner's observations, which must be as unobtrusive as possible, are an important part of the psychological report. The following observational description is typical in a brief psychological assessment report:

Michael is an attractive child with long, straight brown hair and freckles. He seemed a bit anxious during the examination, squirming around in his chair, but not excessively. He tended to give up easily on more difficult tasks, and revealed other signs of low frustration tolerance (sighing deeply, reluctance to try). However, he was fairly cooperative during the examination and mildly interested in the tasks; he showed signs of fatigue toward the end of the session. In general, he was attentive and energetic, responding when told to in a brief, occasionally uncertain manner. He did not smile during the entire time.

Much of what is known about personality dynamics and mental disorders has been obtained from observations of people in clinical settings. Clinical observations are obviously not completely objective: both parties in a clinical situation affect each other's behavior. Consequently, the accuracy of clinical observations and the interpretations given to them should be verified by other people and procedures.

An alert clinical observer notes a variety of details: what the examinee is wearing and whether he or she is well groomed; if and how the examinee shakes hands and looks at the examiner; how the examinee sits, stands, and walks; what facial expressions, body movements, and voice tones are characteristic. These are nonverbal behaviors and, when interpreted properly, can provide better insight into personality than a record limited to what the examinee actually says.

## Nonverbal Behavior

Most people realize that interpersonal communication is not entirely verbal, but they are usually unaware of the extent to which movements of their hands, eyes, and mouth, as well as body postures and voice tones, are interpreted as messages. As suggested by the following quotation, Sigmund Freud was quite aware of these nonverbal cues: "He that has eyes to see and ears to hear may convince himself that no mortal can keep a secret. If his lips are silent, he chatters with his fingertips; betrayal oozes out of him at every pore" (Freud, 1905, page 94).

A great deal of research has been conducted on nonverbal behavior, including *kinesics* (movements of body parts), *proximics* (distance between communicants), and *paralinguistics* (tone of voice, rate of speaking, and other nonverbal aspects of speech). According to the findings of one investigation, 65 to 90 percent of the meaning in interpersonal communications comes from nonverbal cues (Mehrabian & Weiner, 1967). It has been found that certain types of nonverbal cues are more important than others in message transmission. Kinesics are particularly important, followed by proximics, paralinguistics, and even *culturics* (style of dress, culturally based habits or customs, and the like). Most people are probably right more often than wrong in interpreting nonverbal messages, but mistakes occur. The poker-faced gambler and the glad-handed salesman or politician are renowned for their ability to deceive others with nonverbal behavior. Nonverbal behaviors and characteristics are interpreted more accurately when the observer has some knowledge of the specific situation or context in which the behavior occurs. In addition, some people are better than others at interpreting nonverbal behavior, an ability that appears to be related to personality but not to intelligence.

***The PONS***    To assess individual differences in the ability to interpret nonverbal communications, Rosenthal et al. (1979) devised the Profile of Nonverbal Sensitivity (PONS). The PONS consists of a 45-minute film in which viewers are presented with a series of stimuli, such as facial expressions or spoken phrases heard as tones or sounds but not as words. After each stimulus is presented, the viewer selects the most appropriate of two descriptive labels. The authors of the PONS report that men and women who make high scores tend to have fewer friends, but warmer, more honest, and more satisfying sexual relationships than those who make low scores.

Reasoning that sensitivity to nonverbal messages is an important ability for diplomats, David McClelland used the PONS in an applicant screening program for the U.S. Information Agency. Short taped segments from the test were played to USIA job applicants, who were then asked to indicate what emotion was being expressed. It was found that applicants who scored high on the PONS were viewed by their colleagues as significantly more competent than those who scored low (Rosenthal et al., 1979, pages 304–306).

***Unmasking the Face***    Another contribution to the assessment of nonverbal behavior is the Facial Action Coding System (FACS). Designed by Paul Ekman and Wallace Friesen, the FACS material consists of 135 photographs of various facial expressions for training observers in scoring dozens of facial action units. Also useful in training observers to judge emotion from facial expressions are Friesen and Ekman's Pictures of Facial Affect. These are 110 black-and-white pictures expressing fear, anger, happiness, sadness, surprise, or danger (plus a neutral expression).

## Self-observation and Content Analysis

Observing oneself, which most people typically spend quite a bit of time doing, is an appealing data-collection method in both research and clinical contexts. The appeal of the method lies in both its economy and the fact that it is one of very few ways to get at private thoughts and feelings.[1] A problem with self-observations is that they are likely to be even more biased than observations made by others: people are seldom entirely objective in describing their own thoughts and behavior (Wolff & Merrens, 1974). As with observations made by others, however, people can be trained to make more objective, systematic self-observations (Thoreson & Mahoney, 1974). They can learn to distinguish what they are actually feeling, thinking, or doing from what they should or would like to feel, think, or do.

By keeping a continuous written record of one's thoughts, feelings, and actions, a wealth of self-observation data can be accumulated. Unfortunately, it is not always clear what to do with such an abundance of data, that is, how to analyze or interpret it. As seen in the *content analysis* of diaries, autobiographies, letters, drawings, and other personal documents, important insights into personality and behavior can be obtained from interpreting self-observation data (Allport, 1965). But the complexity and laboriousness of content analysis have kept this interpretive approach from being applied routinely in clinical and other applied contexts.

## Biographical Data and Employment Situations

Information supplied by completed application blanks and other self-report forms is useful in clinical and educational contexts, but the most systematic research and applications with biographical data have taken place in employment contexts. Although much of this information is highly factual and objective (applicant's name, birthdate, marital status, and so on), a substantial amount is obtained from self-observations and the respondent's impressions of the interpersonal environment.

*Applications and Recommendations*    One of the first things required of a job applicant is to write a letter of application and/or fill out an application blank. A completed application blank is both a formal request for employment and a brief description of the applicant's fitness for the job. Following a series of identifying questions (name, address, employment desired, and so on), detailed background information (education, physical handicaps, military record, previous employment and experience) is requested. In most cases, a section of the blank is also provided for references.

Whether elicited by letter, telephone, interview, or questionnaire, information from an applicant's listed references can be useful despite some obvious limitations. Letters of recommendation probably have the most serious limitations in that they often provide a biased description of the applicant. Because former employers or other reference sources are reluctant to reveal negative information about a person in writing, one telephone call is sometimes worth a dozen letters of recommendation. In fact, praise is so common in letters of recommendation that personnel administrators and other selection officials often become overly sensitized to anything less than very positive statements concerning the applicant. There is also a tendency to interpret short letters as indicative of disapproval and longer letters as more complimentary.

[1]Some others are hypnosis, narcoanalysis, and free association.

***Biographical Inventories***    A completed application blank provides a human resources (personnel) department with an efficient, inexpensive way of determining whether an applicant meets the minimum requirements for a job. If not filed away and forgotten, it can also serve as an information guide for any subsequent interviews of the applicant. Furthermore, the background, experience, and other information provided by a completed application form can be numerically weighted and used to predict quality of work, absenteeism, turnover, and other criteria of job performance. More formal *biographical inventories,* or biodata forms, which are comprised of a variety of items pertaining to the life history of the applicant (such as family relationships, friendships, extracurricular activities, and interests), have been designed and used by Exxon, the U.S. Office of Personnel Management, and other production and service organizations. A great deal of research on these longer forms of weighted application blanks has been conducted during the past three decades (see Owens, 1976). Catalogs of life history items, from which personnel administrators or recruiters may construct their own biographical inventories, have even been prepared (Glennon, Albright, & Owens, 1966).

Biographical inventories not only have substantial content validity; they are also effective predictors of performance in a variety of job contexts ranging from unskilled work to high-level executive responsibilities. However, legal problems are associated with requests for certain kinds of information (age, sex, ethnicity, religion, marital status, number of children) on application blanks and biographical inventories and in interviews. This is unfortunate, because information of this kind is often highly predictive of job performance. Although data provided by application forms and biographical inventories have fairly high validity, applicants may object to certain items as being too personal or otherwise offensive (Rosenbaum, 1973). Therefore, one might expect answers to these kinds of items (about personal finances, family background, and other intimate details) to be less accurate than less sensitive information.

## INTERVIEWS

Interviewing is one of the oldest and most widely used methods of personality assessment. Not only does it yield much the same kind of data as observations, but information is obtained on what a person says as well as what he or she does. The interviewee's nonverbal behavior, including body postures and poise, gestures, eye movements, and the quality and pattern of speech, is important and should be noted. The major emphasis in interviewing, however, is on the content of the verbal statements made by the interviewee. For this reason, an interview may be defined as a "face-to-face verbal interchange in which one person, the interviewer, attempts to elicit information or expressions of opinion or belief from another person or persons" (Maccoby & Maccoby, 1954, page 449). The information obtained in an interview consists of details of the interviewee's background or life history, in addition to data concerning feelings, attitudes, perceptions, and expectations.

Interviews are used in many different contexts and for a variety of purposes. In research contexts, they are used for polling, surveys, and to obtain in-depth information on personality and behavior to test some hypothesis or theoretical proposition. In employment situations, interviews are used for employee selection and screening, evaluation or appraisal, troubleshooting, and termination. In clinical contexts, intake interviews of patients and their relatives are essential in collecting case history information for making medical and/or psychological diagnoses (diagnostic interviews). In addition, therapeutic interviews are a part of the psychological treatment process, and exit interviews are designed to determine whether an institutionalized individual is ready to be released.

Whatever the context and purposes of interviewing may be, it requires skill and sensitivity and may be quite time consuming and laborious. It is as much an art as a science, and some interviewers are more effective than others in establishing rapport and getting interviewees to open up. An interviewer's approach varies with the purpose and context of the interview, but, as in any interpersonal situation, the outcomes depend on the personality and actions of both participants. Thus, an interview is not a one-way, question-and-answer situation in which the interviewer remains unaffected; in almost every case it is a dynamic, two-way interchange in which the participants mutually influence each other.

Interviewing can be an end in itself, but it may also function as a "get acquainted" or warming-up process designed as a lead-in to other assessment procedures. Most clinical and counseling psychologists like the face-to-face closeness of an interview because it enables them to get a "feel" for the patient or client and his or her problems and characteristics. Clinical psychologists, personnel psychologists, employment counselors, and other human service professionals usually believe that the time and expense of an interview are justified because personal information obtained in this way is not available by any other means. Applicants, counselees, and patients usually express feelings of being more involved when interviewed than when they are merely asked to fill out paper-and-pencil questionnaires or application blanks and are not given an opportunity to communicate their problems, needs, opinions, and circumstances in a face-to-face manner.

## Interviewing Techniques and Structure

A personal interview can take place anywhere, but it is usually better to conduct it in a quiet room free from distractions. Both the interviewer and the interviewee should be comfortably seated and facing each other. Because interviewing is a complex interpersonal skill and to some extent a function of the interviewer's interpersonal style, effective interviewing is not easily taught. Attention to the following recommendations, however, can improve one's interviewing skills.

Professional interviewers are usually friendly but neutral, interested but not prying in reacting to interviewees. They are warm and open, accepting interviewees for what they are without showing approval or disapproval. They do not begin with leading questions of the "How often do you beat your wife?" type and do not ask questions that imply a certain answer (for example, "You still do that, don't you?"). By properly timing and varying the nature of the questions according to the situation, good interviewers are able to develop a conversation that flows from topic to topic. Pauses or silences cause them no discomfort: they allow the interviewee sufficient time to answer a question completely, and they listen to the answer without interrupting. In addition, they pay attention not only to what the interviewee says, but also to the manner in which it is said. Realizing that the interviewer's behavior (activity level, amount and speed of talking, and the like) tends to be imitated by the interviewee, interviewers are patient and comfortable and do not hurry the interviewee. Skilled interviewers also check their understandings, impressions, and perceptions of the interviewee's answers to clarify them and make certain that they do not misunderstand, or they may ask direct questions to fill in gaps. Effective interviewers are, however, not voyeurs who relentlessly probe or relish the discussion of certain topics and consciously or unconsciously reinforce the interviewee's statements concerning those matters.

Although the characteristics of good interviewers described above are generally applicable, specific techniques vary with the theoretical orientation (behavioral, client centered, psychoanalytic, and so on) of the interviewer, as well as with the goals and stage of the interview. Most interviewers outside clinical contexts, as well as many clinicians, are fairly eclectic in their orientation, following no particular theory of personality but applying relevant concepts from a variety of theories.

**Structured versus Unstructured Interviews**   The degree to which an interview is *structured* should depend primarily on the goals of the interview, but it is also important to consider the characteristics of the participants. Some interviewees respond more readily to a relatively unstructured, open-ended approach; others provide more relevant information when the interviewer follows an *interviewing guide* and asks very structured questions. Interviewers may also feel more comfortable and accomplish more by asking a series of questions similar to those found on an application blank or personal history form. Less experienced interviewers typically find it easier to handle a structured interview, the results of which can be more easily quantified for purposes of analysis. But many experienced interviewers prefer greater flexibility in the content and timing of interview questions, in other words, less structure.

More skill and time are required to conduct an interview in an unstructured or open-ended manner in which the interviewer can follow up interesting leads or concentrate on details of greater significance. To accomplish this, the interviewer encourages the interviewee to feel free to talk about his or her problems, interests, behaviors, or whatever else seems relevant to the goals of the interview. Those goals also affect the amount of structure in an interview. When answers to a large number of specific questions are needed, as in an employment selection situation, a fairly structured approach is appropriate. When the goal is to obtain an in-depth picture of personality or to define the nature of certain problems and their causes, less structure is called for. Whether highly structured or relatively open ended, the sequence of questions should usually proceed from general to specific and from less personal to more personal topics. Most professional interviewers are able to vary their approach with the personality of the person being interviewed and the objectives of the interview. They begin by asking a series of nonthreatening, open-ended questions to establish rapport and get the conversation going, and then become more specific in questioning as the interview proceeds.

**Interview Topics and Questions**   The specific questions asked depend on the purposes of the interview, but it is helpful to plan an interview by outlining the topics to be covered, if not the specific questions to be asked. A topical outline for a life history interview is given in Table 11–1. A complete life history interview, whether conducted in a clinical, social service, employment, or research context, requires obtaining the kinds of information listed in this table. Not all of these topics need be covered in a specific situation: the interviewer can concentrate on areas considered most important. In any event, the specific interview questions, framed in language with which the interviewee is familiar and comfortable, can be developed from the outline in Table 11–1.

**TABLE 11–1   Information to Obtain in a Life History Interview**

What are the interviewee's name, address, and date and place of birth?

What is the purpose of the interview (employment, psychodiagnostic, vocational counseling, personal counseling, etc.)?

How can the interviewee's family (parents, siblings, other family members) and sociocultural group be described?

What is the interviewee's medical history (present health, health history, major health problems)?

What is the interviewee's developmental history (physical, intellectual, speech, emotional, social; irregularities of problems in development)?

What education and training has the interviewee had (schools attended, performance level, adjustment to school), and what are his or her plans for further education and training?

What jobs or positions has the interviewee held, and how well did he or she perform? Were there any particular problems?

Has the interviewee ever been in trouble with the law (what, when, where, why)?

What is the interviewee's marital history [marriages, marital problems and divorce(s), children]?

What are the interviewee's self-perceptions? Is he or she self-accepting or dissatisfied with self? Why?

What are the interviewee's attitudes toward his or her past, present, and future life?

## Clinical Interviews

In clinical interviews conducted for intake purposes at a social agency or mental hospital, diagnostic interviews to determine the causes and correlates of an individual's problems, and therapeutic interviews (counseling, psychotherapy), it is recommended that, among other things, the interviewer should do the following:

Assure the interviewee of the confidentiality of the interview.

Convey a feeling of interest and warmth (rapport).

Try to put the interviewee at ease.

Try to get in touch with how the interviewee feels (empathy).

Be courteous, patient, and accepting.

Encourage the interviewee to express his or her thoughts and feelings freely.

Adjust the questions to the cultural and educational background of the interviewee.

Avoid psychological or psychiatric jargon.

Avoid leading questions.

Share personal information and experiences with the interviewee (self-disclosure) if appropriate and timed accurately.

Use humor sparingly, and only if appropriate and not insulting.

Listen without overreacting emotionally.

Attend not only to what is said, but also to how it is said.

Take notes or make a recording as inconspicuously as possible.

Many of these recommendations are not restricted to clinical interviews but apply to many other types of verbal interchanges as well.

When conducted properly, a diagnostic or therapeutic interview can provide a great deal of information about a person: the nature, duration, and severity of his or her problems; how the problems are manifested (inwardly or outwardly); what past influences are related to present difficulties; the interviewee's resources and limitations for coping with the problems; the kinds of psychological assistance the interviewee has had in the past; and the kinds of assistance that are expected and might be of help now.

**Behavioral Interviewing**    Behavioral interviewing is a type of clinical interviewing in which the focus is on obtaining information to plan a program of behavior modification. As discussed later in the chapter, this entails describing, in objective behavioral terms, the problem behaviors of the interviewee as well as the antecedent conditions and reinforcing consequences. To conduct such an interview successfully, the interviewee must be encouraged (and taught if necessary) to respond in specific behavioral terms, rather than in the more customary language of motives or traits. After obtaining the necessary information to develop a behavior modification program, the program must then be explained to the person, and he or she must be motivated to follow it.

**Stress Interviewing**    The usual rule of cordiality toward the interviewee is suspended in a *stress interview.* The goal of stress interviewing, which is used in clinical, selection, and interrogation contexts, is to determine the ability of the person to cope or solve a specific problem under emotionally stressful conditions. Stress interviewing may also be appropriate when time is short or when the interviewee is very repetitive, emotionally unresponsive, or quite defensive. An attempt is made to produce a valid emotional response—to get beneath the superficial social mask (*persona*) of the interviewee—by asking probing, challenging questions in a kind of police interrogation atmosphere. A great deal of professional expertise is obviously required to make a stress interview appear realistic and not let it get out of control.

**Methode Clinique and Morality Research**    The clinical method of interviewing, in which the interviewer asks probing questions to test the limits or obtain in-depth information about a person, was employed extensively by Sigmund Freud, Jean Piaget, and many other famous psychologists. The use of clinical interviewing in research, referred to as the *methode clinique,* requires considerable skill.

An example of a research instrument involving the use of the *methode clinique* is Lawrence Kohlberg's Moral Judgment Scale. Kohlberg (1969, 1974) maintained that the development of personal morality progresses through three ascending levels, consisting of two stages each. At the lowest level (*premoral level*), moral judgments are guided either by punishment and obedience or by a kind of naive pleasure–pain philosophy. At an intermediate level (*morality of conventional rule conformity*), morality depends either on the approval of other people ("good boy–good girl" morality) or on adherence to the precepts of authority. In the first stage of the last level (*morality of self-accepted moral principles*), morality is viewed in terms of acceptance of a contract or democratically determined agreement. In the second stage of the last level, the individual has developed an internal set of principles and a conscience that directs his or her judgment and behavior.

The Moral Judgment Scale is administered by presenting nine hypothetical moral dilemmas and obtaining the examinee's judgments and reasons for the judgments pertaining to each dilemma. One such dilemma, the case of Heinz and the druggist, is as follows:

In Europe, a woman was near death from a special kind of cancer. There was one drug that the doctors thought might save her. It was a form of radium that a druggist in the same town had recently discovered. The drug was expensive to make, but the druggist was charging ten times what the drug cost him to make. He paid $200 for the radium and charged $2000 for a small dose of the drug. The sick woman's husband, Heinz, went to everyone he knew to borrow the money, but he could only get together about $1000 which is half of what it cost. He told the druggist that his wife was dying, and asked him to sell it cheaper or let him pay later. But the druggist said, "No, I discovered the drug and I'm going to make money from it." So Heinz got desperate and broke into the man's store to steal the drug for his wife. (Kohlberg & Elfenbein, 1975)

Scoring the examinee's moral judgments and reasons for the judgments concerning stories such as this one consists of making rather subjective evaluations of those responses in terms of Kohlberg's stages.

## Personnel Interviews

Almost all production and service organizations use interviews, not only for selecting, classifying, and placing employees, but also for counseling, troubleshooting, termination (exit interview), and research. Because the interviewing process is expensive and time consuming, it is reasonable to wonder if it is the most efficient procedure for obtaining data on job applicants. Much of the information from a structured interview, which is the preferred approach in most employment settings, can be obtained from an application blank or questionnaire. But job applicants are often more willing to reveal matters of significance in the personal atmosphere of an interview than in writing. In most organizational settings, for all but the lowest-level jobs a personnel interview is the final step in the employee selection process.

A variety of information about an applicant is usually available to employment interviewers, including that supplied by the completed application form, letters of recommendation, test scores, and the like. The interviewer's task is to integrate the information obtained from all these sources and the personal interview to make a recommendation or job decision.

An employment interviewer must be cautious in asking questions concerning private matters, not only because they may place the interviewee under an emotional strain, but also because it may be illegal to ask them. Examples of questions that are and are not legally permissible are given in Box 11–1.

**Box 11–1**

**Permitted and Nonpermitted Employment Questions**

Interpretive guidelines issued by the Equal Employment Opportunity Commission indicate that it is permissible to ask the following questions in an employment interview:

How many years experience do you have?

(To a housewife) Why do you want to return to work?

What are your career goals?

Who have been your prior employers?

Why did you leave your last job?

Are you a veteran? Did the military provide you with job-related experience?

If you have no phone, where can we reach you?

What languages do you speak fluently?

Can you do extensive traveling?

Who recommended you to us?

What did you like or dislike about your previous jobs?

What is your educational background? What schools did you attend?

What are your strong points? Weaknesses?

Do you have any objection if we check with your former employer for references?

*Continues*

## Reliability and Validity of Interviews

Interviewing is an important psychological tool, but it shares with observational methods problems of reliability and validity. Reliability demands consistency, but interviewers vary in their appearance, approach, and style and, consequently, the impression they make on interviewees. These differing impressions result in differences in behavior: with one interviewer a person may be friendly and outgoing, whereas with another he or she becomes hostile and remote. In addition, the interviewer's perceptions of the interviewee can be distorted by his or her own experiences and personality.

The reliability of an interview is usually determined by comparing the ratings given to the interview's responses by two or more judges. The magnitude of an interrater reliability

On the other hand, it is considered legally unacceptable to ask the following questions in an employment interview:

What is your age?

What is your date of birth?

Do you have children? If so, how old are they?

What is your race?

What church do you attend?

Are you married, divorced, separated, widowed, or single?

Have you ever been arrested?

What kind of military discharge do you have?

What clubs or organizations do you belong to?

Do you rent or own your own home?

What does your wife (husband) do?

Who lives in your household?

Have your wages ever been attached or garnisheed?

What was your maiden name (female applicants)?

coefficient computed from these ratings varies with the specificity of the questions asked and the rated behaviors; it is usually higher for structured and semistructured than for unstructured interviews (Schwab & Heneman, 1969; Bradley & Caldwell, 1977; Disbrow, Doerr, & Caulfield, 1977). Even when the questions are fairly objective and specific and asked in a structured format, however, the interrater reliabilities are usually no higher than .80.

When conducting an interview, the interviewer is the assessment instrument. Consequently, many of the reliability problems of interviews are related to the characteristics and behavior of the interviewer. Because the interviewer is almost always in charge in an interviewing situation, his or her personality and biases are usually more important than those of the interviewee in determining what kinds of information are obtained. The socioemotional tone of an interview is determined more by the interviewer's actions than by those of the interviewee: the interviewer talks more, and the length of the interviewee's answers is directly related to the length of the questions asked by the interviewer. In addition to being overly dominant, the interviewer may fail to obtain complete, accurate information by asking the wrong questions, by not encouraging complete answers or not allowing enough time for them, and by recording the responses incorrectly.

Other shortcomings of interviewers are the tendency to give more weight to first impressions and to be affected more by unfavorable than by favorable information about an interviewee. Errors that affect ratings also occur in interviewers' judgments. An example is the *halo effect* of making judgments—both favorable and unfavorable—on the basis of a "general impression" or a single prominent characteristic of the interviewee. This effect occurs when a person who is actually superior (or inferior) on only one or two characteristics is given an overall superior (or inferior) evaluation. In addition, the *contrast error* of judging an average interviewee as inferior if the preceding interviewee was clearly superior, or as superior if the preceding interviewee was clearly inferior, can occur.

Because an interviewer's impressions are influenced by the neatness, posture, and other nonverbal behaviors of the interviewee, as well as the latter's verbal responses, prospective interviewees would do well to prepare themselves both mentally and physically for an interview. In the case of an employment interview, the interviewee should have some knowledge of the organization and its philosophy. The interviewee should be prepared to give a synopsis of his or her background and aspirations, but refrain from making controversial comments or engaging in bad habits such as smoking or nailbiting during the interview (see Box 11–2).

A consistent finding of research pertaining to the validity of the interview in employment selection or clinical diagnosis is that it is overrated (Arvey, 1979; Reilly & Chao, 1982). Interviews can be made more valid, but they must be carefully planned or structured, and the interviewers need to be extensively trained. The results of an interview are also more valid when the interviewer focuses on specific (job or clinical) information and when responses are evaluated question by question, preferably by at least two evaluators, rather than as a whole. To facilitate this process, the entire interview should be electronically recorded for later playback and evaluation. In this way, the task of interpreting an interviewee's responses can be separated more effectively from the actual interviewing process. But even a videotape recording, and especially an audiotape recording, of an interview are not sufficient. Spoken words and pictures are not always clear, and the emotional tone and contextual variables are frequently missed in an electronic recording. For this reason, an alert human observer who takes good notes is needed to supplement an electronic recording of an interview.

## RATING SCALES AND CHECKLISTS

Information obtained from observations and interviews, whether formally or informally, can be recorded in a variety of ways. Because of the large mass of data produced in lengthy observational and interviewing sessions, the findings are almost always summarized in some form. Together with a condensed written description, a rating scale or checklist is a useful device for summarizing observations and interview responses. Unlike the items on a checklist, which require only a yes–no decision, rating scale items require the respondent to make an evaluative judgment on an ordered series of categories.

### Rating Scales

The rating scale, which was introduced by Francis Galton during the latter part of the nineteenth century, is a popular assessment device in schools, employment settings, and many other contexts. Ratings may be made either by the ratee (the person being rated) or another rater and are generally considered to be less precise than personality inventories and more

## Box 11–2

## Don'ts for Employment Interviews and Resumé Bloopers

### Major "Don'ts" for Interviews

Don't ask "How long is this going to take?"

Don't say "I'm a people person."

Don't say "I left my last three positions because my boss picked on me."

Don't ask "How much vacation am I going to get?"

Don't say "I'm not sure what I want to do."

Don't ask "Can you sign my unemployment card?"

Don't wear a blue metallic cocktail dress.

Don't wear short shorts.

Don't leave your tattoo exposed.

Don't fall asleep.

Don't bring your children.

Don't bring a Pepsi.

Don't bring your beeper.

### Some Favorite Resumé Bloopers

"My career objection is."

"Experienced in private relations . . . "

"Skilled in proolreading . . . "

"I want to work for a company where I can be depreciated."

"I have WordPurpose and Locust skills . . . "

"I want a position to pay my bills . . . "

Compiled by Snelling Temporaries.

superficial than projective techniques. Nevertheless, various types of rating scales are used extensively in assessing a wide range of behavioral and personality characteristics.

**Numerical Scale**  On a *numerical scale*, the person, object, or event is assigned one of several numbers corresponding to particular descriptions of the characteristics being rated. All that is required is for the ratings to be made on an ordered scale on which different numerical values are assigned to different locations. Figure 11–5 is an illustration of an instrument containing 15 numerical ratings scales, which can be used to rate oneself or someone else. Responses are scored on five personality variables: agreeableness, conscientiousness, extroversion, neuroticism, and openness. Scores on each variable range from 0 to 18.

**Semantic Differential**   A type of numerical rating scale that has frequently been used in research on personality and social psychology is the *semantic differential*. Osgood, Suci, and Tannenbaum (1957) devised this method for their studies of the connotative (personal) means that concepts such as "father," "mother, "sickness," "sin," "hatred," and "love" have for different people. To begin, a person rates a series of concepts on several 7-point, bipolar adjectival scales. For example, the concept "MOTHER" might be rated by making a checkmark on the appropriate line segment on each of the following three scales:

| | | |
|---|---|---|
| BAD | _____ : _____ : _____ : _____ : _____ : _____ : _____ | GOOD |
| WEAK | _____ : _____ : _____ : _____ : _____ : _____ : _____ | STRONG |
| SLOW | _____ : _____ : _____ : _____ : _____ : _____ : _____ | FAST |

After all concepts of interest have been rated on the various scales, responses to each concept are scored on several *semantic dimensions* and compared with responses to the remaining concepts. The main connotative meaning (semantic) dimensions that have been determined by factor analysis of ratings of a series of concepts on a large number of these adjectival scales are evaluation, potency, and activity. A *semantic space* may then be constructed by plotting a person's scores on the rated concepts on each of these three dimensions. Concepts falling close to each other in the semantic space presumably have similar connotative meanings for the rater.

**Graphic Rating Scale**   Another popular type of rating scale is a *graphic rating scale,* an example of which is:

How well does this person cooperate in a group?

| Never cooperates | Usually does not cooperate | Cooperates about half the time | Usually cooperates | Always cooperates |
|---|---|---|---|---|

The rater marks an **X** or check mark on each of a series of lines such as this containing descriptive terms or phrases pertaining to a certain characteristic or trait. Typically, a verbal description of the lowest degree of the characteristic is given at the extreme left end, a verbal description of the highest degree of the characteristic is given at the extreme right, and intermediate points on the line contain descriptions referring to intermediate degrees of the characteristic.

**Standard Rating Scale**   On a *standard rating scale,* the rater supplies or is supplied with a set of standards for evaluating the persons being rated (the *ratees*). An example of a standard rating scale is the *man-to-man* (or *person-to-person) scale,* which is constructed for rating individuals on a specified trait such as "leadership ability." The rater is asked to

---

**Five-Variable Personality Ratings**

*Directions:* For each item, check the number between the pair of adjectives corresponding to your description of yourself.

| 1. | affectionate | 1  2  3  4  5  6  7 | reserved |
|----|--------------|---------------------|----------|
| 2. | calm | 1  2  3  4  5  6  7 | worrying |
| 3. | careful | 1  2  3  4  5  6  7 | careless |
| 4. | conforming | 1  2  3  4  5  6  7 | independent |
| 5. | disorganized | 1  2  3  4  5  6  7 | well-organized |
| 6. | down-to-earth | 1  2  3  4  5  6  7 | imaginative |
| 7. | fun-loving | 1  2  3  4  5  6  7 | sober |
| 8. | helpful | 1  2  3  4  5  6  7 | uncooperative |
| 9. | insecure | 1  2  3  4  5  6  7 | secure |
| 10. | prefer routine | 1  2  3  4  5  6  7 | prefer variety |
| 11. | retiring | 1  2  3  4  5  6  7 | sociable |
| 12. | ruthless | 1  2  3  4  5  6  7 | soft-hearted |
| 13. | self-disciplined | 1  2  3  4  5  6  7 | weak-willed |
| 14. | self-pitying | 1  2  3  4  5  6  7 | self-satisfied |
| 15. | suspicious | 1  2  3  4  5  6  7 | trusting |

---

*Scoring formulas for the five variables are:

Agreeableness = 5 + Item 12 + Item 15 − Item 8
Conscientiousness = 13 − Item 3 + Item 5 − Item 13
Extroversion = 13 − Item 1 − Item 7 + Item 11
Neuroticism = 13 + Item 2 − Item 9 − Item 14
Openness = Item 4 + Item 6 + Item 10 − 3

**FIGURE 11–5**   Five-Variable Personality Rating Scales.

think of five people falling at different points along a hypothetical continuum of leadership ability. Then the rater compares each ratee with these five individuals and indicates which of them is most like the ratee in leadership ability.

***Behaviorally Anchored Scales***   Developed by Smith and Kendall (1963) and based on Flanagan's (1954) critical incidents technique, *behaviorally anchored scales* represent attempts to make the terminology of rating scales more descriptive of actual behavior and hence more objective. Understandably, terms such as *anxiety, self-confidence, aggressiveness,* and other nouns or adjectives used in traditional trait-oriented rating scales may be interpreted differently by different raters. This is particularly true when raters receive little or no training in how to interpret such terms. A tongue-in-cheek illustration of a behaviorally anchored scale for rating five employee performance factors is given in Figure 11–6.

A behaviorally anchored rating scale is constructed by convening a group of individuals who possess expert knowledge of a particular job or situation. Then, through discussion and painstaking deliberation, these individuals attempt to reach a consensus on a series of behaviorally descriptive critical incidents from which an objective, highly reliable rating scale can be constructed. Behavioral descriptions that survive repeated reevaluation by the group, or by other groups, may then be prepared as a series of items to be rated. One might expect that the emphasis on observable behavior and the concentrated group effort in devising behaviorally anchored scales would make such scales psychometrically superior to

### Guide to Employee Performance Appraisal

#### Performance Degrees

| Performance factors | Far exceeds job requirements | Exceeds job requirements | Meets job requirements | Needs some improvement | Does not meet minimum requirements |
|---|---|---|---|---|---|
| Quality | Leaps tall buildings with a single bound | Must take running start to leap over buildings | Can only leap over a short building or medium with no spires | Crashes into buildings when attempting to jump over them | Cannot recognize buildings at all, much less jump |
| Timeliness | Is faster than a speeding bullet | Is as fast as a speeding bullet | Not quite as fast as a speeding bullet | Would you believe a slow bullet | Wounds self with bullets when attempting to shoot gun |
| Initiative | Is stronger than a locomotive | Is stronger than a bull elephant | Is stronger than a bull | Shoots the bull | Smells like a bull |
| Adaptability | Walks on water consistently | Walks on water in emergencies | Washes with water | Drinks water | Passes water in emergencies |
| Communication | Talks with God | Talks with the angels | Talks to himself | Argues with himself | Loses those arguments |

**FIGURE 11–6**   Tongue-in-Cheek Behaviorally Anchored Rating Scale for Employee Appraisal.
(Adapted from *The Industrial-Organizational Psychologist, 1980, 17*(4), p. 22, and used with permission.)

other types of rating scales. Furthermore, the fact that the scale-construction process requires group involvement and consensus, and hence a greater likelihood of group acceptance, would seem to be an advantage. However, according to research findings, behaviorally anchored rating scales are not necessarily superior to graphic rating scales (Schwab, Heneman, & De Cotiis, 1975).

**Forced-choice Scale**    In a *forced-choice rating scale,* raters are presented with two or more descriptions and told to indicate which one best characterizes the person to be rated. If there are three or more descriptions, raters may also be asked to indicate which is least descriptive of the ratee. When there are four descriptions, for example, an item consists of two equally desirable and two equally undesirable statements. The rater is told to select the statement that is most descriptive and the one that is least descriptive of the ratee. Only one desirable statement and one undesirable statement actually discriminate between high and low ratees on the criterion, but the raters presumably do not know which statements these are. A hypothetical example of a four-statement forced-choice item for rating "leadership" follows:

_____ Assumes responsibility easily.

_____ Doesn't know how or when to delegate.

_____ Has many constructive suggestions to offer.

_____ Doesn't listen to others' suggestions.

Can you tell which statement is keyed as "desirable" and which one is keyed as "undesirable?"

**Errors in Rating**    Raters sometimes find the forced-choice format cumbersome, but it is considered fairer than the person-to-person rating technique. The forced-choice technique also has the advantage of controlling for certain errors in rating, such as constant errors, the halo effect, contrast error, and proximity error. *Constant errors* occur when the assigned ratings are higher (*leniency* or *generosity error*), lower (*severity error*), or more often in the average category (*central tendency error*) than they should be. The *halo effect* refers to the tendency of raters to respond on the basis of the general impression made by the ratee or to overgeneralize by giving favorable ratings to all traits merely because the ratee is outstanding on one or two. A halo effect may also be negative, in which case one bad characteristic spoils the ratings on all other characteristics. Related to the halo effect is the *logical error* of assigning similar ratings on characteristics that the rater perceives as logically related.

The term *contrast error* has been used in at least two senses. In one sense it refers to the tendency to assign a higher rating than justified if the immediately preceding ratee received a very low rating or to assign a lower rating than justified if the preceding ratee received a very high rating. In a second sense, *contrast error* refers to the tendency of a rater to compare or contrast the ratee with the rater in assigning ratings on certain behaviors or traits. Finally, the *proximity error* occurs when the rater tends to assign similar ratings to a person on items that are placed close together on the printed page. If a person is consistently rated high, low, or average on the majority of a set of items situated close together on the printed page, the person may receive similar ratings on other items near these items.

***Improving Ratings***   It is not easy to make reliable and valid judgments of people under any circumstances and especially so when the behaviors or characteristics are poorly defined or highly subjective. Not only are personal biases likely to affect ratings, but raters are often not sufficiently familiar with ratees to make accurate judgments. Training in how to make ratings more objective—by being aware of the various kinds of errors that can occur in rating, becoming more familiar with the persons and traits being rated, and omitting items that the rater feels unqualified to judge—can improve the accuracy of ratings. Combining the responses of several raters is also a recommended way of balancing out the response biases of individual raters. Finally, careful attention to the design of rating scales—defining the points (anchors) clearly with precise behavioral descriptions of the characteristics to be rated—can also improve the validity of ratings.

***Standardized Rating Scales***   Although a large number of rating scales are homemade devices designed for use in specific applied research settings, many standardized scales for assessing the behavior of children and adults are commercially available. Scales for rating the developmental status and behaviors of mentally retarded, learning disabled, emotionally disturbed, and physically handicapped children are especially popular. Scales for rating anxiety, depression, hostility, and other clinical symptoms are also widely used. The following scales are representative:

> Behavior Rating Profile (pro.ed)
>
> Conners' Rating Scales (The Psychological Corporation)
>
> Derogatis Psychiatric Rating Scale (NCS Assessments)
>
> Pupil Rating Scale Revised: Screening for Learning Disabilities (The Psychological Corporation)
>
> Revised Hamilton Rating Scale for Depression (Western Psychological Services)
>
> Waksman Social Skills Rating Scale (Psychological Assessment Resources)

## Checklists

A *checklist* is a relatively simple, highly cost effective, and fairly reliable method of describing or evaluating a person. They are more easily constructed than rating scales or personality inventories and are often just as valid; checklists can be administered as self-report of observer-report instruments. Respondents are instructed to mark the words or phrases in a list that apply to the person being evaluated, who may be themselves or someone else. When a number of respondents evaluate the same person on a checklist, the person's score on each item can be set equal to the number of respondents who checked it.

Useful checklists for appraising job performance in certain employment situations have been constructed from a set of critical on-the-job incidents. Checklists for special purposes or for use in specific contexts can also be prepared in clinical, research, and other situations (see Figure 11–7). A problem with such homemade instruments is that they are rarely adequately standardized or validated, reliability data are meager, and therefore it is uncertain whether the checklist is serving its intended purposes. For this reason, it is wise to consider one of the many commercially available checklists before constructing one. Checklists of adaptive behavior, developmental progress, health problems, personal characteristics, personal history, personal problems, and psychopathological symptoms are all commercially available. For example, a number of checklists, including the Child Behavior Checklist (Achenbach & Edelbrock, 1983) and the Revised Behavior Problem Checklist (Quay & Peterson, 1983), have been designed to identify behavioral problems in children. At the adolescent and adult levels are instruments such as the Personal History Checklists and Personal Problems Checklists (from Psychological Assessment Resources) and the Personal Experiences Checklists (from Western Psychological Services). Two of the most popular and time-honored checklists of problems and characteristics are the Mooney Problem Checklist and the Adjective Check List.

**Mooney Problem Checklists**   One of the oldest of all published checklists, this series consists of four forms: J (for junior high school pupils), H (for high school pupils), C (for college students), and A (for adults). The 210 to 330 problems on each form are grouped into the areas of health and physical development, home and family, boy and girl relations, morals and religion, courtship and marriage, economic security, school or occupation, and social and recreational. Examinees are instructed to underline those problems of some concern to them, circle the number of the problems of most concern, and then write a summary of their personal problems. The Mooney checklists can be scored on the number of problems in each area, but no national norms have been published. Responses are either interpreted impressionistically or compared with locally obtained norms. The manual reports test–retest reliability coefficients of .90 or higher for ranks (order of importance) of the problem areas for each examinee. The case for the validity of the Mooney checklists, as with problem checklists in general, is usually made on the basis of content.

---

*Directions:* Make a checkmark on the dashed line for every item that is descriptive of you.

| | |
|---|---|
| ____ 1. achievement oriented | ____ 11. emotionally explosive |
| ____ 2. aggressive | ____ 12. fast worker |
| ____ 3. ambitious | ____ 13. hard worker |
| ____ 4. competitive | ____ 14. highly motivated |
| ____ 5. constant worker | ____ 15. impatient |
| ____ 6. dislikes wasting time | ____ 16. likes challenges |
| ____ 7. easily angered | ____ 17. likes to lead |
| ____ 8. easily aroused to action | ____ 18. likes responsibility |
| ____ 9. easily frustrated | ____ 19. restless |
| ____ 10. efficient | ____ 20. tries hard to succeed |

**FIGURE 11–7**   Checklist for Identification of Type A Personality.

**Adjective Check List**   In contrast to the nonnormative approach of the Mooney Problem Checklists, the Adjective Check List (ACL) consists of 300 adjectives arranged alphabetically from *absent-minded* to *zany*. Examinees take 15 to 20 minutes to mark those adjectives that they consider to be self-descriptive. These responses may then be scored on the 37 scales described in the 1983 manual: 4 modus operandi scales, 15 need scales, 9 topical scales, 5 transactional analysis scales, and 4 origence–intellectence (creativity and intelligence) scales. Scores on the modus operandi scales (total number of adjectives checked, number of favorable adjectives checked, number of unfavorable adjectives checked, communality) pertain to the manner in which the respondent has dealt with the checklist. The need scales (scales 5 to 19) are based on Edwards's (1954) descriptions of 15 needs in Murray's (1938) need-press theory of personality. Each of the topical scales (scales 20 to 28) assesses a different topic or component of interpersonal behavior (for example, counseling readiness, personal adjustment, creative personality, and masculine attributes). The transactional analysis scales (scales 29 to 33) are described as measures of the five ego functions in Berne's (1966) transactional analysis. The origence–intellectence scales (scales 34–37) are described as measures of Welsh's origence–intellectence (creativity and intelligence) dimensions of personality.

For purposes of interpretation and counseling, raw scores on the ACL are converted to standard $T$ scores. As an illustration, the 37 $T$ scores and the associated profile of the cases described in Report 11–1 are given in Table 11–2. The $T$ scores, interpreted with reference to norms, are based on samples of 5236 males and 4144 females in 37 states, listed in the manual. Profiles and associated interpretations for six sample cases, one of which is summarized in Report 11–1, are also provided. The internal consistency reliabilities of most of the 37 scales are reasonably high, but test–retest reliability data are limited. The manual reports test–retest reliability coefficients for the separate scales ranging from .34 for the high-origence, low-intellectence scale to .77 for the aggression scale (median of .65) and also describes many uses of the ACL and research investigations in which it has been used.

Reviews of the ACL have been fairly positive, concluding that the instrument is well developed (Teeter, 1985; Zarske, 1985). The scales are significantly intercorrelated and therefore should not be interpreted as independent factors. A factor analysis that this author conducted on the 15 need scales (scales 5 to 19) yielded three factors: Self-confidence or Ego Strength, Goal Orientation, and Social Interactiveness or Friendliness. The ACL has been used primarily with normal adolescents and adults, and its validity in psychodiagnosis and treatment planning has not been determined. It has been found most useful in research on the self-concept.

## Q-sorts and the Rep Test

Q-sorts are similar to rating scales, but they also possess certain features of checklists. The *Q-sort technique,* which was pioneered by Stephenson (1953), requires the respondent to sort a set of descriptive statements into a series of piles ranging from "most characteristic" to "least characteristic" of himself (herself) or an acquaintance. The respondent is asked to arrange the statements so that a specified number will fall in each pile and result in a normal distribution of statements across piles.

Q-sort statements may be written specifically for a certain investigation, but standard decks of statements are available. A commercially distributed set is the California Q-Sort

## TABLE 11–2   Scales and Sample *T* Scores on the Adjective Check List

| Scale name and designation | T scores for case in Report 11–1 |
|---|---|
| *Modus Operandi* | |
| 1. Total number of adjectives checked (No. Ckd) | 37 |
| 2. Number of favorable adjectives checked (Fav) | 62 |
| 3. Number of unfavorable adjectives checked (Unfav) | 59 |
| 4. Communality (Com) | 68 |
| **Need Scales** | |
| 5. Achievement (Ach) | 57 |
| 6. Dominance (Dom) | 50 |
| 7. Endurance (End) | 53 |
| 8. Order (Ord) | 57 |
| 9. Intraception (Int) | 57 |
| 10. Nurturance (Nur) | 44 |
| 11. Affiliation (Aff) | 53 |
| 12. Heterosexuality (Het) | 46 |
| 13. Exhibition (Exh) | 44 |
| 14. Autonomy (Aut) | 49 |
| 15. Aggression (Agg) | 58 |
| 16. Change (Cha) | 58 |
| 17. Succorance (Suc) | 41 |
| 18. Abasement (Aba) | 56 |
| 19. Deference (Def) | 49 |
| **Topical Scales** | |
| 20. Counseling readiness (Crs) | 55 |
| 21. Self-control (S-Cn) | 48 |
| 22. Self-confidence (S-Cfd) | 59 |
| 23. Personal adjustment (P-Adj) | 53 |
| 24. Ideal self (Iss) | 64 |
| 25. Creative personality (Cps) | 63 |
| 26. Military leadership (Mls) | 52 |
| 27. Masculine attributes (Mas) | 54 |
| 28. Feminine attributes (Fem) | 69 |
| **Transactional Analysis** | |
| 29. Critical parent (CP) | 62 |
| 30. Nurturing parent (NP) | 48 |
| 31. Adult (A) | 56 |
| 32. Free child (FC) | 46 |
| 33. Adapted child (AC) | 41 |
| **Origence–Intellectence** | |
| 34. High origence, low intellectence (A-1) | 47 |
| 35. High origence, high intellectence (A-2) | 64 |
| 36. Low origence, low intellectence (A-3) | 44 |
| 37. Low origence, high intellectence (A-4) | 63 |

**REPORT 11–1    Case Description Accompanying Adjective Check List Scores in Table 11–2**

This 19-year-old undergraduate student majoring in biology maintained an A– grade average and planned to go to graduate school. She was brought up in a close-knit, large family, and had warm feelings about her parents and her childhood. Before college, she had always lived in small towns or semirural areas. Coming to an urban college required quite an adjustment, but she liked the excitement and stimulation of city life. She retained her religious beliefs and regularly attended church. She viewed herself as a political and economic conservative. Her life-history interviewer described her in the following way:

> She is an intelligent, vivacious, attractive young woman, enthusiastic about her life at the university. Although she views herself as introverted, her behavior is more extroverted; she was talkative, outgoing, candid, and not hesitant to assume a leadership role. Her parents were strict, expected the children to assume responsibilities, and placed a high value on academic achievement. She described her mother as a demanding, extremely shy woman who participated in social activities from a sense of duty. She said her father was somewhat intimidating, but affectionate; she feels closer to him now than she did when she was growing up. Being at school—away from home and the relative isolation of that environment—is very exciting.

Scores on her ACL profile are in agreement with the case history data and staff evaluations. Moderate elevations occur on the scales for Achievement, Self-confidence, and Personal Adjustment and scores of 60 or greater on the scales for Ideal Self, Creative Personality, and A-2 (high origence, high intellectence). The ACL profile also revealed scores of 60 or greater on the scales for Favorable, Communality, Femininity, Critical Parent, and A-4 (low origence, high intellectence). Although the staff rating of 54 on Femininity was above average for the sample of 80 students included in this project, it is not as high as the score of 69 on her self-descriptive ACL. Because she had scores greater than 50 on both Masculinity and Femininity, she is in the androgynous cell in the interaction diagram between the two scales. The profile also reveals elevated scores on *both* Favorable and Unfavorable, which suggests she is more complex, internally differentiated, and less repressive than her peers.

Revised (Adult Set), consisting of 100 cards containing statements descriptive of personality; a Child Set is also available.

Certain investigations of changes in self-concept resulting from psychotherapy or other interventions have required the research subjects to make before-and-after Q-sorts of a series of statements to describe their feelings and attitudes (for example, Rogers & Dymond, 1954). If the real- and ideal-self sorts are more alike after than before intervention, it is concluded that the intervention experience was effective.

Rather than having them sort statements, people may be asked to sort a set of individuals into various categories. Illustrative of this approach is the Role Construct Repertory (Rep) Test. According to Kelly (1955), people are like scientists in that they conceptualize or categorize their experiences in what appears to them a logical way. Unfortunately, many people perceive or construe the world incorrectly and thereby develop a faulty system of constructs. The aim of the Rep Test is to identify the system of personal constructs that a person uses to interpret his or her experiences. The examinee sorts into various conceptual, self-selected categories those people who are important to him or her in certain ways. Performance on the Rep Test is analyzed by noting how many constructs are used by the respondent, what those constructs are, what characteristics of people are emphasized by those constructs (physical, social, and so on), and what people are most like or most different from the respondent. Interpreting the results of the Rep Test in terms of the respondent's system of personal constructs, which serves as an internal frame of reference for perceiving and understanding the world, is a laborious, subjective process. This fact, plus meager evidence for the validity of the test, has resulted in infrequent use of the Rep Test in clinical and research programs.

## BEHAVIOR ANALYSIS AND ASSESSMENT

The term *behavior modification* refers to a set of psychotherapeutic procedures based on learning theory and research and designed to change inappropriate behavior to more personally and/or socially appropriate behavior. The inappropriate behaviors may be excesses, deficits, or other inadequacies of action that are correctable through behavioral techniques such as systematic desensitization, counterconditioning, and extinction. Among maladaptive behaviors that have received special attention by behavior modifiers are specific fears (or phobias), smoking, overeating, alcoholism, drug addiction, underassertiveness, bedwetting, chronic tension and pain, and sexual inadequacies. Although these target behaviors have typically been rather narrowly defined, more cognitively inclined behavior therapists have also tackled less specific problems, such as negative self-concept and identity crisis. Furthermore, the target behaviors consist not only of nonverbal movements, but also of verbal reports of thoughts and feelings.

### Behavior Analysis

Behavior therapists have attempted to understand behavior by identifying its antecedents, including both the social learning history and current environment, and the results or consequences of that behavior. A fundamental principle of behavior modification, based on laboratory studies of operant learning, is that behavior is controlled by its consequences. So, in designing a program to correct problem behavior, one must identify not only the conditions that precede and trigger it, but also the reinforcing consequences that sustain it. Following this approach, the process of behavior modification is preceded by a *functional analysis* of the problem behavior(s). This analysis consists of an A–B–C sequence in which A stands for the antecedent conditions, B the problem behavior, and C the consequences of that behavior. B is modified by controlling for A and altering C. The antecedents and consequences of the target behavior may be overt, objectively observable conditions or covert mental events reported by the person whose behavior is to be modified.

## Behavioral Assessment

Behavioral assessment has multiple functions, including (1) identification of target behaviors, alternative behaviors, and causal variables; (2) design of intervention strategies; and (3) reevaluation of target and causal behaviors (Haynes, 1990). Various procedures are employed for these purposes, including observations, interviews, checklists, rating scales, and questionnaires completed by the patient or by a person acquainted with the patient. On occasion, behavior modifiers have even used responses to projective techniques as samples of behavior (see Maloney & Ward, 1976).

The observational procedures employed in a behavior analysis involve taking note of the frequency and duration of the target behaviors and the particular contingencies (antecedents and consequences) of their occurrence. Depending on the context and the age of the patient, behavior observations can be made and recorded by teachers, parents, nurses, nursing assistants, or any other person who is acquainted with the patient.

## Self-observation and Self-monitoring

Perhaps the easiest and most economical way to determine how frequently and under what conditions a particular target behavior occurs is *self-observation.* Although self-observation is not always reliable, people can be trained to make accurate and valid observations of their own behavior (Kendall & Norton-Ford, 1982). In self-observation for purposes of behavior analysis and modification, the person is instructed to carry at all times materials such as index cards, a note pad, a wrist counter, and a timer to keep a record of occurrences of the target behavior and the time, place, and circumstances under which it occurs. The self-observational procedure, referred to as *self-monitoring,* can be fairly reliable when the patient is carefully trained. Interestingly, the very process of self-monitoring (observing and tabulating occurrences of specific behaviors in which one engages) can affect the occurrence of those behaviors, sometimes in a therapeutic way (Ciminero, Nelson, & Lipinski, 1977). For example, heavy smokers tend to smoke less when they keep a record of how often, how long, and in what circumstances they smoke.

***Behavioral Interviewing***   Behavioral interviewing is a type of clinical interviewing in which the focus is on obtaining information to plan a behavior modification program. This entails objectively describing the problem behaviors, as well as the antecedent conditions and the reinforcing consequences to the interviewee. Successfully conducting such an interview requires that the interviewee be encouraged (and taught if necessary) to respond in terms of specific behaviors, rather than in the more customary language of motives and traits. After obtaining the necessary information to develop a program of behavior modification, it must be explained to the person and he or she must be motivated to stick with the program.

***Other Psychometric Techniques***   Several additional procedures for behavioral assessment are described by Haynes and Wilson (1979), Kendall and Korgeski (1979), Hersen and Bellack, (1982), Ciminero, Calhoun, and Adams (1986), Ollendick and Green (1990), and Haynes (1990). The specific assessment procedures and instruments vary with the therapeutic techniques and goals. A representative approach begins by measuring the frequency and intensity of the target behavior(s), determining what triggers the behavior (antecedents), and noting the effects of the behavior. Many questionnaires, checklists, and inventories, some of which are commercially available, may be employed in behavior analysis. Examples are the Fear Survey Schedule and the Beck Depression Inventory. Unfortunately, there is no standard, generally recommended battery of assessment instruments for this purpose. The great majority of psychometric instruments administered in behavior analysis are somewhat makeshift devices that are inadequately standardized and frequently fail to meet the reliability and validity requirements of good psychological assessment instruments and procedures.

## SUMMARY

The temperamental, emotional, and stylistic characteristics referred to as personality variables are neither as stable nor as precisely measurable as cognitive variables. Attempts to assess these characteristics go back to antiquity, but a genuine scientific approach did not get underway until the late nineteenth and early twentieth centuries.

Although certain instruments have been designed on a purely empirical basis, many assessment devices have been constructed in the context of some theory of personality. Psychoanalytic, trait-factor, and phenomenological theories have been particularly influential in this regard. More recently, behavior theory has also stimulated the development of a number of instruments and procedures for assessing characteristic behaviors.

Observations and interviews are the most widely used, but not necessarily the most valid, methods for assessing personality. Observations may be controlled or uncontrolled, and interviews structured or unstructured. Observing and interviewing can be made more objective by training observers and interviewers. It is also important to collect observational and interview data as unobtrusively as possible and to pay attention to both the verbal and nonverbal components of interpersonal communication.

Special observational procedures include anecdotal records, time sampling, incident sampling, and situational testing. A special type of interviewing is stress interviewing, an approach that requires a great deal of training in order to be effective. Interviews are conducted for various purposes, but certain kinds of interview questions are considered illegal in personnel selection.

Various types of rating procedures—numerical scales, graphic scales, standard scales, behaviorally anchored scales, forced-choice scales—have been employed in psychological assessments. Of the various types, graphic rating scales are probably the most popular. A numerical rating scale of particular interest is the semantic differential, which is used to determine the connotative meanings that selected concepts or constructs have for people.

Errors in rating, including constant errors (leniency or generosity error, severity error, central tendency error), the halo effect, the logical error, the contrast error, and the proximity error, can be reduced by careful training of raters and the use of certain formats in constructing rating scales.

A checklist of personal characteristics or problems is a popular, efficient method of recording observations of oneself and others. Checklists of various kinds are commercially available, including those for adaptive behavior, mental status, depression, anxiety, personal problems, personal history, health problems, marital evaluation, sexual abuse, preschool behavior, and for a more general analysis of personality.

Numerous behavior assessment instruments have been constructed for use in behavior analyses preceding the application of behavior modification procedures. These instruments are designed to reveal a person's social learning history and the antecedents and consequences of certain maladaptive target behaviors. Administration of several such instruments, in addition to extensive observation (self and other) and interviewing, is a diagnostic first step in planning a behavior modification program.

## QUESTIONS AND ACTIVITIES

1. Describe the major concepts of trait theory, psychoanalytic theory, phenomenological (self) theory, and social learning theory. Which theories have made the most significant contributions to personality assessment? Which theory is most appealing to you in terms of its explanatory power and congruence with your own personal theory of human personality?

2. Defend physiognomy and graphology as legitimate areas of investigation and application in personality assessment. Why are they more reputable than phrenology and astrology?

3. Show the personality description on page 276 to several of your friends. How many agreed that it is a fairly accurate description of their personalities? Why do you think this is so?

4. Select a person in one of your classes as a subject for observation, preferably someone whom you do not know and toward whom you have neutral feelings. Observe the person over a period of three or four class meetings, inconspicuously recording what he or she does and says. Try to be as objective as possible, looking for consistent, typical behaviors, as well as noting responses that occur infrequently. At the end of the observation period, write a two- to three-page characterization of the person. Without having access to any other information about this person (what other students say about the person, how well he or she does in college, and the like), how would you describe his or her personality and characteristic behavior? Finally, check your observations against those of other people who know or have observed this person. After this experience of close observation using a time sampling technique, how do you feel about objective observation as a method of assessing personality? Is it valid and useful?

5. Ask six people, one at a time, to make facial expressions indicative of each of the following emotions: anger, disgust, fear, happiness, sadness, and surprise. Make notes on the facial expressions, differentiating among the various emotions. Did your "actors" find the task difficult? Was there appreciable consistency from person to person in the expressions characterizing a particular emotion? Were certain emotions easier to express and more consistently expressed than others?

6. Review the discussion of interviewing procedures in this chapter and other interviewing guidelines available to you. Then conduct a structured personal interview of someone whom you do not know well. Write up the results as a formal report, giving identifying information, a summary of the interview findings, and recommendations pertaining to the interviewee.

7. Consult a dictionary or thesaurus and select a sample of 50 adjectives referring to traits or characteristics of personality. Select a mixture of positive and not-so-positive terms that are not synonyms or antonyms. Make multiple copies of the alphabetized list of terms, including a short blank line in front of each adjective, and administer the list to a sample of students. Ask the students to check each adjective that they believe to be generally descriptive of themselves. Summarize the results, comparing them with what you already know about the persons from other reports and observations.

8. Run all four programs in category H ("Checklists, Rating Scales, and Rankings") of the set of *Computer Programs for Psychological Assessment*. Compare your results with those of your fellow students.

# 12

# PERSONALITY ASSESSMENT: INVENTORIES AND PROJECTIVE TECHNIQUES

Rating scales, checklists, and related psychometric devices have contributed to the assessment and understanding of human personality. They have not, however, received as much professional attention as the instruments discussed in the present chapter. The origins of the instruments considered in Chapter 11 are, in the main, different from those discussed here. Although a number of rating scales and checklists originated in clinical situations, the majority were designed for educational and employment purposes. Personality inventories have also been used extensively in nonclinical situations, but, like projective techniques, the most popular ones have focused on personality adjustment and psychopathology. The design and applications of personality inventories and projectives have been extended to include the evaluation and investigation of normal personality. Both types of instrument—and projectives in particular—are, however, concerned mainly with the identification of emotional disorders and the diagnosis of psychopathology.

There are dissimilarities in both construction and application between personality inventories and projective techniques. Designers and users of inventories have concentrated more on the psychometric qualities of these instruments, whereas those who construct and administer projective techniques tend to be less concerned with reliability, validity, and norms and more with the richness of impressionistic interpretation and the clinical analysis of responses. Nevertheless, personality inventories and projectives serve similar purposes, sometimes for screening applications in educational and employment contexts but more often for psychodiagnosis in mental health clinics, hospitals, and counseling centers.

## PERSONALITY INVENTORIES

Inventories of adjustment and temperament, more generally referred to as *personality inventories,* consist of items concerning personal characteristics, thoughts, feelings, and behavior. As on an interest inventory, a rating scale, or a checklist, respondents mark those items on a personality inventory that they judge to be descriptive of themselves. Such an instrument usually yields scores on several variables, although some, such as the Beck Depression Inventory and the Beck Hopelessness Scale, measure a single variable.

## Truthfulness in Responding

Truthfulness in responding can be a serious problem on personality inventories. Not only may respondents be unwilling to tell the truth, but they may not even know the truth about themselves and therefore give wrong answers. Research has found that people can respond to personality inventories in a distorted fashion when instructed to do so, but that, perhaps for fear of being detected or for whatever reason, they do not lie or fake as much in counseling or job-placement situations as might be suspected (Schwab & Packard, 1973). Special validation scoring keys have been designed to detect dissimulation or faking on some inventories. These keys do not always reveal when an examinee is lying, but they are very effective in certain situations.

Intentional deception, either to make oneself appear worse ("fake bad") or better ("fake good") than is actually the case, is not the only factor affecting the accuracy of responses to a personality inventory. Response tendencies or sets, such as acquiescence, social desirability, overcautiousness, and extremeness, also influence score validity. Of particular concern are the response sets of *acquiescence* (the tendency to agree rather than disagree when in doubt) and *social desirability* (the tendency to respond in a more socially acceptable manner). As with faking good and faking bad, special scoring keys have been devised on certain inventories to detect or compensate for these response sets. Typically, a person's scores on such *validity scales* are inspected before evaluating scores on other (content or diagnostic) scales. But personality inventories that are scored on validity scales may still be susceptible to faking and response sets, leading to incorrect interpretations of scores on the content scales. For this reason, it is best to use scores on personality inventories as aids in decision making only when the examinees have nothing to gain by failing to answer thoughtfully and truthfully.

## Norms, Reliability, and Validity

Scores on personality inventories are usually interpreted with reference to a set of norms based on the responses of selected groups of people. Because the standardization samples are sometimes very small and unrepresentative of the intended (target) population, such norms must be interpreted cautiously. Furthermore, scores and norms for some personality inventories, particularly those consisting of items having a forced-choice format, are *ipsative*. When scores are ipsative, a person's score on one scale is affected by his or her scores on the remaining scales: it is impossible to make all high scores or all low scores, because the scores compensate for one another. This creates problems in comparing the scores of different people on a particular scale or variable.

The fact that affective variables appear to be more influenced than cognitive variables by situational factors causes measures of personality to be more unstable than measures of ability. Together with difficulties in defining personality characteristics and designing acceptable measures of them, the instability of personality measurements typically results in these measures having lower reliabilities than scores on tests of ability or achievement.

In addition to modest reliabilities, personality inventories have fairly limited validities. Faking and response sets contribute to the low validities of many inventories used in clinical diagnosis and classification. Another factor affecting the validity of personality inventories is the susceptibility of users to the "jingle fallacy" of believing that sets of items (scales) with similar names measure the same variable. This can occur, for example, when the "anxiety" and "hostility" scales of one inventory have only moderate correlations with similarly labeled scales on another inventory. Moreover, a high correlation between scales on two different inventories may be illusory because of a common response set.

## Early Inventories

The first personality inventory of any importance, the Personal Data Sheet, was constructed during World War I by R. S. Woodworth to screen U.S. Army recruits for emotional disorders. This single-score instrument consisted of 116 yes–no questions concerning abnormal fears, obsessions, compulsions, tics, nightmares, and other feelings and behaviors. Four illustrative items from the Personal Data Sheet are:

Do you feel sad and low-spirited most of the time?

Are you often frightened in the middle of the night?

Do you think you have hurt yourself by going too much with women?

Have you ever lost your memory for a time? (DuBois, 1970, pages 160–163)

Another early personality inventory scored on a single variable was the A–S Reaction Study, a multiple-choice instrument designed by G. W. and F. H. Allport in 1928 to measure the disposition to be ascendant or submissive in everyday social relationships.

The first multiscore, or multiphasic, adjustment inventory was the Bernreuter Personality Inventory (1931). It consisted of 125 items to be answered "yes," "no," or "?" by high school students, college students, or adults in 25 minutes or so. By assigning different numerical weights to different items, six scores were obtained: Neurotic Tendency, Self-sufficiency, Introversion–Extroversion, Dominance–Submission, Sociability, and Confidence.

Many other personality inventories have been published since 1930. Supplementing the logical–rational procedure of selecting items on the basis of content validity are the statistical procedures of factor analysis and criterion keying. A combination of these methods has been applied in constructing certain inventories. For convenience, illustrative personality inventories will be described under three separate headings: content validated, factor analyzed, and criterion keyed.

## Content-validated Inventories

Items on content-validated inventories were selected because they seemed to the developer(s) to measure certain personality traits or characteristics that were considered important. The content-validated approach has also been referred to as the "rational" or "a priori" method of instrument construction. This approach is often guided, at least to some extent, by a formal or informal theory of personality. Illustrative of inventories associated with certain conceptions or theories of personality are the Edwards Personal Preference Schedule and the Myers–Briggs Type Indicator.

***Edwards Personal Preference Schedule***   The Edwards Personal Preference Schedule (EPPS), consisting of 225 pairs of statements pertaining to individual likes and feelings, is one of the most extensively researched of all personality inventories. An example of an item on the EPPS is:

A.  I like to do things by myself.
B.  I like to help others do things.

Each forced-choice pair of statements on the EPPS pits two psychogenic needs against each other, and the examinee indicates which statement is more descriptive of himself (herself). In an effort to control for the social desirability response set, the two statements comprising an item were selected to be approximately equal in social desirability.

Based on Henry Murray's need system, the EPPS is scored for the 15 needs listed as scales 5 to 19 in Table 11–2; consistency and profile stability scores are also computed. Percentile and *T* score norms for each scale are based on over 1500 students in 29 colleges and approximately 9000 adults in 48 states; separate norms for high school students are also available. Split-half reliabilities of the various scores on the EPPS range from .60 to .87, and test–retest reliabilities from .74 to .88.

As with all forced-choice inventories, scores on the EPPS are *ipsative* rather than *normative* and must be interpreted accordingly. By endorsing statements pertaining to certain needs, the respondent simultaneously rejects statements concerned with other needs. The result is that, rather than being independent of other need scales, a person's score on one need is relative to his or her scores on other needs. The fact that scores on the various need scales are not statistically independent on forced-choice inventories such as the EPPS creates problems of score interpretation and data analysis.

Even though the forced-choice format of the EPPS controls to some extent for the social desirability response set (Feldman & Corah, 1960; Wiggins, 1966), many examinees find this format awkward and difficult. In addition, the validity of the EPPS scales as measures of psychological needs is questionable. For example, the correlations of EPPS need scales with scores on other measures of similar variables are not very high.

**Myers–Briggs Type Indicator**    The Myers–Briggs Type Indicator (MBTI) is composed of a series of two-choice items concerning preferences or inclinations in feelings and behavior. There are four forms (G, F, K, and J), with 126 to 290 items per form. Based on Carl Jung's theory of personality types, the MBTI is scored on four bipolar scales: Introversion–Extroversion (I–E), Sensing–Intuition (S–N), Thinking–Feeling (T–F), and Judging–Perceptive (J–P). Combinations of scores on these four two-part categories yield 16 possible personality types. Thus, an ENFP type is a person whose predominant modes are Extrovert, Intuition, Feeling, and Perceptive, whereas an ISTJ type is a person whose predominant modes are Introvert, Sensing, Thinking, and Judging. Unfortunately, the fact that no measures of test-taking attitude are provided can lead to mistakes in diagnosis and screening.

Percentile norms for the four indicator scores, based on small samples of high school and college students, are given in the MBTI manual (Myers & McCaulley, 1985). Split-half reliabilities of the four indicators are reported as being in the .70s and .80s, and a number of small-scale validity studies are also described. Although the conceptualization of personality in terms of types is not viewed favorably by many U.S. psychologists, Consulting Psychologists Press has published an impressive array of materials on the Myers–Briggs Type Indicator. These include various interpretive guides, books, workshop materials, and related assessments. Computer-generated profiles of scores and several types of reports can be prepared, and other resources and services for users are also available.

## Factor-analyzed Inventories

The common goal of researchers who apply factor-analytic techniques to the analysis of personality has been to isolate a relatively small number of personality factors or traits that can account for variations in scores on different inventories and then to construct a measure of each factor. The first published application of factor analysis to the study of personality was made by Webb (1915), who had groups of male students rate 40 qualities they considered to have "a general and fundamental bearing on the total personality."

J. P. Guilford, whose psychometric research activities began in the late 1930s and early 1940s (Guilford, 1940; Guilford & Martin, 1943), deserves credit for being the first psychologist to construct a personality inventory by using factor-analytic techniques. Construction of his initial inventories, the Guilford–Martin Inventory of Factors, the Guilford–Martin Personnel Inventory, and the Inventory of Factors STDCR, was influenced by Jung's introversion–extroversion types and involved correlating scores on a large number of existing personality tests. Guilford's results and tests were carefully reviewed by Louis and Thelma Thurstone, who then constructed their own personality inventory, the Thurstone Temperament Schedule. This 140-item inventory was scored on seven traits (Active, Vigorous, Impulsive, Dominant, Stable, Sociable, Reflective), but the reliabilities of the trait measures were not high.

***Guilford–Zimmerman Temperament Survey*** Following the Thurstones' analysis of his data, Guilford reanalyzed the data and published a 10-factor composite of his three earlier inventories. Known as the Guilford–Zimmerman Temperament Survey (GZTS), the inventory was designed for high school through adult levels and scored on 10 trait scales: General Activity, Restraint, Ascendance, Sociability, Emotional Stability, Objectivity, Friendliness, Thoughtfulness, Personal Relations, and Masculinity. Three verification keys for detecting false and careless responding were also provided. Percentile and standard score norms for the 10 scales, which have moderate reliabilities, are based mainly on samples of college students. Although still in print, the GZTS has never been as popular as the more clinically oriented Minnesota Multiphasic Personality Inventory.

***Cattell's Questionnaires*** The most comprehensive series of inventories for assessing personality in both children and adults was designed by R. B. Cattell. Cattell began his personality research with a list of approximately 18,000 personality–descriptive adjectives that had been obtained by Allport and Odbert (1936) from dictionaries. By combining terms having similar meanings, the list was first reduced to 4500 "real" traits and then to 171 trait names; subsequent factor analyses of scores on these trait dimensions produced 31 surface traits and 12 source traits of personality. Cattell devised a number of measures of these traits and four others isolated in his later work, but his major product was the 16 Personality Factor Questionnaire (16 PF).

The fifth edition of the 16 PF consists of 185 three-choice items, including 10 to 15 items for each of the 16 primary factor scales (Russell & Karol, 1994). Overall readability of the inventory is at the fifth-grade level, and total testing time is 35 to 50 minutes. In addition to the 16 primary factors, the 16 PF can be scored, by hand or computer, on five second-order factors and three response-style indexes (see Report 12–1). These indexes—Impression Management, Infrequency, and Acquiescence—provide a preliminary check on the validity of the responses.

**REPORT 12–1   Basic Interpretive Report for 16 PF Fifth Edition from the *16 PF Fifth Edition Basic Interpretive Report.***

```
Basic Interpretive Report                    NAME: Jody A. Good
Profile                                      DATE: January 22, 1996


                                             Norms: Combined
```

```
                     Response Style Indices

        Index                   RS
        Impression Management    6    within expected range
        Infrequency              0    within expected range
        Acquiescence            64    within expected range

        All response style indices are within the normal range.
```

### Global Factors

```
Sten Factor                Left Meaning 1 2 3 4 5 6 7 8 9 10 Right Meaning

  7  Extraversion              Introverted                7     Extraverted
  8  Anxiety                   Low Anxiety                  8   High Anxiety
  3  Tough-Mindedness          Receptive        3             Tough-Minded
  7  Independence              Accommodating              7     Independent
  5  Self-Control              Unrestrained          5         Self-Controlled

                                            low  average  high
```

### 16PF Profile

```
Sten Factor                   Left Meaning 1 2 3 4 5 6 7 8 9 10 Right Meaning

  8  Warmth(A)                      Reserved                8    Warm
  5  Reasoning(B)                   Concrete          5          Abstract
  3  Emotional Stability(C)         Reactive       3            Emotionally Stable
  7  Dominance(E)                   Deferential              7   Dominant
  7  Liveliness(F)                  Serious                 7   Lively
  6  Rule-Consciousness(G)          Expedient              6    Rule-Conscious
  5  Social Boldness(H)             Shy              5          Socially Bold
  7  Sensitivity(I)                 Utilitarian            7    Sensitive
  6  Vigilance(L)                   Trusting              6     Vigilant
  6  Abstractedness(M)              Grounded             6      Abstracted
  7  Privateness(N)                 Forthright             7    Private
  9  Apprehension(O)                Self-Assured              9  Apprehensive
  7  Openness to Change(Q1)         Traditional            7    Open to Change
  4  Self-Reliance(Q2)              Group-Oriented   4          Self-Reliant
  5  Perfectionism(Q3)              Tolerates Disorder  5       Perfectionistic
  6  Tension(Q4)                    Relaxed              6      Tense

                                             low  average  high
```

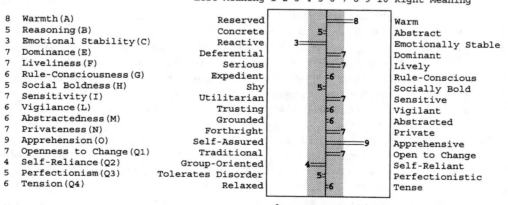

## REPORT 12–1 Continued

Basic Interpretive Report
Criterion Scores

NAME: Jody A. Good
DATE: January 22, 1996

The following scores are predictions based upon empirical research with the 16PF Fifth Edition and other criterion measures. This research is discussed in the 16PF Fifth Edition Administrator's Manual.

### Self-Esteem and Adjustment

At the present time, this individual may be hesitant in the face of challenges, or experiencing feelings of insecurity. Sometimes, however, the presentation of low self-esteem can simply reflect considerable humility. Self-Esteem is low-average (4).

Mr. Good tends to be uneasy or restless, and may be find it hard to focus his attention and energy. He tends to be easily upset and may have difficulty coping with demanding situations. Emotional Adjustment is low (2).

Mr. Good may feel at ease in most social situations. He may participate socially but may not go out of his way to initiate interactions. Social Adjustment is average (5).

### Social Skills

The following six scales pertain to the ways in which information is communicated in social environments. The scales are broadly divided into two categories: nonverbal communication (Emotional Scales) and verbal communication (Social Scales). Within each category, communication skills are discussed at three more specific levels: the ability to send information (Expressivity), to receive and interpret messages (Sensitivity), and to control information (Control). Although a person may be more or less skilled in certain areas, overall social competence is reflected in a general balance among the six scales below.

Like most adults, Mr. Good often may be effective at conveying his feelings, including via use of emotional cues. At other times, he may be less able to express himself to others. Emotional Expressivity is average (5).

This person is likely to enjoy observing and interpreting people's gestures, moods, and nonverbal interactions. Thus, he probably feels skilled in understanding emotional cues expressed by others. Additionally, he may be personally affected by others' emotional states. Emotional Sensitivity is high (8).

Mr. Good shows a tendency to express his feelings outright; control of emotional displays may be somewhat low. Because his expression of mood and feelings tends to be straightforward, others are less likely to misinterpret his emotional state. However, he may find it hard to suppress strong emotions even when it might be prudent to do so. Emotional Control is low-average (4).

Mr. Good seems to be as outgoing and verbally expressive as the average person. He may be just as likely to initiate conversations as he is to let others direct conversations. Social Expressivity is average (6).

Mr. Good is likely to be observant of social behaviors and manners. He may evaluate the appropriateness of his own actions, possibly to the point of being overly self-conscious. However, monitoring social interaction may assist him in being

## REPORT 12–1    Continued

Basic Interpretive Report                                   NAME: Jody A. Good
Criterion Scores continued                                  DATE: January 22, 1996

sensitive to social cues and situations.  Social Sensitivity is high (9).

Social conversations may be natural and forthright at times, or tailored to the
demands of a given situation.  He is as likely to direct the topic of conversation
as he is simply to participate or to observe.  Social Control is average (6).

Mr. Good is sometimes able to understand a situation from another's perspective, but
at other times may disregard another person's feelings or point of view.  This
tendency is typical of most adults.  Empathy is average (6).

### Leadership and Creativity

In a group of peers, potential for leadership is predicted to be average (5).

At the client's own level of abilities, potential for creative functioning is
predicted to be average (6).

Should this individual choose to pursue creative endeavors, his rate of output is
predicted to be average (5).

In addition to the profile shown in Report 12–1, the computer-generated Basic Interpretive Report for the 16 PF contains a profile and narrative interpretation of each of the
second-order Global Factors; interpretations of three criterion scores (Self-esteem and
Adjustment, Social Skills, Leadership and Creativity); a profile and narrative interpretation
of Vocational Activities based on Holland's (1985) hexagonal model; and item summary
statistics. The items on the fifth edition of this questionnaire reflect modern language usage
and were screened for ambiguity as well as gender, race, and cultural bias. Normative data
are based on the 1990 U.S. Census, and combined gender norms are available. Administrative indexes for assessing response bias include Impression Management (IM), Acquiescence (ACQ), and Infrequency (INF). In addition to improved construction and norms, the
16 PF Fifth Edition scales have higher reliabilities than those of their predecessors. Internal
consistency reliabilities range from .64 to .85, with an average of .74; test–retest reliabilities average around .80 over a 2-week interval and .70 over a 2-month interval.

Four inventories designed by Cattell as downward extensions of the 16 PF are the High
School Personality Questionnaire (for ages 12 to 18), the Children's Personality Questionnaire (for ages 8 to 12), the Early School Personality Questionnaire (for ages 6 to 8), and the
Preschool Personality Questionnaire (for ages 4 to 6). These questionnaires have some reliability problems, but they are generally well constructed and have proved useful in educational and research contexts. Cattell also designed several single-score instruments, for
example, the IPAT Anxiety Scale and the IPAT Depression Scale, as measures of more general factors of personality. By factor analyzing 16 PF items related to psychological disorders, he obtained 12 new factors; a new inventory, the Clinical Analysis Questionnaire, was
then constructed to assess scores on these 12 factors in clinical populations.

***Eysenck Personality Questionnaire*** This revision of the Eysenck Personality Inventory and the Junior Eysenck Personality Inventory represents a more parsimonious conception of personality than the inventories of Guilford and Cattell. Two earlier inventories, the Maudsley Personality Inventory and the Eysenck Personality Inventory, were scored on the dimensions of Neuroticism (N) and Extraversion (versus Introversion) (E) that emerged from Hans Eysenck's factor-analytic research. A measure of Psychoticism (P) and a Lie Scale (L) were added in constructing the Eysenck Personality Questionnaire (EPQ). The EPQ has a wide age range (7 through adulthood) and takes only 10 to 15 minutes to complete.

Test–retest reliabilities of the N, E, P, and L scales of the EPQ range from .78 to .80 over a 1-month interval; internal consistency coefficients are in the .70s and .80s. Norms on the two forms (A and B), based on U.S. college students and adults, are appropriate for individuals aged 16 years and above. Norms on the Junior EPQ were obtained from samples of 7- to 15-year-old children. The EPQ and its predecessors have been used extensively in personality research, although less frequently in clinical and other applied contexts. Eysenck (1965, 1981) used scores on the E and N factors in particular to predict how people react in certain experimental situations. He also related personality patterns to body type: for example, introverts are taller and leaner than extroverts.

***Perspective on Factor Analysis*** Many other personality inventories have been constructed using factor-analytic methods. Regardless of the mathematical sophistication of these methods, however, most psychometricians do not believe that factor analysis identifies true or real dimensions of personality. What it does reveal are internal consistencies and differences among test items and scales, thereby clarifying the relationships among personality constructs or variables.

Because the criterion-related validities of personality inventories constructed by factor analysis tend to be either low or unknown, these inventories are generally less helpful than content-validated and criterion-keyed instruments in making behavioral predictions and decisions in clinical and other applied psychological contexts. Nevertheless, many psychologists find applications of factor analysis to the construction of personality inventories and to basic research on the nature of human personality appealing. There is fairly general agreement that many personality inventories measure at least the extroversion–introversion and neuroticism (emotionality) factors described by Eysenck. In addition, the evidence for a five-factor model of personality is impressive. Goldberg (1980) designated these five factors as extroversion or surgency, agreeableness, conscientiousness, emotional stability, and culture; Costa and McCrae (1986) labeled them neuroticism, extroversion, openness, agreeableness, and conscientiousness. Costa and McCrae defined the five personality factors, which appear to be highly consistent across various groups of people and different situations, as follows:

> *Neuroticism:* worry versus calm, insecure versus secure, self-pitying versus self-satisfied
>
> *Extroversion:* sociable versus retiring, fun loving versus sober, affectionate versus reserved
>
> *Openness:* imaginative versus down to earth, preference for variety versus preference for routine, independent versus conforming

*Agreeableness:* soft-hearted versus ruthless, trusting versus suspicious, helpful versus uncooperative

*Conscientiousness:* well organized versus disorganized, careful versus careless, self-disciplined versus weak willed

**NEO Personality Inventory**    Assessment of personality in terms of the five-factor model is provided by the NEO Personality Inventory–Revised (NEO-PI–R) and an abbreviated version, the NEO Five-Factor Inventory (NEO-FFI). The NEO-PI–R, which consists of 243 items to be rated on a 5-point scale, takes about 30 minutes to complete. There are only 60 items on the NEO-FFI, which requires only 10 to 15 minutes to complete. Both inventories are scored for the three N–E–O *domains* (factors) of Neuroticism (N), Extroversion (E), and Openness to Experience (O), plus Agreeableness (A) and Conscientiousness (C). Each of these five domains is further subdivided into six scorable *facets,* as follows:

*Neuroticism:* Anxiety, Hostility, Depression, Self-consciousness, Impulsiveness, Vulnerability

*Extroversion:* Warmth, Gregariousness, Assertiveness, Activity, Excitement Seeking, Positive Emotions

*Openness to Experience:* Fantasy, Aesthetics, Feeling, Actions, Ideas, Values

*Agreeableness:* Trust, Modesty, Compliance, Altruism, Straightforwardness, Tendermindedness

*Consciousness:* Competence, Self-discipline, Achievement Striving, Dutifulness, Order, Deliberation

The internal consistency reliability coefficients of scores on the domain scales range from .86 to .95 for NEO-PI–R and from .74 to .80 for NEO-FFI. As might be expected because the scales are shorter, internal consistency coefficients of scores on the facet scales are lower (.56 to .90 for NEO-PI–R). Test–retest reliabilities computed over a 6-month period range from .86 to .91 for the domain scales and from .66 to .92 for the facet scales on the original NEO-PI. Evidence for the validity of these inventories is somewhat scanty, but correlations with other personality inventories, experts' ratings, and sentence-completion test scores are reported in the manual.

## The MMPI and Other Criterion-keyed Inventories

Analogous to the Strong Interest Inventory, criterion-keyed personality inventories are composed of items or scales that differentiate between two or more criterion groups. An early instrument of this kind was the A–S Reaction Study, which consisted of items that differentiated between groups of people who had been rated by their peers as ascendant or submissive. The most famous criterion-keyed inventory of personality, however, is the Minnesota Multiphasic Personality Inventory (MMPI), which was constructed by S. R. Hathaway and J. C. McKinley in the early 1940s.

***Description of the MMPI***    The MMPI was designed to assess personality characteristics indicative of psychological abnormality. The 550 statements on the inventory, answered "True," "False," or "Cannot say," are concerned with attitudes, emotions, motor disturbances, psychosomatic symptoms, and other reported feelings and behaviors indicative of psychiatric problems. Each of the nine scales on which the MMPI is scored consists of items that distinguish between the responses of a specified psychiatric patient group and a control group of normal people. The scales were cross-validated by comparing responses of psychiatric patients with those of various normal groups. The nine clinical scales, together with the Si (Social Introversion) scale and the four validity scales (*?, L, F, K*) are described in Table 12–1. Many special scales (for example, accident proneness, anxiety, ego strength, originality) were developed from the MMPI item pool during the course of thousands of research investigations over 40 years. Most of these special scales have rarely been used, two noteworthy exceptions being the Taylor Manifest Anxiety Scale and the Welsh A Scale.

Before attempting to interpret scores on the clinical or special scales of the MMPI, scores on the four validity scales should be inspected. The first of these, the raw question (*?*) score, is the total number of items the examinee answered "cannot say" or did not answer. A high question score is interpreted as defensiveness in responding. The raw lie (*L* or "fake good") score is the number of items answered in such a way as to place oneself in a more favorable light. The infrequency (*F* or "fake bad") score is the number of items answered so as to place oneself in a less favorable light. Why should a person wish to fake bad? To avoid something unpleasant, such as going to prison, military service, or many other kinds of responsibilities. Also, disability awards are available for persons diagnosed as having psychiatric disorders.

The *K* score, a fraction of which is applied as a correction factor to the raw scores on clinical scales 1, 4, 7, 8, and 9, is a measure of overcriticalness or overgenerosity in evaluating oneself. High scorers on the *K* scale tend to deny personal inadequacies and deficiencies in self-control; low scorers are willing to say socially undesirable things about themselves.

***The MMPI–2***    The MMPI was first published in 1943, so by the 1980s the norms and some of the item content were out of date. A revision of the inventory was undertaken for several reasons: to provide new, up-to-date norms; to broaden the item pool with content not represent in the original version; to revise and reword the language of some of the existing items that were dated, awkward, or sexist; and to provide separate forms of the inventory for adults and adolescents. All 550 items on the original MMPI were retained in the Adult and Adolescent revised versions, but 14 percent of them were changed because of dated language or awkwardness of expression. Words or phrases that were more characteristic of the 1940s (streetcar, sleeping powder, drop the handkerchief, and the like) were omitted, and other modifications were made to update statements (for example, "I like to take a bath" became "I like to take a bath or shower"). As on the original form, items on the revised MMPI were written at a sixth-grade level. The Adult Version (MMPI–2) contains 154 new experimental items designed to assess certain areas of psychopathology (such as eating disorders, Type A personality, and drug abuse) that are not well represented in the original MMPI. The Adolescent Version (MMPI–A) contains 104 new items concerned specifically with adolescent problems. In addition, the tendency for normal adolescents in a temporary state of turmoil to score like adult psychopaths on the original MMPI was corrected.

**TABLE 12–1   Descriptions of Validity and Clinical Scales on the Original MMPI**

**Validity (Test-taking Attitude) Scales**
*? (Cannot Say)*   Number of items left unanswered.
*L (Lie)*   Fifteen items of overly good self-report, such as "I smile at everyone I meet." (Answered True)
*F (Frequency or Infrequency)*   Sixty-four items answered in the scored direction by 10 percent or less of normals, such as, "There is an international plot against me." (True)
*K (Correction)*   Thirty items reflecting defensiveness in admitting to problems, such as, "I feel bad when others criticize me." (False)

**Clinical Scales**
*1 or Hs (Hypochondriasis)*   Thirty-three items derived from patients showing abnormal concern with bodily functions, such as, "I have chest pains several times a week." (True)
*2 or D (Depression)*   Sixty items derived from patients showing extreme pessimism, feelings of hopelessness, and slowing of thought and action, such as, "I usually feel that life is interesting and worthwhile." (False)
*3 or Hy (Conversion Hysteria)*   Sixty items from neurotic patients using physical or mental symptoms as a way of unconsciously avoiding difficult conflicts and responsibilities, such as, "My heart frequently pounds so hard I can feel it." (True)
*4 or Pd (Psychopathic Deviate)*   Fifty items from patients who show a repeated and flagrant disregard for social customs, an emotional shallowness, and an inability to learn from punishing experiences, such as, "My activities and interests are often criticized by others." (True)
*5 or Mf (Masculinity–Femininity)*   Sixty items from patients showing homoeroticism and items differentiating between men and women, such as, "I like to arrange flowers." (True, scored for femininity.)
*6 or Pa (Paranoia)*   Forty items from patients showing abnormal suspiciousness and delusions of grandeur or persecution, such as, "There are evil people trying to influence my mind." (True)
*7 or Pt (Psychasthenia)*   Forty-eight items based on neurotic patients showing obsessions, compulsions, abnormal fears, and guilt and indecisiveness, such as, "I save nearly everything I buy, even after I have no use for it." (True)
*8 or Sc (Schizophrenia)*   Seventy-eight items from patients showing bizarre or unusual thoughts or behavior, who are often withdrawn and experiencing delusions and hallucinations, such as, "Things around me do not seem real" (True) and "It makes me uncomfortable to have people close to me." (True)
*9 or Ma (Hypomania)*   Forty-six items from patients characterized by emotional excitement, overactivity, and flight of ideas, such as, "At times I feel very 'high' or very 'low' for no apparent reason." (True)
*0 or Si (Social Introversion)*   Seventy items from persons showing shyness, little interest in people, and insecurity, such as, "I have the time of my life at parties." (False)

*Source:* After Sundberg (1977). The items quoted are simulated MMPI items. The MMPI scale names and abbreviations are from Minnesota Multiphasic Personality Inventory. Copyright © by the Regents of the University of Minnesota, 1942, 1943 (renewed 1970). Reproduced by permission of the University of Minnesota Press. (Minnesota Multiphasic Personality Inventory and MMPI are registered trademarks of the University of Minnesota, Minneapolis, Minnesota.)

Designed to be more suitable for nonclinical as well as clinical uses, MMPI–2 consists of 567 true–false questions at an eighth-grade level and takes about 90 minutes to complete. The four validity scales and the ten basic clinical scales are scored from the first 370 items, whereas the supplementary content and research scales are scored on items 371 to 567 (see Table 12–2). Many of the scales are carryovers from the original MMPI.

## TABLE 12–2   MMPI–2 Scales

### Basic Validity and Clinical Scales

*Validity*
L  Lie
F  Infrequency
K  Defensiveness
?  Cannot Say

*Clinical*
(1) *Hs*  Hypochondriasis
(2) *D*   Depression
(3) *Hy*  Conversion Hysteria
(4) *Pd*  Psychopathic Deviate
(5) *Mf*  Masculinity–Femininity
(6) *Pa*  Paranoia
(7) *Pt*  Psychasthenia
(8) *Sc*  Schizophrenia
(9) *Ma*  Hypomania
(0) *Si*  Social Introversion

### Content Scales

ANX  Anxiety
FRS  Fears
OBS  Obsessiveness
DEP  Depression
HEA  Health Concerns
BIZ  Bizarre Mentation
ANG  Anger
CYN  Cynicism
ASP  Antisocial Practices
TPA  Type A
LSE  Low Self-esteem
SOD  Social Discomfort
FAM  Family Problems
WRK  Work Interference
TRT  Negative Treatment Indicators

### Content Component Scales

*Fears Subscale*
FRS1  Generalized Fearfulness
FRS2  Multiple Fears

*Depression Subscales*
DEP1  Lack of Drive
DEP2  Dysphoria
DEP3  Self-depreciation
DEP4  Suicidal Ideation

*Health Concerns Subscales*
HEA1  Gastrointestinal Symptoms
HEA2  Neurological Symptoms
HEA3  General Health Concerns

*Bizarre Mentation Subscales*
BIZ1  Psychotic Symptomatology
BIZ2  Schizotypal Characteristics

*Anger Subscales*
ANG1  Explosive Behavior
ANG2  Irritability

*Cynicism Subscales*
CYN1  Misanthropic Beliefs
CYN2  Interpersonal Suspiciousness

*Antisocial Practices Subscales*
ASP1  Antisocial Attitudes
ASP2  Antisocial Behavior

*Type A Subscales*
TPA1  Impatience
TPA2  Competitive Drive

*Low Self-esteem Subscales*
LSE1  Self-doubt
LSE2  Submissiveness

*Social Discomfort*
SOD1  Introversion
SOD2  Shyness

*Family Problems*
FAM1  Family Discord
FAM2  Familial Alienation

*Negative Treatment Indicators*
TRT1  Low Motivation
TRT2  Inability to Disclose

*Continued*

**TABLE 12–2    Continued**

**Supplementary Scales**

| | |
|---|---|
| *TRIN* | True Response Inconsistency |
| *VRIN* | Variable Response Inconsistency |
| *FB* | Back F |
| *A* | Anxiety |
| *R* | Repression |
| *Es* | Ego Strength |
| *MAC–R* | MacAndrew Alcoholism–Revised |
| *O–H* | Overcontrolled Hostility |
| *Do* | Dominance |
| *Re* | Social Responsibility |
| *Mt* | College Maladjustment |
| *GM* | Gender Role—Masculine |
| *GF* | Gender Role—Feminine |
| *PK* | Post-traumatic Stress Disorder–Keane |
| *PS* | Post-traumatic Stress Disorder–Schlenger |
| *MDS* | Marital Distress Scale |
| *APS* | Addiction Potential Scale |
| *AAS* | Addiction Admission Scale |

*Social Introversion Subscales*

| | |
|---|---|
| $Si_1$ | Shyness/Self-consciousness |
| $Si_2$ | Social Avoidance |
| $Si_3$ | Alienation—Self and Others |

**Harris-Lingoes Subscales**

| | |
|---|---|
| $D_1$ | Subjective Depression |
| $D_2$ | Psychomotor Retardation |
| $D_3$ | Physical Malfunctioning |
| $D_4$ | Mental Dullness |
| $D_5$ | Brooding |
| $Hy_1$ | Denial of Social Anxiety |
| $Hy_2$ | Need for Affection |
| $Hy_3$ | Lassitude–Malaise |
| $Hy_4$ | Somatic Complaints |
| $Hy_5$ | Inhibition of Aggression |
| $Pd_1$ | Familial Discord |
| $Pd_2$ | Authority Problems |
| $Pd_3$ | Social Imperturbability |
| $Pd_4$ | Social Alienation |

| | |
|---|---|
| $Pd_5$ | Self-alienation |
| $Pa_1$ | Persecutory Ideas |
| $Pa_2$ | Poignancy |
| $Pa_3$ | Naivete |
| $Sc_1$ | Social Alienation |
| $Sc_2$ | Emotional Alienation |
| $Sc_3$ | Lack of Ego Mastery, Cognitive |
| $Sc_4$ | Lack of Ego Mastery, Conative |
| $Sc_5$ | Lack of Ego Mastery, Defective Inhibition |
| $Sc_6$ | Bizarre Sensory Experiences |
| $Ma_1$ | Amorality |
| $Ma_2$ | Psychomotor Acceleration |
| $Ma_3$ | Imperturbability |
| $Ma_4$ | Ego Inflation |

**Wiener–Harmon Subtle–Obvious Subscales**

| | |
|---|---|
| *D-O* | Depression, Obvious |
| *D-S* | Depression, Subtle |
| *Hy-O* | Hysteria, Obvious |
| *Hy-S* | Hysteria, Subtle |
| *Pd-O* | Psychopathic Deviate, Obvious |
| *Pd-S* | Psychopathic Deviate, Subtle |
| *Pa-O* | Paranoia, Obvious |
| *Pa-S* | Paranoia, Subtle |
| *Ma-O* | Hypomania, Obvious |
| *Ma-S* | Hypomania, Subtle |

**Special Indexes**

Welsh Codes (based on MMPI-2 and MMPI norms)
F-K Dissimulation Index
Percentage True and False
Average Profile Elevation

**Setting-specific Indexes**

Megargee Classification
Pain Classification
Henrichs Rules
Goldberg Index
Cooke's Disturbance Index

The MMPI–2 is scored on the same clinical scales as the MMPI, but the $T$ scores for eight of the clinical and other (content) scales have been made uniform so that a given $T$ score is now comparable from scale to scale. Uniform $T$ scores were determined because, due to differences in score distributions, the traditional $T$ scores on different scales were not strictly comparable. These differences are removed by uniform $T$ scores, which, unlike normalized $T$ scores, retain the general shape of the raw-score distributions.

To provide a more representative sample of U.S. adults than the original MMPI, the MMPI–2 was standardized on 2600 U.S. residents aged 18 to 90 (1138 males and 1462 females). The standardization sample was selected according to 1980 census data on geographical distribution, ethnic and racial composition, age and educational levels, and marital status. Reliability data reported in the MMPI–2 manual (Hathaway & McKinley, 1989) are based on relatively small samples (82 men and 111 women); test–retest coefficients for scores on the basic scales range from .58 to .92. Some of the low reliability coefficients, coupled with the fairly sizable standard errors of measurement, indicate that differences in scores on the various scales should be interpreted cautiously.

***Interpretation of MMPI–2 Profiles***    Figure 12–1 is a profile of scores on the MMPI–2 obtained by the 60-year-old businessman described in Report 12–2. Although a generally high profile on the clinical scales suggests serious psychological problems, a high $T$ score on a given clinical scale is not necessarily indicative of the disorder with which the scale is labeled. For this and other reasons, the clinical scales are now referred to by their numerical designations. Rather than being based on a single score, a psychiatric diagnosis or personality analysis is made on the basis of the pattern displayed by the entire group of scores.

## REPORT 12–2    Interpretative Report of Scores on MMPI–2 Profile in Figure 12–1

Mr. A was seen in a medical outpatient service complaining of a variety of abdominal pains and distress. He is a 60-year-old businessman, white, married, with 2 years of college. Little evidence could be found for an organic basis for his complaints, and he was referred for psychological assessment.

The profile he obtained on the MMPI–2 is shown in Figure 12–1; the code is 12-670 39/845/LK:F. All the traditional validity indicators are below the mean and suggest that he was very cooperative with the test. There is no evidence of defensiveness or of intention to distort his self-presentation on the inventory. His L and K scores fell in the ranges that raise the possibility that he was deliberately faking a poor adjustment, but his score on the F scale does not indicate that this is true. The correlates of these validity indicators suggest that this man is open, conventional, likely to display his problems, but is not in the midst of a serious emotional crisis.

On scale 1, his highest clinical score, he earned a $T$ score of 66. A score in the high range on this scale suggests that he is rather self-centered and demanding, pessimistic and defeatist in his view of the future, and likely to overreact to any real problems. It is likely Mr. A will have numerous physical complaints that will shift to different places on his body.

His second highest score is on scale 2 and it falls in the moderate range. This score also suggests that he is pessimistic and discouraged about the future. He is dissatisfied with himself or the world, is worrying and moody. His temperament is introverted, but he is a responsible and modest individual.

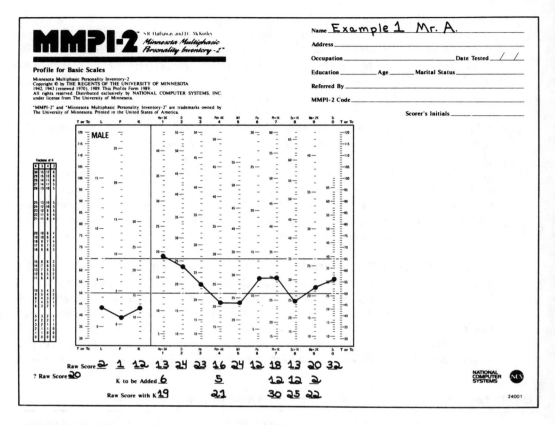

**FIGURE 12–1**  Sample Profile of Scores on MMPI–2.   See Report 12–2.
[From *Minnesota Multiphasic Personality Inventory–2,* copyright © The Regents of the University of Minnesota, 1942, 1943 (renewed 1970, 1989). All rights reserved.]

Three other scores fall within the moderate range: scales 6, 7, and 0. These scores also characterize Mr. A as responsible, hard-working, and reserved.

Individuals with 12/21 profiles show an exaggerated reaction to physical disorders, are prone to fatigue, and are often shy, irritable, seclusive, and depressed. Visceral pain, over-concern with bodily functions, and lack of insight are prominent features.

The scale-by-scale analysis of this man's profile highlights some hypochondriacal and depressive trends in an introverted, moody, and hard-working man. The code-type characteristics are present, but only to a moderate degree, as would be expected for profile elevations of this magnitude.

These characterizations are clearly borne out in the background information about Mr. A. He was married at the age of 25 to his present wife; there have been no marital difficulties. However, Mrs. A has recently quit her job, which resulted in a loss in the family income. They have one child, a son age 25, who is living away from home.

Mr. A has consulted his family physician very frequently in the last year and has made three visits to a Veterans Administration outpatient clinic in the last few months. In addition to his abdominal symptoms, Mr. A has had problems sleeping, complains of chronic fatigue, a loss of interest in sex, and recurring fears of death. He has also lost considerable weight and has had difficulty concentrating in his work. Sedatives have not been helpful. The present diagnostic impression is that Mr. A is suffering from dysthymia (moderate depression) with hypochondriacal features.

---

Several systems for coding score profiles on the MMPI have been devised, those of Hathaway and Welsh being the most popular. The coding process begins by arranging the numerical designations of the nine clinical scales and the Social Introversion scale (Scale 0), from left to right, in descending order of their $T$ scores. Performing this ranking process for the scores profiled in Figure 12–1 yields 1267039845. Both Hathaway's and Welsh's profile coding systems require placing a prime (′) after the number of the last scale having a $T$ score of 70 or greater and a dash (–) after the number of the last scale having a $T$ score of 60 or greater. The numerical designations of scales having $T$-score values within 1 point of each other are underlined, and scores on the $L$, $F$, and $K$ scales are placed after the profile code. The complete Welsh code for the profile in Figure 12–1 is 12–670 39/845/LK:F.

A number of interpretive computer programs based on a set of rules for configural or pattern analysis of MMPI and MMPI–2 scores have been developed. Despite the seeming expertise and plausibility of many computer-based interpretations, one must be careful not to overmechanize the process of profile interpretation. Like people, computers make mistakes, but one may be inclined to trust the latter over the former.

In interpreting an MMPI or MMPI–2 profile, special attention is given to scales having high $T$ scores (above 65 or 70). Scale 2 is considered to be a measure of depression and scale 7 a measure of anxiety, tension, or alertness to unknown danger. Because depression and anxiety are common symptoms of mental disorder, psychiatric patients typically have high scores on scale 2, scale 7, or both. High scores on scales 2 and 7 point to a combination of anxiety and depression. Other patterns of high scores indicate other symptoms. For example, high scores on scales 4 and 9 suggest impulsiveness, low frustration tolerance, rebelliousness, and hostile aggression. High scores on scales 6 and 8 point to withdrawal, apathy, and paranoid delusions.

Special terms have become associated with certain patterns of high scores on the MMPI clinical scales. Scales 1, 2, and 3 are referred to as the "neurotic triad," because high scores on these scales are so often related to psychoneurotic problems. When the $T$ scores on all three scales are above 70, but scale 2 is lower than scales 1 and 3, the picture is referred to as a "conversion V" and associated with a diagnosis of conversion hysteria. At the other end of the profile, scales 6, 7, 8, and 9 are referred to as the "psychotic tetrad" because of their association with psychotic problems. A configuration in which the $T$ scores on scales 6 through 9 are all above 70, but the $T$ scores on scales 7 and 9 are lower than those on scales 6 and 8, is referred to as a "paranoid valley" and suggests a diagnosis of paranoid schizophrenia.

Like the Stanford–Binet in intelligence testing, the MMPI has been a parent instrument for a number of other personality inventories. One of these offspring was the Minnesota Counseling Inventory (MCI), which was based on the MMPI and the older Minnesota Personality Scale. In contrast to the psychiatric orientation of the MMPI, the MCI was designed to measure personality adjustment in normal high school boys and girls. The MCI is now out of print, having been superseded by the California Psychological Inventory.

***California Psychological Inventory***   Of the many empirically validated, MMPI-like inventories for normal individuals, the most popular and extensively researched is the California Psychological Inventory (CPI). Designed by Harrison Gough, half of the 480 true–false statements on the original version of this inventory of adolescent and adult personality characteristics were taken from the MMPI and the remaining half were new. Unlike the MMPI clinical scales, which are concerned primarily with maladjustment and psychiatric disorders, the CPI scales assess more positive, normal aspects of personality.

*CPI Scales*   The original CPI is scored for the starred (*) scales listed in Table 12–3, three of which, Well-being, Good Impression, and Communality, are validity scales. The first two validity scales were constructed from items that tended to be responded to in a certain way by normal people who were either asked to fake bad (Well-being) or fake good

**TABLE 12–3   Basic Scales on the California Psychological Inventory, Revised Edition**

| Interpersonal Style and Manner of Dealing with Others | Cognitive and Intellectual Functioning |
|---|---|
| *Dominance | *Achievement via Conformance |
| *Capacity for Status | *Achievement via Independence |
| *Sociability | *Intellectual Efficiency |
| *Social Presence | |
| *Self-acceptance | **Thinking and Behavior** |
| Independence | *Psychological-mindedness |
| Empathy | *Flexibility |
|  | *Femininity–Masculinity |
| **Internalization and Endorsement of Normative Conventions** | |
|  | **Special Scales and Indexes** |
| *Responsibility | Managerial Potential |
| *Socialization | Work Orientation |
| *Self-control | Leadership Potential Index |
| *Good Impression | Social Maturity Index |
| *Communality | Creative Potential Index |
| *Tolerance | |
| *Well-being | |

*Scales on original version of California Psychological Inventory.
*Source:* Reprinted by permission of Consulting Psychologists Press.

(Good Impression), whereas the Communality score is simply a count of highly popular responses. Eleven of the 15 remaining scales, like those on the MMPI, were selected by comparing the responses of different groups of people; the other four scales—Social Presence, Self-acceptance, Self-control, Flexibility—were content validated.

*Norms, Reliability, and Validity*   The CPI has been more extensively standardized than any other criterion-keyed inventory, and, with the exception of the MMPI, it is the most thoroughly researched inventory of personality. The standard score norms on the CPI are based on the responses of 6000 males and 7000 females of varying ages and socioeconomic status. The test–retest reliability coefficients for all scales except Psychological-mindedness and Communality range from .57 to .77 for high school students over a period of 1 year. Coupled with the fact that the correlations among CPI scales are rather high, the relatively low reliabilities point to problems of differentiating among an examinee's scores on different CPI scales. The situation is somewhat better with respect to differentiating among the mean scale scores of different groups of people. Megargee (1972) summarized the results of various studies and discussed the questions of profile interpretation and interactions among the CPI scales. Most of the validity coefficients for single scales are low, but the usefulness of the CPI as a predictor of grades, delinquency, dropouts, parole violations, and other criteria can be improved by combining scores on several scales by means of multiple-regression equations.

*Revised CPI*   The revised version of the CPI, published in 1986, consists of 462 items retained or reworded from the original 480-item CPI. Two new scales, Empathy and Independence, were added to the original 18 scales. The Revised CPI can also be scored on the five Special Scales and Indexes listed in Table 12–3.

Another way of classifying the Revised CPI scales is in terms of three conceptual groups. The first group, the folk-concept measures, consists of the 18 original scales plus the Empathy and Independence scales. The second group of measures includes the special purpose scales, indexes, and regression equations developed by Gough and others (Social Maturity, Type A Living Style, and others). The third group represents a theoretical model containing three major themes: role, character, and competence. Vectors 1, 2, and 3 (v.1, v.2, v.3) assess these three themes (see Figure 12–2). The role, or interpersonal orientation, theme (internality versus externality), which is the interpersonal presentation of self inherent in the Capacity for Status, Dominance, Self-acceptance, Sociability, and Social Presence scales, is measured by the 34-item structural scale v.1. The character theme (norm favoring versus norm questioning), which involves interpersonal values of the sort assessed by the Responsibility, Socialization, and Self-control scales, is measured by the 36-item structural scale v.2. The competence, or realization, theme is assessed by combining scores on Achievement via Conformance, Achievement via Independence, Intellectual Efficiency, Well-being, and Tolerance to yield scores on the 58-item structural scale v.3. The three structural scales have zero correlations with each other, but they are significantly related to the folk-concept scales.

Scores on v.1 and v.2 were classified separately for 1000 males and 1000 females to create the fourfold typology shown in Figure 12–3. Note the descriptions of the alpha, beta, gamma, and delta personality types in the four quadrants of this figure. As depicted in Figure 12–2, the third structural scale (v.3) is divided into seven competence levels;

**Three Major Vectors**

Interpersonal orientation
(from externality to internality)
Normative perspective
(from norm-favoring to norm-questioning)
Realization
(from lower to higher levels)

**Results in Four Types . . .**

Alphas
(externally oriented, norm-favoring)
Betas
(internally oriented, norm-favoring)
Gammas
(externally oriented, norm-questioning)
Deltas
(internally oriented, norm-questioning)

**And Seven Levels**

1 . . . . 2 . . . . 3 . . . . 4 . . . . 5 . . . . 6 . . . . 7

| | |
|---|---|
| 1 = poor integration and little or no realization of the positive potential of the type | 7 = superior integration and realization of the positive potential of the type |

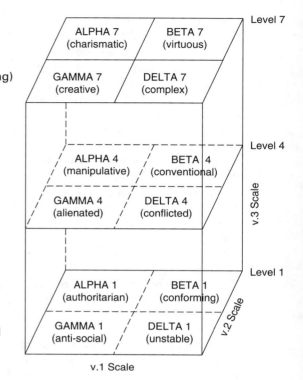

FIGURE 12–2   Structure of the Revised CPI.
(Reprinted by permission of Consulting Psychologists Press.)

Figure 12–3 is a cross section at level 4 of v.3. Level 1 is described as "poor integration and little or no realization of the positive potential of the type," and level 7 of v.3 as "superior integration and realization of the positive potential of the type" (the type being alpha, beta, gamma, or delta). Levels 2 through 6 are assigned descriptions intermediate between these two extremes. Thus, various scores on v.1, v.2, and v.3 can be combined to produce a total of 4 types × 7 levels = 28 personality configurations.

***Personality Inventory for Children***   Because of the low reading comprehension of most children, self-report inventories are less reliable and less valid when used with children. Although there are numerous inventories, such as the Children's Personality Questionnaire, on which children rate themselves, instruments on which adults rate children are perhaps more valid. An example is the Personality Inventory for Children (PIC). This MMPI-based inventory of 660 true–false items concerning child behavior can be completed by a parent, usually the mother, or other caregiver.

The PIC was standardized on 2400 normal boys and girls ranging in age from 6 to 16 years and 200 normal boys and girls aged 3 to 5 years. It is scored on 16 primary scales, including three validity scales (Lie, *F* or deviant responding, and Defensiveness), 12 clinical scales, and a screening scale (Adjustment) to identify children needing psychological evaluation. Scores on 17 experimental scales may also be determined. The clinical scales

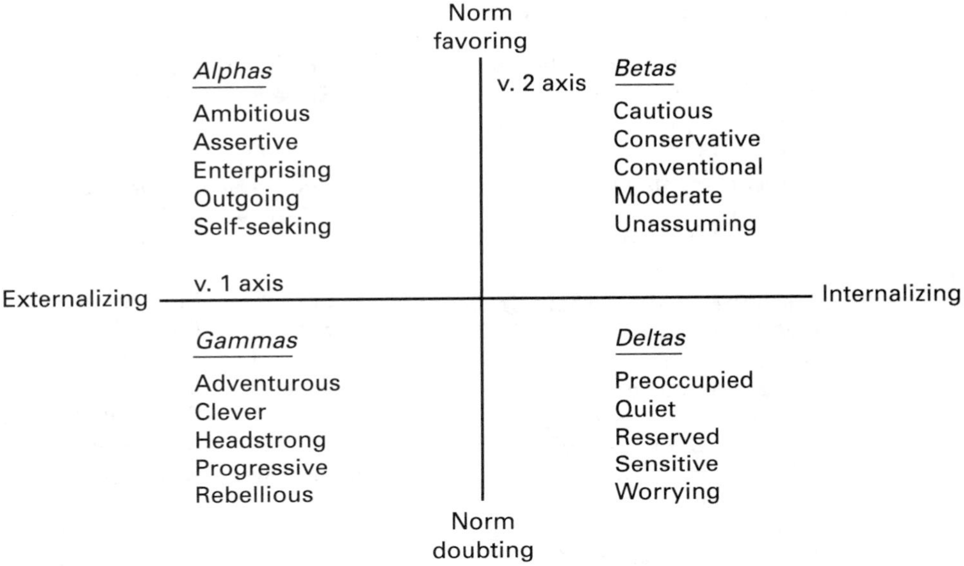

Norm
favoring

| | | |
|---|---|---|
| *Alphas* | v. 2 axis | *Betas* |
| Ambitious | | Cautious |
| Assertive | | Conservative |
| Enterprising | | Conventional |
| Outgoing | | Moderate |
| Self-seeking | | Unassuming |

Externalizing ——— v. 1 axis ————————————— Internalizing

| | |
|---|---|
| *Gammas* | *Deltas* |
| Adventurous | Preoccupied |
| Clever | Quiet |
| Headstrong | Reserved |
| Progressive | Sensitive |
| Rebellious | Worrying |

Norm
doubting

**FIGURE 12–3** Theoretical Model for the v.1 and v.2 Structural
Scales of the California Psychological Inventory.  The Figure Depicts the Role (v.1)
and Character (v.2) Type Quadrants at Level 4 (Average) on Competence (v.3).
(Reprinted by permission of Consulting Psychologists Press, Inc., from the Manual of the
California Psychological Inventory, Revised Edition, copyright 1987.)

were designed to identify certain emotional and interpersonal problems, in addition to assessing the child's cognitive development and the psychological climate of the family. Score profiles may be plotted separately by sex and age group (3 to 5 and 6 to 16 years) and interpreted by computer (Wirt & Lachar, 1981).

A Revised Form PIC, in which items are rearranged into four parts to provide meaningful results without the parent having to respond to all 600 items, was published in 1982. A recent extension of the PIC is the Personality Inventory for Youth, a self-report inventory designed for 9- to 18-year-olds. Containing 270 items, the PIY is scored on 9 clinical scales, 24 subscales, and several validation scales.

***Millon Clinical Multiaxial Inventory***   The Millon Clinical Multiaxial Inventory–III (MCMI–III) was designed to assess personality disorders and clinical syndromes related to DSM–IV and coordinated with Theodore Millon's theory of personality (Millon, Millon, & Davis, 1994). In revising the MCMI–II to produce the MCMI–III, 95 of the 175 items were reworded or replaced for closer alignment of the inventory with the DSM–IV. Of the 24 diagnostic scales on the MCMI–III, 14 are personality pattern scales that coordinate with DSM–IV Axis II disorders, and 10 are clinical syndrome scales related to DSM–IV Axis I disorders. In addition, there are three modifying indexes and a validity index to detect careless, confused, or random responding (see Table 12–4).

The MCMI–III can be administered in approximately 25 minutes to adults 18 years and older in clinical situations where people are evaluated for emotional, behavioral, or personal

**TABLE 12–4   MCMI–III Scales**

| | |
|---|---|
| **1. Modifier Indexes (Correction Scales)** | Scale 7 — Compulsive |
| Scale X — Disclosure | Scale 8A — Passive-Aggressive (Negativistic) |
| Scale Y — Desirability | |
| Scale Z — Debasement | Scale 8B — Self-Defeating |
| **2. Severe Personality Pathology Scales** | **4. Clinical Syndrome Scales (DSM–IV, Axis I)** |
| Scale S — Schizotypal | |
| Scale C — Borderline | Scale A — Anxiety |
| Scale P — Paranoid | Scale H — Somatoform |
| **3. Clinical Personality Pattern Scales (DSM–IV, Axis II)** | Scale N — Bipolar: Manic |
| | Scale D — Dysthymic |
| Scale 1 — Schizoid | Scale B — Alcohol Dependence |
| Scale 2A — Avoidant | Scale T — Drug Dependence |
| Scale 2B — Depressive | Scale R — Post-Traumatic Stress Disorder |
| Scale 3 — Dependent | |
| Scale 4 — Histrionic | **5. Severe Syndrome Scales** |
| Scale 5 — Narcissistic | Scale SS — Thought Disorder |
| Scale 6A — Antisocial | Scale CC — Major Depression |
| Scale 6B — Aggressive (Sadistic) | Scale PP — Delusional Disorder |

difficulties. It can be scored with a set of handscoring templates or by means of the MICROTEST Q System computer software available from NCS Assessments. Raw scores on the various scales are weighted and converted to *base rate scores*, which take into account the incidence of a particular characteristic or disorder in the general population. By determining the occurrence of a particular personality disorder or trait in a specific population, one can transform raw scores in such a way as to maximize the ratio of the number of correct classifications (valid positives) to the number of incorrect classifications (false positives).

In addition to scoring MCMI–III, NCS Assessments provides a treatment-oriented narrative report including statements on the validity of the responses, interpretations for both DSM–IV Axis I and Axis II disorders, comments regarding noteworthy responses made by examinees, parallel DSM–IV multiaxial diagnoses, and therapeutic implications. A capsule summary section of the report reviews the severity of the symptoms and briefly describes indications on DSM–IV Axes I and II and related treatment considerations.

The manual for MCMI–III describes standardization data from various samples (Millon, Millon, & Davis, 1994). The normative sample consisted of 1000 males and females representing a wide variety of psychiatric diagnoses. Average test–retest and internal consistency reliabilities of the scales are quite good for a personality inventory. Alpha coefficients range from .66 to .89 for the personality scales and .71 to .90 for the clinical syndrome scales; test–retest reliabilities range from .84 to .96 for the clinical syndrome scales.

## Jackson's Inventories

More recent efforts to construct personality inventories have taken place in an atmosphere of renewed interest in research on personality and a greater appreciation of its complexities. Rather than relying on a single approach—content (rational), theoretical, factor analytic, or empirical—the development of new personality assessment instruments has involved a combination of procedures. Representative of this increased level of sophistication in personality test construction are the inventories designed by D. N. Jackson. Jackson began with detailed descriptions of the characteristics to be measured. Next, a large pool of items was written or collected and administered to a sizable representative sample of people. Using the trait descriptions prepared at the outset, judges' ratings of the examinees on these traits were also obtained. In analyzing the data, the item responses of separate samples of examinees were subjected to different item analyses. A statistical, computer-based procedure was employed to ensure that correlations among the items constituting a given scale were high and that correlations among different scales were low. Consequently, the reliabilities of differences among scores on the various subtests were high enough to permit differentiation among subtest scores.

*Personality Research Form*   Based on Henry Murray's trait theory of personality and focusing on areas of normal functioning rather than psychopathology, the Personality Research Form (PRF) is a true–false inventory designed for grade 6 through adulthood. It takes 35 to 75 minutes to complete, depending on the form (A, B, AA, BB, or E). Each of the 15 scales on Forms A and B and the 22 scales on Forms AA, BB, and E consists of 20 true–false items. Many of these scales bear the same names as those listed in Table 11–2. In addition to the content scales, all forms are scored on an Infrequency scale consisting of rarely marked items. Forms AA, BB, and E are also scored on a Social Desirability Scale.

The PRF was standardized on 1000 male and 1000 female college students. Internal consistency and test–retest reliability coefficients for scores on the 14 content scales common to all five forms cluster around .80, but the reliabilities of the six additional content scales on Forms AA, BB, and E are in the .50s. Validity coefficients obtained by correlating the content scales with behavior ratings and a specially devised trait-rating form are in the .50s. Evidence for the convergent and discriminant validity of the PRF using peer ratings and data from hundreds of studies bearing on the validity of the PRF are reported in the manual.

*Jackson Personality Inventory*   Like the PRF, the Jackson Personality Inventory–Revised (JPI–R) (Jackson, 1994) was designed to assess normal personality in adolescents and adults. The JPI–R consists of 300 true–false items and takes 35 to 45 minutes to complete. It has a more social or interpersonal orientation than the PRF, providing a method of predicting behavior in a variety of practical settings (business/industrial, educational, recreational), as well as clinical and counseling situations. The construction methodology for the JPI was even more sophisticated than that for the PRF: separate item analyses were conducted on a large item pool administered to two samples of people to maximize content variance in relation to social desirability variance, to maximize item variance, and to minimize the overlap among scales.

The JPI–R is scored on 15 content scales, aggregated into five clusters: Analytic (Complexity, Breadth of Interest, Innovative, Tolerance), Emotional (Empathy, Anxiety,

Cooperativeness), Extroverted (Sociability, Social Confidence, Energy Level), Opportunistic (Social Astuteness, Risk Taking), and Dependable (Organization, Traditional Values, Responsibility).

The JPI–R was standardized on three groups of people: 367 male and 740 female college students in 23 North American institutions, 629 male and 264 female blue-collar workers, and 555 senior executives enrolled in a professional development program. Means and standard deviations, as well as T score equivalents of raw scores on the 15 content scales for each group, are given in the manual. Internal consistency reliability coefficients for the separate scales range from .66 to .85. No validity coefficients are reported in the manual, but moderate correlations between scores on the 15 JPI scales with ratings on the same traits are listed (.38 with peer ratings, .56 with self-ratings, .70 with relevant adjective checklist variables). The manual also cites significant correlations of the JPI–R scales with other criteria (occupational preference, attitude toward marijuana use, and so on). Like the Personality Research Form, the Jackson Personality Inventory and the JPI–R have good potential. In a review of the JPI, Dyer (1985) concluded that the inventory is most appropriate for research on personality correlates of occupational criteria and specific teacher learning situations or styles.

**Basic Personality Inventory**   Having a somewhat different orientation from the Personality Research Form and the Jackson Personality Inventory, which were designed to assess "normal" personalities, is the Basic Personality Inventory (BPI). The BPI is intended to be used with both clinical and normal populations to identify sources of maladjustment and personal strengths in juveniles and adults. It consists of 240 true–false items written at a fifth-grade level and can be completed in approximately 35 minutes. It is scored on the following 12 basic scales: Hypochondriasis, Anxiety, Depression, Thinking Disorder, Denial, Impulse Expression, Interpersonal Problems, Social Introversion, Alienation, Self-depreciation, Persecutory Ideas, amd Deviation (Critical Item Scale).

The maladjustment orientation of the BPI has made it more applicable in psychological, psychiatric, and counseling practices in juvenile and adult correctional facilities and in other organizational contexts concerned with behavioral or conduct disorders. The BPI manual provides separate profiles for groups of psychiatric patients with symptoms ranging from anorexia to suicidal behavior and hallucinations (Jackson et al., 1989). The norms used for the adult profiles described in the manual were obtained from mail surveys or interviews of 709 men and 710 women selected at random from telephone directories and voters' records in the United States and Canada. The internal consistency and test–retest reliabilities of the scales on the BPI are moderate to high in both clinical and nonclinical samples (Holden et al., 1988; Jackson et al., 1989). Information on the validity of the BPI is not as adequate as one might wish, but the instrument appears to have promise for clinical use in the fields of health psychology and juvenile delinquency in particular.

## PROJECTIVE TECHNIQUES

*Projective technique* is a term coined by Lawrence Frank (1939) for psychological assessment procedures in which respondents project their inner needs and feelings onto ambiguous stimuli. The stimuli are relatively unstructured materials and/or tasks that a person is asked to describe, tell a story about, complete, or respond to in some other manner. In contrast to the more direct personality inventories and rating scales, projective techniques are usually less obvious in intent and therefore presumably less subject to faking and response sets. Because the stimulus materials or tasks are relatively unstructured in content and open ended in terms of the responses elicited, it is assumed that the structure imposed by the respondent is a reflection, or *projection,* of his or her individual perceptions of the world. It is also assumed that less structured materials are more likely to reveal important facets of personality than more structured ones.

According to their proponents, projective techniques can tap deeper layers of personality, of which even the respondent may be unaware. Projectives do not, however, provide an "open Sesame" to the unconscious or an X-ray of the mind. Furthermore, lack of structure is a two-edged sword that can result in a wealth of data that are difficult to interpret. Because of scoring problems, most projective techniques fail to meet conventional standards of reliability and validity. The validity coefficients of these instruments are generally low, reflecting situational factors as well as subjectivity in scoring and interpretation.

Because projectives attempt to get at unconscious processes, interpretation of responses to the test materials has been greatly influenced by psychoanalytic theory. It is not surprising that the greatest increase in the use of projectives took place from 1940 to 1960, a time when psychoanalytic thinking exerted a particularly strong influence on personality theory and research. In addition to being influenced by psychoanalysis and other psychodynamic theories, psychologists who interpret projective test protocols usually try to form an overall impression of the examinee's personality by searching for consistencies and outstanding features in the pattern of responses.

Administering and scoring a typical projective test requires more training and sensitivity than for a self-report inventory. Even so, psychologists who are presumably well trained in projectives frequently disagree in their interpretations of responses to them. The interpretations described in the following sections and analyses of responses to projectives in general should be viewed as hypotheses or possibilities, rather than confirmed fact. Consider, for example, the following suggested interpretations of figure drawings:

*Large size:* emotional expansiveness or acting-out behavior

*Small size:* emotional constriction, withdrawal or timidity

*Erasures around buttocks and/or long eyelashes on male figure:* latent homosexuality

*Overworking of lines:* tension and aggressive behavior, possible delusional thinking

*Distorted or omitted facial or other body features:* conflict pertaining to that feature or organ

These interpretations may seem plausible, but they are based to a large extent on stereotypes or illusory correlations and are more often wrong than right. Clinical psychologists and psychiatrists should not make the mistake of concluding that something is true simply because it appears reasonable. Rather, they should view both their own interpretations of responses to projectives and those made by other people only as plausible possibilities or reasonable hypotheses that may or may not be confirmed by other sources of information concerning a person.

## Word Associations and Construction Techniques

Various projective techniques have been devised to detect less obvious motives, conflicts, problems, and other covert intrapersonal characteristics. Of these, semistructured techniques such as word associations and sentence completions are perhaps closest to self-report inventories in terms of design, format, and objectivity.

*Word Associations*    The method of word association was introduced by Francis Galton (1879) and first applied clinically by Carl Jung (1910) to detect neurotic conflicts. A series of words is read aloud to a person, who has been instructed to respond to each one with the first word that comes to mind. Clinical applications of the technique involve interspersing selected emotionally loaded words or words of special significance to the person within a set of neutral words. In addition to significant associations and delays in responding, the degree to which certain words are emotionally arousing may be determined by measuring skin conductance, muscle tension, respiration rate, blood pressure, pulse rate, voice tremors, or other physiological reactions to the stimulus words.

As with all projective techniques, responses on a word-association test should be interpreted against a backdrop of other information concerning the person. A general principle that has guided psychoanalytic interpretations of language is that nouns are more likely than verbs to be disguised expressions of needs and conflicts. This is so because, according to Freudian theory, it is easier to alter the object of a desire (a noun) than its direction (a verb). Words may also be used as stimuli in a polygraph (lie detector) test designed to detect high emotional responses to certain words associated with a crime.

Many clinical psychologists prefer to construct their own word lists, but standardized lists are available. An example is the Kent–Rosanoff Free Association Test, a standard list of 100 words and associations to them given by 1000 adults. The Kent–Rosanoff, which was published originally in 1910, is one of oldest psychological tests in use.

*Sentence Completions*    Asking a person to complete specially prepared incomplete sentences is a flexible, easily administered projective technique first described by Payne (1928). A variety of sentence fragments or *stems* related to possible areas of emotional arousal and conflict can be constructed. The following stems are illustrative:

My greatest fear _____

I only wish my mother had _____

The thing that bothers me most is _____.

It is assumed that the respondent's wishes, desires, fears, and attitudes are reflected in the way he or she completes the sentences.

Despite the fact that they are more obvious than many other projective techniques, sentence completions are considered one of the most valid of all projective techniques for diagnostic and research purposes (Goldberg, 1965). The reliability and validity of sentence completions are higher when the responses are scored and interpreted objectively rather than impressionistically. As with the MMPI and other criterion-keyed instruments, empirical keys can be constructed for both word associations and sentence completions.

Sentence-completion tests may be constructed for a particular clinical case or personality research study, but a half-dozen or so instruments of this kind are commercially available. Examples are the Activity Completion Technique, the Bloom Sentence Completion Survey, the Geriatric Sentence Completion Form, and the Rotter Incomplete Sentences Blank. The 60 sentence stems of the Activity Completion Technique cover the areas of Family, Interpersonal, Affect, and Self-Concept. Both the Student and Adult forms of the Bloom Sentence Completion Test consist of 40 stems covering eight areas (age mates or other people, physical self, family, psychological self, self-directedness, education and work, accomplishment, and irritants). The 30-item Geriatric Sentence Completion Form, designed for older adults, is scored on four content domains: physical, psychological, social, and temporal orientation. Finally, the 40 sentence fragments on each of the three forms of the Rotter blank (high school, college, and adult) are scored in three categories: conflict or unhealthy responses, neutral responses, and positive or healthy responses.

**_Rosenzweig Picture-Frustration Study_**   Another projective device on which examinees construct verbal responses to partially verbal stimuli is the Rosenzweig Picture-Frustration Study (Rosenzweig, 1978). Each of the three forms (child, adolescent, adult) of this instrument consists of 24 cartoons; each cartoon depicts an individual in a frustrating situation. The examinee is asked to indicate, by writing in the balloon over the frustrated person's head, a verbal response that might have been made by this anonymous person (Figure 12–4). Responses are scored according to the direction of aggression and the type of aggression expressed. Included under direction of aggression are extraggression (outwardly, toward the environment), intraggression (inwardly, toward oneself), or imaggression (avoidance or nonexpression of aggression). Included under type of aggression are obstacle dominance or O-D (the frustrating object stands out), etho defense or E-D (the examinee's

**FIGURE 12–4**   Item from Rosenzweig Picture-Frustration Study. (Copyright 1964 by Saul Rosenzweig. Reproduced by permission.)

ego predominates to defend itself), and need persistence or N-P (the goal is pursued despite the frustration). Scores are interpreted in terms of frustration theory and available norms on the instrument. The Rosenzweig Picture-Frustration Study has been used in a large number of research investigations worldwide on the nature of frustration and its relationships with other variables (see Rosenzweig, 1978).

***Projective Drawings***    Procedures requiring oral or written responses to words and sentences are only one of many construction tasks that qualify as projective techniques. Other nonverbal materials that have been employed are clay paints, building materials, and colored chips. Handwriting analysis, although it has not received wide acceptance among psychologists, also has proponents (Holt, 1974). Even more popular have been drawings of people and other objects, such as the Draw-a-Person Test (Machover, 1971) and the House–Tree–Person Technique.

On the Draw-a-Person Test, an examinee's drawings of people of the same and the opposite sex are interpreted in terms of the placement of various features of the drawings (sex, quality, position, clothing, and so forth). Specialists in the technique maintain that there is a tendency for people to project impulses that are acceptable to them onto the same-sex figure and impulses that are unacceptable to them onto the opposite-sex figure. Particular aspects of the drawings are considered to be indicative of certain personality characteristics or psychopathological conditions. Large eyelashes on persons in the drawings are said to indicate hysteria; many clothing details suggest neurosis; large drawings point to acting out of impulses; and dark, heavy shading suggests strong aggressive impulses. Small drawings, few facial features, or a dejected facial expression point to depression; few body periphery details indicate suicidal tendencies; and few physical features suggest psychosis or organic brain damage (Kaplan & Sadock, 1989). To Machover (1949, 1951), a disproportionately large or small head—the center of intellectual power, control of body impulses, and social balance—was indicative of functional difficulties in those areas. Although many of these interpretive signs and generalizations were reportedly based on clinical experience and may make psychoanalytic and even common sense, they have not held up under close scrutiny. Some evidence has been found for a relationship between the judged quality of the drawings and overall psychological adjustment (Lewinsohn, 1965; Roback, 1968), but research has not supported most of Machover's interpretive hypotheses.

## Inkblot Tests

***Rorschach Psychodiagnostic Technique***    The Swiss psychiatrist Hermann Rorschach was not the first person to use inkblots to study personality, but he did provide the first widely accepted set of blots and a standard approach to administration and response interpretation.

The stimulus materials for the Rorschach Psychodiagnostic Technique, which was published originally in 1921, are ten $5\frac{1}{2}$- by $9\frac{1}{2}$-inch cards. Each card contains one bilaterally symmetrical, black-and-white (five cards), red-and-gray (two cards), or multicolored (three cards) inkblot against a white background similar to the one in Figure 12–5. The cards are

**FIGURE 12–5**   Inkblot Similar to Those on the Rorschach
Psychodiagnostic Technique.

presented individually and viewed at no greater than arm's length, but turning the card is
permitted. Examinees are told to report what they see in the blot or what it might represent.
A young woman in her senior year of college gave the following response to the inkblot in
Figure 12–5 ten seconds after it was shown:

My first impression was a big bug, a fly maybe. I see in the background two facelike figures pointing
toward each other as if they're talking. It also resembles a skeleton, the pelvis area. I see a cute little
bat right in the middle. The upper half looks like a mouse.

After all cards have been presented, the examiner may start over with Card I and ask
the examinee what features (shape, color, shading, and so on) of the card determined his or
her responses. Following this *inquiry* period, there may be a further period of *testing the
limits* to discover whether the examinee can see certain things in the cards.

A number of scoring methods for the Rorschach have been proposed, the most recent
being Exner's (1991, 1993) comprehensive system. Every response given to a blot may be
scored on several categories:

*Location:* Where it was seen—the whole blot (*W*), a common detail (*D*), an uncommon detail (*Dd*), or, if the white space on the card was used, *WS, DS,* or *DdS.*

*Determinant:* What aspects of the blot determine the response—form (*F*), color (*C*),
shading–texture (*T*), shading–dimension (*V*), shading–diffuse (*Y*), chromatic color
(*C*), achromatic color (*C′*), movement (*M*), or combinations of these.

*Content:* Anatomy (*An*), blood (*Bl*), clouds (*Cl*), fire (*Fi*), geography (*Ge*), nature
(*Na*), and so forth.

*Popularity:* Whether the response is a popular (*P*) or an original (*O*) one.

The number of responses in each category and certain ratios computed from them guide the interpretation of the test protocol as a whole. For example, several good "whole" (W) responses are considered indicative of integrated or organized thinking, whereas color responses suggest emotionality and impulsivity; many detailed responses indicate compulsivity; white-space responses point to oppositional tendencies; and movement responses reveal imagination. The ratio of the number of human movement responses to the number of color responses (*experience balance*) is said to be related to the degree to which a person is thought-minded rather than action oriented. The ratio of the number of form responses to the number of color responses is an index of the extent to which the respondent is controlled by cognition rather than emotion. Also important in evaluating a Rorschach protocol is the accuracy of responses, that is, how well the responses fit the respective parts of the blots (good, poor, and indeterminate). Delays in responding may be interpreted as anxiety, a small number of color and movement responses as depression, and several shading responses as self-control. Many original responses having poor form and other indicators of confused thinking suggest a psychotic process.

One of the most reliable scores on the Rorschach, and a rough index of mental ability, is a simple count of the total number of responses to the 10 inkblots. Responses may also be interpreted in terms of content, but the process is very subjective. For example, unreal characters such as ghosts and clowns are interpreted as indicative of an inability to identify with real people, and masks are interpreted as role playing to avoid exposure. Food is interpreted as dependency needs or emotional hunger, death as loneliness and depression, and eyes as sensitivity to criticism.

Thousands of articles have been published on the Rorschach Technique, but it has not fared well in reliability and validity studies. Considering the length of time required to administer and score the test, it is unsatisfactory when judged by conventional psychometric criteria. It remains popular among clinical psychologists and psychiatrists, however, and will probably continue to be so until a demonstrably superior method for the in-depth analysis of personality is devised.

***Holtzman Inkblot Technique***   The Holtzman Inkblot Technique (HIT) represents an attempt to construct a more objective and valid inkblot test than the Rorschach. The two parallel forms of the HIT (A and B) consist of 45 blots each, and the examinee is limited to one response per blot. Each of the blots was selected on the basis of high split-half reliability and an ability to differentiate between normal and pathological responses. The HIT blots are more varied than those on the Rorschach: some are asymmetrical, and some have colors and different visual textures. The HIT can be scored on the 22 response categories developed by computer analysis of hundreds of test protocols. The percentile norms for these 22 scores are based on eight groups of people, normal and pathological, ranging in age from 5 years to adulthood.

The procedures for constructing and standardizing the HIT were more like those for a personality inventory than other projective techniques, so it is not surprising that its reliability is higher than that of the Rorschach. As with the Rorschach, however, a great deal of work on the validity of the HIT remains to be done. The validity of projectives in general for helping to make decisions about people has not been adequately demonstrated, but in spite of its limitations the Holtzman Inkblot Technique is one of the few instruments in this category that come even close to meeting the psychometric standards for a good test.

## Apperception Tests

Less structured than word associations and incomplete sentences, but more structured than inkblots, are pictures or other materials about which the respondent is asked to tell a story. The majority of these *apperception tests* employ pictures of people or animals as stimuli, but one (the Hand Test) is composed of pictures of hands and another (the Auditory Apperception Test) consists of auditory stimuli. Nearly all apperception tests call for open-ended response, but at least one (the Iowa Picture Interpretation) has a multiple-choice format. Directions for the various picture-story tests are similar: The examinee is asked to tell a story about each picture, including what is going on at the moment, what led up to it, and what the outcome might be.

***Thematic Apperception Test***　　Among projectives, next in popularity to the Rorschach in terms of research citations and clinical usage, is the Thematic Apperception Test (TAT). The TAT consists of 30 black-and-white picture cards (four overlapping sets of 19 cards each for boys, girls, men, and women) depicting people in ambiguous situations, plus one blank card. The usual procedure for administering the TAT begins by asking the examinee to tell a complete story about each of the 10 or so picture cards selected as appropriate for his or her age and sex. The examinee is asked to devote approximately 5 minutes to each story, telling what's going on now, what thoughts and feelings the people in the story have, what events led up to the situation, and how it will turn out. For example, one of the pictures shows a young woman in the foreground and a weird old woman with a shawl over her head grimacing in the background. The following story was told by a young college woman in response to this picture:

This is a woman who has been quite troubled by memories of a mother she was resentful toward. She has feelings of sorrow for the way she treated her mother; her memories of her mother plague her. These feelings seem to be increasing as she grows older and sees her own children treating her the same way as she treated her mother. She tries to convey the feeling to her children, but does not succeed in changing their attitudes. She is living the past in her present, because this feeling of sorrow and guilt is reinforced by the way her children are treating her.

From stories such as this, a skilled examiner obtains information about the dominant needs, emotions, sentiments, complexes, and conflicts of the storyteller and the pressures to which he or she is subjected. As revealed by this story, responses to TAT pictures can be especially useful in understanding the relationships and difficulties between a person and his or her parents.

When interpreting TAT stories, it is assumed that respondents project their own needs, desires, and conflicts into the stories and characters. Interpretation of the stories is a fairly subjective, impressionistic process centering on an analysis of the needs and personality of the main character (the *hero* or *heroine*), who presumably represents the examinee, and the environmental forces (*press*) impinging on the main character. The frequency, intensity, and duration of the story are all taken into account in the interpretation.

The following are illustrative of the TAT responses or signs that certain psychologists consider indicative of mental disorders of various kinds: Slowness or delays in responding may indicate depression; stories by men that involve negative comments about women or affection for other men may point to homosexuality; overcautiousness and preoccupation with details are suggestive of obsessive-compulsive disorder.

Although the usual methods of scoring and interpreting TAT stories are highly impressionistic, scores determined by one of the more systematic procedures are fairly reliable and can be interpreted in terms of norms based on standardization studies (see Bellak, 1993). Asking a person to tell stories about pictures would also seem to have potentially greater validity in personality assessment than asking for responses to inkblots. The content of TAT stories is, however, influenced by the particular environmental context in which the test is taken, and the test does not always differentiate between normal and mentally disordered persons (Eron, 1950). Furthermore, many psychologists maintain that amorphous stimuli such as inkblots are more effective than picture stories in revealing unconscious conflicts and repressed desires. This claim has never been adequately verified, and the validity of picture stories is less disputed than that of responses to inkblots. Even so, the TAT has not proved to be as popular as the Rorschach for purposes of psychiatric diagnosis.

**Modifications of the TAT**   The TAT has been used with a range of ethnic and chronological age groups, and various modifications have been constructed for blacks, children, and older adults. On the assumption that blacks identify more closely with pictures of other blacks than with pictures of whites, 21 of the original TAT pictures were redrawn with black figures and published as the Thompson Modification of the TAT. Two other special versions of the TAT are the Senior Apperception Technique and the Children's Apperception Test.

*Senior Apperception Technique*   The 16 stimulus pictures on this test, which was designed specifically for older adults, reflect themes of loneliness, uselessness, illness, helplessness, and lowered self-esteem, in addition to positive and happier situations. As in the case of the Gerontological Apperception Test (Wolk & Wolk, 1971), a similar instrument, responses to the pictures on the Senior Apperception Technique reflect serious concerns over health, getting along with other people, and being placed in a nursing or retirement home. Both tests have been criticized for inadequate norms and possible stereotyping of the elderly.

*Children's Apperception Test (CAT)*   Based on the assumption that young children (3 to 10 years) identify more closely with animals than with humans, the CAT consists of 10 pictures of animals in various situations. An extension of the test to older children, the CAT–H, is composed of pictures of humans in situations paralleling those of the CAT animal pictures. The stories on both the CAT and CAT–H are interpreted from the viewpoint of psychodynamic theory, specifically in terms of conflicts, anxiety, and guilt. A checklist, the Haworth Schedule of Adaptive Mechanisms, is available to assist in interpreting CAT and CAT–H stories.

**Other Apperception Tests**   Unfortunately, the lack of representativeness and variety of the stimulus materials and the lack of psychometric rigor in design, standardization, and validation for which the TAT has been criticized also apply to the modifications described. Somewhat sounder from a psychometric viewpoint than the Children's Apperception Test are the Michigan Picture Test and the Children's Apperceptive Story-Telling Test.

The Michigan Picture Test–Revised (MPT–R) is one of the best picture story tests for older children (8 to 14 years old), because in developing it a genuine effort was made to meet the requirements of adequate standardization and reliability. Seven of the 15 pictures (one blank) on the MPT–R are appropriate for both sexes, four are exclusively for girls, and four are exclusively for boys. Responses to the social and emotional situations depicted in the pictures are scored for a Tension Index (needs for love, extropunitiveness–intropunitiveness, succorance, superiority, submission, and personal adequacy), Direction of Force (whether the central figure acts or is acted upon), and Verb Tense (tense of verbs used by examinee). Although the interscorer reliability coefficients for the MPT–R are moderately high and the results of cross-validation studies have been reported, evidence for the validity of the test is inadequate.

More recently published than the Michigan Picture Test is the Children's Apperceptive Story-Telling Test (CAST). Based on Adlerian theory and designed to evaluate the emotional functioning of children aged 6 through 13, CAST consists of 31 colorful pictures to which children make up stories (Figure 12–6) (Schneider, 1989; Schneider & Perney, 1990). The test was constructed to be racially sensitive and was standardized on a sample of 876 U.S. children selected as representative. It is scored on four factors: adaptive, nonadaptive, immature, and uninvested. Internal consistency and test–retest reliability coefficients of the factor scores are in the .80s and .90s. Some evidence for the content, criterion-related, and construct validity, including score profiles for several clinical groups of children (attention deficit, conduct, anxiety, opposition, and depressive disorders), are reported in the manual.

### Problems with Projectives

As shown by this brief overview, on the whole projective techniques leave much to be desired from a strictly psychometric viewpoint. Their shortcomings include problems of administration, scoring, and standardization. The lack of objectivity in scoring and the

**FIGURE 12–6** Sample Materials on the Children's Apperceptive Story-telling Test.
(Reprinted by permission of pro.ed.)

paucity of representative normative data are particularly troublesome to specialists in psychometrics. Nevertheless, repeated criticism has not dampened the enthusiasm of clinical psychologists and psychiatrists for projective techniques. For example, a survey of the members of the Society for Personality Assessment found that the Rorschach and the TAT were ranked second and fourth, respectively, in terms of usage among all psychometric instruments (Piotrowski, Sherry, & Keller, 1985). Other popular projectives included the Sentence Completion, the Draw-a-Person Test, the House–Tree–Person Technique, the Bender–Gestalt Test, and the Children's Apperception Test.

It appears that clinicians, like many laypersons, view projective techniques as possessed of a kind of mystique, making them capable of revealing human personality in greater depth and detail than more consciously controllable and hence fakable personality inventories, rating scales, and interviews. Whatever the reasons may be, research indicates that most people place more faith in personality descriptions based on projective techniques than they do on interpretations based on scores from personality inventories (Snyder, 1974). Perhaps soap operas, murder mysteries, and other "human-interest" programs on television and in the other media have made people more suspicious of others and more inclined to accept deep, convoluted explanations of behaviors that are usually explicable in terms of fairly ordinary human motives.[1]

## PHYSIOLOGICAL, PERCEPTUAL, AND COGNITIVE MEASURES

A definition of personality that includes both affective and cognitive factors has been advocated by certain psychologists for many years. Although measurement specialists have tended to separate the two domains, interest in combined cognitive and affective instruments has grown. Furthermore, dissatisfaction with traditional, self-report techniques for assessing personality has led to a greater emphasis on less obvious but more structured physiological, perceptual, cognitive, and behavioral measures. These indirect, relatively objective indexes of personality are favored because the responses are not so much under conscious control, cannot be easily faked, and are not influenced as much by response sets as are scores on traditional assessment procedures.

### Physiological Measures

Many types of instruments have been applied to the measurement of physiological responses produced by stressful or arousing stimuli. Among these are responses obtained by a polygraph, which measures blood pressure, respiration rate, and the electrical resistance of the skin (galvanic skin response, or GSR). Changes in blood chemistry, brain waves, pupillary diameter, finger and penile volume, muscle tension, and voice tone or tremors have also been analyzed. These reactions, which are regulated by the autonomic,

---

[1]Noteworthy in this context is that, when they were presented with flattering descriptions of themselves reported devised by astrologers, even skeptics of astrology began to think that "maybe there's something in this astrology business after all" (Glick, Gottesman, & Jolton, 1989). Furthermore, when presented with a generalized description of their personality, like the one on page 276, most people consider the bogus description as more accurate than an individualized personality description based on a bona fide test (Myers, 1995, p. 492).

reticular, and other parts of the nervous system, are frequently used as indexes of emotional arousal. They are, however, rather imprecise measures of response intensity and reveal little or nothing about the specific emotion or feeling being experienced. An occasional investigation has found certain physiological or biochemical differences between emotions such as fear and anger (for example, Levenson, 1992), but research has generally failed to reveal any reliably distinctive physiological response patterns associated with different emotions or personality characteristics. It may be that further research involving biofeedback of physiological status, for example, will yield information of value in personality assessment, but it is unlikely that such methods will replace paper-and-pencil inventories and other traditional assessment procedures.

Polygraph tests have been used extensively in industry to screen out dishonest workers and by government to detect security risks. Despite their wide usage, it has been estimated that polygraph tests are accurate in only about 65 percent of the cases and that they are more likely to declare innocent people guilty than to find guilty people innocent (Lykken, 1983; Kleinmuntz & Szucko, 1984). Since the passage in 1988 of federal legislation banning the use of polygraph tests in job interviews in government and the private workplace, a number of questionnaires and other paper-and-pencil instruments have been devised to detect cheating and other forms of dishonesty in job situations.

## Perceptual and Cognitive Measures

A significant amount of research has found moderate relationships between personality characteristics and certain aspects of perception and cognition. For example, it has been demonstrated that, compared with extroverts, introverts are more vigilant, more sensitive to pain, more easily bored, more cautious, and more disrupted by overstimulation (Wilson, 1978). Speed of responding on several perceptual and learning tasks (for example, word recognition, identification of incomplete figures, dark adaptation, and conditioning) is also related to personality (Eysenck, 1962; Eysenck & Rachman, 1965). The majority of these tasks are, however, rather crude measures, and they show no immediate signs of replacing traditional personality assessment devices.

***Field Independence and Dependence***    One of the most systematic series of investigations of the relationships between personality and perception was conducted by Herman Witkin and his colleagues (Witkin et al., 1973; Witkin & Goodenough, 1977). Three tests (Body Adjustment Test, Rod and Frame Test, and Embedded Figures Test) were used in these studies to classify individuals as field independent or field dependent. On the Body Adjustment Test, the subject (person) is seated in a chair located in a tilted room and directed to adjust the chair to a true vertical position. On the Rod and Frame Test, the person is seated before a luminous rod situated in a luminous square frame in a darkened room and instructed to adjust the rod to the true vertical position when the rod and frame are tilted in opposite directions. On the Embedded Figures Test, the speed with which simple figures can be found in a series of complex forms is determined (Figure 12–7). According to Witkin, these three tests measure much the same thing: the ability to differentiate aspects or parts of a complex, confusing whole. People who are able to find the upright position accurately and the embedded figures quickly are *field independents;* those who have difficulty finding the upright position and locating the embedded figures are *field dependents.*

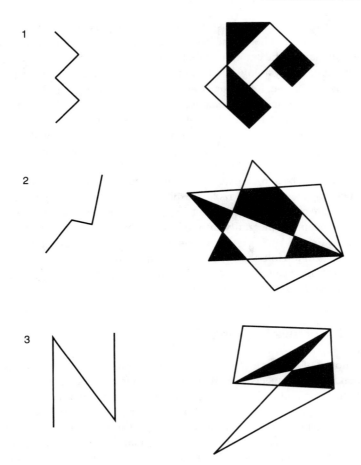

**FIGURE 12–7**    Sample Embedded Figures Test Item.    People Who Have
Difficulty Locating the Figures at the Left in the Complex Patterns at the Right
May Be Characterized as Field Dependent.
(From Witkin et al., "Field Dependent and Field Independent Cognitive Styles and Their
Educational Implications," *Review of Educational Research, 47,* 1–64. Copyright 1977
by The American Educational Research Association. Adapted by permission of
the publisher.)

Of particular interest is the fact that field independents and field dependents tend to have
different personalities. Witkin's description of a typical field-independent person is that of a
secure, independent, more psychologically mature, self-accepting individual who is active in
dealing with the environment, tends to use intellectualization as a defense mechanism, and
is more aware of his or her inner experiences. On the other hand, a typical field-dependent
person is less secure, psychologically immature, passive, less attuned to inner experiences,
and tends to use repression and denial as defenses. Sex and sociocultural differences in these
two perceptual styles have also been found. Boys are typically more field independent than
girls, and members of hunting and foraging cultures are more field independent than those

living in sedentary, agricultural societies (Witkin & Berry, 1975). In terms of child-rearing practices, the parents of field independents are usually less restrictive and less authoritarian than those of field-dependent children.

Witkin's research program represents only one of many areas of investigation concerned with the relationships of personality to the ways in which people attend to, process, store, and use information from the environment to solve problems. It has also been found that people differ in the broadness of the categories employed in classifying their experiences, a variable that is related to other personality characteristics (Block et al., 1981). The findings of numerous investigations in which cognitive, affective, and perceptual variables were combined indicate that cognition and affect are actually inseparable, interwoven processes.

**Cognitive Styles**    The term *cognitive style* has been applied to the collection of strategies or approaches to perceiving, remembering, and thinking that a person comes to prefer in attempting to understand and cope with the world. Among the cognitive styles that have received particular research attention are the reflective versus impulsive style and the internal versus external locus of control style. Both the reflective–impulsive and the internal versus external locus of control dimensions are correlated with numerous personal and sociocultural variables.

The *reflective versus impulsive* style, as measured by the Matching Familiar Figures Test (Kagan et al., 1964) (Figure 12–8), is concerned with whether, when faced with a problem or task, a person tends to be slow and accurate (reflective) or quick and inaccurate (impulsive) in finding a solution.

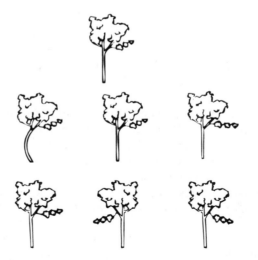

**FIGURE 12–8**    Sample of Types of Items on the Matching Familiar Figures (MFF) Test.    On This Item the Examinee Is Instructed to Select Which of the Six Pictures in the Second or Third Rows Is Identical to the Picture at the Top. (From Jerome Kagan, "Reflection–Impulsivity: The Generality and Dynamics of Conceptual Tempo," *Journal of Abnormal Psychology, 71,* 17–24. Copyright © 1966 by the American Psychological Association. Reprinted by permission of the author.)

The *internal versus external locus of control* style, as measured by Rotter's (1966) I–E Scale, is concerned with whether people believe that rewards in life are the consequences of their own behavior (internal locus of control) or are controlled by forces outside themselves (external locus of control). The following are examples of items on the I–E Scale:

1A. Many of the unhappy things in people's lives are partly due to bad luck.

1B. People's misfortunes result from the mistakes they make.

2A. No matter how hard you try, some people just don't like you.

2B. People who can't get others to like them don't understand how to get along with others.

3A. In the case of the well-prepared student, there is rarely if ever such a thing as an unfair test.

3B. Many times exam questions tend to be so unrelated to course work that studying is really useless.

4A. Becoming a success is a matter of hard work; luck has little or nothing to do with it.

4B. Getting a good job depends mainly on being in the right place at the right time.

5A. The average citizen can have an influence in government decisions.

5B. This world is run by the few people in power, and there is not much the little guy can do about it.
(Reprinted with permission from Rotter, 1966)

You should be able to tell which statement in each pair indicates an internal locus of control and which indicates an external locus of control.


## SUMMARY

Personality inventories and projective techniques have traditionally been used in clinical contexts to identify personal problems and to diagnose psychopathology. However, a number of inventories and projectives have been designed for or extended to the analysis of normal personality.

The first personality inventory of note was the Woodworth Personal Data Sheet, but numerous single-score and multiscore inventories have been constructed since that instrument made its debut during World War I. These inventories measure the respondent's standing on certain adjustment, temperament, trait, or psychiatric variables. The items and scales on some personality inventories are based on a rational or theoretical frame of reference. Item selection and scoring for certain inventories are determined by the results of factor analysis or empirical studies of the ability of items to differentiate among various criterion groups.

Examples of inventories based on personality theory are the Edwards Personal Preference Schedule and the Myers–Briggs Type Indicator. Among the inventories based on the results of factor analysis are the Guilford–Zimmerman Temperament Survey, the 16 Personality Factor Questionnaire, and the Eysenck Personality Questionnaire.

The most famous personality inventory, and the one on which the greatest amount of research has been conducted, is the Minnesota Multiphasic Personality Inventory (MMPI). The MMPI, which is a criterion-keyed inventory, was designed to differentiate among various groups of people by analyzing differences in the responses on nine clinical scales of normals and patients having specific psychiatric diagnoses. The MMPI may be scored on many other scales as well, including four validating scales (*?, L, F, K*). Validating scales on the MMPI and other personality inventories are scored to determine whether the items have been answered properly and to adjust scores on content scales for faking and response sets. The MMPI–2, an updated and restandardized version of the MMPI, was published in 1986.

The criterion-keyed procedure by which the MMPI was constructed was also employed in preparing the California Psychological Inventory, the Personality Inventory for Children, and related instruments. Other more noteworthy personality inventories designed on the basis of criterion keying, as well as on theory and sophisticated psychometric procedures, include the Millon Clinical Multiaxial Inventory and the Jackson Personality Inventory.

The most unstructured of all personality assessment devices are projective techniques. Various kinds of projective techniques have been devised, including word associations, sentence completions, drawing human figures, responses to inkblots, and making up stories to pictures. Proponents of projective techniques maintain that inventories and other self-report instruments fail to get at deeper layers of personality because people either do not know or will not reveal their characteristics and problems. Since the scoring of projectives is usually very impressionistic or subjective, difficulties have been encountered in determining the validity of these instruments.

The two most popular projective techniques are the Rorschach Psychodiagnostic Technique and the Thematic Apperception Test. Also noteworthy are the Rosenzweig Picture-Frustration Study, the Rotter Incomplete Sentences Blank, the Holtzman Inkblot Technique, and various picture-story tests for children, seniors, and nonwhite ethnic groups.

Efforts have been made to devise methods of assessing personality that are less fakable than self-report instruments and more valid than projectives. The majority of these physiological, perceptual, cognitive, and behavioral tests are, unfortunately, somewhat crude, or at least narrow, measures of personality. For the present, these "objective" tests show no signs of replacing traditional personality assessment methods—observations, interviews, checklists, rating scales, personality inventories, and projective techniques.

The results of research on perceptual and cognitive styles, in particular field independence or dependence, reflectivity–compulsivity, and internal–external locus of control, demonstrate that cognition and affect are interactive rather than independent processes and that cognitive and affective assessment instruments overlap in what they measure. These research investigations have been concerned with determining the relationships of personality variables to the perceptual–cognitive processes of attending to, encoding, and using information.

## QUESTIONS AND ACTIVITIES

1.  Write five true–false items pertaining to personality characteristics that you think would be answered "true" more often by fakers than nonfakers. Then write five items that you believe would be answered "false" more often by fakers than nonfakers.

2.  Arrange to take the California Psychological Inventory, the Jackson Personality Inventory, or another personality inventory and have your scores interpreted by a qualified person. Are your scores consistent with your own assessment of yourself? What criticisms of the inventory do you have to offer?

3.  Compare personality inventories with projective techniques. Describe both the positive and negative features of both kinds of instrument and the conditions under which each is most appropriate to administer.

4.  Construct a 10-item self-concept inventory using a true–false format. On five of the statements the keyed answer should be "true," and on the other five statements it should be "false." Administer your Self-concept Inventory to several students, and compute their total scores (0 to 10) as the number of responses given in the keyed direction. Were the scores generally low or generally high? How variable were they? What evidence is there for the reliability and validity of your Self-concept Inventory?

5.  Construct an alphabetized list of 25 nouns pertaining to subjects of interest to people in your age group: college, grades, graduation, failure, sex, marriage, religion, mother, father, career, health, and so on. Read your list to 12 acquaintances and ask each person to respond to each word on the list as quickly as possible with the first word that comes to mind. Record the response time (in seconds) and the response to each word. Summarize the results in terms of the number of responses of a given kind made to each word, average response times, and insights provided into the personalities of the respondents. Review the section on word associations in this chapter before drawing any conclusions.

6.  Construct 10 incomplete sentences pertaining to matters of concern to college students. Type (double space) the sentence fragments on a sheet of paper and make several copies. Administer your sentence-completion test to a group of college students; instruct them to complete every sentence fragment with a word or phrase that has a personal meaning or refers to a matter of concern to them. Study the responses given to the sentence fragments, and try to analyze them in terms of the personalities of the respondents. Write a report summarizing your findings.

7.  Construct two incomplete stories that you believe will reveal something about the respondent's personality when he or she is asked to complete the stories. Try out your stories on several of your classmates or friends. Does the content of the completed stories suggest anything significant about the respondent's personality? Do you consider this technique of personality assessment to be reliable and valid? Why or why not?

8.  Have each of several people draw a picture of a person on a clean sheet of paper. Then have them turn the sheet over and draw a picture of a person of the opposite sex. Collect the drawings, and tell the participants that you are going to have the drawings interpreted by an expert personality analyst and that you will give them the interpretations later. Sometime later, present the following personality description (Forer, 1949) to each participant:

    You have a strong need for other people to like you and for them to admire you. You have a tendency to be critical of yourself. You have a great deal of unused capacity, which you have not turned to your advantage. While you have some personality weaknesses, you are generally able to compensate for them. Your sexual adjustment has presented some problems for you. Disciplined and controlled on the outside, you tend to be worrisome and insecure inside. At times you have serious doubts as to whether you have made the right decision or done the right thing. You prefer a certain amount of change and variety, and become dissatisfied when hemmed in by restrictions and limitations. You pride yourself on being an independent thinker and do not accept others' opinions without satisfactory proof. You have found it unwise to be too frank in revealing yourself to others. At times you are extroverted, affable, social, while at other times you are introverted, wary, reserved. Some of your aspirations tend to be pretty unrealistic.

    Be sure to scramble the sentences in the interpretation so that the order will be different for different people. Ask each person to read the description and tell you whether it is highly accurate, accurate, somewhat accurate and somewhat inaccurate, inaccurate, or very inaccurate as a description of his or her personality. Tabulate the results, interpret them as well as you can, and report them to your course instructor. After the exercise has been completed, inform the participants of the deception and hope that they react to this debriefing information with good humor!

9. Construct an inkblot picture by putting a large drop of black ink in the middle of an $8\frac{1}{2}$- by 11-inch sheet of white paper. Fold the sheet in half so that the ink is inside, crease the sheet in the middle and press it flat. Then open up the sheet and let the blot dry. Repeat the process with other sheets of paper until you obtain five fairly detailed, preferably symmetrical inkblots. Then administer your inkblot test to several people. Instruct them to tell you what they see in each blot, where on the blot they see it, and what it was about the blot (shape, color, texture, or other quality) that caused them to give that response. Record the response(s) made by each person to each inkblot, and then see if you can tell anything about the various personalities from their responses to the five inkblots. Compare the results with your personal knowledge of the individual and any other test results that are available. Summarize your findings in a report.

10. Look through several popular magazines and either cut out or photocopy five pictures of people in ambiguous situations. It should not be immediately obvious what the people in the pictures are doing or thinking. Present the pictures, one at a time, to several people, and ask them to tell a story about each picture. Tell them that they should include in their stories what is going on now, what led up to it (what happened before), and how it will turn out. Interpret the stories in terms of common themes, the actions and feelings of the main characters, the pressures and frustrations occurring in the stories, whether the stories are generally pleasant or unpleasant, and whether the endings are upbeat or downbeat (comedic or tragic). Are there common elements in all the stories? Can you tell anything from these stories about the personality, attitudes, and feelings of the storyteller?

11. Run all the computer programs in Category I ("Personality Inventories and Projective Techniques") of *Computer Programs for Psychological Assessment*.

# Part Four

# Applications, Issues, and Developments

# 13

# PSYCHOLOGICAL ASSESSMENT IN APPLIED SETTINGS

Tests and other psychological assessment instruments and procedures are used extensively for research purposes, not only in psychology and education but in many other professions and contexts as well. For example, an anthropologist planning to conduct a field study in a primitive society might take along a set of Rorschach inkblots, a Draw-a-Person Test, and other assorted test materials to obtain information on the cognitive abilities and personality characteristics of the members of that society. Likewise, a medical researcher might decide to administer a personality inventory or rating scale as part of a study of factors affecting the occurrence and prognosis of a particular disease or disorder.

Psychometric psychologists contribute their expertise in test selection and design, in addition to statistical analysis, as members of research teams in many different situations. This is true because, whatever the research area may be, psychological measures of various kinds can serve as independent, control, concomitant, moderator, or dependent variables. First and foremost, psychologists are observers, investigators, and explorers of human behavior—activities that entail research even if not in a formal sense. Of course, psychological assessment is not limited to research uses. Otherwise, many students who dislike research courses would never become professional psychologists! To an even greater extent than in research studies, testing provides valuable data in applied areas such as educational and employment selection and placement, psychodiagnosis and treatment planning, or in any situation that involves making decisions about people, programs, and procedures.

Previous chapters in this book have been concerned with the methodology and tools of psychological testing and assessment. Applications of testing are certainly not overlooked in those chapters, but they are not dealt with at length. The purpose of this chapter is to remedy that deficiency with a more detailed consideration of psychological assessment in several applied contexts: educational, occupational, clinical, health, legal, and environmental. The discussion is by no means exhaustive, since entire books have been written on the applications of psychological testing to any one of these areas. Instead, the focus is on a few situations within each of these areas in which psychological assessment instruments have been found useful. Applications of psychological testing in all these areas have been criticized, often vociferously and unremittingly, but consideration of such criticisms will be postponed until Chapter 14.

## ASSESSMENT IN EDUCATIONAL CONTEXTS

The main reason why tests are administered in schools, colleges, and other educational institutions is to evaluate the extent to which students have accumulated specific knowledge and skills, either in or out of formal academic settings. The knowledge should involve not only simple recall of memorized facts, but also some degree of comprehension and an ability to apply what has been learned to various situations and circumstances. Likewise, the learned skills, which include cognitive, psychomotor, and social skills, should be generalizable or transferrable to other areas of life. In the process of assessing these abilities not only are individual people (students, teachers, administrators, and the like) evaluated, but also groups of people (classes, schools, school districts, representative samples of the residents of states and countries) and the programs or intervention procedures by which changes in knowledge and ability are brought about.

In this part of the chapter we shall consider four areas on which educational assessment has concentrated in recent years: neuropsychological functioning, student competency, teacher competency, and the evaluation of educational and other intervention programs. An analysis of efforts in these four areas should provide a useful overview of the manner in which psychological assessment instruments have been applied in schools, colleges, and adult education programs. Our survey begins with neuropsychological assessment, a topic that might also have been considered in the section on clinical testing. However, the emphasis here will be on neuropsychological testing in special education, rather than in the diagnosis of mental disorders.

### Neuropsychological Disabilities

The Binet–Simon Intelligence Scale, the grandfather of tests for measuring cognitive abilities, was designed primarily for testing mentally handicapped children. The term *handicapped,* however, has been used in a more general sense to refer to people who have physical, mental, cultural, or even emotional disabilities. Because procedures for testing nonhandicapped or normal individuals are frequently unsuitable or unfair in testing the handicapped, special methods and tests have been devised. A number of these tests, in particular tests for the physically handicapped, are described in Chapters 6 and 7. Here we consider instruments and procedures for assessing one subgroup of the handicapped—the neuropsychologically impaired.

Scores on various kinds of tests can contribute to the identification and diagnosis of neuropsychological disorders. Among these instruments are intelligence tests, neuropsychological batteries, memory tests, language tests, visuospatial tests, executive measures, tests of psychomotor functoning, and personality tests (Butler, Retzlaff, & Vanderploeg, 1991). Several test publishers, including Psychological Assessment Resources, The Psychological Corporation, and Western Psychological Services, market entire series of neuropsychological assessment instruments. These single tests and test batteries have been designed specifically for neuropsychological screening and/or the assessment of organic brain damage.[1]

---

[1]A growing use of neuropsychological tests is in the differential diagnosis of memory loss due to dementia, delirium, and depression. Psychologists who specialize in the diagnosis and treatment of older adults and in research on this age group employ many tests of this type. For example, tests of memory, perceptual abilities, and abstract reasoning are used to differentiate between dementia and the pseudo-dementia of depression.

As advanced as medical technology may be, damage to the central nervous system is not always detectable with CAT, EMR, or PET scans and other medical instruments and procedures, but its effects may still be expressed in behavioral and cognitive disturbances. Proficiency in diagnosing and treating deficits in neuropsychological abilities requires a long training program and extensive experience, and even then it is often as much of an art as a science.

Neuropsychological abilities include sensation, motor speed and strength, perception and perceptual-motor integration, language, attention, abstracting ability, flexibility of thought, orientation, and memory (Grant & Reed, 1982). Brain-injured children experience deficits in one or more of these abilities. Thus, a brain-injured child is a

child who before, during, or after birth has received an injury to or suffered an infection of the brain. As a result of such organic impairment, defects in the neuromotor system may be present or absent; however, such a child may show disturbances in perception, thinking, and emotional behavior, either separately or in combination. These disturbances prevent or impede a normal learning process. (Strauss & Lehtinen, 1947, page 4)

Because brain-injured children are typically more hyperactive, impulsive, distractible, and emotionally unstable than normal children, special preparations must be made when testing them. Not only should such children be informed of the examination several days in advance, but noise and other sources of distraction in the testing room should be kept to a minimum. Perceptual-motor deficits, coordination defects, short attention span, and uncooperativeness are more common in brain-injured children. Because these problems contribute to difficulties in testing such children, careful preparation, patience, and understanding by examiners are necessary.

***Perceptual-Memory Tests***   Distortions of both perception and memory are characteristic of brain-injured persons. Among the single tests that tap perceptual and memory functions are the Bender Visual Motor Gestalt Test, the Memory for Designs Test, and the Benton Revised Visual Retention Test. These three tests are usually administered as supplements to individual intelligence tests or other longer psychological examinations.

The Bender Visual Motor Gestalt Test consists of nine geometric designs on 4- by 6-inch white cards. The examinee is directed to copy each design, as it is presented. The level of maturation of visuomotor abilities, which are associated with linguistic and intellectual functions, is indicated by the responses. Notable departures of the copies from the originals, or errors, are interpreted in terms of perceptual deficits. Children 8 years or older and of normal intelligence usually make no more than two errors. Errors in making the drawings that suggest organic brain damage include shape distortions; rotating designs; problems with integrating designs; disproportionate, overlapping, or fragmented drawings; and perseverations. The Bender was restandardized and norms for ages 5 through 10 years were published in 1975. Scores on the test are highly correlated with IQ up to ages 9 to 10 (Koppitz, 1975; also see Lacks, 1984).

The Memory for Designs Test (MFD) is similar to the Bender except that the examinee attempts to draw copies of 15 geometric designs from memory. Research findings indicate that the MFD, which can be administered in 10 minutes to individuals aged $8\frac{1}{2}$ through 60 years, can contribute to the identification of organic brain damage (Graham & Kendall, 1960). Also consisting of a set of geometric designs (10 each in three forms) is the Benton Revised Visual Retention Test: the examinee is asked to draw each design from memory after seeing it briefly. The Benton takes about 5 minutes to administer and, like the Bender and the MFD, is based on the assumption that impairments in visual perception, visual memory, and visuoconstructive abilities result from neurological deficits.

Other measures that have been used to detect brain damage are tests involving hidden figures, the detection of patterns, and sustained attention or concentration. Screening instruments such as the Quick Neurological Screening Test–Revised and the Stroop Neuropsychological Screening Test provide preliminary indexes that suggest whether a child should be referred for a complete neurological examination. Tests designed to identify or diagnose aphasia, as well as problems with face recognition, form discrimination, and other specific neuropsychological disabilities are also available. However, a comprehensive assessment of neuropsychological functioning requires administration of a battery of specialized tests.

***Comprehensive Batteries for Assessing Memory***    Deficits in memory and learning are diagnostic signs of specific learning disabilities, traumatic brain injury, neurological disorders, attention deficit hyperactivity disorder (ADHD), and serious emotional disturbance. Because memory and learning are not unitary capacities, a battery of tests is often needed to identify the presence of specific deficits. Such batteries cannot take the place of intelligence tests, which assess a wider range of cognitive functions, but they may provide supplementary data and diagnostic clues.

Three popular memory assessment batteries are the Test of Memory and Learning (TOMAL), the Wide Range Assessment of Memory and Learning (WRAML), and the Memory Assessment Scales (MAS). TOMAL and WRAML are designed for children and adolescents, whereas the MAS is for adults. All three batteries are highly reliable measures of memory and learning functions. The MAS manual, for example, provides profiles of scores for patients with neurological disorders such as dementia, closed head injury, left hemisphere lesions, and right hemisphere lesions.

***Neuropsychological Test Batteries***    Although conventional intelligence tests such as the Wechsler series are helpful in identifying neuropsychological deficits, a series of tests such as those comprising the Halstead–Reitan Neuropsychological Test Battery, the Reitan–Indiana Neuropsychological Test Battery, the Luria–Nebraska Neuropsychological Battery, or the Contributions to Neuropsychological Assessment has traditionally been administered to measure neuropsychologically based adaptive abilities that are not assessed by intelligence tests.

The Halstead–Reitan Neuropsychological Test Battery contains the first five tests listed in Table 13–1, but several of the remaining six psychometric procedures may also be included in the total battery. These tests and procedures tap a number of sensory abilities, perceptual-motor speed and dexterity, expressive and receptive language functions, memory, concept formation, and abstract reasoning. Any of these abilities may be affected by damage to or dysfunction of the central nervous system or damage to the sense receptors and muscles. A related battery of tests, the Reitan–Indiana Neuropsychological Battery for Children (Reitan, 1964), also includes a variety of sensorimotor and perceptual tests for several sensory modalities and response modes. Among the more complex tests included in the battery are the Category Test and the Trail Making Test. On the Category Test the examinee deduces general principles from information presented on slides. On the Trail Making Test, he or she draws lines to connect numbered and lettered circles (from 1 to A, from 2 to

**TABLE 13–1    Tests and Procedures of the Halstead–Reitan Test Battery**

**Category Test.** The examinee tries to find the rule for categorizing pictures of geometric shapes. This test measures abstract reasoning and concept formation.

**Tactual Performance Test.** The blindfolded examinee places blocks in an appropriate cutout on an upright board with the dominant hand, then the nondominant hand, then both hands. This test measures kinesthetic and sensorimotor ability, as well as incidental memory.

**Speech Sounds Perception Test.** The examinee attempts to pick from four choices the written version of taped nonsense words. This test measures attention and auditory–visual synthesis.

**Seashore Rhythm Test.** The examinee indicates whether paired musical rhythms are the same or different. This test measures attention and auditory perception.

**Finger-tapping Test.** The examinee taps a telegraph keylike lever as quickly as possible for 10 seconds. This test measures motor speed.

**Grip Strength.** The examinee squeezes a dynamometer as hard as possible; separate trials are given with each hand. This test measures grip strength.

**Trail Making (Parts A and B).** The examinee connects numbers (Part A) or numbers and letters in alternating order (Part B) with a pencil line under pressure of time. This test measures scanning ability, mental flexibility, and speed.

**Tactile Form Recognition.** The examinee tries to recognize simple shapes (e.g., a triangle) placed in the palm of the hand. This test measures sensory-perceptual ability.

**Sensory–Perceptual Exam.** The examinee responds to a simple bilateral sensory task (e.g., detecting which finger has been touched or which ear has received a brief sound). This test measures sensory–perceptual ability.

**Aphasia Screening Test.** The tasks on this test include naming a pictured item (e.g., fork), repeating short phrases, and copying. This test measures expressive and receptive language abilities.

**Supplementary.** WAIS–R, WRAT–R, MMPI, memory tests such as the Wechsler Memory Scale or the Rey Auditory Verbal Learning Test may also be administered.

*Source:* Adapted from Robert J. Gregory, *Psychological testing: History, principles, and applications* (2nd ed.). Copyright © 1996 by Allyn & Bacon.

B, and so on, alternating numbers and letters). Administration of all tests in the Halstead–Reitan Battery requires 6 to 8 hours.

The Luria–Nebraska Neuropsychological Battery, which is based on the diagnostic techniques pioneered by A. R. Luria, was designed to assess cerebral dominance; tactile, visual, and motor functions; perception and reproduction of pitch and rhythm; receptive and expressive speech; reading, writing, and arithmetic; memory; concept formation; and other intellectual processes. Both forms (I and II) of the battery can be scored by computer, but Form I can also be scored by hand. Like the Halstead–Reitan, the Luria–Nebraska is administered for more extensive neuropsychological screening for brain damage. Although the Luria–Nebraska takes only about one-third as much time to administer as the Halstead–Reitan, it has been criticized for relying too heavily on language skills and for failing to detect aphasia and certain other neuropsychological disorders adequately.

Contributions to Neuropsychological Assessment is a test battery that emphasizes a flexible, sequential approach to neuropsychological assessment. The battery consists of three Tests of Orientation and Learning and nine Perceptual and Motor Tests. The patient's specific complaint and questions arising during the examination determine which tests are administered. These tests were developed over a period of 20 years and have been fairly extensively standardized and validated on brain-diseased and brain-injured patients.

**Computer-based Neuropsychological Assessment**   Advances in neurophysiology and cognitive psychology, together with improvements in computer technology and psychometric methodology during the past two decades, have led to an increased use of computers for administering, scoring, and interpreting neuropsychological tests. Neuropsychological testing has become faster, more flexible, and more focused; not only the accuracy of responses, but also their speed and even their intensity can be determined by means of computer-based assessment.

Among the many neuropsychological tests with computer-based versions are the Category Test and the Wisconsin Card Sorting Test. Computer software for components of the Halstead–Reitan Neuropsychological Battery and the Luria–Nebraska Neuropsychological Battery is also available. Even more recent than tests that can be given by a human examiner or a computer are instruments that are administered exclusively by computer. An example of a test of this kind is MicroCog: Assessment of Cognitive Functioning. Designed to assess cognitive functioning in adults aged 18 to 80 years, MicroCog comes in a Standard Form requiring 50 to 60 minutes testing time and a Brief Form requiring 30 minutes. The nine tests comprising MicroCog were standardized on 810 adults reportedly representative of the U.S. national population, with separate norms for nine age groups as well as norms adjusted for educational level. Validity data for various clinical groups (depression, dementia, schizophrenia, alcoholism, epilepsy, mixed psychiatric, lupus, and others) and correlations with the WAIS–R, the Wechsler Memory Scale–Revised, and other neuropsychological tests are reported in the manual.

**Diagnosing Learning Disabilities**   Not all children who score at or above the mean on general intelligence tests do well in school. In addition to those who have pronounced physical handicaps, emotional disturbances, or low motivation are children of average or better intelligence who apparently have none of these problems but still experience difficulties in reading, arithmetic, spelling, writing, and/or other basic academic skills. Examples are the reading disability known as *dyslexia* and the impairment in learning arithmetic referred to as *dyscalculia*. The term *learning disability* or *specific learning disability* has been applied to such conditions, and the emphasis has been on identifying and diagnosing learning problems that cannot be explained by mental retardation, cultural deprivation, mental disorder, or sensory loss.

Research on learning disabilities and the construction of psychometric instruments for use in diagnosis and remediation programs were prompted by Public Law 94-142, the Education for All Handicapped Children Act, in 1975. This act mandated that handicapped children be evaluated for mental, behavioral, and physical disabilities and that appropriate educational opportunities be provided to them. Subsequent legislation (PL 99-457 and PL 102-119) provided funds for the states to evaluate children who are delayed in cognitive, language, motor, socioemotional, or adaptive skills.

The diagnosis of learning disabilities is multidisciplinary, involving a teacher or other specialist who is knowledgeable in the field of the suspected handicap, the child's regular teacher, and at least one person qualified to conduct diagnostic evaluations of children by using valid psychometric instruments. To warrant a diagnosis of *specific learning disability,* a discrepancy between ability and achievement in one or more of the following areas must be found: oral expression, listening comprehension, written expression, basic reading skill, reading comprehension, mathematics calculation, or mathematical reasoning. Following team evaluation of the child, an individualized educational plan (IEP), including short- and long-term objectives and procedures for achieving them, is prepared.

Eligibility criteria for providing learning disability services vary from state to state. One guideline for identifying learning disabled children in the state of California, for example, is that the child's ability level (as measured, for example, by a general intelligence test) should be at least 1.5 standard deviations above his or her level of achievement (as measured by a standardized achievement test). More complex regression models for defining a critical discrepancy between actual and expected achievement warranting a diagnosis of learning disability are discussed by Reynolds (1984–1985).

Children diagnosed as learning disabled, whose actual performance levels do not keep pace with their estimated potential, are frequently inattentive and deficient in linguistic skills. This is true most often in reading, which is a foundation skill for scholastic achievement. Classroom teachers may be able to detect such conditions through careful observation or administration of a group intelligence test and more specialized instruments, such as the McCarthy Screening Test, the Pupil Rating Scale, and the Slingerland Screening Tests for Identifying Children with Specific Language Disability. However, administration of a comprehensive battery of tests to determine the nature and extent of a child's learning disability and his or her educational needs requires the skills of a trained psychologist.

A variety of cognitive, perceptual, motoric, and even affective measures may be included in a battery of tests for diagnosing learning disabilities. These include an individual intelligence test such as the SB–IV, WPPSI–R, or WISC–III; an achievement test battery, such as the Peabody Individual Achievement Test–Revised, the Kaufman Test of Educational Achievement, or the Woodcock–Johnson Psycho-Educational Battery–Revised; and one or more special tests, such as the Bender Visual Motor Gestalt Test or the Benton Visual Retention Test, the Goodenough–Harris Drawing Test, the Porch Index of Communicative Ability in Children, the Diagnostic Arithmetic Test, the Frostig Developmental Test of Visual Perception, the Gray Oral Reading Tests, and the Southern California Sensory Integration Tests. Because many children with learning disabilities have social and emotional problems, instruments designed to assess social and emotional functioning (for example, Conners' Rating Scales or Personality Inventory for Children) may also be administered.

## Evaluating Student Competencies

American public schools and their students are in trouble. As summarized in Table 13–2, the results of 20 years of evaluation by the National Assessment of Educational Progress (NAEP) of the knowledge and skills of young Americans reveals persisting deficiencies in reading, writing, science, mathematics, history, civics, and other subject areas. Scholastic achievement is low among white, black, and Hispanic students alike, and particularly so in

**TABLE 13–2   Highlights of Findings from 20 Years of NAEP**

Students can read at a surface level, getting the gist of material, but do not read analytically or perform well on challenging reading assignments.

Small proportions of students write well enough to accomplish the purposes of different writing tasks; most do not communicate effectively.

Only small proportions of students develop specialized knowledge needed to address science-based problems, and the pattern of falling behind begins in elementary school.

Students' grasp of the four arithmetic operations and beginning problem solving is far from universal in elementary school; by the time students near high school graduation, half cannot handle moderately challenging mathematics material, including computation with decimals, fractions, and percents.

Students have a basic understanding of events that have shaped U.S. history, but they do not appear to understand the significance and connections of those events.

Similarly, students demonstrate an uneven understanding of the Constitution and U.S. government and politics; their knowledge of the Bill of Rights is limited.

*Source:* Reprinted with permission of the National Assessment of Educational Progress.

the last two groups. Black and Hispanic students in the United States have, since the 1970s, improved in reading, mathematics, and science, but their performance remains significantly below that of white students.

***Testing Students for Academic Competency***   National concern with the low test scores of U.S. high school graduates has led to the requirement in most states that students pass a *functional literacy,* or minimum competency, test before being awarded a high school diploma. Florida's 240-item competency exam, which was developed in response to the concern that too many children were being "socially promoted," was designed to measure basic skills in the three R's applied to real-life situations (making change, writing checks, calculating interest, and the like). Students take the examination first in the eleventh grade and are given four chances to pass. Those who do not pass it by the end of the twelfth grade receive a certificate of completion to show that they attended high school, but it does not have the same status as a diploma.

Despite compromises and efforts to make it more acceptable, minimum competency or functional literacy testing has been the subject of continuing debate. Because substantially larger percentages of black than white students failed the Florida examination for high school students, the test was alleged to be discriminatory against minorities. In the case of *Debra P.* v. *Turlington* (1984), it was alleged that the Florida examination was racially biased, that sufficient time had not been given for the students to prepare, and that using the test to group students for remediation purposes would reinstate segregation in the public schools of that state. The court also concluded in this case that a minimum competency test could be used only when students' entire education had been received in integrated schools. On the other side are critics who feel that passing an eighth-grade-level test is an inadequate standard for high school graduation and that minimum competency may well become the norm. Two other dangers of minimum competency testing are that teachers may end up teaching to the test and that enforcers of the requirement will continue to be besieged by the outraged parents of children who have failed the tests.

Despite these problems, using tests to assess competency in basic skills and requiring specified minimum scores for high school graduation seems to be here to stay. In many states, accountability through evaluation of student performance is an annual event resulting in the publication in local newspapers of test score averages by school and grade level. Efforts to make such evaluation more useful in educational decision making and resource allocation are indicated by calls for reporting scores on the NAEP tests by state and locality, rather than simply averages for the nation as a whole. There has also been a great deal of discussion among governmental leaders and professionals concerning the possibility and procedures for establishing national educational standards and constructing national tests in English, mathematics, science, history, and geography to be administered on a national level in the fourth, eighth, and twelfth grades. Such a set of standards and the accompanying tests would presumably provide a source of motivation, a guide for improving learning in the public schools, and a way of determining the extent of progress in reaching the standards.

***Value-added Testing***    Related to accountability and competency testing is the concept of value-added education and the associated process of value-added testing. In *value-added testing,* students' achievements in academic subjects and life skills, such as analyzing a newspaper column, a mathematical table, or a television advertisement, are assessed before and after a certain period of formal education and study. The difference between pre- and post-course test scores is a measure of the value added by the educational experience. Value-added testing is mandated by law and controlled by state coordinating boards in certain states, and individual institutions in several other states have incorporated value-added testing into their academic procedures. For example, entering students at Northeast Missouri State University take either the ACT Freshman College Entrance Examination or the ACT College Outcome Measures Project. The latter requires students to analyze newspaper advertisements, articles, and speeches to demonstrate their mastery of life skills. Retesting at the end of the sophomore year, when students still have sufficient time to make up deficiencies, reveals how much they have learned in the general education curriculum.

## Teachers and Testing

Testing in the schools is conducted by school psychologists, guidance counselors, and directors of special education, but most often by the classroom teachers themselves. Teachers are involved with formal and informal evaluations of students from their very first day in the classroom. Such evaluations entail not only observations, classwork, homework, and teacher-made tests, but also standardized tests. The extensive use of standardized tests in the schools frequently leads to errors of administration, scoring, and interpretation. Many of these errors are attributable to a lack of training, a lack of concern, or both on the part of test users. Consequently, it is a matter of some importance for teachers, guidance counselors, and others who have testing responsibilities in the schools to be properly trained and informed.

***Teacher Training in Testing***    The majority of prospective teachers have some exposure to educational testing during their college education, but in most cases it is fairly superficial. Many teachers do not understand what is being measured by the tests that they administer, nor do they know the meanings of the standard scores entered into a student's permanent record. They often draw sweeping conclusions on the basis of a single test score, failing to take into account the child's developmental history, social competency, or home environment. Therefore, it is essential for more attention to be paid to this aspect of teacher training. For example, teachers need to realize that scores on tests of intelligence and special abilities should be interpreted in terms of the probabilities that the examinees will succeed in particular vocations or programs of study. Far too often test scores are viewed as fixed measures of mental status on the one hand or completely meaningless on the other.

***Testing the Teachers***   Increasing public concern over the quality of education in the United States has led to another form of involvement of teachers with testing. Almost all 50 states have implemented some form of teacher evaluation system. Most states require a passing score on a specified test for students to enter teacher training programs, and almost all states use tests for teacher certification. Tests are also administered for purposes of recertification and the allocation of merit pay.

Custom-built tests are administered for teacher certification purposes in certain states, whereas other states use tests designed by commercial testing organizations. In the latter category are the National Teacher Examinations (NTE), the Pre-Professional Skills Test (PPST), and the California Basic Educational Skills Test (CBEST). These examinations cover basic skills in reading, writing, and mathematics, knowledge of the subject matter the applicant plans to teach, and knowledge of professional education (curriculum theory, psychology of instruction, and the like). In addition to the tests, several states have implemented formal observation systems for beginning teachers. In these states, beginning teachers are given assistance in teaching for a trial period, after which a recommendation made to state officials determines whether the candidate will receive regular certification.

Results of national opinion polls indicate that a majority of the general public is in favor of using competency tests for teacher certification or licensing. In addition, both of the nation's two largest organizations of teachers, the National Education Association and the American Federation of Teachers, support the testing of all beginning teachers to ensure that they meet a reasonable standard of competency. Supporters of a national test for prospective teachers argue that it would be an indicator of teacher quality and would professionalize the teaching force. By improving the quality of teachers, such a test would also result in raising teachers' salaries and improving schools (Doyle & Hartle, 1985).

Teacher competency tests have not gone unchallenged, and legal battles concerning the matter have taken place in several states. A continuing problem concerns the passing standard on the tests: if it is set reasonably high, then a large number of minority candidates are likely to fail; if it is set too low, individuals of low ability will enter the teaching profession. In addition, certain professional educators have expressed dissatisfaction with the nature of the examinations. Some authorities believe that a blend of tests using computer technology, direct observations of classroom performance, portfolios with documentation of teaching performance and other items, as well as standardized paper-and-pencil tests, will ultimately be employed to evaluate both prospective teachers for hiring and experienced teachers for recertification, promotion, tenure, and merit pay.

## Program Evaluation

In addition to evaluating student and teacher competencies, tests are often used to evaluate the effectiveness of educational programs and other interventions. Psychological and educational assessment plays an important role in evaluating instruction and in determining the effectiveness of psychological treatments and other procedures designed to change behaviors, cognitions, and attitudes. Such programs should not be designed unilaterally by specialists in psychometrics and research, but in collaboration with educators, human service personnel, health personnel, and other professionals in the area of intervention. The contributions of measurement specialists, however, are the important ones of recommending and/or designing instruments to evaluate program outcomes.

Difficulties in measuring change and other technical problems in evaluating the effectiveness of behavioral interventions resulted in the creation of a new kind of specialty— *program evaluation.* The goal of program evaluation is to make judgments concerning the utility or value of educational, psychosocial, and other social intervention programs. Various guides or models of program evaluation have been proposed, including the CIPP (context, input, process, product) model, discrepancy evaluation, and adversary evaluation. Numerous books and articles have been written on the topic of program evaluation, and only a brief description of one approach can be given here.

The comprehensive model proposed by Rossi and Freeman (1993) characterizes the overall process of program evaluation in terms of four successive stages: planning, monitoring, impact assessment, and economic efficiency assessment. During the first, or *program planning,* stage, the extent of the problem (for example, drug dealing and use in the schools), the goals, and the target population of the program are identified. After the goals and target population have been specified, a decision is made as to whether the program can be properly implemented. Once a decision has been made to go ahead, the *program monitoring* stage begins. During this stage, implementation or operation of the program is continually monitored to see whether it is providing the designated resources and services to the target population.

At the third, or *impact assessment,* stage, the actual outcomes are evaluated to see if the goals of the program have been met. Various statistical and nonstatistical procedures are applied to determine whether the outcomes are significant and in the predicted direction. Other unintended or unexpected outcomes are also evaluated at the impact assessment stage, but, even when statistically significant, they may not be of sufficient practical significance. Consequently, it is the purpose of the fourth stage—*economic efficiency assessment*—to determine whether the results of a program are worth the costs incurred in implementing it. This is a matter of cost–benefit analysis, in which the costs of the program are weighed against its potential benefits to the individual and society. For example, even if the program works, it may be that the monetary and other resources required to implement it could be used more effectively elsewhere. When the results of a cost–benefit analysis favor the program, it is a signal to go ahead and put the program in place. Even after the program has been initiated, its effectiveness should be evaluated and reviewed periodically.

Although various models of program evaluation differ in their details, they all attempt to determine the goals, resources, procedures, and management of the program in order to judge its merit. Indicative of the level of interest in these efforts and public support for them is the existence of centers for research and development in educational evaluation and other types of program evaluation at prominent U.S. universities. The findings of studies conducted at these centers provide a more rational basis for answering questions concerning the processes and outcomes of various types of social programs.

## ASSESSMENT OF CONSUMER BEHAVIOR

Psychological assessment in industrial and organizational contexts contributes to a variety of activities, including the selection of employees, training new employees and retraining old ones, and the continuing appraisal of all employees. The uses of tests to help to make evaluations and decisions concerning workers are among the activities of personnel psychologists, a topic considered in some detail in Chapter 5. Psychological assessment also contributes to the decision-making processes in another business-oriented area—consumer psychology.

*Consumer psychology* is concerned with identifying attitudes, interests, opinions, values, personality traits, and life-styles associated with preferences for and purchases of certain products and services. A particular focus of consumer psychology is *psychographics,* which attempts to describe the characteristic patterns of temperament, cognition, and behavior that differentiate between diverse human components of the marketplace. The results of psychographic research may contribute to segmenting a particular market according to consumer personality and behavioral characteristics and then designing advertising, packaging, and promotional messages and materials that will be appealing and motivating to that market. Two popular approaches in psychographic studies are AIO inventories and VALS (values and life-styles).

*AIO Inventories* consist of statements of the activities, interests, and opinions of specified groups of people. Illustrative of this approach are the following items on an AIO inventory administered to a sample of 18 to 24-year-old men who both drank and drove (Lastovicka et al., 1987):

It seems like no matter what my friends and I do on a weekend, we almost always end up at a bar getting smashed.

A party wouldn't be a party without some liquor.

I've been drunk at least five times this month.

Being drunk is fun.

The chances of an accident or losing a driver's license from drinking and driving are low.

Drinking helps me to have fun and do better with girls.

A few drinks will have no noticeable effect on my coordination and self-control.

*VALS*™2, from SRI International in Menlo Park, California, is based on the dimensional concepts of self-orientation and resources. Consumers are viewed as being motivated by one of three *self-orientations*: principle, status, and action. The choices of *principle-oriented* consumers are guided by abstract, idealized criteria, rather than by feelings, events, or the behaviors or opinions of other people. *Status-oriented* consumers, on the other hand, are interested in products and services that indicate success to their peers. Finally, *action-oriented* consumers are motivated toward social or physical activity, variety, and risk taking.

The *resources* dimension of the VALS 2 system refers to the psychological, physical, demographic, and material means and capacities that are available to consumers. These resources include education, income, self-confidence, health, eagerness to buy, intelligence, and energy level. Resources, which are on a continuum from minimal to abundant, generally decrease in old age, when depression, financial reverses, and physical or psychological impairment are more likely to set in.

The three self-orientations and the minimal to abundant resources dimension of VALS 2 define eight segments of adult behavior and decision making (see Figure 13–1).

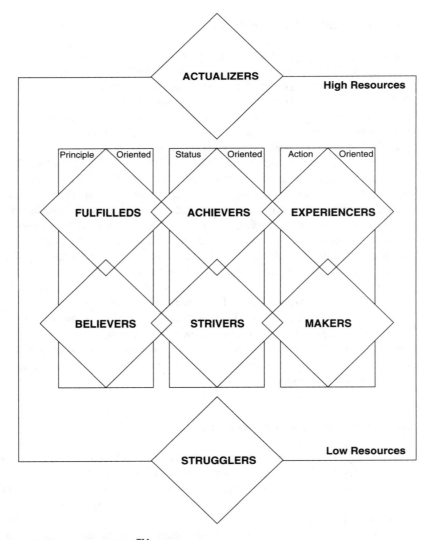

**FIGURE 13–1**    VALS<sup>TM</sup>2 Network.
(*Source:* © 1995 SRI International, VALS<sup>TM</sup>2. All rights reserved. Unauthorized reproduction prohibited.)

Approximately equal proportions of the population are represented by each segment, which is a viable marketing target. *Actualizers,* who have abundant resources and are a combination of the principle, status, and action orientations, are at the top of the VALS 2 hierarchical segmentation system. Of the two segments with the greatest amount of principle orientation, *Fulfilleds* have more abundant resources than *Believers.* Of the two primarily status oriented segments, *Achievers* have more resources than *Strivers.* Of the two primarily action oriented segments, *Experiencers* have more abundant resources than *Makers.* At the bottom of the resources hierarchy are the *Strugglers,* whose lives are constricted and difficult and who are therefore cautious consumers.

## ASSESSMENT IN CLINICAL CONTEXTS

Although clinical psychologists usually spend more time on treatment, consultation, research, teaching, and other activities than on psychological assessment, a substantial majority of clinicians find objective tests such as the MMPI and projective tests such as the Rorschach useful in psychodiagnosis and treatment planning. Clinical assessment for purposes of identifying and diagnosing disorders of behavior and cognition and for planning treatments or other intervention procedures takes place in a variety of settings. These include private offices, mental health clinics, mental hospitals, Veterans Administration medical centers, schools, custodial institutions, and forensic settings. Clinical psychologists are called on to conduct psychological evaluations in mental health settings for purposes of diagnosis, treatment, and residential placement; in medical settings as an aid in evaluating the psychological aspects of illness; in psychotherapeutic settings as an aid in planning and evaluating the effectiveness of psychotherapy and chemotherapy; in educational settings as an aid in formulating proper remediation measures; in legal settings to assist courts in sanity hearings and planning rehabilitation measures; and in various settings to conduct evaluations required by law, such as cases involving state or federal compensation.

Once the need for clinical assessment has been recognized, goals can be set and decisions made concerning the kinds of data needed to attain these goals. The general goals of clinical assessment are to provide an accurate description of the patient's (client's) problem(s), to determine what interpersonal and environmental factors precipitated and are sustaining the problem(s), and to make predictions concerning outcomes with and without intervention. Obtaining the kind of information required in clinical settings often necessitates a thorough case study.

### Mental Status Examination and Clinical Case Study

Clinical psychologists are frequently called on to conduct a *mental status examination* to obtain in-depth information about a person's emotional state (affect and mood), intellectual and perceptual functioning (attention, concentration, memory, intelligence, and judgment), style and content of thought processes and speech, level of insight into mental status and personality problems, and psychomotor activity, as well as the person's general appearance, attitude, and insight into his or her condition. Of course, all this information is not obtained from psychological testing alone. Careful observations and detailed interviews of the person and those who know him or her well are also required. In conducting a thorough case study, information on the client's background and characteristics is obtained from the client and significant other persons, and follow-up data are collected over a period of time. Information on the family, culture, health history, developmental history, educational history, economic history, legal history, and the person's activities and thoughts may all be elicited. After the assessment data have been obtained and integrated, a report summarizing the findings concerning the person's strengths and weaknesses is prepared, and recommendations for clinical, educational, or vocational interventions may be made.

When a case study is conducted to determine the cause(s) of a specific psychological problem, hypotheses or conclusions pertaining to causation may be formulated and specific recommendations made concerning treatment (psychotherapy, drugs or other medical treatment, special education, and so on). A follow-up assessment to evaluate the effectiveness of the prescribed treatment program should also be conducted after an appropriate time interval.

Despite its yield of potentially useful information for constructing an overall picture as well as an in-depth understanding of the individual, a clinical case study has some notable weaknesses. These include the introspective nature of the data (memory is rarely completely accurate), the fact that the person conducting the study is frequently biased in selecting and evaluating certain kinds of data or measurements, and the extent to which the findings are generalizable across situations or circumstances encountered by the person. Employing a variety of assessments in a systematic sample of situations and being aware of the likelihood of bias in selection and evaluation can help reduce, if not eliminate, misinterpretations and overgeneralizations.

## Psychodiagnosis

*Psychodiagnosis* is the process of examining a person from a psychological viewpoint to determine the nature and extent of a mental or behavioral disorder. In the traditional *medical model* of mental disorders, the psychodiagnostician observes, interviews, and tests the patient to determine the presence or absence of certain psychological (and physical) symptoms. The diagnostician then compares the patient's symptoms with standard descriptions of abnormal behavior to determine in which category of disorders the patient best fits. The end result of this process is to give the patient a psychiatric classification, as specified in the *Diagnostic and Statistical Manual of Mental Disorders–IV* (American Psychiatric Association, 1994). In addition to diagnosing the disorder, a *prognosis,* or prediction of probable outcome, is made.

The ability to make accurate psychodiagnoses requires extensive training and experience, and even then the probability of making a mistake is not small. Arkes (1994) describes a number of errors made in psychodiagnosis and other clinical judgments. One source of error is basing clinical judgments on the number of times a certain sign or indicator and a specific disorder have occurred together, but overlooking the fact that they have failed to occur together even more often. Another source of error is the *hindsight bias* of believing that, after an event has already occurred, one could have predicted it if asked to do so. A third source of error in clinical judgments is overconfidence in one's judgments, despite evidence to the contrary. Because of selective perception, selective remembering, insufficient experience, inadequate follow-up, and faulty logic, clinicians make errors in diagnosis.

## Case Conference

A written report is only one way in which the results of a psychometric evaluation are communicated to those who have a legitimate right to know. Clinical-case conferences or consultations in mental health contexts and parent–teacher or parent–counselor conferences in school settings may occur both before and after a psychological evaluation. When conducting a posttest conference with a person who is unsophisticated in psychological terminology, such as a typical parent, the examiner should describe, in language appropriate to the listener, the test results and whatever conclusions can reasonably be drawn from them. In general, qualitative rather than quantitative descriptions and interpretations should be employed. The purpose and nature of the tests, why these particular tests were selected, and the limitations of the tests and results should also be discussed. Descriptive statements, rather than labels, and score ranges that take into account the standard error of measurement, rather than specific scores, should be used. Consultation also involves a discussion of options and decisions for treatment, remediation, rehabilitation, or other intervention and the provision of information on referral sources. Following the consultation, the examiner should send a copy of the examination report to the referral source and other responsible parties.

## Marital and Family Assessment

An estimated 2,362,000 marriages were performed and 1,191,000 divorces were granted in the United States in 1994 (National Center for Health Statistics, 1995). Although these figures show that there were more marriages than divorces, many of the marriages led to separation in a relatively short time. Furthermore, thousands of people have children but are never married, and numerous one-parent families exist. As heard in speeches and discussions in the public forum, it is recognized that a crisis has arisen with regard to the stability of marriages and families in the United States. The consequence of marital and family disruption is that a large percentage of the population lives a rootless existence, devoid of traditional values. These individuals find companionship and tutoring in antisocial models who contribute to crime and perpetuate the cycle of instability, violence, and poverty in their own descendants.

Realizing that marital problems are in many cases family problems that involve not only a husband and a wife but children and other members of the family unit as well, the traditional field of marriage counseling has of necessity been superseded in many instances by family counseling. The family is seen as a dynamic social system in which the intercommunications and other activities of all members of the family contribute to marital discord, intrafamilial conflict, and unstable marriages and families, as well as mutual gratification and happiness. Pathology is typically not limited to a single family member, in that "no person is an island unto himself." The family is a dynamic system in which the problems, difficulties, and unhappiness of each member affect the well-being and functioning of the family as a whole. Just as there are pathological individuals, families may themselves become disturbed and require the services of a trained therapist.

A number of psychological assessment instruments have proved useful in identifying, diagnosing, and making prognoses concerning marital and family problems. Instruments are available for premarital advising, identifying sources and possible solutions for family disagreements and problems, and helping victims of divorce, either parents or children, to pick up the pieces and get on with their lives. Traditional inventories and projectives such as the MMPI, the 16 PF, the Rorschach, and the TAT are frequently administered to analyze marital and family problems. Also available are checklists, such as the Marital Evaluation Checklist, and inventories, such as the Marital Attitude Evaluation, the California Marriage Readiness Evaluation, the Marriage Adjustment Inventory, and the Marital Satisfaction Inventory, as well as special projectives, such as the Family Relations Test: Children's Version and the Family Apperception Test. Another useful psychometric instrument, the Family Environment Scale, was designed to assess the social climate of family systems and how the characteristics of the family interact. This questionnaire can be used to identify family strengths and problems and important issues for family treatment. All these instruments must, of course, be supplemented by sensitive interviewing and observations of couples and family members in face-to-face social interactions.

## ASSESSMENT IN HEALTH AND LEGAL CONTEXTS

Two areas in which there has been an increased demand for psychological services during the past decade are those concerned with health-related and legal matters. Both areas have attracted the attention of research psychologists and other professionals who are interested in developing psychometric instruments for research and applications in these areas. A number of universities have instituted graduate programs in health and legal psychology, and measurement and research pertaining to issues in these areas are extensive.

### Health Psychology

*Health psychology* has been defined as the "educational, scientific, and professional contributions of the discipline of psychology to the promotion and maintenance of health, the prevention and treatment if illness, and the identification of etiological and diagnostic correlates of health, illness, and related dysfunction" (Matarazzo, 1980, page 815). Interest in the role of attitudes, self-efficacy, and other psychological factors or personality variables in health is not limited to so-called psychosomatic disorders, such as duodenal ulcers and migraine headaches, but includes cardiovascular disorders, cancer, and other life-threatening illnesses. Psychologists are called upon not only to identify psychological factors that are related to various medical conditions and to help to diagnose specific disorders, but also to assist in planning intervention or treatments. The field of *behavioral medicine*, a subspecialty of health psychology, has made significant contributions to the treatment and management of patients by behavior modification techniques and other procedures.

Several health-related personality inventories are available for assisting in the formulation of comprehensive treatment plans for adult medical patients. Among these are the Jenkins Activity Survey for identifying coronary-prone Type A personalities, the Eating Disorders Inventory–2 for assessing behavior traits associated with anorexia and bulimia, and the Millon Behavior Health Inventory for assisting in the formulation of comprehensive treatment plans for adult medical patients. The number of commercially available checklists, rating scales, and other questionnaires concerned with health-related matters has increased markedly in recent years. Included among these are instruments designed to identify health problems in general and specific health areas, questionnaires of opinions and beliefs pertaining to health, measures of stress and ways of coping with it, measures of pain perception and control, and measures of anxiety, depression, substance abuse, violence, and suicide potential. As defined by certain instruments, *health* connotes more than just the absence of disease; it means *positive wellness* and a focus on attaining a good *quality of life*.

Among the important topics of research in health psychology are the roles of stress, learned helplessness, depression, information processing, and coping with illness. For example, a sense of helplessness has been found to be an important factor in the coronary-prone personality (Glass & Carver, 1980). According to Dana (1984), a feeling of personal efficacy or confidence that the internal and external environments can be understood and predicted and therefore controlled is the single most important mediator of psychological health. One instrument designed to measure the extent of control or responsibility felt toward one's health is the Health Locus of Control Scale (Wallston, Maides, & Wallston, 1976).

Related to the notion of control is the idea of personal efficacy, which is the opposite of helplessness and has been found to be an important factor in physical health. A number of theoretical models have been devised to assist in understanding the development and consequences of feelings of helplessness and personal efficacy. For example, considerable research on the topic has been stimulated by attribution theory, which seeks to explain how people decide, on the basis of samples of an individual's behavior, what the specific causes of that behavior are (Abramson, Garber, & Seligman, 1980). Two examples of instruments for assessing attributions in the domain of personal health are the Attributional Styles Questionnaire (Peterson et al., 1982) and the Health Attribution Test (by J. Achterberg and G. F. Lawlis, Institute of Personality and Ability Testing, 1988).

Another variable that has played a central role in the field of health psychology is *stress*. Several years ago, Dana (1984) pointed to the need for more comprehensive measurement of life stress, including identification of the specific stressors, reactions to stress, and an inventory of potential mediators of stress. Dana also noted that a workable model of psychological health, good functioning, or human wellness is needed. Available measures based on various definitions of effective functioning, derived from theories of self-actualization, ego development, and psychosocial development, represent a good beginning, but better measures of coping abilities, resistance to stress, and self-efficacy are required. Among the commercially available instruments with the word *stress* in the title are the Daily Stress Inventory and the Parenting Stress Index. Other stress-related instruments are the Coping Resources Inventory and the Hassles and Uplifts Scale. Related to the measurement of stress or stress reactions is the field of *behavioral toxicology*, which is concerned with the assessment of performance under adverse environmental circumstances.

## Legal Psychology

*Legal psychology* is that branch of psychology concerned with matters of law enforcement. Psychologists who are employed in law-enforcement contexts are typically clinicians who possess a wide range of skills and perform a variety of tasks. They may use tests, questionnaires, and interviewing procedures to help select law-enforcement personnel. They may serve as human relations experts and staff developers who give workshops and in other ways train police officers in techniques of intervening in crises such as domestic arguments and hostage taking. They may counsel or conduct group and individual psychotherapy with officers and their families. They may also contribute to the evaluation of staff development programs in law-enforcement contexts and conduct research on the training and treatment of law-enforcement personnel.

Equally important in terms of social significance is the branch of legal psychology known as *forensic psychology*. It is concerned primarily with evaluating defendants in court cases to determine whether they are competent to stand trial and whether they are dangerous and/or likely to be recidivists. In court cases, psychologists may be asked by either the prosecution or the defense to examine the plaintiff for signs of mental disorder, dangerous or violent behavior, incompetency to stand trial or to handle his or her own affairs, inability to serve as a suitable parent in a child custody hearing, or for many other purposes. Among the questions asked of forensic psychologists by legal representatives and officials are the following (Lanyon, 1986):

Is this person insane?

What is the likelihood that this person will engage in dangerous or violent behavior?

Who should assume custody of this child?

Why did this person commit homicide?

What are the personal characteristics of a particular murderer who has not been apprehended?

How can sex offenders be identified from psychological evaluations, and can their future behavior be predicted?

How can one tell whether a particular client will be defensive or honest in testifying?

Not only the defendant but also other persons (witnesses and others) associated with a legal dispute may require examination by a psychologist. The psychologist may be asked for an opinion concerning an unknown or apprehended criminal, whether a child will be better off if placed with one of the parents or with another person, and even how potential jurors are likely to vote. For example, an expert in personality analysis may be called upon to assist in the process of jury selection in criminal or civil trials.

***Competency and Insanity***    The opinions and recommendations of psychologists in matters dealing with the issue of competency (competency to stand trial, civil commitment, understanding of Miranda rights, and related issues) have been increasingly sought in recent years. Competency to stand trial has to do with whether a defendant understands the charges against him or her and can assist in his or her own defense.[2] As stated by the U.S. Supreme Court in *Dusky* v. *United States* (1960), the defendant must possess "sufficient present ability to consult with his lawyers with a reasonable degree of rational . . . [and]

[2]A kind of partial competency—*testamentary capacity*—refers specifically to competency to make a will. An individual who possesses testamentary capacity, which is legally determined, knows the nature and extent of his or her property, that he or she is making a will, and who his or her natural beneficiaries are.

factual understanding of the proceedings against him." This means that usually, but not always, persons who are mentally retarded, psychotic, or suffering from debilitating neurological disorders are considered incompetent to stand trial. Incompetency is, however, not synonymous with *insanity*. Whereas legal insanity pertains to the mental state of the defendant at the time the crime was committed, the condition of incompetency is a continuing one. A person may be found "competent to stand trial" and yet adjudged "not responsible by reason of insanity."

The M'Naughten Rule, the Durham decision, and the Model Penal Code have all influenced legal tests for insanity in the United States (Blau, 1984; *Durham* v. *United States,* 1954; Smith & Meyer, 1987). Although the great majority of states permit insanity pleas, several states have completely abolished such pleas. The standard of legal insanity applied most frequently by the judicial system in the United States is the Model Penal Code proposed by the American Law Institute (ALI) and adopted in 1972. As cited by Smith and Meyer (1987), the ALI definition states that

A person is not responsible for criminal conduct, i.e., [is] insane if, at the time of such conduct, as a result of mental disease or defect, he lacks substantial capacity either to appreciate the criminality (wrongfulness) of his conduct, or to conform his conduct to the requirement of the law (American Law Institute, 1956).

Among the procedures and tools employed by psychologists in assessing competency are interviewing guides and competency screening instruments such as the Georgetown Screening Interview for Competency to Stand Trial (Bukatman, Foy, & De Grazia, 1971), the Competency Screening Test (Lipsitt, Lelos, & McGarry, 1971), the Competency Assessment Instrument (McGarry et al., 1973), and the Georgia Court Competency Test (Wildman et al., 1980). The Rogers Criminal Responsibility Scales (Rogers, 1984, 1986) may be administered to determine criminal responsibility according to the degree of psychological impairment that is significant in determining insanity under the ALI standard. The five scales on this instrument assess Patient Reliability, Organicity, Psychopathology, Cognitive Control, and Behavioral Control at the time of the crime that the patient is alleged to have committed. Neuropsychological tests may also be administered to defendants in insanity pleas.

***MMPI and Rorschach***   Two of the most commonly administered tests in forensic contexts are the MMPI and Rorschach. In addition to its many other applications in jurisprudence, the MMPI contributes to the identification of defensiveness (unwillingness to tell the truth) and provides information pertaining to additional matters of personal behavior that are of concern in court trials. The Rorschach is another workhorse in legal settings, but neither the MMPI nor the Rorschach permits unqualified answers and opinions concerning legal affairs. According to some authorities (for example, Lanyon, 1986), what is required are more question-specific instruments, for example, instruments that can assess the effects of particular brain injuries on criminal behavior. Obviously, psychologists who design and use such instruments should be familiar with the law, as well as being capable test designers and clinicians.

***Sex and Violence***   With respect to sexual offenses, the Clarke Sex History Questionnaire for Males (Langevin, 1983), which reportedly assesses types and strength of sexually anomalous behavior, may be of help to a forensic psychologist.

Although no test has been developed that, by itself, can predict violent behavior, the MMPI can contribute to forecasting dangerous or violent behavior. A number of behavioral indicators, such as a recent history of violence, substance abuse, breakup of a marriage or love relationship, discipline or termination at work, and access to weapons such as guns can also contribute to the prediction of violent behavior (Hall, 1987). A combination of personal history and test data can be used to derive an estimate of the probability of violent behavior. Determining the potential for violent behavior is important, not only in parole hearings and other matters concerning convicted criminals, but also in the selection and promotion of police officers and other peace-keepers.

Violence may be expressed toward adults or children, but in recent years the legal system and society as a whole have become sensitized to allegations of physical abuse of children. In cases of alleged mistreatment of children, observations, interviews, figure drawing tests, and doll play can contribute to the determination or prediction of physical or sexual abuse of children.

***Child Custody*** Child custody evaluations may entail parent interviews focusing on child-rearing practices, as well as administration of tests of intelligence and personality. Measures of parents' knowledge and attitudes concerning child-rearing practices may also contribute to decisions in child custody cases. Gordon and Peck's (1989) Custody Quotient, which yields ratings on 10 parenting factors, can be helpful in this regard.

Evaluation of children in custody cases may involve administration of standardized psychometric instruments such as the Comprehension subtest of the WPPSI–III or WISC–R, storytelling tests, and the Bricklin Perceptual Scales (Bricklin, 1984). The latter instrument focuses on understanding the child's perceptions of his or her parents in four areas: competence, supportiveness, follow-up consistency, and possession of admirable personality traits. It is customary to talk with the child and perhaps employ other techniques (doll play and figure drawings concerning family living situations, sentence-completion tests, and others) to determine whether the child has a preference regarding his or her future living and visitation arrangements. It must be acknowledged, however, that the stated preferences and reports of preschoolers with average or below-average intelligence are frequently not very reliable and are influenced too much by recent events to be taken at face value.

## ENVIRONMENTAL ASSESSMENT

Because situational factors play an important role in determining behavior, combining environmental assessments with measures of ability and personality should improve the prediction of behavior in specific situations. Data obtained on environmental characteristics may also prove useful in comparing different situations. The effect of the situation on the person, however, does not constitute a one-way street. Different people react to the same situation in different ways, and they select and structure situations in terms of their own personalities. The relationship between the person and the environmental context is reciprocally interactive, or *transactive,* with the person both affecting and being affected by the environment.

Situations may exert either a weak or a strong influence on the behavior of a person. An example of a strong situation is a religious service, in which expected behaviors are clearly prescribed. Another strong situation is when a person is in a different culture or social group and does not know quite how to behave: the uncertainty is usually resolved by observing and modeling the behavior of other people in that situation.

A weak situation is one in which the physical and social environments have relatively small effects on a person's behavior. For example, when a person is at home with close relatives or partying with two or three close friends, a greater range of behaviors is acceptable. In such circumstances, personal or individual characteristics play a more important role than environmental ones in determining behavior.

Efforts to construct more effective measures of personality might be more successful if they began with a conceptual model of how personality dispositions and environmental (situational) variables interact. Then measures of both sets of variables could be developed to permit a true interactional assessment (McReynolds, 1979). Certainly, some situations fit or match particular personalities better than others, and effective person–situation measures must assess the extent of the congruence. In any event, the development of valid measures of person–situation interaction requires the combined efforts of specialists in psychometrics and environmental psychology.

Psychologists are only on the threshold of devising techniques for analyzing and assessing the dynamic, two-way interactions between persons and environments. However, the work of Rudolf Moos and his associates (Moos, 1976, 1979; Moos & Moos, 1986) on environmental assessment is indicative of how social environments may be conceptualized and evaluated and how the degree of congruence between actual and preferred environments might be measured.

Recognizing that the ways in which people perceive environments affect their behaviors in those environments and that the environments are, in turn, influenced by personal perceptions, Moos directed his efforts toward understanding and assessing human milieus. His assessments of the "personalities" of social environments and their influences on individual functioning may be described in terms of three broad dimensions: (1) the nature and intensity of personal relationships, (2) personal growth and self-enhancement influences, and (3) system maintenance and change. In general, people are more satisfied and comfortable, less irritable and depressed, and experience greater self-esteem in environments that they perceive as highly relationship oriented.

Moos maintains that an analysis of environments in terms of these three dimensions can lead to the formulation of criteria for an ideal environment and optimal methods for instituting environmental changes. To provide a means for assessing these dimensions, he constructed a number of Social Climate Scales. Each scale consists of 90 to 100 items and yields 7 to 10 scores covering the three dimensions. Based on the assumption that people can distinguish different dimensions of social environments, the items on each scale are answerable in 15 to 20 minutes by persons who are functioning in or cognizant of the particular social environment.

Measures of the following social environments were devised by Moos and his collaborators: classroom, community-oriented programs, correctional institutions, family, group, military, university residence, ward atmosphere, and work. Different forms of these instruments (Social Climate Scales) measure perceptions of the actual social environment (Form R), perceptions of the ideal social environment (Form I), and the expectations of a person regarding a particular social environment (Form E); short forms (Form S) requiring 5 to 10 minutes to complete are also available. A number of other measures of the characteristics of particular social environments are available. Among these are the Environmental Response Inventory, the Classroom Environmental Index, the College Characteristics Index, the Elementary and Secondary School Index, the High School Characteristics Index, the Organizational Climate Index, and the Effective School Battery. Unfortunately, none of these instruments is based on a satisfactory taxonomy of situations relevant to persons. Such a taxonomy would undoubtedly contribute to the design of better measures of situational variance, which might be combined with measures of personality to predict individual and group behavior.

## SUMMARY

This chapter is an overview of the applications of psychological assessment in educational, industrial and organizational, clinical, health, legal, and environmental contexts. In educational situations, achievement tests are used to determine the extent to which students have attained the objectives of instruction, to diagnose students' strengths and weaknesses in the subject matter, and to evaluate teachers and educational programs. Diagnostic testing for educational purposes may involve neuropsychological evaluation of handicapped children, including children with sensorimotor and learning disabilities. A variety of psychometric devices, including perceptual-motor tests, memory–learning tests, and neuropsychological test batteries, are used in diagnosing neuropsychological disorders. Batteries of tests are also administered to diagnose learning disabilities stemming from other conditions.

Requiring students to pass a minimum competency test before being awarded a high school diploma and requiring teachers to pass a professional competency test before being hired or retained are common practices in the United States. Some colleges and universities have also implemented a value-added approach to the assessment of changes in knowledge and skills during the undergraduate years. Finally, tests and related instruments are used extensively to evaluate educational programs or curricula and to determine the effectiveness of other intervention procedures and programs.

Consumer psychology is concerned with the marketing of goods and services and, in particular, the identification of consumer characteristics for purposes of market segmentation. AIO and VALS 2 are approaches used in marketing according to the personality characteristics of potential customers.

Clinical psychologists administer tests and other psychometric instruments for screening, psychodiagnosis, treatment planning, and research in mental health clinics and other settings. Of particular importance are mental status examinations, which assess the intellectual, perceptual-motor, and emotional status of patients by means of in-depth interviews, questionnaires, rating scales, and related psychometric procedures. After a psychodiagnostic examination of a person has been completed, a clinical case conference is held to explain the results to family members and others who have a right to know.

Both health psychologists and legal psychologists are trained to perform a variety of tasks in medical or law-enforcement contexts. Health psychologists analyze the role of psychological factors in physical illness and assist in planning and implementing prescribed treatments for such conditions. Among the many activities of legal or forensic psychologists are the psychological evaluation of offenders and other parties in judicial cases concerned with questions of competency to stand trial, responsibility for criminal acts, and the custody of minors.

Environmental assessment is concerned with analyzing the psychological environments of people and determining how a person's environment affects his or her sense of well-being and functioning. Particularly noteworthy among various environmental assessment instruments are Moos's Social Climate Scales.

## QUESTIONS AND ACTIVITIES

1. List arguments for and against competency testing of (a) high school students, (b) prospective school teachers, and (c) experienced teachers.

2. Consult the yellow pages of several large city telephone directories, which can be found in most college or university libraries, for advertisements about psychological services. Look under various headings, including "psychologists," "psychiatrists," "psychotherapists," "physicians," "counselors," "therapists," "marriage counselors," "education," "clinics," or any other headings that occur to you as relevant. What information is given to assist people who require such services? In addition to telephone directories, the County Medical Society, the Mental Health Center, and other local organizations may provide you with a list of psychological service providers.

3. Differentiate between the legal concepts of competency and insanity. What psychological assessment instruments or techniques can contribute to decisions concerning competency and insanity?

4. List 12 different roles that psychologists may perform in law-enforcement settings. Which of these are most useful and valid?

5. Many articles and programs in the media have dealt with the problem of child abuse and procedures for detecting and confirming its existence in particular cases. What are some of the techniques used by psychologists to determine if a child has been abused? How valid are these techniques, and what are their dangers and other shortcomings?

6. How successful has the use of psychology been in the marketing mix (advertising and selling)? What ethical problems might arise in using psychology and psychologists to identify particular markets for products and services and to induce people to purchase them?

# 14

# CRITICISMS AND ISSUES IN TESTING

As witnessed by the number and variety of instruments described in the preceding chapters, the field of psychological assessment has expanded rapidly during this century. The widespread administration of group tests of achievement, intelligence, and special abilities in education, business, and government has contributed to the growth of psychological assessment. However, organized labor, maintaining that occupational selection and promotion should be based on experience and seniority rather than measured abilities, has typically been unsupportive of testing. Opposition to standardized testing in educational contexts, in particular the use of college entrance examinations and intelligence testing in the schools, has also been outspoken.

## NATURE AND CONSEQUENCES OF CRITICISMS OF TESTING

The bulk of criticism of psychological and educational testing during the past several decades has been concerned with either the content and applications of tests or the social consequences of relying on test scores to make decisions about people. Testing in general has been attacked on the one hand for invasion of the right to privacy and, on the other hand, for its secretiveness or confidentiality. Ability tests in particular have been faulted for limitations and bias in what they purport to measure. Perhaps because their applications are less extensive and less crucial, personality assessment instruments have not been attacked as much by the general public. The relatively poor measurement characteristics of many personality tests, however, have not escaped scrutiny by psychologists and nonpsychologists alike. Among the nonpsychologists who have denounced personality testing are certain writers and parents who object to particular questions or approaches used in the assessment of personal characteristics, attitudes, and behavior.

With respect to their applications, it has been argued that, rather than fostering equality of opportunity, tests have led to maintenance of the status quo and a legitimizing of undemocratic practices by educational institutions, business organizations, and government. More specifically, it has been claimed that tests are often useless as predictors of behavior, that they are unfair to minority groups, that the results are frequently misinterpreted and misused, and that they promote a narrow and rigid classification of people according to supposedly static characteristics.

Criticisms of psychological and educational testing have frequently created more heat than light, although some of the concerns have stimulated a reevaluation of testing practices. Certain criticisms have led to changes of a technical nature, whereas others have prompted a reexamination of the ethics of testing and proposals for an ethical code that would apply to the publishers, distributors, and users of tests.

Legal and ethical issues concerned with the administration of psychological tests and the use of test results were discussed briefly in Chapter 1. As noted there, according to the Family Rights and Privacy Act, test scores and interpretations kept by educational institutions may be made available to other people only with the *informed consent* of the student or an adult who is legally responsible for the former. Even when informed consent has been granted, test information may be *privileged* in that only certain persons (parents, personal attorney, physician, psychologist, and others) have the right of access to the results.

The concept of privileged communication also applies to both test and nontest information. Privileged communication is, however, an all or none affair: a psychologist who is authorized by a client to reveal specific information pertaining to a case must reveal all available information that is relevant to the case when requested by the court. Furthermore, whenever a psychologist feels that a client represents a clear and present danger to himself, herself, or others, this information can be released to responsible persons without the client's consent. In fact, because the good of society as a whole supersedes the individual's right to privacy and privileged communication, a psychologist may be legally obligated to reveal this information (see *Tarasoff* v. *Regents of University of California,* 1983).

Whether the administration of psychological tests represents a serious invasion of privacy has been debated at length. Some authorities (for example, Marland, 1969) have maintained that if the responses to test questions are of sufficient social value then people may have to endure some invasion of privacy. As important as respect for individual rights concerning confidentiality of test scores and invasion of privacy may be, these rights must be balanced against the need for evaluative information of high quality.

Ideally, the results of psychological assessments are treated conscientiously and with an awareness of the limitations of the instruments and the needs and rights of examinees. Unfortunately, the ethical standards of psychological examiners are not always as high as they should be. An awareness of this problem led the American Psychological Association and other professional organizations to adopt codes of ethics pertaining to testing and to impose sanctions against the violation of these codes (American Psychological Association, 1981, 1992; American Educational Research Association et al., 1985). This represents a step forward in psychological assessment and the practice of psychology in general.

## COLLEGE ENTRANCE EXAMINATIONS

Large-scale testing programs, in which tests are administered to thousands of students each year, have been the special targets of criticism during the past four decades. It has been said, for example, that too much school time is spent administering tests that measure only a few of the variables pertinent to academic achievement and other accomplishments. Of all large-scale testing programs, the most influential and most often attacked are those involving college and university entrance examinations. The Scholastic Assessment Test (SAT), the American College Tests (ACT), and various other instruments fall in this category, but of these it is the SAT that has been the target of the most unrelenting criticism.

It has been alleged that college admissions officers assign too much weight to SAT scores and not enough weight to interview data as indicators of creativity or exceptionality. As revealed by the results of a study by Willingham & Breland (1982), there appears to be some truth in this allegation: this study found that three times as much weight was given to high school grades and SAT scores as to personal qualities or extracurricular accomplishments.

Other research indicates that letters of recommendation do not carry as much weight in admissions as might be expected (Ravitch, 1983–1984). Due to lack of confidentiality or a concern about it and a strong interest on the part of the letter writer in having the applicant accepted, almost all such letters tend to be laudatory. For this reason, it has been said that "One telephone call is worth a dozen letters of recommendation." The same leniency error, in addition to variability in grading standards from school to school, affects the accuracy of high school grades as predictors of performance in college. Personal interviews continue to be of some value in admissions, but they are also limited by the prejudices of the inter- viewer and the ability of applicants to present themselves effectively.

Despite the fact that few colleges require the submission of SAT scores with an appli- cation, the great majority of undergraduate institutions have retained either the SAT or the ACT for admissions and placement purposes. Scores on these tests can also serve as an early warning system and as diagnostic guides for remedial work. The SAT is one of the most carefully designed of all available tests, having high reliability and substantial valid- ity for predicting college grades. These features, however, have not protected the SAT from the rash of criticism to which it has been subjected since the 1950s.

## Multiple-choice Tests

During the 1960s, there were many critics of college entrance examinations and other nationally administered educational tests (for example, Black, 1962; Hoffman, 1962). Of these critics, the most vocal and influential was Banesh Hoffman, who argued that multi- ple-choice tests (1) favor shrewd, nimble-witted, rapid readers; (2) penalize subtle, creative, more profound persons; (3) are concerned only with the answer and not with the quality of thought behind it or the skill with which it is expressed; and (4) have a generally bad effect on education and the recognition of merit. These allegations, however, relied mainly on hypothetical examples and emotionally loaded arguments rather than solid evidence.

Hoffman's criticisms and those of other writers did not go unchallenged. After exam- ining the basic assumptions of various critics of educational testing, Dunnette (1963) con- cluded that most of the assumptions were erroneous and fallacious and due either to a lack of information or a refusal to recognize that tests are the most accurate means available for identifying merit. Other authorities (for example, Chauncey & Dobbin, 1963) admitted that tests have limitations but that, when properly used, they can help improve instruction.

Attacks on standardized tests did not disappear with the 1960s, nor were they limited to nonpsychologists. For example, McClelland (1973) argued for discontinuing the use of all multiple-choice tests. He felt that it was preferable to develop other measures, such as those for assessing the capacity to learn quickly, rather than continuing to use measures of what a person already knows as a way of demonstrating his or her capabilities.

One criticism of multiple-choice tests that is difficult to prove or disprove, but which has wide educational and social implications, is that such tests are not only poor measures of ability and achievement, but that they also encourage inferior teaching and improper study habits. For this reason, a report by the National Assessment of Educational Progress that standardized tests requiring brief answers are a significant factor in the superficiality of students' reading skills demanded attention. The report called for teachers to be wary of excessive reliance on objective tests and to reinstate the traditional essay examination, which requires students to explain and support their answers (David, 1981). The effective use of essay items demands that scorers evaluate not only the content of answers, but also the style or skill with which answers are expressed. Writing out an answer to a question does not improve the ability to express oneself in writing unless constructive feedback on the form as well as the content of the answer is provided.

The criticism that multiple-choice tests provide only a glimpse of a student's knowledge at a superficial level and fail to reveal what the student can do with that knowledge has prompted a movement toward *performance-based testing,* or *authentic assessment,* in the public schools. Consisting of open-ended questions and hands-on problem solving in mathematics, science, and certain other subject-matter areas, performance-based tests stress reasoning, analysis, and writing. On such tests, students earn credit not only by obtaining the right answer, but also by demonstrating how they arrived at the answer. Students may also be required to work in small groups, conducting experiments and sharing interpretations of results or producing something through collective efforts. Despite enthusiasm for the new tests, the issues of validity, fairness, cost–benefit ratio, and scoring reliability with respect to performance-based testing remain to be resolved (Educational Testing Service, 1992).

## Nader–Nairn Criticisms of ETS

The most publicized campaign against standardized tests, and college and university entrance examinations in particular, during the 1980s was directed by consumer advocate Ralph Nader and his "raiders." In speeches and written reports, Nader criticized the SAT, the GRE, the LSAT, and other standardized tests of ability for not measuring imagination, idealism, determination, and other human attributes that he considered important for the advancement of civilization. Nader maintained that the use of these tests has resulted in the restriction of students' career choices and misallocation of a great deal of professional talent.

Allan Nairn (1980), an associate of Nader, alleged that scores on the SAT and other ETS tests rank people by social class rather than aptitude, a fact that Nairn accused ETS of trying to suppress. The result, Nairn argued, is the denial of educational opportunities to lower-class students and hence preservation of the status quo in higher education. Nairn also concluded that the SAT is a poor predictor of college grades and should be abandoned in favor of various diagnostic measures of skill and competency. He called for a full disclosure of the questions and answers to the SAT and an admission that the test does not measure any construct so general as "scholastic aptitude."

ETS responded at length to the Nader–Nairn attack (Educational Testing Service, 1980a, 1980b), concluding that tests do not deny opportunities to children of poor and working-class families and that the SAT in particular is not a poor predictor of academic performance. ETS officials admitted that no test is a perfect predictor of either academic or life success nor is it a measure of a person's value or worth. The SAT and other scholastic ability tests were never intended to measure innate ability, but rather to assess skills learned in a wide range of school-type activities.

The Nader–Nairn attack on ETS has been extended and expanded by the National Center for Fair and Open Testing (FairTest), a testing watchdog organization in Cambridge, Massachusetts. FairTest maintains that SAT items are often biased and unfair toward minority groups and women and, consequently, that the tests deprive these groups of equal educational opportunities. Another concern of FairTest is that it is unethical to require students to take experimental sections on the SAT, the GRE, and other ETS tests consisting of items that are not scored but are used for tryout purposes. It called on ETS to obtain examinees' consent before having them complete experimental sections of the SAT. FairTest's "Bill of Rights" also emphasizes that test takers have a right to receive sound test-taking information and tips on test-taking strategies, accurately timed tests administered under quiet conditions, privacy of scores and other personal data, due process for any challenge to the test, and access to data concerning the test's accuracy (Weiss, Beckwith, & Schaeffer, 1989).

Students and their parents have a legal right in most states to information regarding performance on psychological or educational tests, but this does not necessarily mean that actual scores should be reported. Rather, test results should be communicated in such a way that they are not misunderstood or misused and to assist rather than hinder examinees. This caution applies primarily to tests administered to children for diagnostic purposes in clinical or educational contexts. On the other hand, scores on college entrance examinations are routinely reported to the test takers, as well as to institutions to which students indicate that their scores should be sent. In addition, New York State's truth-in-testing law requires that students who take the SAT or other college admissions tests be given copies of the actual questions and correct answers, as well as copies of their own answer sheets, within a reasonable period of time after taking the test. Two other provisions of the New York State law, which was enacted in 1979, are that (1) test takers must be told at the time of application how their scores will be computed, what the tester's contractual obligation to them is, and how scores on the test are affected by coaching and various demographic factors; and (2) the test contractor must file information on and studies of the test's validity with the state commission on education. The law also requires that complete editions of the tests be published so that students can practice taking them.

Critics of testing wish to expand the full-disclosure provisions of the New York law to other states and to include other examinations, to encourage the use of novel tests to lessen cultural bias, and to make the testing industry more accountable to consumers. Although over 24 state legislatures, in addition to the federal government (H.R. 3564 and H.R. 4949), have considered laws similar to the one in New York State, the only other state to enact a special statute regulating college entrance examinations is California. This law, referred to as the Dunlop Act, requires only that representative samples of tests be provided to the California State Department of Education. State legislatures in both New York and California have considered additional legislation to tighten regulations pertaining to testing, but only in New York have those efforts met with success.

The New York State statute and other pending truth-in-testing legislation affect not only the SAT, the ACT, and other undergraduate admissions tests, but also tests for admission to graduate and professional schools. Although the Law School Admission Council and the Graduate Management Admission Council approved disclosure of the results of their tests (LSAT and GMAT), the American Association of Medical Colleges and the American Dental Association expressed strong opposition to truth-in-testing legislation. The former organization, arguing that the New York law violates the copyright on the

MCAT, obtained an injunction in 1979 against implementation of the law. In 1990, a federal court found that the New York State statute, which requires publication of materials from the Medical College Admission Test, violates federal copyright law. Despite this ruling, disclosure of test materials continues to be standard practice by testing organizations. Current procedures designed to ensure fair and open testing are an accepted part of test construction, administration, and scoring at Educational Testing Service, the American College Testing Program, and other organizations that design and market tests.[1]

Concern over truth-in-testing legislation led to improvements in monitoring test questions for cultural or socioeconomic bias. Careful internal review by the ETS professional staff has eliminated bias (ethnic group, gender, and so on) from almost all of the 50,000 or so items included on ETS tests each year. Furthermore, the College Entrance Examination Board has adopted a policy of letting students verify their SAT scores and of public disclosure of SAT items 1 year after the tests have been administered. Test takers can challenge items on the SAT and other ETS tests and how those examinations are administered.

## Effects of Coaching on Test Scores

Prospective applicants to undergraduate or graduate colleges and professional schools are understandably interested in improving their scores on qualifying examinations. A result of the increasing importance of large-scale nationwide testing has been the publication of coaching booklets and the establishment of schools that purport to increase a person's score on a particular test or standardized tests in general. Whether coaching has a significant effect on scores on the SAT and other entrance examinations has been a topic of discussion for many years. It is an important issue, for if it were demonstrated that coaching can improve test scores, then young people who could not afford it would be deprived of the same opportunity as their more affluent peers.

The results of earlier studies on coaching had indicated that its effects are quite variable, depending on the similarity of the coached material to the test material, the examinee's level of motivation and education, and other factors. Evidence concerning the effects of coaching on the SAT was reported some years ago by the College Entrance Examination Board (1971). The findings indicated that short-term, intensive drill on items similar to those on the SAT did not lead to significant gains in scores, especially on the verbal section of the test. However, this conclusion was questioned by a number of people, in particular Stanley H. Kaplan, director of the largest test-coaching organization in the world. In 1979, the Federal Trade Commission (FTC) released a report of a study of the effects of a 10-week coaching program in three of the Kaplan Educational Centers. Admitting that the study had certain methodological flaws, the FTC nevertheless concluded that performance on both the verbal and mathematical portions of the SAT could be improved by coaching courses.

---

[1]With respect to disclosure of psychological test information in court, the 1991 Illinois Confidential Act states that "psychological test materials whose disclosure would compromise the objectivity or fairness of the testing process may not be disclosed to anyone including the subject of the test and is not subject to disclosure in any administrative, judicial or legislative proceeding. However, any recipient who has been the subject of the psychological test shall have the right to have all records relating to that test disclosed to any psychologist designated by the recipient" (*APA Monitor*, February, 1991, page 22).

The FTC study and a review of the results by Slack and Porter (1980) were subsequently evaluated by Educational Testing Service. Reanalyzing the data from the FTC investigation, ETS obtained similar findings: inconsistent and negligible effects of coaching for students at two of the Kaplan schools and increases of 20 to 35 points for both verbal and mathematical scores at a third school. Acknowledging that significant increases in test scores may occur when coaching programs involve many hours of course work and assignments, ETS nevertheless maintained that at least part of the gains found at the third school could be attributed to differences in motivation and other personal characteristics. Getting only two or three more items correct could increase the verbal or math scores as much as 20 to 35 points.

Summaries of studies conducted during the past two decades on the effects of coaching on SAT scores reveal that gains of 15 to 25 points on both the verbal and mathematical sections are typical. Improvements occur mainly on items with complex or confusing formats (Powers, 1986). In general, however, claims by the Princeton Review (Biemiller, 1986) and other organizations of SAT increases of 100 points or more are unwarranted (Powers, 1993).

Scores on college entrance examinations usually improve somewhat with student growth and familiarity with the tests. In particular, taking rigorous academic courses and brushing up on algebra, geometry, and word meanings just before the test can enhance scores. With respect to test-taking procedures, skipping difficult items and coming back to them after completing the rest of the items in that section, looking for "reasonable" answers on items containing long reading passages, making informed guesses, and the like, will not work wonders but may improve scores somewhat (see the suggestions for test taking on page 55).

The latest version of the SAT, SAT I, is reportedly even less susceptible to coaching than its predecessor because of the greater emphasis placed on the interpretation of long passages. The omission of the Antonyms subtest, scores on which can be improved by simple memorization of words and a knowledge of word associations, has also reduced the effects of coaching. Analogies, sentence completions, and long reading passages to be interpreted have been retained, but these tasks require not only word knowledge (vocabulary), but also reasoning abilities that are more difficult to improve by crash coaching.

## Annual Changes in SAT Scores

Test scores are not fixed, unvarying numbers: they are subject to errors of measurement and to genuine changes in abilities and other personal characteristics. School officials are usually alert to annual changes in test scores, and decisions concerning individual instruction, curriculum modifications, and allocation of public funds for instruction are made on the basis of the observed changes. Of particular concern are declines in aptitude and achievement test scores.

During the 1970s, it became increasingly obvious that mean scores on the SAT and other standardized tests of cognitive abilities that were being administered to high school students throughout the United States were declining each year. Although increases in mean SAT scores occurred during the 1950s and 1960s, the mean SAT–Verbal score decreased from 478 in 1963 to 460 in 1970 and 423 in 1980. The decrease on the SAT–M was not quite as large as that on the SAT–V score, but still significant—from a mean of 502 in 1963 to 488 in 1970 and 467 in 1980 (see Figure 14–1). Declines occurred for both sexes, for all ethnic groups, and for both higher- and lower-ability students. Although the total number of students taking the SAT fell only 3 percent from 1972 to 1982, there was a 45 percent reduction in the number of students who scored above 650 on the SAT–V and a 23 percent reduction in the number scoring above 650 on the SAT–M. Similar downward trends occurred in mean scores on the ACT, the Minnesota Scholastic Aptitude Test, the Iowa Tests of Educational Development, and the Comprehensive Test of Basic Skills.

Various explanations have been given for the decline in test scores during the late 1960s and 1970s: less parental attention, concern for, and supervision of children; students not motivated to do well; too much television viewing; society becoming too permissive; and teachers providing less attention to students (Elam, 1978). Other explanations included drugs, sex, lack of economic incentives for obtaining a good education, and spacing of children within families (see Zajonc, 1986).

In a comprehensive review of declines in ability test scores, a special advisory panel failed to find any evidence that they were caused by more difficult tests (Austin & Garber, 1982). Approximately half of the overall declines in scores from 1963 to 1977 were interpreted as being caused by changes in the composition of the sample of students taking the tests. But changes in the economic, ethnic, sex, and social class composition of those who took the SAT had already expressed their effects by 1970. Further test-score declines during the 1970s were, according to the advisory panel, caused by more pervasive social forces. Precisely what these forces were and how much influence each had were not clear, but factors such as less intellectually demanding high school curricula, diminishing educa-

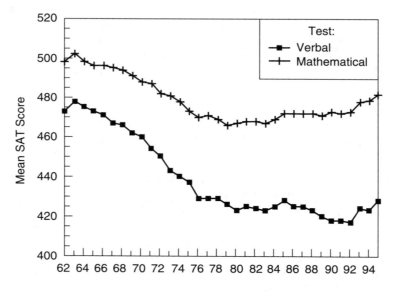

**FIGURE 14–1** Changes in Mean SAT Scores from 1962 through 1995.
(Data from College Entrance Examination Board.)

tional standards, lower abilities of teachers, changes in the role and social structure of U.S. families, television, national disruption during the early 1970s, and lower student motivation were cited. The decline in SAT scores, which for all intents and purposes appeared to have stopped by the mid-1980s, was one of the factors leading to a national debate concerning educational policies.

## Demographic Differences

***Gender***   Over the years, males have consistently outscored females on the SAT–M, but until 1972 females outscored males on the SAT–V; in 1995, the mean score for males (503) was 40 points higher than that for women (463) on the SAT–M and 3 points higher (429 for males, 426 for females) on the SAT–V. These scores were slightly higher than those for 1994, but not significantly so. On the average, males also score slightly higher than females on the ACT (see Figure 14–2). These are overall differences, however, and are not the same for all ethnic groups. For example, black females scored higher than black males on the SAT–V in 1994.

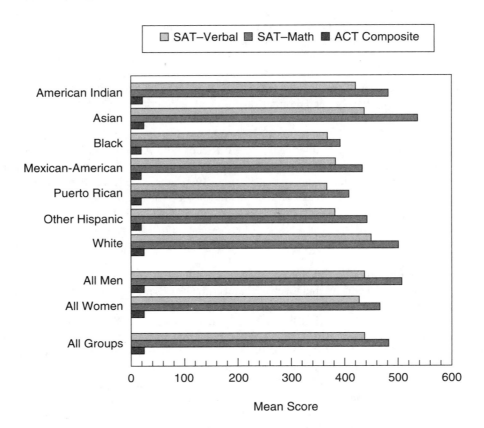

**FIGURE 14–2**   Mean SAT and ACT Scores by Ethnic Group and Gender in 1995. (Data provided by Educational Testing Service and American College Testing Program.)

Critics have long charged that the SAT underestimates the college grades of women and is therefore biased against them (Shea, 1994). According to Bob Schaeffer of FairTest (Chavez, 1993, page A23),

The very nature of the SAT, a fast-paced, high-pressure, multiple-choice test with a high premium on guessing, is a game in which boys excel. Who knows what the cultural or biological reasons are, but girls are more inclined to try and think through a problem, weigh all the options. And that puts them at a strategic disadvantage.

As a result of the gender gap in SATs, it has been alleged that young women are less likely than young men to be awarded college scholarships. ETS officials countered that the differences between the average SAT scores of men and women reflect genuine educational differences and that the predictive validity of the test is as high for one sex as the other. In any event, in most states college scholarships are not awarded on the basis of SAT scores alone, but include other criteria, such as grade-point average and performance in other activities.

The causes of gender differences in SATs, which are the reverse of the differences in high school and college freshman year grade-point averages, are not entirely clear. Authorities are uncertain whether to blame the tests, the schools, biological factors, or other environmental variables. One possible factor is that, on the average, the socioeconomic status of girls who took the SAT in the 1980s was lower than that of boys. Another hypothesis is that during the 1980s teenage girls were more worried about dating and possible pregnancies and less committed to schoolwork than they had been in the 1970s (Cordes, 1986). Whatever, the causes of sex differences in SAT scores may be, they appear to be declining: since 1987 women have gained 6 points on men on both sections of the SAT (Shea, 1994).

**Ethnicity**  For the past decade, the relative standings of Asian-Americans, African-Americans, Mexican-Americans, Puerto Ricans, and Anglo-Americans on the SAT have remained fairly constant. As shown in Figure 14–2, except for the scores of Asians on the SAT–M in 1995, the mean scores of minority groups were lower than those of whites on both the SAT–M and SAT–V. The mean scores of blacks were approximately 100 points lower than those of whites on the SAT–V and SAT–M in that year. Critics charge that the black–white difference is a result of the SAT being biased against blacks, but similar rankings of blacks, Hispanics, and whites have been obtained on the reading, mathematics, and science tests of the National Assessment of Educational Progress. The lower mean SAT scores for minorities are undoubtedly due, at least in part, to lower family incomes and lower parental educational levels. Whatever the causes may be, the test scores of blacks and Hispanics have increased slightly in recent years.

Related to, but obviously not specific to, the issue of ethnic group differences in scores on college admissions tests is the requirement that student athletes make a minimum total score of 700 on the SAT or 17 on the ACT and a minimum grade-point average of 2.0. This requirement, which was enacted as Proposition 48 by the NCAA in 1983, was modified in 1992 to a minimum GPA of 2.5. The higher required GPA was phased in over a 5-year period, and reduced to as low as 2.0 for students whose SAT or ACT scores are higher than those required by Proposition 48. Some opponents of the revised requirements mandated by the NCAA have described them as discriminatory against minorities, but most representatives of colleges in Division I of the NCAA felt that student athletes can meet the requirements (Robbins & Almond, 1992).

***Area of Residence*** Students from large cities who took the SAT in 1994 averaged approximately 12 points lower than the national mean on the verbal and 10 points lower than the mean on the mathematical portions of the SAT. In contrast, the mean verbal scores of suburban students were approximately 17 points higher and their mean mathematical scores approximately 20 points higher than the national average (Chavez, 1993). These urban–suburban differences are, of course, confounded with socioeconomic status and ethnicity.

For some years, the U.S. Department of Education has used SAT scores in annual state-by-state comparisons of educational quality. But because of the differing percentages of students in each state who take the SAT, such comparisons are subject to misinterpretation. For example, only 4 percent of high school seniors in Mississippi took the SAT in 1989, on which they obtained a mean total score of 1001. But Mississippi's schools rank close to last among the states on various criteria. In that same year, the 67 percent of high school seniors in New Jersey who took the SAT made a mean total SAT score of 894. ETS has cautioned that, because of differences in the percentages of students from various states who take the SAT, not much can be made of state-by-state comparisons of mean scores. A much fairer state-by-state comparison can be made with the NAEP scores, but there are also serious problems in interpreting the differences in mean scores on the NAEP tests.

Despite the many criticisms and the recognized limitations of the SAT, it is an objective, rigorous measure of cognitive ability that can be used in conjunction with grades and other more subjective evaluations of performance. Because of grade inflation and the uncertain meanings of other performance criteria, over three-fourths of 4-year colleges in the United States continue to use the test for admissions purposes. Over a million students took the SAT in 1995, a number that tends to increase every year (College Bound Seniors, 1995). Because it appears that the SAT will be with us for some time, psychologists and educators should continue to evaluate the test and the effects of using it.

## OTHER ISSUES IN EDUCATIONAL TESTING

Although matters pertaining to the SAT and other national testing programs have received more attention in the media, a number of other issues concerning testing in and for the schools are noteworthy. Among these are requiring students to pass a minimum competency test in order to graduate from high school and requiring prospective teachers to pass a test of professional knowledge and skills to receive a license or credential. These two topics were considered in some detail in Chapter 13, but a few additional points should be made about testing teachers.

Currently, almost all states require some form of standardized testing of would-be teachers and somewhat over half require students to pass tests to earn a certain score on a standardized test before they can major in education. Unfortunately, the failure rate on these tests, especially among minorities, is high. In addition, the validity of many of the tests as measures of the knowledge and skills important to teaching has been questioned. The majority of the tests contain not only questions pertaining to professional competence, but also items to assess general academic knowledge and communication skills. Such is the case with the National Teacher Examinations (NTE), the most popular of the teacher tests. The NTE in particular has been criticized for some years, and a successor to this examination was introduced by Educational Testing Service in 1992. Unlike its predecessor, the new test does not rely exclusively on multiple-choice items; it also includes computer simulation, interactive video, and classroom observation. It is hoped that the new version of the NTE will be more effective and more acceptable than the old one, but it is undoubtedly overly optimistic to expect any test to be exempt from criticism. People will continue to complain about competency or selection tests on which they or their relatives and friends do not do as well as expected and that they view as inadequate indicators of job performance.

## Cheating on Tests

As test scores have become more important not only in determining the future educational and professional careers of individuals, but also in the political arena for assessing schools and other institutions, the temptation to cheat appears to have increased. Administration of *secure* tests involves standard procedures, such as verifying personal identification, seating examinees in a certain way, careful proctoring, and counting tests and answer sheets to minimize cheating, but none of these procedures entirely eliminates cheating. Pressures from parents, teachers, peers, and themselves to do well may lead students to steal copies of tests, copy answers from other students, and cheat in other ways.

In addition to directly observing cheating on tests or being told by other people that specific students cheated, circumstantial evidence of cheating may be obtained by observing (1) similar patterns of wrong answers by students who sat close to each other during the test and (2) very large numbers of erasures on answer sheets, primarily from changing wrong answers to right ones. The last technique was used in California during the mid-1980s to confirm suspicions that dramatic increases in test scores in some schools were caused by teachers themselves altering students' answers to items on the California Assessment Program (CAP) tests. The answer sheets from the CAP tests, which measured basic skills in reading, writing, and mathematics and were administered annually in the third, sixth, eighth, and twelfth grades of California public schools, were scored by electronic data scanners. The scanners not only scored the answer sheets but also counted erasures. Using this procedure in combination with confirmatory clerical work, it was found that in several dozen Los Angeles schools the percentage of erasures on the answer sheets was significantly higher than the expected 3 percent. Although the resulting furor and associated media coverage precipitated strong protests by the teachers' union and refusals by some teachers to handle the CAP tests, these events led to an investigation of both direct and indirect cheating and tampering with the CAP and CTBS tests.

Tampering by teachers with students' answer sheets could not be convincingly denied, but why did they do it? The general answer to this question seems to be that test scores have come to be used so extensively in U.S. society—not only to evaluate individuals, but also schools, school districts, stages, and even neighborhoods[2]—that the pressure on teachers and schools for their students to do well is enormous. Not only have the social pressures on everyone connected with the schools resulted in cheating by students and test tampering by teachers, but the latter frequently "teach to the test." Teaching to and tampering with tests is understandable when one considers the extensive publicity given to test scores by schools,

---

[2]Real estate agents often cite high test scores in their sales pitches to prospective home-buyers with school-age children.

the need to justify increased public expenditures on education, and incentives in which additional funds are allocated to schools when their students score higher on standardized tests.

The time-worn circle in which the state superintendent is badgered by politicians, district superintendents by the state superintendent, school principals by the district superintendent, teachers by principals, students by teachers and parents, and politicians, principals, and teachers by parents leads to a situation in which someone is "always on your back." Principals and other school administrators, who do not have tenure and may be demoted or transferred if students score too low on standardized tests, are particularly susceptible to pressure. Being only human, they may direct this pressure toward teachers in order to have their schools show up well in the annual roster of test score averages of schools published in local newspapers.

Students, teachers, and school administrators all require some source of motivation in order to improve the low level to which public education has sunk in many sections of the United States and some means of evaluating the effectiveness of their efforts. However, the atmosphere of paranoia that reportedly permeated the ranks of teachers and administrators in the Los Angeles School District during the test-tampering scandal of 1986–1988 was not beneficial to education in general or to educational testing in particular.

## Lake Wobegon Effect

In 1988 it was reported that 70 percent of the students, 90 percent of the 15,000 school districts in the United States, and all 50 states were scoring above the national norms on norm-referenced achievement tests administered in elementary schools (Cannell, 1988). This report led to the term "Lake Wobegon effect," after Garrison Keilor's fictional Minnesota community "where all children are above average." Cannell's findings were supported by the results of a study conducted by the U.S. Department of Education: 57 percent of elementary school students scored above the national median in reading and 62 percent above the national median in mathematics. In another survey, conducted by the Friends of Education, it was found that 83 percent of 5143 elementary school districts, 73 percent of 4501 secondary school districts, and all but two states (Louisiana and Arizona) were "above average" in achievement test scores (Cannell, 1989).

One explanation for the Lake Wobegon effect is that it is a consequence of the tests not being renormed often enough. Another explanation is that it is caused by teachers' coaching students on test questions, allowing them more than the allotted time to take the test, and even altering the completed answer sheets.

Publishers of the standardized achievement tests cited in these studies (CTB/McGraw-Hill, Riverside Publishing Company, and The Psychological Corporation) responded that it is expensive to renorm tests as frequently as might be desirable and that improved tests scores may actually indicate that the schools are getting better. Nevertheless, test publishers could undoubtedly do more to emphasize to users of their tests when (the date) and on what samples of students their tests were standardized. In particular, it should be made clear whether any groups (for example, special education students or those with limited English proficiency) were excluded from the norming samples.

Most school officials did not respond in writing or print to Cannell's findings and criticisms, but one school assessment expert asserted that it is unethical and unwarranted to assume that cheating has occurred when test scores increase. This official defended the right of teachers to examine the content of a test in order to determine in which skill areas students need to improve, but not to "teach to the test" (Landers, 1989).

It is widely recognized that scores tend to creep upward when a particular test battery is used in a school over a period of years. One reason for the increase may be that teachers are teaching to the test, but a likelier explanation is that they are teaching *from* the test (Lenke, 1988). Teachers make a note of the areas of the test in which scores are low and attempt to improve students' knowledge and skills in those areas. This is, of course, an appropriate instructional strategy and should not be labeled as cheating. One could also argue that the problem is with norm-referenced tests and that the results of criterion-referenced testing would yield more meaningful information concerning academic strengths and weaknesses and be less subject to misinterpretation. Be that as it may, politicians, parents, and others will undoubtedly continue to demand year-to-year and school-to-school comparative test data to assist in educational decision making.

## National Educational Standards and Tests

The nationwide concern that U.S. children are not as well educated in science and mathematics as children in many other countries goes back at least as far as the launching of the first Soviet Sputnik in 1957. More recently, the results of internally administered achievement tests have reawakened that concern by revealing that U.S. children are behind their counterparts in most other industrialized nations, and in mathematics and science in particular (Stevenson & Stigler, 1992; International Assessment of Educational Progress, 1989).

In the light of these international comparisons and other test statistics, the federal government and its advisers began formulating national standards in mathematics, science, English, history, and geography. To determine the extent to which such standards are being met, it was proposed that tests in these five subject-matter areas (the American Achievement Tests) be constructed and administered to students in the fourth, eighth, and twelfth grades. The U.S. public deserves to know how well its schools are doing their job and whether children in the United States measure up to those in other countries (Merl, 1991). The existence of national educational standards and tests would presumably help to restore public confidence in American education.

Although these plans were greeted with some degree of enthusiasm on the part of professional educators and measurement specialists, as well as political leaders and the general public, formulating and implementing the plans proved difficult. Some critics argued that we need to focus on improving the schools, rather than simply developing more tests that reveal the low estate of U.S. students and education. A related concern is the expense of constructing and administering the national tests and acting on the findings to improve instruction. Pointing to the fact that national standards and tests are already in place in Japan, France, England, Germany, and certain other countries, it seems to many Americans that some kind of national achievement tests should be devised, whether or not the individual states of school districts choose to administer them. However, this hope has dimmed in recent years as a result of wholesale cost-cutting measures by the federal government and a decentralizing political philosophy that would turn more of the educational responsibilities of the federal government over to the states. In addition to competency testing in the school grades, there is currently a movement underway to develop a national test for determining the extent to which college students have acquired the skills in critical thinking, problem solving, and communication needed in order "to compete in a global economy and exercise the rights and responsibilities of citizenship" (Zook, 1993, page A3). Proposals for such a National Postsecondary Student Assessment, which have been spurred by the demand for accountability in higher education, are controversial. However, some sort of evaluative procedure to determine whether the large sums of money being spent on higher education are effective in equipping young adults with the analytic skills required in the workplace will probably be developed in the near future. The development of such a test or tests will be expensive, but certainly not as costly as having a nation full of poorly educated college graduates.

## Intelligence Testing in the Schools

The relationships of educational experience, socioeconomic status, ethnicity, nationality, gender, nutrition, and numerous other psychosocial and biological variables to scores on tests of cognitive abilities have been considered in hundreds of research investigations over the past several decades (see Chapter 8). A continuing question is whether the variables measured by intelligence tests are genetically determined, rather than being shaped primarily by environment and experience. The significance of this question and the social and educational implications of the answer have resulted in legal action in certain states. At issue are the utility and bias of intelligence tests. Are these tests useful and fair to all groups of children, or are they biased against certain ethnic groups?

Among the legal cases that have dealt with administration of intelligence tests in schools are *Stell* v. *Savannah–Chatham County* (1963), *Hobson* v. *Hansen* (1967), *Diana* v. *State Board of Education* (1970), *Guadalupe* v. *Tempe Elementary School District* (1972), *Larry P.* v. *Riles* (1979), *Parents in Action on Special Education (PASE)* v. *Joseph P. Hannon* (1980), and *Georgia State Conferences of Branches of NAACP* v. *State of Georgia* (1985). A decision that was later reversed by the U.S. Circuit Court of Appeals was handed down in the case of *Stell* v. *Savannah–Chatham County*: the court concluded that, since the IQs of black children were lower than those of white children, requiring both groups to integrate in the same schools would be mutually disadvantageous. In *Hobson* v. *Hansen* the court ruled that group tests of ability discriminate against minority children and hence could not be used to assign students to different ability "tracks." In *Diana* v. *State Board of Education,* the court ruled that traditional testing procedures could not be used for the placement of Mexican-American children in educable mentally retarded (EMR) classes in California and that special provisions (for example, bilingual assessment) had to be used to test minority children. The court's decision in *Guadalupe* was to have students tested in their primary language and to eliminate unfair portions of the test. Furthermore, it was decreed that IQ scores must be at least two standard deviations below the mean and that other determiners, such as measures of adaptive behavior, must be included in making decisions on whether children should be classified as mentally retarded.

In his book *Bias in Mental Testing,* Jensen (1980) asserted that neither verbal nor nonverbal tests of intelligence are biased in any meaningful way against native-born minorities in the United States. Jensen maintained that tests of intelligence and other cognitive abilities have predictive validity for all ethnic groups and that the tests are not responsible for differences among those groups. As reflected in the case of *Larry P.* v. *Riles* (1979), Judge Robert Peckham of the Federal District Court of San Francisco disagreed with Jensen. After concluding that IQ tests denied the five black plaintiffs in a class action suit equal protection under the law, Judge Peckham ordered a continuation of his earlier ban on IQ testing for the placement of blacks in California public school classes for EMR children. Thus, it was ruled that individually administered tests of intelligence are biased against blacks and that the California State Department of Education could not use these tests for educational diagnosis or placement of black children. Contributing to this decision was the fact that a disproportionate number of black children had been assigned to EMR classes, which Judge Peckham labeled "dead-end education." Consequently, it was stipulated that the proportion of black children in EMR classes should match their proportion in the general population of schoolchildren. In 1986, Judge Peckham reissued his ruling prohibiting the use of IQ tests in the public schools of California, even when parental consent had been obtained. The court's decision in *Larry P.,* however, did not ban the use of all intelligence testing in California public schools; such tests continued to be administered for certain purposes.

Less than a year after the decision in *Larry P.* v. *Riles* was handed down, another federal judge, John F. Grady, rendered a very different decision in a similar case in Illinois. In this case, *Parents in Action on Special Education (PASE)* v. *Hannon* (1980), it was decreed "that the WISC, WISC–R, and Stanford–Binet tests, when used in conjunction with the statutorily mandated '[other criteria] for determining an appropriate educational program for a child' (under Public Law 94-142) . . . do not discriminate against black children" (page 883). As a result, intelligence tests continued to be administered for special class placement in Illinois public schools and in the schools of many other states. Similar to the decision in *PASE* v. *Hannon,* the court ruled in *Georgia NAACP* v. *State of Georgia* (1985) that intelligence tests do not discriminate against black children. Also contrary to the ruling in the *Larry P.* case, it was concluded in the Georgia decision that the presence of disproportionate numbers of black children in EMR classes does not constitute proof of discrimination. Finally, in September 1992, Judge Peckham lifted the ban on intelligence testing in California public schools on the grounds that it was unfair to black parents who wanted the tests to be used in the class placement of their learning disabled children (Bredemeier, 1991). This ruling effectively nullified his earlier (1986) prohibition against the use of intelligence tests in the public schools of California. A review of these and other court cases concerned with intelligence testing in the schools reveals that the judicial decisions have varied from state to state and with the political climate of the times.

Although the use of intelligence tests may sometimes encourage discrimination and even contribute to a self-fulfilling prophecy, a number of psychologists and educators maintain that there are advantages to using intelligence tests for placement purposes. Many children who are referred by teachers as in need of special education are found not to be so when such tests are administered. In fact, if the tests were not used, more minority children would probably be assigned to special education classes. And even those who are placed in such classes on the basis of low test scores often profit from special education to such an extent that their IQs are raised and they become ineligible for those services. Finally, we might ask what happens to children who need special education but are not identified because intelligence tests are not used. How many schoolchildren fall further behind each year because they are deprived of an education appropriate to their abilities by being placed in regular classes?

## EMPLOYMENT TESTING AND BIAS

Equal in importance to issues surrounding the use of tests in schools and colleges is the question of the fairness of these instruments for purposes of job selection, placement, and promotion. As a result of the growing concern over civil rights, the matter became increasingly important during the 1960s. Because employment tests had been validated principally on members of the dominant white culture, it was reasonable to ask whether they had any validity for blacks and other minorities. Such was the situation in the *Myart* v. *Motorola* (1964) case, in which the issue was whether a test that was being used for selection purposes was racially discriminatory.

### Equal Employment Opportunity Legislation

The Civil Rights Act of 1964 came in the wake of the Motorola case and other criticisms of psychological testing. Title VII of this act specifically prohibited discrimination on the basis of race, color, national origin, sex, or religion. A Supreme Court ruling on Title VII occurred in the case of *Griggs et al.* v. *Duke Power Company* (1971), which was concerned with a suit brought against the Duke Power Company by black employees. The suit challenged Duke Power's earlier requirement of a high school diploma and new hiring and promotion policies requiring designated minimum scores on the Wonderlic Personnel Test and the Bennett Test of Mechanical Comprehension. Chief Justice Warren Burger, who wrote the majority opinion in this case, concluded that "If an employment practice which operates to exclude Negroes cannot be shown to be [significantly] related to job performance, the practice is prohibited" (*Griggs et al.* v. *Duke Power Company,* 1971, page 60). But Justice Burger also stated that

nothing in the [Civil Rights] Act precludes the use of testing or measuring procedures; obviously they are useful. What Congress has forbidden is giving these devices and mechanisms controlling force unless they are demonstrably a reasonable measure of job performance. Congress has not commanded that the less qualified be preferred over the better qualified simply because of minority origins. Far from disparaging job qualifications as such, Congress has made such qualifications the controlling factor, so that race, religion, nationality, and sex become irrelevant. (*Griggs et al.* v. *Duke Power Company,* 1971, page 11)

The intent of the Supreme Court decision in *Griggs et al.* v. *Duke Power Company* and two subsequent cases, *United States* v. *Georgia Power* (1973) and *Albemarle Paper Co.* v. *Moody* (1975), was to require employers to demonstrate that the skills measured by their selection tests and other hiring procedures are job related. In the case of *Washington* v. *Davis* (1976), the court expanded the criterion against which selection tests could be validated to include performance in job-training programs. An immediate effect of these court decisions was a reexamination and in some cases a discontinuance of certain job-selection tests. Nevertheless, Congress subsequently concluded that Title VII of the Civil Rights Act of 1964 had not been adequately enforced and that discrimination against minorities and women was continuing. This conclusion led to a revision of the Civil Rights Act—the Equal Employment Opportunity Act of 1972.

The Equal Employment Opportunity Coordinating Council (EEOCC), which was established by the Equal Employment Opportunity Act, subsequently prepared a set of *The Uniform Guidelines on Employee Selection Procedures*. These guidelines described procedures for employers, labor organizations, and employment agencies to follow in showing

that any selection procedure which operates to disqualify or otherwise adversely affect members of any racial, ethnic, or sex group at a higher rate than another group, has been validated in accord with these guidelines, and that alternative employment procedures of equal validity which have less of an adverse effect are unavailable. (Equal Employment Opportunity Commission, 1973, page 20)

The guidelines further state that, to be considered a valid predictor of performance, the test or combination of tests should normally account for at least half the reliably measurable skills and knowledge pertaining to the job.

Clearly, the implication of the EEOC guidelines was that employment managers need to conduct validation studies of all their selection procedures, not just psychological tests, to determine if they are significantly related to job success. Using more subjective selection procedures rather than tests is an unsatisfactory alternative. In fact, the court ruled in *Watson* v. *Fort Worth Bank and Trust* (1988) that subjective employment devices such as interviews can be validated and that employees may claim adverse impact resulting from promotion practices based on interviews. Costly though it may be, interviews and other methods that are less objective than tests must be subjected to scrutiny by means of appropriate validity studies.

In the case of *Albemarle Paper Co.* v. *Moody* (1975), after finding the company's testing program inadequate, the court maintained that, even if a test is valid but adversely affects the employment of certain groups, the organization should make every effort to find a less biased selection device. The legal definition of *adverse impact* follows the four-fifths rule, according to which a condition of adverse impact is viewed as being present if one group has a selection rate that is less than four-fifths (80%) of that of the group with the highest selection rate. For example, if 100 whites and 100 blacks apply for a job and 60 whites (the highest group) are hired, then a condition of adverse impact may be said to exist if fewer than $(\frac{4}{5})60 = 48$ blacks are also hired. Under the EEOC guidelines, employers are required to adopt selection techniques having the least adverse impact.

The 1978 revision of the EEOC Guidelines on Employee Selection (Equal Employment Opportunity Commission, 1978) was not as strict as the original version of the guidelines in requiring employees to conduct differential validity studies. Like their predecessor, the revised guidelines were designed to require employers to justify the use of tests and other selection procedures that exclude disproportionate numbers of minority group members and women. The guidelines describe three validation methods on which employers may rely: criterion-related validity, content validity, and construct validity. But they are not clear on how large the validity coefficients should be. In addition, although the revised guidelines state that using tests is legitimate when the scores are related to job performance, they do not specify what is meant by "job-related criteria."

Job relatedness is an important concept in this context, because the use of tests that have an adverse impact is often justified on the basis of the claim that they are job related.

The failure of the EEOC guidelines to make clear what is meant by "job-related criteria" and other problems of clarity in the guidelines prompted many business and service organizations to suspend the use of job-selection tests altogether. The guidelines are considered by many authorities to be technically outdated, and in many cases the required validity studies are too expensive and of questionable value.

Another interesting court case concerned with fair employment practices was *Wards Cove Packing Company* v. *Antonio* (1989). The plaintiffs in this case were Filipino and Eskimo workers in salmon canneries in Alaska, who claimed that the company was keeping them out of better paying jobs such as machinery repair. The judicial decision in this case is important because it shifted the burden of proof to the employee to show that the psychological test being used for promotion purposes was not valid and reliable. Concern over this decision, which reversed a central theme of the *Griggs* v. *Duke Power Company* case, led to the Civil Rights Act of 1991. This act clarified the condition that the burden of proof lies with the employer. Another important provision of the act effectively outlawed the use of differential cutoff scores by race, gender, or ethnic background, the impact of which was a shift away from the quota system that had been in effect for over two decades. In short, it was stipulated that

It shall be an unlawful employment practice for a respondent in connection with the selection or referral of applicants or candidates for employment or promotion to adjust the scores of, use different cutoff scores, or otherwise alter the results of employment related tests on the basis of race, color, religion, sex, or national origin.

Other recent lawsuits related to educational and employment selection have been concerned with the effects of affirmative action or quotas in denying university admission to Asian- and Caucasian-Americans who possess the requisite qualification. Although the court has upheld selection or admissions procedures that favor underrepresented groups (for example, *United States* v. *City of Buffalo,* 1985), proposals to do away with legislatively mandated affirmative action requirements in schools and in the workplace have become quite significant during the 1990s.

## Test Fairness

As the EEOC guidelines imply, psychological and educational tests standardized on white samples are unacceptable for use in selecting blacks and other minority group applicants. The use of such tests with groups other than those on which they were standardized raises the issue of test fairness. The concept of fairness in psychological and educational assessment has a more statistical meaning than implied by the EEOC guidelines. The traditional point of view in psychological measurement is that the *fairness* of a test for different groups depends on whether applicants with the same probability of doing well on the performance criterion have the same likelihood of being selected. According to this definition, even if the mean test score of one group is lower than that of another, the test is not necessarily unfair. Blacks or other minorities in the United States may attain lower average scores than whites on employment tests, but it reveals nothing about the fairness of the tests in the technical sense. Regardless of any difference in mean test scores for two different groups, a job-selection test is said to be fair if it predicts job success equally well for all applicant groups.

After calling attention to a statistical flaw in the traditional (equal regression) definition of test fairness, Thorndike (1971) proposed an alternative definition. Thorndike's *constant ratio* definition specifies that qualifying scores on a test should be established in such a way that different groups of applicants are selected in proportion to the number of each group capable of attaining an acceptable level on the performance criterion. For example, if 30 percent of all white applicants and 20 percent of all black applicants are judged capable of performing a given job, then qualifying scores on a selection test should be set in such a way that 30 percent of white applicants and 20 percent of black applicants are hired.

Another definition of test fairness was proposed by Cole (1973). Separate cutoff scores would be established for the two or more different groups of applicants in such a way that the probability of selection is the same for potentially successful applicants in each group. Assume, for example, that two different groups are composed of 50 and 100 applicants each. If it has been previously determined that 50 percent of all applicants can perform the job satisfactorily, then $50\% \times 50 = 25$ applicants in the first group and $50\% \times 100 = 50$ applicants in the second group should be selected. A similar quota selection procedure was suggested by Dunnette and Borman (1979). In the Dunnette and Borman proposal, however, the percentage of applicants to be selected is determined beforehand; then separate regression equations are applied to each group.

The revised EEOC guidelines admit that test fairness is not a fixed concept and that experts disagree on its meaning. Whatever definition of fairness may be preferred, the relative seriousness of errors of incorrectly rejecting and incorrectly accepting applicants must be taken into account. This implies that the fairness of a test is a relative matter, depending on whether it is considered more serious to reject an applicant who would have succeeded (*false negative*) or to accept an applicant who will fail (*false positive*). Social conscience may dictate that the former error is more serious, whereas considerations of safety and profit point to the latter error as being of greater concern.

Even when the test as a whole is considered fair, it is possible for individual items to be unfair or biased toward a particular group. For example, certain items may present a stereotyped view of minorities and women according to occupation, education, family, and recreation or in other ways (Tittle, 1984). To identify and guard against item bias, test publishers typically conduct judgmental reviews to detect stereotyping and unfamiliarity of test content to certain groups. Various statistical procedures have also been devised to determine the presence of item bias, including the use of transformed item-difficulty indexes, biserial correlations to determine item discriminations, item characteristic curves, and variants of chi square such as the Mantel–Haenszel statistic (Cole & Moss, 1989).

Construction of item characteristic curves is one of the most descriptive ways of detecting item bias. According to this approach, a test item is unbiased if its characteristic curve is the same for the groups being compared. In other words, examinees of equal ability, regardless of the group to which they belong, have equal probabilities of getting the item right. Experimental studies in which the content of a test is varied to determine if different groups respond differently and factor-analytic studies to determine whether the responses of different groups yield the same factors have also been conducted to investigate test and item bias (Tittle, 1984; Cole & Moss, 1989).

A kind of compromise solution to the problem of item bias was worked out in 1984 when Educational Testing Service agreed to an out-of-court settlement of a suit charging social bias on insurance licensing examinations in Illinois. According to the terms of the settlement, it was agreed that, in constructing the insurance examinations, ETS would first use items on which blacks and whites scored most alike. This approach, referred to as the "Golden Rule settlement" after the insurance company involved in the suit, was subsequently applied in a number of other states. Be that as it may, the Golden Rule settlement was subsequently the subject of considerable debate and opposition (*Educational Measurement,* 1987, *6*(2); Anrig, 1987; Denton, 1988).

## Race Norming

Another practice that was adopted to make the results of selection tests color-blind is *race norming,* in which applicants' test scores are compared only with those of their own ethnic group. Such a practice was used by the U.S. Department of Labor with scores on the General Aptitude Test Battery (GATB) as part of the affirmative action policy of that agency. Separate percentile norms were determined for whites, blacks, and Hispanics, and only the in-group percentile ranks of applicants were reported to prospective employers. Race norming was not limited to the federal government: at one time more than 30 states race-normed their employment tests.

The charge of reverse discrimination allegedly represented by the practice of race norming led to a moratorium on the use of the GATB by the federal government. This decision was made to allow time to improve the ability of the GATB to predict job performance or to decide whether use of this test battery should be discontinued altogether (Adler, 1991; Hacker, 1991). Because the Civil Rights Act of 1991 bans any form of "score adjustment" on the basis of "race, color, religion, sex, or national origin" (Public Law No. 102-166, Section 106), the use of separate subgroup norms for employment selection purposes is now illegal.

## Validity Generalization

As noted in Chapter 5, a test devised in one situation or on one sample of people may not be of equal validity in other situations or with other samples. Because of the problem of "shrinkage" of the predictor–criterion correlation from one situation or sample to another, job-selection tests should be cross-validated to make certain they are valid in different contexts or with different groups of employees.

The fact that different tests seem to work best as predictors of job success in different situations implies that, for each job, it is necessary to determine which tests and prediction equations work best in predicting job performance. As documented in several publications by Schmidt and his colleagues (for example, Schmidt & Hunter, 1977, 1978, 1981), however, many job-selection tests have a substantial degree of cross-situational generality, or *validity generalization.* Some measures, such as job-replica tests and measures of skills fundamental to the job, are more likely to retain their validity despite situational or sample changes. With these kinds of tests, it may not be necessary to conduct new validity studies with every change in the situation or in the persons who are being evaluated.

## Integrity Testing

Theft is a big problem in U.S. business and industry, with perhaps billions of dollars in materials and products being stolen each year. Consequently, corporation executives are alert to any legal means for detecting dishonesty among employees or applicants.

For years, polygraph (lie detector) tests, which typically measure heart rate, respiration rate, blood pressure, and changes in skin resistance, were used by business and industrial organizations to identify thieves and deceivers among their employees. However, in 1988 the U.S. Congress passed the Employee Polygraph Protection Act, which banned most uses of polygraphs in preemployment interviews in government and the private sector. Subsequently, a number of paper-and-pencil tests of honesty or integrity were introduced. Some states have also contemplated banning these tests, although a task force of the American Psychological Association concluded that "honesty tests, when used appropriately and in conjunction with additional selection procedures, have demonstrated useful levels of validity as selection procedures." ("APA Task Force . . . ," 1991, page 6).

The practice of integrity testing in business and industry remains controversial, and there are many unresolved issues and unanswered questions regarding the construct of honesty and the testing of integrity. The matter continues to be discussed at length in the professional literature, which will hopefully clarify the issues and improve the psychometric qualities of the instruments and the social sensitivity with which they are used (Camara & Schneider, 1994, 1995; Lillienfeld, Alliger, & Mitchell, 1995; Ones, Viswesvaran, & Schmidt, 1995).

## ISSUES IN PERSONALITY ASSESSMENT

Like measures of cognitive abilities, measures of personality have been criticized by psychologists and nonpsychologists alike. Some of the most extreme negative comments about these instruments are in books by Whyte (1956) and Gross (1962, 1965) on the applications of personality tests in business and industry.

White and Gross were not alone in finding fault with personality assessment instruments. Indicative of the feelings of some of the lay public was the burning of certain attitude scales and other questionnaires and tests by order of the Houston School Board in 1959. The bonfire was a consequence of the strenuous protest by a group of Houston parents who objected to the fact that, as a part of a research study, their children had been required to respond to items such as

> I enjoy soaking in the bathtub.
>
> A girl who gets into trouble on a date has no one to blame but herself.
>
> If you don't drink in our gang, they make you feel like a sissy.
>
> Sometimes I tell dirty jokes when I would rather not.
>
> Dad always seems too busy to pal around with me. (Nettler, 1959, page 682)

The resulting furor caused the Houston School Board to order the burning of the answer sheets to six tests and inventories that had been administered to 5000 ninth graders.

How a situation like this could have developed is understandable when one realizes that the general public is not always sympathetic to scientific interest in research on human behavior. It has also been alleged that some items on personality tests, particularly those that deal with sex, religion, and morals, may be both personally offensive and potentially destructive to the character of children.

Another event concerning psychological testing and social science research in general that led to strong emotional reactions was Project CAMELOT. Financed by the U.S. government, this project was designed to study the causes of counterrevolution and counterinsurgency in Latin America. Both the Latin American public and certain U.S. congressmen reacted rather heatedly when they became aware of the project, precipitating a congressional investigation of psychological testing in government, industry, and education. One issue aired at length during the inquiry was administration to job applicants of personality test items concerning sex and religion, such as (1) My sex life is satisfactory; (2) I believe in God; (3) I don't get along very well with my parents. The congressional hearings did not result in a discontinuance of such tests, but the political concern associated with the hearings prompted psychologists and other assessment specialists to pay more attention to the ethics of psychological assessment.

More recently, a similar situation regarding the administration of a true–false personality test occurred in the case of *Soroka* v. *Dayton–Hudson Corporation* (1991). The dispute concerned Psychscreen, a personality inventory developed from the MMPI and the CPI that the Target Stores' management had administered to applicants for the position of security guard. This inventory had been used previously for screening applications for positions in law enforcement, air-traffic control, and nuclear power plants—in which security was of the utmost importance. Legal council for the plaintiff argued that the following kinds of items on Psychscreen were discriminatory with regard to religious and sexual preferences:

I believe in the second coming of Christ.

I believe there is a devil and a hell in afterlife.

I am very strongly attracted to members of my own sex.

I have never indulged in any unusual sex practices. (Hager, 1991, page A-20)

Attorneys for Dayton–Hudson Corporation argued that such questions were effective in identifying emotionally unstable persons, who could not be expected to perform effectively in the position of security guard. However, the appellate court, concluding that questions on religion and sex violate a job seeker's right to privacy, ruled in favor of the plaintiff.

Appealing this ruling to the California Supreme Court, the American Psychological Association pointed out that items such as those on PsychScreen should not be considered singly but rather collectively in evaluating their effectiveness in detecting emotional instability. Still, it can be argued that questions concerning sexual and religious preferences, which may contribute slightly to the prediction of job performance but almost certainly are not directly job relevant, have no place on employment screening tests.

## Validity

Questions of what is measured by personality tests, whether these things are worth measuring, and how best to interpret and apply the results have received extensive scrutiny during the past few decades. The psychometric qualities of personality assessment instruments, and projective tests in particular, often leave much to be desired. Criterion-keyed inventories may have somewhat higher validities than other instruments or procedures, but their validity coefficients often decline markedly over time and situations.

Improvements are needed not only in the reliability and validity of personality tests, but also in the theoretical underpinnings of these tests and the criteria against which they are validated. The disease model of mental disorders and the associated diagnostic classification system (DSM–IV) (American Psychiatric Association, 1994), which have influenced the development of many personality assessment procedures, are in many respects ambiguous and unreliable. Another matter of concern is the misinterpretation of the results of personality assessments. Errors of interpretation can occur through failure to consider the base rate, or frequency of the event (criterion) to be predicted. Misinterpretations also result from what is referred to as "clinical insight" or "intuition," but which is often only a collection of superficial stereotypes, truisms, and overgeneralizations.

Despite the impressive array of techniques employed in personality assessment, many of these techniques represent relatively crude attempts to measure behavior and cognition. For this reason they should be viewed primarily as research devices, rather than as finished psychometric tools. To be fair, personality inventories and projectives have sometimes contributed to selection decisions: one example is the use of the MMPI in the successful selection program of the Peace Corps (Hobbs, 1963). Combining measures of cognitive abilities with measures of temperament and motivation may also increase the predictability of job-performance criteria. Gottfredson (1994) suggested that employment selection may be improved by identifying the less cognitive elements of job performance and administering measures of these elements (for example, certain personality traits) along with aptitude tests. She maintained that such noncognitive predictors may reduce adverse impact from using cognitive predictors alone and at the same time enhance the validity of those predictors. Gottfredson admitted, however, that the contribution made by affective variables, over and above that made by a cognitive test battery alone, in forecasting occupational performance is probably fairly small in most instances.

The problem of the validity of personality tests cannot be resolved without better research and development, but such efforts should be undertaken with a socially responsible attitude and a respect for the rights of individuals (see Messick, 1989). Test users should also possess a solid understanding of statistical and other technical matters pertaining to test design, reliability, validity, and norms. And even so, it is important for psychological examiners to keep records of their hits and misses and other indicators of success and failure resulting from the use of test results. In the long run, this kind of information serves as a check on the validity of tests in achieving their stated purposes.

## Ethnic and Gender Bias

Related to both ethical issues and the question of test validity is the matter of whether personality tests are biased against a particular race, gender, or other demographic group. For example, Gynther and Green (1980) maintained that significant differences between the scores of blacks and whites on the original MMPI led to incorrect diagnoses and treatments. Pritchard and Rosenblatt (1980) countered, however, that such differences are exaggerated and that the MMPI is as valid for one ethnic group as another. As noted in Chapter 12, in revising the MMPI an effort was made to eliminate both ethnic-group and gender bias.

Although there has been relatively little systematic research on the personality test scores of different ethnic, social-class, or nationality groups in recent years, research on gender bias has flourished. A traditional response to gender differences in test scores has been to provide separate norms for males and females, but efforts have been made to construct test items that are not biased toward either sex. Such efforts are routine in constructing periodically revised ability tests such as the SAT and the GRE. With regard to affective instruments, the development of MMPI–2 and the 1994 edition of the Strong Interest Inventory, in particular, involved painstaking efforts to eliminate gender bias.

## Clinical versus Statistical Prediction

One of the most important reasons for obtaining test data is to predict behavior. Unfortunately, personality assessments tend to have rather low predictive validities, which, when coupled with their uses in screening and clinical diagnosis, has prompted a substantial amount of research on ways to improve their validities. The statistical (or actuarial) approach to data collection and behavior prediction consists of applying a statistical formula, a set of rules, or an actuarial table to assessment data. This can be done by a human being or, what has become common practice in recent years, by a computer following an interpretive program. In contrast, the clinical, or impressionistic, approach involves making intuitive judgments or drawing conclusions on the basis of subjective impressions combined with a theory of personality. One of the most famous examples of the impressionistic approach, provided by the psychoanalyst Theodore Reik, is given in Box 14–1. Impressionistic interpretations such as this are made not only on the basis of interviews, biographical data, and other clinical information; personality ratings, test scores, and other statistically based data may also be used.

An early review of research comparing the clinical and statistical approaches to prediction concluded that in 19 out of 20 studies the statistical approach was either superior or equal in effectiveness to the clinical approach (Meehl, 1954). Eleven years later, after summarizing data from some 50 studies in which the two approaches had been compared, Meehl (1965) concluded that the statistical approach was more efficient in two-thirds of the studies and just as efficient as the clinical approach in the remaining one-third. A subsequent review by Sines (1970) concurred with Meehl's conclusion: in all but one of the 50 studies reviewed by Sines the actuarial (statistical) approach was found to be superior to the clinical approach in predicting various kinds of behavior.

Although the studies summarized by Meehl and Sines provided impressive support for the conclusion that personality diagnoses and behavior predictions are more accurate when a statistical rather than a clinical approach is employed, Lindzey (1965) demonstrated that an expert clinician can sometimes make highly accurate diagnoses. By using only the information obtained from administering the Thematic Apperception Test, a clinical psychologist proved to be 95 percent accurate in detecting homosexuality. The statistical approach of employing only certain objective scores obtained from the TAT protocols was significantly less accurate.

Other studies have also found that, under certain circumstances, trained practitioners employing data from a variety of sources (case history, interview, test battery, and so on) are

**Box 14–1**

**A Clinical (Impressionistic) Interpretation**

After a few sentences about the eventful day, the patient fell into a long silence. She assured me that nothing was in her thoughts. Silence from me. After many minutes she complained about a toothache. She told me that she had been to the dentist yesterday. He had given her an injection and then had pulled a wisdom tooth. The spot was hurting again. New and longer silence. She pointed to my bookcase in the corner and said, "There's a book standing on its head."

Without the slightest hesitation and in a reproachful voice I said, "But why did you not tell me that you had an abortion?" I had said it without an inkling of what I would say and why I would say it. It felt as if, not I, but something in me had said that. The patient jumped up and looked at me as if I were a ghost. Nobody knew or could know that her love, the physician, had performed an abortion on her. The operation, especially dangerous because of the advanced state of her pregnancy was, of course, kept very secret because abortion in the case of gentiles was punishable by death in Germany. To protect the man she still loved, she had decided to tell me all except this secret. (Reik, 1948, pages 263–264)

better predictors than actuarial formulas (for example, Goldberg, 1970; Holt, 1970; Wiggins & Kohen, 1971). Debate over the relative effectiveness of the clinical and statistical approaches to personality assessment has subsided, but support for both approaches remains strong.

## Heredity versus Environment

The extent to which test scores and personality in general are influenced by heredity and environment has been the topic of dispute for the better part of this century. The issue is far from settled, although contemporary psychologists recognize that all behavior is a product of both influences acting in concert. Correlational statistics computed from scores on inventories and other measures of personality obtained from people having different degrees of kinship reveal modest but significant contributions of hereditary factors (Figure 14–3). For example, research on concordance rates for various personality characteristics in identical twins has provided evidence for a significant hereditary influence in introversion–extroversion, activity level, anxiety, dependence, dominance, emotionality, sociability, and certain other traits (Thomas & Chess, 1977; Worobey, 1986; Torgerson, 1985; Riese, 1988; Floderus-Myrhed et al., 1980; Royce & Powell, 1983; Buss & Plomin, 1984, 1986). Evidence for a genetic influence in schizophrenia and bipolar (manic-depressive) disorders is also impressive (Kallman & Jarvik, 1959; Gottesman & Shields, 1973, 1982). The effects of heredity on personality are, however, far from simple: they vary with age, gender, and other individual differences.

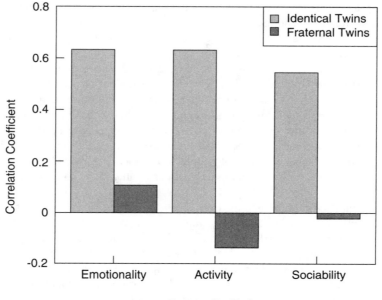

**FIGURE 14–3**  Average Correlations of Parental Ratings of Identical and Fraternal Twins on Emotionality, Activity Level, and Sociability. (Data from Buss & Plomin, 1984.)

After summarizing evidence for the persistence of various personality characteristics throughout childhood, Thomas and Chess (1977) underscored the fact that hereditary characteristics both influence and are influenced by personal experiences. Parents, other people, and the nonhuman environment all react differently to children having different physical and temperament traits. These reactions can, in turn, influence the child's genetically-based characteristics, thereby demonstrating the interplay between heredity and environment in shaping personality.

## Traits versus Situations

The emphasis on situations, as opposed to traits, as determiners of behavior goes back to the Hartshorne and May (1928) studies of children's character. Four decades later, Mischel (1968) summarized evidence for the conclusion that, although behavioral correlates of cognitive abilities are fairly consistent across different situations, personal–social behavior is highly dependent on the specific situation. Mischel concluded that inferences regarding personality dynamics or traits are less useful than knowledge of the situation itself in predicting behavior. He argued that assessments of generalized traits of personality are not particularly helpful because such traits are frequently not generalized across situations. Rather than analyzing personality into a complex of traits or factors, Mischel (1986) proposed a social-learning approach. This approach emphasizes that people learn to make different responses in different situations, and the accuracy with which a person's behavior in a specific situational context can be predicted must take into account the learning history of that person in similar situations.

It is certainly true that social norms, roles, and other group-related conditions can exert powerful effects on people and override temperament or personal style as determiners of individual thoughts and actions. When a social situation remains fairly constant, people tend to suppress their idiosyncrasies and adjust their behavior and thinking to the expectations, rewards, and punishments provided by other people in that situation. It has been amply demonstrated by research in social psychology and by candid television programs that when in Rome all kinds of people "do as the Romans do." Acceptance of this truism does not imply, however, that individual personality plays no role whatsoever in determining behavior.

Evidence pertaining to the trait-situation controversy is not all in favor of situationism. A number of investigators (for example, Bem & Allen, 1974; Block, 1977; Underwood & Moore, 1981; Chaplin & Goldberg, 1984) have found that the consistency of traits across situations is itself an individual difference variable. Regardless of the external circumstances, some people are more consistent than others in their behavior, and they are aware of how consistently they behave. In an investigation by Bem and Allen (1974), people who believed themselves to be fairly consistent in friendliness and conscientiousness tended to be so; those who identified themselves as less consistent tended to be that way.

Research has also demonstrated that some behaviors are more consistent than others. Certain behaviors are narrowly situation specific, whereas other behaviors that do not require specific eliciting stimuli occur in a wide range of situations and hence are more reflective of broad personality variables (Funder & Colvin, 1991).

Reviewing Mischel's position and subsequent evidence, a reasonable conclusion is that there is little support for a strict situationist viewpoint regarding personality. Rather, it is best to emphasize that behavior is a joint product of personality characteristics and the particular situation in which the behavior occurs. In certain (strong) situations, the features of the situations themselves are more important in determining how people behave; in other (weak) situations, personality characteristics are more influential. More generally, behavior is determined by the interaction between personality characteristics and the nature of the situation in which an individual finds himself. Furthermore, people with certain personality traits tend to seek out situations having certain characteristics. Not only are people affected by specific situations, but they also choose the situations that will affect them. To develop more effective measures of personality, we need to begin by formulating a conceptual model of the interactions, or *transactions,* between personality dispositions and situational characteristics. Then measures of both sets of variables can be constructed to make possible a true "interactional assessment" (McReynolds, 1979).

## SUMMARY

The content and applications of standardized tests of ability and personality have been under attack for much of this century. Standardized tests have been criticized as being invalid indicators of what they are purported to measure, as invading the individual's right to privacy, as unfair to both advantaged and disadvantaged students, and as fostering poor study habits and unethical social and economic practices. Ethical issues in testing are of great concern to psychologists, educators, and other informed persons, and codes of conduct that incorporate psychological assessment have been drafted by professional organizations. Congressional hearings during the 1960s stimulated much discussion and some action on the matters of invasion of privacy and confidentiality in the administration of tests and the treatment of test results.

Multiple-choice items like those on college and professional school entrance examinations have been severely criticized. Interest in truth-in-testing legislation is indicative of the demand for the testing industry to become more open and responsible to the public. Also of concern with respect to ability testing have been annual declines in scores on the SAT and other nationally administered tests of ability and the effects of coaching on test scores. Surveys have revealed that testing in schools is extensive, but that teachers, parents, and students usually lack sufficient information and training to interpret test scores accurately. Competency testing of both high school students and teachers has gained momentum in recent years.

Legislation and litigation concerning civil rights and equal employment opportunity has led to the regulation of test usage in business and industry. Federal guidelines for employee selection procedures list the characteristics that test and nontest measures should possess in order to be acceptable and valid techniques for employee selection and placement. The question of the fairness of tests for minority and disadvantaged groups led to new definitions of *fairness*. Legal and technical issues stemming from consideration of the concepts of fairness and differential prediction have alerted professional psychologists, employment managers, and the general public to the need for more responsible use of tests and other assessment procedures.

Personality tests and other affective measures, especially when administered in school and employment situations, have been criticized as representing invasions of privacy, as being irrelevant or poor predictors of behavior, and even as suggesting immoral acts. Psychologists recognize the limitations of these kinds of instruments and, by and large, criticism has had the salutary effect of increasing care in the design of new affective assessment instruments and promoting further research on personality assessment. Such research has led to an emphasis on the interaction between heredity and environment and between personality traits and situational variables in determining behavior. Other research on affective measurement has pointed to the superiority of the statistical to the clinical approach in the collection and interpretation of personality assessment data.

## QUESTIONS AND ACTIVITIES

1. Discuss specific objections to standardized tests in general and multiple-choice tests in particular.
2. Describe criticisms of the Scholastic Aptitude Test and the responses of the College Entrance Examination Board and Educational Testing Service to these criticisms.
3. Why might "truth-in-testing" legislation encourage teachers to "teach to the test"?
4. Review legislation enacted by the U.S. Congress and decisions by the Supreme Court pertaining to employment testing in business and industry, beginning with Title VII of the Civil Rights Act of 1964.

5. In the Glossary, the fairness of an achievement test is defined as "the extent to which the items on a test are a representative sample of what examinees know," whereas the fairness of an aptitude test is defined as "the extent to which scores on the test are equally predictive of the criterion performance of different groups." Thorndike maintained, however, that tests are fair if "the qualifying scores [on the test are] set at levels that . . . qualify applicants in the two groups in proportion to the fraction of the two groups reaching a specific criterion performance." Why do different definitions of test fairness exist, and what are the implications of the various definitions?

6. What is *clinical prediction,* and how does it differ from *statistical prediction*? Which is more effective and why?

7. Refer to the 30 paired scores in Table A–2 of Appendix A. Assume that $X$ is a score on a job-selection test and $Y$ is a job-performance rating. Further assume that the 30 paired scores were obtained from a majority group of applicants for the job, whereas the following 20 paired scores were obtained from a minority group of applicants.

| X | Y | X | Y | X | Y | X | Y |
|---|---|---|---|---|---|---|---|
| 40 | 64 | 34 | 41 | 52 | 46 | 50 | 39 |
| 62 | 48 | 48 | 44 | 42 | 38 | 32 | 30 |
| 40 | 32 | 56 | 64 | 18 | 26 | 68 | 42 |
| 52 | 40 | 48 | 36 | 46 | 34 | 60 | 60 |
| 36 | 31 | 24 | 54 | 64 | 65 | 44 | 48 |

Now assume that 50 percent of the majority group applicants, 25 percent of the minority group applicants, and 40 percent of all applicants perform the job satisfactorily ($Y = 50$ or higher). Is the test fair according to the traditional definition of fairness? According to Thorndike's definition? According to Cole's definition? What are the percentages of false positives and false negatives in each group, and how do they affect the fairness of the test?

8. Investigate the test-coaching schools, test-coaching courses, and published materials on test coaching available in your geographical area. Try to locate a half-dozen or so students who have been coached or prepared for the SAT, the GRE, or some other nationally administered test for a fee. Was the coaching worthwhile? Did it help the students to improve their scores on the test? What evidence, if any, was cited for the beneficial effects of coaching?

9. Write one or two personality test items (true–false format) that are biased toward men, women, blacks, whites, Americans, Asians, and more highly educated people.

10. Run program 2 ("Attitudes toward Intelligence Testing") and program 3 ("Attitudes toward Personality Testing") in Category G of *Computer Programs for Psychological Assessment.* Compare your responses to the questionnaires with those of your classmates.

# 15

## COMPUTER-BASED ASSESSMENT AND OTHER DEVELOPMENTS

Despite criticism both within and outside the profession of psychology, psychological assessment has continued to expand and diversify. New tests, inventories, and scales, coupled with methodological advances in constructing administering, scoring, and interpreting psychometric instruments, attest to the dynamic state of the field. Many factors have contributed to this growth, including expansion of the population, the spread of social services and opportunities to a larger segment of the population, and the consequent need for more efficient methods for selecting, placing, and diagnosing people in employment, educational, and clinical contexts. The growth of testing has also been facilitated by progress in designing and programming high-speed computing machinery. From the start of their commercial availability in the mid-1950s, computers have been used to analyze responses and scores on tests. They have literally reshaped the field of psychological measurement, and there is every reason to believe that they will continue as a potent force in psychometrics in the future.

## CHARACTERISTICS OF COMPUTERS

A contemporary digital computer, with its microelectrode, solid-state circuitry packed in one or more carry-out boxes, is a marked improvement over the vacuum-tube monsters of the 1950s. Large miniframe computers, as well as somewhat smaller minicomputers, became more generally available in the 1960s and 1970s, but the extension of computer technology to private homes and small offices awaited the introduction of microcomputers.

### Hardware and Software

A digital computer consists essentially of three units: an input unit, a central processing unit, and an output unit. A variety of devices is used to enter information or data into the central processing unit (CPU): typewriter keyboard, optical scanner, magnetic tape or disk reader, and light-sensitive or heat-sensitive cathode ray tube (CRT), as well as punched card or paper tape readers in older computers and voice input in newer ones. Information from the CPU can be sent to a CRT screen, to magnetic tape or disk, or to a fast paper printer. The CPU, which is the heart of a computer, also consists of three units: a storage (memory) unit for storing instructions (programs) and data, an arithmetic–logical unit for performing calculations and making logical decisions, and a control unit for following the instructions given in the stored programs. The control unit directs the flow of information from the input unit, uses data from the storage unit, prompts the arithmetic–logical unit to make decisions and perform needed computations, and then sends the results to the output unit(s).

## Microcomputers

In a microcomputer, the microprocessor, consisting of an integrated network of thousands of microscopic circuits etched on the surface of a thin layer of silicon, combines the functions of the arithmetic–logical unit. Programmable microcomputers first became available with APPLE in 1975, followed in rapid succession by many other brands in the 1980s.

Two types of primary storage are available in microcomputers: a read-only memory (ROM) for storing directions on how the microprocessor should process input information and a random-access memory (RAM) for temporary storage of information entered by tape or permanent storage device (electromagnetic tape or disk). Typical permanent storage devices for microcomputers are portable $3\frac{1}{2}$- or $5\frac{1}{4}$-inch diameter floppy disks and fixed hard disks located in the computer itself. A standard high-density floppy disk has a storage capacity of 1.44 million characters and can be randomly accessed at any point on its surface in a matter of milliseconds. Typical hard disks, on the other hand, have storage capacities of several million characters.

## Computer Programs

The rapid speed, compact size, and relatively modest prices of microcomputers have made it feasible to employ them in many situations involving testing and other psychological and educational activities. But a microcomputer, or any other computer for that matter, is not very useful without an appropriate selection of software—the programs that tell it what to do. A computer program consists of a series of instructions on how to enter data or other information, what operations to perform on the data, and where to send the results after the data have been processed. A program can be entered into the computer by means of a typewriter keyboard or a magnetic disk drive. It may be written in any number of computer languages, such as BASIC, COBOL, FORTRAN, Pascal, and C+, and translated by the computer into its own machine language by a special program known as a compiler or an interpreter.

The short program in Figure 15–1, written in BASIC, is designed to score any objective test containing true–false, multiple-choice, or short-answer items. The user first types in the number of items on the test and the keyed (correct) response to each item. Then an

```
10  REM Program TESTSCORE. Score tests of 500 items or less.
20  DIM KEE$(500), ANS$(500)
30  REM Enter scoring key for test.
40  CLS
50  INPUT "Total number of items"; N
60  PRINT
70  FOR I = 1 TO N
80  PRINT "Correct answer to item"; I; "?"
90  LINE INPUT KEE$(I)
100 NEXT I
110 REM Enter examinee's name and responses. Score is computed.
120 CLS
130 PRINT "Examinee's name?"
140 LINE INPUT NAM$
150 SCORE = 0
160 FOR I = 1 TO N
170 PRINT "Answer to item"; I; "?"
180 LINE INPUT ANS$(I)
190 IF ANS$(I) = KEE$(I) THEN SCORE = SCORE +1
200 NEXT I
210 REM Examinee's name and test score printed.
220 PRINT
230 PRINT "Name of Examinee:"; NAM$
240 PRINT "Score = "; SCORE
250 PRINT
260 PRINT "Do you want to score another anwer sheet--y or n?"
270 ANS$ = INKEY$
280 IF ANS$ = "" THEN 270
290 IF ANS$ = "y" OR ANS$ = "yes" THEN 110
300 END
```

**FIGURE 15–1**  Computer Program for Scoring Objective Tests.

examinee's name and his or her responses to the items are entered, after which the total score (number right) is calculated by the microprocessor. After the examinee's name and score are printed on the computer screen, the program asks for the name and responses of the next examinee.

One feature of the simple program in Figure 15–1 that should be emphasized is that it is interactive. This means that there is continuous interaction between the computer and the user. In *interactive mode,* the computer asks questions or waits for instructions, and the user responds by typing and entering an appropriate response. Interactive mode contrasts with *batch mode,* in which the responses of all examinees have been recorded on a floppy disk or other permanent storage input medium and are entered line by line without any further action on the part of the user. Interactive mode makes possible the administration, scoring, and interpretation of a test in a single session in which the examinee is actively responding to a series of questions on the computer screen. For this reason, it is usually preferable to batch mode for the purposes of psychological assessment. However, batch mode is more efficient when one faces the onerous chore of simply scoring a large number of answer sheets.

## TEST CONSTRUCTION, ADMINISTRATION, AND SCORING

A functional flow chart of the testing process is shown in Figure 15–2 (Baker, 1989). Computers can be of assistance at all stages of this process, including test construction, administration, scoring, analysis, reporting and interpreting results.

### Test Construction

The most common application of computers in test construction consists of word-processing programs to assist in typing the items, formatting, checking for errors in spelling and syntax, and so forth. Test construction is facilitated even more by a combination of word-processing and graphics programs that support the preparation of tests comprised of words and drawings. These program packages contain banks or pools of test items that can be accessed by entering certain keywords indicating the content and psychometric characteristics desired in the test. Item banks, from which items can be selected and retrieved in designing tests, are available from textbook publishers for particular subjects and curricula.

### Adaptive Testing

It is fairly simple to write a program that follows the traditional test-administration procedure in which the same items are presented to all examinees. Historically, this procedure was not followed precisely on all tests, for example, on various individually administered

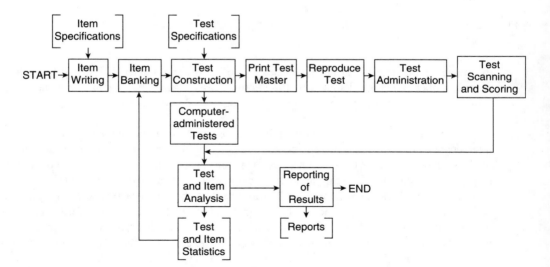

**FIGURE 15–2**  Functional Flow Chart of the Process of Testing.
(Reprinted from *Educational Measurement (3rd ed.),* edited by Robert L. Linn. Copyright 1989. Used by permission of American Council on Education and The Oryx Press, 4041 N. Central at Indian School Rd., Phoenix, AZ 85012.)

tests of intelligence and personality. In general, however, little flexibility was permitted in determining which items to administer. This traditional approach is particularly inefficient with achievement tests, because examinees must answer many items that are either too easy or too difficult for them. Adapting the content of the test (that is, which items are administered) to the ability level of the examinee eliminates the necessity for administering many very easy or very difficult items, thereby saving time and effort.

Item banks or pools for interactive or adaptive tests (also known as branched, sequential, tailored, or routing tests) can be assembled by computers programmed to follow one of the item-response methodologies (latent trait theory, item characteristic curve theory, Rasch mode, and so on). In adaptive testing, it is important for certain assumptions of item-response theory (IRT) to be met. Two assumptions are that (1) all items in a pool measure a single aptitude or achievement dimension and (2) the items are independent; that is, a person's response to one item does not depend on his or her response to any other item. Satisfaction of the first assumption, that of unidimensionality, can be verified by factor-analytic procedures and is more likely to be met by item pools or tests derived by factor analysis. The second assumption is met if the items are not interlocked or interrelated in some way.

The adaptive procedure for administering a test of achievement or aptitude works in the following way. Applying an appropriate statistical model and item-response methodology, a pool of test items scaled in terms of their difficulties, and perhaps discrimination and guessing parameters as well, is assembled for administration by computer. An estimate of the examinee's ability level dictates which item(s) are administered first. Alternatively, items of medium difficulty level may be administered initially (see Figure 15–3). Which items are subsequently administered depends on the examinee's responses to previous items. Testing continues until the estimate of error or level of accuracy in the responses reaches a specified level.

A person's score on an adaptively administered test is determined not merely by counting the number of items answered currently, but by taking into account the statistical characteristics (difficulty, discrimination, and guessing parameters) of the items. Instead of making the presentation of a specific item contingent on the examinee's response to an immediately preceding item, administration and scoring of the test can be made easier by considering the examinee's responses to a subset of previously presented items in deciding which item(s) to present next.

Because not all items in the pool are administered to every examinee, adaptive testing is more efficient than conventional testing. Only about half as many items are administered to a specific examinee as in the traditional testing practice, with no loss of information and equivalent reliability and validity. Furthermore, research has shown that scores on computerized adaptive tests are highly comparable to scores on equivalent paper-and-pencil tests (Henley et al., 1989; Kapes & Vansickle, 1992; Mead & Crasgow, 1992). In fact, Vansickle and Kapes (1993) reported greater reliability and decreased administration time for a computer-based version than for a paper-and-pencil version of the Strong–Campbell Interest Inventory.

Test security is also easier to maintain in the case of computer-assisted adaptive tests, which insiders affectionately refer to as "CATS." One disadvantage of CATS is that examinees are not permitted to review and perhaps change their answers after their initial choices have been made. Another disadvantage, at least when testing individuals or small groups, is the initial investment cost and the expense of maintaining the computer hardware and updating the software (Schoonman, 1989).

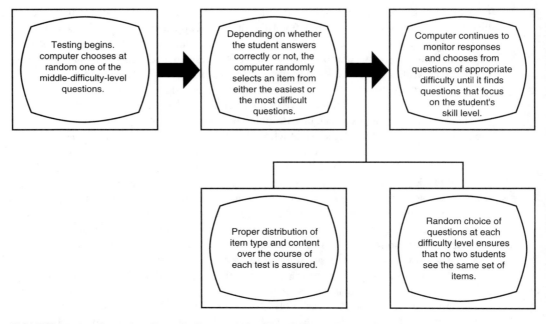

**FIGURE 15–3** Question Branch Patterns for The College Board Computerized Placement Tests.   The Four Placement Tests in This Series—Reading Comprehension, Sentence Skills, Arithmetic, and Algebra—Are Adaptive Tests Administered on IBM-PC or Compatible Computers.
(Reprinted by permission of The College Entrance Examination Board.)

Until recently, the uses of adaptive testing in assessing general intelligence and special abilities were somewhat limited. Now, the Educational Testing Service, the U.S. Army, and various other organizations offer computerized, adaptive versions of ability tests such as the Scholastic Assessment Test (SAT), the Armed Services Vocational Aptitude Battery (ASVAB), and the Graduate Record Examination (GRE). It is expected that before long CATS versions of the SAT and other college admissions and placement tests, as well as job and military selection tests, will be administered at sites throughout the world.

Other illustrations of computerized adaptive tests produced by ETS are the Praxis tests of basic reading, writing, and mathematics skills for prospective teachers; licensing examinations for nursing candidates under a program of the National Council of State Boards of Nursing; and certification exams for manufacturing employees in cooperation with the American Production and Inventory Control Society (Jacobson, 1993). In the future, the use of sound, graphics, simulations, modems, "free-response" items, and input–output devices such as voice encoders and decoders will increase the versatility of test content and the flexibility and ease with which such tests are administered. Not only the correctness or incorrectness of the responses given by examinees, but the quality, speed, and intensity with which they are made may be evaluated.

Considering the high enthusiasm for CATS, it is unfortunate that all is not rosy with the system. Concern over the security of computer-based testing with the GRE has resulted from the ease with which representatives of the Kaplan Educational Centers who took the GRE were able to memorize most of the test questions and report them to the test-coaching firm (Wallace, 1994; Jacobson, 1995). Computerized adaptive testing entails administering a smaller number of questions to a specific examinee than conventional testing. But if test security requires that the item pool be changed each time a different small group of persons is tested, even more items will be needed than with conventional testing of large groups. Since computerized versions of the GRE were scheduled for total replacement of paper-and-pencil versions of the test by 1996–1997, the problem of security became especially acute in the light of efforts to update New York State's truth-in-testing law. Under the proposed updating of the law, testing agencies would be required to disclose the item pools that they had used in computerized tests during the preceding year, together with the correct answers and the rules used to determine test scores. Furthermore, examinees could immediately review all questions that they had been given and the corresponding answers during four 4-week periods each year (Jacobson, 1994).

## Stratadaptive Testing

Although adaptive testing procedures have been used more extensively in the measurement of achievement and aptitude, applications of adaptive testing methodology to assess personality have also been explored. A promising approach is stratified adaptive testing, in which the pool of test items is divided into subsets by difficulty level. Whether the test is designed to assess cognitive abilities or personality traits, responding to an item on such a *stratadaptive test* in a certain way (by giving the keyed answer) leads to the presentation of another item at a higher stratum. Responding incorrectly (not giving the keyed answer) results in presentation of an item at a lower stratum. Testing may continue until a ceiling stratum—a level at which the examinee answers no items in the keyed direction—is reached.

Suppose, for example, that level of extroversion is to be assessed. A person who endorses an item in the keyed direction for extroversion in one stratum goes on to an item pertaining to extroversion at the next higher stratum (next higher level of the characteristic). Various termination and scoring rules are possible. For example, the process of presenting items at successively higher strata might continue until the examinee fails to endorse an extroversion item at a given level; his or her score would then be determined by the highest level reached and by the item endorsed on that level. Similarly, a person who failed to endorse an item in the direction keyed for extroversion in one stratum would be presented an extroversion item at the next lower level, and so on, until he or she endorsed an item in the extroversion direction or there were no more strata. In each stratum, items would be arranged in such a way that the most discriminating items were presented first.

## Response Sets and Guidelines for Administration

Another possibility in the computerized assessment of personality is to supplement special scales for detecting response sets and faking with measures of the latency and strength of responding on a computer-administered personality test or interest inventory. For example, research findings indicate that people who have a tendency to respond in a more socially desirable manner may respond more rapidly than other people to test items on personality or interest inventories. It seems that people who are eager to present themselves in a more favorable light are able to identify the most socially desirable alternative quickly and consequently spend less time thinking about the answer (George & Skinner, 1990; Holden & Fekken, 1988; Holden, Fekken, & Cotton, 1991; Holden & Kroner, 1992).

In addition to the method (conventional, adaptive, and others) of selecting the items to be presented, certain cautions concerning the equipment for presenting test items should be exercised in administering a test by computer. Six recommendations in the *Guidelines for Computer-based Tests and Interpretations* (American Psychological Association, 1986) pertaining to computerized test administration are as follows:

The environment in which the testing terminal is located should be quiet, comfortable, and free from distraction.

Test items presented on the display screen should be legible and free from noticeable glare.

Equipment should be checked routinely and should be maintained in proper working condition.

Test performance should be monitored, and assistance to the test taker should be provided, as is needed and appropriate.

Test takers should be trained on proper use of the computer equipment.

Reasonable accommodations must be made for individuals who may be at an unfair disadvantage in a computer testing situation.

## Test Scoring and Reporting

Test-scoring machines have been available for much of this century. The machines of yesteryear were sensitive only to magnetic marks on paper, so special magnetic pencils were required for marking answer sheets. Most of the test-scoring machines of today are optical scanners that are sensitive to marks made with ordinary pencils.

A computer is not needed for rapid and efficient scoring of tests, but it provides flexibility and further statistical analysis, interpretation, and storage of test scores and other personal data. In addition to local scoring by an optical scanner, answer sheets can either be mailed or transmitted by modem to a central scoring service.

The amount of programming needed to use a desktop optical scanner is fairly simple and includes a wide range of features, such as item weighting, part scoring, item analysis and flagging, and a printout of various kinds of data, statistics, and graphs. In addition to raw and converted scores, frequency distributions and histograms, test statistics (arithmetic means, standard deviations, internal consistency reliabilities), and item statistics (difficulty and discrimination indexes, distributions of responses to options, and the like) are reported.

Test scoring, score analysis, and score reporting may all be accomplished by using an optical scanner connected to a microcomputer containing appropriate assessment system software. However, software packages that construct tests according to certain specifications, score them, and analyze and report the results are complex and expensive. Perhaps the best example of such a general-purpose system is MicroCAT (from Assessment Systems

Corporation), which makes possible the construction, administration, scoring, and analysis of tests designed from item-response or classical testing perspectives and administered by adaptive or conventional procedures. Even more complex and versatile than MicroCAT are second-generation microcomputer systems having several megabytes of internal memory, advanced graphics, desktop publishing features, and video-display features such as windows. By means of networks of computers situated throughout the country, nationwide test scoring and analysis, as well as on-line testing, are being implemented.

### Open-ended and Essay Items

Although the process of programming a computer to administer and score objective tests is fairly straightforward, computerized administration and scoring of responses to open-ended or interlocking questions are more difficult. Efforts to design computer programs for the automated administration of tests of cognitive abilities and personality have met with some success, but much remains to be done. Evaluating responses to essay-type items, such as writing samples in particular, poses problems for a computer, but here too progress is being made.

## OTHER APPLICATIONS OF COMPUTERS IN PSYCHOLOGICAL ASSESSMENT

The uses of computers in psychological assessment are not limited to test construction, administration, scoring, reporting, and statistical analysis. Computers can also be used to interview clients in clinical and employment contexts, interpret the results of psychological assessments, and even provide personal counseling.

### Interviewing by Computer

Psychodiagnostic interviewing has been automated by storing in a computer a set of questions and instructions so that the computer asks a question, receives an answer, and decides (conditionally branches) what question to ask next. Such branching strategies have been applied effectively in patient data systems by numerous psychiatric hospitals, including that of the University of Wisconsin and the Salt Lake City Veterans Administration Hospital.

Computer interviewing for purposes of obtaining case histories, conducting behavioral assessments, focusing on specific problems, identifying target symptoms, and assisting in psychiatric diagnosis has been growing in recent years. Representative of computer software packages for psychodiagnostic interviewing and report preparation are the Diagnostic Interview for Children and Adolescents (from Multi-Health Systems), the Giannetti On-Line Psychosocial History (GOLPH) (Giannetti, 1987; from NCS Assessments), and the Quickview Social History (from NCS Assessments). The last of these collects information on the client's developmental, familial, educational, mental, occupational, legal, and military history, as well as identifying demographic data, financial information, and symptoms of disorder. Also available is software that enables clinicians to develop their own interviews (for example, Q-Fast from StatSoft) or to modify existing interviews (for example, Psychosocial History Report from Psychometric Software).

As with other psychometric applications of computers, the advantages of interviewing by computer are efficiency, flexibility, and reliability. Computer-based interviewing saves professional time, permits a broader coverage of topics, and is more flexible than a series of questions asked by a human interviewer. In general, there is a high degree of agreement between information obtained by computer interviewing and information elicited by standard psychiatric interviews and questionnaires. Most people do not object to being interviewed by a computer and, in fact, may be more willing to divulge personal information, particularly of a sensitive nature, to an impersonal, nonjudgmental computer than to a human interviewer (Rosenfeld et al., 1989; Farrell, 1993). Some disadvantages of computer-based interviewing are that it may be necessary to abbreviate or bypass the system in crisis cases, it has limited utility with children and adults of low mentality, and it may not be flexible enough to use with the wide range of problems and symptoms found in psychiatric patients (Haynes, 1984). Other potential disadvantages of computer-based interviewing are difficulties in handling anything other than structured, verbal information and an inability to tailor the wording of questions to the person and the context (Erdman, Klein, & Greist, 1985). A sequential, unstructured interview in which successive questions are determined by the interviewee's responses to previous questions is more difficult to program than a structured interviewing procedure in which the same questions are asked of every interviewee.

## Computer-based Test Interpretation

Even more complex than using computers to administer and score tests or to conduct interviews is automated interpretation of the results. The first computer-based test interpretation (CBTI) programs were developed in the early 1960s at the Mayo Clinic, the Hartford Institute of Living, and the University of Alabama (Swenson & Pearson, 1964; Rome et al., 1962; Glueck & Reznikoff, 1965). These programs were designed to score, profile, and interpret MMPI responses that had been hand-recorded on optical-scan answer sheets. Subsequently, Fowler (1966–1976) developed a more complex program for automated interpretation of the MMPI. By the mid-1970s, Johnson and Williams (1975) had designed a large-scale computer-based test interpretation system for patients at the Salt Lake City Veterans Administration Hospital. By 1977, an improved on-line system for interpreting the MMPI was available for use with microcomputers.

Hundreds of CBTI programs and services are now commercially available, including programs that score and interpret the results of tests of cognitive abilities, neuropsychological functioning, and personality. Report 12–1 was generated by a computer program designed to interpret the 16 PF, and Report 12–2 was generated by a program for interpreting the MMPI-2. Many companies provide computerized test interpretation and reporting services, as well as hardware and software for computer-based testing. The names and addresses of some of these companies are given in Appendix E. This list should in no way be construed as an endorsement of these companies; some of the products and services are satisfactory, others are not.

The programs that generate CBTI reports represent either a distillation of clinical experience or a conglomeration of statistical relationships between what people say on an inventory or other psychometric device and what they actually do or are. In the clinical approach, the diagnostic program essentially mimics the clinical judgments of experienced or expert psychodiagnosticians, whereas in the statistical or actuarial approach the reported interpretative statements are based on significant differences between the responses of two contrasting groups of people—those independently diagnosed as belonging to one diagnostic group and those belonging to another.

Whether the program follows the more popular clinical approach or the statistical–actuarial approach, the rules or algorithms used in generating CBTI reports range in difficulty from (1) a simple procedure in which a given score or score range is connected to a set of short interpretative paragraphs all the way through (2) a complex set of if–then decision rules in which a particular pattern of subscores leads to a given interpretive statement. However, even the most complex interpretations are usually not as individualized as those devised impressionistically by a clinical or counseling psychologist. The algorithms and decision trees followed in various CBTI programs result in the same data producing the same set of verbal statements. The reader of such a report may be impressed by its scientific aura, but may also find the interpretative statements too long and repetitious. For this reason, the trend has been toward simpler narrative reports that are easy to read. Decrying this trend, Conoley, Plake, and Kemmerer (1991) warn that it probably compromises the validity of CBTI reports. On the other hand, inclusion of an extensive amount of detailed interpretative information in a report should also serve as a warning flag. As a broad rule of thumb, Murphy and Davidshofer (1994) suggest that the more a CBTI report says about a person the less likely it is to be true.

Most CBTI programs are designed to take the age, gender, and other demographic information about the examinee into account, but no program considers all the examinee's personal attributes. Consequently, psychological examiners typically supplement these reports with additional interpretive statements gleaned from their own observations and experiences. Thus, they concur with the recommendation in the *Guidelines for Computer-Based Tests and Interpretations* that

Computer-generated interpretive reports should be used only in conjunction with professional judgment. The user should judge for each test taker the validity of the computerized test report based on the user's professional knowledge of the total context of testing and the test taker's performance and characteristics. (American Psychological Association, 1986, page 12)

CBTI reports are not an adequate substitute for clinical judgment, and a trained clinician should review the report and perhaps fine-tune it with information obtained from other sources. Nevertheless, embellishing or altering a computer-based interpretation in any way should not be done routinely, but only for good and compelling reasons.

Computers have been resisted by those clinicians who consider them a threat to their control over decision making. But the importance of the counselor or therapist is rarely diminished when a computer administers, scores, and provides an initial interpretation of the results. Research findings indicate that CBTI reports are not viewed as more accurate or valid than clinical judgment (Andrews & Gutkin, 1991; Honacker, Hector, & Harel, 1986). Despite their aura of scientific certainty, it would appear that computers are trusted no more than, and typically not as much as, a sensitive clinician to identify one's characteristics and problems and point to the right direction for success and solutions.

## Problems and Standards in Computer-based
## Test Interpretation

Computers, and especially microcomputers, possess many advantages for psychological assessment. In addition to being extremely efficient, they are adaptable to individual differences in mental and physical characteristics and provide prompt scoring and interpretation of assessment results. There are, however, some serious problems with the use of computers in testing. Among these are the cost of the system and the inadequacy of software, as well as the fact that computer-based test interpretations may be inappropriate with certain groups of people—young children, the mentally retarded, people in crisis situations, and severe psychotics. The problem of maintaining confidentiality when computers collect and store personal information also exists. People have a legal right to control the release of their test scores and other personal information, a right that may be too easily violated when such information is stored on a computer. Clearly, CBTI reports should be kept confidential, with both the examiner and the record-keeper acting in accord with the examinee's right to privacy and control over his or her own personal data.

With respect to computer-based test scoring and interpretation services, because of their proprietary nature it is almost impossible to know whether the interpretations generated by the programs applied in these services are valid or not (Conoley, Plake, & Kemmerer, 1991; Moreland, 1990; Snyder, Widiger, & Hoover, 1990). From the available information, it seems safe to say that few of the algorithms used in these programs have been adequately validated and many of the interpretations are based on inadequate norms. Reliability is also a problem with some programs. For these reasons, customers of computer-based psychometric services should require proof that the service providers adhere to the usual standards of reliability, validity, and representative norms as do publishers of paper-and-pencil tests.

On the vendor side, developers of CBTI products and organizations that provide CBTI services should make certain that users of their products are qualified psychodiagnosticians. At the very least, users of such products should be required to provide proof of competency in administering and interpreting the computer-based test(s) without assistance from a computer (Conoley, Plake, & Kemmerer, 1991). Providers of CBTI software should also make certain that their programs are adequately validated and standardized, that they follow the *Guidelines for Computer-based Tests and Interpretations,* and that supporting information is made available, with all applicable documentation, to qualified reviewers. Reviews of CBTI products are published in professional journals such as *Computers in Human Behavior, Computers in Human Services, Computers in Psychiatry/Psychology, Computer Use in Social Services,* and the *Journal of Counseling and Development.*

Finally, students in the human service professions should receive adequate computer-based assessment training, more than that required by the "computer-literate" qualification for college graduation. Such training has become increasingly important as new forms of assessment based on administration, scoring, and interpretation by computers are developed. Because the human service professions have traditionally been nontechnically oriented and usually attract students having minimal knowledge and experience with computers, this requirement is important, but admittedly difficult to realize in practice.

## Computer-based Counseling and Guidance

Related to the use of computers in psychological and educational testing is computer-based counseling. Because many students experience learning problems that require academic counseling, it is not surprising that a number of computer programs have been devised for this purpose. An early example is the Computer-Assisted Study Skills Instruction System (CASSI) (Sampson, 1981). Using this system, students completed assigned lessons and were then assisted in applying to their academic studies the concepts that they learned.

Career counseling and guidance is another school-related area in which computers have been used extensively. Computer-assisted guidance systems are designed to help students to explore their interests, values, attitudes, and abilities and to make realistic career decisions. In addition to possessing the advantages of speed and reliability, these systems have access to much more occupational information than any guidance counselor working alone could ever be expected to. For example, the examinee might be asked to indicate which of several occupational activities he or she would most like to pursue. The computer would then search its massive memory bank for information pertaining to occupations of which those activities are a part. Two computer-based career guidance programs, SIGI PLUS and DISCOVER, are described in Chapter 10.

Computers have also been programmed to assist in personality counseling, and a variety of software is available. One of the first such programs was designed by Cassel and Blum (1970) to identify and counsel potentially delinquent youth. Potential delinquents were first identified from their scores on an eight-part Ego-Ideal and Conscience Development Test and then exposed to Computer Assist Counseling to teach them more socially appropriate behavior patterns. Programs utilizing other approaches to counseling (client centered, psychoanalytic, cognitive, and others) have been developed since the late 1960s. Illustrative of attempts to combine counseling with assessment is PLATO DCS (Wagman, 1980), which followed a cognitive framework and a logical pattern modeled after the computer. Further progress in computer-assisted counseling for personal problems awaits the construction of programs that have the ability to interpret natural language and to respond not only to what is said but also to how it is said.

## Computers and Diagnostic Tools

With respect to the applications of computers in psychodiagnosis, data on thousands of human problems occurring in a variety of person–situation contexts can be stored in a computer's memory and referred to on request. For every clinical problem or case described by the assessor, the computer may suggest several possible explanations or assessment strategies for further exploration. Advances in computer simulation of medical cases suggest that computers might also be programmed to simulate various psychological disorders, providing a framework for increased understanding and treatment of the disorders. Once enough information on the diagnostic signs has been stored in a computer's memory, it may play a central role in periodic psychological checkups of people. Research on using expert systems to make medical diagnosis, in which the approaches (heuristics) followed by experts are incorporated into a computer program, suggests that these speculations may not be far afield (Michaelsen, Michie, & Boulanger, 1985).

Routine use of computers to make educational and psychological diagnoses may not occur for many years, but currently on the drawing board are machines that will herald a dramatic shift from the role of number cruncher to that of knowledge processor and problem solver. These computers will be able to generate open-ended questions and, by being programmed to recognize a set of key words and phrases, evaluate the typed or spoken responses. Computers with the capacity to analyze complex verbal responses will be able to recognize many possible right answers and score them intelligently. By attaching various input and output devices (audio- and videocassettes; light-, heat-, and touch-sensitive screens; joysticks, dials, psychophysical transducers, and so on) to a computer, the administration of tests to both normal and handicapped individuals and the interpretation of responses to a variety of cognitive and affective stimuli is becoming possible. In classrooms of the future, computers will administer interactive diagnostic tests, keep a record of every student's performance, and track errors to identify patterns and problems. Feedback will be immediate and on-screen, confirming right answers, correcting wrong answers, and suggesting instructional materials that can correct errors.

## OTHER CURRENT DEVELOPMENTS AND FUTURE PROSPECTS

As witnessed by the large number of psychometric instruments cited in recent editions of *Tests, Tests in Print,* and other sources, the quantity of new instruments has continued to increase. Many of these instruments fail to meet the requirements of adequate standardization, reliability, and validity, but improvements in the assessment of abilities, personality, and other psychological processes have been noteworthy.

### Theory-based Assessment

In the past, tests of cognitive abilities have been constructed primarily on an empirical, utilitarian basis. In the case of tests of intelligence and special aptitude, less concern was shown with content and more with whether the statistical evidence indicated that the tests performed as they were supposed to. In the future, however, tests of abilities will probably be based more on theories of cognition, learning, and instruction. The field of intelligence testing is being reshaped by the research of cognitive and physiological theorists. Attempts are being made to identify the cognitive stages or components and the physiological structures and processes involved in human learning, thinking, and problem solving. Information-processing analyses of performances that contribute to proficiency in various tasks are conducted by comparing the techniques employed by experts with those of novices. Such analyses are leading to an increased understanding of what is involved in highly competent performance.

### Individualized Instruction

Because tests are designed to measure individual differences in cognitive and affective variables, it seems reasonable to capitalize on these differences by using test scores to allocate people to occupations or educational curricula that are deemed most appropriate to their abilities and interests. The fact that the effectiveness of a particular type of instructional program depends to some degree on the learner's pattern of cognitive abilities is widely recognized and has been the topic of much research. Individualized approaches to instruction envisioned by certain educational planners consider each student's unique pattern of abilities and interests in planning his or her educational experiences. This instructional strategy is modular: the student works through only those learning modules from which, according to the results of psychodiagnostic testing, he or she can benefit. Computers can be of assistance at every stage of an individualized instructional process: in diagnosing the needs of the learner, in presenting the instructional material, in reevaluating the learner's status and needs, and in redesigning the instructional program.

## Computer-assisted Instruction

Computer-assisted instruction is not new, but technological advances in computing machinery and programming have made it even more feasible now than in the past. In computer-assisted instruction (CAI), a computer acts as a private tutor in guiding the learner through the lesson in small steps, asking questions, and keeping a record of correct and incorrect responses. The learner proceeds at his or her own rate, reading the statements of information and responding to questions based on that information. Instructional materials may also be presented by colored slides, computer graphics, sound recordings, and other media. Learners usually type their responses into the computer, although other response modes include touching a light-pen or finger to the CRT screen and voicing answers. A joystick connected to a computer can also facilitate the measurement of perceptual-motor skills. Whatever the response may be and however it is made, it will be evaluated by the computer and confirmed or disconfirmed. If the response is correct, the computer acknowledges this and perhaps rewards the learner in some other way and then proceeds with the regular program. If the response is incorrect, the computer informs the learner of the fact and why, perhaps offers some encouragement, and may then branch to an alternative remedial procedure in the program.

Proponents of computer-assisted instruction may not express the same revolutionary fervor as they did in the 1960s, but CAI is still being used to teach a wide range of information and skills—from learning a foreign language to flying a helicopter—in educational and other organizational contexts. An advantage of CAI is that learners can proceed at their own rate and receive immediate feedback regarding the correctness or adequacy of their responses. Major disadvantages include high cost, poorly designed programs, and negative reactions on the part of some learners.

## Educational Diagnosis Revisited

One needed improvement in cognitive assessment is for tests that are more diagnostic in nature, a goal that can only be realized with multiscore instruments. Consequently, psychometric seers look forward to less emphasis on single-score tests for predicting educational or vocational performance and greater emphasis on multiscore instruments designed with diagnostic purposes in mind. These diagnostic tests of cognitive abilities may well be of the criterion-referenced (absolute assessment) type, rather than the more traditional norm-referenced (relative assessment) type. Their use may be coupled with dynamic (authentic) assessment, using a test–teach–test format in which initial testing is followed by practice on the test materials and then retesting. The number of prompts, cues, or other instructional aids required to produce a significant change in scores from initial to final testing will be a measure of ability in the particular skill area being assessed.

The proposed diagnostic tests are likely to be individualized and adaptive, including a brief challenge test, probes to identify the component skills of an area in which the student has problems, construction of a profile of the learner's strengths and weaknesses, and presentation of remedial instruction. The tests will be aimed primarily at helping students to learn and succeed, rather than simply yielding scores for institutional decision making, and will guide instruction and self-development on a continuing basis, rather than merely comparing performances among test takers. For many years, aptitude test batteries such as the DAT and the ASVAB and interest inventories such as the SII and the KOIS have been administered in the schools to provide assistance to students in making academic and vocational decisions. A related, but more sophisticated and extensive product and service developed by the American College Testing Program promises to have greater utility than the older aptitude and interest instruments. This product, designated as the *Work Keys Systems,* translates national standards for high school graduation into workplace skills. Using a common language to describe the pattern of strengths and weaknesses in a person's cognitive abilities, the Work Keys Systems consists of a series of criterion-referenced skills scales for measuring abilities and other work skills. Work Keys skills include applied mathematics, applied technology, learning, listening, locating information, managing resources, motivation, observing, reading for information, speaking, teamwork, and writing. A person's performance on skills tests in these areas is compared with the skill level required for a particular job, resulting in a skills profile for that job. This information can then be used to identify deficiencies, provide feedback to students who take the tests, and train them in the skills needed for particular jobs (Custer, 1994).

## Personality Assessment

Compared with the technical sophistication of ability testing, personality inventories and other affective measuring instruments are relatively crude. The potential value of accurate personality assessment is obvious, and recent progress in the psychometrically sophisticated design of certain inventories of personality characteristics and interests suggests that general improvements in affective assessment are forthcoming. New methodologies and research on the cognitive processes involved in clinical judgments are contributing to that progress.

Over a decade ago, Ziskin (1986) listed a number of signs of the unhealthy state of clinical psychology: the lack of an adequate system for classifying mental disorders, contamination of data by situational effects, evidence that clinical skills do not improve with practice, difficulties in differentiating between normal and psychopathological behavior, and problems with computer interpretation of data. Unfortunately, these signs are still visible. Ziskin advocated treating this "illness" with a broader approach to computer use in clinical diagnosis, including not only the MMPI and similar instruments, but also demographic data and information from structured interviews. He also predicted that in the future greater emphasis will be placed on personal assets (such as good looks), psychosocial stress, and structured interviewing. Finally, clinicians should be more aware of the fact that there are limits to what can be discovered about people by means of psychological assessment.

Because of their adaptability to changing circumstances and the existence of highly capable proponents such as James Butcher and John Exner, it is unlikely that work horses such as the MMPI or the Rorschach will be replaced anytime soon. Newer uses for these tests will be discovered, and newer tests will force a continuing reevaluation of these and other time-honored clinical instruments. Some years ago Weiner (1983) predicted a bright future for psychodiagnosis. He also cautioned, however, that the realization of such a future demands "continued careful research on psychodiagnostic methods and the expert application of psychological test findings . . ." (page 456). This still seems like good advice.

Almost a decade later, Matarazzo (1992) continued to see a bright future for clinical psychodiagnosis. An illustration is the construction of tests to identify and analyze more specific forms of psychopathology, such as panic reactions and depressive disorders. Matarazzo also predicted that newer and better measures of personal competence in adapting to one's environment, including scales of quality of life and adaptive behavior, will be devised. Even more intriguing to Matarazzo than the future of personality assessment were expected developments in physiological measures of intelligence, including indexes derived from intrinsic and evoked brain potentials (EEG and PET) and nerve conduction velocity. Changes in brain potentials have also been found to be associated with scores on measures of personality traits such as introversion–extroversion.

Whatever the future may hold for personality and clinical assessment, there will be a continuing need to evaluate the effectiveness of psychometric instruments and procedures in these areas. Then as now, the major questions concerning any attempt to assess personality will focus on the validity of the instruments and procedures for doing so. To what extent do the assessment methods fulfill their intended purposes in research, clinical diagnosis, treatment planning, and evaluation of the effectiveness of interventions?

Unlike Nostradamus, psychologists are not known for their ability to peer into the future. Even so, the author still believes that exciting and productive times lie ahead for psychological testing and assessment and for those who would make it their life's work. The current situation in this field is quite different from what it was at the beginning of this century—when it was reportedly viewed as the only way in which psychologists could make a living outside the classroom and the laboratory. Today, testing is no longer the bread and butter of psychology, but it certainly remains and will continue to be a significant portion of the meat and potatoes!

## SUMMARY

Psychological testing and assessment continue to grow and undoubtedly will remain an important part of applied psychology well into the next century. The increasing automation of psychological assessment and interviewing by means of computers, and especially microcomputers, has made the administration and scoring of tests and other psychometric devices, as well as the interpretation of test results, more objective and efficient. Computer-based testing is at least as motivating and the results are just as acceptable to examinees as tests administered by traditional procedures.

Adaptive testing, in which the sequence of questions presented to an examinee varies with his or her estimated standing on the specified variable and responses to previous items, substantially reduces the time to administer a test. The use of computers for presenting test items and evaluating answers makes adaptive testing an efficient, albeit more expensive, alternative to the traditional approach of presenting the same items to all examinees.

Substantial progress in computer-based interviewing and test interpretation has been made during the past three decades. Computer-based test interpretation, which began with the work on interpretive scoring of the MMPI at the Mayo Clinic in the early 1960s, has expanded to include the scoring and interpretation of dozens of cognitive and affective instruments by hundreds of commercial organizations.

In addition to their uses in test administration, scoring, and interpretation, psychologists and educators have made extensive use of computers for analyzing research data, for controlling stimulus inputs and response outputs in experiments, and for simulating experiments, environments, and behavior patterns. Two other areas in which computers have been applied with noteworthy success are computer-assisted instruction and computer-based academic and personal counseling. Future computers, which will have parallel architecture and run advanced programs based on expert systems and artificial intelligence, will increase the versatility of psychological assessment procedures far beyond the traditional objective-test format. Theories of cognition and research on the psychophysiological bases of memory, learning, and thinking will also continue to influence the fields of psychological assessment and educational instruction and evaluation.

Although computers have made and will certainly continue to make important contributions to psychological and educational assessment, a number of problems have been encountered. Such problems as cost and "computerphobia" (or "cyberphobia") are perhaps less serious than the problem of confidentiality, which arises when masses of personal data on individuals are stored on computers to which unauthorized persons may have access. Recognition of the growing importance of computers in social science research and applications and consequently the potential for misuse has led to the formulation of guidelines and standards for using computers in psychological practice and research.

Recent developments in psychological testing and assessment include revisions of older psychometric instruments and the development of many new ones, the growth of competency testing in educational and employment contexts, continuing efforts to link assessment to instruction, extensions of psychometric theory and methodology, and efforts to create a clearer interface between assessment, research, and theories of cognition, personality, and psychophysiology.

## QUESTIONS AND ACTIVITIES

1. Run the test-scoring program in Figure 15–1 on a microcomputer, using the fictitious names and letter (a, b, c, d) responses of 10 examinees to 10 test items. Make up your own scoring key. You are also encouraged to extend the program, for example, to compute the mean, standard deviation, and standard $T$ scores of your 10 examinees.

2. How have digital computers in general, and microcomputers in particular, changed the nature of psychological and educational assessment during the past two decades? What further changes in testing are likely to occur as a result of continuing improvements in technology and in the methodology of psychological assessment in the future?

3.  What is *adaptive testing?* What is *stratadaptive testing?* In what ways is adaptive testing superior to traditional testing procedures?

4.  Using information gained from reading or your personal experiences, compare programmed instruction, including computer-assisted instruction, with conventional methods of instruction (lecture, discussion, reports, tests, and others). What are the advantages and disadvantages of computer-assisted instruction compared with other methods of instruction?

5.  Because psychological counseling has traditionally been viewed as involving an interpersonal relationship between a counselor and a counselee, how is it possible to be "counseled" by a non-human, inanimate computer? In what areas and with what kinds of problems is computer-based counseling most likely to be most effective?

6.  Discuss the ethical issues involved in the use of computers in various stages of psychological assessment: test development, test scoring, test interpretation, and test use. What steps should be taken to make certain that computer technology is used wisely and ethically in psychological assessment?

7.  What changes do you foresee for psychological testing and assessment during the next 50 years? What new kinds of tests and methodologies are likely to be developed? What role will automation (computers in particular) play in these changes?

# Appendix A

## MEASUREMENT AND STATISTICS

Any kind of physical measurements (of size, weight, coloration, and so on) made on living things will vary across individual members of a species. Human beings differ physically from each other in many ways—in height, weight, blood pressure, visual acuity, and so on. Individual differences in these physical variables, in addition to cognitive abilities, personality traits, and behaviors, are appreciable. Among other things, people differ in their abilities, interests, attitudes, and temperaments. Some of these individual differences can be measured more precisely than others, as reflected in the type of measurement scale.

### SCALES OF MEASUREMENT

The measurement of physical and psychological variables may be characterized by degree of refinement or precision in terms of four levels or scales: nominal, ordinal, interval, and ratio. Measures on a *nominal scale* are used merely to describe or name, rather than to indicate the order or magnitude of something. Examples of nominal measurement are the numbers on athletic uniforms or numerical designations of demographic variables such as sex (for example, male = 1, female = 2) and ethnicity (white = 0, black = 1, other = 2). Such numbers are a convenient way of describing individuals or groups, but it makes no sense to compare the numbers in terms of direction or magnitude. Somewhat more refined than nominal measurement is measurement on an *ordinal scale*. Numbers on an ordinal scale refer to the ranks of objects or events on some order of merit. For example, numbers designating the order of finishing in a race or other contest are on an ordinal scale. A third level of measurement is an *interval scale,* on which equal numerical differences correspond to equal differences in whatever characteristic is measured. The Celsius scale of temperature is an example of an interval scale. For example, the difference between 40°C and 60°C is equal to the difference between 10° and 30°C, both numerically and in terms of temperature (heat). Standard scores on intelligence test are also considered to be interval-level measurements.

The highest, or most refined, level of measurement is a *ratio scale.* This type of scale has the characteristics of an interval scale as well as a true zero: a value of 0 on a ratio scale signifies a complete absence of whatever is being measured. Measurements made on a ratio scale allow numerical ratios to be interpreted in a meaningful way. Height, for example, is measured on a ratio scale. So if John is 6 feet tall and Paul is 3 feet tall, it is correct to say that John is twice as tall as Paul. Many physical variables are measured on ratio scales, but most psychological characteristics are not. Scores on psychological tests represent measurement on an ordinal or, at most, an interval scale. For this reason, even if Frank's score on an intelligence test is 150 and Jim's score is 50, one cannot conclude that Frank is three times as intelligent as Jim. But if the scores on the test are interval-level measures and Amy makes an IQ score of 100, it can be said that the difference in intelligence between Frank and Amy $(150 - 100)$ is equal to the difference in intelligence between Amy and Jim $(100 - 50)$.

## FREQUENCY DISTRIBUTIONS

The range and distribution of individual differences in physical and mental characteristics may be depicted by means of a frequency distribution of scores on a test or some other psychometric instrument. In its simplest form, a *frequency distribution* is a list of possible scores and the number of people who made each score. Assume that, on a five-item test, one point is given for each correct answer. Then the possible scores are 0, 1, 2, 3, 4, and 5. If 25 people take the test, the frequency distribution of their scores might look something like this:

| Score | Frequency |
|-------|-----------|
| 5 | 1 |
| 4 | 4 |
| 3 | 9 |
| 2 | 6 |
| 1 | 3 |
| 0 | 2 |

Note that 2 people got all five items wrong, 9 people got three items right, and 1 person got all five items right.

### Score Intervals

When the range of scores on a test is large, say 25 points or more, it may be convenient to group them into intervals. To illustrate, intelligence quotient (IQ) scores on the Wechsler Adult Intelligence Scale (WAIS) range from approximately 43 to 152. Computations made on these scores may be simplified by grouping them into intervals of IQ points, starting with the interval 43–47 and counting up through the interval 148–152 (see column 1 of Table A–1). This gives 22 intervals instead of the 110 intervals (IQs from 43 through 152) that would result if an interval were allotted to every possible score. Using the smaller number of intervals has little effect on the accuracy of the statistics computed from the

**TABLE A–1  Frequency Distribution of Full-scale IQs on WAIS**

| IQ interval | Number of examinees (frequency) |
|---|---|
| 148–152 | 1 |
| 143–147 | 0 |
| 138–142 | 3 |
| 133–137 | 12 |
| 128–132 | 26 |
| 123–127 | 64 |
| 118–122 | 145 |
| 113–117 | 165 |
| 108–112 | 224 |
| 103–107 | 274 |
| 98–102 | 278 |
| 93–97 | 255 |
| 88–92 | 220 |
| 83–87 | 135 |
| 78–82 | 107 |
| 73–77 | 55 |
| 68–72 | 49 |
| 63–67 | 18 |
| 58–62 | 11 |
| 53–57 | 6 |
| 48–52 | 3 |
| 43–47 | 1 |

*Source:* Data from D. Wechsler, *The Measurement and Appraisal of Adult Intelligence,* 4th ed. Baltimore: Williams & Wilkins, 1958, page 253.

frequency distribution of WAIS–IQ scores, and it is a more efficient way of describing the scores.

## Histogram and Frequency Polygon

A frequency distribution of scores can be plotted graphically as a histogram or a frequency polygon. To construct a *histogram,* the exact limits of the score intervals must first be determined. The *exact limits* of an interval are computed by subtracting .5 from the lower limit and adding .5 to the upper limit of the interval. For example, the exact limits of the interval 43–47 in Table A–1 are 42.5–47.5, and the exact limits of the interval 148–152 are 147.5–152.5. After the exact limits of all intervals have been computed, the frequency corresponding to each interval is plotted as a vertical bar with a width spanning the exact limits and a height proportional to the number of scores falling on the interval. Figure A–1 is a histogram of the frequency distribution in Table A–1.

A frequency distribution can also be represented by a series of connected line segments. In Figure A–2, the points corresponding to the frequencies and midpoints of the score intervals in Table A–1 have been joined to form a *frequency polygon.*

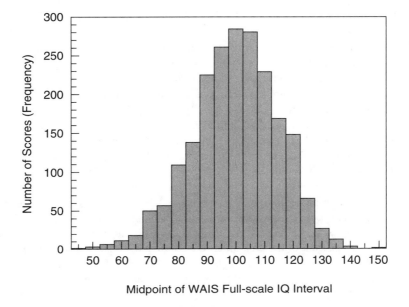

FIGURE A–1   Histogram of Frequency Distribution in Table A–1.

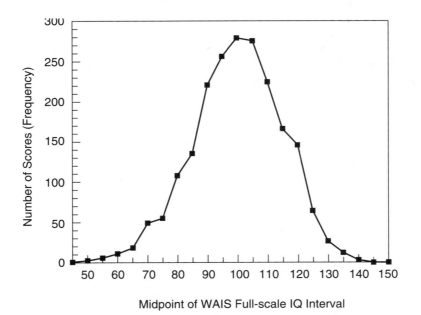

FIGURE A–2   Frequency Polygon of Frequency Distribution in Table A–1.

## Normal Curve

Although the frequency polygon in Figure A–2 is not a smooth curve, it is similar to a symmetrical, bell-shaped curve. More people made scores of approximately 100 (actually 98–102) than any other score, and successively fewer people made scores lower or higher than 100. If the frequency polygon were perfectly symmetrical, smooth, and bell-shaped, it would look like Figure A–3.

The graph in Figure A–3, which can be described by a mathematical equation, is called a *normal curve*. The scores on the base axis of this curve are *standard scores (z scores)*, the computation of which is described in Chapter 4. These z scores serve as a convenient, standard method of expressing and comparing the scores of the same person on two or more tests or the scores of two or more people on the same test.

A certain percentage of the area under the curve in Figure A–3 lies between any two z scores. This percentage may correspond to the percentage of a group of people whose raw test scores, when converted to z scores, fall within the range of the two z scores. For example, 19.15 percent of the area under the curve and, consequently, 19.15 percent of a normal distribution of test scores, falls between $z = 0$ and $z = .5$ (or $z = 0$ and $z = -.5$). On the other hand, only 1.66 percent of the area under a normal curve lies between $z = +2.0$ and $z = +2.5$ (or $z = -2.0$ and $z = -2.5$).

The theoretical range of z scores in a normal distribution is minus infinity ($-\infty$) to plus infinity ($+\infty$), but over 99 percent of the area under the normal curve (or 99 percent of a normal distribution of test scores) falls between z scores of $-3.00$ and $+3.00$. When converting a raw test score to a z score, the result, of course, is not always one of the 13 z scores listed on the horizontal axis of Figure A–3. A special table or computer program must be used to determine the percentage of the area falling between any two values of z (see Appendix B).

During the late nineteenth and early twentieth centuries, there was much speculation concerning whether the normal curve expressed an inherent law of nature. The reason for this belief was that the frequency distributions of measurements made on many characteristics of living organisms are approximately normal in shape. In fact, much of the mathematical

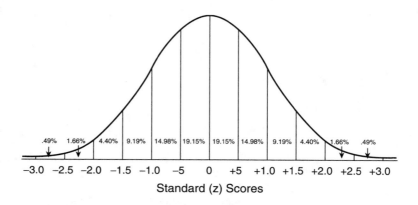

Standard (z) Scores

**FIGURE A–3**  Standard Normal Distribution.

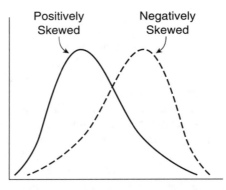

**FIGURE A–4** Skewed Frequency Distributions.

theory of statistical inference, which is so important in psychological and educational research, is based on the assumption of a normal distribution of measurements. You should be careful, however, not to glorify the normal curve. Although many tests are constructed in such a way that their scores are approximately normally distributed, the frequency distributions of other test scores are very asymmetrical, or skewed. A common situation is a *positively skewed* distribution of scores (few high scores and many low scores), representing the results of a test that was perhaps too difficult. Less common is a *negatively skewed* distribution (many high scores and few low scores), which occurs when a test is too easy (Figure A–4).

## MEASURES OF CENTRAL TENDENCY

In addition to plotting the distribution of a set of test scores, it is convenient to have some measure of the typical or average score. Three kinds of averages may be computed: mode, median, and arithmetic mean.

### Mode

The *mode* of a set of test scores is the score obtained by the largest number of people. In the five-item test referred to previously, more people (nine) made a score of 3 than any other score, so the mode is 3. When test scores are grouped into intervals, the mode is the midpoint of the interval containing the largest number of scores. The score interval 98–102 in Table A–1 contains the largest number of scores (278); the midpoint of that interval $(98 + 102)/2 = 100$, is the mode of that frequency distribution.

As seen in the frequency polygon in Figure A–2, the mode is the score corresponding to the highest point in a frequency distribution. Figure A–2 pictures a *unimodal* distribution having one peak. Sometimes a frequency distribution has more than one peak; it is *bimodal* if it has two peaks, and *multimodal* if it has more than two.

## Median

The *median* (Mdn) of a set of scores is the middlemost score, that is, the score below which half the scores fall. The median of 7, 6, 9, 5, and 3 is 6, because 6 is in the middle when these five scores are ranked from highest to lowest. When the number of scores is even, the median is defined as the mean of the two middlemost scores.

It takes a few steps to compute the median of a frequency distribution, but it can be found fairly quickly by interpolating within the interval in which it falls. To illustrate the procedure, the median of the frequency distribution in Table A–1 will be computed. The total number of scores is 2052, so the median is the IQ score below and above which .5(2052) = 1026 scores fall. By successively adding the frequencies in column 2 of Table A–1, we find that there are 860 scores up through the interval 93–97 and 1138 scores up through the interval 98–102. Expressed in terms of the exact upper limits of the intervals, we say that 860 scores fall below 97.5 and 1138 scores fall below 102.5. Because the median is the score below which 1026 scores fall, it is between 97.5 and 102.5. To find the exact median, we form the ratio $(\text{Mdn} - 97.5)/(102.5 - 97.5) = (1026 - 860)/(1138 - 860)$. Solving this equation yields a value of 100.49 for the median.

The procedure described for finding the median of a frequency distribution may be simplified as

$$\text{Mdn} = L + \frac{w(.5n_t - n_b)}{n_i} \tag{A.1}$$

In this formula, $L$ is the lower exact limit and $w$ the width of the interval containing the median, $n_t$ is the total number of scores in the distribution, $n_b$ is the number of scores falling below the interval containing the median, and $n_i$ is the number of scores falling on the interval containing the median.

## Summation Operator

Before considering the procedure for computing the arithmetic mean, you should become familiar with the special symbol $\Sigma$. This symbol, the Greek letter capital sigma, is a shorthand way of designating the mathematical operation of summation. Thus, $\Sigma X = X_1 + X_2 + X_3 + \cdots + X_n$. To illustrate, consider the three scores $X_1 = 2$, $X_2 = 4$, and $X_3 = 1$. The sum of these scores is $\Sigma X = 2 + 4 + 1 = 7$. Similarly, the sum of squares of the three scores $\Sigma X^2 = X_1^2 + X_2^2 + X_3^2 = 2^2 + 4^2 + 1^2 = 4 + 16 + 1 = 21$.

The sum of the products of two variables, $X$ and $Y$ is expressed as $\Sigma XY = X_1Y_1 + X_2Y_2 + X_3Y_3$. If $Y_1 = 3, Y_2 = 5, Y_3 = 2$ and the $X$ values are the same as those in the preceding problem, $\Sigma XY = 2(3) + 4(5) + 1(2) = 6 + 20 + 2 = 28$.

## Arithmetic Mean

Although the mode is easy to compute, it is greatly affected by the shape of the frequency distribution of scores. The median, which is less affected by the shape of the frequency distribution, is the preferred measure of central tendency when the distribution is highly asymmetrical, or skewed. But because the median is cumbersome to work with in statistical theory, the arithmetic mean is the most popular measure of central tendency (average). The arithmetic mean of a set of scores ($X$'s) is determined by adding the scores and dividing the resulting sum by the number of scores:

$$\overline{X} = \Sigma\, X/n \qquad\qquad\qquad\qquad\text{(A.2)}$$

The mean of the $X$ scores in the preceding problem is $7/3 = 2.33$.

When scores are grouped in the form of a frequency distribution, the mean can be found more quickly by (1) multiplying the midpoint ($X_i'$) of each interval by the frequency ($f_i$) on that interval, (2) adding these $fX'$ products, and (3) dividing the resulting sum of products by the total number of scores ($n$):

$$\overline{X} = \Sigma\, fX'/n \qquad\qquad\qquad\qquad\text{(A.3)}$$

To illustrate, in the five-item problem described earlier, the arithmetic mean is $[2(0) + 3(1) + 6(2) + 9(3) + 4(4) + 1(5)]/25 = 63/25 = 2.52$. As an exercise, you should verify that the arithmetic mean of the frequency distribution in Table A–1 is 99.96.

## PERCENTILES, DECILES, AND QUARTILES

The median is sometimes referred to as the 50th percentile, because 50 percent of the scores fall below the median. A frequency distribution may be divided into 100 percentiles: the *pth percentile* is the value below which $p$ percent of the scores fall. For example, the 25th percentile is the value below which 25 percent of the scores fall, and the 75th percentile is the value below which 75 percent of the scores fall. Any percentile can be computed by a procedure similar to that described previously for finding the median.

In addition to percentiles, a frequency distribution may be divided into tenths (*deciles*), fifths (*quintiles*), or fourths (*quartiles*). The fourth decile (or 40th percentile) is the value below which four-tenths of the scores fall, and the third quartile (or 75th percentile) is the value below which three-fourths of the scores fall. Note that the 50th percentile, the fifth decile, and the second quartile are all equal to the same numerical value.

## MEASURES OF VARIABILITY

A measure of the average or central tendency does not, by itself, provide an adequate analytic description of a sample of scores. Groups of scores differ not only in their averages, but also in their degree of variability (spread), symmetry, and peakedness. Three measures of variability will be described: the range, the semi-interquartile range, and the standard deviation.

### Range and Semi-interquartile Range

The simple *range,* defined as the highest score minus the lowest score, is the easiest measure of variability to compute. The range of the scores in the five-item problem described previously is $5 - 0 = 5$, and the range of the IQ scores in Table A–1 is $152 - 43 = 109$.

Because it is markedly affected by a single very high or very low score, in most cases the range is a poor measure of variability. A modified type of range known as the *semi-interquartile range* is sometimes used as an index of variability when the distribution of scores is highly skewed. The semi-interquartile range, or $Q$, is computed as one-half the difference between the 75th percentile (third quartile) and the 25th percentile (first quartile).

As an exercise, you should verify that, for the frequency distribution in Table A–1, the first quartile is 90.41, the third quartile is 110.33, and the semi-interquartile range is 9.96. The two quartiles may be found by the same sort of linear interpolation procedure that was used to compute the median. Because the first quartile is the score below which .25(2052) = 513 scores fall, we interpolate within the interval 87.5 to 92.5. To find the third quartile, which is the .75(2052) = 1539th score, we interpolate within the interval 107.5 to 112.5. Thus, the first quartile is found by solving the following expression for $Q_1$: $(Q_1 - 87.5)/(92.5 - 87.5)$ = (513 − 385)/(605 − 385). Likewise, the third quartile is found by solving for $Q_3$ in the expression $(Q_3 - 107.5)/(112.5 - 107.5) = (1539 - 1412)/(1636 - 1412)$.

## Standard Deviation

The most common measure of variability, the *standard deviation*, is appropriate when the arithmetic mean is the reported average. The standard deviation of a sample of scores may be computed from

$$s = \sqrt{\frac{\Sigma X^2 - (\Sigma X)^2/n}{n - 1}} \tag{A.4}$$

For example, to find the standard deviation of 7, 6, 9, 5, and 3, we begin by computing $\Sigma X = 30$ and $\Sigma X^2 = 200$. Therefore, $\Sigma X^2 - (\Sigma X)^2/n = (200 - 30^2/5)/4 = 5$, which is the *variance* of our five numbers. Extracting the square root of the variance yields 2.24, the standard deviation.

By setting $\Sigma X = \Sigma f(X')$ and $\Sigma X^2 = \Sigma f(X'^2)$, where $f$ is the frequency and $X'$ the midpoint on an interval, we can use formula A.4 to compute the standard deviation of a frequency distribution. As an exercise, you should show that the standard deviation of the five-item problem referred to previously is 1.26 and the standard deviation of the frequency distribution in Table A–1 is 14.85.

## CORRELATION AND LINEAR REGRESSION

The method of correlation has been employed extensively in the analysis of test data, and it is also very important in classical test theory. Correlation is concerned with determining the extent to which two sets of measures, such as intelligence test scores and school marks, are related. The magnitude and direction of the relationship between two variables is expressed as a numerical index known as the *correlation coefficient*. Of the many different types of correlation coefficient, the Pearson *product–moment coefficient*, or *r*, is the most popular. It ranges in value from −1.00 (a perfect inverse relationship) to +1.00 (a perfect direct relationship).

## Computing the Product–Moment Coefficient

Table A–2 illustrates the initial computations in determining the correlation coefficient between 30 pairs of $X$–$Y$ scores. Let $X$ be an ability test score and $Y$ a job performance rating. Thus, person 1 scored 44 on the ability test and 69 on the performance rating, whereas the corresponding scores for person 2 are 38 and 46. The column headings indicate the steps in computing $r$:

1.  Compute $X^2$, $Y^2$, and $XY$ for each person (columns 4, 5, and 6).

**TABLE A–2   Computing Sums for Determining Product–Moment Correlation**

| (1)<br>Person | (2)<br>X | (3)<br>Y | (4)<br>$X^2$ | (5)<br>$Y^2$ | (6)<br>XY |
|:---:|:---:|:---:|:---:|:---:|:---:|
| 1 | 44 | 69 | 1,936 | 4,761 | 3,036 |
| 2 | 38 | 46 | 1,444 | 2,116 | 1,748 |
| 3 | 56 | 51 | 3,136 | 2,601 | 2,856 |
| 4 | 54 | 44 | 2,916 | 1,936 | 2,376 |
| 5 | 66 | 53 | 4,356 | 2,809 | 3,498 |
| 6 | 52 | 49 | 2,704 | 2,401 | 2,548 |
| 7 | 46 | 43 | 2,116 | 1,849 | 1,978 |
| 8 | 36 | 35 | 1,296 | 1,225 | 1,260 |
| 9 | 44 | 37 | 1,936 | 1,369 | 1,628 |
| 10 | 60 | 69 | 3,600 | 4,761 | 4,140 |
| 11 | 22 | 31 | 484 | 961 | 682 |
| 12 | 72 | 47 | 5,184 | 2,209 | 3,384 |
| 13 | 56 | 45 | 3,136 | 2,025 | 2,520 |
| 14 | 52 | 41 | 2,704 | 1,681 | 2,132 |
| 15 | 50 | 39 | 2,500 | 1,521 | 1,950 |
| 16 | 64 | 65 | 4,096 | 4,225 | 4,160 |
| 17 | 40 | 36 | 1,600 | 1,296 | 1,440 |
| 18 | 28 | 59 | 784 | 3,481 | 1,652 |
| 19 | 68 | 70 | 4,624 | 4,900 | 4,760 |
| 20 | 48 | 53 | 2,304 | 2,809 | 2,544 |
| 21 | 32 | 51 | 1,024 | 2,601 | 1,632 |
| 22 | 74 | 63 | 5,476 | 3,969 | 4,662 |
| 23 | 42 | 54 | 1,764 | 2,916 | 2,268 |
| 24 | 50 | 52 | 2,500 | 2,704 | 2,600 |
| 25 | 40 | 49 | 1,600 | 2,401 | 1,960 |
| 26 | 58 | 48 | 3,364 | 2,304 | 2,784 |
| 27 | 62 | 60 | 3,844 | 3,600 | 3,720 |
| 28 | 54 | 64 | 2,916 | 4,096 | 3,456 |
| 29 | 60 | 55 | 3,600 | 3,025 | 3,300 |
| 30 | 30 | 33 | 900 | 1,089 | 990 |
| Sums | 1,498 | 1,511 | 79,844 | 79,641 | 77,664 |

2. Add the $X, Y, X^2, Y^2$, and $XY$ columns (columns 2 through 6) and substitute these sums into the following formula:

$$r = \frac{n \sum XY - (\sum X)(\sum Y)}{\sqrt{[n \sum X^2 - (\sum X)^2][n \sum Y^2 - (\sum Y)^2]}} \qquad \text{(A.5)}$$

Since $\sum X = 1498$, $\sum Y = 1511$, $\sum X^2 = 79,844$, $\sum Y^2 = 79,641$, and $\sum XY = 77,664$,

$$r = \frac{30(77,664) - (1498)(1511)}{\sqrt{[30(79,844) - (1498)^2][30(79,641) - (1511)^2]}}$$

$$= .524$$

## Meaning of Correlation

The method of correlation is useful in the field of psychological testing for a number of reasons, among which is the fact that correlation implies predictability. The accuracy with which a person's score on measure $Y$ can be predicted from his or her score on measure $X$ depends on the magnitude of the correlation between the two variables. The closer the correlation coefficient is to an absolute value of 1.00 (either $+1.00$ or $-1.00$), the smaller is the average error made in predicting $Y$ scores from $X$ scores. For example, if the correlation between tests $X$ and $Y$ is close to $+1.00$, it can be predicted with confidence that a person who makes a high score on variable $X$ will also make a high score on variable $Y$, and a person who makes a low score on $X$ will make a low score on $Y$. On the other hand, if the correlation is close to $-1.00$, it can be predicted with confidence that a person who scores high on $X$ will score low on $Y$ and a person who scores low on $X$ will score high on $Y$. The closer the value of $r$ is to $+1.00$ or $-1.00$, the more accurate these predictions will be; the closer $r$ is to .00, the less accurate they will be. When $r = .00$, predicting a person's score on one variable from his or her score on the other variable is no better than chance.

It is important to remember that correlation implies prediction, but it does not imply causation. The fact that two variables are related does not mean that either is necessarily a cause of the other. Both variables may be influenced by a third variable, and the correlation between the first two is a reflection of this common cause. For example, it can be demonstrated that the mental ages of a group of children with a wide range of chronological ages is positively correlated with their shoe sizes. Neither mental age nor shoe size is a cause of the other, but rather the positive correlation between these two variables is due to the influence of a third variable—maturation or physical growth—on both mental age and shoe size. The fact that two variables are significantly correlated facilitates predicting performance on one from performance on the other, but it provides no direct information on whether the two variables are causally connected.

## Simple Linear Regression

The product–moment correlation coefficient, which is a measure of the *linear* relationship between two variables, is actually a by-product of the statistical procedure for finding the equation of the straight line that best fits the set of points representing the paired *X–Y* values. To illustrate the meaning of this statement, the *X–Y* pairs of values listed in Table A–2 are plotted as a *scattergram* in Figure A–5. Clearly, all 30 points do not fall on the same straight line, but a line can be fitted through the points in such a way that the sum of the squared vertical distances of the points from the line is as small as possible. A formula for finding this *least-squares regression line* is

$$Y_{pred} = r \frac{s_y}{s_x}(X - \overline{X}) + \overline{Y} \tag{A.6}$$

where $\overline{X}$ and $\overline{Y}$ are the means and $s_x$ and $s_y$ the standard deviations of the $X$ and $Y$ variables. For the data in Table A–2, $\overline{X} = 49.93$, $\overline{Y} = 50.37$, $s_x = 13.19$, $s_y = 11.04$, and $r = .52$. Entering these numbers into formula A.6 and simplifying yields the linear equation $Y_{pred} = .44X + 28.64$. Using this equation, a person's score on variable $Y$ can be predicted with better than chance accuracy from his or her score on variable $X$. For example, as illustrated by the dashed lines in Figure A–5, if $X = 42$, $Y_{pred} = .44(42) + 28.64 = 47.12$. This means that, if a person makes a score of 42 on the $X$ variable, the best estimate of his or her score on the $Y$ variable is approximately 47.

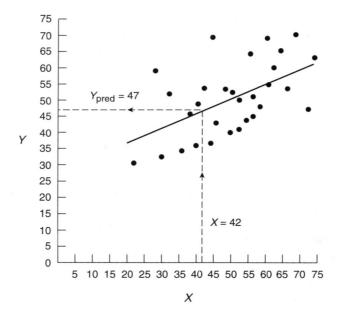

**FIGURE A–5** Scattergram of Scores in Table A–2, Showing Regression Line and Illustration.

## ADVANCED STATISTICS

### Multiple Regression

Simple linear regression analysis involving one independent ($X$) variable can be extended to two or more independent variables. Let $Y$ be the criterion variable and $X_1, X_2$, and $X_3$ be the independent variables. Then

$$d = 1 - r_{12}^2 - r_{13}^2 - r_{23}^2 + 2r_{12}r_{13}r_{23}$$

$$B_1 = \frac{r_{y1}(1 - r_{23}^2) - r_{y2}(r_{12} - r_{13}r_{23}) - r_{y3}(r_{13} - r_{12}r_{23})}{d} \tag{A.7}$$

$$B_2 = \frac{r_{y2} - r_{y3}r_{23} - B_1(r_{12} - r_{13}r_{23})}{(1 - r_{23}^2)} \tag{A.8}$$

$$B_3 = r_{y3} - B_1 r_{13} - B_2 r_{23} \tag{A.9}$$

To find the regression equation, substitute the values of the $B_i$'s in the following formula:

$$Y_{\text{pred}} = s_y \Sigma \frac{B_i}{s_i}(X_i - \overline{X}_i) + \overline{Y} \tag{A.10}$$

A multiple correlation coefficient can be computed with the formula

$$R = \sqrt{\Sigma \, B_i r_{yi}} \tag{A.11}$$

Furthermore, to test the statistical significance of each of the $B$ weights, we find the standard errors of each $B$ weight by means of the following formulas:

$$se_1 = \sqrt{\frac{(1 - R^2)(1 - r_{23}^2)}{d(n - p)}} \tag{A.12}$$

$$se_2 = \sqrt{\frac{(1 - R^2)(1 - r_{13}^2)}{d(n - p)}} \tag{A.13}$$

$$se_3 = \sqrt{\frac{(1 - R^2)(1 - r_{12}^2)}{d(n - p)}} \tag{A.14}$$

Each of the $t$ values can then be computed as $t = B_i/se_i$, with degrees of freedom equal to $n - p$.

In these formulas, $n$ is the number of scores and $p$ is the number of independent variables plus 1. If there are only two independent variables, $B_3$ and $se_3$ are not computed, and all other expressions involving a subscript 3 become 0.

### Factor Analysis

The major purpose of *factor analysis* is to reduce the number of variables in a group of measures by taking into account the overlap (correlations) among them. In the field of psychological testing, the problem is to find a few salient factors that can account for the major part of the variance of a group of scores on different tests. The many different procedures for extracting these factors from test scores are all based on a fundamental theorem: The observed (total) variance of a test $(s_{obs}^2)$ is equal to the sum of the variance due to factors that the test has in common with other tests $(s_{com}^2)$, the variance specific to the test itself $(s_{spe}^2)$, and the variance produced by errors of measurement $(s_{err}^2)$. Consequently, formula 5.1 may be rewritten as

$$s_{obs}^2 = s_{com}^2 + s_{spe}^2 + s_{err}^2 \qquad \text{(A.15)}$$

In formula A.15, what was referred to in Chapter 5 as the true variance of a test $(s_{tru}^2)$ is partitioned into common-factor variance and specific-factor variance. The portion of the observed variance due to common factors is called the test's *communality,* whereas the portion of the observed variance due to specific factors is its *specificity.* From these definitions and formulas 5.2 and A.15, we may write the equation

$$\text{reliability} = \text{communality} + \text{specificity} \qquad \text{(A.16)}$$

One component of this equation, the communality of a test, is obtained from the results of a factor analysis involving the test. Then, if the test's reliability is known, its specificity can be found by subtraction. An illustrative factor analysis should clarify these matters.

One way to begin a factor analysis of the scores of $n$ people on a group of tests is to compute the correlations among all the tests and cast them into the form of a matrix. This has been done in Table A–3 with the average correlations among the 11 WAIS–R subtests for nine ages ($n = 1880$). Notice that the matrix is symmetrical; that is, the correlations in a given row are identical to those in the corresponding column. In addition, there are no entries on the diagonal running from the upper-left corner to the lower-right corner of the matrix.

The decision as to what values to place on the diagonal of the matrix—the reliabilities of the tests, estimates of their communalities, or all 1.00's—depends on the particular factor-analysis procedure or theory followed by the researcher. In one type of factoring procedure, the *centroid method,* estimates of the communalities of the tests are placed on the

**TABLE A–3    Matrix of Average Correlations among WAIS–R Subtests**

| Subtest | 1 | 2 | 3 | 4 | 5 | 6 | 7 | 8 | 9 | 10 | 11 |
|---------|---|---|---|---|---|---|---|---|---|----|----|
| 1. Information | | .46 | .81 | .61 | .68 | .66 | .52 | .50 | .50 | .39 | .44 |
| 2. Digit Span | .46 | | .52 | .56 | .45 | .45 | .37 | .37 | .43 | .33 | .42 |
| 3. Vocabulary | .81 | .52 | | .63 | .74 | .72 | .55 | .51 | .52 | .41 | .47 |
| 4. Arithmetic | .61 | .56 | .63 | | .57 | .56 | .48 | .46 | .56 | .42 | .45 |
| 5. Comprehension | .68 | .45 | .74 | .57 | | .68 | .52 | .48 | .48 | .40 | .44 |
| 6. Similarities | .66 | .45 | .72 | .56 | .68 | | .54 | .50 | .51 | .43 | .46 |
| 7. Picture Completion | .52 | .37 | .55 | .48 | .52 | .54 | | .51 | .54 | .52 | .42 |
| 8. Picture Arrangement | .50 | .37 | .51 | .46 | .48 | .50 | .51 | | .47 | .40 | .39 |
| 9. Block Design | .50 | .43 | .52 | .56 | .48 | .51 | .54 | .47 | | .63 | .47 |
| 10. Object Assembly | .39 | .33 | .41 | .42 | .40 | .43 | .52 | .40 | .63 | | .38 |
| 11. Digit Symbol | .44 | .42 | .47 | .45 | .44 | .46 | .42 | .39 | .37 | .38 | |

diagonal of the correlation matrix. On the other hand, the *principal axis method* requires placing 1.00's on the diagonal. Without belaboring the question of what diagonal entries are best, it should be emphasized that the choice affects both the number of factors extracted and the obtained weights (*factor loadings*) of each test on each factor.

***Factoring the Correlation Matrix*** The immediate result of a typical factor analysis is an original (unrotated) factor matrix such as that in columns A, B, and C of Table A–4. Observe that factor analysis has reduced the number of variables or psychological dimensions from 11, which is the total number of subtests on the WAIS–R, to 3, the number of common factors extracted. The decimal numbers in each column of the factor matrix are the loadings of the 11 WAIS–R subtests on that factor. For example, the Information subtest has a loading of .82 on factor A, but loadings of only $-.31$ and $-.14$ on factors B and C. Each factor loading is the correlation between a particular subtest and that factor. The square of the loading of a given subtest on a factor is the proportion of the total variance of the subtest scores that can be accounted for by that factor. Thus, $(.82)^2 = .67$ means that 67 percent of the variance of the scores on the Information subtest can be accounted for by factor A. But only $(-.31)^2 = .10$, or 10 percent, of the Information subtest scores can be accounted for by factor B. Similarly, $(-.14)^2 = .02$, or 2 percent, of Information subtest scores can be accounted for by factor C.

The sum of the cross products of the corresponding factor loadings of any two subtests in Table A–4 is an estimate of the correlation between those two subtests. For example, the correlation between the Information and Digit Span subtests is estimated from the loadings in the original factor matrix to be $.82(.65) + (-.31)(-.11) + (-.14)(.59) = .48$. This is a fairly close approximation to the actual correlation of .46 (see Table A–3). The accuracy with which the correlation matrix is reproduced by estimates determined from the factor

**TABLE A–4   Original and Rotated Factor Matrices**

| Subtest | Original factor matrix | | | Rotated factor matrix | | | Communality |
|---|---|---|---|---|---|---|---|
| | A | B | C | A′ | B′ | C′ | |
| Information | .82 | −.31 | −.14 | .81 | .21 | .29 | .78 |
| Digit Span | .65 | −.11 | .59 | .27 | .11 | .83 | .78 |
| Vocabulary | .86 | −.31 | −.10 | .82 | .22 | .34 | .84 |
| Arithmetic | .78 | −.08 | .24 | .49 | .28 | .59 | .67 |
| Comprehension | .80 | −.28 | −.16 | .79 | .23 | .26 | .74 |
| Similarities | .81 | −.19 | −.16 | .75 | .30 | .25 | .71 |
| Picture Completion | .73 | .25 | −.26 | .48 | .64 | .11 | .66 |
| Picture Arrangement | .68 | .10 | −.22 | .51 | .49 | .13 | .52 |
| Block Design | .74 | .42 | .06 | .26 | .72 | .38 | .74 |
| Object Assembly | .64 | .60 | −.08 | .14 | .85 | .19 | .77 |
| Digit Symbol | .64 | .13 | .36 | .23 | .37 | .61 | .56 |

loadings depends on the extent to which the obtained factors account for the total variance among the subtests.

**Rotating the Factors**    A process known as *factor rotation* may be applied to the original factor matrix to increase the number of high and low positive loadings in the columns of the factor matrix. The result is a simpler configuration of factor loadings, thereby facilitating interpretation of the factors. Depending on the particular rotation method selected, either uncorrelated (*orthogonal*) or correlated (*oblique*) factors may be obtained. Some factor analysts prefer orthogonal rotation, while others like oblique rotation. The rotated factor matrix in Table A–4 (columns A′, B′, and C′) was produced by orthogonal rotation of the original factor matrix, so the rotated factors are uncorrelated.

**Interpreting the Rotated Factors**    After completing all the statistical computations required by factoring and rotation, we are ready to examine the pattern of high and low loadings of each test on every factor. The higher a particular loading is, the more important the factor is on the given test. As shown in Table A–4, the Information, Vocabulary, Comprehension, and Similarities subtests have loadings of over .70 on factor A′. Because these are verbal subtests, factor A′ might be labeled a *verbal* factor. Several other subtests also have appreciable loadings on factor A′, so this factor actually comes close to what is meant by a *general cognitive factor* (*g*). The Picture Completion, Picture Arrangement, Block Design, and Object Assembly subtests also have moderate to high loadings on factor B′. Considering the kinds of tasks comprising these four subtests, factor B′ may be labeled a *spatial–perceptual* or *spatial imagery* factor. The Digit Span, Arithmetic, and Digit Symbol subtests, all three of which involve numbers, have moderate to high loadings on factor C′. Therefore, a good name for factor C′ might be *numerical facility.*

**Communality and Specificity**    The last column in Table A–4 contains the communalities of the 11 subtests, computed as the sum of squares of the rotated factor loadings on a given subtest. For example, the communality of the Information subtest is $(.81)^2 + (.21)^2 + (.29)^2 = .78$, so 78 percent of the variance of the scores on the Information subtest can be accounted for by factors A′, B′, and C′. If the reliability of the Information subtest is known, formula A.16 can be used to compute the subtest's specificity. Also, subtracting the communality from 1.00 yields the proportion of the total subtest variance that is attributable to a combination of specific factors and error variance. For the Information subtest, this figure is $1.00 - .78 = .22$; that is, 22 percent of the total variance of the scores on the Information subtest can be explained by specific factors and errors of measurement.

## SUMMARY

A statistical analysis of test scores begins with the construction of a frequency distribution of the number of people making each score or whose scores fall within a specified interval. Frequency distributions may be represented pictorially as histograms or frequency polygons. The normal curve is a theoretical frequency polygon that is basic to much test theory, and it is used for a variety of purposes. Nonnormal, asymmetrical frequency distributions may be skewed to the right (positively skewed) or to the left (negatively skewed).

Three measures of the central tendency or average of a group of scores—the mode, median, and mean—may be computed from raw scores or from a frequency distribution. The mode is the most frequently occurring score, the median is the value below which 50 percent of the scores fall, and the arithmetic mean is the sum of the scores divided by the number of scores. Three measures of variability or spread of a group of scores are the range, the semi-interquartile range, and the standard deviation. Of these, the standard deviation is the most popular and the most appropriate measure of variability when the arithmetic mean is the reported average. For comparison and interpretive purposes, raw scores can be converted to standard z scores, percentiles, and other transformed scores.

The product–moment correlation coefficient, which is a number between −1.00 (perfect negative correlation) and +1.00 (perfect positive correlation), is a measure of the magnitude and direction of the relationship between two variables. A significant correlation between two variables facilitates the prediction of a person's score on one variable from his or her score on the other variable. A high correlation between two variables should not, however, be construed as implying a causal connection between them. Although causation implies correlation, correlation does not imply causation.

Correlations among variables may be used in simple and multiple linear regression analyses to make predictions of scores on a dependent ($Y$ or criterion) variable from scores on one or more independent ($X$ or predictor) variables. Correlational procedures are also used in factor analysis to determine the dimensions or factors that different tests have in common. Factor analysis of the scores obtained by a large sample of people on a group of tests or items consists of extracting the factors, rotating the factor axes, and interpreting the resulting factors. Factors are interpreted by inspecting the loadings of the various tests on the factor. Computation of the communality (common factor variance) and specificity (specific factor variance) can also contribute to the factor interpretation process.

## QUESTIONS AND ACTIVITIES

1. Consider the following frequency distribution of scores obtained by a group of 50 students on a test:

| Test Score Interval | Number of Students |
|---|---|
| 96–100 | 6 |
| 91–95 | 8 |
| 86–90 | 15 |
| 81–85 | 10 |
| 76–80 | 7 |
| 71–75 | 4 |

Construct a histogram and a superimposed frequency polygon of this frequency distribution. Then compute the arithmetic mean, median, standard deviation, 25th percentile, 75th percentile, and semi-interquartile range.

2. Using the table in Appendix B, find the percentage of the area under the normal curve falling below each of the following z scores: −2.575, −2.33, −1.96, −1.645, .00, 1.645, 1.96, 2.33, and

2.575. Next, find the z scores below which 10, 20, 30, 40, 50, 60, 70, 80, and 90 percent of the area under the normal curve falls.

3. Consider the following pairs of X, Y scores for 30 people:

| X | Y | X | Y | X | Y | X | Y | X | Y |
|---|---|---|---|---|---|---|---|---|---|
| 32 | 46 | 28 | 23 | 37 | 28 | 36 | 21 | 42 | 27 |
| 35 | 26 | 32 | 20 | 27 | 13 | 31 | 14 | 39 | 46 |
| 20 | 8 | 45 | 24 | 37 | 22 | 35 | 18 | 34 | 16 |
| 41 | 42 | 29 | 13 | 23 | 34 | 43 | 47 | 33 | 30 |
| 25 | 28 | 46 | 40 | 30 | 31 | 34 | 27 | 29 | 26 |
| 38 | 25 | 40 | 37 | 36 | 39 | 39 | 32 | 24 | 7 |

Compute the following statistics: arithmetic means and standard deviations of X and Y, product–moment correlation between X and Y, and regression line for predicting Y from X. Make a graphical plot (*scattergram*) of the X, Y points, and draw the regression line of Y on X.

4. Whenever the frequency distribution of a group of scores is markedly skewed in either a positive (to the right) or negative (to the left) direction, the median is considered to be a better, less biased measure of central tendency than the arithmetic mean. Why?

5. Run program 7 ("Multiple Regression Analysis") in category A ("Programs on Basic Statistical Methods") of the computer programs accompanying this textbook. Use the following information:

Criterion variable ($Y$): Average grade in computer programming course.

Predictor variable (1): Analogies Test score.

Predictor variable (2): Average grade in high school.

Predictor variable (3): Score on Inventory of Interest in Computers.

$$r_{12} = .396 \qquad \overline{Y} = 73.8 \qquad s_y = 9.1$$

$$r_{13} = .215 \qquad \overline{X}_1 = 49.5 \qquad s_1 = 17.0$$

$$r_{23} = .345 \qquad \overline{X}_2 = 61.1 \qquad s_2 = 19.4$$

$$r_{y1} = .583 \qquad \overline{X}_3 = 29.7 \qquad s_3 = 3.7$$

$$r_{y2} = .546 \qquad N = 100$$

$$r_{y3} = .365$$

Using the B coefficients in column 4 of the printout and the value of the intercept, write the regression equation for predicting computer course grades from the other three (predictor) variables. Evaluate the $t$ ratios for testing the significance of the three predictor variables and the $F$ ratio for evaluating the significance of the multiple correlation coefficient ($R$). Ask your instructor to help you to interpret the results if you have problems.

6. The following is an SPSS/PC + computer program for a factor analysis of the average intercorrelations of the WISC–III subtests for all ages. Run this program on a microcomputer that has the SPSS/PC + software and print the results.

```
DATA LIST MATRIX FREE
  /INF SIM ARI VOC COM DIS PIC COD PIA BLD OBA SYS MAZ.
SET PRINTER=ON.
VARIABLE LABELS INF 'INFORMATION' /SIM 'SIMILARITIES'
  /ARI 'ARITHMETIC' /VOC 'VOCABULARY' /COM 'COMPREHENSION'
  /DIS 'DIGIT SPAN' /PIC 'PICTURE COMPLETION' /COD 'CODING'
  /PIA 'PICTURE ARRANGEMENT' /BLD 'BLOCK DESIGN'
  /OBA 'OBJECT ASSEMBLY' /SYS 'SYMBOL SEARCH' /MAZ 'MAZES'.
```

```
N 200.
BEGIN DATA.
1.
 .66 1.
 .57 .55 1.
 .70 .69 .54 1.
 .56 .59 .47 .64 1.
 .34 .34 .43 .35 .29 1.
 .47 .45 .39 .45 .38 .25 1.
 .21 .20 .27 .26 .25 .23 .18 1.
 .40 .39 .35 .40 .35 .20 .37 .28 1.
 .48 .49 .52 .46 .40 .32 .52 .27 .41 1.
 .41 .42 .39 .41 .34 .26 .49 .24 .37 .61 1.
 .35 .35 .41 .35 .34 .28 .33 .53 .36 .45 .38 1.
 .18 .18 .22 .17 .17 .14 .24 .15 .23 .31 .29 .24 1.
END DATA.
FACTOR READ=COR TRIANGLE
 /VARIABLES=INF TO MAZ.
FINISH.
```

Using the factor loadings of the rotated factor matrix and the reliability coefficients given in the following table, compute the communality and specificity of each subtest and interpret the factors. Refer to the section on factor analysis in this appendix and the descriptions of the WISC–III subtests given in Chapter 7.

| Subtest | Average Reliability | Subtest | Average Reliability |
|---|---|---|---|
| Information | .84 | Vocabulary | .87 |
| Similarities | .81 | Comprehension | .77 |
| Arithmetic | .78 | Digit Span | .85 |
| Picture Completion | .77 | Object Assembly | .69 |
| Coding | .79 | Symbol Search | .76 |
| Picture Arrangement | .76 | Mazes | .72 |
| Block Design | .87 | | |

7. Solve exercises 1, 2, 3, and 5 using the appropriate programs in category A ("Basic Statistical Methods") on the diskette of *Programs for Psychological Testing and Assessment*. On exercise 1, use the interval midpoints for the raw scores.

# Appendix B

## AREAS UNDER THE NORMAL CURVE

To find the proportion of the area under the normal curve below the specific $z$ value, find $z$ in the first column and first row of the table. The decimal number at the intersection of the appropriate row and column is the corresponding proportion of the area under the curve. For example, to find the area below $z = 1.57$, find the intersection of 1.5 in the first column and .07 in the first row. The resulting value is .9418, so 94.18 percent of the area under the curve falls below $z = 1.57$. Conversely, to find the value of $z$ below which a specified proportion of the area under the curve falls, we begin by locating that proportion in the body of the table. Then we find the $z$ value in the corresponding row and column. For example, to find the value of $z$ below which 67 percent of the area under the curve falls, we begin by locating .6700 in the body of the table. It is at the intersection of the row labeled .4 and the column labeled .04, so the corresponding $z$ value is .44.

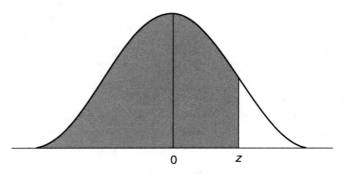

| z | .00 | .01 | .02 | .03 | .04 | .05 | .06 | .07 | .08 | .09 |
|---|-----|-----|-----|-----|-----|-----|-----|-----|-----|-----|
| −3.0 | .0013 | .0013 | .0013 | .0012 | .0012 | .0011 | .0011 | .0011 | .0010 | .0010 |
| −2.9 | .0019 | .0018 | .0018 | .0017 | .0016 | .0016 | .0015 | .0015 | .0014 | .0014 |
| −2.8 | .0026 | .0025 | .0024 | .0023 | .0023 | .0022 | .0021 | .0021 | .0020 | .0019 |
| −2.7 | .0035 | .0034 | .0033 | .0032 | .0031 | .0030 | .0029 | .0028 | .0027 | .0026 |
| −2.6 | .0047 | .0045 | .0044 | .0043 | .0041 | .0040 | .0039 | .0038 | .0037 | .0036 |
| −2.5 | .0062 | .0060 | .0059 | .0057 | .0055 | .0054 | .0052 | .0051 | .0049 | .0048 |
| −2.4 | .0082 | .0080 | .0078 | .0075 | .0073 | .0071 | .0069 | .0068 | .0066 | .0064 |
| −2.3 | .0107 | .0104 | .0102 | .0099 | .0096 | .0094 | .0091 | .0089 | .0087 | .0084 |
| −2.2 | .0139 | .0136 | .0132 | .0129 | .0125 | .0122 | .0119 | .0116 | .0113 | .0110 |
| −2.1 | .0179 | .0174 | .0170 | .0166 | .0162 | .0158 | .0154 | .0150 | .0146 | .0143 |
| −2.0 | .0228 | .0222 | .0217 | .0212 | .0207 | .0202 | .0197 | .0192 | .0188 | .0183 |
| −1.9 | .0287 | .0281 | .0274 | .0268 | .0262 | .0256 | .0250 | .0244 | .0239 | .0233 |
| −1.8 | .0359 | .0351 | .0344 | .0336 | .0329 | .0322 | .0314 | .0307 | .0301 | .0294 |
| −1.7 | .0446 | .0436 | .0427 | .0418 | .0409 | .0401 | .0392 | .0384 | .0375 | .0367 |
| −1.6 | .0548 | .0537 | .0526 | .0516 | .0505 | .0495 | .0485 | .0475 | .0465 | .0455 |
| −1.5 | .0668 | .0655 | .0643 | .0630 | .0618 | .0606 | .0594 | .0582 | .0571 | .0559 |
| −1.4 | .0808 | .0793 | .0778 | .0764 | .0749 | .0735 | .0721 | .0708 | .0694 | .0681 |
| −1.3 | .0968 | .0951 | .0934 | .0918 | .0901 | .0885 | .0869 | .0853 | .0838 | .0823 |
| −1.2 | .1151 | .1131 | .1112 | .1093 | .1075 | .1056 | .1038 | .1020 | .1003 | .0985 |
| −1.1 | .1357 | .1335 | .1314 | .1292 | .1271 | .1251 | .1230 | .1210 | .1190 | .1170 |
| −1.0 | .1587 | .1562 | .1539 | .1515 | .1492 | .1469 | .1446 | .1423 | .1401 | .1379 |
| −0.9 | .1841 | .1814 | .1788 | .1762 | .1736 | .1711 | .1685 | .1660 | .1635 | .1611 |
| −0.8 | .2119 | .2090 | .2061 | .2033 | .2005 | .1977 | .1949 | .1922 | .1894 | .1867 |
| −0.7 | .2420 | .2389 | .2358 | .2327 | .2296 | .2266 | .2236 | .2206 | .2177 | .2148 |
| −0.6 | .2743 | .2709 | .2676 | .2643 | .2611 | .2578 | .2546 | .2514 | .2483 | .2451 |
| −0.5 | .3085 | .3050 | .3015 | .2981 | .2946 | .2912 | .2877 | .2843 | .2810 | .2776 |
| −0.4 | .3446 | .3409 | .3372 | .3336 | .3300 | .3264 | .3228 | .3192 | .3156 | .3121 |
| −0.3 | .3821 | .3783 | .3745 | .3707 | .3669 | .3632 | .3594 | .3557 | .3520 | .3483 |
| −0.2 | .4207 | .4168 | .4129 | .4090 | .4052 | .4013 | .3974 | .3936 | .3897 | .3859 |
| −0.1 | .4602 | .4562 | .4522 | .4483 | .4443 | .4404 | .4364 | .4325 | .4286 | .4247 |
| −0.0 | .5000 | .4960 | .4920 | .4880 | .4840 | .4801 | .4761 | .4721 | .4681 | .4641 |
| 0.0 | .5000 | .5040 | .5080 | .5120 | .5160 | .5199 | .5239 | .5279 | .5319 | .5359 |
| 0.1 | .5398 | .5438 | .5478 | .5517 | .5557 | .5596 | .5636 | .5675 | .5714 | .5753 |
| 0.2 | .5793 | .5832 | .5871 | .5910 | .5948 | .5987 | .6026 | .6064 | .6103 | .6140 |
| 0.3 | .6179 | .6217 | .6255 | .6293 | .6331 | .6368 | .6406 | .6443 | .6480 | .6517 |
| 0.4 | .6554 | .6591 | .6628 | .6664 | .6700 | .6736 | .6772 | .6808 | .6844 | .6879 |
| 0.5 | .6915 | .6950 | .6985 | .7019 | .7054 | .7088 | .7123 | .7157 | .7190 | .7224 |
| 0.6 | .7257 | .7291 | .7324 | .7357 | .7389 | .7422 | .7454 | .7486 | .7517 | .7549 |
| 0.7 | .7580 | .7611 | .7642 | .7673 | .7704 | .7734 | .7764 | .7794 | .7823 | .7852 |
| 0.8 | .7881 | .7910 | .7939 | .7967 | .7995 | .8023 | .8051 | .8078 | .8106 | .8133 |
| 0.9 | .8159 | .8186 | .8212 | .8238 | .8264 | .8289 | .8315 | .8340 | .8365 | .8389 |

| z | .00 | .01 | .02 | .03 | .04 | .05 | .06 | .07 | .08 | .09 |
|---|------|------|------|------|------|------|------|------|------|------|
| 1.0 | .8413 | .8438 | .8461 | .8485 | .8508 | .8531 | .8554 | .8577 | .8599 | .8621 |
| 1.1 | .8643 | .8665 | .8686 | .8708 | .8729 | .8749 | .8770 | .8790 | .8810 | .8830 |
| 1.2 | .8849 | .8869 | .8888 | .8907 | .8925 | .8944 | .8962 | .8980 | .8997 | .9015 |
| 1.3 | .9032 | .9049 | .9066 | .9082 | .9099 | .9115 | .9131 | .9147 | .9162 | .9177 |
| 1.4 | .9192 | .9207 | .9222 | .9236 | .9251 | .9265 | .9279 | .9292 | .9306 | .9319 |
| 1.5 | .9332 | .9345 | .9357 | .9370 | .9382 | .9394 | .9406 | .9418 | .9429 | .9441 |
| 1.6 | .9452 | .9463 | .9474 | .9484 | .9495 | .9505 | .9515 | .9525 | .9535 | .9545 |
| 1.7 | .9554 | .9564 | .9573 | .9582 | .9591 | .9599 | .9608 | .9616 | .9625 | .9633 |
| 1.8 | .9641 | .9649 | .9656 | .9664 | .9671 | .9678 | .9686 | .9693 | .9699 | .9706 |
| 1.9 | .9713 | .9719 | .9726 | .9732 | .9738 | .9744 | .9750 | .9756 | .9761 | .9767 |
| 2.0 | .9772 | .9778 | .9783 | .9788 | .9793 | .9798 | .9803 | .9808 | .9812 | .9817 |
| 2.1 | .9821 | .9826 | .9830 | .9834 | .9838 | .9842 | .9846 | .9850 | .9854 | .9857 |
| 2.2 | .9861 | .9864 | .9868 | .9871 | .9875 | .9878 | .9881 | .9884 | .9887 | .9890 |
| 2.3 | .9893 | .9896 | .9898 | .9901 | .9904 | .9906 | .9909 | .9911 | .9913 | .9916 |
| 2.4 | .9918 | .9920 | .9922 | .9925 | .9927 | .9929 | .9931 | .9932 | .9934 | .9936 |
| 2.5 | .9938 | .9940 | .9941 | .9943 | .9945 | .9946 | .9948 | .9949 | .9951 | .9952 |
| 2.6 | .9953 | .9955 | .9956 | .9957 | .9959 | .9960 | .9961 | .9962 | .9963 | .9964 |
| 2.7 | .9965 | .9966 | .9967 | .9968 | .9969 | .9970 | .9971 | .9972 | .9973 | .9974 |
| 2.8 | .9974 | .9975 | .9976 | .9977 | .9977 | .9978 | .9979 | .9979 | .9980 | .9981 |
| 2.9 | .9981 | .9982 | .9982 | .9983 | .9984 | .9984 | .9985 | .9985 | .9986 | .9986 |
| 3.0 | .9987 | .9987 | .9987 | .9988 | .9988 | .9989 | .9989 | .9989 | .9990 | .9990 |

# Appendix C

## AMERICAN COMMERCIAL SUPPLIERS OF PSYCHOLOGICAL AND EDUCATIONAL ASSESSMENT MATERIALS

Addison–Wesley Testing Service, 2725 Sand Hill Road, Menlo Park, CA 94025.

American Association on Mental Deficiency, 5201 Connecticut Avenue, N.W., Washington, DC 20015.

American College Testing Program (ACT), P.O. Box 168, Iowa City, IA 52243.

American Guidance Service (AGS), 4201 Woodland Road, P.O. Box 99, Circle Pines, MN 55014-1796. Tel 800/328-2560.

American Orthopsychiatric Association, Inc., 1790 Broadway, New York, NY 10019.

Assessment Systems Corporation, 2233 University Avenue, Suite 200, St. Paul, MN 55114-1629. Tel 612/647-9220.

Behavior Science Systems, Inc., P.O. Box 1108, Minneapolis, MN 55440.

Consulting Psychologists Press, Inc. (CPP), 3803 East Bayshore Road, P.O. Box 10096, Palo Alto, CA 94303. Tel. 800/624-1765.

CPPC, 4 Conant Square, Brandon, VT 05733. Tel. 800/433-8234.

C.P.S., Inc., P.O. Box 83, Larchmont, NY 10538. Tel. 800/433-8324.

CTB/McGraw-Hill, 20 Ryan Ranch Road, Monterey, CA 93940. Tel. 800/538-9547.

Denver Developmental Materials, P.O. Box 20037, Denver, CO 80220.

DLM Resources, One DLM Park, Allen, TX 75002. Tel. 800/527-4747.

Educational and Industrial Testing Service (EdITS), P.O. Box 7234, San Diego, CA 92167. Tel. 619/222-1666.

Educational Testing Service (ETS), Princeton, NJ 08540.

Evaluation Research Associates, P.O. Box 6503, Teall Station, Syracuse, NY 13217.

GED Testing Service, One Dupont Circle, N.W., Washington, DC 20036.

Grune & Stratton, Inc., 465 South Lincoln Drive, Troy, MO 63379.

Harcourt Brace Jovanovich, 757 Third Avenue, New York, NY 10017.

Hawthorne Educational Services, Inc., 800 Gray Oak Drive, Columbia, MO 65201. Tel. 800/542-1673.

Hilson Research, Inc., P.O. Box 150239, Kew Gardens, NY 11415-0239. Tel. 800/926-2258.

Houghton Mifflin, 110 Tremont Street, Boston, MA 02107.

Industrial Psychology International Ltd., 111 North Market Street, Champaign, IL 61820. Tel. 800/747-1119.

Institute for Personality and Ability Testing (IPAT), P.O. Box 1188, Champaign, IL 61824-1188. Tel. 800/225-4728.

London House, 9701 West Higgins Road, Suite 770, Rosemont, IL 60018. Tel. 708/292-1900.

Marshal S. Hiskey, 5640 Baldwin, Lincoln, NB 68507.

Martin M. Bruce, 50 Larchwood Road, Box 248, Larchmont, NY 10538. Tel. 914/834-1555.

Metritech, Inc., 4106 Fieldstone Road, P.O. Box 6489, Champaign, IL 61826-6479. Tel. 800/747-4868.

National Educational Laboratory Publishers, Inc., 813 Airport Boulevard, Austin, TX 78702.

NCS Assessments, P.O. Box 1416, Minneapolis, MN 55440. Tel. 800/627-7271.

Personnel Press, 191 Spring Street, Lexington, MA 02173.

pro.ed, 8700 Shoal Creek Boulevard, Austin, TX 78757-6897. Tel. 512/451-3246.

Psychological and Educational Publications, Inc., 1477 Rollins Road, Burlingame, CA 94010-2316. Tel. 800/523-5775.

Psychological Assessment Resources, Inc. (PAR), P.O. Box 998, Odessa, FL 33556. Tel. 800/331-TEST.

Psychological Corporation (The), 555 Academic Court, San Antonio, TX 78204-2498. Tel. 800/228-0752.

Psychological Publications, Inc., 290 Conejo Ridge Avenue, Suite 100, Thousand Oaks, CA 91361. Tel. 800/345-TEST.

Psychological Test Specialists, Box 9229, Missoula, MT 59807.

Psychologists and Educators, Inc., P.O. Box 513, Chesterfield, MO 63006.

Psychometric Affiliates, Box 807, Murfreesboro, TN 37133-0807. Tel. 615/898-2565.

Publishers Test Service, CTB/McGraw-Hill, 20 Ryan Ranch Road, Monterey, CA 93940. Tel. 800/538-9547.

Reitan Neuropsychology Laboratories, 2920 South 4th Avenue, Tucson, AZ 85713-4819. Tel. 602/882-2022.

Riverside Publishing Company (The), 8420 Bryn Mawr Avenue, Chicago, IL 60631. Tel. 800/323-9540.

Scholastic Testing Service, Inc. (STS), 480 Meyer Road, P.O. Box 1056, Bensenville, IL 60106-1617. Tel. 800/642-6STS.

Science Research Associates (SRA), 155 North Wacker Drive, Chicago, IL 60606.

Sigma Assessment Systems, Inc., P.O. Box 610984, Port Huron, MI 48061-0984. Tel. 800/265-1285.

Slosson Educational Publications, Inc., P.O. Box 280, East Aurora, NY 14052-0280. Tel. 800/828-4800.

SOI Systems, P.O. Box D, Vida, OR 97488. Tel. 503/896-3936.

Special Child Publications, P.O. Box 33548, Seattle, WA 98133.

SRA/London House, 9701 Higgins Road, Rosemont, IL 60018. Tel. 800/221-8378.

Stoelting, Oakwood Centre, 620 Wheat Lane, Wood Dale, IL 60191. Tel. 708/860-9700.

U.S. Employment Service, Division of Program Planning and Operations, U.S. Department of Labor, 601 D Street, N.W., Washington, DC 20213.

U.S. Military Entrance Processing Command Testing Directorate, 2500 Green Bay Road, North Chicago, IL 60064.

Western Psychological Services (WPS), 12031 Wilshire Boulevard, Los Angeles, CA 90025-1251. Tel. 800/648-8857.

Wide Range, Inc., P.O. Box 3410, Wilmington, DE 19804-0250. Tel. 800/221-WRAT.

Wonderlic Personnel Test, Inc., 1509 North Milwaukee Avenue, Libertyville, IL 60048-1380. Tel. 800/963-7542.

# Appendix D

## COMPUTER PROGRAMS FOR PSYCHOLOGICAL ASSESSMENT

**MAIN MENU PROGRAM CATEGORY**

A. Basic Statistical Methods
B. Test Construction, Administration, and Scoring
C. Item Analysis, Sampling, and Norms
D. Reliability and Validity
E. Problem Solving and Thinking
F. Special Abilities or Aptitudes
G. Inventories of Interests, Attitudes, and Values
H. Checklists, Rating Scales, and Rankings
I. Personality Inventories and Projective Techniques

**Category A: Basic Statistical Methods**

1. Frequency Distributions and Associated Graphs
2. Descriptive Statistics
3. Percentiles and Percentile Ranks
4. Normal Deviates and Normal Probabilities
5. Scatter Diagram and Regression Line Plot
6. Correlation Coefficient and Regression Equation
7. Multiple Regression Analysis

**Category B: Test Construction, Administration, and Scoring**

1. Constructing an Objective Test
2. Administering and Scoring an Objective Test
3. Constructing a Rating Scale or Checklist

4. Correcting for Guessing on an Objective Test
5. Scoring a Rating Scale or Checklist
6. Scoring Ranking Items
7. Grade Assignment by the Modified Cajori Technique
8. Randomly Generated Arithmetic Tests
9. A Spelling and Word Usage Test

## Category C: Item Analysis, Sampling, and Norms

1. Difficulty and Discrimination Indexes for Test Items
2. Difficulty and Discrimination Indexes of Criterion-referenced Items
3. Item Characteristic Curves and Item-Response Curves
4. Point-Biserial Correlation
5. Selecting Random Samples and Permutations
6. Selecting Stratified Random Samples
7. Multistage Cluster Sampling
8. Standard Scores and Percentiles

## Category D: Reliability and Validity

1. Spearman–Brown Reliability Formulas
2. Kuder–Richardson Reliability Coefficients
3. Coefficient Alpha
4. Agreement Index and Kappa Coefficient
5. Intraclass Coefficient
6. Concordance Coefficient
7. Reliability and Standard Error of Difference Scores
8. Standard Errors of Measurement and Estimate

## Category E: Problem Solving and Thinking

1. Concept Formation Test
2. Insight Problems
3. Luchins Waterjar Problems
4. Number Series
5. Tower of Hanoi Problems

## Category F: Special Abilities or Aptitudes

1. Anagrams
2. Clerical Speed and Accuracy Test
3. Digit Span Test

4. Hearing Acuity Test
5. Phi Phenomenon
6. Searching for Numbers
7. Visual Perimeter Test

## Category G: Inventories of Interests, Attitudes, and Values

1. Vocational Interests, Personality, and Careers
2. Attitudes Toward Intelligence Testing
3. Attitudes Toward Personality Assessment
4. Math and Science Attitude Inventories
5. College Course and Instructor Evaluation
6. Educational Values Inventory

## Category H: Checklists, Rating Scales, and Rankings

1. Ranking Adjectives for Real and Ideal Selves
2. Rating Professor's Personality
3. Checklist for Type A Behavior
4. Checklist for Comparing Self with Others

## Category I: Personality Inventories and Projective Techniques

1. Altruism Inventory
2. Five-factor Personality Inventory
3. Sensation Seeking Scale
4. Word Association Test
5. Sentence Completion Test
6. Dot Pattern Test
7. Projective Line Drawings

# Appendix E

## SUPPLIERS OF COMPUTER-BASED PRODUCTS AND SERVICES FOR PSYCHOLOGICAL ASSESSMENT

AI Software, Inc., P.O. Box 724, Wakefield, RI 02880-0723. Tel. 800/272-2250.

American College Testing, 2201 North Dodge Street, Iowa City, IA 52243. Tel. 319/337-1000.

American Guidance Service, 4201 Woodland Road, P.O. Box 99, Circle Pines, MN 55014-1796. Tel. 800/328-2560.

Assessment Systems Corporation, 2233 University Avenue, Suite 200, St. Paul, MN 55114-1629. Tel. 612/647-9220.

Behavior Data Systems Ltd., 3008 North Third Street, Suite 303, Phoenix, AZ 85012. Tel. 214/243-8543.

Behaviordyne, Inc., P.O. Box 10994, Palo Alto, CA 94303-0992. Tel. 415/857-0111.

Caldwell Report, 1545 Sawtelle Blvd, Suite 14, Los Angeles, CA 90025. Tel. 310/478-3133.

Century Diagnostics, Inc., 2101 E. Broadway, Suite 22, Tempe, AZ 85282. Tel. 602/966-6006.

CFKR Career Materials, Inc., 11860 Kemper Road, Unit 7, Auburn, CA 95603. Tel. 916/880-2357.

Clinical Psychometric Research, P.O. Box 619, Riderwood, MD 21139. Tel. 301/321-6165.

Computerized Psychological Diagnostics, Inc., 1101 Dove Street, Suite 225, Newport Beach, CA 92660. Tel. 714/833-7931.

Conover Company Ltd., 1050 Witzel Avenue, Oshkosh, WI 54901. Tel. 414/231-4667.

Consulting Psychologists Press, Inc., 3803 East Bayshore Road/P.O. Box 10096, Palo Alto, CA 94303. Tel. 800/624-1765.

Cool Springs Software, 4 Moonmaiden Court, Walkersville, MD 21793. Tel. 301/845-8719.

Educational and Industrial Testing Service, P.O. Box 7234, San Diego, CA 92167. Tel. 619/222-1666.

Functional Assessment & Training Consultants, P.O. Box 141152, Austin, TX 78714. Tel. 512/836-1222.

Happ Electronics, Inc., 3680 North Main Street, Oshkosh, WI 54901. Tel. 414/231-5128.

Hilson Research, Inc., P.O. Box 150239, Kew Gardens, NY 11415-0239. Tel. 800/926-2258.

Institute for Personality & Ability Testing, Inc., P.O. Box 1188, Champaign, IL 61824-1188. Tel. 800/225-4728.

Integrated Professional Systems, Inc., 5211 Mahoning Avenue, Suite 135, Youngstown, OH 44515. Tel. 216/799-3282.

Life Science Associates, One Fenimore Road, Bayport, NY 11705. Tel. 516/472-2111.

Metritech, Inc., 4106 Fieldstone Road, P.O. Box 6489, Champaign, IL 61826-6479. Tel. 800/747-4868.

Multi-Health Systems, Inc., 908 Niagara Falls Boulevard, North Tonawanda, NY 14120-2060. Tel. 800/456-3003.

NCS Assessments, 5605 Green Circle Drive, P.O. Box 1416, Minneapolis, MN 55443. Tel. 800/NCS-7271.

NFER-Nelson Publishing Company Ltd., 2 Oxford Road East, Windsor, Berkshire, SL4 1DF ENGLAND.

Planet Press, P.O. Box 3477, Newport Beach, CA 92663-3418. Tel. 714/650-5135.

Precision People, Inc., 3452 North Ride Circle South, Jacksonville, FL 32217. Tel. 904/262-1096.

pro.ed, 8700 Shoal Creek Boulevard, Austin, TX 78757-6897. Tel. 512/451-3246.

Psychological Assessment Resources, Inc., P.O. Box 998, Odessa, FL 33556. Tel. 800/331-TEST.

Psychological Corporation (The), 555 Academic Court, San Antonio, TX 78204-2498. Tel. 800/228-0752.

Psychological Psoftware Company, 12486 Brickellia, San Diego, CA 92129. Tel. 619/484-8877.

Psychologistics, Inc., P.O. Box 033896, Indialantic, FL 32903. Tel. 407/259-7811.

Psychometric Software, Inc., 927 East New Haven Avenue, Suite 314, Melbourne, FL 32902-1677. Tel. 407/729-6390.

Reason House, 204 East Joppa Road, Suite 10, Towson, MD 21204. Tel. 410/321-7270.

Risk & Needs Assessment, Inc., P.O. Box 32818, Phoenix, AZ 85064-4401. Tel. 602/234-2888.

Riverside Publishing Company (The), 8420 Bryn Mawr Avenue, Chicago, IL 60631. Tel. 800/767-TEST.

Scholastic Testing Service, Inc., 480 Meyer Road, P.O. Box 1056, Bensenville, IL 60106-1617.

Selby MillSmith, 30 Circus Mews, Bath BA1 2PJ, Avon, ENGLAND. Tel. (225) 446655.

Sigma Assessment Systems, Inc., P.O. Box 610984, Port Huron, MI 48061-0984. Tel. 800/265-1285.

Slosson Educational Publications, Inc., P.O. Box 280, East Aurora, NY 14052-0280. Tel. 800/828-4800.

Southern Micro Systems, P.O. Box 2097, Burlington, NC 27216. Tel. 919/584-5552.

StatSoft, 2325 East 13th Street, Tulsa, OK 74104. 918/583-4149.

Test Agency, Cournswood House, North Dean, High Wycombe, Bucks HP14 4NW ENGLAND. Tel. 44-24-024-3384.

University Associates, 8517 Production Avenue, San Diego, CA 92121-2280. Tel. 619/578-5900.

Vocational Research Institute, 1528 Walnut Street, Suite 1502, Philadelphia, PA 19102. Tel. 800/874-5387.

Western Psychological Services, 12031 Wilshire Boulevard, Los Angeles, CA 90025-1251. Tel. 800/648-8857.

Wide Range, Inc., P.O. Box 3410, Wilmington, DE 19804-0250. Tel. 800/221-WRAT.

Wonderlic Personnel Test, Inc., 1509 North Milwaukee Avenue, Libertyville, IL 60048-1380. Tel. 800/963-7542.

# GLOSSARY

**ABC approach.** Behavioral assessment approach, involving the identification of the antecedent events (A) and consequences (C) of the behavior (B). The behavior is modified by controlling for A and changing C.

**Ability test.** A test that measures the extent to which a person is capable of performing a certain task or occupation.

**Academic aptitude.** The ability to learn school-type tasks; also called *scholastic aptitude*. Many intelligence tests are basically measures of academic aptitude.

**Accommodation.** In J. Piaget's theory of cognitive development, the modification of schema as the result of experience.

**Achievement.** The degree of success or accomplishment in a given area or endeavor; a score on an achievement test.

**Acquiescence response set (style).** Tendency of a person to answer affirmatively ("yes" or "true") to personality test items and in other alternative response situations.

**Adaptive behavior.** The extent to which a person is able to interact effectively and appropriately with the environment.

**Adaptive testing.** Testing procedure, usually computer based, in which the specific items presented vary with the estimated ability or other specified characteristics of the examinee and his or her responses to previous items.

**Adjustment.** Ability to cope in social situations and achieve satisfaction of one's needs.

**Affective assessment.** Measurement of noncognitive (nonintellective) variables or characteristics. Affective variables include temperament, emotionality, interests, attitudes, personal style, and other behaviors, traits, or processes typical of an individual. See *Cognitive assessment*.

**Age equivalent score.** See *Age norm*.

**Age norm.** Median score on an aptitude or achievement test made by children of a given chronological age.

**Age scale.** A test on which the items are grouped by age level.

**Alternate-forms reliability.**   An index of reliability (*coefficient of equivalence*) determined by correlating the scores of individuals on one form of a test with their scores on another form.

**Analogies test.**   A test that requires the examinee to determine a relationship, similarity, or difference between two or more things. Example: "Roses are to red as violets are to (a) blue, (b) green, (c) orange, (d) yellow."

**Anchor test.**   A common set of items on each of several forms of a test used to equate scores on the several forms.

**Anecdotal record.**   A written record of behavioral observations of a specified individual. Care must be taken to differentiate between observation and interpretation if the record is to be objective.

**Apgar rating.**   A rating score, determined at 1 minute and at 5 minutes after birth, for evaluating neonates. A rating of 0 to 2 is assigned to measurements of heart rate, respiration, muscle tone, reflexes, and color. A sum of ratings between 7 and 10 is normal for newborns.

**Aptitude.**   Capability of learning to perform a particular task or skill. Traditionally, aptitude was thought to depend more on inborn potential than on experience and practice.

**Aptitude test.**   A measure of the ability to profit from additional training or experience, that is, become proficient in a skill or other ability.

**Arithmetic mean.**   A measure of the average or central tendency of a group of scores. The arithmetic mean is computed by dividing the sum of the scores by the number of scores.

**Assessment.**   Appraising the presence or magnitude of one or more personal characteristics. Assessing human behavior and mental processes includes such procedures as observations, interviews, rating scales, checklists, inventories, projectives techniques, and tests.

**Assessment center.**   Technique, used primarily in the selection of executive personnel, for assessing the personality characteristics and behavior of a small group of individuals by having them perform a variety of tasks during a period of a few days.

**Assimilation.**   In J. Piaget's theory of cognitive development, the process of fitting new experiences into preexisting mental structures.

**Assortative mating.**   Nonrandom mating between individuals possessing similar characteristics.

**Attitude.**   Tendency to react positively or negatively to some object, person, or situation.

**Attitude scale.**   A paper-and-pencil instrument consisting of a series of statements concerning an institution, situation, person, or event. The examinee responds to each statement by endorsing it or indicating his or her degree of agreement or disagreement with it.

**Audiometer.**   An instrument for measuring auditory acuity that presents pure tones of varying intensities and frequencies in the normal range of hearing. Hearing is tested in each ear. The results are plotted as an audiogram, a graph of the examinee's auditory acuity at each frequency and for each ear.

**Aunt Fanny error.**   Accepting as accurate a trivial, highly generalized personality description that could pertain to almost anyone, even one's Aunt Fanny.

**Automated assessment.**   Use of test-scoring machines, computers, and other electronic or electromechanical devices to administer, score, and interpret psychological assessments.

**Average.**   Measure of central tendency of a group of scores; the most representative score.

**Bandwidth.**   L. J. Cronbach's term for the range of criteria predictable from a test; the greater the number of criteria that a test can predict, the broader its bandwidth. See *Fidelity.*

**Barnum effect.**   Accepting as accurate a personality description phrased in generalities, truisms, and other statements that sound specific to a given person but are actually applicable to almost anyone. Same as *Aunt Fanny error.*

**Basal age.**   The highest year level on an intelligence test, as on older editions of the Stanford–Binet, at and below which an examinee passes all subtests.

**Base rate.**   Proportion of individuals in a specified population having a certain characteristic, condition, or behavior.

**Battery of tests.**   A group of aptitude or achievement tests measuring different things, but standardized on the same sample, thus permitting comparisons of a person's performance in different areas.

**Behavior analysis.**   Procedures that focus on objectively describing a particular behavior and identifying the antecedents and consequences of that behavior. Behavior analysis may be conducted for research purposes or to obtain information in planning a behavior modification program.

**Bias.**   Any one of a number of factors that cause scores on psychometric instruments to be consistently higher or lower than they would be if measurement were accurate. Illustrative of factors that result in bias is the *leniency error,* the tendency to rate a person consistently higher than he or she should be rated.

**Bimodal distribution.**   A frequency distribution having two modes (maximum points). See *Frequency distribution; Mode.*

**Case study.**   Detailed study of an individual, designed to provide a comprehensive, in-depth understanding of behavior and personality. Information for a case study is obtained from biographical, interview, observational, and test data.

**Ceiling age.**   The minimum age or year level on a test, such as the Stanford–Binet, at which an examinee fails all subtests. See *Basal age.*

**Central tendency.**   Average, or central, score in a group of scores; the most representative score (for example, the arithmetic mean, median, mode).

**Classification.**   The use of test scores to assign a person to one category rather than another.

**Clinical (impressionistic) approach.**   Approach to behavioral prediction and diagnosis in which psychologists or psychiatrists assign their own judgmental weights to the predictor variables and then combine them in a subjective manner to make diagnoses and prognoses.

**Cluster sampling.**   Sampling procedure in which the target population is divided into sections or clusters. The number of units selected at random from a given cluster is proportional to the total number of units in the cluster.

**Coaching.**   Short-term instruction designed to improve the test scores of prospective test takers. The instructional activities include practice on various types of items and test-taking strategies.

**Coefficient alpha.**   An internal-consistency reliability coefficient, appropriate for tests comprised of dichotomous or multipoint items; the expected correlation of one test with a parallel form containing the same number of items.

**Coefficient of equivalence.**   A reliability coefficient (correlation) obtained by administering two different forms of a test to the same people. See *Alternate-forms reliability.*

**Coefficient of internal consistency.**   Reliability coefficient based on estimates of the internal consistency of a test (for example, split-half coefficient and alpha coefficient).

**Coefficient of stability.**   A reliability coefficient (correlation) obtained by administering a test to the same group of examinees on two different occasions. See *Test–retest reliability.*

**Coefficient of stability and equivalence.**   A reliability coefficient obtained by administering two forms of a test to a group of examinees on two different occasions.

**Cognition.**   Having to do with the processes of intellect; remembering, thinking, problem solving, and the like.

**Cognitive assessment.**   Measurement of intellective processes, such as perception, memory, thinking, judgment, and reasoning. See *Affective assessment.*

**Cognitive style.**   Strategy or approach to perceiving, remembering, and thinking that a person seems to prefer in attempting to understand and cope with the world (for example, field independence–dependence, reflectivity–impulsivity, and internal–external locus of control).

**Communality.**   Proportion of variance in a measured variable accounted for by variance that the variable has in common with other variables.

**Component processes.**   According to Sternberg's theory, the cognitive processes or mental components, including metacomponents, performance components, acquisition components, retention components, and transfer components.

**Composite score.**   The direct or weighted sum of the scores on two or more tests or sections of a test.

**Computer-assisted instruction (CAI).**   Individualized instructional procedures in which a computer is used to present the material to be learned, to ask questions, and to evaluate answers.

**Concordance reliability.**   Several raters or scorers make numerical judgments of the amount of a characteristic or behavior shown by a large sample of people. Then a *coefficient of concordance,* an index of agreement among the judgments of the corers or raters, is computed.

**Concrete operations stage.**   In J. Piaget's theory of cognitive development, the stage (7 to 11 years of age) during which a child develops organized systems of operations by the process of social interaction, with a corresponding reduction in self-centeredness.

**Concurrent validity.**   The extent to which scores obtained by a group of people on a particular psychometric instrument are related to their simultaneously determined scores on another measure (criterion) of the same characteristic that the instrument is supposed to measure.

**Confidence interval.**   A range of values within which one can be fairly certain (usually 95 or 99 percent confident) that a person's true score (or difference between scores) on a test or a criterion variable falls. See *Standard error of measurement* and *Standard error of estimate.*

**Construct validity.**   The extent to which scores on a psychometric instrument designed to measure a certain characteristic are related to measures of behavior in situations in which the characteristic is supposed to be an important determinant of behavior.

**Content analysis.**   Method of studying and analyzing written (or oral) communications in a systematic, objective, and quantitative manner to assess certain psychological variables.

**Content validity.**   The extent to which a group of people who are experts in the material with which a test deals agrees that the test or other psychometric instrument measures what it was designed to measure.

**Contrast error.**   In interviewing or rating, the tendency to evaluate a person more positively if an immediately preceding individual was given a highly negative evaluation or to evaluate a person more negatively if an immediately preceding individual was given a highly positive evaluation.

**Convergent thinking.**   Using facts and reason to produce a single correct answer.

**Convergent validity.**   Situation in which an assessment instrument has high correlations with other measures (or methods of measuring) the same construct. See *Discriminant validity.*

**Correction for attenuation.**   Formula used to estimate what the validity coefficient of a test would be if both the test and the criterion were perfectly reliable.

**Correction for guessing.**   A formula, applied to raw test scores, to correct for the effects of random guessing by examinees. A popular correction-for-guessing formula requires subtracting a portion of the number of items the examinee answers incorrectly from the number he or she answers correctly.

**Correlation.**   Degree of relationship or association between two variables, such as a test and a criterion measure.

**Correlation coefficient.**   A numerical index of the degree of relationship between two variables. Correlation coefficients usually range from $-1.00$ (perfect negative relationship), through .00 (total absence of a relationship), to $+1.00$ (perfect positive relationship). Two common types of correlation coefficient are the product–moment coefficient and the point-biserial coefficient.

**Creativity test.**   A test that assesses original, novel, or divergent thinking.

**Criterion.**   A standard or variable with which scores on a psychometric instrument are compared or against which they are evaluated. The validity of a test or other psychometric procedure used in selecting or classifying people is determined by its ability to predict a specified criterion of behavior in the situation for which people are being selected or classified.

**Criterion contamination.**   The effect of any factor on a criterion such that the criterion is not a valid measure of an individual's accomplishment. Aptitude test scores may be used to predict grades in school, but when teachers use scores on an aptitude test to decide what grades to assign to students, the grades are not a valid criterion for validating the aptitude test; the criterion has become contaminated.

**Criterion-referenced test.**   A test that has been designed with very restricted content specifications to serve a limited range of highly specific purposes. The aim of the test is to determine where the examinee stands with respect to certain educational objectives. See *Norm-referenced test.*

**Criterion-related validity.**   The extent to which a test or other assessment instrument measures what it was designed to measure, as indicated by the correlation of test scores with some criterion measure of behavior.

**Critical incident.**   A behavior that is considered critical to effective performance on a job, for example, "cleans up work area before leaving" or "treats customers cordially."

**Cross validation.**   Readministering an assessment instrument that has been found to be a valid predictor of a criterion for one group of persons to a second group of persons to determine whether the instrument is also valid for that group. There is almost always some shrinkage of the validity coefficient on cross validation, since chance factors spuriously inflate the validity coefficient obtained with the first group of examinees.

**Crystallized intelligence.**   R. B. Cattell's term for mental ability (knowledge, skills) acquired through experience and education.

**Culture-fair test.**   A test composed of materials to which all sociocultural groups have presumably been exposed. The test does not penalize any sociocultural group because of lack of relevant experience. Attempts to develop culture-fair tests have not proved very successful.

**Cutoff score (cutting score).**   All applicants falling below the cutoff score on a criterion are rejected, and all applicants falling at or above the cutoff score are accepted. The cutoff score depends on the validity of the test, the selection ratio, and other factors.

**Derived score.**   A score obtained by performing some mathematical operation on a raw score, such as multiplying the raw score by a constant and/or adding a constant to the score. See *Standard scores; T scores; z score.*

**Developmental quotient (DQ).**   An index, roughly equivalent to a mental age, for summarizing an infant's behavior as assessed by the Gesell Developmental Schedules.

**Deviation IQ.**   Intelligence quotient (IQ) score obtained by converting raw scores on an intelligence test to a score distribution having a mean of 100 and a fixed standard deviation, such as 16 for the Stanford–Binet or 15 for the Wechsler tests.

**Diagnostic interview.**   An interview designed to obtain information on a person's thoughts, feelings, perceptions, and behavior; used in making a diagnostic decision about the person.

**Diagnostic test.**   An achievement test composed of a number of areas or skills constituting a certain subject, with the purpose of diagnosing an individual's relative strengths and weaknesses in the areas. Diagnostic tests are available in reading, arithmetic, and spelling.

**Discriminant validity.**   Situation in which a psychometric instrument has low correlations with other measures of (or methods of measuring) different psychological constructs.

**Distracter.**   Any of the incorrect options on a multiple-choice test item.

**Divergent thinking.**   Creative thinking that involves more than one solution to a problem.

**Down syndrome (mongolism).**   A disorder characterized by a flattened skull; thickened skin on eyelids; short, stubby fingers and toes; coarse, silky hair; short stature; and moderately low intelligence. An extra chromosome is found in the twenty-first position in karyotypes of Down syndrome cases.

**Dynamic assessment.**   A test–teach–test approach to assessment in which a person is tested (pretested), then given practice on the test materials, and finally tested again (posttested). The change in performance level from pretest to posttest is a measure of learning potential (see *Zone of potential development*).

**Ectomorph.**   In Sheldon's somatotype system, a person with a tall, thin body build; related to the cerebrotonic (thinking, introversive) temperament type.

**Educable mentally retarded (EMR).**   Children characterized by a mild degree of mental retardation (IQ = 51–69). Such children are capable of obtaining a third- to sixth-grade education and can learn to read, write, and perform elementary arithmetic operations.

**Ego.**   According to psychoanalytic theory, that part of the personality (the "I" or "me") that obeys the reality principle and attempts to mediate the conflict between the id and superego.

**Electroencephalograph (EEG).**   Electronic apparatus designed to detect and record brain waves from the intact scalp.

**Electromyograph (EMG).**   Electronic apparatus designed to measure muscular activity or tension.

**Empirical scoring.**   A scoring system in which an examinee's responses are scored according to a key constructed from responses made by people in certain criterion groups, such as schizophrenics or physicians. This scoring procedure is employed with various personality and interest inventories.

**Endomorph.**   In Sheldon's somatotype system, a person having a rotund body shape (fat); related to the viscerotonic (relaxed, sociable) temperament.

**Equilibration.**   In J. Piaget's theory of cognitive development, the process by which a child comes to know and understand the environment by interacting with it. Equilibration involves the processes of assimilation and accommodation.

**Equipercentile method.**   Traditional method of converting the score units on one test to the score units on a parallel test. The scores on each test are converted to percentile ranks, and a table of equivalent scores is produced by equating the score at the *p*th percentile on the first test to the score at the *p*th percentile on the second test.

**Equivalent forms.**   See *Parallel forms.*

**Essay test.**   A test on which examinees are required to compose rather lengthy answers to a series of questions. The answers are evaluated subjectively by the teacher or another evaluator. See *Objective test.*

**Estimated learning potential (ELP).**   An estimate of a child's ability to learn, derived from measures obtained in the System of Multicultural Pluralistic Assessment (SOMPA). The ELP takes into account not only the child's IQ on the Wechsler Intelligence Scale for Children–Revised or the Wechsler Preschool and Primary Scale of Intelligence, but also family size, family structure, socioeconomic status, and degree of urban acculturation.

**Evaluation.**   To judge the merit or value of an examinee's behavior from a composite of test scores, observations, and reports.

**Exceptional child.**   A child who deviates significantly from the average in mental, physical, or emotional characteristics.

**Expectancy effect.**   Effect of teacher expectations on the IQ scores of pupils; more generally, the effect of a person's expectations on another person's behavior.

**Expectancy table.**   A table giving the frequency or percentage of examinees in a certain category (score interval) on a predictor variable (test) who would be expected to fall in a certain category (score interval) on the criterion variable.

**Experiential intelligence.**   According to Sternberg, the ability to cope effectively with novel tasks.

**Extrovert.**   C. G. Jung's term for people who are oriented, in thought or social orientation, toward the external environment and other people rather than toward their own thoughts and feelings.

**Face validity.**   The extent to which the appearance or content of the materials (items and the like) on a test or other psychometric instrument is such that the instrument appears to be a good measure of what it is supposed to measure.

**Factor.**   A dimension, trait, or characteristic of personality revealed by factoring the matrix of correlations computed from the scores of a large number of people on several different tests or items.

**Factor analysis.**   A mathematical procedure for analyzing a matrix of correlations among measurements to determine what factors (constructs) are sufficient to explain the correlations.

**Factor loadings.**   In factor analysis, the resulting correlations (weights) between tests (or other variables) and the extracted factors.

**Factor rotation.**   A mathematical procedure applied to a factor matrix for the purpose of simplifying the matrix for interpretation purposes by increasing the number of high and low factor loadings in the matrix. Factor rotation may be either *orthogonal,* in which case the resulting factors are at right angles to each other, or *oblique,* in which the resulting factor axes form acute or obtuse angles with each other.

**Fairness.**   On an aptitude test, the extent to which scores are unbiased, that is, equally predictive of the criterion performances of different groups.

**False negative.**   Selection error or diagnostic decision error in which an assessment procedure incorrectly predicts a maladaptive outcome (for example, low achievement, poor performance, or psychopathology).

**False positive.**   Selection error or diagnostic decision error in which an assessment procedure incorrectly predicts an adaptive outcome (for example, high achievement, good performance, or absence of psychopathology).

**Fantasy stage.**   The earliest stage in the development of interests, in which a child's interest orientations are not based on an accurate perception of reality.

**Fidelity.**   The narrowness of the bandwidth of a test or other measuring instrument. A test with high fidelity is a good predictor of a fairly narrow range of criteria. See *Bandwidth.*

**Field dependence.**   A perceptual style in which the perceiver relies primarily on cues from the surrounding visual environment, rather than kinesthetic (gravitational) cues, to determine the upright position in the rod-and-frame test.

**Field independence.**   A perceptual style in which the perceiver depends primarily on kinesthetic (gravitational) cues, rather than visual cues from the surrounding environment, to determine the upright position in the rod-and-frame test.

**Fluid intelligence.**   R. B. Cattell's term for inherent, genetically determined mental ability, as seen in problem solving or novel responses.

**Forced-choice item.**   Item on a personality or interest inventory, arranged as a dyad (two options), a triad (three options), or a tetrad (four options) of terms or phrases. The respondent is required to select an option viewed as most descriptive of the personality, interests, or behavior of the person being evaluated and perhaps another option perceived to be least descriptive of the personality, interests, or behavior of the person being evaluated. Forced-choice items are found on certain personality inventories (for example, the Edwards Personal Preference Schedule), interest inventories (Kuder General Interest Survey), and rating forms to control for response sets.

**Formal operations.**   The final stage (11 to 15 years) in J. Piaget's cognitive development sequence, in which the child can now use logic and verbal reasoning and perform higher-level, more abstract mental operations.

**Formative evaluation.**   Evaluation of performance for the purpose of improving instruction or determining areas of strength and weakness for purposes of enrichment or remedial instruction. See *Summative evaluation.*

**Four-fifths rule.**   Selection rule that any procedure resulting in a selection rate for any race, gender, or ethnic group that is less than four-fifths (80%) of that of the group with the highest rate has an adverse impact and is consequently illegal.

**Frequency distribution.**   A table of score intervals and the number of cases (scores) falling within each interval.

***g* factor.**   The single general factor of intelligence postulated by Spearman to account for the high correlations among tests of intelligence.

**Generalizability theory.**   A theory of test scores and the associated statistical formulation that conceptualizes a test score as a sample from a universe of scores. Analysis of variance procedures are used to determine the generalizability from score to universe value, as a function of examinees, test items, and situational contexts. A generalizability coefficient may be computed as a measure of the degree of generalizability from sample to population.

**Grade norm.**   The average of the scores on a test made by a group of children at a given grade level.

**Graphic rating scale.**   A rating scale containing a series of items, each consisting of a line on which the rater places a check mark to indicate the degree of a characteristic that the ratee is perceived as possessing. Typically, at the left extremity of the line is a brief verbal description indicating the lowest degree of the characteristic, and at the right end is a description of the highest degree of the characteristic. Brief descriptions of intermediate degrees of the characteristic may also be located at equidistant points along the line.

**Graphology.**   The analysis of handwriting to determine the character or personality of the writer.

**Group test.**   A test administered simultaneously to a group of examinees by one examiner. See *Individual test.*

**Guess-who technique.**   Procedure for analyzing group interaction and the social stimulus value of group members, in which children are asked to "guess who" in a classroom or other group situation possesses certain characteristics or does certain things.

**Halo effect.**   Rating a person high on one characteristic merely because he or she rates high on other characteristics.

**Heritability index ($h^2$).**   Ratio of the test score variance attributable to heredity to the variance attributable to both heredity and environment.

**Hierarchical model.**   P. E. Vernon's tree model of intelligence, consisting of a general factor at the highest level, two major group factors (verbal–educational and practical–mechanical–spatial) at the second level, and a number of minor group factors at a third level.

**Ideal self.**   In C. R. Rogers' phenomonological theory, the self a person would like to be, as contrasted with the person's *real self.*

**Idiographic approach.**   Approach to personality assessment and research in which the individual is viewed as a lawful, integrated system in his or her own right. See *Nomothetic approach.*

**In-basket technique.**   A procedure for evaluating supervisors or executives in which the candidate is required to indicate what action should be taken on a series of memos and other materials of the kind typically found in a supervisor's or executive's in-basket.

**Incident sampling.**   In contrast to *time sampling*, an observational procedure in which certain types of incidents, such as those indicative of aggressive behavior, are selected for observation and recording.

**Individual test.**   A test administered to one examinee at a time.

**Informed consent.**   A formal agreement made by a person, or the person's guardian or legal representative, with an agency or someone else to permit use of the person's name and/or personal information (test scores and the like) for a specified purpose.

**Insanity.**   A legal term for a disorder of judgment or behavior in which a person cannot distinguish between right and wrong (McNaghten Rule) or cannot control or manage his or her actions and affairs.

**Intelligence.**   Many definitions of this term have been offered, such as "the ability to judge well, understand well, and reason well" (A. Binet) and "the capacity for abstract thinking" (L. M. Terman). In general, what is measured by intelligence tests is the ability to succeed in school-type tasks.

**Intelligence quotient (IQ).**   A derived score, used originally in scoring the Stanford–Binet Intelligence Scale. A ratio IQ is computed by dividing the examinee's mental age (MA), as determined from a score on an intelligence test, by his or her chronological age (CA), and multiplying the resulting quotient by 100. A deviation IQ is computed by multiplying the $z$ score corresponding to a raw score on an intelligence test by the standard deviation of the deviation IQs and adding 100 to the product.

**Intelligence test.**   A psychological test designed to measure an individual's aptitude for scholastic work or other kinds of activities involving verbal ability and problem solving.

**Interest inventory.**   A test or checklist, such as the Strong Interest Inventory or the Kuder General Interest Survey, designed to assess individual preferences for certain activities and topics.

**Interlocking items.**   Test items on which a response to one item is affected by or is contingent upon responses to other items on the test.

**Internal consistency.**   The extent to which all items on a test measure the same variable or construct. The reliability of a test computed by the Spearman–Brown, Kuder–Richardson, or Cronbach–alpha formulas is a measure of the test's internal consistency.

**Interrater (interscorer) reliability.**   Two scorers assign numerical ratings or scores to a sample of people. Then the correlation between the two sets of numbers is computed.

**Interval scale.**   A measurement scale on which equality of numerical differences implies equality of differences in the attribute or characteristic being measured. The scale of temperature (Celsius or Fahrenheit) and, presumably, standard score scales ($z$, $T$, and others) are examples of interval scales.

**Interview.**   A systematic procedure for obtaining information by asking questions and, in general, verbally interacting with a person (the interviewee).

**Intraclass reliability.**   An index of agreement among the ratings assigned by a group of raters (judges) to a characteristic or behavior of a person.

**Introvert.** Carl Jung's term for orientation toward the self; primarily concerned with one's own thoughts and feelings rather than with the external environment or other people; preference for solitary activities.

**Inventory.** A set of questions or statements to which people respond (for example, by indicating agreement or disagreement); designed to provide a measure of personality interest, attitude, or behavior.

**Ipsative measurement.** Test item format (for example, forced choice) in which the variables being measured are compared with each other, so a person's score on one variable is affected by his or her scores on other variables measured by the instrument.

**Item.** One of the units, questions, or tasks of which a psychometric instrument is composed.

**Item analysis.** A general term for procedures designed to assess the utility or validity of a set of test items.

**Item characteristic curve.** A graph, used in item analysis, in which the proportion of examinees passing an item is plotted against total test scores.

**Item difficulty index.** An index of the easiness or difficulty of an item for a group of examinees. A convenient measure of the difficulty of an item is the percentage ($p$) of examinees who select the correct answer.

**Item discrimination index.** A measure of how effectively an item discriminates between examinees who score high on the test as a whole (or on some other criterion variable) and those who score low.

**Item-response (characteristic) curve.** Graph showing the proportion of examinees who get a test item right, plotted against an internal (total test score) or external criterion of performance.

**Item sampling.** Procedure for selecting subsets of items from a total item pool; different samples of items are administered to different groups of examinees.

**Job analysis.** A general term for procedures used to determine the factors or tasks making up a job. A job analysis is usually considered a prerequisite to the construction of a test for predicting performance on a job.

**Kuder–Richardson formulas.** Formulas used to compute a measure of internal-consistency reliability from a single administration of a test having 0–1 scoring.

**Language test.** A test composed of verbal or numerical items, that is, items involving the use of language. See *Nonverbal test*.

**Latent trait theory.** Any one of several theories (for example, item characteristic curve theory or Rasch model) and associated statistical procedures that relate item and test scores to estimated standing on some hypothetical latent ability trait or continuum; used in item analysis and test standardization.

**Leaderless group discussion (LGD).** Six or so individuals (for example, candidates for an executive position) are observed while discussing an assigned problem to determine their effectiveness in working with the group and reaching a solution.

**Learning disability.**   Difficulty in learning to read, write, spell, or perform arithmetic or other academic skills by a person whose score on an intelligence test (IQ) is average or above.

**Leniency error.**   Tendency to rate an individual higher on a positive characteristic and less severely on a negative characteristic than he or she actually should be rated.

**Likert scale.**   Attitude scale in which respondents indicate their degree of agreement or disagreement with a particular proposition concerning some object, person, or situation.

**Linear regression analysis.**   Procedure for determining the algebraic equation of the best-fitting line for predicting scores on a dependent variable from one or more independent variables.

**Local norms.**   Percentile ranks, standard scores, or other norms corresponding to the raw test scores of a relatively small, local group of examinees.

**Locus of control.**   J. B. Rotter's term for a cognitive–perceptual style characterized by the typical direction (internal or self versus external or other) from which individuals perceive themselves as being controlled.

**Looking-glass theory.**   After C. H. Cooley, the idea that the self is formed as a result of the individual's perception of how others view her or his person and behavior.

**Man-to-man scale.**   Procedure in which ratings on a specific trait (for example, leadership) are made by comparing each person to be rated with several other people whose standings on the trait have already been determined.

**Mastery test.**   See *Criterion-referenced test.*

**Matching item.**   A test item requiring examinees to indicate which of several options in one list is (are) the correct match(es) or answer(s) for each of the several options in another list.

**Measurement.**   Procedures for determining (or indexing) the amount or quantity of some construct or entity; assignment of numbers to objects or events.

**Median.**   Score point in a distribution of scores below and above which 50 percent of the scores fall.

**Mental age (MA).**   A derived score on an intelligence test such as the Stanford–Binet. An examinee's mental age corresponds to the chronological age of a representative sample of children of the same chronological age whose average score on the test was equal to the examinee's score. See *Intelligence quotient.*

**Mental age grade placement.**   An index of the grade level at which a person is functioning mentally.

**Mentally gifted.**   A person who is significantly above average in intellectual functioning, variously defined as an IQ of 130 or 140 and above.

**Mentally retarded.**   A person who is significantly below average in intellectual functioning, variously defined as an IQ of 70 or 75 and below.

**Mesomorph.**   W. H. Sheldon's term for a person having an athletic physique; correlated with a somatotonic temperament (active, aggressive, energetic).

**Mode.**    The most frequently occurring score in a group of scores.

**Moderator variable.**    Demographic or personality variable (for example, age, sex, cognitive style, compulsivity) affecting the correlation between two other variables (for example, aptitude and achievement).

**Multilevel test.**    A test designed to be appropriate for several age levels; a separate test is constructed for each level.

**Multiple abstract variance analysis (MAVA).**    Statistical procedure, devised by R. B. Cattell, for determining the relative effects of heredity and environment on a particular personality characteristic.

**Multiple-choice item.**    A test item consisting of a stem (statement, question, phrase, or the like) and several response options (usually three to five), only one of which is correct.

**Multiple correlation coefficient ($R$).**    A measure of the overall degree of relationship, varying between $-1.00$ and $+1.00$, of several variables with a single criterion variable. The multiple correlation of a group of scholastic aptitude tests with school grades is typically around .60 to .70, a moderate degree of correlation.

**Multiple cutoff.**    Selection strategy in which applicants are required to make at least specific minimum scores on several selection criteria in order to be accepted (employed, admitted, and so on).

**Multiple-regression analysis.**    Statistical method for analyzing the contributions of two or more independent variables in predicting a dependent variable.

**Multitrait–multimethod matrix.**    Matrix of correlation coefficients resulting from correlating measures of the same trait by the same method, different traits by the same method, the same trait by different methods, and different traits by different methods. The relative magnitudes of the four types of correlations are compared in evaluating the construct validity of a test.

**National norms.**    Percentile ranks, standard scores, or other norms based on a national sample. See *Local norms; Norms.*

**Neuropsychological assessment.**    Measurement of cognitive, perceptual, and motor performance to determine the locus, extent, and effects of neurological damage and malfunction.

**Nominal scale.**    The lowest type of measurement, in which numbers are used merely as descriptors or names of things, rather than designating order or amount.

**Nomination technique.**    Method of studying social structure and personality in which students, workers, or other groups of individuals are asked to indicate with which persons in the group they would like to do a certain thing or whom they feel possess(es) certain characteristics.

**Nomothetic approach.**    Search for general laws of behavior and personality that apply to everyone.

**Nonverbal behavior.**    Any communicative behavior that does not involve making word sounds or signs. It includes movements of large (macrokinesics) and small (microkinesics) body parts, interpersonal distance or territoriality (proximics), tone and rate of voice sounds (paralinguistics), and communications imparted by culturally prescribed matters relating to time, dress, memberships, and the like (culturics).

**Nonverbal test.** A test that does not necessitate the use of spoken or written words, but requires the examinee to construct, manipulate, or respond to test materials in other nonverbal ways.

**Norm group.** Sample of people on whom a test is standardized.

**Normal distribution.** A smooth, bell-shaped frequency distribution of scores, symmetric about the mean and described by an exact mathematical function. The test scores of a large group of examinees are frequently distributed approximately in this way.

**Normalized scores.** Scores obtained by transforming raw scores in such a way that the transformed scores are normally distributed with a mean of 0 and a standard deviation of 1 (or some linear function of these numbers).

**Norm-referenced test.** A test whose scores are interpreted with respect to norms obtained from a representative sample of examines. See *Criterion-referenced test*.

**Norms.** A list of scores and the corresponding percentile ranks, standard scores, or other transformed scores of a group of people on whom a test has been standardized.

**Objective test.** A test scored by comparing an examinee's responses to a list of correct answers (a key) prepared beforehand, in contrast to a subjectively scored test. Examples of objective test items are multiple-choice and true–false.

**Oblique rotation.** In factor analysis, a rotation in which the factor axes are allowed to form acute or obtuse angles with each other. Consequently, the factors are correlated.

**Observation method.** Observing behavior in a controlled or uncontrolled situation and making a formal or informal record of the observations.

**Odd–even reliability.** The correlation between total scores on the odd-numbered and total scores on the even-numbered items of a test, corrected by the Spearman–Brown reliability formula. See *Spearman–Brown formula*.

**Omnibus test.** A test consisting of a variety of items designed to measure different aspects of mental functioning. The Otis–Lennon School Ability Test and the Henmon–Nelson Test of Mental Ability are omnibus tests. See *Spiral omnibus test*.

**Operation.** In J. P. Guilford's structure-of-intellect model, one of five possible types of mental processes (cognitive, memory, divergent thinking, convergent thinking, and evaluation). In J. Piaget's theory of cognitive development, an *operation* is any mental action that is reversible (can be returned to its starting point) and integrated with other reversible mental actions.

**Ordinal scale.** Type of measurement scale on which the numbers refer merely to the ranks of objects or events arranged in order of merit (for example, numbers referring to order of finishing in a contest).

**Orthogonal rotation.** In factor analysis, a rotation that maintains the independence of factors; that is, the angles between factors are kept at 90° and hence the factors are uncorrelated.

**Out-of-level testing.**    Administering a test designed primarily for one age or grade level to examinees below or above that level.

**Parallel forms.**    Two tests that are equivalent in the sense that they contain the same kinds of items of equal difficulty and are highly correlated. The scores made on one form of the test are very close to those made by the same persons on the other form.

**Parallel forms reliability.**    An index of reliability determined by correlating the scores of individuals on parallel forms of a test.

**Participant observation.**    A research technique, used primarily by cultural anthropologists, in which an observer attempts to minimize the intrusiveness of his or her person and observational activities by becoming part of the group being observed, for example, by dressing and acting like other members of the group.

**Percentile.**    The test score at or below which a specified percentage of scores fall.

**Percentile band.**    A range of percentile ranks within which there is a specified probability that an examinee's true score on a test will fall.

**Percentile norms.**    A list of raw scores and the corresponding percentages of the test standardization group whose scores fall below the given percentile.

**Percentile rank.**    The percentage of scores falling below a given score in a frequency distribution or group of scores; the percentage corresponding to the given score.

**Performance test.**    A test on which the examinee is required to manipulate various physical objects; performance tests are contrasted with paper-and-pencil tests. Examples are the performance scale of the Wechsler Intelligence Scale and the Arthur Point Scale of Performance.

**Personality.**    The sum total of all the qualities, traits, and behaviors that characterize a person and by which, together with his or her physical attributes, the person is perceived as an individual.

**Personality assessment.**    Description and analysis of personality by means of various techniques, including observing, interviewing, administering checklists, rating scales, personality inventories, and projective techniques.

**Personality inventory.**    A self-report inventory or questionnaire consisting of statements concerning personal characteristics and behaviors. On a true–false inventory, the respondent indicates whether each item is self-descriptive; on a multiple-choice or forced-choice inventory, the respondent selects the words, phrases, or statements that are self-descriptive.

**Phrenology.**    Discredited theory and practice relating affective and cognitive characteristics to the configuration (bumps) of the skull.

**Pluralistic model.**    In the System of Multicultural Pluralistic Assessment (SOMPA), a combination made up of the Student Assessment Materials and the Parent Interview. A child's scores on the various measures are interpreted by comparing them with the scores of other children having a similar sociocultural background.

**Point-biserial coefficient.** Correlation coefficient computed between a dichotomous variable and a continuous variable; derived from the product–moment correlation coefficient.

**Point scale.** A test on which points (0, 1, or 2, for example) are assigned for each item, depending on the accuracy and completeness of the answer.

**Power test.** A test with ample time limits so all examinees will have time to attempt all items. Many of the items are difficult, and they are often arranged in order from easiest to most difficult.

**Predictive validity.** Extent to which scores on a test are predictive of performance on some criterion measured at a later time; usually expressed as a correlation between the test (predictor variable) and the criterion variable.

**Preoperational period.** In J. Piaget's theory of cognitive development, the egocentric period of development (3 to 7 years) when the child acquires language and other symbolic representations.

**Projective technique.** A relatively unstructured personality assessment technique in which the person responds to materials such as inkblots, ambiguous pictures, incomplete sentences, and other materials by telling what he or she perceives, making up stories, or constructing and arranging sentences and objects. Theoretically, because the material is fairly unstructured, the structure imposed on it by the examinee represents a projection of his or her own personality characteristics (needs, conflicts, sources of anxiety, and the like).

**Psychometrics.** Theory and research pertaining to the measurement of psychological (cognitive and affective) characteristics.

**$Q$ technique (sort).** Personality assessment procedure that centers on sorting decks of cards ($Q$ sorts) containing statements that may or may not be descriptive of the sorter.

**Quartile.** A score in a frequency distribution below which either 25 percent (first quartile), 50 percent (second quartile), 75 percent (third quartile), or 100 percent (fourth quartile) of the total number of scores fall.

***r.*** A symbol for the Pearson product–moment correlation coefficient.

**Random sample.** A sample of observations (for example, test scores) drawn from a population in such a way that every member of the target population has an equal chance of being selected in the sample.

**Range.** A crude measure of the spread or variability of a group of scores computed by subtracting the lowest score from the highest score.

**Rapport.** A warm, friendly relationship between examiner and examinee.

**Rasch model.** One-parameter (item difficulty) model for scaling test items for purposes of item analysis and test standardization. The model is based on the assumption that indexes of guessing and item discrimination are negligible parameters. As with other latent-trait models, the Rasch model relates examinees' performances on test items (percentage passing) to their estimated standings on a hypothetical latent ability trait or continuum.

**Ratio IQ.** An intelligence quotient obtained by dividing an examinee's mental age score on an intelligence test (such as the older Stanford–Binet) by his or her chronological age and multiplying the quotient by 100. See *Deviation IQ.*

**Ratio scale.**   A scale of measurement, having a true zero, on which equal numerical ratios imply equal ratios of the attribute being measured. Psychological variables are typically not measured on ratio scales, but height, weight, energy, and many other physical variables are.

**Raw score.**   An examinee's unconverted score on a test, computed as the number of items answered correctly or the number of correct answers minus a certain portion of the incorrect answers.

**Readiness test.**   A test that measures the extent to which a person possesses the skills and knowledge necessary to learn a complex subject.

**Realistic stage.**   Final stage in the development of vocational interests, usually occurring during late adolescence or early adulthood. At this stage the individual has a realistic notion about what particular occupations entail and the vocation he or she would like to pursue.

**Regression equation.**   A linear equation for forecasting criterion scores from scores on one or more predictor variables; a procedure often used in selection programs or actuarial prediction and diagnosis.

**Regression toward the mean.**   Tendency for test scores or other psychometric measures to be closer to the mean on retesting; the more extreme the original score is, the closer it will be to the mean on retesting.

**Reliability.**   The extent to which a psychological assessment device measures anything consistently. A reliable instrument is relatively free from errors of measurement, so the scores obtained on the instrument are close in numerical value to the true scores of examinees.

**Reliability coefficient.**   A numerical index, between .00 and 1.00, of the reliability of an assessment instrument. Methods for determining reliability include test–retest, parallel forms, and internal consistency.

**Representative sample.**   A group of individuals whose characteristics are similar to those of the population of individuals for whom a test is intended.

**Response sets (styles).**   Tendencies for individuals to respond in relatively fixed or stereotyped ways in situations where there are two or more response choices, such as on personality inventories. Tendencies to guess, to answer true (acquiescence), and to give socially desirable answers are some of the response sets that have been investigated.

**Scatter diagram.**   A cluster of points plotted from a set of $X$–$Y$ values, in which $X$ is the independent variable and $Y$ the dependent variable.

**Schema.**   In J. Piaget's theory of cognitive development, a mental structure (grasping, sucking, shaking, and so on) that is modified (accommodated) as a result of experience.

**Scholastic aptitude test.**   Any test that predicts the ability of a person to learn the kinds of information and skills taught in school. The abilities measured by these tests (for example, the Scholastic Aptitude Test) are similar to those measured by general intelligence tests.

**Scoring formula.**   A formula used to compute raw scores on a test. Common scoring formulas are $S = R$ and $S = R - W/(k - 1)$, where $S$ is the score, $R$ is the number right, $W$ is the number wrong, and $k$ is the number of options per item.

**Screening.**   A general term for any selection process, usually not very precise, by which some applicants are accepted and others are rejected.

**Secure test.**   A test administered under conditions of tight security to make certain that only persons who are supposed to take the test actually take it and that copies of test materials are not removed from the examination room(s) by examinees.

**Selection.**   The use of tests and other devices to select those applicants for an occupation or educational program who are most likely to succeed in that situation. Applicants who fall at or above the cutoff score on the test are selected (accepted); those who fall below cutoff are rejected.

**Selection ratio.**   The proportion of applicants who are selected for a job or training (educational) program.

**Self-fulfilling prophecy.**   Tendency for a person's expectations and attitudes concerning future events or outcomes to affect their occurrence; the tendency for children to behave in ways in which parents or teachers expect them to behave.

**Self-report inventory.**   A paper-and-pencil measure of personality traits or interests, comprised of a series of items that the respondent indicates as characteristic (true) or not characteristic (not true) of himself or herself.

**Semantic differential.**   A rating scale for evaluating the connotative meanings of selected concepts. Each concept is rated on a 7-point, bipolar adjectival scale.

**Semi-interquartile range ($Q$).**   A measure of the variability of a group of ordinal-scale scores, computed as half the difference between the first and third quartiles.

**Sensorimotor stage.**   The first stage in J. Piaget's theory of cognitive development (0 to 2 years), during which the child learns to exercise simple reflexes and to coordinate various perceptions.

**Sentence completion test.**   A projective test of personality consisting of a series of incomplete sentences that the examinee is instructed to complete.

**Sequential processing.**   Mental process in which a series of items is processed sequentially, in serial order. An example of a sequential task is attempting to recall a series of numbers. See *Simultaneous processing*.

**Sequential testing.**   Testing procedure in which an examinee's answers to previous items determine which items will be presented next; also referred to as *adaptive* or *tailored testing*.

**Simultaneous processing.**   Mental process in which several bits or pieces of information are synthesized or integrated simultaneously. See *Sequential processing*.

**Situation(al) test.**   A performance test in which the person is placed in a realistic but contrived situation and directed to accomplish a specific task. Situation tests have been used to assess personality characteristics such as honesty and frustration tolerance.

**Skewness.**   Degree of asymmetry in a frequency distribution. In a positively skewed distribution, there are more scores to the left of the mean (low scores); this is true when the test is too difficult for the examinees. In a negatively skewed distribution, there are more scores to the right of the mean (high scores); this is true when the test is too easy for the examinees.

**Snellen chart.**   A chart containing letters of various sizes, designed to measure visual acuity at a distance.

**Social desirability response set.**   Response set or style affecting scores on a psychological assessment instrument. Refers to the tendency for an examinee to answer in what he or she perceives as the more socially desirable direction, rather than answering in a manner that is truly characteristic or descriptive of him or her.

**Sociogram.**   Diagram consisting of circles representing individuals in a group, with lines drawn indicating which people chose (accepted) each other and which people did not choose (rejected) each other. Terms used in referring to particular elements of a sociogram are *star, clique, isolate,* and *mutual admiration society.*

**Sociometric technique.**   Method of determining and describing the pattern of acceptances and rejections in a group of people.

**Somatotype.**   Classification of a body build (physique) in W. H Sheldon's three-component system (endomorphy, mesomorphy, ectomorphy).

**Spearman–Brown formula.**   A formula for estimating the internal consistency reliability of a test by correlating separate scores on two split halves. See *Odd-even reliability* and *Split-half coefficient.*

**Special children.**   Children having physical, psychological, cognitive, or social problems that make the fulfillment of their needs and potentials more difficult than for other children.

**Specific learning disability.**   See *Learning disability.*

**Specificity.**   The proportion of the total variance of a test that is due to factors specific to the test itself.

**Speeded test.**   A test consisting of a large number of fairly easy items, but having a short time limit so that almost no one finishes the test in the allotted time. Many tests of clerical, mechanical, and psychomotor ability are speeded.

**Spiral omnibus test.**   A test consisting of a variety of items arranged in order of ascending difficulty. Items of a given type or content appear throughout the test, intermingled with other types of items of similar difficulty, in a spiral of increasing difficulty.

**Split-half coefficient.**   An estimate of reliability determined by applying the Spearman–Brown formula for $m = 2$ to the correlation between two halves of the same test, such as the odd-numbered items and the even-numbered items.

**Standard deviation.**   The square root of the variance; used as a measure of the dispersion or spread of a group of scores.

**Standard error of estimate.**   Degree of error made in estimating a person's score on a criterion variable from his or her score on a predictor variable.

**Standard error of measurement.** An estimate of the standard deviation of the normal distribution of test scores that an examinee would theoretically obtain by taking a test an infinite number of times. If an examinee's obtained test score is $X$, then the chances are two out of three that he or she is one of a group of people whose true scores on the test fall within one standard error of measurement of $X$.

**Standard scores.** A group of scores, such as $z$ scores, $T$ scores, or stanine scores, having a desired mean and standard deviation. Standard scores are computed by changing raw scores to $z$ scores, multiplying the $z$ scores by the desired standard deviation, and then adding the desired mean of the transformed scores to the product.

**Standardization.** Administering a carefully constructed test to a large, representative sample of people under standard conditions for the purpose of determining norms.

**Standardization sample.** Subset of a target population on which a test is standardized.

**Standardized test.** A test that has been carefully constructed by professionals and administered with standard directions and under standard conditions to a representative sample of people for the purpose of obtaining norms.

**Stanine.** A standard score scale consisting of the scores 1 through 9; stanine scores have a mean of 5 and a standard deviation of approximately 2.

**Statistic.** A number used to describe some characteristic of a sample of test scores, such as the arithmetic mean or standard deviation.

**Stratified random sampling.** A sampling procedure in which the population is divided into strata (for example, men and women; blacks and whites; lower class, middle class, upper class) and samples are selected at random from the strata; sample sizes within strata are proportional to strata sizes.

**Stress interview.** Interviewing procedure in which the interviewer applies psychologically stressful techniques (critical and hostile questioning, frequent interruptions, prolonged silences, and so on) to break down the interviewee's defenses or to determine how the interviewee reacts under pressure.

**Structured interview.** Interviewing procedure in which the interviewee is asked a predetermined set of questions.

**Subtest.** A portion or subgroup of items on a test (for example, a group of items measuring the same function or a set of items at the same age level or difficulty level).

**Summative evaluation.** Evaluation at the end of an instructional unit or course of study to provide a sum total or final product measure of achievement.

**_T_ scores.** Converted, normalized standard scores having a mean of 50 and a standard deviation of 10. $Z$ scores are also standard scores with a mean of 50 and a standard deviation of 10, but in contrast to $T$ scores they are not normalized.

**Target behaviors.** Specific, objectively defined behaviors observed and measured in behavioral assessments. Of particular interest are the effects of antecedent and consequent events on these behaviors.

**Target population.**   The population of interest in standardizing a test or other assessment instrument; the norm group (sample) must be representative of the target population if valid interpretations of (norm-referenced) scores are to be made.

**Taylor–Russell tables.**   Tables for evaluating the validity of a test as a function of the information contributed by the test beyond that provided by chance alone.

**Test.**   Any device used to evaluate the behavior or performance of a person. Psychological tests are of many kinds—cognitive, affective, and psychomotor, for example.

**Test anxiety.**   Anxiety in a testing situation.

**Test–retest reliability.**   A method of assessing the reliability of a test by administering it to the same group of people on two different occasions and computing the correlation (*coefficient of stability*) between their scores on the two occasions.

**Trainable mentally retarded (TMR).**   Children in the moderately retarded range of IQs (approximately 36 to 50), who usually cannot learn to read and write but can perform unskilled tasks under supervision.

**Transfer hypothesis (of ability differentiation).**   G. A. Ferguson's hypothesis that the different abilities isolated by factor analysis are the results of overlearning and differential positive transfer in certain areas of learning.

**True score.**   The hypothetical score that is a measure of an examinee's true knowledge of the test material. In test theory, an examinee's true score on a test is the mean of the distribution of scores that would result if the examinee took the test an infinite number of times.

**Unobtrusive observations.**   Observations made without interfering with or otherwise influencing the behavior to be observed.

**Validity.**   The extent to which an assessment instrument measures what it was designed to measure. Validity can be assessed in several ways: by analysis of the instrument's content (*content validity*), by relating scores on the test to a criterion (*predictive and concurrent validity*), and by a more thorough study of the extent to which the test is a measure of a certain psychological construct (*construct validity*).

**Validity generalization.**   The applicability of validity evidence to situations other than those in which the evidence was obtained.

**Variability.**   The degree of spread or deviation of a group of scores around their average value.

**Variable.**   In contrast to a *constant,* any quantity that can assume more than one state or numerical value.

**Variance.**   A measure of variability of test scores, computed as the sum of the squares of the deviations of raw scores from the arithmetic mean, divided by one less than the number of scores; the square of the standard deviation.

**Verbal test.**   A test with verbal directions requiring oral or written word and/or number answers.

**Word-association test.**   A projective test on which the examinee responds to each of several words presented by the examiner with the first word that comes to mind. Unusual responses or slow responding to certain words may be indicative of conflicts or other emotional problems associated with those words.

**z score.**   Any one of a group of derived scores varying from $-\infty$ to $+\infty$, computed from the formula $z = $ (raw score – mean)/standard deviation for each raw score. In a normal distribution, over 99 percent of the cases lie between $z = -3.00$ and $z = +3.00$.

**Zone of potential development.**   The difference (distance) between a child's actual developmental level—his or her completed development as might be assessed by a standardized test—and his or her potential development—the degree of competence he or she can attain with assistance.

# ANSWERS TO QUANTITATIVE EXERCISES

## Chapter 3

**4.** Uncorrected score = number right = 30
Corrected score = rights − (wrongs/3) = 30 − (16/3) = 25
If items are true–false: uncorrected score = number right = 30, and corrected score = rights − wrongs = 14.

**5.** The sum of the absolute values of the differences between the keyed ranks and John's ranks is 12. Using formula 3.1a, we find his score is 3.5, which rounds to 4. In Jenny's case, the sum of the absolute values of the differences is 6, and her score rounds to 5.

**6.** Test $X$:

| Grade | Range | Number |
|-------|-------|--------|
| A | 44 and above | 2 |
| B | 38–43 | 7 |
| C | 31–37 | 12 |
| D | 25–30 | 6 |
| F | 24 and below | 3 |

Test $Y$:

| Grade | Range | Number |
|-------|-------|--------|
| A | 44 and above | 3 |
| B | 33–43 | 5 |
| C | 22–32 | 13 |
| D | 11–21 | 7 |
| F | 10 and below | 2 |

## Chapter 4

**1.** Since $.27 \times 75 = 20.25$, there are 20 people in the upper group and 20 people in the lower group. Therefore, $p = (18 + 12)/40 = .75$ and $D = (18 − 12)/20 = .30$. The item is in the acceptable ranges of both $p$ and $D$.

**2.** $U = 30$, $L = 20$, $U_p = 20$, and $L_p = 10$, so $p = (20 + 10)/50 = .80$ and $D = 20/30 − 10/20 = .17$.

**3.**

| Item | 1 | 2 | 3 | 4 | 5 | 6 | 7 | 8 | 9 | 10 |
|------|---|---|---|---|---|---|---|---|---|----|
| $p$ | .50 | .45 | .45 | .55 | .40 | .75 | .50 | .50 | .60 | .40 |
| $D$ | .40 | .30 | .30 | .50 | .60 | .30 | .20 | .20 | .40 | .60 |

Table 4–1 gives the optimum mean $p$ value of a four-option multiple-choice item as .74. Taking $\pm.20$ around this value, acceptable items should be in the $p$ range of .54 to .94. The $D$ value of acceptable items should be .30 or higher. According to these criteria, only items 4, 6, and 9 are acceptable. The remaining seven items should be revised or discarded.

**5.** George's $z$ score on the arithmetic test is $z_a = (65 - 50)/10 = 1.50$; his $z$ score on the reading test is $z_r = (80 - 75)/15 = .33$. His $Z$ scores on the two tests are $Z_a = 65$ and $Z_r = 53$. George is slightly better in arithmetic than he is in reading.

**6.**

| % Rank | $z$ | $T$ | CEEB | Stanine | Deviation IQ |
|--------|-----|-----|------|---------|--------------|
| 10 | −1.28 | 37 | 372 | 2 | 81 |
| 20 | −.84 | 42 | 416 | 3 | 87 |
| 30 | −.52 | 45 | 448 | 4 | 92 |
| 40 | −.25 | 48 | 475 | 4 | 96 |
| 50 | .00 | 50 | 500 | 5 | 100 |
| 60 | .25 | 52 | 525 | 6 | 104 |
| 70 | .52 | 55 | 552 | 6 | 108 |
| 80 | .84 | 58 | 584 | 7 | 113 |
| 90 | 1.28 | 63 | 628 | 8 | 119 |

**7.**

| Score interval | Midpoint | Frequency | Cumulative frequency below midpoint | Percentile rank | $z$ | $Z$ | $z_n$ | $T$ |
|----------------|----------|-----------|-------------------------------------|-----------------|-----|-----|-------|-----|
| 96–98 | 97 | 1 | 29.5 | 98.33 | 2.00 | 70 | 2.13 | 71 |
| 93–95 | 94 | 2 | 28 | 93.33 | 1.54 | 65 | 1.50 | 65 |
| 90–92 | 91 | 3 | 25.5 | 85.00 | 1.08 | 61 | 1.04 | 60 |
| 87–89 | 88 | 5 | 21.5 | 71.67 | .63 | 56 | .57 | 56 |
| 84–86 | 85 | 5 | 16.5 | 55.00 | .17 | 52 | .13 | 51 |
| 81–83 | 82 | 5 | 11.5 | 38.33 | −.29 | 47 | −.29 | 47 |
| 78–80 | 79 | 4 | 7 | 23.33 | −.75 | 43 | −.73 | 43 |
| 75–77 | 76 | 2 | 4 | 13.33 | −1.21 | 38 | −1.11 | 39 |
| 72–74 | 73 | 2 | 2 | 6.67 | −1.66 | 33 | −1.50 | 35 |
| 69–71 | 70 | 1 | .5 | 1.67 | −2.12 | 29 | −2.13 | 29 |

## Chapter 5

**1.** $r_{oe} = .226$, $r_{11} = .369$, $\text{KR}_{20} = .61$, $\text{KR}_{21} = .58$

**2.** $s_{err} = 4.00$

95% confidence interval for $X = 40$ is 32.16–47.84
95% confidence interval for $X = 50$ is 42.16–57.84
99% confidence interval for $X = 60$ is 52.16–67.84

**3.** Substituting in formula 5.9, we have

$$m = \frac{.90(1 - .80)}{.80(1 - .90)} = \frac{.18}{.08} = 2.25$$

Multiplying $n$ by $m$ gives $40 \times 2.25 = 90$. Therefore, 50 more items of the same general type as those on the test must be added to the test to increase its reliability coefficient to .90.

**4.**

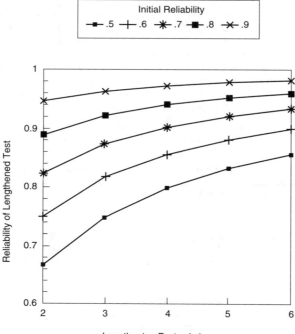

Initial Reliability

—■— .5  —+— .6  —✳— .7  —■— .8  —✕— .9

Reliability of Lengthened Test

Lengthening Factor (*m*)

**Reliability of a lengthened test as a function of initial reliability ($r_{11}$) and lengthening factor (*m*).** Reliability increases as a test is lengthened, the amount of increase being greater when the initial reliability is lower. The increase in reliability as a function of lengthening gradually levels off as the test is increasingly lengthened.

**5.** Agreement index = .75 and kappa = .138. Because neither of these values is statistically significant, it cannot be concluded that this criterion-referenced test is reliable.

**6.** $s_{est} = s\sqrt{1 - r^2} = .5\sqrt{1 - .60^2} = .5\,(8) = .4$. Therefore, the chances are approximately two out of three that the examinee's obtained criterion score will fall within .4 of his or her predicted score on the criterion variable.

**7.**

Criterion Variable (Y)

|  |  | 28–34 | 35–41 | 42–48 | 49–55 | 56–62 | 63–70 |
|---|---|---|---|---|---|---|---|
| *Predictor Variable* | 71–78 |  |  | 1 (100) |  |  | 1 (50) |
|  | 63–70 |  |  |  | 1 (100) |  | 2 (67) |
|  | 56–62 |  |  | 2 (100) | 2 (67) | 1 (33) | 1 (17) |
|  | 49–55 |  | 2 (100) | 1 (67) | 2 (50) |  | 1 (17) |
|  | 42–48 |  | 1 (100) | 1 (80) | 2 (60) |  | 1 (20) |
|  | 35–41 |  | 2 (100) | 1 (50) | 1 (25) |  |  |
|  | 28–34 | 1 (100) |  |  | 1 (67) | 1 (33) |  |
|  | 21–27 | 1 (100) |  |  |  |  |  |

## Chapter 7

1. $IQ = 100(MA/CA) = 100(77/105) \approx 73$

## Chapter 8

4. $h^2 = .54$, implying that 54% of the variance in IQ scores is attributable to genetic factors.

## Chapter 9

9. Yes. $s_{est} = 10\sqrt{2 - .90 - .85} = 5$, and $2 \times 5 = 10$ is equal to the difference between the two $T$ scores.

## Chapter 10

7.

| Statement | Scale value (median) | Ambiguity index (Q) |
|---|---|---|
| D | 8.96 | 1.14 |
| N | 5.19 | 1.22 |
| X | 2.50 | 1.01 |

## Chapter 14

7. The regression equation for predicting $Y$ from $X$ is $Y_{pred} = .44X + 28.34$ for the majority group and $Y_{pred} = .43X + 24.57$ for the minority group; the corresponding correlation coefficients are .52 and .47. The correlation coefficient suggests that the test may be a slightly more accurate predictor for the majority group than for the minority group, but not significantly so. Thus, it may be concluded that the test is not appreciably biased according to the traditional definition of fairness.

If we assume that 50 percent of the majority group and 25 percent of the minority group can perform the job, then $.50(30) = 15$ examinees in the majority group and $.25(20) = 5$ examinees in the minority group should be selected if the test is fair. If the cutoff score is set at $X = 52$, then 7 minority group members and 15 majority group members will be selected; if it is set at $X = 53$, then 5 minority and 13 majority group members will be selected. According to Thorndike's definition, the first cutoff score would slightly favor the minority group and the second would slightly disfavor the majority group.

If we assume that 40 percent of the entire group of 50 examinees is capable of performing the job, then $.40(30) = 12$ majority group members and $.40(20) = 8$ minority group members should be selected if the test is fair according to Cole's definition. Any cutoff score that yields a total number of selectees close to 20 will tend to favor the majority group according to this definition. Thus, using this procedure, the test is slightly biased toward the majority group.

Combining the scores of the majority and minority groups yields a correlation between $X$ and $Y$ of $r = .517$, and the regression equation $Y_{pred} = .46X + 25.639$. Now, if the cutoff score is set at $X = 50$, the number of false positive and false negative errors in each group will be as follows:

| | False positives | False negatives |
|---|---|---|
| Majority group | 6 (20%) | 6 (20%) |
| Minority group | 5 (25%) | 2 (10%) |

These percentages are based on the total number of applicants in each group. The total percentage of errors is 5 points greater for the majority group than for the minority group, but the percentage of false positives is greater in the minority group and the percentage of false negatives is greater in the majority group. In this case, the question of bias is complex, depending on which kind of error is considered more serious.

## Appendix A

**1.**

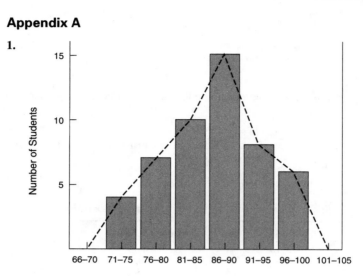

Test Score Interval

$$\overline{X} = 86.40, \text{Mdn} = 86.83, \text{Mode} = 88, s = 7.17$$
$$P_{25} = Q_1 = 80.50 + 5\,(12.5 - 11)\,/10 = 81.25$$
$$P_{75} = Q_3 = 90.5 + 5\,(37.5 - 36)\,/8 = 91.44$$
$$Q = (Q_3 - Q_1)\,/2 = (91.44 - 81.25)\,/2 = 5.10$$

**2.** .5%, 1%, 2.5%, 5%, 50%, 95%, 97.5%, 99%, 99.5%
$-1.28, -.84, -.52, -.25, .00, .25, .52, .84, 1.28$

**3.** $\overline{X} = 34.00, s_x = 6.58$
$\overline{Y} = 27.00, s_y = 11.03$
$r_{y.x} = .54, Y_{\text{pred}} = .91X - 3.78$

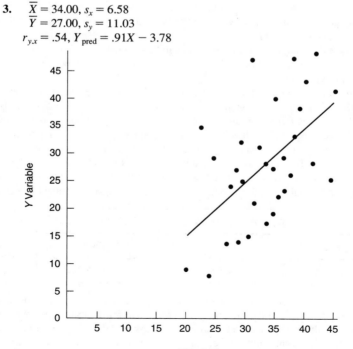

**5.** $Y_{pred} = .225X_1 + .152X_2 + .401X_3 + 41.488$

$t_1 = 5.22, t_2 = 3.87, t_3 = 2.07, df = 96$

All three of the $t$ values are statistically significant; hence each of the three predictor variables makes a significant contribution to the prediction of the criterion. $R = .693$, $F = 29.65$, $df = 3, 96$; the overall $F$ ratio and hence the multiple correlation coefficient ($R$) are statistically significant.

**6.**

| Subtest | Factor 1 | Factor 2 | Communality | Specificity |
|---|---|---|---|---|
| Information | .743 | .325 | .658 | .192 |
| Similarities | .691 | .390 | .630 | .180 |
| Arithmetic | .734 | .191 | .575 | .196 |
| Vocabulary | .783 | .328 | .720 | .140 |
| Comprehension | .644 | .371 | .553 | .217 |
| Digit Span | .646 | .033 | .419 | .361 |
| Picture Completion | .263 | .692 | .548 | .222 |
| Picture Arrangement | .308 | .605 | .461 | .269 |
| Block Design | .374 | .725 | .666 | .184 |
| Object Assembly | .182 | .778 | .638 | .062 |
| Coding | .459 | .180 | .243 | .477 |
| Mazes | .102 | .660 | .446 | .274 |

# REFERENCES

Abrahams, N. M., Neumann, I., & Gilthens, W. H. (1971). Faking vocational interests: Simulated vs. real life motivation. *Personnel Psychology, 24*(1), 5–12.

Abramson, L. Y., Garber, J., & Seligman, M. E. P. (1980). Learning helplessness in humans. In J. Garber & M. E. P. Seligman (eds.), *Human helplessness* (pp. 3–34). New York: Academic Press.

Achenbach, T. M., & Edelbrock, C. (1983). *Manual of the Child Behavior Checklist and Revised Child Behavior Profile.* Burlington, VT: University of Vermont, Department of Psychiatry.

Adler, T. (1991, May). Tug-of-war develops over use of GATB. *APA Monitor,* p. 14.

Aiken, L. R. (1973). *Readings in psychological and educational testing.* Boston: Allyn & Bacon.

Aiken, L. R. (1979a). Attitudes toward mathematics and science in Iranian middle schools. *School Science and Mathematics, 79,* 229–234.

Aiken, L. R. (1979b). Relationships between item difficulty and discrimination indexes. *Educational and Psychological Measurement, 39,* 821–824.

Aiken, L. R. (1980). Problems in testing the elderly. *Educational Gerontology, 5,* 119–124.

Aiken, L. R. (1983a). *The case for oral achievement testing.* ERIC Document Reproduction Service No. ED 222 578 & TM 820 755.

Aiken, L. R. (1983b). Determining grade boundaries on classroom tests. *Educational and Psychological Measurement, 3,* 759–762.

Aiken, L. R. (1985). Three coefficients for analyzing the reliability and validity of ratings. *Educational and Psychological Measurement, 45,* 131–142.

Aiken, L. R. (1988). KAPPO: A program for assessing the reliability of criterion-referenced tests. *Applied Psychological Measurement, 12*(1), 104.

Ajzen, I., & Fishbein, M. (1977). Attitude–behavior relations: A theoretical analysis and review of empirical research. *Psychological Bulletin, 84,* 888–918.

*Albemarle Paper Company* v. *Moody.* 10 FEP 11 1181 (1975).

Allard, G., Butler, J., Faust, D., & Shea, M. T. (1995). Errors in hand scoring objective personality tests: The case of the Personality Diagnostic Questionnaire. *Professional Psychology: Research and Practice, 26,* 304–208.

Allison, D. E. (1984). The effect of item-difficulty sequence, intelligence, and sex on test performance, reliability, and item difficulty and discrimination. *Measurement and Evaluation in Guidance, 16,* 211–217.

Allport, G. W. (1937). *Personality: A psychological interpretation.* New York: Holt, Rinehart & Winston.

Allport, G. W. (1961). *Pattern and growth in personality.* New York: Holt, Rinehart & Winston.

Allport, G. W. (ed.) (1965). *Letters from Jenny.* New York: Harcourt Brace Jovanovich.

Allport, G. W., & Odbert, H. S. (1936). Trait-names, a psycholexical study. *Psychological Monographs, 47*(1).

Altus, W. D. (1966). Birth order and its sequelae. *Science, 151,* 44–49.

American College (1978). *Test wiseness: Test taking skills for adults.* New York: McGraw-Hill.

American Educational Research Association, American Psychological Association, & National Council on Measurement in Education (1985). *Standards for educational and psychological testing.* Washington, DC: American Psychological Association.

American Law Institute (1956). *Model penal code.* Tentative Draft Number 4.

American Psychiatric Association (1994). *Diagnostic and statistical manual of mental disorders* (4th ed.). Washington, DC: Author.

American Psychological Association (1981). Ethical principles of psychologists. *American Psychologist, 36,* 633–638.

American Psychological Association (1987). *General guidelines for providers of psychological services.* Washington, DC: Author.

American Psychological Association (1992). Ethical principles of psychologists and code of conduct. *American Psychologist, 47,* 1597–1611.

American Psychological Association, Committee on Professional Standards & Committee on Psychological Tests and Assessment. (1986). *Guidelines for computer-based tests and interpretations.* Washington, DC: Author.

Ames, L. B., et al. (1979). *The Gesell Institute's child from one to six: Evaluating the behavior of the preschool child.* New York: Harper & Row.

Andreasen, N. C. (1987). Creativity and mental illness: Prevalence rates in writers and their first-degree relatives. *American Journal of Psychiatry, 144*(10), 1288–1297.

Andrews, L. W., & Gutkin, T. B. (1991). The effects of human versus computer authorship on consumers' perceptions of psychological reports. *Computers in Human Behavior, 7,* 311–317.

Anrig, G. R. (1987). "Golden Rule": Second thoughts. *APA Monitor, 18*(8), 3.

APA task force releases final report on integrity testing (1991, May/June). *Psychological Science Agenda, 4*(3), 1, 6. Washington, DC: American Psychological Association.

Archer, R. P., Maruish, M., Imhof, E. A., & Piotrowski, C. (1991). Psychological test usage with adolescent clients: 1990 survey findings. *Professional Psychology: Research and Practice, 22,* 247–252.

Arkes, H. R. (1994). Clinical judgment. In R. J. Corsini (ed.), *Concise encyclopedia of psychology* (2nd ed., pp. 237–238). New York: Wiley.

Arvey, R. D. (1979). Unfair discrimination in the employment interview: Legal and psychological aspects. *Psychological Bulletin, 86,* 736–765.

Austin, G. R., & Garber, H. (eds.) (1982). *The rise and fall of national test scores.* New York: Academic Press.

Baker, F. B. (1989). Computer technology in test construction and processing. In R. L. Linn (ed.), *Educational measurement* (3rd ed., pp. 409–423). New York: Macmillan.

Baller, W. R., Charles, D. C., & Miller, E. L. (1967). Midlife attainment of the mentally retarded: A longitudinal study. *Genetic Psychology Monographs, 75,* 235–329.

Baltes, P. B., & Schaie, K. W. (1974). The myth of the twilight years. *Psychology Today, 7*(10), 35–40.

Barba, C. V. (1981). Mental development after dietary intervention: A study of Philippine children. *Journal of Cross-cultural Psychology, 12,* 480–488.

Bayley, N., & Oden, M. M. (1955). The maintenance of intellectual ability in gifted adults. *Journal of Gerontology, 10,* 91–107.

Bell, A., & Zubek, J. (1960). The effect of age on the intellectual performance of mental defectives. *Journal of Gerontology, 15,* 285–295.

Bellak, L. (1993). *The T.A.T., C.A.T., and S.A.T. in clinical use.* Des Moines, IA: Longwood Division, Allyn & Bacon.

Belmont, L., & Marolla, F. A. (1973). Birth order, family size, and intelligence. *Science, 182,* 1096–1101.

Bem, D. J., & Allen, A. (1974). On predicting some of the people some of the time: The search for cross-situational consistencies in behavior. *Psychological Review, 81,* 506–520.

Benjamin, L. T., Cavell, T. A., & Shallenberger, W. R. (1984). Staying with initial answers on objective tests: Is it a myth? *Teaching of Psychology, 11*, 133–141.

Berne, E. (1966). *Principles of group treatment*. New York: Oxford University Press.

Biemiller, L. (1986, January 8). Critics plan assault on admissions tests and other standard exams. *Chronicle of Higher Education*, pp. 1, 4.

Binet, A., & Simon, T. (1916). *The development of intelligence in children* (trans. E. S. Kite). Baltimore: Williams & Wilkins.

Black, H. (1962). *They shall not pass*. New York: Morrow.

Blau, T. H. (1984). *The psychologist as expert witness*. New York: Wiley.

Block, J. (1977). Recognizing the coherence of personality. In D. Magnusson & N. S. Endler (eds.), *Interactional psychology: Current issues and future prospects*. New York: LEA/Wiley.

Block, J., et al. (1981). The cognitive style of breadth of categorization: Longitudinal consistency of personality correlates. *Journal of Personality and Social Psychology, 40*, 770–779.

Bloom, B. S., Hastings, J. T., & Madaus, G. F. (1971). *Handbook of formative and summative evaluation of student learning*. New York: McGraw-Hill.

Bloom, B. S., & Krathwohl, D. R. (1956). *Taxonomy of educational objectives: Handbook I. The cognitive domain*. New York: David McKay.

Bogardus, E. S. (1925). Measuring social distances. *Journal of Applied Sociology, 9*, 299–308.

Bolton, B. (1985). Work Values Inventory. In D. J. Keyser & R. C. Sweetland (eds.), *Test critiques* (Vol. II, pp. 835–843). Kansas City, MO: Test Corporation of America.

Botwinick, J. (1977). Intellectual abilities. In J. E. Birren & K. W. Schaie (eds.), *Handbook of the psychology of aging*. New York: Van Nostrand Reinhold.

Bouchard, T. J., Jr., et al. (1983, June). *Family resemblance for psychological interests*. Paper presented at meeting of International Congress on Twins Research, London.

Bouchard, T. J., & McGue, M. (1981). Familial studies of intelligence: A review. *Science, 212*, 1055–1059.

Bouchard, T. J., Jr., Lykken, D. T., McGue, M., Segal, N. L., & Tellegen, A. (1990). Sources of human psychological differences: The Minnesota Study of Twins Reared Apart. *Science, 250*, 223–228.

Bowman, M. L. (1989). Testing individual differences in Ancient China. *American Psychologist, 44*, 576–578.

Bradley, R. H., & Caldwell, B. M. (1977). Home observation for measurement of the environment: A validation study of screening efficiency. *American Journal of Mental Deficiency, 81*, 417–420.

Brazelton, T. B. (1973). *Neonatal Behavioral Assessment Scale*. Philadelphia: Lippincott.

Brazelton, T. B. (1984). *Neonatal Behavioral Assessment Scale* (2nd ed.). Philadelphia: Lippincott.

Bredemeier, M. (1991). IQ test ban for blacks called unconstitutional. *California Association of School Psychologists Today*, Nov./Dec., 22–23.

Bricklin, B. (1984). *Bricklin Perceptual Scales*. Furlong, PA: Village.

Bridgman, C. S., & Hollenbeck, G. P. (1961). Effect of simulated applicant status on Kuder Form D occupational interest scores. *Journal of Applied Psychology, 45*, 237–239.

Brigham, C. C. (1923). *A study of American intelligence*. Princeton, NJ: Princeton University Press.

Brigham, C. C. (1930). Intelligence tests of immigrant groups. *Psychological Review, 37*, 158–165.

Brody, N. (1992). *Intelligence* (2nd ed.). San Diego, CA: Academic Press.

Broman, S. H., Nichols, P. L., Shaughnessy, P., & Kennedy, W. (1987). *Retardation in young children*. Hillsdale, NJ: Erlbaum.

Brown, W. R., & McGuire, J. M. (1976). Current psychological assessment practices. *Professional Psychology, 7*, 475–484.

Bruvold, W. H. (1975). Judgmental bias in the rating of attitude statements. *Educational and Psychological Measurement, 35*, 605–611.

Bukatman, B. A., Foy, J. L., & De Grazia, E. (1971). What is competency to stand trial? *American Journal of Psychiatry, 127*, 1225–1229.

Burket, G. R. (1973). Empirical criteria for distinguishing and validating aptitude and achievement measures. In D. R. Green (ed.), *The aptitude–achievement distinction*. Monterey, CA: CTB/McGraw-Hill.

Buros, O. K. (ed.) (1970). *Personality tests and reviews*. Highland Park, NJ: Gryphon Press.

Buros, O. K. (1975a). *Reading tests and reviews II*. Highland Park, NJ: Gryphon Press.

Buros, O. K. (1975b). *Vocational tests and reviews*. Highland Park, NJ: Gryphon Press.

Buros, O. K. (ed.) (1978). *The eighth mental measurements yearbook*. Vols. 1 and 2. Highland Park, NJ: Gryphon Press.

Buss, A. H., & Plomin, R. (1984). *Temperament: Early developing personality traits*. Hillsdale, NJ: Erlbaum.

Buss, A. H., & Plomin, R. (1986). The EAS approach to temperament. In R. Plomin & J. Dunn (eds.), *The study of temperament: Changes, continuities and challenges* (pp. 67–79). Hillsdale, NJ: Erlbaum.

Busse, E. W., & Maddox, G. (1985). *The Duke longitudinal studies of normal aging*. New York: Springer.

Butler, M., Retzlaff, P., & Vanderploeg, R. (1991). Neuropsychological test usage. *Professional Psychology: Research and Practice, 22*, 510–512.

Camara, W. J., & Schneider, D. L. (1994). Integrity tests: Facts and unresolved issues. *American Psychologist, 49*, 112–119.

Camara, W. J., & Schneider, D. L. (1995). Questions of construct breadth and openness of research in integrity testing. *American Psychologist, 50*, 459–460.

Campbell, D. P. (1965). A cross-sectional and longitudinal study of scholastic abilities over twenty-five years. *Journal of Counseling Psychology, 12*, 55–61.

Campbell, D. P. (1971). *Handbook for the Strong Vocational Interest Blank*. Stanford, CA: Stanford University Press.

Campbell, D. P., & Fiske, D. W. (1959). Convergent and discriminant validation by the multitrait–multimethod matrix. *Psychological Bulletin, 56*, 81–105.

Campbell, D. P., & Hansen, J. C. (1981). *Manual for the Strong–Campbell Interest Inventory* (3rd ed.). Stanford, CA: Stanford University Press.

Canfield, A. A. (1951). The "sten" scale—a modified C-scale. *Educational and Psychological Measurement, 11*, 295–297.

Cannell, J. J. (1988). Nationally normed elementary school testing in America's public schools: How all 50 states are testing above the national average (with commentaries). *Educational Measurement Issues and Practice, 7*(1), 3–24.

Cannell, J. J. (1989). *The Lake Wobegon Report: How public educators cheat on achievement tests*. Albuquerque, NM: Friends for Education.

Carlson, J. S., Jensen, C. M., & Widaman, K. F. (1983). Reaction time, intelligence and attention. *Intelligence, 7*, 329–344.

Carroll, J. B. (1973). The aptitude–achievement distinction: The case of foreign language aptitude and proficiency. In D. R. Green (ed.), *The aptitude–achievement distinction*. Monterey, CA: CTB/McGraw-Hill.

Carver, R. P. (1974). Two dimensions of tests: Psychometric and edumetric. *American Psychologist, 29*, 512–518.

Cascio, W. F., & Ramos, R. A. (1986). Development and application of new method for assessing job performance in behavioral economic terms. *Journal of Applied Psychology, 71*, 20–28.

Cassell, R. N., & Blum, L. P. (1970). *Computer Assist Counseling (COASCON) for the prevention of delinquent behavior among teenagers and youth*. Milwaukee: Department of Educational Psychology, University of Wisconsin—Milwaukee.

Castro, J. G., & Jordan, J. E. (1977). Facet theory attitude research. *Educational Researcher, 6*, 7–11.

Cattell, R. B. (1963). Theory of fluid and crystallized intelligence: A critical experiment. *Journal of Educational Psychology, 54*, 1–22.

Chaplin, W. F., & Goldberg, L. R. (1984). A failure to replicate the Ben and Allen study of individual differences in cross-situational consistency. *Journal of Personality and Social Psychology, 47,* 1074–1090.

Charles, D. C., & James, S. T. (1964). Stability of average intelligence. *Journal of Genetic Psychology, 105,* 105–111.

Chase, C. (1990–1991). Essay test scoring: Expectancy and handwriting quality. *Psychology, A Journal of Human Behavior, 27*(4), 38–41.

Chauncey, H., & Dobbin, J. E. (1963). *Testing: Its place in education today.* New York: Harper & Row.

Chavez, S. (1993, August 19). SAT scores remain level in California. *Los Angeles Times,* pp. A1, A23.

Christiansen, K., & Knussman, R. (1987). Sex hormones and cognitive functioning in men. *Neuropsychobiology, 18,* 27–36.

Chun, K. T., Cobb, S., & French, J. R. P. (1976). *Measures for psychological assessment.* Ann Arbor, MI: Institute for Social Research, University of Michigan.

Ciminero, A. R., Calhoun, K. S., & Adams, H. E. (eds.) (1986). *Handbook of behavioral assessment* (2nd ed.). New York: Wiley.

Ciminero, A. R., Nelson, R. O., & Lipinski, D. P. (1977). Self-monitoring procedures. In A. R. Ciminero, K. S. Calhoun, & H. E. Adams (eds.), *Handbook of behavioral assessment.* New York: Wiley.

Clarizio, H. F. (1982). Piagetian assessment measures revisited: Issues and application. *Psychology in the Schools, 19,* 421–430.

Cole, N. S. (1973). Bias in selection. *Journal of Educational Measurement, 10,* 237–255.

Cole, N. S., & Moss, P. A. (1989). Bias in test use. In R. L. Linn (ed.), *Educational measurement* (3rd ed., pp. 201–219). New York: Macmillan.

College bound seniors. 1995 profile of SAT program test takers. (1995). Princeton, NJ: College Entrance Examination Board and Educational Testing Service.

College Entrance Examination Board (1971). *Report of the Commission on Tests.* New York: Author.

Comrey, A. L., Bacher, T. E., & Glaser, F. M. (1973). *A source book for mental health measures.* Los Angeles: Human Interaction Research Institute.

Conoley, C. W., Plake, B. S., & Kemmerer, B. E. (1991). Issues in computer-based test interpretative systems. *Computers in Human Behavior, 7,* 97–102.

Conoley, J. C., & Impara, J. C. (eds.) (1995). *The twelfth mental measurements yearbook.* Lincoln: Buros Institute of Mental Measurements of the University of Nebraska—Lincoln.

Conoley, J. C., & Kramer, J. J. (eds.) (1989). *The tenth mental measurements yearbook.* Lincoln: Buros Institute of Mental Measurements of the University of Nebraska—Lincoln.

Converse, P. E., Dotson, J. D., Hoag, W. J., & McGee III, W. H. (1980). *American social attitudes data sourcebook, 1947–78.* Cambridge, MA: Harvard University Press.

Cooley, H. H. (1922). *Human nature and the social order.* New York: Scribner.

Cooley, W. W., & Lohnes, P. R. (1968). *Predicting development of young adults.* Project TALENT Five-year Follow-up Studies, Interim Report 5, American Institutes for Research. Washington, DC: U.S. Office of Education.

Cordes, C. (1986, June). Test tilt: Boys outscore girls on both parts of the SAT. *APA Monitor,* pp. 30–31.

Costa, P. T., Jr., & McCrae, R. R. (1986). Personality stability and its implications for clinical psychology. *Clinical Psychology Review, 6,* 407–423.

Crites, J. O. (1969). Interests. In R. L. Ebel (ed.), *Encyclopedia of educational research* (4th ed., pp. 678–685). New York: Macmillan.

Cronbach, L. J. (1951). Coefficient alpha and the internal structure of tests. *Psychometrika, 16,* 297–334.

Cronbach, L. J. (1970). *Essentials of psychological testing* (3rd ed.). New York: Harper & Row.

Cronbach, L. J., & Drenth, P. J. D. (eds.) (1972). *Mental tests and cultural adaptation.* The Hague: Mouton.

Cronbach, L. J., & Gleser, G. C. (1965). *Psychological tests and personnel decisions.* Urbana: University of Illinois Press.

Cronbach, L. J., Gleser, G. C., Nanda, H., & Rajaratnam, N. (1972). *The dependability of behavioral measures: Theory of generalizability for scores and profiles.* New York: Wiley.

Cronin, J., Daniels, N., Hurley, A., Kroch, A., & Webber, R. (1975). Race, class, and intelligence: A critical look at the IQ controversy. *International Journal of Mental Health, 3*(4), 46–132.

Crowl, T. K., & McGinitie, W. H. (1974). The influence of students' speech characteristics on teachers' evaluations of oral answers. *Journal of Educational Psychology, 66,* 304–308.

Custer, G. (1994, September). School-to-work transition is eased by testing system. *APA Monitor,* p. 7

Dana, R. H. (1984). Personality assessment: Practice and teaching for the next decade. *Journal of Personality Assessment, 48,* 46–56.

Darley, J. B., & Hagenah, T. (1955). *Vocational interest measurement.* Minneapolis: University of Minnesota Press.

Das, J. P., Naglieri, J. A., & Kirby, J. P. (1994). *Assessment of cognitive processes: The PASS theory of intelligence.* Boston: Allyn and Bacon.

David, P. (1981, November 27). Multiple-choice tests under fire: United States. *Times Education Supplement, 3413:*11.

Davidshofer, C. (1985). Review of Jackson Vocational Interest Survey. In J. V. Mitchell, Jr. (ed.), *The ninth mental measurements yearbook* (Vol. 1, pp. 739–740). Lincoln: Buros Institute of Mental Measurements of the University of Nebraska—Lincoln.

*Debra* v. *Turlington, 644* F.2d 397 (1981); 730F.2d 1406 (1984).

DeMille, R. (1962). Intellect after lobotomy in schizophrenia. *Psychological Monographs, 76*(16), 1–18.

Denton, L. (1988, August). Board votes to oppose Golden Rule technique. *APA Monitor,* p. 7.

Diamond, E. E. (1979). Sex equality and measurement practices. *New Directions for Testing and Measurement, 3,* 61–78.

*Diana* v. *State Board of Education,* C-70 37 RFT (N.D. Cal 1970).

Diekhoff, G. M. (1984). True–false tests that measure and promote structured understanding. *Teaching of Psychology, 11,* 99–101.

Disbrow, M. A., Doerr, H. O., & Caulfield, C. (1977, March). *Measures to predict child abuse.* Final report of Grant MC-R530351, Maternal and Child Health. Washington, DC: National Institute of Mental Health.

Dolliver, R. H., Irvin, J. A., & Bigley, S. E. (1972). Twelve-year follow-up of the Strong Vocational Interest Blank. *Journal of Counseling Psychology, 19,* 212–217.

Donahue, D., & Sattler, J. M. (1971). Personality variables affecting WAIS scores. *Journal of Consulting and Clinical Psychology, 36,* 441.

Donlon, T. F. (ed.) (1984). *The College Board technical handbook for the scholastic aptitude and achievement tests.* New York: College Entrance Examination Board.

Doppelt, J. E., & Wallace, W. L. (1955). Standardization of the Wechsler Adult Intelligence Scale for older persons. *Journal of Abnormal and Social Psychology, 51,* 312–330.

Dorr-Bremme, D. W., & Herman, J. L. (1986). *Assessing student achievement: A profile of classroom practices* (CSE Monograph 11). Los Angeles: University of California, Center for the Study of Evaluation.

Doyle, D. P., & Hartle, T. W. (1985, June 4). Toward a national teachers' test. *Los Angeles Times,* p. II-5.

Doyle, K. O., Jr. (1974). Theory and practice of ability testing in Ancient Greece. *Journal of the History of the Behavioral Sciences, 10,* 202–212.

Dreger, R. M., & Miller, K. S. (1960). Comparative psychological studies of Negroes and whites in the United States. *Psychological Bulletin, 57,* 1–5.

DuBois, P. H. (1970). *The history of psychological testing.* Boston: Allyn & Bacon.

Duckworth, D., & Entwhistle, N. J. (1974). Attitudes to school subject: A repertory grid technique. *British Journal of Educational Psychology, 44,* 76–83.

Dunnette, M. D. (1963). Critics of psychological tests: Basic assumptions; how good? *Psychology in the Schools, 1,* 63–69.

Dunnette, M. D., & Borman, W. C. (1979). Personnel selection and classification systems. *Annual Review of Psychology, 30,* 477–525.

*Durham* v. *United States,* 214 F.2d 862 (D.C. Cir. 1954).

*Dusky* v. *United States,* 362 U.S. 402 (Apr. 18, 1960).

Dyer, C. O. (1985). Jackson Personality Inventory. In D. J. Keyser & R. C. Sweetland (eds.), *Test critiques* (Vol. II, pp. 369–375). Kansas City, MO: Test Corporation of America.

Ebel, R. L. (1979). *Essentials of educational measurement* (3rd ed.). Upper Saddle River, NJ: Prentice Hall.

Educational Testing Service (1965). *ETS builds a test.* Princeton, NJ: Author.

Educational Testing Service. (1980a). *Test use and validity: A response to charges in the Nader/Nairn Report on ETS.* Princeton, NJ: Author.

Educational Testing Service (1980b). *Test scores and family income: A response to charges in the Nader/Nairn Report on ETS.* Princeton, NJ: Author.

Educational Testing Service (1992). *What we can learn from performance assessment for the professions.* ETS Conference on Education and Assessment. Princeton, NJ: Author.

Edwards, A. L. (1954). *Manual—Edwards Personal Preference Schedule.* New York: The Psychological Corporation.

Edwards, A. L. (1957). *Techniques of attitude scale construction.* Upper Saddle River, NJ: Prentice Hall.

Eisdorfer, C. (1963). The WAIS performance of the aged: A retest evaluation. *Journal of Gerontology, 18,* 169–172.

Ekstrom, R. B., French, J. W., & Harman, H. H. (1979). Cognitive factors: Their identification and replication. *Multivariate Behavior Research Monographs.* Ft. Worth, TX: Society for Multivariate Experimental Psychology.

Elam, S. M. (ed.) (1978). *A decade of Gallup polls of attitudes toward education: 1969–1978.* Bloomington, IN: Phi Delta Kappa.

Embretson, S. E. (1987). Toward development of a psychometric approach. In C. S. Lidz (ed.), *Dynamic assessment: An interactive approach to evaluating learning potential* (pp. 135–164). New York: Guilford Press.

Equal Employment Opportunity Commission (1973, August 23). *The uniform guidelines of employee selection procedures.* Discussion draft. Washington, DC: Author.

Equal Employment Opportunity Commission, Civil Service Commission, Department of Labor and Department of Justice (1978). Adoption by four agencies of Uniform Guidelines on Employee Selection Procedures. *Federal Register, 43*(166), 38290–38315.

Erdman, P. E., Klein, M. J., & Greist, H. (1985). Direct patient computer interviewing. *Journal of Consulting and Clinical Psychology, 53,* 760–773.

Eron, L. (1950). A normative study of the TAT. *Psychological Monographs, 64* (Whole No. 315).

Esquivel, G. B., & Lopez, E. (1988). Correlations among measures of cognitive ability, creativity, and academic achievement for gifted minority children. *Perceptual and Motor Skills, 67,* 395–398.

*ETS test collection catalog, Vol. 5* (1991). Phoenix, AZ: Oryx Press.

Evans, W. (1984). Test wiseness: An examination of cue-using strategies. *Journal of Experimental Education, 52,* 141–144.

Exner, J. E. (1991). *The Rorschach: A comprehensive system. Vol. 2. Current research and advanced interpretation.* New York: Wiley.

Exner, J. E. (1993). *The Rorschach: A comprehensive system. Vol. 1. Basic foundations* (3rd ed.). New York: Wiley.

Eyde, L., et al. (1993). *Responsible test use: Case studies for assessing human behavior.* Washington, DC: American Psychological Association.

Eysenck, H. J. (1962). Conditioning and personality. *British Journal of Psychology, 53,* 299–305.

Eysenck, H. J. (1965). The effects of psychotherapy. *International Journal of Psychiatry, 1,* 97–178.

Eysenck, H. J. (1971). *The IQ argument.* New York: Library Press.

Eysenck, H. J. (ed.) (1981). *A model for personality.* New York: Springer.

Eysenck, H. J. (1984). Recent advances in the theory and measurement of intelligence. *Early Child Development and Care, 15,* 97–115.

Eysenck, H. J. (1987). Speed of information processing, reaction time, and the theory of intelligence. In P. A. Vernon (ed.), *Speed of information-processing and intelligence* (pp. 21–67). Norwood, NJ: Ablex.

Eysenck, H. J., & Rachman, S. (1965). *The causes of neurosis.* San Diego, CA: Robert R. Knapp.

Fabiano, E. (1989). *Index to tests used in educational dissertations.* Phoenix, AZ: Oryx Press.

Farrell, A. D. (1993). Computers and behavioral assessment: Current applications, future possibilities, and obstacles to routine use. *Behavioral Assessment, 13,* 159–170.

Feldman, M. J., & Corah, N. L. (1960). Social desirability and the forced choice method. *Journal of Counseling Psychology, 24,* 480–482.

Feuerstein, R., et al. (1987). Prerequisites for assessment of learning potential: The LPAD model. In C. S. Lidz (ed.), *Dynamic assessment: An interactive approach to evaluating learning potential* (pp. 35–51). New York: Guilford Press.

Fewer firms testing employee literacy (1992, August 12). *Los Angeles Times,* p. D–5.

Fish, L. J. (1941). *One hundred years of examinations in Boston.* Dedham, MA: Transcript Press.

Flanagan, J. C. (1954). The critical incident technique. *Psychological Bulletin, 51,* 327–358.

Flanagan, J. C., Tiedeman, D. V., & Willis, M. G. (1973). *The career data book.* Palo Alto, CA: American Institutes for Research.

Fleishman, E. A. (1954). Dimensional analysis of psychomotor abilities. *Journal of Experimental Psychology, 48,* 437–454.

Fleishman, E. A. (1972). On the relation between abilities, learning, and human performance. *American Psychologist, 27,* 1017–1032.

Floderus-Myrhed, B., Pedersen, N., & Rasmuson, I. (1980). Assessment of heritability for personality based on a short form of the Eysenck Personality Inventory: A study of 12,898 twin pairs. *Behavior Genetics, 10,* 153–162.

Forer, B. R. (1949). The fallacy of personal validation: A classroom demonstration of gullibility. *Journal of Abnormal and Social Psychology, 44,* 118–123.

Fowler, R. D. (1966–1976). *Roche MMPI computerized interpretation service.* Nutley, NJ: Roche Psychiatric Institute.

Frank, L. K. (1939). Projective methods for the study of personality. *Journal of Psychology, 8,* 389–413.

Frankenberger, W. (1984). A survey of state guidelines for identification of mental retardation. *Mental Retardation, 22,* 17–20.

Franklin, M. R., & Stillman, P. L. (1982). Examiner error in intelligence testing: Are you a source? *Psychology in the Schools, 19,* 563–569.

Fremer, J., Diamond, E. E., & Camara, W. J. (1989). Developing a code of fair testing practices in education. *American Psychologists, 44,* 1062–1067.

French, J. L., & Hale, R. L. (1990). A history of the development of psychological and educational testing. In C. R. Reynolds & R. W. Kamphaus (eds.), *Handbook of psychological and educa-*

*tional assessment of children: Intelligence and achievement* (pp. 3–28). New York: Guilford Press.

Freud, S. (1905, reprinted 1959). Fragment of an analysis of a case of hysteria. In *Collected papers,* Vol 3. New York: Basic Books.

Fulton, M., Thomson, G., Hunter, R., Raab, G., Laxen, D., & Hepburn, W. (1987). Influence of blood lead on the ability and attainment of children in Edinburgh. *Lancet, 1,* 1221–1226.

Funder, D. C., & Colvin, C. R. (1991). Some behaviors are more predictable than others. *The Score* (Newsletter of Division of the American Psychological Association), *13*(4), 3–4.

Galton, F. (1879). Psychometric experiments. *Brain, 2,* 149–162.

Gardner, H. (1983). *Frames of mind: The theory of multiple intelligences.* New York: Basic Books.

Geiger, M. A. (1990). Correlates of net gain from changing multiple-choice answers: Replication and extension. *Psychological Reports, 67,* 719–722.

Geiger, M. A. (1991a). Changing multiple-choice answers: Do students accurately perceive their performance? *Journal of Experimental Education, 59,* 250–257.

Geiger, M. A. (1991b). Changing multiple-choice answers: A validation and extension. *College Student Journal, 25,* 181–186.

George, M. S., & Skinner, H. A. (1990). Using response latency to detect inaccurate responses in a computerized lifestyle assessment. *Computers in Human Behavior, 6,* 167–175.

*Georgia State Conferences of Branches of NAACP* v. *State of Georgia.* Eleventh Circuit Court of Appeals, No. 84-8771 (1985).

Gerlach, V. S., & Sullivan, H. J. (1967). *Constructing statements of outcomes.* Inglewood, CA: Southwest Laboratory for Educational Research & Development.

Gerow, J. R. (1980). Performance on achievement tests as a function of the order of item difficulty. *Teaching of Psychology, 7,* 93–94.

Gesell, A., & Amatruda, C. S. (1941). *Developmental diagnosis.* New York: Paul B. Hoeber.

Getzels, J. W., & Jackson, P. W. (1962). *Creativity and intelligence: Explorations with gifted students.* New York: Wiley.

Ghiselli, E. E. (1973). The validity of aptitude tests in personnel selection. *Personnel Psychology, 26,* 461–477.

Giannetti, R. A. (1987). The GOLPH psychosocial history: Response-contingent data acquisition and reporting. In J. N. Butcher (ed.), *Computerized psychological assessment* (pp. 124–155). New York: Basic Books.

Glass, D. C., & Carver, C. S. (1980). Helplessness and the coronary-prone personality. In J. Garber & M. E. P. Seligman (eds.), *Human helplessness.* New York: Academic Press.

Glennon, J. R., Albright, L. E., & Owens, W. A. (1966). *A catalog of life history items.* Washington, DC: American Psychological Association, Richardson Foundation for the Scientific Affairs Committee, Division 14.

Glick, P., Gottesman, D., & Joltan, J. (1989). The fault is not in the stars. Susceptibility of skeptics and believers in astrology to the Barnum effect. *Personality and Social Psychology Bulletin, 15,* 572–583.

Glovrozov, P. A. (1974, July). Testing pupils orally. *Soviet Education, 16,* 95–105.

Glueck, B. C., & Reznikoff, M. (1965). Comparison of computer-derived personality profile and projective psychological test findings. *American Journal of Psychiatry, 121,* 1156–1161.

Goddard, H. H. (1920). *Human efficiency and levels of intelligence.* Princeton, NJ: Princeton University Press.

Goldberg, L. R. (1970). Man vs. model of man: A rationale, plus some evidence for a method of improving on clinical inferences. *Psychological Bulletin, 73,* 422–432.

Goldberg, L. R. (1980, April). *Some ruminations about the structure of individual differences: Developing a common lexicon for the major characteristics of human personality.* Paper presented at the annual meeting of the Western Psychological Association, Honolulu, HI.

Goldberg, P. (1965). A review of sentence completion methods in personality assessment. *Journal of Projective Techniques and Personality Assessment, 29,* 12–45.

Goldman, B. A., & Busch, J. C. (eds.) (1978). *Directory of unpublished experimental mental measures* (Vol. 2). New York: Human Sciences Press.

Goldman, B. A., & Busch, J. C. (eds.) (1982). *Directory of unpublished experimental mental measures* (Vol. 3). New York: Human Sciences Press.

Goldman, B. A., & Mitchell, D. F. (eds.) (1990). *Directory of unpublished experimental mental measures* (Vol. 5). Dubuque, IA: William C. Brown.

Goldman, B. A., & Osborne, W. L. (eds.) (1985). *Directory of unpublished experimental mental measures* (Vol. 4). New York: Human Sciences Press.

Goldman, B. A., & Saunders, J. L. (eds.) (1974). *Directory of unpublished experimental mental measures* (Vol. 1). New York: Human Sciences Press.

Goldstein, G., & Hersen, M. (1990). Historical perspective. In G. Goldstein & M. Hersen (eds.), *Handbook of psychological assessment* (2nd ed., pp. 3–17). New York: Pergamon.

Gordon, E. (1967). *A three-year longitudinal predictive validity study of the Musical Aptitude Profile. Studies in the psychology of music* (Vol. 5). Iowa City: University of Iowa Press.

Gordon, R., & Peck, L. A. (1989). *The Custody Quotient.* Dallas, TX: Willington Institute.

Gottesman, I. I., & Shields, J. (1973). *Schizophrenia and genetics: A twin study vantage point.* New York: Academic Press.

Gottesman, I. I., & Shields, J. (1982). *Schizophrenia: The epigenetic puzzle.* New York: Cambridge University Press.

Gottfredson, G. D., Holland, J. L., & Gottfredson, L. S. (1975). The relation of vocational aspirations and assessments to employment reality. *Journal of Vocational Behavior, 7,* 135–148.

Gottfredson, L. S. (1994). The science and politics of race-norming. *American Psychologist, 49,* 955–963.

Gottfredson, L. S., & Becker, H. J. (1981). A challenge to vocational psychology: How important are aspirations in determining male career development? *Journal of Vocational Behavior, 18,* 121–137.

Gould, S. J. (1981). *The mismeasure of man.* New York: W. W. Norton.

Graham, F. K., & Kendall, B. X. (1960). Memory-for-Designs Test: Revised general manual (Monograph). *Perceptual and Motor Skills, 11,* 147–188.

Granick, S., & Patterson, R. D. (1972). *Human aging, II: An eleven year follow-up biomedical and behavioral study.* Washington, DC: U.S. Government Printing Office.

Grant, D., & Reed, R. (1982). Neuropsychological testing. In W. C. Wiederholt (ed.), *Neurology for non-neurologists* (pp. 143–155). New York: Academic Press.

Green, J. A. (1975). *Teacher-made tests* (2nd ed., pp. 122–135). New York: Harper & Row.

Green, K. (1984). Effects of item characteristics on multiple-choice item difficulty. *Educational and Psychological Measurement, 44,* 551–561.

Green, K. E. (1991). Measurement theory. In K. E. Green (ed.), *Educational testing: Issues and applications* (pp. 3–25). New York: Garland Publishing.

Greene, H. A., Jorgensen, A. N., & Gerberich, J. R. (1954). *Measurement and evaluation in secondary school* (2nd ed.). New York: David McKay.

*Griggs et al.* v. *Duke Power Company.* 401 U.S. 424, 3FEP175 (1971).

Gross, M. L. (1962). *The brain watchers.* New York: Random House.

Gross, M. L. (1965). Testimony before House Special Committee on Invasion of Privacy of the Committee on Government Operations. *American Psychologist, 20,* 958–960.

Grotevant, H. D., Scarr, S., & Weinberg, R. A. (1977). Patterns of interest similarity in adoptive and biological families. *Journal of Personality and Social Psychology, 35,* 667–676.

*Guadalupe* v. *Tempe Elementary School District,* Stipulation and Order (January 24, 1972).

Guilford, J. P. (1940). *An inventory of factors.* Beverly Hills, CA: Sheridan Supply.

Guilford, J. P. (1954). A factor analytic study across the domains of reasoning, creativity, and evaluation. I. Hypothesis and description of tests. *Reports from the Psychology Laboratory.* Los Angeles: University of Southern California.

Guilford, J. P. (1967). *The nature of human intelligence.* New York: McGraw-Hill.

Guilford, J. P. (1974). *Structure-of-Intellect Abilities*. Orange, CA: Sheridan Psychological Services.

Guilford, J. P. (1981). Higher-order structure-of-intellect abilities. *Multivariate Behavioral Research, 16,* 411–435.

Guilford, J. P. (1985). The structure-of-intellect model. In B. B. Wolman (ed.), *Handbook of intelligence: Theories, measurements and applications.* New York: Wiley.

Guilford, J. P., & Fruchter, B. (1973). *Fundamental statistics in psychology and education* (5th ed.). New York: McGraw-Hill.

Guilford, J. P., & Hoepfner, R. (1971). *The analysis of intelligence.* New York: McGraw-Hill.

Guilford, J. P., & Martin, H. G. (1943). *The Guilford–Martin Inventory of Factors (GAMIN): Manual of directions and norms.* Beverly Hills, CA: Sheridan Supply.

Guilford, J. P., & Tenopyr, M. L. (1968). Implications of the structure-of-intellect model for high school and college students. In W. B. Michael (ed.), *Teaching for creative endeavor* (pp. 25–45). Bloomington: Indiana University Press.

Guttman, L. (1944). A basis for scaling quantitative data. *American Sociological Review, 9,* 139–150.

Gynther, M. D., & Green, S. B. (1980). Accuracy may make a difference, but does a difference make for accuracy? *Journal of Consulting and Clinical Psychology, 48,* 268–272.

Hack, M., & Breslau, N. (1985). Very low birth weight infants: Effects of brain growth during infancy on intelligence quotient at 3 years of age. *Pediatrics, 77,* 196–202.

Hacker, H. K. (1991, June 6). Adjusted federal employment tests stir controversy. *Los Angeles Times,* p. A-5.

Hager, P. (1991, October 29). Court bans psychological tests in hiring. *Los Angeles Times,* p. A-20.

Haier, R. J. (1991). Cerebral glucose metabolism and intelligence. In P. A. Vernon (ed.), *Biologic approaches to the study of human intelligence.* Norwood, NJ: Ablex.

Hall, H. V. (1987). *Violence prediction: Guidelines for the forensic practitioner.* Springfield, IL: Charles C Thomas.

Hamersma, R. J., Paige, J., & Jordan, J. E. (1973). Construction of a Guttman facet designed cross-cultural attitude–behavior scale toward racial ethnic interaction. *Educational and Psychological Measurement, 33,* 565–576.

Hammill, D. D., Brown, L., & Bryant, B. R. (1992). *A consumer's guide to tests in print* (2nd ed.). Austin, TX: pro.ed.

Hampson, E. (1990). Variations in sex-related cognitive abilities across the menstrual cycle. *Brain and Cognition, 14,* 26–43.

Haney, D. A. (1985, February 3). Creative people: Their inner drive awes researchers. *Los Angeles Times,* I-2, 9.

Hanna, G. S., & Johnson, P. R. (1978). Reliability and validity of multiple-choice tests developed by four distractor selection procedures. *Journal of Educational Research, 71,* 203–206.

Hansen, Jo-Ida C., & Campbell, D. P. (1985). *Manual for the SVIB–SCII* (4th ed.). Stanford, CA: Stanford University Press.

Harmon, L. W., Hansen, Jo-Ida C., Borgen, F. H., & Hammer, A. L. (1994). *Strong Interest Inventory: Applications and technical guide.* Palo Alto, CA: Consulting Psychologists Press.

Harrell, T. W., & Harrell, M. S. (1945). Army General Classification Test scores for civilian occupations. *Educational and Psychological Measurement, 5,* 229–342.

Harrington, R. G. (ed.) (1986). *Testing adolescents.* Kansas City, MO: Test Corporation of America.

Harrison, P. L., et al. (1988). A survey of tests used for adult assessment. *Journal of Psychoeducational Assessment, 6,* 188–198.

Harrow, A. J. (1972). *A taxonomy of the psychomotor domain: A guide for developing behavioral objectives.* New York: David McKay.

Hartshorne, H., & May, M. A. (1928). *Studies in the nature of character. Vol. 1: Studies in deceit.* New York: Macmillan.

Hathaway, S. R., & McKinley, J. C. (1989). *MMPI–2.* Minneapolis: University of Minnesota Press.

Hattie, J. (1980). Should creativity tests be administered under test-like conditions? An empirical study of three alternative conditions. *Journal of Educational Psychology, 72,* 87–98.

Haynes, S. N. (1984). Computer-assisted assessment. In R. J. Corsini (ed.), *Encyclopedia of psychology* (pp. 263–264). New York: Wiley.

Haynes, S. N. (1990). Behavioral assessment of adults. In G. Goldstein & M. Hersen (eds.), *Handbook of psychological assessment* (2nd ed., pp. 423–463). New York: Pergamon.

Haynes, S. N., & Wilson, C. C. (1979). *Behavioral assessment.* San Francisco: Jossey–Bass.

Hebb, D. O. (1949). *The organization of behavior.* New York: Wiley.

Henley, S. J., Klebe, K. J., McBride, J. R., & Cudeck, R. (1989). Adaptive and conventional versions of the DAT: The first complete battery comparison. *Applied Psychological Measurement, 13,* 363–372.

Herrnstein, R. J., & Murray, C. (1994). *The bell curve.* New York: The Free Press.

Hersen, M., & Bellack, A. S. (eds.) (1982). *Behavioral assessment: A practical handbook* (2nd ed.). New York: Pergamon.

Hier, D. B., & Crowley, W. F., Jr. (1982). Spatial ability in androgen-deficient men. *New England Journal of Medicine, 306,* 1202–1205.

Hirsch, N. D. M. (1926). A study of natio-racial mental differences. *Genetic Psychology Monographs, 1,* 231–406.

Hiskey, M. (1966). *Hiskey–Nebraska Test of Learning Aptitude.* Lincoln, NE: Union College Press.

Hobbs, N. (1963). A psychologist in the Peace Corps. *American Psychologist, 18,* 47–55.

*Hobson* v. *Hansen,* 269 F. Suppl. 401 (D.D.C. 1967).

Hoffman, B. (1962). *The tyranny of testing.* New York: Crowell-Collier.

Holden, R. R., & Fekken, G. C. (1988). *Using reaction time to detect faking on a computerized inventory of psychopathology.* Paper presented at Annual Convention of Canadian Psychological Association, Montreal.

Holden, R. R., & Kroner, D. G. (1992). Relative efficacy of differential response latencies for detecting faking on a self-report measure of psychopathology. *Psychological Assessment, 4,* 170–173.

Holden, R. R., Fekken, G. C., & Cotton, D. H. G. (1991). Assessing psychopathology using structured test-item response latencies. *Psychological Assessment, 3,* 111–118.

Holden, R. R., Fekken, G. C., Reddon, J. R., Helmes, E., & Jackson, D. N. (1988). Clinical reliabilities and validities of the Basic Personality Inventory. *Journal of Consulting and Clinical Psychology, 56,* 766–768.

Holland, J. L. (1985). *Making vocational choices: A theory of careers: A theory of vocational personalities and work environments* (2nd ed.). Upper Saddle River, NJ: Prentice Hall.

Holt, A. (1974). *Handwriting in psychological interpretations.* Springfield, IL: Charles C Thomas.

Holt, R. R. (1970). Yet another look at clinical and statistical prediction: Or, is clinical psychology worthwhile? *American Psychologist, 25,* 337–349.

Honacker, L. M., Hector, V. S., & Harel, T. H. (1986). Perceived validity of computer versus clinician-generated MMPI reports. *Computers in Human Behavior, 2,* 77–83.

Horn, J. L. (1979). The rise and fall of human abilities. *Journal of Research and Development in Education, 12,* 59–78.

Horn, J. L., & Cattell, R. B. (1966). Refinement and test of the theory of fluid and crystallized intelligence. *Journal of Educational Psychology, 57,* 253–276.

Horn, J. L., & Donaldson, G. (1976). On the myth of intellectual decline in adulthood. *American Psychologist, 31,* 701–719.

Hsu, T.-C., Moss, P. A., & Khampalikit, C. (1984). The merits of multiple-answer items as evaluated by using six scoring formulas. *Journal of Experimental Education, 52,* 152–158.

Hughes, H. H., & Converse, H. D. (1962). Characteristics of the gifted: A case for a sequel to Terman's study. *Exceptional Children, 29,* 178–183.

Hunt, C. B. (1980). Intelligence as an information processing concept. *British Journal of Psychology, 71,* 449–474.

Hunt, E. (1983). On the nature of intelligence. *Science, 219,* 141–146.

Hunt, E. (1987). The next word on verbal ability. In P. A. Vernon (ed.), *Speed of information-processing and intelligence* (pp. 347–392). Norwood, NJ: Ablex.

Hunt, E., & Lansman, M. (1983). Individual differences in intelligence. In R. Sternberg (ed.), *Advances in the psychology of human intelligence.* Hillsdale, NJ: Erlbaum.

Hunt, J. McV. (1961). *Intelligence and experience.* New York: Ronald Press.

International Assessment of Educational Progress (1989). *A world of differences: An international assessment of math and science.* Princeton, NJ: Educational Testing Service.

Jackson, D. N. (1984). *Multidimensional Aptitude Battery manual.* Port Huron, MI: Research Psychologists Press.

Jackson, D. N. (1994). *Jackson Personality Inventory–Revised manual.* Port Huron, MI: Sigma Assessment Systems.

Jackson, D. N., Helmes, E., Hoffmann, H., Holden, R. R., Jaffe, P. G., Reddon, J. R., & Smiley, W. C. (1989). *Basic Personality Inventory manual.* Port Huron, MI: Sigma Assessment Systems.

Jacobson, R. L. (1993, September 15). New computer technique seen producing a revolution in educational testing. *Chronicle of Higher Education,* pp. A22–A23, A26.

Jacobson, R. L. (1994, August 3). Computerized testing runs into trouble. *Chronicle of Higher Education,* pp. A16–A17.

Jacobson, R. L. (1995, January 6). Shortfall of questions curbs use of computerized graduate exam. *Chronicle of Higher Education,* p. A23.

Jamison, K. R. (1984). Manic-depressive illness and accomplishment: Creativity, leadership, and social class. In F. K. Goodwin & K. R. Jamison (eds.), *Manic-depressive illness.* New York: Oxford University Press.

Jensen, A. R. (1969). How much can we boost IQ and scholastic achievement? *Harvard Educational Review, 39,* 1–123.

Jensen, A. R. (1980). *Bias in mental testing.* New York: Free Press.

Jensen, A. R. (1981). *Straight talk about mental tests.* New York: Free Press.

Jensen, A. R., & Sinha, S. N. (1991). Physical correlates of human intelligence. In P. A. Vernon (ed.), *Biological approaches to the study of human intelligence.* Norwood, NJ: Ablex.

Jessell, J. C., & Sullins, W. L. (1975). Effect of keyed response sequencing of multiple-choice items on performance and reliability. *Journal of Educational Measurement, 12,* 45–48.

Johnson, J. H., & Williams, T. (1975). The use of on-line computer technology in a mental health admitting system. *American Psychologist, 3,* 388–390.

Johnson, O. G. (1976). *Tests and measurements in child development: Handbook II.* San Francisco: Jossey–Bass.

Johnson, O. G., & Bommarito, J. W. (1971). *Tests and measurements in child development.* San Francisco: Jossey–Bass.

Jones, H. E., & Conrad, H. S. (1933). The growth and decline of intelligence: A study of a homogeneous group. *Genetic Psychology Monographs, 13,* 223–298.

Jordan, J. E. (1971). Construction of a Guttman facet designed cross-cultural attitude-behavior scale toward mental retardation. *American Journal of Mental Deficiency, 76,* 201–219.

Jung, C. G. (1910). The association method. *American Journal of Psychology, 21,* 219–269.

Kagan, J. (1966). Reflection–impulsivity: The generality and dynamics of conceptual tempo. *Journal of Abnormal Psychology, 71,* 17–24.

Kagan, J., Rosman, B. L., Day, D., Albert, J., & Phillips, W. (1964). Information processing in the child: Significance of analytic and reflective attitudes. *Psychological Monographs, 78* (Whole No. 578).

Kallman, F. J., & Jarvik, L. (1959). Individual differences in constitution and genetic background. In J. E. Birren (ed.), *Handbook of aging and the individual.* Chicago: University of Chicago Press.

Kansup, W., & Hakstian, A. R. (1975). Comparison of several methods of assessing partial knowledge in multiple-choice tests: Scoring procedures. *Journal of Educational Measurement, 12,* 219–230.

Kapes, J. T., Borman, C. A., & Frazier, N. (1989). An evaluation of the SIGI and DISCOVER micro-computer-based career guidance systems. *Measurement and Evaluation in Counseling and Development, 22,* 126–136.

Kapes, J. T., & Vansickle, T. R. (1992). Comparing paper–pencil and computed-based version of the Harrington–O'Shea Career Decision Making System. *Measurement and Evaluation in Counseling and Development, 25*(1), 5–13.

Kaplan, H. I., & Sadock, B. J. (1989). *Comprehensive textbook of psychiatry,* No. V. Baltimore: Williams & Wilkins.

Keating, D. P. (ed.) (1976). *Intellectual talent: Research and development.* Baltimore, MD: Johns Hopkins University Press.

Kelderman, H., Mellenberg, C. J., & Elshout, J. J. (1981). Guilford's facet theory of intelligence: An empirical comparison of models. *Multivariate Behavioral Research, 16,* 37–61.

Kellaghan, T., & MacNamara, J. (1972). Family correlates of verbal reasoning ability. *Developmental Psychology, 7,* 49–53.

Kelly, E. L., & Fiske, D. W. (1951). *The prediction of performance in clinical psychology.* Ann Arbor: University of Michigan Press.

Kelly, G. A. (1955). *The psychology of personal constructs.* New York: Norton.

Kendall, P. C., & Korgeski, G. P. (1979). Assessment and cognitive–behavioral interventions. *Cognitive Therapy and Research, 1,* 1–21.

Kendall, P. C., & Norton-Ford, J. D. (1982). *Clinical psychology: Scientific and professional dimensions.* New York: Wiley.

Keyser, D. J., & Sweetland, R. C. (eds.) (1984–1994). *Test critiques* (Vols. I–X). Austin, TX: pro.ed.

Kidd, J. W. (1983). The 1984 A.A.M.D. definition and classification of mental retardation: The apparent impact of the CEC-MR positron. *Education and Training of the Mentally Retarded, 18,* 243–244.

Kilbride, H. W., Johnson, D. L., & Streissguth, A. P. (1977). Social class, birth order, and newborn experience. *Child Development, 48,* 1686–1688.

Kimura, D., & Hampson, E. (1993). Neural and hormonal mechanisms mediating sex differences in cognition. In P. A. Vernon (ed.), *Biological approaches to the study of human intelligence* (pp. 375–397). Norwood, NJ: Ablex.

Kleinmuntz, B., & Szucko, J. J. (1984). A field study of the fallibility of polygraphic lie detection. *Nature, 308,* 449–450.

Klimko, I. P. (1984). Item arrangement, cognitive entry characteristics, sex, and test anxiety as predictors of achievement examination performance. *Journal of Experimental Education, 52,* 214–219.

Klineberg, O. (1963). Negro–white differences in intelligence test performance. *American Psychologist, 18,* 198–203.

Knobloch, H., & Pasamanick, B. (eds.) (1974). *Gesell and Amatruda's developmental diagnosis* (3rd ed.). New York: Harper & Row.

Kohlberg, L. (1969). Stage and sequence: The cognitive–developmental approach to socialization. In D. Goslin (ed.), *Handbook of socialization: Theory and research.* Chicago: Rand McNally.

Kohlberg, L. (1974). The development of moral stages: Uses and abuses. *Proceedings of the 1973 Invitational Conference on Testing Problems* (pp. 1–8). Princeton, NJ: Educational Testing Service.

Kohlberg, L., & Elfenbein, D. (1975). The development of moral judgments concerning capital punishment. *American Journal of Orthopsychiatry, 45,* 614–639.

Koppitz, E. M. (1975). *The Bender–Gestalt test for young children: Research and application, 1963–1973.* New York: Grune & Stratton.

Kramer, J. J., & Conoley, J. (1992). *The eleventh mental measurements yearbook.* Lincoln: Buros Institute of Mental Measurements of the University of Nebraska—Lincoln.

Krathwohl, D. R., Bloom, B. S., & Masia, B. B. (1964). *Taxonomy of educational objectives: Handbook II, The affective domain.* New York: David McKay.

Kretschmer, E. (1925). *Physique and character.* New York: Harcourt Brace Jovanovich.

Krug, S. E. (1993). *Psychware sourcebook* (4th ed.). Champaign, IL: MetriTech.

Kuder, G. F. (1963). A rationale for evaluating interests. *Educational and Psychological Measurement, 23,* 3–12.

Lacks, P. (1984). *Bender–Gestalt screening for brain dysfunction.* San Antonio, TX: The Psychological Corporation.

Landers, S. (1989, December). Test score controversy continues. *APA Monitor,* p. 10.

Langevin, R. (1983). *Sexual strands: Understanding and treating sexual anomalies in men.* Hillsdale, NJ: Erlbaum.

Lanyon, R. I. (1986). Psychological assessment procedures in court-related settings. *Professional Psychology: Research and Practice, 17,* 260–268.

*Larry P.* v. *Riles,* 495 F. Supp. 926 (N.D. Cal. 1979), appeal docketed, No. 80-4027 (9th Cir., Jan. 17, 1980).

Larson, G. E., & Saccuzzo, D. P. (1989). Cognitive correlates of general intelligence: Toward a process theory of *g. Intelligence, 13,* 5–32.

Lastovicka, J. L., et al. (1987). A lifestyle typology to model young male drinking and driving. *Journal of Consumer Research, 14,* 257–263.

Lee, E. S. (1951). Negro intelligence and selective migration: A Philadelphia test of the Klineberg hypothesis. *American Sociological Review, 16,* 227–233.

Lenke, J. M. (1988, April). Controversy fueled by district and state reports of achievement test results . . . "Lake Wobegon—or Not?" *The Score,* pp. 5, 13 (Newsletter of Division 5 of the American Psychological Association).

Levenson, R. W. (1992). Autonomic nervous system differences among emotions. *Psychological Science, 3,* 23–27.

Levine, M. (1976). The academic achievement test: Its historical context and social functions. *American Psychologist, 31,* 228–238.

Levy, P., & Goldstein, H. (1984). *Tests in education: A book of critical reviews.* New York: Academic Press.

Lewinsohn, P. M. (1965). Psychological correlates of overall quality of figure drawings. *Journal of Consulting Psychology, 29,* 504–512.

Lewis, M., & McGurk, H. (1972). Evaluation of infant intelligence: Infant intelligence scores—true or false? *Science, 1178*(4066), 1174–1177.

Lieberman, M. A. (1965). Psychological correlates of impending death: Some preliminary observations. *Journal of Gerontology, 20,* 71–84.

Lieberman, M. A., & Coplan, A. S. (1969). Distance from death as a variable in the study of aging. *Developmental Psychology, 2,* 71–84.

Lillienfeld, S. O., Alliger, G., & Mitchell, K. (1995). Why integrity testing remains controversial. *American Psychologist, 50,* 457–458.

Lindzey, G. (1965). Seer versus sign. *Journal of Experimental Research on Personality, 1,* 17–26.

Linn, M. L., & Hyde, J. S. (1989). Gender, mathematics, and science. *Educational Researcher, 18*(8), 17.

Linn, R. L. (1992). Achievement testing. In M. C. Alkin (ed.), *Encyclopedia of Educational Research* (6th ed., pp. 1–12). New York: Macmillan.

Lipsitt, P. D., Lelos, D., & McGarry, A. L. (1971). Competency for trial: A screening instrument. *American Journal of Psychiatry, 128,* 105–109.

Little, E. B. (1962). Overcorrection for guessing in multiple-choice test scoring. *Journal of Educational Research, 55,* 245–252.

Little, E. B. (1966). Overcorrection and undercorrection in multiple-choice test scoring. *Journal of Experimental Education, 35,* 44–47.

Loehlin, J. C. (1989). Partitioning environmental and genetic contributions to behavioral development. *American Psychologist, 44,* 1285–1292.

Lubin, B., Larsen, R. M., & Matarazzo, J. D. (1984). Patterns of psychological test usage in the United States: 1935–1982. *American Psychologist, 39,* 451–452.

Lucas, A., Morley, R., Cole, T. J., Lister, G., & Leeson-Payne, C. (1992). Breast milk and subsequent intelligence quotient in children born preterm. *Lancet, 339,* 261–264.

Lundeberg, M. A., & Fox, P. W. (1991). Do laboratory findings on test expectancy generalize to classroom outcomes? *Review of Educational Research, 61,* 94–106.

Lyerly, S. B. (ed.) (1978). *Handbook of psychiatric rating scales* (2nd ed.). Rockville, MD: National Institute of Mental Health.

Lykken, D. T. (1983, April). Polygraph prejudice. *APA Monitor,* p. 4.

Lynn, R. (1982). IQ in Japan and the United States shows a growing disparity. *Science, 297,* 222–223.

Lynn, R. (1987). The intelligence of the mongoloids: A psychometric, evolutionary and neurological theory. *Personality and Individual Differences, 8,* 813–844.

Maccoby, E. E., & Maccoby, N. (1954). The interview: A tool of social science. In G. Lindzey (ed.), *Handbook of social psychology* (pp. 449–487). Reading, MA: Addison–Wesley.

Machover, K. (1949, 1951, 1971). *Personality projection in the drawing of the human figure.* Springfield, IL: Charles C Thomas.

MacKinnon, D. W. (1962). The nature and nurture of creativity talent. *American Psychologist, 17,* 484–495.

MacPhee, D., Ramey, C. T., & Yeates, K. O. (1984). Home environment and early cognitive development: Implications for intervention. In A. W. Gottfried (ed.), *Home environment and early cognitive development. Longitudinal research.* Orlando, FL: Academic Press.

Maloney, M. P., & Ward, M. P. (1976). *Psychological assessment: A conceptual approach.* New York: Oxford University Press.

Marland, S. P. (1969). A customer counsels the testers. *Proceedings of the 1968 Invitational Conference on Testing Problems,* pp. 101–112. Princeton, NJ: Educational Testing Service.

Martin, E., & McDuffee, D. (1981). *A sourcebook of Harris national surveys: Repeated questions, 1963–76.* Chapel Hill: University of North Carolina, Institute for Research in Social Science.

Matarazzo, J. D. (1980). Behavioral health and behavioral medicine: Frontiers for a new health psychology. *American Psychologist, 35,* 807–817.

Matarazzo, J. D. (1992). Psychological testing and assessment in the 21st century. *American Psychologist, 47,* 1007–1018.

May, R. B., & Thompson, J. M. (1989). Test expectancy and question answering in prose processing. *Applied Cognitive Psychology, 3,* 261–269.

McArthur, C., & Stevens, L. B. (1955). The validation of expressed interests as compared with inventoried interests: A fourteen-year follow-up. *Journal of Applied Psychology, 39,* 184–189.

McCabe, S. P. (1985). Career Assessment Inventory. In D. J. Keyser & R. C. Sweetland (eds.), *Test critiques* (Vol. II, pp. 128–137). Kansas City, MO: Test Corporation of America.

McClelland, D. (1973). Testing for competence rather than for intelligence. *American Psychologist, 28,* 1–14.

McGarry, A. L., et al. (1973). *Competency to stand trial and mental illness.* Washington, DC: U.S. Government Printing Office.

McMichael, A. J., Baghurst, P. A., Wigg, N. R., Vimpani, G. V., Robertson, E. F., & Roberts, R. J. (1988). Port Pirie cohort study: Environmental exposure to lead and children's abilities at the age of four years. *New England Journal of Medicine, 319,* 468–475.

McNemar, Q. (1942). *The revision of the Stanford–Binet scale.* Boston: Houghton Mifflin.

McNemar, Q. (1964). Lost: Our intelligence? Why? *American Psychologist, 19,* 871–882.

McReynolds, P. (1979). The case for interactional assessment. *Behavioral Assessment, 1,* 237–247.

McReynolds, P. (1986). History of assessment in clinical and educational settings. In R. O. Nelson & S. C. Hayes (eds.), *Conceptual foundations of behavioral assessment* (pp. 42–80). New York: Guilford Press.

Mead, A. D., & Crasgow, F. (1992). *Effects of administration: A meta-analysis.* Unpublished manuscript, University of Illinois, Champaign.

Mednick, S. A. (1962). The associative basis of the creative process. *Psychological Review, 69,* 1220–1232.

Meehl, P. E. (1954). *Clinical versus statistical prediction.* Minneapolis: University of Minnesota Press.

Meehl, P. E. (1965). Seer over sign: The first good example. *Journal of Experimental Research in Personality, 11,* 27–32.

Megargee, E. I. (1972). *The California Psychological Inventory Handbook.* San Francisco: Jossey–Bass.

Mehrabian, A., & Weiner, M. (1967). Decoding of inconsistent communication. *Journal of Personality and Social Psychology, 6,* 109–114.

Merl, J. (1991, May 26). National school testing faces many roadblocks. *Los Angeles Times,* pp. A1, A34–35.

Messick, S. (1989). Validity. In R. L. Linn (ed.), *Educational measurement* (3rd ed., pp. 13–103). New York: Macmillan.

Michaelsen, R. H., Michie, D., & Boulanger, A. (1985). The technology of expert systems. *Byte, 10*(4), 303–312.

Millman, J., & Pauk, W. (1969). *How to take tests.* New York: McGraw-Hill.

Millon, T., Millon, C., & Davis, R. (1994). *Manual for the MCMI–III.* Minneapolis, MN: NCS Assessments.

Mischel, W. (1968). *Personality and assessment.* New York: Wiley.

Mischel, W. (1986). *Introduction to personality* (4th ed.). New York: Holt, Rinehart & Winston.

Mitchell, J. V., Jr. (ed.) (1983). *Tests in print III.* Lincoln: Buros Institute of Mental Measurements of the University of Nebraska—Lincoln.

Mitchell, J. V., Jr. (ed.) (1985). *The ninth mental measurements yearbook.* Lincoln: Buros Institute of Mental Measurements of the University of Nebraska—Lincoln.

Moos, R. H. (1976). *The human context.* New York: Wiley.

Moos, R. H. (1979). *Evaluating educational environments.* San Francisco, CA: Jossey–Bass.

Moos, R. H., & Moos, B. S. (1986). *Family Environment Scale: Manual* (2nd ed.). Palo Alto, CA: Consulting Psychologists Press.

Moreland, K. L. (1990). Some observations on computer-assisted psychological testing. *Journal of Personality Assessment, 55,* 820–823.

Murphy, K. R., & Davidshofer, C. O. (1994). *Psychological testing: Principles & applications* (3rd ed.). Upper Saddle River, NJ: Prentice Hall.

Murphy, L. L., Conoley, J. C., & Impara, J. C. (eds.) (1994). *Tests in print IV.* Lincoln: University of Nebraska and Buros Institute of Mental Measurements.

Murray, H. A. (and collaborators). (1938). *Explorations in personality.* New York: Oxford University Press.

*Myart* v. *Motorola,* 110 Cong. Record 5662-64 (1964).

Myers, D. G. (1995). *Psychology* (4th ed.). New York: Worth.

Myers, I. B., & McCaulley, M. H. (1985). *Manual: A guide to the development and use of the Myers–Briggs Type Indicator.* Palo Alto, CA: Consulting Psychologists Press.

Naglieri, J. A. (1989). A cognitive processing theory for the measurement of intelligence. *Educational Psychologist, 24,* 185–206.

Naglieri, J. A., Das, J. P., & Jarman, R. F. (1990). Planning, Attention, Simultaneous, Successive cognitive processes as a model for assessment. *School Psychology Review, 19,* 423–442.

Nairn, A., & Associates. (1980). *The reign of ETS: The corporation that makes up minds.* Washington, DC: Learning Research Project.

National Center for Health Statistics. (1995). Annual summary of births, marriages, divorces, and deaths: United States, 1994. *Monthly Vital Statistics Report, 43*(13). Hyattsville, MD: Public Health Service (produced October 23, 1995).

Needleman, H. L., Gunnoe, C., Leviton, A., & Perie, H. (1978). Neuropsychological dysfunction in children with "silent" lead exposure. *Pediatric Research, 12,* 1374 (Abstract).

Needleman, H. L., Schell, A., Bellinger, D., Leviton, A., & Allred, E. N. (1990). The long-term effects of exposure to low doses of lead in childhood. *New England Journal of Medicine, 322*(2), 83–88.

Nettler, G. (1959). Test burning in Texas. *American Psychologist, 14,* 682–683.

Newland, T. E. (1969). *Manual for the Blind Learning Aptitude Test: Experimental edition.* Urbana, IL: T. Ernest Newland.

Nisbet, J. D. (1957). Intelligence and age: Retesting after twenty-four years' interval. *British Journal of Educational Psychology, 27,* 190–198.

Oden, M. H. (1968). The fulfillment of promise: 40-year follow-up of the Terman gifted group. *Genetic Psychology Monographs, 77*(1), 3–93.

Ollendick, T. H., & Green, R. (1990). Behavioral assessment of children. In G. Goldstein & M. Hersen (eds.), *Handbook of psychological assessment* (2nd ed., pp. 403–422). New York: Pergamon.

Ones, D. S., Viswesvaran, C., & Schmidt, F. L. (1995). Integrity tests: Overlooked facts, resolved issues, and remaining questions. *American Psychologist, 50,* 456–457.

Osgood, C. E., Suci, G. J., & Tannenbaum, P. H. (1957). *The measurement of meaning.* Urbana: University of Illinois Press.

Osipow, S. H. (1983). *Theories of career development* (3rd ed.). New York: Appleton-Century-Crofts.

Owens, R. E., Hanna, G. S., & Coppedge, F. L. (1970). Comparison of multiple-choice tests using different types of distractor selection techniques. *Journal of Educational Measurement, 7,* 87–90.

Owens, W. A., Jr. (1953). Age and mental abilities: A longitudinal study. *Genetic Psychology Monographs, 48,* 3–54.

Owens, W. A., Jr. (1966). Age and mental abilities: A second adult follow-up. *Journal of Educational Psychology, 57,* 311–325.

Owens, W. A. (1976). Background data. In M. D. Dunnette (ed.), *Handbook of industrial and organizational psychology.* Chicago: Rand McNally.

Palmore, E. (1982). Predictors of the longevity difference: A 25-year follow-up. *Gerontologist, 225,* 513–518.

Palmore, E., & Cleveland, W. (1976). Aging, terminal decline, and terminal drop. *Journal of Gerontology, 31*(1), 76–86.

*Parents in Action on Special Education (PASE)* v. *Joseph P. Hannon,* No. 74C 3586 (N.D. III. 1980).

Paterson, D. G., et al. (1930). *Minnesota Mechanical Ability Tests.* Minneapolis: University of Minnesota Press.

Payne, A. F. (1928). *Sentence completions.* New York: New York Guidance Clinic.

Pellegrino, J. W., & Varnhagen, C. K. (1985). Intelligence: Perspectives, theories, and tests. In T. Husén & T. N. Posthlethwaite (eds.), *The international encyclopedia of education, 5,* 2611–2618. New York: Wiley.

Peterson, C. J., et al. (1982). The Attributional Style Questionnaire. *Cognitive Therapy and Research, 6*, 287–300.

Piotrowski, C., & Keller, J. W. (1989). Psychological testing in outpatient mental health facilities: A national study. *Professional Psychology: Research and Practice, 20*, 423–425.

Piotrowski, C., Sherry, D., & Keller, J. W. (1985). Psychodiagnostic test usage: A survey of the Society for Personality Assessment. *Journal of Personality Assessment, 49*, 115–119.

Plake, B. S., et al. (1982). Effects of item arrangement, knowledge of arrangement, test anxiety and sex on test performance. *Journal of Educational Measurement, 19*, 49–57.

Platt, J. R. (1961). On maximizing the information obtained from science examinations. *American Journal of Physics, 29*, 111–122.

Plomin, R. (1988). The nature and nurture of cognitive abilities. In R. J. Sternberg (ed.), *Advances in the psychology of human intelligence* (Vol. 4). Hillsdale, NJ: Erlbaum.

Plomin, R. (1989). Environment and genes: Determinants of behavior. *American Psychologist, 44*, 105–111.

Plomin, R. (1990). *Nature and nurture: An introduction to human behavior genetics.* Pacific Grove, CA: Brooks/Cole.

Popham, W. J. (1981). *Modern educational measurement.* Upper Saddle River, NJ: Prentice Hall.

Powers, D. E. (1986). Relations of test item characteristics to test preparation/test practice effects: A quantitative summary. *Psychological Bulletin, 100*, 67–77.

Powers, D. E. (1993). Coaching for the SAT: A summary of the summaries and an update. *Educational Measurement Issues and Practice, 12*(2), 24–30.

Prediger, D. J., & Hanson, G. R. (1976). Holland's theory of careers applied to men and women: Analysis of implicit assumptions. *Journal of Vocational Behavior, 8*, 167–184.

Preston, R. C. (1964). Ability of students to identify correct responses before reading. *Journal of Educational Research, 58*, 181–183.

Pritchard, D. A., & Rosenblatt, A. (1980). Racial bias in the MMPI: A methodological review. *Journal of Consulting and Clinical Psychology, 48*, 263–267.

Quay, H. C., & Peterson, D. R. (1983). *Interim manual for the Behavior Problem Checklist.* Unpublished manuscript, University of Miami.

Rabinowitz, W. (1984). Study of Values. In D. J. Keyser & R. C. Sweetland (eds.), *Test critiques* (Vol. I, pp. 641–647). Kansas City, MO: Test Corporation of America.

Raju, N. S., Normand, J., & Burke, M. J. (1990). A new approach for utility analysis. *Journal of Applied Psychology, 75*, 3–12.

Raudenbush, S. W. (1984). Magnitude of teacher expectancy effects on pupil IQ as a function of the credibility of expectancy induction: A synthesis of findings from experiments. *Journal of Educational Psychology, 76*, 85–97.

Ravitch, D. (1983–1984, Winter). The uses and misuses of tests. *College Board Review,* pp. 23–26.

Reik, T. (1948). *Listening with the third ear* (pp. 263–264). New York: Grove Press.

Reilly, R. R., & Chao, G. T. (1982). Validity and fairness of some alternative employee selection procedures. *Personnel Psychology, 35*, 1–62.

Reimanis, G., & Green, R. F. (1971). Imminence of death and intellectual decrement in the aging. *Developmental Psychology, 5*, 270–272.

Reitan, R. M. (1964). *Manual for administering and scoring the Reitan–Indiana Neuropsychological Battery for Children (aged 5 through 8).* Indianapolis: Indiana University Medical Center.

Reynolds, C. R. (1984–1985). Critical measurement issues in learning disabilities. *Journal of Special Education, 18*(4), 452–476.

Reynolds, C. R., Chastain, R. L., Kaufman, A. S., & McLean, J. E. (1987). Demographic characteristics and IQ among adults: Analysts of the WAIS–R standardization sample as a function of the stratification variables. *Journal of School Psychology, 25*, 323–342.

Riegel, K. F., & Riegel, R. M. (1972). Development, drop, and death. *Developmental Psychology, 6,* 306–319.

Riese, M. (1988). Temperament in full-term and preterm infants: Stability over ages 6–24 months. *Journal of Developmental and Behavioral Pediatrics, 9,* 6–11.

Roback, H. (1968). Human figure drawings: Their utility in the clinical psychologist's armamentarium for personality assessment. *Psychological Bulletin, 70,* 1–19.

Robbins, D., & Almond, E. (1992, January 9). NCAA tightens academic rules for student-athletes. *Los Angeles Times,* pp. A1, A23.

Robinson, J. P., Athanasiou, R., & Head, K. B. (1974). *Measures of occupational attitudes and occupational characteristics.* Ann Arbor: Institute for Social Research, University of Michigan.

Robinson, J. P., Rush, J. G., & Head, K. B. (1973). *Measures of political attitudes.* Ann Arbor: Institute for Social Research, University of Michigan.

Robinson, J. P., Shaver, P. R., & Wrightsman, L. S. (1991). *Measures of personality and social psychological attitudes.* New York: Academic Press.

Roe, A. (1956). *The psychology of occupations.* New York: Basic Books.

Roe, A., & Klos, D. (1969). Occupational classification. *Counseling Psychologist, 1,* 84–92.

Roe, A., & Siegelman, M. (1964). *The origin of interest.* Washington, DC: American Personnel and Guidance Association.

Rogers, C. R., & Dymond, R. F. (eds.) (1954). *Psychotherapy and personality change.* Chicago: University of Chicago Press.

Rogers, R. (1984). *Rogers Criminal Responsibility Scales.* Odessa, FL: Psychological Assessment Resources.

Rogers, R. (1986). *Conducting insanity evaluations.* Odessa, FL: Psychological Assessment Resources.

Rokeach, M. (1973). *The nature of human values.* New York: Free Press.

Rome, H. P., et al. (1962). Symposium on automation techniques in personality assessment. *Proceedings of the Staff Meetings of the Mayo Clinic, 37,* 61–82.

Rosenbaum, B. (1973). Attitude toward invasion of privacy in the personnel selection process and job applicant demographic and personality correlates. *Journal of Applied Psychology, 58,* 333–338.

Rosenfeld, P., Doherty, L. M., Vincino, S. M., Kantor, J. et al. (1989). Attitudes assessment in organizations: Testing three microcomputer-based survey systems. *Journal of General Psychology, 116,* 145–154.

Rosenthal, R., et al. (1979). *Sensitivity to nonverbal communication: The PONS test.* Baltimore, MD: Johns Hopkins University Press.

Rosenthal, R., & Jacobson, L. (1968). *Pygmalion in the classroom.* New York: Holt, Rinehart & Winston.

Rosenzweig, S. (1978). *Aggressive behavior and the Rosenzweig Picture–Frustration Study.* New York: Praeger.

Ross, C. C., & Stanley, J. C. (1954). *Measurement in today's schools* (3rd ed.). Upper Saddle River, NJ: Prentice Hall.

Rossi, P. H., & Freeman, H. E. (1993). *Evaluation: A systematic approach* (5th ed.). Beverly Hills, CA: Sage Publications.

Rotter, J. B. (1954). *Social learning and clinical psychology.* Upper Saddle River, NJ: Prentice Hall.

Rotter, J. B. (1966). Generalized expectancies for internal versus external control of reinforcement. *Psychological Monographs, 80*(1, Whole No. 609).

Rowley, G. L. (1974). Which examinees are most favoured by the use of multiple-choice tests? *Journal of Educational Measurement, 11,* 15–23.

Royce, J. R., & Powell, A. (1983). *Theory of personality and individual differences: Factors, systems, and processes.* Upper Saddle River, NJ: Prentice Hall.

Russell, M., & Karol, D. (1994). *The 16 PF Fifth Edition administrator's manual.* Champaign, IL: Institute for Personality and Ability Testing.

Ryan, J., Prefitera, A., & Powers, L. (1983). Scoring reliability on the WAIS–R. *Journal of Consulting and Clinical Psychology, 51,* 149–150.

Sameroff, A. J. (ed.) (1978). Organization and stability of newborn behavior: A commentary on the Brazelton Neonatal Behavioral Assessment Scale. *Monographs of the Society for Research in Child Development, 43*(5–6, Serial No. 177).

Sampson, J. P. (1981). CASSI: A computer-assisted approach to improving study skills. *NASPA Journal, 18,* 42–147.

Sampson, J. P., Jr., & Reardon, R. C. (eds.) (1990). Evaluating computer-assisted career guidance systems [Special issue]. *Journal of Career Development, 17,* 79–149.

Sattler, J. M., Hillix, W. A., & Neher, L. A. (1970). Halo effect in examiner scoring of intelligence test responses. *Journal of Consulting and Clinical Psychology, 34,* 172–176.

Sattler, J. M., & Winget, B. M. (1970). Intelligence testing procedures as affected by expectancy and IQ. *Journal of Clinical Psychology, 26,* 446–448.

Savitz, F. R. (1985). Effects of easy examination questions placed at the beginning of science multi-choice examinations. *Journal of Instructional Psychology, 12,* 6–10.

Scarr, S., & Weinberg, R. A. (1976). I.Q. test performance of black children adopted by white families. *American Psychologist, 31,* 726–739.

Scarr, S., & Yee, D. C. (1980). Heritability and educational policy: Genetic and environmental effects on IQ, aptitude and achievement. *Educational Psychologist, 15,* 1–22.

Schaie, K. W. (1983). The Seattle Longitudinal Study: A twenty-one year exploration of psychometric intelligence in adulthood. In K. W. Schaie (ed.), *Longitudinal studies of adult psychological development* (pp. 64–135). New York: Guilford.

Schaie, K. W., & Hertzog, C. (1983). Fourteen-year cohort-sequential analyses of adult intellectual development. *Developmental Psychology, 19,* 531–543.

Schaie, K. W., & Hertzog, C. (1986). Toward a comprehensive model of adult intellectual development: Contributions of the Seattle Longitudinal Study. In R. J. Sternberg (ed.), *Advances in the psychology of human intelligence* (Vol. 3, pp. 79–118). Hillsdale, NJ: Erlbaum.

Schaie, K. W., & Strother, C. R. (1968). A cross-sequential study of age changes in cognitive behavior. *Psychological Bulletin, 70,* 671–680.

Schmidt, F. L., & Hunter, J. E. (1977). Development of a general solution to the problem of validity generalization. *Journal of Applied Psychology, 62,* 529–540.

Schmidt, F. L., & Hunter, J. E. (1978). Moderator research and the law of small numbers. *Personnel Psychology, 31,* 215–232.

Schmidt, F. L., & Hunter, J. E. (1981). Employment testing: Old theories and new research findings. *American Psychologist, 36,* 1128–1137.

Schmidt, S. R. (1983). The effects of recall and recognition test expectancies on the retention of prose. *Memory and Cognition, 11,* 172–180.

Schmitt, N., & Robertson, I. (1990). Personnel selection. *Annual Review of Psychology, 41,* 289–391.

Schneider, M. F. (1989). *Children's Apperceptive Story-telling* Test. Austin, TX: pro.ed.

Schneider, M. F., & Perney, J. (1990). Development of the Children's Apperceptive Story-telling Test. *Psychological Assessment: A Journal of Consulting and Clinical Psychology, 2,* 179–185.

Schoonman, W. (1989). *An applied study of computerized adaptive testing.* Amsterdam: Swete & Zeitlinger.

Schwab, D. P., & Heneman, H. A. (1969). Relationship between interview structure and interview reliability in employment situations. *Journal of Applied Psychology, 53,* 214–217.

Schwab, D. P., Heneman, H. A., III, & De Cotiis, T. A. (1975). Behaviorally anchored rating scales: A review of the literature. *Personnel Psychology, 28,* 549–562.

Schwab, D. P., & Packard, G. L. (1973). Response distortion on the Gordon Personal Inventory and the Gordon Personal Profile in the selection context: Some implications for predicting employee behavior. *Journal of Applied Psychology, 58,* 372–374.

Scribner, S., & Cole, M. (1973). Cognitive consequences of formal and informal schooling. *Science, 182,* 553–559.

Sears, R. R. (1977). Sources of life satisfactions of the Terman gifted men. *American Psychologist, 32,* 119–128.

Seashore, C. E. (1939). *Psychology of music.* New York: McGraw-Hill.

Selltiz, C., Wrightsman, L. S., & Cook, S. W. (1976). *Research methods in social relations* (3rd ed.). New York: Holt, Rinehart & Winston.

Serlin, R. C., & Kaiser, H. F. (1978). Method for increasing the reliability of a short multiple-choice test. *Educational and Psychological Measurement, 38,* 337–340.

Shaha, S. H. (1984). Matching test: Reduced anxiety and increased test effectiveness. *Educational and Psychological Measurement, 44,* 869–881.

Shaw, M. W., & Wright, J. M. (1967). *Scales for the measurement of attitudes.* New York: McGraw-Hill.

Shea, C. (1994, September 7). "Gender gap" on examinations shrank again this year. *Chronicle of Higher Education,* p. A54.

Sheldon, W. H., Stevens, S. S., & Tucker, W. B. (1940). *The varieties of human physique.* New York: Harper & Row.

Siegler, I. C., McCarty, S. M., & Logue, P. E. (1982). Wechsler Memory Scale scores, selective attribution, and distance from death. *Journal of Gerontology, 37,* 176–181.

Simpson, E. J. (1966). The classification of educational objectives, psychomotor domain. *Illinois Teacher of Home Economics, 10,* 110–114.

Sines, J. O. (1970). Actuarial versus clinical prediction in psychopathology. *British Journal of Psychiatry, 116,* 129–144.

Skodak, M., & Skeels, H. M. (1949). A final follow-up study of one hundred adopted children. *Journal of Genetic Psychology, 75,* 85–125.

Slack, W. V., & Porter, D. (1980). The Scholastic Aptitude Test: A critical appraisal. *Harvard Educational Review, 50,* 154–175.

Slate, J. R., & Jones, C. H. (1990). Student error in administering the WISC–R: Identifying problem areas. *Measurement and Evaluation in Counseling and Development, 23,* 137–140.

Smith, P. C., & Kendall, L. M. (1963). Retranslation of expectations: An approach to the construction of unambiguous anchors for rating scales. *Journal of Applied Psychology, 47,* 149–155.

Smith, S. R., & Meyer, R. G. (1987). *Law, behavior, and mental health.* New York: New York University Press.

Snyder, C. R. (1974). Acceptance of personality interpretations as a function of assessment procedures. *Journal of Consulting Psychology, 42,* 150.

Snyder, D. K., Widiger, T. A., & Hoover, D. W. (1990). Methodological considerations in validating computer-based test interpretations: Controlling for response bias. *Psychological Assessment, 2,* 470–477.

Snyderman, M., & Rothman, S. (1987). Survey of expert opinion on intelligence and aptitude testing. *American Psychologist, 42,* 137–144.

Society for Industrial & Organizational Psychology, Inc. (1987). *Principles for the validation and use of personnel selection procedures* (3rd ed.). College Park, MD: Author.

Sokal, M. M. (ed.) (1987). *Psychological testing and American society 1890–1930.* New Brunswick, NJ: Rutgers University Press.

*Soroka* v. *Dayton–Hudson Corp.* 91. L.A. Daily Journal D.A.R. 13204 (Cal. Ct. App. 1991).

Spearman, C. E. (1927). *The abilities of man.* London: Macmillan.

Speath, J. L. (1976). Characteristics of the work setting and the job as determinants of income. In W. H. Sewell, R. M. Sauser, & D. L. Featherman (eds.), *Schooling and achievement in American society.* New York: Academic Press.

Stanley, J. C., Keating, D. P., & Fox, L. H. (eds.) (1974). *Mathematical talent: Discovery, description, and development.* Baltimore, MD: Johns Hopkins University Press.

Starch, D., & Elliott, E. C. (1913). Reliability of grading work in mathematics. *School Review, 21,* 254–259.

*Stell* v. *Savannah–Chatham County Board of Education.* 210 F Supp. 667, 668 (S.D. Ga. 1963), rev'd 333 F.2d 55 (5th Cir. 1964), cert. denied, 379 U.S. 933 (1964).

Stephenson, W. (1953). *The study of behavior: Q-technique and its methodology.* Chicago: University of Chicago Press.

Sternberg, R J. (1981). Testing and cognitive psychology. *American Psychologist, 36,* 1181–1189.

Sternberg, R. J. (1982). Thinking and learning skills: A view of intelligence. *Education Digest, 47,* 20–22.

Sternberg, R. J. (1985). *Beyond IQ: A triarchic theory of human intelligence.* New York: Cambridge University Press.

Sternberg, R. J. (1986). *The triarchic mind: A new theory of human intelligence.* New York: Viking.

Sternberg, R. J. (1988). Mental self-government: A theory of intellectual styles and their development. *Human Development, 31,* 197–224.

Sternberg, R. J. (1989). Domain-generality versus domain-specificity: The life and impending death of a false dichotomy. *Merrill–Palmer Quarterly, 35,* 115–130.

Stevenson, H. W., & Stigler, R. W. (1992). *The learning gap: Why our schools are failing and what we can learn from Japanese and Chinese education.* New York: Summit Books.

Stewart, D. M. (1995, January 14). Scholastic Assessment Test. *Los Angeles Times,* p. B17.

Stoch, M. B., & Smythe, P. M. (1963). Does undernutrition during infancy inhibit brain growth and subsequent intellectual development? *Archives of Disorders of Childhood, 38,* 546–552.

Stoloff, M. L., & Couch, J. V. (eds.) (1992). *Computer use in psychology: A directory of software* (3rd ed.). Washington, DC: American Psychological Association.

Stott, D. H. (1983). Brain size and "intelligence." *British Journal of Developmental Psychology, 1*(3), 279–287.

Strang, H. R. (1980). Effect of technically worded options on multiple-choice test performance. *Journal of Educational Research, 73,* 262–265.

Strauss, A. A., & Lehtinen, L. E. (1947). *Psychopathology and education of the brain-injured child,* Vol. 1. New York: Grune & Stratton.

Strong, E. K., Jr. (1955). *Vocational interests 18 years after college.* Minneapolis: University of Minnesota Press.

Sundberg, N. D. (1977). *Assessment of persons.* Upper Saddle River, NJ: Prentice Hall.

Super, D. E. (1973). The Work Values Inventory. In D. G. Zytowski (ed.), *Contemporary approaches to interest measurement.* Minneapolis: University of Minnesota Press.

Super, D. E., & Bohn, M. J., Jr. (1970). *Occupational psychology.* Belmont, CA: Wadsworth.

Super, D. E., & Crites, J. O. (1962). *Appraising vocational fitness.* New York: Harper & Row.

Sweetland, R. C., & Keyser, D. J. (eds.) (1991). *Tests* (3rd ed.). Austin, TX: pro.ed.

Swenson, W. M., & Pearson, J. S. (1964). Automation techniques in personality assessment: A frontier in behavioral science and medicine. *Methods of Information in Medicine, 3,* 34–36.

Swiercinsky, D. P. (ed.) (1985). *Testing adults.* Kansas City, MO: Test Corporation of America.

*Tarasoff* v. *Regents of University of California,* 17 Cal. 3d 425 (1983).

Taylor, H. C., & Russell, J. T. (1939). The relationship of validity coefficients to the practical effectiveness of tests in selection: Discussion and tables. *Journal of Applied Psychology, 23,* 565–578.

Taylor, J. A. (1953). A personality scale of manifest anxiety: *Journal of Abnormal and Social Psychology, 48,* 285–290.

Teeter, P. A. (1985). Review of Adjective Check List. In J. V. Mitchell, Jr. (ed.), *The ninth mental measurements yearbook* (Vol. I, pp. 50–52). Lincoln: Buros Institute of Mental Measurements of the University of Nebraska—Lincoln.

Terman, L. M., & Merrill, M. A. (1973). *Stanford-Binet Intelligence Scale: 1972 norms edition.* Boston: Houghton Mifflin.

Terman, L. M., & Oden, M. H. (1959). *The gifted group at mid-life. Genetic studies of genius. V.* Stanford, CA: Stanford University Press.

Thatcher, R. W., Lester, M. L., McAlaster, R., Horst, R., & Ignasias, S. W. (1983). Intelligence and lead toxins in rural children. *Journal of Learning Disabilities, 16,* 355–359.

Thomas, A., & Chess, S. (1977). *Temperament and development.* New York: Brunner/Mazel.

Thomas, G. E., Alexander, K. L., & Eckland, B. K. (1979). Access to higher education: The importance of race, sex, social class, and academic credentials. *School Review, 87,* 133–156.

Thomas, R. G. (1985). Review of Jackson Vocational Interest Survey. In J. V. Mitchell, Jr. (ed.), *The ninth mental measurements yearbook* (Vol. I, pp. 740–742). Lincoln: Buros Institute of Mental Measurements of the University of Nebraska—Lincoln.

Thompson, B. (1994). Guidelines for authors. *Educational and Psychological Measurement, 54,* 837–847.

Thoreson, C. E., & Mahoney, M. J. (1974). *Behavioral self-control.* New York: Holt, Rinehart & Winston.

Thorndike, E. L. (1912). The permanence of interests and their relation to abilities. *Popular Science Monthly, 81,* 449–456.

Thorndike, R. L. (1963). The prediction of vocational success. *Vocational Guidance Quarterly, 11,* 179–187.

Thorndike, R. L. (1971). Concepts of culture-fairness. *Journal of Educational Measurement, 8,* 63–70.

Thorndike, R. L., & Hagen, E. P. (1959). *Ten thousand careers.* New York: Wiley.

Thorndike, R. L., Hagen, E. P., & Sattler, J. P. (1986). *The Stanford–Binet Intelligence Scale: Fourth Edition, Technical manual.* Chicago: Riverside Publishing.

Tidwell, R. (1980). Biasing potential of multiple-choice test distractors. *Journal of Negro Education, 49,* 280–296.

Tittle, C. K. (1984). Test bias. In T. N. Husén & T. Postlethwaite (eds.), *International encyclopedia of education* (pp. 5199–5204). New York: Wiley.

Torgerson, A. M. (1985). Temperamental differences in infants and 6-year-old children: A follow-up study of twins. In J. Strelau, F. Farley, & A. Gales (eds.), *The biological bases of personality and behavior* (Vol. 1). New York: Hemisphere.

Torrance, E. P. (1988). The nature of creativity as manifest in its testing. In R. J. Sternberg (ed.), *The nature of creativity: Contemporary psychological perspectives.* New York: Cambridge University Press.

Tuddenham, R. D., Blumenkrantz, J., & Wilkin, W. R. (1968). Age changes in AGCT: A longitudinal study of average adults. *Journal of Counseling & Clinical Psychology, 32,* 659–663.

Tyler, L. E. (1964). The antecedents of two varieties of interest pattern. *Genetic Psychology Monographs, 70,* 177–227.

Tyler, L. E., & Walsh, W. B. (1979). *Tests and measurements* (3rd ed.). Upper Saddle River, NJ: Prentice Hall.

Underwood, B., & Moore, B. S. (1981). Sources of behavioral consistency. *Journal of Personality and Social Psychology, 40,* 780–785.

U.S. Department of Defense (1992). *Counselor's manual for the ASVAB.* North Chicago, IL: U.S. Military Entrance Processing Command.

U.S. Department of Defense (1993). *ASVAB 18/19 technical manual.* North Chicago, IL: U.S. Military Entrance Processing Command.

U.S. Department of Defense (1994). *Technical manual for the ASVAB 18/19 career exploration programs.* North Chicago, IL: U.S. Military Entrance Processing Command.

*United States* v. *City of Buffalo,* 37 U.S. 628 (W.D.N.Y. 1985).

*United States* v. *Georgia Power Company,* 5 FEP 587 (1973).

Uzgiris, I. C., & Hunt, J. McV. (1975). *Assessment in infancy: Ordinal scales of psychological development.* Urbana: University of Illinois Press.

Vansickle, T. R., & Kapes, J. T. (1993). Comparing paper–pencil and computer-based versions of the Strong–Campbell Interest Inventory. *Computers in Human Behavior, 9*(4), 441–449.

Vernon, P. E. (1960). *The structure of human abilities* (rev. ed.). London: Methuen.

Vernon, P. E. (1979). Intelligence testing and the nature/nurture debate, 1928–1978: What next? *British Journal of Educational Psychology, 49,* 1–14.

Vernon, P. E. (1981). Reaction time and intelligence in the mentally retarded. *Intelligence, 5,* 345–355.

Vernon, P. E. (1985). Intelligence: Heredity–environment determinants. In T. Husén & T. N. Posthlethwaite (eds.), *The international encyclopedia of education* (Vol. 5, pp. 2605–2611). New York: Wiley.

Vernon, P. E. (1987). New developments in reaction time research. In P. E. Vernon (ed.), *Speed of information-processing and intelligence* (pp. 1–20). Norwood, NJ: Ablex.

Wade, T. C., & Baker, T. B. (1977). Opinions and use of psychological tests. *American Psychologist, 32,* 874–882.

Wagman, M. (1980). PLATO DCS: An interactive computer system for personal counseling. *Journal of Experimental Psychology, 72,* 596.

Wallace, A. (1994, December 16). Electronic grad school test challenged. *Los Angeles Times,* p. A29.

Wallach, M. A., & Kogan, N. (1965). *Modes of thinking in young children.* New York: Holt, Rinehart & Winston.

Wallston, K. A., Maides, S., & Wallston, B. S. (1976). Health-related information seeking as a function of health-related locus of control and health value. *Journal of Research in Personality, 10,* 215–222.

*Wards Cove Packing Company* v. *Antonio,* 490, U.S. 642 (1989).

Warnath, G. F. (1975). Vocational theories: Direction to nowhere. *Personnel and Guidance Journal, 53,* 422–428.

*Washington* v. *Davis,* 426 U.S. 229, 12 FEP 1415 (1976).

Watkins, C. E., Jr., Campbell, V. L., & McGregor, P. (1988). Counseling psychologists' uses of the opinions about psychological tests: A contemporary perspective. *Counseling Psychologist, 16,* 476–486.

*Watson* v. *Fort Worth Bank and Trust,* 487 U.S. 977, 108 S. Ct. 277 (1988).

Weaver, S. J. (ed.) (1984). *Testing children.* Kansas City, MO: Test Corporation of America.

Webb, E. (1915). Character and intelligence. *British Journal of Psychology Monograph Supplement,* III.

Webb, J. T., & Meckstroth, B. (1982). *Guiding the gifted child.* Columbus: Ohio Psychology Publishing Co.

Wechsler, D. (1975). Intelligence defined and undefined. *American Psychologist, 30,* 135–139.

Wechsler, D. (1981). *WAIS–R manual.* New York: The Psychological Corporation.

Weinberg, R. A. (1989). Intelligence and IQ: Landmark issues and great debates. *American Psychologist, 44,* 98–104.

Weiner, I. B. (1983). The future of psychodiagnosis revisited. *Journal of Personality Assessment, 47,* 451–461.

Weiss, J., Beckwith, B., & Schaeffer, B. (1989). *Standing up for the SAT.* New York: Simon & Schuster.

Welsh, J. R., Kucinkas, S. K., & Curran, L. T. (1990). *Armed Services Vocational Aptitude Battery (ASVAB), Integrative review of validity studies* (AFHRL-TR-90-22). Brooks Air Force Base, TX: Air Force Human Resources Laboratory.

White, N., & Cunningham, W. R. (1988). Is terminal drop pervasive or specific? *Journal of Gerontology: Psychological Sciences, 43,* P141–P144.

Whyte, W. H., Jr. (1956). *The organization man.* Garden City, NY: Doubleday.

Wiggins, J. S. (1966). Substantive dimensions of self-report in the MMPI item pool. *Psychological Monographs, 80* (Whole No. 630).

Wiggins, N., & Kohen, E. S. (1971). Man versus model of man revisited: The forecasting of graduate school success. *Journal of Personality and Social Psychology, 19,* 100–106.

Wilbur, P. H. (1970). Positional response set among high school students on multiple-choice tests. *Journal of Educational Measurement, 7,* 161–163.

Wildman, R., et al. (1980). The Georgia Court Competency Test: An attempt to develop a rapid, quantitative measure of fitness for trial. Unpublished manuscript, Forensic Services Division, Center State Hospital, Milledgeville, GA.

Willerman, L., Schultz, R., Rutledge, J. N., & Bigler, E. (1989). *Magnetic resonance imaged brain structures and intelligence.* Paper presented to the 19th annual meeting of the Behavior Genetics Association. Charlottesville, VA.

Willingham, W. W., & Breland, H. M. (1982). *Personal qualities and college admissions.* New York: College Entrance Examination Board.

Willson, V. L. (1982). Maximizing reliability in multiple-choice questions. *Educational and Psychological Measurement, 42,* 69–72.

Wilson, G. (1978). Introversion/extroversion. In H. London & J. E. Exner (eds.), *Dimensions of personality* (pp. 217–261). New York: Wiley.

Wilson, R. S. (1985). Risk and resilience in early mental development. *Developmental Psychology, 21,* 795–805.

Wirt, R. D., & Lachar, D. (1981). The Personality Inventory for Children: Development and clinical applications. In P. McReynolds (ed.), *Advances in psychological assessment,* Vol. 5. San Francisco: Jossey–Bass.

Witkin, H. A., & Berry, J. W. (1975). Psychological differentiation in cross-cultural perspective. *Journal of Cross-Cultural Psychology, 6,* 4–87.

Witkin, H. A., & Goodenough, D. R. (1977). Field dependence and interpersonal behavior. *Psychological Bulletin, 84,* 661–689.

Witkin, H. A., Price-Williams, D., Bertini, M., Bjorn, C., Oltman, P. K., Ramirez, M., & Van Meel, J. (1973). *Social conformity and psychological differentiation.* Princeton, NJ: Educational Testing Service.

Wolff, W. T., & Merrens, M. R. (1974). Behavioral assessment: A review of clinical methods. *Journal of Personality Assessment, 38,* 3–16.

Wolk, R., & Wolk, R. (1971). *The Gerontological Apperception Test.* New York: Behavioral Publications.

Worobey, J. (1986). Convergence among assessments of temperament in the first month. *Child Development, 57,* 47–55.

Wright, H. E. (1960). Observational child study. In P. E. Mussen (ed.), *Handbook of research methods in child development.* New York: Wiley.

Yerkes, R. M. (ed.) (1921). Psychological examining in the United States army. *Memoirs of the National Academy of Sciences,* Vol. 15.

Zajonc, R. B. (1976). Family configuration and intelligence. *Science, 192,* 227–236.

Zajonc, R. B. (1986). The decline and rise of scholastic aptitude scores. *American Psychologist, 41,* 862–867.

Zarske, J. A. (1985). Review of Adjective Check List. In J. V. Mitchell, Jr. (ed.), *The ninth mental measurements yearbook* (Vol. I, pp. 52–53). Lincoln: Buros Institute of Mental Measurements of the University of Nebraska—Lincoln.

Zeskind, P. S., & Ramey, C. T. (1981). Preventing intellectual and interactional sequelae of fetal malnutrition: A longitudinal transaction, and synergistic approach to development. *Child Development, 52,* 213–218.

Ziskin, J. (1986). The future of clinical assessment. In B. S. Plake & J. C. Witt (eds.), *The future of testing* (pp. 185–201). Hillsdale, NJ: Erlbaum.

Zook, J. (1993). Two agencies start work on national test of college students' analytical skills. *Chronicle of Higher Education, 39*(29), A23.

Zytowski, D. G. (1976). Predictive validity of the Kuder Occupational Interest Survey: A 12- to 19-year follow-up. *Journal of Counseling Psychology, 23*, 221–233.

# AUTHOR INDEX

# TEST INDEX

# SUBJECT INDEX

ABC approach, 453
ability test, 10, 200, 453
academic ability tests, 137, 160–162
academic aptitude, 453
academic competency, 358–359
accommodation, 190, 453
accountability, 113
achievement, 109, 453
achievement test, 10, 22, 109–135
achievement test batteries, 119–124
acoustic impedance audiometry, 206
acquiescence response set, 32n, 308, 453
adaptation, 190
adaptive behavior, 165, 453
adaptive testing, 408, 453
adjustment, 453
adverse impact, 392
affective assessment, 9, 10, 453
AIO inventories, 362
ambiguity index, 252
analogies test, 454
anchor test, 453
anecdotal record, 279, 454
answer sheets, 39–41
Apgar rating, 454
apperception tests, 337–339
aptitude, 10, 110, 454
aptitude test, 10, 200–228
arithmetic mean, 430–431, 454
art ability tests, 215
assembling and reproducing a test, 37–42
assessment, 454
assessment center, 203, 454
assimilation, 190, 454
assortative mating, 454
attainment, 109
attitudes, 231, 251–259, 454
    methods of measuring, 251–259
    scales, 252–256, 454
audiogram, 206
audiometer, 206, 454
auditory acuity, 204–205
Aunt Fanny error, 454
authentic assessment, 378
automated assessment, 455
average, 455

bandwidth, 201, 455
Barnum effect, 276, 455

basal age, 141, 143, 455
base rate, 102, 455
    scores, 328
basic education tests, 124
battery of tests, 455
behavior analysis, 303, 455
behavior modification, 303
behavioral assessment, 304
behavioral medicine, 367
behavioral toxicology, 368
bias, 455
bimodal distribution, 429, 455
biographical data, 283
biographical inventories, 284
blind analysis, 97
body build, 269
business tests, 131–133

C scale, 81
Cajori method (of grading), 62
case conference, 366
case study, 365, 455
CEEB scores, 80–89
ceiling age, 141, 143, 455
central tendency, measures of, 429–431, 455
centroid method, 187
changing answers (on tests), 54
cheating on tests, 51, 386–387
checklists, 298–300
child custody, 371
classification, 99–100, 455
clerical ability, 213, 214
clinical (impressionistic) approach, 455
clinical contexts, assessment in, 364–367
clinical vs. statistical prediction, 399–400, 404
coaching, 456
    effects on test scores, 380–381
Code of Fair Testing Practices in Education, 16–18
coefficient alpha, 89, 456
coefficient of
    agreement, 93
    concordance, 90
    equivalence, 88, 456
    internal consistency, 88–90, 456
    stability, 87, 456
    stability and equivalence, 88, 456
cognition, 456
cognitive abilities
    biological factors and, 182–186